MARSILIO FICINO

Three Books on Life

medieval & renaissance texts & studies

VOLUME 57

The Renaissance Society of America
Renaissance Texts Series

Volume 11

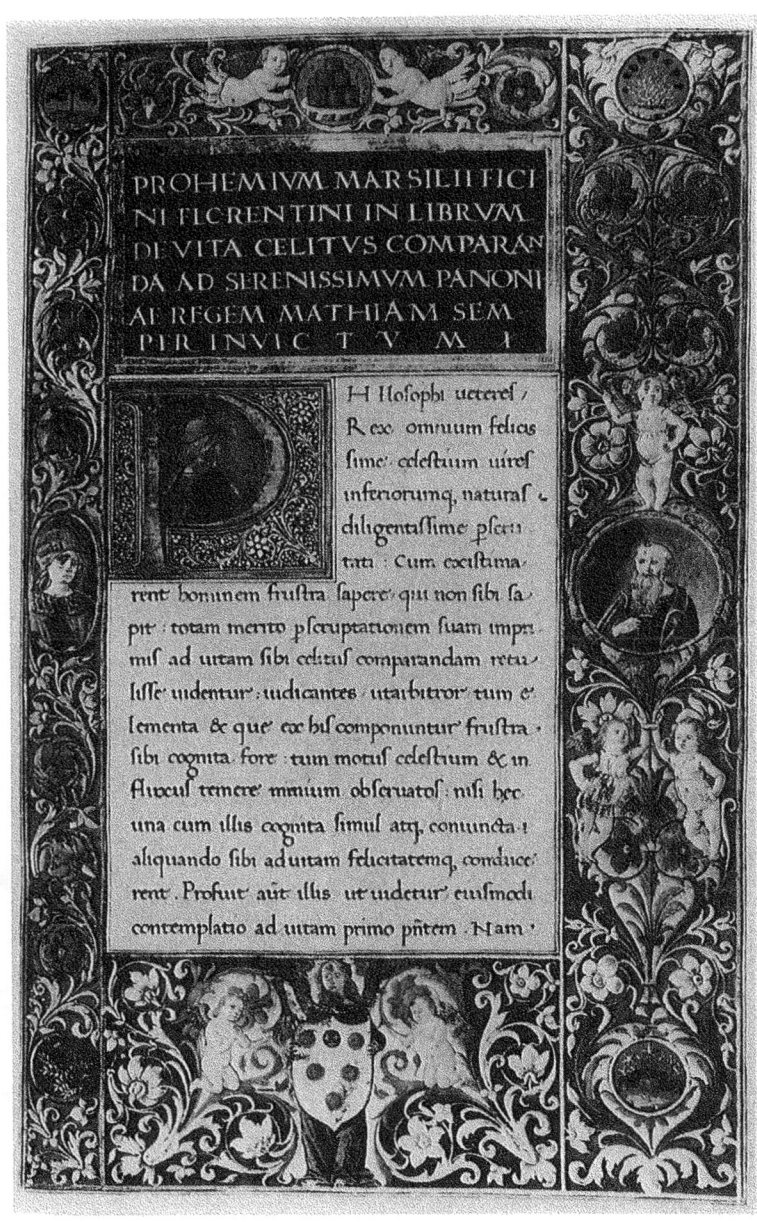

First page of *De vita* 3 from MS Plut. 73, Cod. 39, fol. 77 (80)ʳ [our MS *L*]. In the initial P of the text, Ficino is represented. Reproduced with permission from Pl. XVII, p. 125 of C. Csapodi, et al., *Bibliotheca Corviniana*.

MARSILIO FICINO

Three Books on Life

A Critical Edition and Translation
with Introduction and Notes

by

Carol V. Kaske and *John R. Clark*

MEDIEVAL & RENAISSANCE TEXTS & STUDIES
In conjunction with
The Renaissance Society of America
Tempe, Arizona
1998

Generous grants from Pegasus Limited for the Advancement
of Neo-Latin Studies and from the Hull Fund of Cornell University
have helped defray costs of publication.

© Copyright 1989
Center for Medieval and Early Renaissance Studies
State University of New York at Binghamton

Reprints ©1998, ©2002, ©2006
Arizona Board of Regents for Arizona State University

Paperback © Copyright 2019
Arizona Board of Regents for Arizona State University

published by
Arizona Center for Medieval and Reniassance Studies
Tempe, Arizona
www.acmrs.asu.edu

Library of Congress Cataloging-in-Publication Data
(as printed in the original 1989 edition)

Ficino, Marsilio, 1433–1499.
   Three books on life.
   (MRTS ; v. 57)
   Translation of De triplici vita.
   Bibliography: p.
   Includes index.
   1. Astrology--Early works to 1800. 2. Medicine, Medieval. I. Kaske, Carol V., 1933- . II. Clark, John R., 1947- . III. Title. IV. Series: Medieval & Renaissance texts & studies ; v. 57.
BF1680.F5513   1988b   615.8'99   88-8924
ISBN 978-0-8669-8822-3

In memoriam

James Hutton

1902–1980

Table of Contents

Acknowledgements	xi
List of Abbreviations	xiii
Introduction	
Importance of *De vita*	3
Summary of Contents	4
The Present Edition	4
Editorial Introduction	6
Principles of Translation	13
Scope of the Notes	15
De vita in Ficino's Life and Works	17
Traditional Material and Innovations	31
Habits of Mind	38
Magic	45
Repercussions	55
Notes to the Introduction	71
De vita Text and Translation	
1489 Table of Chapter Headings	92
Sigla	101
Proem	102
Book One	106
Book Two	164
Book Three	236
Apology	394
Commentary Notes	407
Works Cited	461
Indices	
Index to the Introduction	477
Index auctorum et nominum propriorum	485
Index materiae medicae	493

Acknowledgements

The present edition of *De vita* began in 1972 as a group project for a seminar in Renaissance Latin given by the late James Hutton of Cornell University. We are grateful to the third member of the seminar, Earl Delarue, for his initial contributions to our understanding of Book 1. Besides conceiving the project, Professor Hutton checked the first draft of our entire translation along with most of our notes on Book 1 and advised us at all stages of the project up until his death in 1980. As editors, we have experienced the more generous side of the scholarly community. Professor Emeritus Paul Oskar Kristeller of Columbia University first encouraged us to publish the project and to establish a critical text; since then, he has advised and helped us in many ways. The faculty and staff of the Wellcome Institute for the History of Medicine and the Warburg Institute of the University of London extended help and hospitality to Clark during a year in London, 1979-80. Professors D. P. Walker of the Warburg Institute, Michael J. B. Allen of the University of California at Los Angeles, and David Pingree of Brown University have between them checked all of Kaske's translation of Book 3 and some of her notes; Walker, Kristeller, Professor Katharine Park of Wellesley College, and Professor Gerard Cox of the University of Washington as well as Professors Philip H. Holland, R. E. Kaske, and Henry Guerlac of Cornell University have gone through parts of the Introduction and of the translation of Book 1. As readers for the press, Kristeller, Allen, and Professor Brian Copenhaver of Oakland University saved us from many errors; and Copenhaver in particular sifted the Introduction and our notes to Book 3 with a diligence far beyond the call of duty and made innumerable corrections and additions. Robert Johnson and Deborah MacInnes have made valuable suggestions. Any errors which remain are of course our own.

We are grateful for technological assistance to Cornell University, the University of Pennsylvania, and Fordham University, and for monetary assistance to the American Council of Learned Societies, the American Philosophical Society, the English Department and the Humanities Research Grants Committee of Cornell University, and the Wellcome Institute for the History of

Medicine. The following libraries have generously provided us with microfilms and permitted direct access to manuscripts and rare books: in this country, the Houghton Library, Harvard University, Cambridge, Mass.; the Welch Medical Library, the Johns Hopkins University, Baltimore, Md.; the Hanes Collection, University of North Carolina, Chapel Hill, N.C.; the Library of Georgetown University, Washington, D.C.; the Library of the University of Pennsylvania, Philadelphia, Penna.; and the New York Academy of Medicine, New York City; in Europe, the Herzog August Bibliothek, Wolfenbüttel; the Bayerische Staatsbibliothek, Munich; the Staatsbibliothek, Berlin; the Biblioteca Riccardiana and the Biblioteca Laurenziana, Florence; the Stadsbibliotheek, Haarlem; and in London, the Warburg Institute, the Wellcome Institute, and the British Library.

Finally, we record our deep indebtedness to previous scholars, many now beyond reach of this message — Klibansky, Panofsky, and Saxl; D. C. Allen, Chastel, Garin, Kristeller, Marcel, Plessner, Shumaker, Walker, Yates, and Zanier — without whose ground-breaking work on *De vita* this study could never have been written.

List of Common Abbreviations

Allen	Michael J. B. Allen, ed and trans. *Marsilio Ficino: The Philebus Commentary.* Berkeley, 1975.
D. C. Allen	D. C. Allen. *The Star-Crossed Renaissance.* Durham, NC, 1941.
Bouché-Leclercq.	Auguste Bouché-Leclercq. *L'Astrologie grecque.* Paris, 1899; rpt. Brussels, 1963.
Comm. Symp.	Ficino. *In Convivium Platonis*, his *Commentary* on Plato's *Symposium.*
Comm. Tim.	Ficino. *Commentary* on *Timaeus*
Della Torre	Arnaldo della Torre. *Storia dell'Accademia platonica di Firenze. Florence, 1902.*
Galen	Claudius Galenus, *Opera Omnia.* ed. C. G. Kühn. 20 vols. Leipzig, 1821–1833.
Hippocrates	Hippocrates. *Oeuvres completes d'Hippocrate.* ed. and trans. É. Littré. 10 vols. Paris, 1839–1861.
JWCI	*Journal of the Warburg and Courtauld Institutes.*
KP&S	R. Klibansky, E. Panofsky, and F. Saxl. *Saturn and Melancholy.* London, 1964.
Kristeller *Phil MF*	Paul Oskar Kristeller. *The Philosophy of Marsilio Ficino.* New York, 1943.
Kristeller *SF*	Paul Oskar Kristeller. *Supplementum Ficinianum.* 2 vols. 1937, rpt. Florence, 1973.
Letters	*The Letters of Marsilio Ficino.* Translated by members of the Language Department of the School of Economic Science, London. 3 vols. London, 1975–1981.
Marcel	Raymond Marcel. *Marsile Ficin (1433–1499).* Paris, 1958.
Marcel ed. or ed.	*Marsile Ficin: Théologie platonicienne de l'immortalité des âmes.* ed. Raymond Marcel. vols. 1–2, Paris, 1964; vol. 3, Paris, 1970.
OED	*Oxford English Dictionary.* Oxford, 1933.

Op.	*Marsilii Ficini Opera omnia.* Basel, 1575; rpt. Turin, 1959. [Incitations of *Op.*, two numbers are given for letters; thus, 901,2 refers to the second letter on page 901.]
PG	*Patrologiae cursus completus ... Series graeca,* accurante J. P. Migne. Paris, 1857–1866. 161. vols.
PL	*Patrologiae cursus completus ... Series latina,* accurante J. P. Migne. 1st ed. Paris, 1844–1864. 221 vols.
Philostratus *VA*	Flavius Philostratus. *Vita Apollonii.* 2 vols. The Loeb Classical Library, 1912.
Plessner	Martin Plessner, ed. *Marsilius Ficinus: De vita libri tres.* Ed. from the manuscript by Felix Klein-Franke. Hildesheim, 1978.
Pliny *HN*	C. Plinius Secundus. *Naturalis historia.* 10 vols. The Loeb Classical Library, 1938–1962.
Proclus *ET*	*Proclus: The Elements of Theology.* Ed. and trans. E. R. Dodds. Oxford, 1933. 2nd ed., 1963.
Proclus *Plat. Theol.*	*Proclus: Théologie platonicienne.* Ed. and trans. H. D. Saffrey and L. G. Westerink. 4 vols. Paris, 1968–1981.
Shumaker	Wayne Shumaker. *The Occult Sciences in the Renaissance: A Study in Intellectual Patterns.* Berkeley, 1972.
Theol. Plat.	Ficino. *Theologia Platonica.*
Thorndike	Lynn Thorndike. *A History of Magic and Experimental Science.* 2nd ed. 8 vols. New York, 1923–1958.
Walker	D. P. Walker. *Spiritual and Demonic Magic from Ficino to Campanella.* London, 1958, rpt. Notre Dame, Indiana, 1975.
Yates	Frances Yates. *Giordano Bruno and the Hermetic Tradition.* Chicago, 1964.
Zanier	Giancarlo Zanier. *La medicina astrologica e la sua teoria Marsilio Ficino e i suoi critici contemporanei.* Rome, 1977.

INTRODUCTION

INTRODUCTION

Importance of "De vita"

On several roads, *De vita* represents a cultural milestone. It was the first treatise on the health of the intellectual—indeed, says Andrea Corsini, the first on the occupational hazards of any profession.[1] Although it is one of the "strangest and most complex" works to come from Ficino's pen,[2] it was immensely popular in the Renaissance, being rivaled only by his *Consiglio contro la pestilenza*, as Martin Plessner observes, both in simple numbers of editions (nearly thirty) and in the length of time over which it kept appearing (last ed. 1647).[3] This pair of works earned Ficino his place in Sarton's list of seventy-seven best-selling authors of scientific incunabula.[4] The importance of our treatise for the history of Western culture has been attested for English readers in recent decades by detailed treatment in three books written by scholars associated with the Warburg Institute: R. Klibansky, E. Panofsky, and F. Saxl, *Saturn and Melancholy*; D. P. Walker, *Spiritual and Demonic Magic from Ficino to Campanella*; and Frances Yates, *Giordano Bruno and the Hermetic Tradition*. Again, Wayne Shumaker in *The Occult Sciences in the Renaissance* chooses *De vita* as one of three works to summarize as delineations of magic.[5] It had long been appreciated on the continent, as evidenced quantitatively by the many references (like the one quoted above), chapters, and essays devoted to it by Eugenio Garin (see Bibliography), and qualitatively by Putscher's sweeping characterization of it as "einer der wichtigsten Schriften des Neuplatonismus und der Renaissance."[6] I pass over for the sake of this argument the handful of introductions to works (such as the present one) and full-length studies of the author as generically open to the charge of overestimating the importance of their subject. *De vita* is "central to any attempt to understand Ficino," asserts Charles Schmitt, and hence fully deserves an English translation.[7] What Michael J. B. Allen says of his work as a whole, can be said of *De vita* in particular: like the work of Petrarch or Erasmus, its "originality is impossible to define in terms of a single intellectual discipline"; communicating as it frequently did in myths and symbols, using even philosophical terms "as if they were metaphors, . . . for paraphilosophical ends: apology, conversion, intellectual sublimity, and spiritual ecstasy," it caused a revolution more of sensibility than of thought.[8]

Summary of Contents

De vita libri tres rightly announces itself as the first treatise on how to be an intellectual and still keep your health.[1] In Book 1, *De vita sana*, Ficino starts by defending the melancholic humor black bile as the physical basis for that madness which is genius. In the more pharmaceutical part of Book 1 (chaps. 7-26), however, and subsequently in Book 2, he treats black bile in the conventional way as a "monstrum" and a "pestilentia" with no mitigating benefits, and groups it with the occupational hazards of scholars such as insomnia, headaches, and dimness of vision. Uppermost in his mind here and throughout the work are the medical spirits[2] of those patients subject to Saturn, of whom intellectuals, he argues, form the greatest part. A further purpose is a qualified defense of the influence of Saturn on intellectuals. Since art is long, Ficino devotes his second book, *De vita longa*, to how to live a long and healthy life. In both of these books, psychology mingles with prescriptions, and hygiene with pharmacology, while astrology comes in only incidentally. Book 3, *De vita coelitus comparanda*, occupying the last half of the work, is both more philosophical and more occult. Ficino forgets about black bile, though still reverting occasionally to prescriptions. Instead, he elaborates those "celestial causes" mentioned in 1.4 into an astrology extending to talismans and quasi-religious singing, dancing, and suffumigations, whereby he promises to put both the Magus and his patient in touch with their personal stars and the Anima Mundi. With a nervousness betrayed in the introductory and valedictory addresses and in 3.25, Ficino eloquently defends the naturalness of his magic by appeal to his cherished belief that the heavenly bodies are animated with an impersonal spirit which in turn pervades all men. He thus steers around the heresies of determinism and idolatry.

There is no need to summarize further the contents of *De vita*. Synopses of the work are readily available in Klibansky, Panofsky, and Saxl, 3.2.2, pages 266-67, and Walker, pages 3-84, and somewhat less accurate ones in D. C. Allen,[3] Yates, chapter 4, and Shumaker, chapter 3.3; and much can be gathered from the 1489 Table of Chapter Headings which we have printed with the Latin text.

The Present Edition

Although this work represents a collaborative effort, with constant consultation, cooperation, disagreement, compromise, and gratitude, some division of labor can be identified. Clark is solely responsible for the critical edition of the Latin text as printed, and Kaske takes similar responsibility for the English translation. The notes have been a cooperative venture and resist any

such facile division of accountability. In general terms, Kaske is responsible for the longer and more explanatory notes, while Clark was able to locate some of the more inaccessible authors. The Introduction, however, with the exception of Clark's "Editorial Introduction," represents the work and expresses the views of Kaske. Alternating conceptual sections with factual ones, it has brought more of the polyglot literature on *De vita* (though not, regrettably, that in Dutch and Polish) than is usually read by English-speaking scholars, to bear on a first-hand reading of the texts. It attempts to highlight Ficino's most distinctive and influential ideas in the treatise and to explain both their internal coherence and their external polemical purpose. It has also laid down some background for the beginning student.

Our Precursors

Our relation to previous editions and translations of *De vita* should be spelled out. When we began our edition, *De vita* had never been edited in modern times, only reprinted as part of the notoriously corrupt Basel, 1576, *Opera omnia*. These corruptions distort meaning; for example, they make Ficino confess (ungrammatically, *magicum* being an adjective) that his magic is "illicit," *magicum illicitum* (3.26, *Op.*, p. 571), when all he really said was that it used "a magical lure," *magicum illicium* (below, 3.26.92). Several editions had been announced in this century, but in the course of years nothing had come of them, and two would-be editors were known to be deceased and another presumed so.[1] An edition of the Venice text of 1498 by the late Martin Plessner did appear in 1978, edited posthumously from his manuscript by Felix Klein-Franke (see "Editorial Introduction," n. 19). It gives no translation. Plessner's notes to the *Picatrix* and other Arabic sources — though both full of inaccurate page numbers and difficult to correlate with a Latin text which lacks proper pagination — are uniquely valuable because he was an established scholar of this difficult field. We have been able to use some of his notes, as he himself intended, and as we hope that others will be able to develop and add to ours.[2] When we began our translation, *De vita* had never been translated into English; but when this edition was almost completed, a translation by Charles Boer appeared, of which we have not availed ourselves.[3] Boer supplies no Latin text or textual apparatus; and his translation, as one reviewer says, "makes the production of a good scholarly edition and translation even more imperative."[4]

We have striven to the best of our ability to present such a scholarly edition and translation. Although our thinking on *De vita* had for the most part crystallized long before, we owe many corrections and additions, as the notes partly reveal, to four recent or still forthcoming essays on Ficino's magic by Brian Copenhaver. To do justice to a work so encyclopedic as *De vita* would ideally

require the services of a committee embracing historians of science, of the medical profession, of philosophy, and of religion. Some of the ideal committee is represented in the Acknowledgements. Ficino is to his researchers as the elephant to the blind men; each takes the part for the whole. We are by training philologians, but since determining what the words meant in their particular time, place, and context represents the first step, some priority can be claimed for our sort of labor. We hope that the rest of the ideal committee will correct and build upon what we have done.

Editorial Introduction

Manuscripts

The manuscript tradition of *De vita libri tres*[1] is closely associated with the method of the work's composition. The three books of *De vita* were originally three separate treatises: *De vita sana* or *De cura valetudinis eorum qui incumbunt studio litterarum*,[2] *De vita longa*,[3] and *De vita coelitus comparanda*. *De vita sana* was completed by late 1480 and circulated in manuscript form.[4] It soon became attached to the beginning of Book VII of Ficino's *Epistolae*, as can be seen from the Proem to that book: "The seventh book of our Epistles has at its head an epistle which deals with caring for the health of men of letters" (*Op.*, p. 841,1).[5] When this treatise was separated from the *Epistolae* and became *De vita* 1, the proem was left unchanged and the lacuna was filled by an additional note:

> I promised you just now, reader, that at the head of this seventh book there would be an epistle dealing with the health of men of letters. This epistle of ours, however, has grown to such an extent that it no longer wants to be the head of such a small body but rather a whole separate body of its own. And so it has now taken the better course, detached itself, and successfully grown into the book *De vita*.[6]

Five manuscript copies of this earlier version of *De vita sana* have survived. Four of these manuscripts (*BDGR*) are of Ficino's *Epistolae* and contain *De vita sana* following the Proem to *Epistolae VII*. The fifth manuscript (*A*) reveals its similar origin by containing the first two epistles of *Epistolae VII* immediately after *De vita sana*. These five manuscripts contain an earlier version of *De vita sana* before it was revised, primarily by certain additions to the text, for incorporation into *De vita libri tres*.

There are no extant manuscripts of *De vita longa* alone. This treatise was composed during August 1489, when Ficino said that he had read Arnald of Villanova's *De retardanda senectute*.[7] In September 1489 he dedicated *De vita longa* to Filippo Valori (*Op.*, p. 903,2). Shortly afterward *De vita libri tres* was published.

De vita coelitus comparanda, which was to become *De vita* 3, was completed before *De vita longa*. It was originally part of Ficino's commentary on Plotinus and is preserved in one manuscript (*P*) as a *Commentary* on Plotinus' *Enneads* 4, Book 3, chapter 11.[8] By 10 July 1489, Ficino had separated this work from his Plotinus Commentary and dedicated it to Matthias Corvinus, King of Hungary:

> Now, among the books of Plotinus destined for the great Lorenzo de' Medici I had recently composed a commentary (numbered among the rest of our commentaries on him) on the book of Plotinus which discusses drawing favor down from the heavens. With all this in mind, I have just decided to extract that one (with the approval of Lorenzo himself) and dedicate it especially to your Majesty.
> (Proem to Book 3.24-28, dated 10 July 1489)

Some revisions may have been made to this text, since Ficino later says that he completed work on *De vita coelitus comparanda* on 1 August 1489.[9] The Plotinus manuscript (*P*), although dated 12 November 1490, seems to contain an unrevised text of the first six chapters of *De vita* 3.[10]

When Ficino decided to combine his three treatises into one, he added various passages in Books 2 and 3 to connect the three books (2.2.20-23, 2.8.49, 2.16.36-37, 2.18.120-121, 2.20.34-38, 3.4.16-19, 3.5.1-4, 3.11.116-117, 3.13.58-60, 3.14.59-62), a second preface to Book 3, a dedicatory preface of *De vita libri tres* to Lorenzo de' Medici, and two *apologiae*, dated 15 and 16 September respectively. In his dedicatory epistle Ficino maintains the fiction that the order of his books represents their order of composition. The passages which Ficino interspersed throughout the text itself lead to confusing statements about the order of the work's composition, since he has placed *De vita longa* as the second book, although the evidence from his *Epistolae* would place it third according to date.

Two manuscripts survive of the entire *De vita libri tres*, but both postdate the first edition. The more important of the two extant manuscripts (*L*), a presentation copy from Filippo Valori to Lorenzo de' Medici, furnishes a *terminus post quem* of 4 April 1490, since in his dedicatory epistle (printed in Kristeller *SF* 1: 22) Valori refers to the sudden death of King Matthias Corvinus of Hungary. This would date the manuscript four months later than the

editio princeps (3 December 1489). There are a number of parallels between the *L* manuscript and the text of the first edition. Both, for instance, omit the chapter numbers for *De vita* 1. The first edition prefixes a page of *errata* to its text, implying that its original copy was faulty. The manuscript, however, repeats the original faulty readings. Of greater interest are the readings in the manuscript which suggest that its archetype contained an unrevised version of the first eight chapters of *De vita* 2, with its lengthy omissions and marginal additions by another hand, as well as lengthy omissions and additions in the first three chapters of *De vita* 3, which are parallel to those variants in the Plotinus manuscript (*P*).[11]

The other complete manuscript of *De vita* (*H*) was part of the library of Raphael de Marcatellis, Abbot of St. Bavon's, Ghent. Like many of Raphael's books, his *De vita* was copied from an edition.[12] Its readings are very similar to those of the Basel c. 1497 edition and provide no independent evidence.

There are two additional manuscripts (*MMo*), both now in Munich, which contain excerpts from *De vita*. The one (*M*) is a manuscript of Ficino's *Epistolae IX-XII*, preceding the printed edition of the *Epistolae* (1495), and the scattered pieces of *De vita* which it contains serve as an independent, though largely inconsequential, source for the text. The other manuscript (*Mo*) is a miscellany of alchemical treatises; and the pieces from *De vita* 3, copied from one of the early editions, furnish no evidence for the state of the text.[13]

Editions

The *editio princeps* (Florence 1489) takes pride of place in the history of the text and provides the base text for the present edition. Other editions, especially those printed during Ficino's lifetime, were also collated in order to determine if Ficino had revised any part of his text. By using the catalogue in Paul Oskar Kristeller's monumental *Supplementum Ficinianum* 1: LXIV-LXVI, it was possible to eliminate certain editions. The Bologna edition of 1490, as Kristeller had suspected, proved to be identical to the Bologna 1501 edition, which, in turn, had been dependent on the Venice 1498 edition.[14] The reason for the forged date remains unclear. The Florence 1499 and Strasburg 1500 editions turned out to be ghosts.[15] The undated Paris edition of Jean Petit has been placed after 1511 on the basis of the printer's mark.[16] The edition of Georg Wolff and Johann Philippi, Paris c. 1494, may have been the second printing of *De vita*, but it is heavily dependent upon the *editio princeps*, without, however, incorporating the readings of the *errata* page which had been prefixed to the Florence edition.

Johann Amerbach seems to have been responsible for two editions of *De vita* at Basel, c. 1489-1495 and c. 1497.[17] I have collated the text of the more com-

mon c. 1497 edition, whose readings represent a branch of the text which was to lead to that of the *Opera omnia* of 1561 and 1576. In 1529 at Basel, a man named Andreas Leenius prepared a new edition of *De vita*, combining it for the first time with Ficino's *Epidemiarum antidotus*. On the title page Leenius says that he has freed *De vita libri tres* from errors and mold (*De vita libri tres recens iam a mendis situque vindicati*). We are not told on what basis Leenius concluded that the text he had was so corrupt. By thus "correcting" the text, Leenius was responsible for the numerous variants and accretions to the *De vita* text, especially in the rewording of so many chapter titles. The Basel edition of c. 1497, because of a number of similar readings, may have been the copy of the text which Leenius corrupted rather than corrected. These changes in the text were to lead to so many of the corrupt readings in the *De vita* text as printed in the Basel *Opera omnia* editions, which scholars have been forced to use for want of a better, readily accessible text.[18]

As a check on the readings of the first edition, I have also collated the Venice 1498 edition, which represents a text different from the Basel branch yet faithful to the *editio princeps*.[19] Finally, I have collated the text of *De vita* in the *Opera omnia* of Basel 1576, which, though corrupt, has been the standard text for so long.[20]

Manuscript descriptions

L   Florence: Biblioteca Medicea-Laurenziana Plut. 73,39. On parchment; written in early 1490; fols. 173; 260 x 165 (163 x 80) mm. A dedicatory epistle from Filippo Valori to Lorenzo de' Medici (fol. 2; printed in Kristeller *SF* 1: 22). Proem to *De vita libri tres* (fols. 4-5). Proem to *De vita* 1 (fol. 6). *De vita* 1 (fols. 6v-37v). Chapters are not numbered. Proem to *De vita* 2 (fol. 39v). *De vita* 2 (fols. 39v-78r). Chapter 3 is lacking. Proem to *De vita* 3 (fols. 80-81r). *Verba ad Lectorem* is lacking. *De vita* 3 (fols. 81-167v). *Apologia* (fols. 167v-172v). *Quod necessaria sit* . . . (fols. 172v-174v). Verses of Amerigo Corsini (fol. 174v).

There were at least two scribes at work on the manuscript (*pace* Bandini, *Catalogus codicum latinorum Bibliothecae Mediceae Laurentianae* 3 [Florence, 1774-78], p. 74, n. 1). The second scribe is responsible for fols. 40r-49v (*De vita* 2.1-8), with its surprisingly large number of omissions and marginal additions to the text. The second, or possibly a third, scribe is also responsible for fols. 80r-174v (the Proem and text of *De vita* 3). In addition to the corrections to the text made by the original scribes, the hand of a near contemporary corrector can also be identified, although the similarities between the hands do not always permit definite ascription. Although it is a deluxe manuscript, with several folia adorned with elaborate border decorations

and illuminated initials, the text itself is marred by scribal errors, erasures, expunctions, cross-outs, and erroneous variants. The manuscript was executed at the expense of Filippo Valori for Lorenzo de' Medici.[21]

A   Florence: Biblioteca Medicea-Laurenziana Ashburnham 917. On paper; written in the late fifteenth century; fols. 29; 208 x 135 (150 x 85) mm. This manuscript contains the Proem and text of *De vita* 1, followed by (fol. 28) the epistle to Giovanni Cavalcanti (*Op.*, p. 841, 3) and (fol. 29) the epistle to Bernardo Bembo (*Op.*, p. 842, 2).

B   Berlin: Staatsbibliothek lat. fol. 374. On parchment; written in the late fifteenth century; fols. 249; 261 x 169 (170 x 95) mm. *Epistolarum libri I-VII.* fols. 218r-232r: Proem and text of *De vita* 1.

D   Florence: Biblioteca Medicea-Laurenziana Plut. 90 sup. 43. On paper; written in the late fifteenth century; fols. 384; 274 x 210 (190 x 125) mm. *Epistolarum libri I-VII.* fols. 297v-317v: Proem and text of *De vita* 1.

G   Wolfenbüttel: Herzog August Bibliothek, 73 Aug. 2°. On parchment; written in the late fifteenth century; fols. 297; 295 x 200 (195 x 115) mm. *Epistolarum libri I-VII.* fols. 232v-248r: Proem and text of *De vita* 1. The manuscript was executed at the expense of Filippo Valori for Matthias Corvinus, King of Hungary.[22]

R   Florence: Biblioteca Riccardiana 797. On paper; written in the late fifteenth century; fols. 390; 289 x 215 (195 x 129) mm. *Epistolarum libri I-VII.* fols. 339r-361r: Proem and text of *De vita* 1. At the end of Book IV of the *Epistolae* is written (fol. 253v): "Transcripsit manu propria preclarum hoc opus Sebastianus Salvinus amitinus eiusdem Marsilii Ficini philosophi insignis, theologie professor et artium amicitia ad transcribendum ductus." There are several hands, however, at work in the manuscript.

P   Florence: Biblioteca Medicea-Laurenziana Plut. 82,11. On parchment; written in 1490; fols. 411; 349 x 245 (230 x 135) mm. A continuation of manuscript Plut. 82,10, this manuscript contains Ficino's translation and commentary to Plotinus' *Enneads* Books XXVII-LIV (*Enn.* 4.2-6.9). fols. 13r-59r: *De vita* 3. The first chapter of *De vita* 3 is numbered chapter XI, chapters 2-7 receive no numeration, while chapters 8-26 are numbered VIII-XXVI. *P* then has the chapter title, "De descensu animae, Dionysio, Iove, curriculis vitarum, ordine mundi, consonantia universi" (as in *Op.*, p. 1737, although the *Opera* numbers this chapter XI—or rather it should have, instead of the editorial mistake chapter II). *P* then continues: "Revertimur tandem ad interpretationem Plotini continuam et caput aggredimur duodecimum," and the rest as in the *Opera*. fol. 407: "Ego Lucas Marsilii Ficini amanuensis exscripsi hoc opus et finem imposui in agro Caregio die XII. Novembris 1490." The manuscript was executed at the expense of Filippo Valori for Lorenzo de' Medici.

M   Munich: Staatsbibliothek, Clm 10781. On paper; written in the late

fifteenth century; fols. 261; 295 x 220 (195 x 125) mm. fols. 1–100: *Epistolarum libri IX–XII* (although only to *Op.*, p. 949, 2); fols. 101–261: miscellaneous epistles not by Ficino. The following excerpts from *De vita* can be found: Proem to *De vita libri tres* (fols. 17v–19r). *De vita* 1.26 (fols. 99v–100v).[23] Proem to *De vita* 2 (fols. 16r–16v). Proem to *De vita* 3 (fols. 10v–11r). *Verba ad Lectorem*, but only "Salve hospes etc." (fol. 11v). *Apologia* (fols. 19r–22v). *Quod necessaria sit* . . . (fols. 23r–24r).

Manuscripts examined but not included in this edition

H   Haarlem, The Netherlands: Stadsbibliotheek 187C6. On parchment; written in the late fifteenth or early sixteenth century; double columns. fols. 55 = first fascicle. Proem to *De vita libri tres* (fol. 1). Proem to *De vita* 1 (fol. 1v); Table of Contents (fols. 1v–2r); *De vita* 1 (fols. 2r–10v). Proem to *De vita* 2 (fol. 11r); Table of Contents (fol. 11); *De vita* 2 (fols. 11v–22v). Proem to *De vita* 3 (fol. 23r); *Verba ad Lectorem* (fol. 23); Table of Contents (fols. 23v–24r); *De vita* 3 (fols. 24r–48r). *Apologia* (fols. 48v– 49v). *Quod necessaria sit* . . . (fols. 49v–50r). *Principalium sentenciarum Annotatio* (fols. 50v–55r). The second fascicle contains *Nonus Liber Almansoris cum expositione Syllani* [de Nigris] *de Papia*. At the end is read: "Hunc librum comparavit Raphael [de Marcatellis] episcopus Rosensis abbas Sancti Bavonis monasterii iuxta Gandavum."[24]

Mo   Munich: Staatsbibliothek, Clm 26059. On paper; written in 1508; fols. I–V and 320. A miscellaneous collection of alchemical treatises. fol. 277: "Excerpta ex tertio libro Marsilii Phicini Florentini de vita celitus comparanda compositus ab eodem inter commentaria eiusdem in Plotinum." fols. 277r–284v: *De vita* 3, chapters 1, 3, and 4.

Previous editions collated

w   Florence, 3 December 1489 (Antonio Miscomini), *editio princeps*: Table of Contents, an *Errata* page, *De vita libri tres*, and the verses of Amerigo Corsini.[25]

x   Venice, 1498: Title page, Table of Contents, *De vita libri tres*, the verses of Amerigo Corsini, and *Annotatio Praeclarissimarum Sententiarum*.

y   Basel, c. 1497 (Johann Amerbach): Title page, Table of Contents precede each individual book, *De vita libri tres*, and *Annotatio Principalium Sententiarum*.

z   Basel, 1576 (Henricus Petri), *Opera omnia*; reprinted at Turin, 1959: pp. 493–575: *De vita libri tres*. The Proem to *De vita* 1 is lacking.

Translations

In addition to the nearly thirty editions of Ficino's *De vita*, the work was also translated into German, French, and Italian. A German translation of *De vita* 1 and 2 was done by Johannes Adelphus Müling and published at Strassburg in 1505. Wilhelm Kahl and Dieter Benesch have identified seven more editions of this translation, *Das buoch des lebens*, between 1507 and 1537.[26] *De vita* 3 was not translated, probably, according to Kahl, because of its intrinsic difficulties. Kahl was not impressed by the quality of translation of the first two books either.[27] Dieter Benesch has published two further German translations from manuscripts in the Universitätsbibliothek Heidelberg, which he dates to the early sixteenth century. Codex palatinus germanicus 730, fols. 1–35v, contains a translation of *De vita* 1, and Codex palatinus germanicus 452 contains an incomplete translation of *De vita* 2, chapter 1 to the first third of chapter 18.[28]

There are two French translations: one by Jehan Beaufilz (Paris, 1541) of *De vita* 1 and 2,[29] and the other, a complete translation of *De vita*, *Les trois livres de la vie*, by Guy Lefèvre de la Boderie (Paris, 1582).

An Italian translation by Lucio Fauno was published at Venice in 1548 (reprinted at Como in 1969). In spite of its title, *De le tre vite*, it is only a translation of *De vita* 1 and 2. Alessandra Canavero has also identified a reprinted edition of Fauno at Florence in 1568 and an anonymous Italian translation at Milan in 1701.[30] In addition there is an Italian translation of *De vita* 3 contained in a sixteenth-century manuscript at Modena, Biblioteca Estense, cod. Campori 137 (Gamma D 6,24).[31]

Most recently, Charles Boer has attempted an English translation of the entire *De vita*, based on the *Opera omnia* text. For a critical evaluation of his success and failings, see the recent review by the Ficino scholar, Michael J. B. Allen.[32]

Editorial practice

The base text for the present edition is the *editio princeps* of 1489. The readings of the *errata* page prefixed to the 1489 edition have been silently incorporated into the text, except where the original readings coincide with the variants of the manuscripts (usually *L*) or other editions. The text of *De vita* is a strong one, without widely variant readings among the early editions. Among the manuscripts, however, there is some evidence for an earlier version of the text. This is most evident in the five manuscripts which contain *De vita* 1, and for ease of reference in the *apparatus* I have used the letter *e* to signal readings common to all of these manuscripts (*ABDGR*). When Andreas Leenius "corrected"

the edited text in 1529, the number of variant readings increased, and this can best be seen in the numerous variants of the *Opera omnia* text (*z*). Not all variants have been recorded in the *apparatus*, since this would have led to an unnecessarily cumbersome collection of misprints and mistakes. If the variant, however, can be translated and understood or would give the reader a clearer idea of the condition of the alternate text, it has been given. When a variant reading is signalled in the *apparatus*, it can be understood that all the other texts have the reading as printed. On those rare occasions where the reading of the *editio princeps* (*w*) has not been retained or when only one or two of the texts contain the chosen reading, both the accepted and variant text witnesses have been noted in the *apparatus*.

I have attempted to standardize the spelling throughout, although there is no consistency either between or within the manuscripts and editions themselves. This is especially true for the spelling of various herbs. For example, I have consistently printed *gariophylus*, which seems to have been the more usual reading, although such variants as *cariofilus, chariofilus, chariophilus,* and *gariofilus* occur frequently. There seemed to be little advantage in illustrating the range of spellings. The rules I have tried to follow are those of consistency and clarity for the reader. The same rules applied in expanding abbreviations, printing "v" for the consonantal "u" sound, and in consistently spelling words with an "e," "ae," or "oe," although their use was not consistent in the texts. I have also followed the preference in the text for printing "n" for "m" before labials such as "q" or "t," e.g. *tanquam* for *tamquam, duntaxat* for *dumtaxat*. The paragraphing follows that of the *editio princeps* in so far as possible. Since both indentation and blank spacing can be used to indicate a pause or a shift in thought, it is not always clear whether a new paragraph is meant. I have not indicated changes of punctuation, except where a new interpretation is thereby produced. In the margin of the text I give the pagination of the common 1576 *Opera omnia* text.

Principles of Translation

Since we envision the translation not as a substitute for the Latin text but as a companion to it, I have striven for as close a fidelity to the original as is consistent with formal written English, a fidelity which wavers only in the rare case where the result would be obscure or stilted. I have customarily translated, if not word for word, at least phrase for phrase — with the standard exceptions (e.g., breaking up an interminable sentence), the diversification of words of all work like *afficio*, and the condensation of synonyms employed solely for variety. Reduced to a single technical term are Ficino's characteristic elegant variations, e.g., *domus/domicilium/sedes/habitaculum/aedes* to "zodiacal house"

and *domus/plaga* to "place." If a Latin word has a close transliteration in the *Oxford English Dictionary*, be it ever so rare (as in the choice of "euphrasia" over "eyebright"), I have employed it unless (as in the choice of "cashew nut" over "anacard") it has also a perfect equivalent in common use. As a translation of *homo*, *homines*, "person," "people" has been preferred, as being gender-neutral, to the traditional "man," "men."

In particular, the reader should be warned that "spirit" is used in its special medical sense (see Introduction, "Habits of Mind") except in those rare cases where context renders a theological meaning inescapable (e.g., 1.26, passim, and 3.26.91, "deos, id est, spiritus aliquos super homines," p. 571). The air of spookiness about some quotations involving this word, for example in Garin, is no part of Ficino's intention; if anything, he saw himself as demystifying it. In the first book at least, as in Apuleius, and even sometimes in Cicero, *animus* and *anima* are used interchangeably by Ficino (see end of 1 Proem 1, where the phrases "mea . . . anima" and "animus iste meus" are used interchangeably for the very same entity, and note ad loc.). In his own personal Greek-Latin dictionary (on which see below), Ficino lists as translations of Greek *psyche* both *animus* and *anima*. In Book 3, however, Ficino, like Lucretius, distinguishes them;[1] *animus* denotes precisely "mind" and *anima* refers only to the human soul or to its cosmic analogue the Anima Mundi. Once in Book 3, when it is grammatically co-ordinate with a neuter noun (*corpus*) and with an adjective which has to cover both of them, he does slip into *animum* for "soul" (3.4.15, p. 535); but outside of such grammatical-syntactical constraint, he keeps to the careful distinction between mind (there called *mens*) and soul with which Book 3 opens. Our Index lists all instances of *spiritus* as well as *angelus*, *daemon*, and *deus*, and of *animus* as well as *anima*, so that such distinctions can be verified. Conversely, my spelling of "daemon" has retained the *a* throughout simply to avoid prejudging the question of the being's moral allegiance (see "Repercussions"). The word *humor* loses precision in the course of the work, becoming "moisture" or "fluid" in general rather than precisely one or all of the four humors, because they themselves become less important. As Ficino's dictionary again confirms, *mundus* and *mundanus* denote not "earth" and "this-worldly" but "cosmos" and "cosmic," as indeed I have sometimes translated them. The word *ingenium* seems — on contextual evidence such as terms from which it is distinguished, e.g. *memoria* and *sensus*, 1.12.34 — to be employed by Ficino, more often than not, as his standard word for "intelligence."

Translating Ficino reverifies the oft-stated shaping influence of language upon thought. A Cratylan sense of the word as the thing so pervades Ficino's thought as well as language that puns, polyptoton, and etymological fancies are everywhere. If the English sounds far-fetched, it may be rendering some word-play which can be ascertained by checking the Latin. It is with awareness of the anthropomorphic literal meanings that Ficino uses astrological terms such as

aspicio, the verb corresponding to the technical noun "aspect." Ficino affirms that the stars are living eyes (Apologia, 113-14, *Op.*, p. 574); the parallel is more exact in terms of his optics, which conceived vision Platonically as rays emitted from the eye of the beholder. He exploits the etymology of such terms, as Garin observes, for their animistic implications.[2]

In the same vein, although he often distinguishes carefully, as in his use of *spiritus*, Ficino sometimes equivocates. Now *coelum*, *coelestis*, and *coelitus* always refer to the visible heavens; to denote the heaven wherein dwell God, the angels, and the Ideas, he uses the adjective *supercoelestis*. Equivocation creeps in when Ficino downgrades earthly things—such as the "remediis. . . terrenis" in the First Proem to Book 1--only to substitute the equally corporeal *coelestes*. This equivocation is inherent in the Neoplatonic insertion of the *coelestes* as a mezzanine between the two storeys of Plato's universe. As for the translation of it, the French translator of *De vita* often translates it "corps célestes," but Ficino makes clear in several places, as Walker notes (p. 76), that he means the souls of the stars as well; I have therefore preserved the substantive adjective "celestials" in order to remain as noncommittal as Ficino himself. I have consulted this French translation by Guy Lefèvre de la Boderie throughout, with occasional reference to the German translation of Book 1 by Johannes Adelphus Müling and the Italian translation of Books 1 and 2 by Lucio Fauno—all three dating from the sixteenth century (see Clark's "Editorial Introduction") and more or less inaccurate. In addition to the standard dictionaries of classical and medieval Latin, I have consulted the Greek-Latin dictionary which Ficino copied, *Lessico greco-latino: Laur. Ashb. 1439*, ed. R. Pintaudi, Lessico intellettuale europeo, 15 (Rome, 1977); Maria Bruno, *Il lessico agricolo latino*, 2nd ed. (Amsterdam, 1969); and F. Arnaldi and P. Smiraglia, *Latinitatis italicae Medii Aevi lexicon imperfectum*, 1 (Brussels, 1939), 2 (1951-1953), 3 (1957-1964). Doubtless some errors will be found, but at least the presence of both Latin and English texts enables the reader to perfect the translation for himself.

Scope of the Notes

Except in cases of Cimmerian obscurity, we have not undertaken to supply notes which are purely explanatory, since my lengthy Introduction provides a general background study of Ficino's assumptions and doctrines, accompanied there by examples from the text and by bibliographical footnotes, while some necessarily tentative identifications of some individual herbs, foods, and therapeutic substances can be found in our Index of Materia Medica. Instead, we have generally confined our annotations to authors explicitly cited by Ficino—which includes those identified vaguely (e.g., "Arabs") but seldom those

identified simply as "they." We have not been able to locate all of them; when a name has no note, the reader should assume either that we have tried and failed or that the citation is at second-hand within a larger citation which we have identified, as for example, "Brahmans" within a citation from Philostratus, *Vita Apollonii*. In accord with our principle, the Salernitan physicians who are presumed to underlie the prescriptions in Books 1 and 2 receive little attention because they are hardly ever cited by Ficino, and also because these prescriptions have never seemed to warrant such attention. The density of notation on any given chapter or book will increase according to the interest shown in it by the existing secondary literature, the consensus of which it is our job to summarize and evaluate. In 1.1 ff., we have, for example, cited Guaineri even though Ficino does not, in an effort to assess Ficino's originality as a writer on melancholy, to which Guaineri is considered the principal challenger. In Book 3, as well as in the Introduction ("Magic"), we have summarized and verified what is known of his debt to the *Picatrix*, although he never acknowledged it except to his coterie. To extend this practice and trace all the unacknowledged sources and so assess Ficino's overall originality and determine his individual emphases must be the task of future scholars. As Kristeller cautions about such investigations, "Even very specific coincidences are not sufficient unless channels of transmission have been carefully investigated, because they may be due to common or to intermediary sources."[3] Even when Ficino cites someone, we sometimes suspect that it is only at second hand — an irritating medieval and Renaissance practice not unknown in the present day. Roger Bacon seems to be the unacknowledged and perhaps intermediary source, as Clark's notes show, for a good number of the authorities in Book 2.[4] Ficino's documentation is often slanted to lend an air of ancient authority. For citations of Greek authors, for example, Cicero's works often seem to be the unacknowledged yet proximate source.[5] Nevertheless to second-guess him in every case would be an endless task; hence we usually take him at his word and hereby warn the reader of his oversimplification and our own. Nor have we felt obligated always to note all of Ficino's distortions of the sources. An editor should ascertain the validity of his author's own ascriptions before he or another scholar attempts to go beyond them. We have felt obligated to give only book, chapter, and subsection, if any, but not invariably the page; for the editions we have used, see Bibliography. In the case of Ficino, we have consistently cited from the Basel, 1576, *Opera omnia* because it is available to all in facsimile even though better editions of some individual works are available. Even in cross-references within *De vita*, we have given the page numbers of the *Opera omnia* instead of our own so that the citations of it by previous scholars can also be located in our edition and correlated with our citations.

Faced with the insoluble dilemma of annotators as to whether to cite the best modern edition, an edition available to the author, or an edition available

to and legible by most readers, we have attempted to skirt the whole issue by not quoting from the sources at all, giving only chapter and verse as explained above, so that the reader may take his pick of editions and our edition may remain within a practicable size. When, despite this principle, a lengthy quotation is absolutely necessary, in an effort to spare the reader the linguistic hurdles we have endured, we endeavor to confine our languages to Latin or English. Although we cite the Bible according to the now-prevalent Protestant numbering, we have always checked the Vulgate for variations. Almost everything Ficino cites was available to him in a Latin translation, often his own. We will quote the *Picatrix* by way of the German translation (see "Magic"), since Ficino knew no Arabic and whatever Latin version he must have used has not been entirely determined. With the above exceptions, then, our annotations strive for economy.

Indices

The indices to the Latin text include the religious words *deus, daemon,* and *angelus,* along with the psychological words *anima, animus,* and *spiritus.* They also list all proper names of heavenly bodies. We have appended besides an Index of Materia Medica covering all substances not in common use (e.g., human milk and the milk of pigs but not of cows) in order to give medical and scientific historians a handle on the work. In this index, although any identifications are necessarily conjectural, we have appended brief translations. Since it is in English, the Introduction is indexed separately; our notes to the text are not indexed. The contemporary analytical Table of Chapter Headings forms a rudimentary subject-index.

"De vita" in Ficino's Life and Works

The Author in the Work

The standard biography of Ficino is Raymond Marcel, *Marsile Ficin* (Paris, 1958); there is no biography of Ficino in English. The foundation for all biographical studies of Ficino and his circle is Arnaldo della Torre, *Storia dell'Accademia Platonica di Firenze* (Florence, 1902). Less full but by the same token occasionally more helpful is the chapter "Cenni biografici" of Giuseppe Saitta's *Marsilio Ficino e la filosofia dell'Umanesimo,* 3rd ed. (Bologna, 1954). None of these should be used, however, without the indispensable facts supplied by the articles of Kristeller, especially "Per la biografia di Marsilio Ficino," pp. 191ff.,

in his *Studies in Renaissance Thought and Letters* (Rome, 1956) and the biographical sketches and accounts of the genesis of each work in his *Supplementum Ficinianum*. Kristeller's masterful *Philosophy of Marsilio Ficino* (New York, 1943 [rev. ed. in Italian, Florence, 1953, has the fullest apparatus]) proceeds, as its title implies, logically rather than chronologically.

It seems that Ficino wrote *De vita* out of deep personal motives, some of which conflicted not only with his society but with other motives of his own. Some motives and conflicts are announced and some resolved in the prefatory and concluding addresses to various dedicatees and readers. That the author of the *Platonic Theology* should have turned his attention to clysters and opined that "The contemplation is usually as good . . . as is . . . the blood" (1.2.20-22, *Op.*, p. 496) is a surprise which Ficino himself had anticipated. In his opening Proem to the work as a whole, he explains to Lorenzo the Magnificent, his current patron, that after platonizing for so many years, he has decided to write something to repay his father—who had been a doctor and had wanted his son to be one too (*Op.*, p. 493). Diotifeci Ficino of Figline in Valdarno, also called Diotifeci di Agnolo di Giusto, had been "the favorite physician"—so Ficino claims—of Lorenzo's grandfather Cosimo de' Medici.[1] Marsilio says he had two fathers—Diotifeci and Cosimo, his spiritual father in Plato (p. 493)—and in consequence, by implication, two strings to his own bow.

Besides being a Platonist, Ficino was by this time a priest, having been ordained in 1473; why was he involved with medicine in general and with astral magic in particular? One might reply that medieval physicians were usually in at least minor orders; but in Italy, ever since the thirteenth century, doctors had been drawn primarily from the laity.[2] Ficino raised and answered these questions in his Apologia to the three "Pieros" (p. 573). As to medicine, Ficino's theoretical answer is that a priest should serve mankind, and the greatest gift is *mens sana in corpore sano*; moreover, Christ commanded his disciples to heal the sick, an art in which even animals have some skill. As to astrology, it is inextricable from medicine (further documentation in "Traditions," below). As to astral magic, which was to bring *De vita coelitus comparanda* under the censure of the Church, Ficino's overt explanation is that he does not advocate but only reports it in the course of interpreting Plotinus (Apologia, 55-57, p. 573); this claim will be assessed in "Place of *De vita* in the Canon," and "Repercussions," below; in the meantime, we can infer further personal reasons for his choice of medicine, even suspect medicine, as a profession and a theme.

The young Marsilio learned medicine, along with Aristotelian philosophy, from Niccolo Tignosi of Foligno, a professor at the University of Florence where Ficino got most of his formal education. The apparently interdisciplinary coverage of two subjects by this one professor reflects the close connection between medicine and Aristotelian philosophy in the Italian university.[3] It thus helps to explain Marsilio's combination of medicine with philosophy. In the earliest

dated composition from his pen, he gives his address as Santa Maria Nuova, which was the largest hospital of Florence; from this, Kristeller (tentatively) and Marcel (confidently) infer that not only his father but he himself had a professional connection there.[4] Although both *De vita* and the early biographies make it clear that he practiced, there is no evidence that he ever took his medical degree or, aside from the questionable report of his biographer Corsi, that he ever went to the University of Bologna for these or any other studies.[5] Another friend who must have influenced Ficino towards medicine, as Zanier suggests, was Pierleone Leoni of Spoleto, a physician consulted by Lorenzo de' Medici. Like Ficino he was "curiosissimus" in his learning, to which end he accumulated a rich library in which Ficino could have read such authors as the Arabic physicians and Ramon Lull.[6] Ficino borrowed a book of occult science, the *Picatrix*, from one Georgio Medico, conjecturally identified by Delcorno Branca as that Dr. George the Cyprian to whom Ficino wrote various letters and who was recorded in the *Commentary* on the *Timaeus*.[7] Another medical mentor must have been Matteo Aretino. On 29 April 1490, Ficino asks anxiously for his medical evaluation of *De vita* and his recommendation of him to other physicians (*Op.*, p. 909,2). In a letter in praise of medicine, he salutes in particular one Galileo,[8] Lorenzo Martellini, Tommaso Valeri the addressee, and Antonio Benivieni (*Op.*, p. 646).

Ficino also aims to help those of his own calling—men of letters—to keep their health (1 Proem 1 and 1.1). Similarly, in directing Book 2 to prolongation of life for the elderly, he focuses on what he felt to be his own age-group ("myself already old," 2.14.4, p. 520). To be precise, he had then not quite turned fifty-six.

Ficino's ominous horoscope

Ficino had a very bad horoscope. I believe this accounts in part not only for his peculiar adaptations but for his occasional rejection of astrology, as in the unfinished, unpublished *Disputatio contra iudicium astrologorum* (*SF*, 2: 11–76) and the letter on astrology to Poliziano (*Op.*, p. 958). A person with a bad horoscope could hardly be casual and lukewarm towards astrology: he would have to either reinterpret it to give him some hope or else deny it outright. One letter, that to Preninger already cited for Ficino's age, gives Ficino's complete horoscope and then talks about *De vita*. Moreover, just as this horoscope was sent in answer to an inquiry by Preninger, so, he continues, the *De vita* was assembled and indeed partly written (Book 2) in answer to another inquiry of his (p. 901,2). In Ficino's mind, at least at that moment, *De vita* was associated with his own Saturnine horoscope.

Perhaps because of certain inconsistencies, no Ficino scholar has so far ex-

plored Ficino's horoscope in any detail and in the light of his own astrological views. I can at least make a beginning; for the astrological terms and concepts I will employ, see "Traditions," below. Ficino was born, as he reveals to Preninger, in what he estimates to have been the twenty-first hour of 19 October 1433 (p. 901,2). Diotifeci, for all he was a doctor, had failed to record the hour, so that Ficino had to go by "verba" of his parents—meaning presumably subsequent reminiscences, since they both lived into Marsilio's middle life (Diotifeci died in 1477 or 1478, and the mother Alessandra lived almost as long as Marsilio). The twenty-first hour, counted from sunset of 18 October, would be between 2:00 and 3:00 p.m.; not only this but the position of the Sun "in the ninth place" proves that his was a daytime nativity,[9] for the ninth place is by definition quite high in the sky. Strangely enough, Ficino ignores the traditionally considerable power of his Sun-sign (Scorpio) presumably because in his figure the ascendant outweighs it. He estimates that Saturn was just rising and that it was in Aquarius, one of its two planetary houses. In common parlance, he was born under Saturn. Saturn is therefore his "Significator" (Letter of 7 November 1492, to Filippo Valori, *Op.*, p. 948), and Saturn in Aquarius "the Lord of the figure"—that is, the most dignified planet in the sky at the moment (Letter to Pico, *Op.*, p. 888). Saturn thus wielded a double power over him, since just Aquarius in the ascendant was enough, in Ficino's book, to make one Saturnine (for that was all Plato had, and Plato was Saturnine, *Op.*, p. 763).

Another letter—that to his great friend, the young Giovanni Cavalcanti—while less complete, is more revealing in that it isolates all the features in his horoscope which he deplored:

> Saturn seems to have impressed the seal of melancholy on me from the beginning; set, as he is, almost in the midst of my ascendant Aquarius, he is influenced by Mars, also in Aquarius, and the Moon in Capricorn. He is in square aspect to the Sun and Mercury in Scorpio, which occupy the ninth house. But Venus in Libra and Jupiter in Cancer have, perhaps, offered some resistance to this melancholy nature.[10]

Besides being himself in a powerful position, Saturn received the Moon in Capricorn, one of his houses, and Mars in Aquarius, his other house, which last is to say that the Greater Infortune received the Lesser.[11] Incidentally, the reference to Mars in the Preninger letter (p. 901,2) also requires some elucidation. "Martem in eodem [scilicet Aquario] carcerem duodecima tenuisse" is an elliptical way of saying that Mars was in the twelfth place or mundane house which signifies prisons according to Ficino's authorities (see 1.7.45, *Op.*, p. 499 and n.5); Mars could be already in the twelfth place, not the first, be-

cause he was in that half of Aquarius which had already risen ("ascendisse tunc Aquarium ferme medium," *Op.*, pp. 901,2). The Lesser Infortune also dominates Ficino's nativity in more ways than he mentions: Mars received the Sun and Mercury into one of *his* houses—Scorpio—and had the Part of Fortune in his other house—Aries.[12] As Ficino complains, the Sun and Mercury in Scorpio in the ninth place formed a quartile aspect with Saturn and presumably also with Mars in Aquarius. Any quartile aspect is malefic (though Ptolemy calls it simply discordant), and this double one is called, Saitta informs us, the "Tetragono della Morte."[13] Elsewhere, though in a polemical context, Ficino cheers up and interprets favorably Saturn's role in his nativity.[14]

On the brighter side, says Ficino to Cavalcanti, Venus in Libra and Jupiter in Cancer mitigate Saturn's influence towards melancholy. Venus and Jupiter comprise, along with the usually beneficent Sun, the "Three Graces" or good planets, as Ficino metonymizes them in *De vita* 3.5 *et passim*. If Ficino were correct, they would have been dignified in that Libra is one of the houses of Venus, and Cancer is the exaltation of Jupiter.[15] His facts are wrong here, as he seems later to have realized, but he has hold of a cheering principle. In the Letter to Preninger (*Op.*, p. 901,2), written some time after that to Cavalcanti, Ficino says correctly that Venus was in Virgo and Jupiter in Leo. Even in Leo, however, I propose that Jupiter was still mitigating, for he then opposed Saturn in Aquarius, and Ficino says in *De vita*, "When you fear Mars, set Venus opposite; when you fear Saturn, use Jupiter."[16] Venus in this account also seems to be vocationally favorable in that she was received by Mercury in Virgo; for Ptolemy says that a combination of these planets produces doctors who employ drugs in their treatments. While this auspice is unnoticed here, awareness of it and obsession with his own horoscope seem to have prompted Ficino's exaggerated claim in *De vita* that "Venus herself according to astrologers gives birth equally to the musician and the doctor."[17] But what of the other beneficent planets? Mercury, a planet normally favorable to intellectuals,[18] and the Sun, who "rejoices in the ninth place"[19] were apparently nullified by their maleficent aspect.

Ficino's melancholy

As to its particular content, much of *De vita* (especially of Book 1) is devoted to how one can live with the once-feared melancholy temperament and with the concomitant and once-feared influence of the planet Saturn. This preoccupation, though mingled with other standard topics, is so unusual as to strike a personal note. Not only by age and nativity, as shown above, but by profession and temperament, Ficino was himself Saturnine and melancholic. Still more unusual, and hence more likely to arise from personal concern, are the

claims that Saturn and melancholy are good. This tremulously positive emphasis, coupled with the evidence of the letters, points to a veritable "obsession," as Seznec puts it,[20] with his own melancholy complexion and Saturnine horoscope. On the positive side, some of the remedies for and benefits of a Saturnine temperament according to *De vita* are also adumbrated in the letters, particularly in Ficino's interchange with Cavalcanti (pp. 731–33) in which the younger friend is undoubtedly parroting for the older some of his own ideas. Among the many remedies for Saturn in *De vita*, two which are adumbrated in Ficino's own personal life, as shown in the correspondence, are the influence of Jupiter discussed above, and music.[21] In the ultimate analysis, however, say Klibansky, Panofsky, and Saxl, "the Saturnine man can do nothing . . . better" than to embrace his fate and make the best of it.[22]

The best of Saturn, both in the correspondence and in *De vita*, is that it imparts to the native that natural melancholy which is a determinant of genius: "I see you are again, not unjustly, urging me to sing another hymn of recantation to Saturn," Ficino grumbles to Cavalcanti; "I shall in agreement with Aristotle say that this nature itself is a unique and divine gift." "Aristotle" here is the Pseudo-Aristotle of *Problem* 30.1, which was Ficino's authority for his famous, original, and extended praise of melancholy in *De vita* (esp. 1.6). Already in the *Platonic Theology* (finished in 1474), melancholy had come in for mild praise as facilitating prophecy (13.2, *Op.*, pp. 287, 294). His optimism momentarily supported by tradition, Cavalcanti reminds Ficino that his tenacious memory is from Saturn. Again, Saturn's height above all planets, praised in these and other terms in *De vita* (1.6.23, *Op.*, p. 498; 3.22.65, *Op.*, p. 565) is what makes him excel other men. By analogy with the great age of the god Saturn and his rulership over the Golden Age, Ficino's horoscope fostered, or at least foretold, his revival of the uncorrupted ancients.[23] Cavalcanti mentions also the encouraging "fact," which Ficino elsewhere claims to have learned only recently from Firmicus Maternus (p. 763), that Plato too was Saturnine (p. 732, see also pp. 888, 928).

At a more fundamental level, Cavalcanti denies from the start that any planet can have an evil influence inasmuch as the planets are minds acting out the will of God who is our Father. Ficino will affirm this optimistic view, with some inconsistency, in *De vita* 3.3, p. 534, just as he will endorse it when expressed by Plotinus in *Ennead* 3.1, p. 1609, even though Plotinus is employing it against, not for, astrology. As Klibansky, Panofsky, and Saxl put it, the revealing interchange with Cavalcanti (undated, but placed by them in the mid–70s) seems to mark "the moment at which the views of Proclus and Aristotle" on Saturn, voiced by Cavalcanti, "began [however intermittently] to prevail in his mind against the [negative] views of the medieval astrologers" (p. 256). Accordingly *De vita*, while mentioning Saturn's maleficence as a necessary evil, comes down on the positive side. Although the work represents a single and a different side of Ficino, it was not without foundation in his own personality.

The value and influence of Ficino's doctrine of melancholy

Besides being the first treatise on the health of intellectuals, *De vita* was the first work to give the Platonic notion of the four noble *furores* — itself restored to the West almost singlehandedly by Ficino[24] — a medical basis in the melancholic humor or black bile. What precisely was Ficino's contribution to the theory and the literature of melancholy? Admittedly, his entire idea could be seen as merely an extension of the view that the best temperament consists of a due measure of all four humors. Its germ existed already in the Ps.-Aristotelian *Problem* 30.1, but in the Middle Ages this work had generally been misinterpreted or ignored, except by Pietro d'Abano, Ficino's acknowledged predecessor in the theory and practice of magic (see "Repercussions"). The Middle Ages brought two other notable developments: melancholy received a full-length treatise transmitted to the West by Constantinus Africanus, but one which failed to see in it any particular good for intellectuals;[25] and the melancholy of the lover, along with his other symptoms, attracted considerable attention, some of which was at least sympathetic, as, for example, when the term, "the loverys maladye of hereos" was etymologized as "of heroes," thus connecting the malady with greatness. Moving closer to Ficino in time and spirit, Petrarch both thought of himself as an intellectual and complained of melancholy; but he called it by the traditional name of a vice, *ac(c)edia* or *ac(c)idia*, and so serves only as subject, not as analyst. In the Renaissance, Guaineri, citing *Problem* 30.1, had found that melancholy facilitates inspiration by suspending the senses in an ecstasy.[26] All this is but to say that *De vita*, like many another cultural milestone, did but prompt the age to a turn it was already about to make anyway. Ficino's announcement that it sometimes helps to be a little crazy, backed by his now-established reputation, came as a manifesto of liberation. It broke down the hierarchy of the faculties by emphasizing the contribution of the subrational. It thereby established, for one thing, our notion of the temperamental genius and thus — even though the visual artist may not yet have qualified as an "intellectual"[27] — enhanced our understanding and appreciation of the artistic sensibility. The perhaps overripe fruit of this appreciation was the Romantic exaltation of the artist as hero.

Within its own tradition and period, *De vita* further extended and popularized humoral psychology as a way of sorting out mankind's infinite variety. The Renaissance extension of melancholy into a state of heightened sensitivity opened a new country of the mind for lyric exploration, much as the doctrine of romantic love had done at an earlier period. *De vita* played a great part in this extension, particularly by being the first treatise to reason medically at any length about the paradoxically positive intellectual value of melancholy. In the visual arts, *De vita* influenced the iconography of the four temperaments, particularly that of melancholy, through Dürer's famous engraving, *Melencolia I*. Insofar as Dürer's personification is an intellectual, she goes back to Ficino.[28]

The theme of melancholy in English literature—though it is not the most striking influence of *De vita*, and it gets short shrift from Klibansky, Panofsky, and Saxl—yet holds most interest for English-language readers. England's acceptance of this, as of many another continental trend, was filtered through her characteristic pragmatism. A medical work by Ficino—which could only be *De vita* or his plague-tract or the pair of them, often so printed—is listed in a 1570 catalogue of an English doctor's library. Ficino's translation of the "Platonici," meaning chiefly Iamblichus, Proclus, Synesius, and Psellus, was popular in England.[29] *De vita* must have been associated with them, for it was once (Venice, 1516) printed in its entirety (*pace* the title-page) with them; and its third book was composed immediately after them, and borrowed from them, as we shall see. Of the five Englishmen Jayne mentions as owing a considerable and demonstrable debt to Ficino (namely, Colet, Spenser, Chapman, Raleigh, and Burton),[30] Burton's *Anatomy of Melancholy* is the true heir and English counterpart of our treatise. Burton lists "Ficinus" as his model as a writer of a treatise on melancholy (1.1.3.sub.3). Throughout, he gives a Ficinian degree of emphasis to patients who are scholars (e.g., just above, sub. 2). Granting that Burton revels in citations, it is nevertheless remarkable that in the first quarter of their edition, Dell and Jordan-Smith find eight references to Ficino, after which they throw up their hands with an *et cetera*.[31] Generally speaking, "Ficinus" means *De vita*, Books 1 and 2 being cited by the title *De sanitate tuenda* (1.2.3.sub.15), and Book 3 (as such), not at all. On the subject of love-melancholy, which *De vita* largely ignores,[32] it means the *Commentary* on the *Symposium*.

English treatises on melancholy before Burton include: Timothy Bright, *A Treatise of Melancholy* (1586); Nicholas Breton, *Melancholike Humours* (1600); Samuel Rowlands, *Democritus, or Doctor Merry-man his Medicines Against Melancholy Humours* (1607). Moving over into belletristic literature, one encounters as local embodiments Hamlet, Jaques in *As You Like It*, and the "Melancholic Man" in the Overburian *Characters*. Besides the *Anatomy*, the major English belletristic works obviously written in the melancholic tradition are Marston's *Malcontent* and Milton's *Il Penseroso*.[33] Still farther downstream from Ficino are Young's *Night Thoughts*, Gray's *Elegy Written in a Country Churchyard*, James Thomson's *City of Dreadful Night*, and Keats's "Ode to Melancholy." In the untimely dead poetess of *Huckleberry Finn*, the melancholy character and sensibility are parodied to death. It would have amused her creator to know that the inauspicious horoscope of a baby born in 1433 had prompted the fad.

The Place of "De vita" in the Canon

De vita was adumbrated by some of Ficino's works, especially his first works and those of the years immediately preceding it. Ficino had recently published

one medical work: the brief and, as its vernacular language implies, eminently practical *Consiglio contro la pestilenza* (Florence, 1481). *De vita* refers back to it and was sometimes published with it. Like *De vita*, it too was avowedly written out of an immediate, though not a personal, medical circumstance — the plague which ravaged Florence from 1478 to 1480 (chap. 2, *Op.*, p. 577, and last sentence of chap. 3, p. 578). Although Ficino has recently been charged with unworldliness, he ventured for these few years into another and more practical discipline because it was one which his community needed. The translator of the *Consiglio* into Latin, in which form alone it appears in the Basel *Opera omnia*, subjoins that Ficino cured many on that occasion (p. 473, misnumbered for 576). Such success must have encouraged Ficino to attempt a second medical work, *De vita sana*, later known as *De vita* 1. Except for protests that it was difficult to understand and that the well-tempered melancholy was as hard to locate as was Plato's Republic, no fault seems to have been found in it, and readers such as Preninger began pressing him for a sequel.[1] None of the censure which subsequently attached to *De vita* 3, as we shall see, ever followed *De vita sana*.

The canon includes many translations and commentaries which are doubly significant both as sources and as siblings of this strange work. For example, another and concurrent work with which *De vita* 3 claims the most intimate connection is the *Commentary* on Plotinus. Indeed, if we may believe Ficino's defensive protestations, he follows Plotinus so closely that his own views are not accurately represented and whatever blame or merit there may be in the book attaches to Plotinus not to him. After the composition of Book 1 and during that of Book 3, Ficino was indeed writing his commentary on the *Enneads*. Repeatedly, Book 3 claims to be nothing more than an extract from a commentary on a certain part of it entitled by Ficino, "De favore coelitus hauriendo."[2] Indeed, Ficino's title *De vita coelitus comparanda* imitates the alleged Plotinian title in syntactic pattern and use of the adverb *coelitus*. Some confusion has arisen from the fact that these precise words never appear either in Ficino's translation of Plotinus or in his commentary. Yet we agree with Kristeller and Garin that "De favore coelitus hauriendo" means *Ennead* 4, Book 3, chap. 11. Textual research by Kristeller and Clark has shown that it is on this chapter that *De vita* 3 appears — almost in its entirety, yet with its first six chapters in an obviously earlier state — as a commentary within one MS of Ficino's commentary on Plotinus. I would highlight three further facts. As can be seen from the textual variants in this MS, which Clark labels *P*,[3] the title of Ficino's *Commentary* on *Ennead* 4.3.11, which of course exists as such only there, represents an early version of the title of *De vita* 3.1: "In quo consistat virtus magici operis et imaginum scilicet in eo quod anima mundi," etc., exactly as in 3.1. The unanimity of authorial claim and manuscript evidence is compelling. Secondly, in Ficino's own translation of Plotinus, the marginal title which

Ficino appends to 4.3.11, while not identical, at least leans in the direction of *De vita* 3 in general and 3.1 in particular: "Magica trahit vim proprie ab anima mundi, Diisque mundanis, per haec a superioribus" (second comma mine). Finally, in 3.26, in a passage to be discussed below, the statue-animating passage in the *Asclepius* is said to have formed in its turn the lemma which Plotinus "imitatus est" in "De favore coelitus hauriendo," and Plotinus discusses the animation of statues only in 4.3.11.

In Ficino's eyes, the principal subject of the Plotinian chapter was the animated statues, to which he alludes not in 3.1, for a reason to be explained later, but in chapters 13 and 26. Plotinus does not elsewhere so explicitly advocate the magic of artificial signs or representations, confining himself to natural things, or if artificial, then to prayers, music, and dancing (though there are two mentions of "figures" in 4.4.40). To the chapter seen in this light, Yates and Garin have no trouble finding conceptual parallels in *De vita* 3. Ficino's syncretizing mind saw the statues as evidence of the efficacy of their portable counterparts, figurate astrological talismans, with which Ficino becomes obsessed later in the book (Yates, p. 66). Garin identifies Plotinus's first sentence as the theme of Ficino's entire third book: "And it seems to me that those of the ancient wise men who used to seek the presence of the gods by setting up shrines and statues, rightly observed the very nature of the universe. By this they expressed the opinion that the nature of Soul, although it is everywhere tractable, is then most prone and easy to be led and can be captured most easily of all, if one fashion something easily capable of experiencing it and by experiencing, of sharing some portion of it."[4] Yates prefers to construct conceptual parallels between the overall content of Plotinus's chapter and Ficino's first chapter alone (pp. 64–65). This is less credible in that, first, she has to reverse the order of the points, and second, neither the statues nor any figures made by man are specifically mentioned in 3.1, only natural things. A problem for either scholar is that after 3.1, aside from the animated statues in chapter 13 and a mirror analogy in 3.17, Ficino fails to touch this lemma for 25 chapters, beginning chapter 26 with "But lest we digress too long from interpreting Plotinus, which is what we started to do in the beginning . . . " (*Op.*, p. 570). There are, of course, scattered echoes of the adjacent chapters 10 and 12.

A suggestion which Walker developed from KP&S helps to fill the gap mentioned above. On grounds of the striking similarities in content, Walker suggested that *Enn.* 4.4.30–42 was both the lemma of *De vita* 3 (p. 3, n. 2) and its source (p. 14, n. 5).[5] Indeed, it is a text to which *De vita* might more appropriately have been attached. (Other scholars would start the alleged lemma as early as chapter 26 and end it as late as the last chapter, 45.) That Ficino seldom sticks to his lemma is illustrated by his *Commentary* on the *Philebus*.[6] In this case, all these facts can be accounted for by saying that Ficino jumped to *Ennead* 4.4.26 ff. (as I will hereafter designate the disputed beginning of the

relevant passage) as a source from which to elaborate the magic in his lemma, 4.3.11. For whatever it is worth, his own commentary on 4.4.26-44 contains both a long and largely unprovoked exposition of the medical spirits and their cosmic analogue (on 26, cf. *De vita* 1.2-6, and passim, on which see "Habits," below), and a reference to seminal reasons causing occult qualities in magical substances (on 35, 37, cf. *De vita* 3.1) but nothing else very similar to *De vita* 3.

Ficino's repeated claim to be merely interpreting Plotinus is a complex one, in that, first, the line between commentaries and original works was blurred. Generally helpful is Heitzmann's summary of the whole *Commentary* on Plotinus of which *De vita* once formed a part: it is a commentary not so much on the *Enneads* themselves as on the successive problems broached therein.[7] So congenial to medieval man was the commentary as a literary form that Dante — whose work Ficino knew, translated (the *De monarchia*), and used — had cast an original work, the *Vita nuova*, as a commentary on his own poems. Augustine, one of Ficino's favorite authors, had concluded his famous *Confessions* with a commentary, first, on another commentary (*Conf.* 10-11 on Macrobius's *Commentary* on the *Somnium Scipionis*) and then on the opening chapters of Genesis (*Conf.* 12-13). No one would discount as unficinian a statement in the famous *Commentary* on the *Symposium*; hence Ficino should not have hoped to dissociate himself from *De vita* 3 on the grounds that it is a commentary.

That Ficino's entire claim to be merely interpreting Plotinus is to some extent a pose, becomes clear from their respective treatments of magic and astrology. Neither subject got much respect from Plotinus, and the interest he had in astrology, though greater than that in magic, was often condemnatory (e.g., *Enn.* 3.2). Ficino realized this, for he incorporated into his commentary on such parts of Plotinus (e.g., pp. 1525-26) material from his unpublished treatise *against* astrology (e.g., *SF*, 2: 48-49). On the whole, Plotinus condemned any astrology which, like Ficino's in *De vita*, treats particular stars as causes or influences, deriding genethlialogy with its cardines, dignities, aspects, and attribution of malice to certain planets, and acknowledging only cumulative sidereal forces contributing to and signifying large-scale, not personal, events.[8] Unlike Ficino, he denies the ability of daemonic magic to drive out diseases (2.9) on the grounds that since their aetiology is material, their cure should be so too.[9] Ficino's unusual insertion of a world-spirit analogous to our medical spirits between the World-soul and matter represents his personal addition to Plotinus. Plotinus's references to our astral body or vehicle (ὄχημα) may imply something like a medical spirit in us (*Enn.* 4.3.9; 4.3.15; 4.7.14); but most of his references to πνεῦμα, those falling in 4.7-8, serve only to combat the notion of spirit as originally formulated by the Stoics (see "Habits").[10] Plotinus's contribution was more to the Neoplatonic framework: what is essentially Plotinian in Book 3 is not the actual details of the astrology and magic but the underlying presuppositions and one proximate aim, the aim of

realigning ourselves through the stars and the seminal reasons into that planetary series which we want to join or participate in more fully. All in all, *De vita* 3 is a commentary on *Enneads* 4.3.11 in Ficino's acceptation of the word; it is a coherent scholarly essay "updating" ancient Neoplatonic magic and redirecting it to the practical end of medicine.

Just as Book 1 resembled an immediately preceding work in its medical genre, so Book 3 resembles immediately preceding works in theme. Ficino had been tending toward magic and toward what we now call occult science at least as early as 1488 in his translations of the "Platonici," embracing chiefly Iamblichus, *De mysteriis Ægyptiorum* (*Op.*, pp. 1873 ff.); Proclus, *De sacrificio et magia* (pp. 1928-29); Synesius, *De somniis* (pp. 1968 ff.); and Psellus, *De daemonibus* (pp. 1939 ff.). Copies of the first three are mentioned as accompanying the letter to Preninger about *De vita* of 1489 (p. 901,2). On grounds such as these, Kristeller conjectures that they were all done in 1488, though they were not published until 1497 (*SF*, 1: 132 ff.). All four are cited in *De vita* (see our Index). Like all Neoplatonists, these authors believed in daemons—good, bad, and indifferent, and they communicated their belief to Ficino, who in the earlier Book 1 had used "demon" only once (1.6.34) and in the orthodox bad sense. Much of the daemonic magic which Ficino tries to father upon Plotinus is really drawn, explicitly or implicitly, from these more occult Neoplatonists. The difficult opening passage of Book 3, while reminiscent of *Enneads* 4.3.11 as announced, also follows very closely Synesius, *De insomniis* (3.1, p. 531, and n. ad loc.). The very essence of Proclus's opusculum *De sacrificio* (pp. 1928-29) is reflected in *De vita* 3 not only in the animated statues but in the pervasive notion, exemplified already in the latter part of 3.1, of mixing into one compound related things which are weak in isolation so as to concentrate their astrological efficacy.[11] Like Ficino, these "Platonici" advocated images, but for theurgy—alluring gods into sensible forms the better to worship them; except for divination, a goal which Ficino mentions but disavows in *De vita* (3.26), they scorned materialistic ends such as the bodily health at which Ficino aimed.[12] Other sources such as Al-Kindi, the *Picatrix*, and to some extent the *Chaldean Oracles*, while likewise employing worship as a technique, will account for Ficino's practical aims. The presence of Plotinus and these authors whom he had just translated characterizes Book 3 as a *Medicina Platonica* based on Neoplatonic doctrines of forms, seminal reasons, and the World-soul (KP&S, p. 262).

The *Corpus Hermeticum* was the first work which the young Ficino translated for Cosimo. This collection plus the already translated and recognized Hermetic *Asclepius* formed the original inspiration (or so Yates has argued) for *De vita coelitus comparanda*. They lay down a world-view favorable to magic and astrology and express, as Plotinus does not, that notion of a cosmic spirit through which Ficino was to legitimize both. Besides being cited in his own right,

Hermes was closely connected with Plotinus in Ficino's mind; Ficino judged his Plotinian lemma "De favore coelitus hauriendo" (*Enn.* 4.3.11) to be itself expatiating upon the animated statues of *Asclepius* 24 and 37, so that Ficino's commentary on the former is also, and even more so, a commentary on the latter (*De vita* 3.26). Whether anything else in the *Hermetica*, especially in those Hermetic *logia* translated by Ficino, exercised much of an influence on *De vita*, is currently being debated.[13] It is interesting to note that *Asclepius* 37 had been condemned as heretical by St. Augustine (*DCD* 8.23-24). I quote the statue-animating passage of *Asclepius* 37 in my section entitled "Magic."

Another early work which *De vita* recalls in two parts — Zambelli would say, in its whole conception of magic — is the famous *Commentary* on the *Symposium*, which we know to have been substantially composed in 1469 (Marcel, *MF*, p. 336), although it was not published until the *Platonis opera* in 1484. First, like *De vita* 1.2-6, it says that melancholic blood is always accompanied by fixed and profound thought (7.7); and in a similar vein, that the melancholy lover, though hard to catch, is the most constant (7.9). The humor black bile and the medical spirits are prominent in Ficino's explanation of why the lover is dry, that is, melancholy. A complexion that is naturally melancholy (7.3) facilitates love, be it of the carnal or the contemplative type, and the latter can be one of the four divine frenzies which lift the soul to God. In the *Theologia Platonica*, too, two other divine frenzies, those of poetry and prophecy, are also facilitated by melancholy (13.2, ed., 2: 202-3; 219, *Op.*, p. 287).

Second, the beautiful description of cosmic love as a magician in *De vita* 3.26 (p. 570), clearly echoes *Commentary* on the *Symposium* 6.10 and of course its lemma in the *Symposium*, 203c, along with *Enn.* 4.4.40.[14] Ficino is also adapting: whereas in his early work, the cosmic love, like the human love, was a spiritualized homosexual one of like-for-like, in *De vita* he has made the love one of heterosexual opposites which lasciviously attract. The pairs given in both — the Moon and the tides, the lodestone and iron, etc. — being unlike, lend themselves better to his later, heterosexual metaphor; indeed, the later passage is on all counts the more evocative. Ficino's later version may have been influenced by the speech of Eryximachus earlier in the *Symposium*, 186a-188e, in which cosmic love unites opposites. I would add that, in both passages, it is a love of one part of the world for another, not, as in Dante's famous formulation, the love of a part, the Primum Mobile, for God (*Par.* 33). It may have been his analogy of cosmic to biological love (3.26, p. 570) which endeared to Ficino the notion (ultimately Stoic, also found in Plotinus[15]) that everything — even stones (3.3, p. 535) but especially the heavens — is alive; for it is difficult to picture a being which has no life as loving and generating (cf. *Phil MF*, Index, s.v. "Analogy"). A notion which one misses in *De vita*, if one comes to it fresh from Ficino's *Commentary* on the *Symposium*, is his famous rediscovery, the doctrine of "platonic love," the idea that affection between two friends — a non-

orgasmic love of the sort he attributed to Plato and experienced with Giovanni Cavalcanti—can be spiritually uplifting. Nor does the related notion of love-melancholy ever come up. In view of the fact that other medical writers such as Guaineri had included it along with other manifestations of the disease, its absence is perhaps symptomatic of his old age. Ficino may have felt that he had already diagnosed and cured it in the *Commentary* on the *Symposium*; but this would not have stopped him, for he had a penchant for self-reference and self-quotation. In picturing the beneficent *furores*, which Ficino briefly endorses in *De vita* (1.5, our nn. 4–5), Ficino may tacitly have substituted, as he sometimes did elsewhere, that of the philosopher for that of the less relevant lover. While doctor and patient are supposed to love each other, while cosmic love in 3.26 is ardent and titillating, personal eros in *De vita* is physical and, as such, inadvisable for scholars and generally placed on the level of the bodily functions—permissible in its procreative place and in moderation. Only the latter form of love, when it oversteps these restrictions, is associated with melancholy in *De vita*, and then only by the grossest physical causes (1.7). *De vita's* relative silence about love may be explained by Kristeller's remark that in Ficino's early life the bridge which reconciles distant planes of the universe is love, whereas in the late works, the bridge is Soul, as we see it is in *De vita* 3.1 (*Phil MF*, pp. 106–20, esp. pp. 114–15).

Earlier still, the synthesis of a Platonic with a materialistic outlook in *De vita* as a whole is adumbrated by the young Ficino's interest in the *Timaeus*. Ficino and others state in works datable around 1457 that he has already written something on the *Timaeus*. Marcel thinks this refers to an early draft of the *Commentary* on the *Timaeus*,[16] even though the published form contains allusions to works so late as *De vita*. The chronological priority of this dialogue in Ficino's work hints at another answer to the question with which our biography began. When thrown off balance by a remark such as "The contemplation is generally as good as is the blood," the Ficino scholar should recall that the Platonism Ficino imbibed in his youth was of course medieval and therefore Timaeic (the *Timaeus* being the major dialogue to have received in the Middle Ages a translation both fairly complete and widely current), and that the *Timaeus* is more materialistic and deterministic than Plato's other works, anticipating Ficino, for example, in saying one can have a *mens sana* only *in corpore sano* (86b–87b). From this point of departure, Renaissance Neoplatonism retains a qualified respect for the material world belied by the rest of Plato's *oeuvre*. It thus dignified many worldly pursuits: for example, in its Timaeic doctrine of a beneficent but somewhat autonomous World-soul, it cleared a place for the study of the world's body or natural science.[17]

When all is said and done, *De vita* remains a surprising work; anticipations such as we have noticed only render it credible in retrospect.[18] In nothing is it more surprising than in the fact that it largely contradicts both scattered anti-

astrological remarks and letters and an entire, albeit unfinished and unpublished, treatise, the *Disputatio contra iudicium astrologorum*, or *Disputation against Judicial Astrology*.[19] For this anomaly, I have already assigned a biographical cause, and I will partially explain it in the section "Repercussions" below.

Traditional Material and Innovations

In *De vita* Ficino both accepted and transformed at least two traditions. The doctrine of the four humors underlies the first half of the work; astrology underlies the last. Ficino had learned from Aristotle, Galen, and his own experience that astrology is an indispensable part of medicine.[1] It may therefore be useful to review these older thought-patterns; readers already familiar with them may wish to skip to "Magic." Both medicine and astrology depended to some extent upon the notion of the four cosmic elements and their attendant qualities. The four humors in the body were seen as corresponding to, and thus sympathetically interacting with, the four elements and those qualities of which both sets were made: blood was connected with air and the qualities warm and moist; choler, also called red or yellow bile, with fire as warm and dry; black bile or black choler with earth as cold and dry; and phlegm with water as cold and moist. As C. S. Lewis notes,[2] another pair of elemental qualities, heavy versus light, was sometimes mentioned. Although Ficino predicates this pair of "substance" (in the sense of "consistency," the proportion of matter in a thing's makeup) rather than of "quality" and rephrases it as "dense" or "gross" versus "subtle," "tenuous," or "rare," it is very important to him (e.g., 3.2, *Op.*, p. 534). The proportion in which the humors are blended differed from one individual to another and constituted his "temperament" or "complexion." Thus the words "sanguine," "choleric," "melancholic," and "phlegmatic" came to denote peculiar, but not necessarily morbid, aspects of human physiology and thence also psychology (KP&S, p. 12). They also correlated respectively with the four seasons: spring, summer, autumn, and winter. Attempts to line them up with the stages of life were frequent, though less neat: the sanguine temperament always characterized youth, the melancholic an age past one's prime (KP&S, p. 10). Some writers saw the ideal temperament as the sanguine, others as a balance of all the humors. The views are reconcilable in that "balance" means not equal amounts but a certain proportion in which blood dominates — a proportion which Ficino specifies in *De vita* 1.5 as two parts each of black bile and choler to eight parts of blood (p. 498). It was debated which was the worst — the melancholic temperament, dominated by black bile, or the phlegmatic — but the melancholic usually won out. As we have seen, it is Ficino's achievement to have raised at least some varieties of the melancholic temperament above not only the phlegmatic temperament but even all the rest.[3]

Another way in which to sort out mankind's infinite variety was by astrology. Astrology contradicts the post-Newtonian view of the stars as irrelevant and passive with regard to man — *ein Schauspiel nur*. Instead, it postulates that all heavenly bodies influence the earth just as surely as the Moon pulls the tides. Unlike navigation, which looks to the sky for permanence, exemplified by the North Star and its neighbors, astrology looks to the sky for analogues, in a finer tone, of earthly change. The most changeable things known to ancient astronomy in the heavens proper are the planets; true, the fixed stars form ever-returning constellations which operate as units, but the planets create relationships which are endlessly changing (on this distinction, see 3.1, ad fin., p. 532; 3.17, ad fin., p. 555).

To understand Ficino's astrology we must first understand his astronomy, which is still on the traditional geocentric model commonly known as Ptolemaic. Let us take up the motions of the heavenly bodies in ascending order, not of height but of complexity. The fixed stars, or rather their celestial sphere, simply revolve *en bloc* about the earth from east to west in parallel perfect circles once a day, thus providing a relatively stable grid against which the more complex motions of the nearer bodies are measured. (I am ignoring the trepidation of the spheres, as does Ficino.)

The Sun, like the Moon, is in Ptolemaic astronomy just another planet, albeit an important one. In the present study, I have capitalized the words Sun and Moon to co-ordinate them Ptolemaically with the "other" planets, and the adjectival form of each planet to stress its original astrological meaning. The Sun's combined motions can briefly be summed up as helical. To trace them chronologically, in a given day (say, June 21), although the Sun exhibits approximately the same simple diurnal rotation as the celestial sphere (on June 21 coinciding with the circle traced by the constellation Cancer, known as the Tropic of Cancer), he actually deviates from it at an angle (insofar as one can speak of angles on a sphere) of a fraction of a degree. In a half-year, these deviations total forty-seven degrees of latitude, whereupon they begin to reverse themselves. In a year, the Sun carries out his diurnal rotation against different starry backgrounds and in celestial latitudes varying from the Tropic of Cancer in the north to the Tropic of Capricorn in the south and back again, thus producing the four seasons. Owing to this deviation or obliquity, the Sun cannot quite keep up with any given constellation (such as Cancer), but lags behind it from west to east at a rate of about one longitudinal degree per day for a total of 360° or a full circle in a year. The combination of these pulls — the north-south-north and the west-to-east — yields his second motion, his annual orbit, a great circle called the ecliptic crossing the equator at an angle of 23 1/2 degrees.

The apparent motions of the planets are much more complex than the stellar or solar motions we have just described, though they stay within a belt of eight degrees to either side of the Sun's ecliptic. First, some terminology. This

belt of starry background, called the Zodiac, is divided into twelve equal parts, the signs, corresponding (before the slippage owing to the precession of the equinoxes, which I ignore along with Ficino) to the constellations against which the Sun rises and sets in the different months of the year. The signs are as follows, in the west-to-east direction in which the Sun traverses them: Aries, Taurus, Gemini, Cancer, Leo, Virgo, Libra, Scorpio, Sagittarius, Capricorn, Aquarius, and Pisces. Each is in turn divided into thirty degrees, thus yielding the aforementioned total of 360 degrees of celestial longitude measured eastward around the ecliptic from the first degree of Aries, the beginning of the Zodiacal year. A body's course around this circle of the Zodiac is called its "annual" course, from a root meaning "ring," even if it takes either more or less than the Sun's 365¼ days. Such annual motion of a body towards the East, Ficino describes as "direct"—but with this our terminology gets ahead of our explanation. Like the Sun, the "other" planets too revolve, roughly speaking, in diurnal circles from east to west, though deviating from these much as he does with a resulting lag. The slight obliquities of their orbits not only to the equator and its parallels but to the ecliptic, is what gives the Zodiacal belt its width and allows the Moon to be, as Ficino sometimes pictures her, in the same longitudinal degree as the Sun without actually eclipsing him. Some planets, those we now call by that name, have still a third motion back towards the West, described as "retrograde" (e.g., 3, "Ad lectorem," line 28, p. 530) and said to be caused by epicycles. This retrogradation is easily observed in Venus's change, so fascinating to poets, from an evening (east of the Sun or "eastern") to a morning (west of the Sun or "western") star.

Although astrology in general speaks as if everything in the sky performed its gyrations on the celestial sphere, the order in which the so-called planetary spheres nest is important to Ficino. A traveler starting from the earth, like Dante and Beatrice in the *Paradiso*, would encounter the Moon, Mercury, Venus (the "Chaldean order"; see 3.21 and n. 8 ad loc.), the Sun, Mars, Jupiter, Saturn, the Fixed Stars, and lastly, the Primum Mobile (rarely mentioned by Ficino, e.g., *De vita* 3.1.7-8, *Op.*, p. 531). In Ficino's astrology, the concentric arrangement of the spheres governs both the months of fetal development and the days and hours of the planetary week (e.g., 3.2., ad init., on the two Jovial months of gestation).

So much for the mathematical model of the basic spatial relationships of the universe, as laid down for the most part by Ptolemy; let us now turn to its imagined significance for man, starting with the planets, then their relations, then the relations of these to their Zodiacal background, the signs, and finally, the relation of any and all of them to the horizon of the observer. First, to return to the thought-pattern with which we began, the planets through their elemental qualities govern the four humors: Saturn, being very cold and dry, is always seen as the cause of melancholy; Mars, being very hot and dry, of choler. For

the rest, the picture is complicated and controversial, though less fundamental to *De vita*: Jupiter always and Venus sometimes are seen as causing the sanguine or the balanced temperament because they are hot and moist, but temperately so; the Moon often and Venus sometimes are seen as causing the phlegmatic because of their moisture, although they are hardly cold at all.[4] Re-examining these assumptions, Ficino sometimes doubts that the stars are fire, i.e., that they can themselves be either hot or cold, wet or dry, preferring to believe that they are made of quintessence and thus merely cause those qualities here below (3.19, *Op.*, p. 560). Traditionally and qualitatively, the remaining planets, Mercury and the Sun, are comparatively neutral, though inclined to be dry, reinforcing the qualities of whatever bodies they are associated with (*Tetrabiblos*, 1.5). As "luminaries," the Sun, along with the Moon, of course initiates special relationships denied to the other planets. When he treats the Sun, Ficino invests it with Neoplatonic functions beyond these traditional elemental qualities.

Some miscellaneous intrinsic powers of the planets assumed by Ficino are as follows. Each of seven metals, each day of the week, each hour of the day and each month of fetal development come under the rule of some planet. The planets also influence the vocations of those born under them; for example, Mercury traditionally determines most of the intellectual vocations.[5] Ficino elevates Jupiter and Saturn to patronage of special intellectual vocations. Venus and the Moon are female planets; Mercury is hermaphroditic; the rest are male (see 3.26); and, where possible, I have preserved their sex in their pronouns.

Venus and Jupiter are the lesser and greater "fortunes," i.e., good planets; the Moon also is beneficent, at least insofar as she is warm. To Venus and Jupiter, Ficino adds the Sun, making three "Graces" or good and mutually supportive planets. In traditional astrology, Mars and Saturn are the lesser and the greater "infortunes," i.e., bad planets (e.g., *Tetrabiblos*, 1.5). While occasionally adopting this negative view of them (e.g., Letter to Cardinal John of Aragon, *Op.*, p. 819), in *De vita* Ficino sets out to correct it. One born under either Mars or Saturn (for the denotation of "born under," see below), while for that very reason less fortunate, will necessarily get some good out of him, says Ficino, perhaps thinking of himself, because the planet is the signifier of his horoscope and therefore of himself (*De vita* 3.10, p. 542). Moreover, Saturn bestows steadfastness and perseverance, Mars effective motions. Even to one who believes, as Ficino once did, that Saturn and Mars are intrinsically bad, they are still healthful in the same way that poisons can be, Saturn as an astringent or stupefacient and Mars, like hellebore, as a violent purgative (3.2.57–66, pp. 533–34; 3.10, as above).

As to their relations, one way in which planets combine their influences is to be in conjunction, meaning either on top of one another (an eclipse), or

on the identical celestial longitude, or in process of passing one another within a certain number of degrees called their "orbs." (Planets too near the Sun to be visible, a distance sometimes measured by a radius of 15°, are said to be "under the Sun's rays" or "combust.") Since the sky is treated as a single sphere, distance is angular, measured by degrees of arc; hence other configurations too are classified by the angles at which they face each other across the ecliptic. Of these angles, known as aspects, the trine and sextile (60° and 120°) are beneficent, the quartile (90°) and the diametrical, also known as opposition (180°), maleficent. The influences intrinsic to the planets are modified both by the signs and by the places (on which see below).

The sign's intrinsic properties and influences follow partly from its namesake, partly from its "character" or hieroglyph, partly from its placement relative to other signs. Of particular significance for medicine is the *melothesia*, setting each sign over a part of the body—Aries over the head, and so on to form the frequently-illustrated Zodiacal Man (*De vita* 3.10.43f., p. 543). Again, starting from Aries, the signs are alternately masculine and feminine (see *De vita* 3.26). Each sign corresponds to an element which it shares with two others at angles of 120° with it, thus forming a triangle or "triplicity" across the circle of the Zodiac: Aries, Leo, and Sagittarius are the fiery signs; Taurus, Virgo, and Capricorn, earthy; Gemini, Libra, and Aquarius, airy; and Cancer, Scorpio, and Pisces, watery.

Any given sign offers many other relations to the planets: it is to one planet a debility, but a dignity—namely a house (or domicile) and an exaltation—to two others; each third of it is allotted as a "face" to a different planet; and varying still smaller arcs of it are allotted to different planets as their *termini, fines*, "bounds," or "terms."[6] A planet is "received" by another, as a guest by a host (though the host need not be at home), when it is in a domicile of another; it thereby takes on a tinge of the influence of its host or "dispositor." Angles, or "aspects," can be drawn also from planet to sign. Also important is the sign occupied by the aspected planet.

Astrologically speaking, the birth of an individual (or for some, not Ficino, his calculated conception) is the greatest event of his life: it determines the native's gifts and propensities, and, according to some, even the other events of his life, though not what he makes of them. For this event, the key point is the ascendant, the intersection of the Zodiac with the eastern horizon. When a planet or a sign is rising—in or on the ascendant—at the moment of one's birth, it is called one's Ascendant, and one is said to be born "under" it, as Ficino was born under Saturn. Again, certain angles formed by the Sun, the Moon, and the Ascendant determine what sign holds the native's Part or Lot of Fortune and hence his guardian daemon or genius.[7] Now the signs often straddle the ascendant, as they did in Ficino's horoscope treated above. For measuring such angles of the heavenly bodies as they moved relative to the

horizon hour by hour, astrologers had to formulate another framework—the dodecatropos. Starting from the ascendant, numbering downwards from the eastern horizon and thence up from the western, the ecliptic is again divided into twelve arcs of thirty degrees called *plagae* or places (often in English called "mundane houses," thus inviting confusion with the planetary houses or domiciles) each denoting an area of life. Unlike the signs, these places never move, only their contents do. And their contents move faster; for whereas a sign is traversed irregularly at the very least once in a little more than two days (namely by the Moon) from the West, a place is traversed regularly every two hours by a new group of heavenly bodies from the East. Whatever heavenly bodies were in a given place at the moment of one's birth determines one's fortune in that area of life. Since these are less familiar and treated only allusively by Ficino, I will list them and give some of the various meanings assigned to them: I. Life and Character; II. Wealth; III. Friends, Siblings, or Journeys; IV. Parents, or Treasure and Terminations; V. Children; VI. Servants, Health and Illness, very important for Ficino; VII. Marriage; VIII. Fear and Death; IX. Travels, Dreams, Learning, and Religion; X. Kings, Honors, and Career; XI. Friends and Benefits; XII. Enemies and Misfortunes, or, according to Ficino's different scheme, echoed by Shumaker (p. 5), Prison. Other things being equal, houses II, VI, VIII, and XII are bad (see 3.23, p. 567, though for a physician, the sixth house can be good if it is fortunate). Of particular importance and beneficence are the angles or cardines—namely, the ascendant, the mid-heaven or medium coeli, the descendant, and the imum coeli, which is, as Ficino explains, "the mid-heaven on the other side"—and those places—the "succedent" first, tenth, seventh, and fourth—which a planet traverses in its daily approach to these points. The medium coeli and imum coeli (M. C. and I. C.) are sometimes loosely equated with the zenith and the nadir or with the "cardinal points" of the compass, south and north.

Although newspaper astrology emphasizes the zodiacal Sun-sign, that which formed a background for the Sun on a given day (mentioned, for example, 3.18), Ficino lays more stress on the Ascendant. As chief ruler of moisture, the Moon is important for medicine. She is important for all catarchic or elective astrology (on which see below) by reason of her changeableness, both her phases and her swift annual motion—all around the Zodiac in twenty-eight days. For example, when she occupies a given sign, bleeding from the corresponding member of the human body would be dangerously profuse (3.6, p. 539); but in a couple of days she will be elsewhere and the bleeding from this member easier to control.

According to the use to which it is put, astrology branches into various kinds. Genethliacal astrology or the casting of nativities is specific and predictive, as in the uses of the places described above. In *De vita*, Ficino professes it but subordinates it in various ways, for example, by reiterating that medicine can

prolong life beyond the fatal day predicted by the stars (3 Proem and "Ad lectorem," pp. 529-30; 3.18, p. 557 and our n. 20). Continuing astrology records the total disposition of the heavens at times crucial to us or to them—an eclipse, say, or the vernal equinox. Ficino believes in taking the horoscope of the year and of an individual on his birthday (3.19). A further step would be to take the horoscope of any given moment; thus interrogatory or horary astrology seeks answers to specific personal questions (called "interrogations" or "judgments") in the position of the stars at the time of asking. *De vita* contains no interrogatory astrology. Elsewhere, Ficino appeals to it once, but hypothetically as a proposition that his opponents believe, and therefore they ought to assent to another proposition (*Comm. Plot.* 3.2, chap. 7; *Op.*, pp. 1621-22). Against most astrology insofar as it is specific and/or predictive, Ficino wrote but never completed or published his treatise *Contra iudicium astrologorum* (ed. Kristeller, *SF*, 2: 11-76). Verging on magic is an art which Ficino expounded but often distrusted, both as to its possibility and its morality—the art of actually making things happen by capturing stellar influences in images and then manipulating the former through the latter. The image or talisman, generally an engraved disc of some precious mineral (see 3.16, p. 554), became a receptacle for a stellar influence by the following: a) the sympathetic properties of its material—gold, for example, for the Sun; b) by being made in an hour in which that star is favorable, thus investing the wearer with what might be called a second and more appropriate horoscope, that of the talisman (for garments too have horoscopes, says Ficino in 3.25); and c) according to less orthodox writers, by its representational features such as the "character" of the sign or planet.

General, and hence at the opposite extreme from most of these, are elections and general astrology. The weather and the fates of nations and of all mankind may be either predicted from special celestial events such as eclipses and the vernal equinox (see above and 3.19) by general prognostications or else understood in retrospect, as when Ficino accuses Mars and Saturn of having caused the plague of 1478-79 (*Consiglio contro la pestilenza*, Ricci's Latin trans., *Op.*, p. 577). Elective or catarchic astrology too is merely a matter of timing one's activities to coincide with the predicted dominance of favorable stars, of availing oneself of general, already-existing forces, much as one does when launching a ship with the ebbing of the tide. It contrasts favorably with talismanic magic in its cooperation with nature, being analogous to the way in which God tempered lower to higher things from the beginning (3.15, p. 552). Ficino espouses this art most of the time (e.g., 3.12, last sentence), quailing, as we shall see, only under the imagined glare of the "severe prelate of religion" (3.25, p. 569). "Thinking it superfluous to wish for things that have already happened," Ficino even finds that whatever would have influenced a nativity will also influence an activity, thus applying configurations he learned from

predictions, to elections (3.23, p. 567). For example, the twelfth place or mundane house, which Ficino calls the House of Prisons, would be used in genethliacal astrology to predict whether an individual was destined to be incarcerated, but in Ficino's elective astrology it becomes simply the wrong hour for anyone to begin working (1.7, p. 499). Conversely, by one's activities, one renders oneself receptive to the planet and sign governing that activity; for example, by wearing a piece of Saturn's metal, lead, or by metaphysical thinking (see, for example, 3.22, pp. 564, 566), one renders oneself receptive to Saturn. Thus one can "become a planet's child by choice," as Cassirer put it, utilizing the stars by sympathetic magic and enhancing one's free will rather than discovering its impotence.[8]

Another and more fundamental distinction cutting across that of uses is that of causalistic vs. semiological astrology. Although most thinkers believed that the stars somehow influence things here below, it was possible to skirt the deterministic implications of this by stressing instead their symbolism of things below through the sympathies inherent in a unified cosmos, pictured as a single organism or as a series of mirrors. On this view, prediction and elections remained valid, but talismans would find no influence to contain. Plotinus endorsed semiological astrology; and Ficino occasionally retreats to it when defending Saturn or when under fire for determinism, on which see "Repercussions" below.[9] (More specialized terminology which becomes relevant only once or twice will be defined in notes as it occurs.)

The traditions treated in this chapter can be briefly reviewed by assembling Ficino's departures from them: his exaltation of melancholy and therefore of black bile and Saturn; his exaltation of the Sun and Jupiter as well—all three planets being for him rulers of the intellectual vocations—and of the Moon as important for medicine, and his preferences for elective astrology over interrogatory, and for semiological astrology over causalistic. Though it is always possible that his innovations and redirections are the work of some unknown immediate predecessor (this is a citation-study, not a full source-study), it can still be said that in these respects Ficino is, if not original, at least out of the main stream. His divergence from received tradition is less a function of his subject-matter than a function of his distinctive approach or, perhaps more accurately, his cast of mind, to which let us now turn.

Habits of Mind

Certain recurrent structures of thought hold *De vita* together, explain some of its anomalies and much of its originality, and constitute the Ficinian signature on the subject matter. Readers already familiar with Ficinian modes of thought will perhaps wish to skip to the next section. To begin with, as is well

known, Ficino is more of a synthesizer than a fine discriminator. The most famous manifestation of this is his syncretism. Not being a historical relativist like Valla, he believed in a continuous self-consistent secular tradition of truth, the "ancient theology," parallel to Christian truth. His approach, except in some cases of conflict between a pagan author and Christianity or between two authorities, is therefore to accept all texts at face value without considering qualifying historical circumstances such as genre, cultural context, or polemical purpose, invoking, for example, Philostratus's *Apollonius* romance for scientific information. In subject matter, this habit led to religious syncretism, to belief in several diverse sets of divinities: the Christian, embracing the Trinity, angels, the Virgin Mary, and the saints; the Neoplatonic, embracing the three hypostases generally known as the One, the Mind, and the World-soul, the supramundane or supercelestial gods, the mundane or celestial gods including the movers, souls, or Intelligences of the spheres plus an undefined number of other star-souls, heroes living a semi-divine posthumous existence on the stars, and daemons good, bad, and indifferent, both celestial and sublunary;[1] and astronomical entities lumped under the term "celestials" which are alive and sometimes personal (see below); the last two embraced in one form or another the Olympian gods. Ficino's is a crowded universe, one in which a Wordsworth could have heard old Triton blow his wreathéd horn.

Further, like other astrologers, he generalizes extensively from scanty data—from the influence of the Sun on plants, the Moon on the sea, the North Star on the lodestone—to all sorts of what Putscher calls "Fern- und Doppelwirkungen."[2] One sort which he particularly favors is what Warburg and his followers call the *Schlitterlogik* of astrology, in which the representation—be it word or art object—is the thing, so that, for example, what is done to the image is done to its star (see "Traditions," above) and, I would add, what is true of the namesake is true of the heavenly body. Thus the bites of scorpions are cured under the constellation Scorpio. Thus those Olympian gods who have lent their names to heavenly bodies are spoken of and sometimes magically invoked as real agents. The latter habit has been discussed by Saxl, Garin, Seznec, Plessner, and the present writer, so that only a brief and pointed explanation is needed here. In *De vita*, Ficino confessedly (1 Proem 1; Letter to Poliziano, *Op.*, p. 958) alternates between two modes of discourse: the rhetorical/poetical and the practical. In the former mode, even non-planetary gods are treated as real, because gods are only personifications to begin with (e.g., 1 Proem 1; the encounter with Minerva, goddess of both wisdom and oil, 2.3; the conversations of Venus and Mercury with old men, 2.14–16; and the mythologizing about Bacchus's relation to Apollo, 2.20). In the preponderant practical sections of *De vita*, it is chiefly the souls of the twelve spheres (loosely called the planetary gods, but including such deities as Vesta, the soul of the earth) who are mentioned by name and treated as real. Their truth-value fits neatly

into the physical tradition of the gods as Seznec describes it. Since all believed the planets exerted influence and some believed they were either moved or animated by personal beings, the planets took on the attributes of those Olympian gods after whom they were named.[3] The rare but crucial references to the supercelestials will be discussed in "Repercussions," below. All these apparent superstitions have a deeper intellectual foundation.

Two structures give Ficino's thought in *De vita* at least a poetic unity: analogy and mediation within a hierarchy. They will occupy us for the rest of this section and indeed for much of this introduction. Argument from analogy crowds out argument from those material causes and effects which are the staple of modern science.[4] Black food, for example, increases black bile because of its analogous color. One analogy Ficino shares with medieval and Renaissance thought at large is that between microcosm and macrocosm. In particular, he inclines to analogies of generation, in pursuit of which he sometimes pictures the qualitative action of the heavens as organic action.[5] Usually, however, especially in Book 3, the macrocosm-microcosm analogy is more than rhetorical, more than heuristic; analogy is the very energy that holds the Neoplatonic cosmos together and hence the basis of those sympathies by which sympathetic magic operates. Sympathies based on analogy are the key to *De vita* according to Garin and Zambelli: "the form or image . . . as such takes on itself something of a force or soul from above."[6] Ficino is here expanding a notion from Plotinus.[7] In *De vita*, such analogies — not just of hot, cold, moist, or dry, but of color, activity, and shape or figure — are called "congruitates"; and Ficino says "that figure completes this figure," e.g., a constellation completes an image or a medicine, in order that it may work on us to the fullest (3.17.54, *Op.*, p. 555). Either figure can influence the other — a reciprocality which accounts for some curious confusions of agent and patient in *De vita*. In the beautiful passage in 3.26 discussed above, Ficino explains that his magic works because the likeness inspires love; and in love, the attraction is mutual. This notion of cosmic love seems for Ficino to embrace not only analogies of kinship, imitation, and mutual representation, but those opposites which attract, such as heaven and earth, fire and water (3.26, p. 570).

Cosmic sympathy is described not only as love but as the sympathetic vibration of two lutes and as reverberation whereby a wall gives an echo to a voice. The entire analogous structure of the world, especially its mathematical aspect, is itself expressed by still another analogy or metaphor, *musica mundana*, a rationalized version of the Pythagorean doctrine of the music of the spheres.[8] These are the models which "explain" magic and astrology in Plotinus, Synesius, and Ficino.[9] (In no part of the treatise does Ficino ever use the Greek loan-word *sympathia*, just the concept; in his translations of Plotinus and the "Platonici," he usually translates the Greek word as *compassio*). This analogy underlies Ficino's prescriptions of music to put the operator and his patient

in touch with the stars. For example, Ficino says that since all medical and astronomical combinations work as if by harmony (*musica mundana*), a certain seven classes of substance or activity (one of which is literal *musica instrumentalis*) put us in touch with the seven planets.[10]

Equally fundamental to *De vita*, as Kristeller has shown it to be for others of his works, is Ficino's habit of inserting new mediators into the Great Chain of Being:

> The . . . important principle of mediation . . . is also founded on the hierarchical order of reality. This principle states that wherever there are contrasts or sharp differences in the series of Being we must assume the existence of some intermediary elements. Ficino formulates this principle in the commentary on the *Philebus*: 'From extreme to extreme we cannot proceed without some middle term.'

It is a reflection of the principles which Lovejoy labeled "continuity" and "gradation."[11] More precisely, Ficino conceives of a number of analogous chains corresponding to the seven planets and certain constellations, each of which he calls a "series." And finally, another distinctively Neoplatonic feature, certain corresponding links on the chains are themselves joined horizontally to form entire analogous planes of reality such as those which Pico in his contemporaneous work the *Heptaplus* called the three worlds — terrestrial (comprising elemental and human), celestial, and intelligible or angelic. Scholastic thought, too, in which Ficino was nurtured, characteristically seeks mediators, though not in the form of entire analogous planes of reality. Even apart from Neoplatonic subjects and sources, as in Books 1 and 2, Ficino pursues the principle of mediation within the terrestrial plane, perhaps influenced directly or indirectly by Aristotle's doctrine of the golden mean and certainly influenced by his idea of health as *krasis* or good mixture. For example, he says that green is the color easiest to look at because it is a mean between black and white (2.14.30 f., p. 520, see Ps.-Aristotle, *Problem* 31.19, 959a).

As implied by Pico's example invoked above, the heavenly bodies occupied a place of special importance for the Neoplatonist as an intermediary plane of reality (or subplane if one considers the realm of matter as a whole) inserted between our sensible world and the intelligible world of Plato's Ideas. Our forefathers rightly noticed that the heavenly bodies possess a permanence beyond anything else in that although they move, they always come back the same. They therefore recognized in them a special, incorruptible sort of matter, and hence, the Neoplatonists added, the most faithful copies — almost pictures — of those models, the Ideas, after which all things were made. Ficino's three talismanic images of the universe — the ceiling-painting, the clock, and the mental

image (3.19)—exert magical effects because they are artistic embodiments of the Platonic notion of astronomy as a redemptive science. The heavens, being free from corruption, retain the "archetypal" form they received from the hand of the Creator executing his "Idea." Ficino's brand of Christianity too, which emphasized creation more than atonement, is naturally enamored of whatever retains its pristine form. The visible heavenly bodies thus contributed a mezzanine to Plato's two-storey universe.[12] More precisely, as Ficino puts it, the heavenly bodies copy most directly not the Ideas but the seminal reasons in the World-soul (3.1, *Op.*, p. 532). (The reasons epitomize the mediatorial function of the World-soul: Ficino distinguishes them by their upward and downward functions into exemplary reasons, corresponding in the mind of the World-soul to the Ideas in the Intellect itself, and the more frequently mentioned seminal reasons, the agents of the World-soul's generative activity in matter, wherein they also dwell and give rise to the species.)[13] In addition, as mirrors directed downward, they could serve as cosmic analogues of the human mind. Other intermediaries consist of extra ontological levels borrowed from the Proclan four-tiered universe as Ficino was to outline it in the *Phaedrus* commentary, chapter 11 (pub. 1496 but in the planning stage much earlier). As Allen explains, Ficino postulates "a four-tier model": first, "the obvious and traditional distinction between the animate and sensible worlds"; then, above these, the twofold supercelestial or supermundane world divided into "the gods in the third highest, the intellectual, realm," plus the intelligible world, "the realm of the Ideas in the prime intellect, not of gods (at least in Ficino's present analysis)."[14] In *De vita* 3.17 (see notes ad loc.), Ficino refers to an ontological level reported as having no matter but only color and shape, which corresponds to what he says of the animate world in the *Phaedrus* commentary. I will therefore assume that the Proclan four-tiered universe was the pagan starting point onto which he grafted his modifications, whether personal, Platonic, or Christian. One of Ficino's modifications is to annex the Proclan intellectual gods into the mind of the World-soul as the exemplary reasons, while still keeping them as a distinct level there (see 3.1 and n. 5 ad loc. and "Repercussions").

The most important mediator in the entire work is the medical spirit; the notion is so pervasive as almost to constitute the work's real subject (see Index). It is not particularly Platonic. In medical writers the philosophical function of the medical spirit was as a *tertium quid* to bridge the gap between man's body and soul—the function now filled in modern science by electro-chemical nervous transmission.[15] In an article on another Renaissance physician, D. P. Walker summarizes the history of the doctrine:

> In spite of certain inherent weaknesses and vaguenesses, the theory of medical spirits maintained itself throughout the Middle Ages

in a fairly constant and coherent form, based ultimately on Aristotle and Galen, and systematized by the Arabs.

The doctrine of spirit in the Stoics too is remarkably similar to that in Ficino. Early in his first book, Ficino explains the nature of spirit—a vapor or gas; its physical basis—the subtler blood; its efficient cause—the heat of the heart; its destination and purpose—the brain, where "the soul uses it continually for the exercise of the interior as well as the exterior senses. This is why the blood subserves the spirit; the spirit, the senses; and finally, the senses, reason" (1.2, p. 496). English-speaking readers will recall Donne's lines—

> As our blood labours to beget
> Spirits as like soules as it can,
> Because such fingers need to knit
> The subtile knot which makes us man....
> ("The Exstasie," 61-64)

—lines for which Ficino's explanation provides a probable source. It will be noticed that the noun here is usually plural. Ficino occasionally employs the traditional distinction into three—natural, vital, and animal. Like everything else, spirit has hierarchical grades, each serving as raw material for the next and higher. The highest and most important is the "animal," of or pertaining to soul, which Walker defines as follows:

> Animal spirits ... are contained in the ventricles of the brain, whence through the nervous system they are transmitted to sense-organs and muscles; their functions are motor-activity, sense-perception, and, usually, such lower psychological activities as appetite, *sensus communis*, and imagination. They are the first, direct instrument of the soul.[16]

The natural spirit is responsible for nutrition, growth, and reproduction, and is mentioned as such. The vital spirit is responsible for life, the passions, and, in Ficino, astrologically efficacious song (3.21, p. 563).

In accordance with the macrocosm-microcosm analogy and his habit of postulating intermediaries, Ficino greatly extended the importance of the medical spirits by attributing them (or rather it) also to the cosmos, envisioning a *spiritus mundanus* or world-spirit (3.1; 3.3, et passim) between the world's soul and its body. This extension is introduced only in *De vita coelitus comparanda*. The book opens with an example of inserting mediators into a hierarchy, a Plotinian affirmation of the importance of Soul—meaning here particularly the Anima Mundi—as mediatrix between the world's body and the Mind of

the universe, which is both the mind of God and the receptacle of the Ideas. Ficino then proceeds to improve on Plotinus by postulating between the World-soul and the world's body its own so-called *spiritus mundanus*. "The aid," writes Ficino, "of a more excellent body—a body not a body, as it were—is needed. . . . Spirit is a very tenuous body; as if now it were soul and not body, and now body and not soul" (3.3.11-12, 31-33, p. 535). When attributed to the cosmos, the noun loses its plural and embraces all three functions in the singular. The word *spiritus* is thus used in *De vita* in a special sense, which Ficino always carefully distinguishes from the normal, theological sense as, for example, in the title of 1.26: "Care for the corporeal spirit, cultivate the incorporeal. . . . Medicine takes care of the first, moral discipline, the second" (p. 508). According to Walker, spirit is the most important of the several channels through which Ficino's magic works.

Another way in which the heavenly bodies are a mezzanine between the planes of material and immaterial, man and God, is that they are alive. Ficino's notion of the world-spirit is but a codification of this profoundly poetic notion, which made Ficino's astrology less mechanistic and more vitalistic than most. Neoplatonic scalarism—building on an uncharacteristic statement in the *Timaeus* of Plato himself[17] and extending the doctrine of the mundane gods and the World-soul there enunciated—diffused superhuman life through seemingly nonanthropomorphic entities such as the stars and nature at large by giving to them rational souls of their own. The notion that the heavens are alive occurs also in the *Corpus Hermeticum*[18] and in Plotinus (see below). The immediate exigency for some intelligence in the spheres was their motions.[19] Their divinity follows from hierarchy and analogy: if men have souls, if even beasts have souls of a sort, how much more must the heavens, which generate as we do (not organically but qualitatively)[20] but which are, as Plotinus says in a similar argument, "composed of elements more beautiful and purer" than ourselves?[21]

This doctrine is part of a larger instance of Ficino's preference for more-and-less over either/or thinking: for Ficino as for Spinoza, life can sometimes even bridge the gap between organic and inorganic in that everything is more or less alive—the heavens rather more, stones rather less, being, as it were, the teeth and bones of the world's body.[22] Even stones can reproduce themselves when liberated by natural science from the grossness of their matter (3.3.15-20, p. 535). When it makes no practical difference, however, he sometimes falls into the common dichotomy of organic vs. inorganic (3.1, p. 532).

In summary, many of Ficino's distinctive habits of mind—generalizing from a single datum, analogy, and postulating a new intermediary in a hierarchy—can be seen in his cry: "But O that somewhere we might easily find a Solar or Lunar stone so overpowering in its order, as we have in the lodestone and iron in the order of the Northern Pole-star!" (3.15.18-20, p. 555). This desire for power will lead us to Ficino's doctrines of magic.

Magic

It is only in Book 3 that Ficino's therapy can definitely be classed as magic, namely, insofar as it employs for materialistic ends agents from above or outside of ordinary existence. (In Books 1 and 2 he occasionally prescribes a substance not for its elemental but for its occult properties, which could be classed as verging upon the magical.) Ficino's propensity for magic is proved by his tacit employment of *Picatrix*, which has recently been documented by a weighty combination of external and internal evidence. As early as 1922, three scholars associated with the Warburg Institute—Warburg himself, Fritz Saxl, and Hellmut Ritter—were suggesting that *De vita coelitus comparanda* owed an unacknowledged debt to the *Picatrix*, an Arabic compilation of Hellenistic magic done in eleventh-century Spain, translated into Spanish under the aegis of Alphonso the Wise between 1256 and 1258, and thence by unknown persons at an unknown date into Latin. Although it thus constitutes an important influence of the East on the West, it is hard to trace because it was always a concealed and subversive book, referred to by Rabelais as "le reverend père en diable Picatrix." Subsequent scholars of the Warburg school, along with Thorndike, Garin, and Compagni, have pursued various echoes of it—Yates, Compagni, and Plessner in *De vita* itself.[1] As for external evidence, Daniela Delcorno Branca has recently discovered a letter written at Ficino's dictation by Michele Acciari to Filippo Valori stating that although he could not lend him a manuscript of *Picatrix*, nor did he recommend reading it, all its doctrines which were not either frivolous or "condemned by the Christian religion" were incorporated in *De vita coelitus comparanda*. Garin heralded this remarkable discovery with a claim which in hindsight seems a bit overblown and which he has not repeated: that *De vita coelitus comparanda* is a "traduzione"—his interpretation of Ficino's verb "transtulisse"—of and a substitute for *Picatrix*.[2] Ficino's statement is not, however, that all of *De vita* 3 is from *Picatrix*, but that all that is worthwhile in *Picatrix* is in *De vita* 3, along with much other material, as our notes show.

What Ficino did transfer (our interpretation of "transtulisse") includes notions selected by those habits of mind which constitute his distinctive signature on the material—notions such as that of a world-spiritus or *pneuma* which can be captured in images and of personal beings in the stars who can receive and answer petitions and even accept worship, from those willing to offer it, though Ficino disavows any such intention. Unlike *De vita*, however, *Picatrix* generally assigns an individual *pneuma* to each of the seven planets; and it addresses prayers to the lords of the lunar mansions by their proper names. Only the Arabic text and a German translation thereof, by Ritter and Plessner, have so far been edited. Referring to this, Plessner has traced detailed parallels in his edition of *De vita*, of which those we found convincing have been incorpo-

rated into our notes. Plessner documents the very selectivity Ficino professes in Acciari's letter, by showing that Ficino eschews in 3.18 those talismans which would override free will and those which are destructive (see our n. 26 ad loc.). Plessner's parallels are inevitably weakened by the fact that Ficino could have read neither the original Arabic nor its modern German translation, only the Latin *Picatrix*, in one version as yet unidentified out of many. Working from one of these Latin versions, Perrone Compagni in "Picatrix latinus" has discovered various parallels of which those we found convincing have been incorporated into our notes. To give a conspectus of the indebtedness, the clear borrowings, including most of the citations of "astrologi Arabes," are here assembled as follows: the idea that using various materials especially rich in quintessence or the *spiritus mundi* enables one to enter into relationship with the superior world (3.1, *Op.*, p. 532, though materials especially full of the gifts of the gods are also mentioned in Proclus, *De sacrificio* and *ET*, Proposition no. 145); a definition of Elixir (3.3.20-23, p. 535), albeit a very different one; the placing of that planet which was lord of the geniture as lord also of magical operations for the client (3.2, pp. 533-34, on Saturn and Mars, and this transfer is recommended for any and all planets in 3.23); the explanation of why stones make potent talismans (3.13, p. 549); the description of a decan-image (3.18, p. 556); and many planetary ones (3.18, p. 557; see our notes ad loc.); the pagan praise of the cruciform shape as a "universal talismanic figure"; the ascription of this idea to an "Arabic miscellany," an apt characterization of the *Picatrix* (3.18.18, p. 556; see our notes ad loc.); some hints for his few talismans of the mansions of the Moon (3.18, nn. 21-24; 3.20, n.2); the importance of the user's concentration as a means of linkage with the stellar rays (3.20, p. 561, though this idea, as she admits, receives at least equal stress in Al-Kindi's *De radiis*, chap. 6). *Picatrix* does not, on the other hand, contain Ficino's extensive dietetic passages, although it allows for the psychological effects of diet and claims as does Ficino that the astral influence is really working through it ("Picatrix latinus," pp. 260-61, n. 3). Although Compagni's edited portions are helpful and may be closer to the Latin text Ficino actually used than is the definitive text currently being edited by Pingree, yet because they are only portions, not the complete text, we have made no consistent effort to cite them in our notes along with the editions of Ritter, Plessner, and Pingree. *Picatrix* was an influential but not a predominant source; and it seems never to have been "transferred" verbatim into *De vita*, but rather to have acted as a quarry for Ficino's original syntheses of Neoplatonic theurgy with practical magic and of the cosmic with the medical spirit. A definitive assessment of Ficino's debt to *Picatrix* must wait until we can all read the Latin *Picatrix* in the forthcoming critical edition by David Pingree, soon to be published by the Warburg Institute. He has kindly supplied his versions of the references in most of our notes; the finer subdivisions of his chapter-numbers, or the en-

tire number if different, appear in parentheses after our references to the existing German translation by Ritter and Plessner.³

A Greek approximation to the theory of magic animals, herbs, stones, and figurate talismans in *Picatrix*, and hence another likely source for *De vita* 3, is Proclus's brief *De sacrificio et magia*. As explained above, Ficino translated it and often cites it. Although its agents, like those of *De vita*, are for the most part Neoplatonic daemons, of which more below, it is theurgic in its ends, whereas both the *Picatrix* and *De vita* are materialistic. Ficino's other agents, the corporeal spirits, are not mentioned. Another partial analogue in Proclus is his *Elements of Theology*, Proposition no. 145.⁴

Another source which Ficino acknowledges for his magic is the so-called god-making passage in the Hermetic *Asclepius*, available to Ficino as it had long been to the Middle Ages in the Latin translation of the lost Greek original. Since the claim of "making" gods is retracted in the subsequent sentence to "evoked," I have called it the statue-animating passage. Scott's English translation of it is vitiated by the liberties he has taken with the text, and the exact text which Ficino used is not known; I therefore quote D. P. Walker's English translation of the definitive text:

> (Hermes:) What has already been said about man, although marvellous, is less so than this: that man has been able to discover the divine nature and produce it, is admirable beyond all other marvels. Our first ancestors, then, when they were in grave error concerning the gods, being incredulous and paying no attention to worship and religion, invented the art of making gods. Having done so, they added a virtue appropriate to it, taken from the world's nature, and mixed these; since they could not make souls, they evoked the souls of demons or angels, and put them into images with holy and divine rites, so that through these souls the idols might have the power of doing good and evil . . . (Asclepius:) . . . of what kind is the quality of these terrestrial gods? (Hermes:) It consists, O Asclepius, of herbs, stones and aromas, which have in them a natural divine power. And it is for the following reason that people delight them with frequent sacrifices, with hymns and praises and sweet sounds concerted like the harmony of the heavens: that this heavenly thing, which has been attracted into the idol by repeated heavenly rites, may bear joyously with men and stay with them long.

There is a second statue-animating passage (*Asclepius* 24), which Ficino also cites (see 3.26 and n. ad loc.); it says much the same thing in fewer words. Whether anything else in the *Hermetica* made much of an impression on Ficino is currently being debated. Copenhaver will argue that because the *Hermetica*

are philosophically incoherent, the above quotation supplied isolated and merely doxographic support, whereas the more coherent and more frequently cited "Platonici" in general and the *De sacrificio* in particular are much more fundamental to Ficino's theory of magic.[5]

But to assess the relevance of such sources as these, one of the aims of this chapter, depends on the centrality of their contribution, which in turn depends on the work's rationale. First-hand research into many of the magical texts available to Ficino, especially in view of their complex problems of transmission and evasiveness, would require a separate study such as those which are currently being undertaken by Copenhaver. I will simply cull out of the creative chaos which represents the current state of the subject, a few vague labels which characterize the magic Ficino endorses, that which he eschews, and that which he invokes with reservations, and then apply them to a single limited source-relationship. It is impossible to sum up as I did for astrology the basic assumptions of magic because they differ so much from magician to magician. Some distinctions which have helpfully been applied to Ficino are as follows. Shumaker attempted a rough systematization in his chapter on white magic (chap. 3), dividing it into three increasingly suspect kinds, presumably on the basis of the ontological status of the agents: purely natural and sympathetic magic which works as it were automatically, exemplified by Della Porta's *Magia naturalis* and, I would add, by that mentioned in passing in *Ennead* 4.4.26-44, especially 40-43; celestial or astronomical magic which shifts from natural to ceremonial insofar as prescribed words are addressed to living agents, exemplified by *De vita coelitus comparanda*; and full-fledged ceremonial magic verging upon witchcraft (magic which works by an explicit pact with a bad daemon), exemplified by Agrippa's *De occulta philosophia*. Again, effects of magic may be purely "subjective" or they may be what Walker calls "transitive" effects, physical or psychological, on people not involved in the operation: the former effects are explainable at a pinch by psychology while the latter in theory are hard to explain, in practice tend to be attributed to daemonic magic or witchcraft, and hence are generally avoided by Ficino.[6]

Although, as Walker remarks, people do not usually think logically about magic, especially if they believe in it, nevertheless Ficino obviously tried to do so because of his theoretical and Neoplatonic cast of mind. Ficino contributed to the mainstream of magic a theoretical framework which he seemed to believe would emancipate it from evil powers. Part of this frame was an explanation or explanations of how medical magic works. The first explanation is a version of sympathetic magic. From Plotinus, the *Corpus Hermeticum*, and his own instinctive beliefs, Ficino knew that the universe is one living creature whose parts all aid and travail or rejoice with each other. Within this great macro-microcosm analogy, as we have seen, chiefly within the planetary series or chains of being, Ficino sees endless contributory analogies, called *con-*

gruitates, of substance, quality, or activity, and also (in terms less specific but privileged by Garin) "forms" or "images." For him, analogy can operate as a cause; a lower thing can attract a higher by being analogous to it, appealing to the love of like for like, and when it does, he calls it *illicium,* "a lure," or *esca,* "a bait." Scholars disagree as to whether any go-between (such as Ficino's world-spirit or Neoplatonic daemons) mediates this sympathy or whether it all happens, as Plotinus says, spontaneously, by pre-established harmony (*Enn.* 4.4.41–42; see also Proclus, *ET,* no. 122 and *De sacrificio,* p. 1928) — whether, as Garin paraphrases him, "the form or image . . . as such, takes on itself something of a force or soul from above."[7] Ficino does sometimes invoke this Proclan and Plotinian principle (e.g., 3.17, entire chap., pp. 555–56, and 3.21, p. 562). Ficino also draws Plotinian analogies to mirrors, echoes, and sympathetic vibrations, which he seems to have seen as operating without a medium. Ficino's therapies of Orphic music and dancing, i.e., those which imitate the music or the motion of one or all of the heavens for the sake of obtaining some benefit from them, seem to operate in this way. This then is indeed one way in which Ficino's magic works, that stressed by Garin and Zambelli. It would seem to be compatible with Christian orthodoxy.

For Walker and Zanier, Ficino's magic works chiefly in another way — by the corporeal spirits in man and in the cosmos. The very fact that Ficino imported the world-spirit into the Plotinian cosmos[8] shows that he often felt the need of some medium for astral influence, that "the form as such" was not always potent enough. The cosmic spirit served as mediator by being lower than the World-soul yet high enough to influence the human mind and soul. Ficino wished to Platonize his magic by enlisting such Neoplatonic hypostases — God or the One, the Angelic Mind, the World-soul, souls of the stars and spheres and the daemons attendant upon each — on behalf of magicians working for physical and mental health. His doctrine of a spirit at once procreated by the hypostases yet made of matter solved the problem, for our own medical spirit can interpenetrate with that for the sake of physical health (3.1) as it could not with the World-soul, let alone anything higher. Again, Ficino was interested in mental as well as physical health. Yet he knew that a solid body, even a celestial body like the Moon, could not influence our minds, since that would be determinism (see Aquinas, *SCG* 3.84). As Walker stresses, a cosmic spirit, "a body not a body," could influence our spirits; and through the intermediate faculty upon which the animal spirit impinged, the *vis imaginativa* — for present purposes loosely definable as the first processor of sense-data — it and the magic which controlled it could affect even our mind and our soul.

The contribution of Ficino's doctrine of spirit, then, was central, and so is whatever source most nearly supplied it to him. While Garin should not have denied the importance of the notion of spirit, he was right that it was not so original with Ficino as Walker had supposed. Yet even here, the sources which

Garin cited were not close. In citing Plotinus and Proclus, Garin was evidently thinking of the astral body or etherial vehicle (ὄχημα) which the soul picks up on its prenatal descent through the spheres;[9] but this envelope of the individual is still a far cry from Ficino's pair of answering spirits, individual and cosmic (cf. Zanier, p. 24). The same could be said for Aristotle's statement that the individual spirit is "analogous to that element of which the stars are made," (*De gen. animal.*, 736b 27ff.). Putscher solves the dispute by granting that there was always a cosmic component to the medical spirit, but crediting Ficino with foregrounding it.[10] The explanations of both Walker and Garin are valid, it seems to me; but Walker's is more central. Despite occasional references to spontaneous working of the *congruitates*, Ficino gives a great deal of weight to the spirits, and even the daemons, betraying still further his need of a mediator; and later Ficino's Letter to Poliziano (*Op.*, p. 958) will disavow the artificial images, one example of the doctrine of congruity, while not only Ficino's Plotinus commentary (see "Place," above) but even the anti-astrological treatise of Ficino's rebellious disciple Pico will retain Ficino's doctrine of a cosmic spirit.[11] Both Garin and Walker have grasped what are in effect various attempts to reduce the agent to the lowest common denominator. Garin seems rather to stress Ficino's audacity; Walker, his attempt to be orthodox.

Although I am not an Arabist, and Ficino was not the sort of thinker to rule out one source in favor of another, I would argue that Ficino's doctrine of spirit as the basis of magic must have come most directly from his Arabic sources. Neither Walker nor Klibansky, Panofsky, and Saxl realized how close a precedent for this sort of magic was afforded by *Picatrix* and Al-Kindi's *De radiis*, because they lacked both modern editions and any adequate translations from the Arabic. The Latin translation of the Arabic original, now lost, of Al-Kindi's treatise, beginning "Incipit theorica artium magicarum," was known in the Middle Ages, was criticized by Giles of Rome in his *De erroribus philosophorum*, and was edited in 1974 by M.-T. d'Alverny and F. Hudry.[12] Although, as its title implies, it dwells more on rays than on medical and cosmic spirits, its influence on Ficino will bear further examination. Ficino in his marginalia to another of his magical sources, Proclus's *De sacrificio*, cites Al-Kindi as a parallel to it (see Copenhaver, "Hermes Trismegistus, Proclus," forthcoming, and 3.15, n. 3). *Picatrix* too first discusses the medical spirit (3.4, pp. 186–87), then a few pages later postulates air as a vehicle or medium which carries the *pneumata* of magic objects, themselves impregnated with the influences of the planets, to the *pneuma* of man (3.5, ad init., p. 190, Arabic, p. 180), then a few pages later describes a figurate talisman for capturing cosmic *pneuma* (3.5 [5], pp. 195–96). It thus juxtaposes those concepts of spirit which Ficino was later to synthesize into "spiritual magic," acting as a quarry for Ficino's most important original idea. In addition, interspersed throughout these and other passages of both treatises are carelessly undifferentiated references to spirits in

the ordinary, incorporeal sense—references which could be mistaken for the corporeal spirit, or could have given Ficino the idea of the corporeal spirit while he was sorting out what they actually meant.

True, we now know from recent research on them that the later Greek Stoics, the real inventors of the doctrine, had stated as if in anticipation of Ficino that the continuity between the human medical *pneuma* and the cosmic *pneuma* forms the basis of astrology (Lapidge, p. 175). Although Ficino cites these thinkers elsewhere both individually and as a school, and although he could have gathered from Plotinus's refutation that they too believed in a medical spirit, he never cites them in *De vita*; and their writings, which survive only in fragments, were even less available to Ficino than they are to us; hence there is no evidence that Ficino was aware of the Stoic precedent for this distinctive cluster of ideas, which he fathers on the "Arabes" (3.3). This doctrine is almost as well represented in the "Arabes" which he does cite: the *Picatrix*, acknowledged among his coterie; and Al-Kindi's *De radiis*, chap. 6, "On the Power of Words," cited in 3.21. I therefore believe it was from them that he perfected his own concept. The related idea of the power of the operator's state of mind is present in *Picatrix* and elaborated in Ficinian length and detail in Al-Kindi's chapter. Al-Kindi also expounds in the same chapter the idea of music as a therapy enlisting stellar forces to cure the medical spirit, probably inspired as was Ficino (see "Habits," above) by suggestions and imagery in Plotinus.

Ficino's originality lies in the fact that he strove to sort out the equivocal uses of spirits in the Arabic sources and thus eliminate their idolatry. He also strove to better maintain hierarchy. The yoking of the Platonic with the practical is less violent in *De vita* than in *Picatrix*, wherein, as Pingree quips, the very Neoplatonic hypostases themselves are dragged down not just to their previous "vivification of statues" for "communication between the divine and the human" but to helping "the alleged sage" achieve "health, wealth, and women, and the destruction of his enemies" (p. 15). Ficino knew that bodily ills are unworthy of the direct ministrations of the World-soul and therefore tended to confine his magic to the world-spirit. Whether or not my readers will agree that these "Arabes" are the principal source for these notions, at least all agree that Ficino's explanations are somehow Plotinian in origin with an overlay of Hermes Trismegistus, Iamblichus, Proclus, and the *Picatrix*.

Finally, we must confront the slippery distinction between "black" and "white" magic. Distinctions may be drawn between means—agents or operations—or between ends. Ficino himself in his Apologia (summarized in "Repercussions," below) distinguishes good from bad magic as did the ancients, in Pingree's characterization, chiefly by its purpose (p. 15): he judges his own magic to be good because it is for medicine, other magic to be bad if for theatrical or theurgic purposes. Believing that the end evaluates the means, he prides himself on excluding from *De vita* those talismans in *Picatrix* which are frivolous

or destructive or which interfere with someone else's free will. Although traditional distinctions between magic and religion are currently being debated (see, for examples from a slightly later period, the first chapter of Keith Thomas's *Religion and the Decline of Magic*), Ficino and his contemporaries knew there was a difference and that magic involving religions other than Christianity was black magic. Within Christianity, as Thomas shows, the pious superstitions of the uneducated resembled magic in all but name; but the theologians also protested against them. Within paganism, that Neoplatonic magic which came after Plotinus was indeed religious and had even originated in competition with Christianity, though this last feature may have been unknown to Ficino. It uses ceremonies and prescribed words which are difficult, though not impossible, to separate from its pagan religious ends. Still, Iamblichus himself distinguished magic, of which he of course disapproves, from his own theurgy—Neoplatonic rites to perfect the worshiper and to lure deities into perceivable forms, the better to worship them—not in its materials, which may be similar, but in its aims, which are practical, not religious (Thorndike 1: 310-312). In religious rituals, emphasis falls less on the effect, of whatever sort, and more on the personal relationship of operator and client to the being invoked. Only religion, not magic, appends to the petition, "Thy will be done."

According to some, magic can also be bad if it works by means of daemons, even if it does not worship them. The standard church dogma accords with Aquinas's definition of bad or black magic as that which works by enlisting a "separated" or "intellectual" substance, a personal being (*SCG* 3.104-5, 106). Daemon-free natural or white magic, including what we call sympathetic magic, including a magic which works by similarity or analogy of quality or figure— is explicitly approved by Ficino and would have been by most of his contemporaries, except the likes of the "severe prelate of religion" addressed in 3.25. Elaborating upon Ficino's distinction of means, Walker also distinguishes "demonic magic" from "spiritual magic"—i.e., from Ficino's brand of natural magic which by working through the medical spirits, was able to legitimize operations hitherto considered demonic. Thus Walker rightly sees Ficino as converting daemonic agents into an impersonal and corporeal spirit and basing his magic on it. Garin would presumably find the same advantage in the magic of "lures." Unfortunately, however, Ficino did not draw the line where the Church did, though in the Apologia he pretended to. Ficino's magic is not "demonic" in that he refused to worship them or even have any expressed pact with them, as Walker maintained, but it remains daemonic in its agents. In many parts of *De vita* 3, Ficino did also say that it was his cherished Neoplatonic daemons who did the work (e.g., in parts of 3.1 and 3.26, see "Repercussions"), even agreeing with the *Asclepius* as against Plotinus that it was daemons who animated the statues (3.26, p. 571). This avowal reflects post-Plotinian Neoplatonic magic, which usually (in the *Asclepius* and in Iamblichus and

Proclus, but not in the *Picatrix*) enlists those intermediary spirits—good, bad, or indifferent—which it calls daemons. From Ficino's translations we learn that daemons are in fact the very authors of that very "harmonic agreement and ... sympathy of all things" (*Op.*, p. 1874, Iamblichus, *De mysteriis*, "De ordine superiorum") which Garin and Zambelli say renders them unnecessary. Neoplatonic magic after Plotinus, related as it is to theurgy and hence to religion, becomes liturgical and personal (see Pingree on *Picatrix*, pp. 14-15). Besides scrutinizing its ends, a Neoplatonist also sees the goodness of its agents as determining the goodness of the magic; and he envisions most daemons as good. These daemons, then, were for Ficino the cousins and allies, not the competitors, of that pre-established harmony and that world-spirit he had worked so hard to establish (though in the sequel, they came near to discrediting his entire achievement). This Neoplatonic daemonic magic thus occupies that grey area, precisely where Shumaker locates Ficino's ceremonial magic, between the neat theoretical poles of natural or spiritual versus liturgical or demonic magic. It is for this reason that my translation has chosen to spell the word not "demon" but "daemon," in order to avoid prejudging the question of the being's moral allegiance.

So much for magic in Ficino's writings. Walker suspects and Garin echoes a sixteenth-century report that in practice Ficino ventured to practice a religious sort of magic, whose means and ends he so vehemently disavowed in *De vita*.[13]

At the same time, a word for which one looks in vain in *De vita* is "alchemy," even though it existed in medieval Latin as well as the vernaculars. He mentions transmutation and the Elixir in 3.3.20-23, p. 535, a passage influenced by the unmentionable *Picatrix*. That *De vita* was associated in the minds of later readers with alchemy is indicated by several bibliographical facts. One German translator substituted an overtly alchemical treatise for Book 3 (see Clark's "Editorial Introduction" on translations). Two alchemical treatises were sometimes attributed to Ficino, even though they are in matter and style highly unficinian (Kristeller, *SF*, 1: CLXVI-VII). In one manuscript, excerpts from *De vita* actually merge into an alchemical treatise (= Munich, Clm 26059, see Clark's "Marsilio Ficino among the Alchemists," *Classical Bulletin* 59 [1983]: 50-54). Yet Ficino himself in a letter of the 1480s derides not only alchemy but the very process of transmutation to which he appealed in the abovementioned passage of *De vita*. Writing to Jacopo Antiquari on the subject of bringing back the Golden Age, he says in an elaborate conceit, "In the same measure in which opinion deceives and fortune frustrates those vain men popularly called Alchemists every time they labor to turn base metals into gold, in the same measure the project of those men succeeds according to their wishes who as far as possible subject concupiscence, irascibility, and action to contemplation—so much so that they achieve in place of the rest of the metals gold, that is,

in place of the vilest things, the most precious and in place of the transitory, the eternal" (*Epist.* 7, p. 861). It seems that in some moods Ficino did believe in alchemy, while avoiding the term itself, and in some he expressly did not. This last mood may have been self-censoring on Ficino's part. There had been "a papal bull against the activities of alchemists a century before" Guaineri, although that had not inhibited the latter from speaking freely of alchemy and naming alchemists personally known to him, and other medical treatises had followed suit (Thorndike, 4: 230, 231). The *Picatrix,* too, speaks freely of alchemy. On this topic, Ficino was either skeptical or cautious.

The seminality of *De vita* for subsequent treatises of more or less natural magic is precisely the subject of Walker's book. Ficino is a determining force in the magic of Agrippa and Paracelsus, and even, according to Yates and Garin, in the science of Giordano Bruno and Francis Bacon, to name only his most famous apprentices. Perhaps unfairly passing over such predecessors as William of Auvergne and Albertus Magnus, Zambelli calls *De vita* "the founding charter of the new natural magic" (p. 124). Garin and Yates maintained that Ficino was among the first to exemplify the Renaissance insight that practical application is as dignified as theorizing—"a radical change in the manner in which man was seen."[14] In contrast, says Yates,

> Fundamentally, the Greeks did not *want* to operate. They regarded operations as base and mechanical, a degeneration from the only occupation worthy of the dignity of man, pure rational and philosophical speculation. The Middle Ages carried on this attitude in the form that theology is the crown of philosophy and the true end of man is contemplation.[15]

She is right with regard to medicine in that in the Middle Ages, up to the eleventh century and much later in the North, much of medical therapy, including all surgery and phlebotomy, was delegated to the uneducated barber-surgeon; and he and the equally active apothecary "were looked upon as little more than menials."[16] The vulgar healer, midwife, sorcerer, magician, or witch was of course eminently practical, but he or she had neither social dignity nor professional training. Whether because Ficino's father was both a doctor of medicine and a surgeon (see "The Author in the Work"), or whether because the reunion of theory and practice had already taken place in medicine from other causes in his part of the world, *De vita* gives little evidence of this division of labor. Ficino pictures the doctor as collecting his herbs in person (3.16.72, p. 554); and while he prescribes no surgery except phlebotomy, he does not single out a surgeon or other assistant as performing it, equating "physicus et medicus," with "chirurgicus" (3.26, p. 570). This practical orientation on the part of scientists, as Garin was the first to notice and Yates to

popularize, originated with the Renaissance magicians. *De vita* and his translations of the *Corpus Hermeticum* and of the "Platonici" make Ficino the progenitor of all these. Although survey courses ascribe this insight to Francis Bacon, his was only the culmination of a trend philologically initiated by Ficino, for Bacon "owed a great deal to the teachings of alchemy and magic when he insisted that science was power, and that scientific knowledge is a form of activity which listens to the language of nature in order to dominate her."[17] Another Baconian insight, that practical application should in turn be employed as experiment to correct theory, is anticipated to some extent by Ficino. While typically reverent towards authority, Ficino also appeals rather often for his time to his own medical experience. As Mazzeo says of Paracelsus, "In the Renaissance [the metaphysician or religious sage] is displaced by the magus and the artist. However different, they are both makers and doers who conceive of their very activities as acts of the understanding."[18] All we have said of Ficino's ideas in this and the preceding chapter indicates that his magic is characterized by a practical orientation and a vitalizing but depersonalizing of the agents. The materialistic goal allies him with the *Picatrix* and distinguishes him from both the speculative and contemplative Plotinus and the religious Neoplatonists. The vitalization he shares with Plotinus, the depersonalization with Plotinus and some but not all of the *Picatrix*.[19] In the next and final chapter, we shall see how these ideas interacted with his circumstances.

Repercussions

One of the most interesting chapters in Ficino's life is his troubles with the Church over *De vita*. It is a pity that we do not know more about it.

Before *De vita*, Ficino is now thought to have had no serious conflicts with the Church or his own conscience—unless, indeed, we see that astrological problem which was to come to a head in *De vita* festering as early as the exchange with Cavalcanti about Saturn and the writing of the unpublished *Contra iudicium astrologorum*, traditionally dated about 1477 or 1478. Kristeller and Marcel have proved that the single, distinct "crisis of conscience" is a fabrication of the early biographer Corsi and have questioned either the veracity or the importance of Zanobi Acciaiuoli's report of an early injunction to forswear Plato in favor of Aquinas. There had been only scattered skirmishes off and on throughout his life.[1] He had been personally, not publicly, reproved from time to time; for example, his friend John of Hungary reproached him for reviving pagan authors and for claiming that God, through his horoscope, had destined him to do so, but he answered him firmly and piously (*Op.*, pp. 871-72). Nor is *De vita sana* at issue, for it had been circulating in manuscript for almost a decade without reproach (see Clark's "Editorial Introduction" and my "Author in the Work," above).

But already in Book 3 itself, Ficino betrayed some signs of anxiety. Chapter 25 refutes the actual or anticipated objections, to be discussed below, of a "severe prelate of religion" and appeals to their common ground in Thomas Aquinas. The last words of the book proper, on "how impure was the superstition of the Gentiles," abruptly turn on the very authors he has just been citing with approval. Then the two postscripts at the end—cast in the form of letters to "the three Pieros" and other friends and dated the month after *De vita* was finished (i.e., 15 and 16 September 1489), but several months before it was published (i.e., 3 December 1489)—anticipate specific charges, also discussed below, and complain in vague allegories of attacking monsters. Again, for the printed edition, several protestations of orthodoxy and disclaimers of heresy were added to Book 3 along with much else which was absent both from the early Plotinus-commentary version of it and from the *de luxe* manuscript of the whole which was made shortly after for the eyes of its patron alone (for example, the defensive second preface, "Ad lectorem," p. 530; see in general the textual notes on early parts of 3 to MSS *P* and *L*, and Clark's "Editorial Introduction"). Nevertheless, impelled by some personal conviction, as I have shown, Ficino went ahead and published the controversial book.

By May of the following year, 1490, the fat was in the fire. Various letters (esp. those in *Op.*, pp. 910-12, but see also 904,4; 906,3; 907,1, to his lawyer; and 909,3) indicate that *De vita* was accused of some offence against religion to the Roman Curia.[2] While the attackers hypothesized within *De vita* bring specific charges, we have no record from either party of the actual charges. The real attackers are referred to in the letters in only the most vague and cryptic terms. Then on July 26, Ficino congratulated his bishop, Rainaldo Orsini of Florence, that "the highest Pontiff began to favor your work on my behalf," and that Orsini has saved him "from the voracious jaws of the wolves" (p. 911,2). Finally, on 1 August, Ermolao Barbaro wrote to say that he had saved Ficino and that in fact Pope Innocent VIII spoke kindly of him and desired to see him (p. 912,3). It may be as a further repercussion of this accusation that Ficino never wrote another medical work, although he lived and occasionally wrote for another decade. Indeed, in a late letter to Poliziano (of 1494, with messages also for Pico), Ficino finally, and seemingly once and for all, disowned at least the images, protesting that even in *De vita* he had only narrated as possibilities the opinions of others about them. On the same occasion, in a complete but temporary about-face, he set in doubt the very existence of aspects and constellations as operative units—leaving in this category only the planets (as he had done in the unfinished *Disputatio*, *SF*, 1: 35, 40-42). Given the centrality of celestial images to Ptolemaic astrology, this doubt reflected, as he once acknowledged, even on parts of *De vita* 3.[3] As for the impact of the ecclesiastical criticisms on Ficino's audience at large, under the latitude given them by the replacement of the authorial title *De vita libri tres* with the false

De vita triplici, all published translators of *De vita* but one (the Frenchman Guy Lefèvre de la Boderie; see "Editorial Introduction: Translations") ignore Book 3; and so do some printed editions of it. These are the facts as we know them.

From such facts of publication and reception, I must pause to draw an inference about the genesis of Book 2, *De vita longa*. Although part of the second installment, it was never criticized any more than was Book 1 with which it was to be conspicuously reprinted. The indication is that Ficino wrote Book 2 and tucked it away in the middle, although it was written last, in a somewhat perfunctory attempt to please his audience. Its composition was late, hasty, and derivative, both from Book 1 and from sources such as the unacknowledged Roger Bacon, and it is full of rhetorical padding. Ficino prudently judged that at least one detachable half of the work should be filled up with more of the sort of thing which had so pleased the audience of *De vita sana*; but he placed *De vita coelitus comparanda* at the climax, though it was not written last, because it was the most congenial to him and the most fundamental.

Also relevant is the trouble with the Church recently experienced by Ficino's friend and disciple Giovanni Pico della Mirandola, who had gotten himself imprisoned and his *Conclusiones* condemned for heresy just two years before (1487). At first, the papal commission objected only to a small percentage of the 900 "conclusions" or propositions for debate; then, when the author proved impenitent, it condemned the entire lot. Comparisons and contrasts with Ficino's trouble will prove illuminating in many ways.[4] Twenty-six of the conclusions dealt with magic of one kind or another, though only one — which went much farther than Ficino ever did — was among those specifically condemned. Though eventually pardoned by the succeeding pope, Pico soon renounced magic and such astrology as he had ever believed in, indicting the latter in his own posthumously published *Disputationes adversus astrologiam divinatricem*. It seems likely in view of the evidence assembled by Garin that he did this at the particular instigation of his new mentor, Savonarola.[5] Pico had always been dubious of astrology as well as of talismanic magic, though he had once been enthusiastic about magic of a very different sort, so that in this regard he was a bit more consistent than was Ficino.[6] A few years before even Pico's trouble, in 1482, a debate had been held on the utility of magic, Thorndike reports, at the University of Paris between an M. A. candidate and the Church's spokesman, one Dr. Bernard Basin, who took a very hard line against it.[7]

Of what, then, was *De vita* accused, or lacking that, about what in *De vita* did Ficino feel worried or guilty? Let us examine the objections which Ficino anticipates. In Chapter 25, the "severe prelate of religion" complains that *De vita* derogates from "free will" and "the worship of the one God" (3.25, *Op.*, p. 569) — an error about the patient and an error about the agent, an error about things below and one about things above. As to free will, Ficino replies in effect that to recognize and manipulate the forces of nature through science

is not determinism but an escape from it to relative freedom, whereas not to recognize and manipulate them is abrogation of freedom.[8] I find his defense both enlightened and convincing. He could even turn the tables and charge that his masters Plotinus and Aquinas were more deterministic than he, in that they allowed that the stars caused some events or tendencies here below but conceded to man no worldly remedy. Everything Ficino says about astrology in *De vita* is reconcilable with free will.

Ficino's treatment of the death-day is a case in point. Only once in *De vita*, and tentatively, does he "tell a fortune" and prophesy a person's life-span from the stars, in the Dedication of Book 3 to King Matthias Corvinus of Hungary (p. 529; and then, as it turned out, he got it wrong); usually he consults the stars merely to sketch out general tendencies. Moreover, he asserts that one can prolong one's life by hygiene "beyond what was initially appointed," presumably by, or as known through, one's natal stars (3.18.86 f., p. 557).

The same goes for astrological choice of vocation. Outside *De vita*, in the mostly anti-astrological Plotinus commentary, he simply denies that the stars can make one a theologian or an orator (*Enn.* 3.2, comment 3, p. 1611); whereas in the Letters, as we shall see, he vacillates in his own case as to whether Saturn caused or just prophesied that he should become a renovator of ancient things (pp. 872-73, 948). In *De vita* 3.23, where he tells how to use the stars in the choice of a vocation, namely, by determining the Part of Fortune and thence what the guardian daemon is like,[9] he gives just as much weight to the personal factors of preference and experiment; and one can resist the vocational implications of one's horoscope, though only at the cost of one's happiness. All these statements can be reconciled by saying that the stars seem to tell Ficino about as much about someone's future vocation as an I. Q. test is supposed to do today. It is because of his belief in free will that he locates the psychological effects of the stars in the medical spirits and the *vis imaginativa*, but no higher. For the same reason, Ficino characteristically chooses the elective or catarchic over the predictive types, though under the gaze of the "severe prelate of religion" Ficino momentarily and unnecessarily renounces even "elections." Yet even here, he holds out for the uses of astrology (themselves basically elective) in those areas—agriculture and a few other activities—where it was universally recognized, as for example in almanacs. Aside from this partial recantation, as Garin argues, Ficino's synthesis of catarchic astrology with free will in *De vita*, far from being the uneasy compromise Cassirer feels it to be, is even something of a speculative triumph.[10]

In Ficino's work at large, on the contrary, despite a good deal of attention, the relation of free will to astrology has not been reduced to a consistent system; yet even here, at bottom, whatever astrological causation there may be stops short of the will, as almost everyone agreed and as Ficino had asserted in *Theologia Platonica* (9.4, *Op.*, p. 209). Few astrologers were as thoroughgo-

ing determinists as their opponents would have us believe. In the name of free will (and God's providence and the angels' righteousness), Ficino had started but not finished or published his *Disputatio contra iudicium astrologorum* (ed. Kristeller, *SF,* 2: 11-76) condemning astrology on the grounds that it assumes particular astral causation. In some other works, and especially when speaking theologically, Ficino sometimes defends astrology by retreating to Plotinus's position that the stars mainly signify events, whereas they cause them, if at all, in only the most limited sense. Otherwise, in Ficino's letters and whenever he gets into astrological medicine, he accepts astral causation and hence becomes or at least sounds deterministic (Zanier, p. 49). For example, he vacillates between the two last positions when he writes to John of Hungary (pp. 872-73) and to Filippo Valori (7 Nov. 1482, p. 948), that Saturn, his own signifier, not to say leader, prophesied, not to say made, him a renovator of ancient things. This may be real indecision as D. C. Allen and Cassirer affirm,[11] but it is only between various kinds of astrology; and the semiological and elective astrology can survive the condemnation of predictive astrology voiced in the earlier *Disputatio contra iudicium astrologorum* and the concurrent *Commentary* on Plotinus.[12] Even his occasional and dangerous assertions both in *De vita* (e.g., 3.22, *Op.*, pp. 564, 566, on some of which see Walker, p. 45 and n. 3) and elsewhere (e.g., *Comm. Symp.* 6.4) that through their own souls the stars can influence our souls, do not necessarily extend to the will; for in all three passages, the subject is health and vocational aptitudes and hazards, which are pre-moral; the star-souls in two of them (*Comm. Symp.* 6.4, and *De vita*, p. 566) are loosely identified with angels; and in the last *De vita* reference, Ficino immediately affirms the role of "the election of free will" in instigating the transaction (p. 566, to be discussed further below). Again, even psychological effects can be annexed while still avoiding determinism, by limiting astral influence to the intercourse between the human and the cosmic spirits but no higher. Ficino is consistent, says Garin, at least insofar as he never affirms that any body, even a heavenly one, can influence a soul. Hence Ficino's real vacillation between semiological and causative astrology throughout his works leaves intact his orthodox and sincere belief in free will. Some, though not all, of the crises and contradictions in Ficino's thought have been artificially created and can be integrated when read in the proper sense; and some, according to Kristeller, are only a matter of emphasis, depending on whether he is stressing the body or the soul.[13]

The charge which Ficino in Chapter 25 both anticipates and has trouble answering, and which therefore we may infer to be the one the Curia held against him, is the second—derogating from the worship of the one true God. Irreligion is again the issue in the imagined accusation in the Apologia. I will ultimately support Walker's contention that Ficino incurred this, when all is said and done, by employing daemons as mediators and thus expressing a belief which

he genuinely both cherished and feared as dangerous, if not to his soul, at least to his worldly fortunes.

Let us first establish the ground whereon Ficino was safe, where he could have remained without self-endangerment. I see no evidence, *pace* Walker, that he was ever nervous about his non-verbal Orphic music and dancing, presumably because they were safely explained: the first, provided it is non-verbal, as working through the medical and cosmic spirit; and the second, through a very physical analogy, as yielding to the drift of the celestial motions. Astrology was not so dangerous, for just after the storm blew over he wrote offering astrological counsel to the Pope, showing that he "was not in the least worried about his ordinary astrological practice" (Walker, p. 53). Again, despite his advocating quasi-religious suffumigations and prescribed verbal formulas borrowed from Neoplatonic theurgy, Ficino repeatedly disavows worship (*adoratio*) of any of his agents.[14] Ficino's syncretism of various pantheons (see "Habits") also made him harder for theological watchdogs to pin down, since if he was criticized for believing in one divinity, he could always switch his allegiance to its equivalent in one of the other two systems. When criticized for learning about his personal genius or daemon, he could have pointed to his statement that he was simply using Platonic language to characterize his guardian angel (*De vita* 3.23–24, esp. 23, p. 567).

Again, we have seen that by his habit of postulating intermediaries and its major result, his key notions of the life and spirit of the cosmos, Ficino sometimes manages to blur the distinctions on which both heresies turn: to save the free will of the patient, he usually demotes the apparently psychic effects of astrology to a level just below the human soul, namely, the medical spirit, along with its associated psychic faculty, the *vis imaginativa*; to avoid addressing or utilizing daemons, he occasionally demotes his agent to a level of the cosmos just below its various souls, namely, the world-spirit (e.g., in 3.25). It is therefore relevant, though he does not spell it out, that just after his denial of daemon-worship in the Apologia, he asks the third Piero to defend his doctrine of the spirit or, as he here Plotinically and reductively calls it, the life of the heavens. Although this means it too was under attack, he insists upon it so confidently that there cannot have been much danger in it. In both the individual and the cosmos, another word frequently employed by Ficino is *vis* ("force"); this suggests that we view his cosmic spirit as what we now call "the life-force," just as in the individual we translate the archaic concept of "animal spirits" into "élan vital" or, as Putscher calls it, "Lebensantrieb." There is little danger of worshiping something so impersonal.

Images or figurate talismans were both cherished and feared and hence nervously qualified, retracted, and fathered upon Plotinus. Ficino's warning just after describing the talismans—"We ought not rashly to allow even the shadow of idolatry" (3.18, ad fin.)—glances at "Thou shalt not make a graven image

before the Lord." Also significant is the mild protest of Pico: "neque stellarum imagines in metallis, sed illius, idest Verbi Dei imaginem in nostris animis reformemus."[15] They are part of the issue; but they could not in themselves have caused all the trouble; for they had been advocated by Ficino in the well-received plague-tract (*Op.*, p. 605) as the only protection for the medical personnel and had long been employed in "magyk natureel," as Ussery demonstrates in evaluating Chaucer's fictional physician.[16] He could therefore have gotten away with them in *De vita* if he had played his cards right and used them, as they had been used by practicing physicians, purely empirically, without thinking about how they worked. Girolamo Torella in the next decade continued to recommend them with impunity (Thorndike, chap. 44, 4: 574 ff.). But Ficino's theoretical framework invited people to think about the practice and called attention to an implication which was quite disturbing once followed out. Pietro d'Abano had made a similar mistake in the previous century: his *Conciliator*, an advocate of images within another philosophical framework, and cited by Ficino as such (3.18, p.557), had also fallen under the censure of the church. One of the very talismans recommended by Ficino and Pietro had brought a physician of Montpellier under the censure of that great naysayer Jean Gerson.[17] Others of Ficino's talismans were from the *Picatrix* and hence tarred with the same brush as the "things condemned by the Christian religion" which Ficino himself found in it. The evil of images, in the view of Aquinas (*SCG* 3.92; 104–107), was precisely that, insofar as they contained figures and words, they "could only be effective through being understood by another intelligent being," and only the evil ones would be willing to comply.[18] Insofar as his images were suspect, then, it seems to have been because they were seen as addressed to demons. This accurately represents the Church's position (e.g., Gerson had appealed to it in 1428), and hence her probable grounds for condemning *De vita*.

But, as I will argue, these grounds do not quite represent Ficino's own idea of the distinction between good and bad magic. For one thing, grounding himself on Plotinus, Ficino sometimes explains the figures on images as working automatically, or, as Plotinus puts it, spontaneously (4.4.40, *De vita* 3.17, see nn. ad loc.), thus precluding any need for a demon. This seems to me to constitute a tacit refutation of Aquinas's respected argument summarized above and epitomized in *SCG* 3.105, which Ficino dutifully reports in the very next chapter (3.18 ad fin.). In Chapter 18, he claims to agree with Aquinas; and in one respect, he does. As Copenhaver shows, he seizes upon Aquinas's grudging final exculpation of those talismans adorned only with figures: "figures are like specific forms"; and again, a figure "gives the image its species, not so far as [the figure] is a figure but in so far as [the figure] causes the species of what is artificially made, which acquires power from the stars" (Copenhaver's translation). Thus Ficino enlisted even Aquinas, at least his unguarded parenthe-

sis, to say that talismanic magic did not after all depend on demons.[19] But having devised this shift, which he realized ran counter to the main thrust of Aquinas's argument, he nonetheless, for a reason to be explored below, kept on mentioning demons. Derogating from the worship of the one true God is a charge from which Ficino never fully exculpated himself.

For the Church in general, insofar as she had committed herself on the subject, in view of the tradition of the fall of the angels, any demon was by definition a bad one, or devil, and any other mediating spiritual being was an angel. The obvious conclusion to be drawn was that which had been stated by the Church's spokesman, Dr. Bernard Basin, in his debate on magic at Paris a few years before: "If a person invokes a demon either expressly or tacitly . . . in the belief that the demon is a friend of God, he is . . . a heretic" (Thorndike, 4: 492, 493; D. C. Allen, p. 19). Or as Walker more mildly puts it, granting that good or neutral demons may exist, any address to any demon, other than those prescribed by the Church (e.g., prayers to St. Michael and one's guardian angel) was morally dangerous because a bad demon might cut in.[20] Whereas in Neoplatonism a demon was innocent until proved guilty, in Christianity a demon could not even be proved innocent. Accordingly, in Books 1 and 2 of *De vita*, the single mention of a demon is clearly in the orthodox bad sense of the term (1.6.34, *Op.*, p. 499), and these books were never criticized and were more often reprinted and translated.

On the contrary, in Book 3, although he knew how the Church felt about daemons, Ficino takes pains to insist that daemons are among his agents — even in his chapter titles, including that of the very first chapter. Let us assemble what Ficino says about daemons directly. In *De vita 3*, he mentions them seventy-two times, and most of these are favorable. His Hellenic spelling with an *a* implies and his usage bears out, as we shall see below, that he means the word in its Neoplatonic sense as a neutral, generic term, for beings good, bad, and indifferent, noncommittal as to the crucial question of moral allegiance.

If one were for some reason nevertheless determined to study and manipulate good daemons, Christianity afforded two small areas in which a Neoplatonist and a theologian even so orthodox as Aquinas could operate: the guardian and the planetary angels. As I mentioned in "Habits of Mind," the guardian angel of Christianity is in some respects comparable to the individual genius or guardian daemon of Neoplatonism (see 3.23); and the good daemons/angels, insofar as they have the astronomical, and hence morally neutral, job of instigating the celestial motions, are the equivalent of Intelligences or, in Neoplatonism, their subordinate star-souls. To these, Aquinas allowed prayers or acts of reverence precisely insofar as he did to the saints, i.e., with *dulia* but not with *latria*.[21] This "more-and-less" rather than "either/or" habit of mind, shared to some extent by Neoplatonism and Scholasticism alike, allows

for other divine beings claiming a high degree of reverence, so long as one Being is worshiped supreme and transcendent above them. Thus polytheism in itself is not the issue.

Against this still-stark background, we must acknowlege that while Ficino answered the defender of the faith stoutly and in isolation convincingly, his work does not live up to his profession. To the hypothetical critic in the Apologia who asks, "What has a Christian to do with magic or images?" he replies,

> Nor do I affirm here a single word about profane magic which depends upon the worship of daemons, but I mention natural magic, which, by natural things, seeks to obtain the services of the celestials for the prosperous health of our bodies. . . . Lastly, there are two kinds of magic. The first is practiced by those who unite themselves to daemons by a specific religious rite, and, relying upon their help, often contrive portents. . . . But the other kind of magic is practiced by those who seasonably subject natural materials to natural causes to be formed in a wondrous way.

Of this kind one use is merely spectacular, and must likewise be avoided, but that which joins medicine with astrology must be kept (p. 573). From this, one would get the impression that daemons are not involved, but in fact, Ficino refers to them emphatically and often favorably. What Ficino does not deal with here is the way in which, in Book 3, he reasons about and addresses daemons as well as star-souls, intelligences of spheres or planetary angels, and the World-soul. Ficino is sincere in his denial of worship to daemons; but as we have seen, a Christian was not supposed to address them at all. Although Walker seems to have surmised correctly the attitude of the Church towards daemons, he underestimates their importance for *De vita* 3 when he says Ficino was "anxious to avoid them" (p. 45). This emphasis is characteristic of Ficino's Platonic translations and commentaries; in his *Platonic Theology*, an original work, he does indeed seem anxious to avoid them, as will be explained below.

What led him to mention daemons so often and so favorably as to call his own orthodoxy into question? It is precisely Ficino's mental habit of postulating more mediators into a hierarchy. Daemons fill the same mediating role which they fill in his Platonic and Hermetic translations and commentaries, namely, as "medios inter homines et stellas" (*Op.*, p. 1715). In magic, he says in *De vita*, invoking Iamblichus and apparently in further tacit rebellion against Aquinas, daemons are (or at least were for the pagans) all right in their place, which is as "gradus quosdam ad superiores deos investigandos" (3.26.94, p. 571). A person can even become a daemon if he lives only in intelligence (*Comm. Tim.*, p. 1466). They, along with the heroes or deified supermen, "accommo-

date to their inferiors the universal, simple, immobile gifts of the gods." As mentioned above, they actually are the authors of cosmic "harmonic agreement and . . . sympathy" (Iamblichus, *De mysteriis*, "De ordine superiorum," p. 1874). Consonant with this mediatorial position, in Neoplatonism, contrary to Christian theology, they always have bodies, bodies which are similar in composition to the human medical spirit (*Op.*, pp. 876, 1293, 1503). As immortal but at least emotionally passible beings they fill a rung of the Scale of Nature above mortal, passible man, but below immortal, impassible gods (*Comm. Symp.* 6.3, ed. Marcel, 202-203). As Allen says (*Platonism*, pp. 8-28, esp. p. 16), even more than does Aquinas, Ficino stresses the inherent goodness of daemons as a species; and although he mentions Satan, he vacillates as to whether there was one single decisive fall of the angels. (According to the *Commentary* on the *Phaedrus* there was such a fall, and this may be the allegorical meaning of the reference in the Apologia to the "Dragon . . . drawing after him one third of the stars"; but according to a letter, each individual daemon or intermediary spirit decides at some personal crisis, like each human being, whether he is to be good or evil, influenced by how far he is enslaved to his body.)[22] It must be that at least by 1489, having just translated the "Platonici" (see "Place of *De vita* in the Canon"), perhaps even as early as the translation of the *Corpus Hermeticum* or the *Commentary* on the *Symposium,* Ficino had imbibed a sincere belief in such Neoplatonic daemons, as will appear more fully below. The unworshipful, businesslike relationship with daemons which he sets up in *De vita* he never to my knowledge renounced, and I will show that in his eyes, this means of contact justified their use.

Another line of defense in the Apologia is the reiterated disclaimer that images are only Plotinus's idea, not his own, and so by implication are the daemons which they are sometimes employed to evoke. We have assessed the general validity of this claim on philological grounds in a previous chapter ("Place"); now we should assess its polemical purpose. It will be recalled that Plotinus in his isolated remark about the statues (*Enn.* 4.3.11) was praising a very different kind of magic from Ficino's, if indeed it is magic at all; indeed, he was not very interested in either astrology or magic; and his attitude, when expressed, was complex. For daemons, Ficino's disclaimer has more validity in that, like any Neoplatonist, Plotinus does of course mention them.[23] A commentary, even of Ficino's personal and rambling sort, is different from an original work. The indices reveal that in the veritably or ostensibly derivative works, the word demon/daemon is employed frequently and in the distinctively Neoplatonic neutral sense; whereas in the original works, it is employed but rarely, and then mostly in an unfavorable sense. In an original work when he wants to praise daemons, he throws up a local smoke-screen; in the *Theologia Platonica*, for instance, it is only *quidam*, "some people," who say that those spirits who lead the just to their eternal reward are called good daemons (18.10, *Op.*,

p. 418). Somewhat more boldly, in the Letter to Braccio Martelli cited above, he makes clear that he and his friends believe in the Neoplatonic ones; before laying down doctrines about them, he lists authorities—Plotinus (probably meaning *Enn.* 3.4), Porphyry, and Origen (probably meaning the *Contra Celsum*)—and then simply asserts that these thinkers, like Plato himself, agree with the Christian religion (*Epist.* 8, p. 875). Ficino suspected that it was only under cover of someone else's ideas that he had managed to speak of them with impunity. He therefore pretended that *De vita* 3, where he spoke of them freely in his own words, was nothing more than a commentary. Up to 1489, Ficino had almost exclusively singled out pagan works to translate and comment (Romans, Dionysius the Areopagite, and Athenagoras are contemporary or later; only the epistle "De raptu Pauli ad tertium coelum" is before *De vita*, and it is brief [*Op.*, pp. 697–706]; a commentary on the Gospels is supposed to have been written before 1474 but has not survived). For Ficino, it appears that the commentary as a literary form allowed him to say things which he believed but which he could not as a Christian, and latterly as a priest, have said *in propria persona*. But the authorities saw through the smoke-screen and understood the voice to be his own.

Ficino was so sincerely enamored of daemons as to take this risk, I conjecture, because of another and subtler scruple: one that was partly Christian, partly Neoplatonic. Ficino also felt worried or guilty about invoking, and thus seeming to worship, supercelestial gods (3.1, 3.15, 3.21, 3.22, 3.23, 3.26, to be discussed below). Although he does not bring up this particular issue as he does that of daemons in the defensive sections of *De vita*, I will argue that he was skirting an error which was undoubtedly the second one he mentions there, the same one to which the daemons also exposed him, derogating from the worship of the one true God. True, Ficino like many other astrologers regarded the heavenly bodies as living beings with Olympian names (see "Habits"); and like many other Neoplatonists he called metaphysical principles gods (for example, the seminal reasons in 3.26, *Op.*, p. 571). True, not everything which smacks of polytheism or idolatrous worship to postmedieval minds like our own would have done so in 1489 to the minds of Ficino or of the Church. For example, the Old Testament too has a habit of calling all superhuman beings "gods." The Christian God himself is multiple insofar as He is a Trinity and a thinker of thoughts; and thus Christian Platonism found it easy to dictate, as Allen says, that the intelligibles, the Ideas, be equated with "the Ideas in God's Mind" thus annexing the second hypostasis to the first (*Platonism*, p. 252); indeed, Plotinus had invited such an equation in *Ennead* 5.8.9 ad fin. by allowing plurality in Mind. As Walker says, the Church's offering of *dulia* though not *latria* to the saints and to guardian angels might have seemed to Ficino extendable to their approximate Neoplatonic equivalents, daemons and daemonized heroes. When Ficino goes about to list the errors of cer-

tain pagans, he castigates not polytheism but lack of due subordination of such beings to the one God.[24] Nevertheless, we do know that, for her part, the Church through her self-appointed spokesmen, such as the Byzantine George Scholarios and the Roman George of Trebizond, had persecuted the Byzantine Platonist Gemisthus Pletho because he allegedly believed in and revived the worship of, among others, the supercelestial gods.[25]

Ficino would have at the same time known of Pletho's fate and yet sympathized with him and agreed with his reasoning. Pletho's religion, as well as its precursors, the theurgy of Iamblichus and especially of the *Chaldean Oracles* (of which more below), would have attracted Ficino as a poet but repelled him as a Christian and distracted him as a physician.[26] Surely any Neoplatonist would be glad to hear Iamblichus's announcement that the Ideas were knowable by means less rigorously intellectual than those laid down by Plato. Supercelestial gods, like daemons, filled another link in the Chain of Being, albeit a very exalted one; and Pletho's reasoning about them may help to explain their seductive appeal. According to Pletho, following Proclus (*ET*, Prop. no. 113), the Neoplatonic principles of continuity and gradation or insertion of mediators into a hierarchy demanded that right under the One God there should be many partial gods of one sort or another to mediate this world's diversity. Both Pletho and Proclus, Masai explains, are engaging the problem of the one and the many, explaining how a world so diverse as ours could arise from a creator who is the One, by postulating subordinate gods responsible each for a different segment of it.[27] Now it is true that in his *Platonic Theology*, Ficino solves this problem in the Christian manner forged by Aquinas, namely by putting the Ideas of these segments in the mind of God and explaining that He can know diversity without being Himself diverse.[28] It was doubtless such pronouncements which forced Masai to concede that Pletho's key doctrine was without appeal to Italian Platonists such as Ficino (p. 373). But I think it did appeal and that it was renounced only with a struggle and what the Curia, though not Ficino, regarded as a further heresy; besides, as I have argued above, an original work like the *Platonic Theology* is not necessarily Ficino's last and only word on what is admittedly a complex metaphysical problem, since a translation or commentary seems at times to have provided him with a safe forum from within which to utter unorthodox beliefs. Another similarity is that Pletho's comment on the oracle "Ne spiritum conspurces," Μὴ πνεῦμα μολύνῃς . . . (Des Places no. 104 = Kroll p. 64), which equates *pneuma* (πνεῦμα) with the aetherial vehicle or *idolum*, a topic of interest to Ficino, also discusses in Ficinian terms the supercelestial gods (pp. 35–36). It required a heresy as dire as the pagan rites of Mistra were reported to be to drive Ficino to fall into the opposite tactical blunder of parading as he did his use of daemons.

It is because of such sympathy, I propose, that Ficino does occasionally allude to these supercelestial gods. He means in particular the intelligibles of

Proclus.[29] Ficino vacillates about them as agents of his magic somewhat as he does about the daemons, though for reasons we will examine below, he usually disavows direct access to them, whereas he usually, by stated preference, endorses the daemons. In 3.15, doubtless thinking of Pletho's troubles, he leaves the question to others whether the supercelestials can be attracted through the celestials (*Op.*, p. 552, see also 3.1, p. 531, mentioned below, and 3.13, p. 549). In 3.22, however, in pursuance of his orthodox and, as I have argued, whole-hearted belief in free will, he more boldly and centrally invokes the supercelestial gods despite their idolatrous implications: the supercelestial divinities can be induced by the patient's direct emotional or deliberate contact with them to free him from the very fate to which their supposed agents — the mundane, planetary gods and their attendant daemons — have bound him through astrological causation (*Op.*, pp. 565-66). This proves that Ficino believed, contrary to what he says elsewhere, that they could be invoked directly, not only without the celestial gods but in opposition to them. If he were speaking as a Christian, he would say, as Dante did, that astrological determinism can be overcome not by the supercelestials but with the innate strength of free will and the help of divine grace (*Purgatorio* 17-18). As is indicated by his ascription of this notion to Iamblichus, and of a preceding related notion to Chaldeans, Egyptians, and Platonists, the means is Iamblichan higher theurgy; indeed, its rank above, rather than continuity with, lower kinds of magic is more Iamblichan than Ficino usually gets. Again, later in the same chapter (3.22), he disavows sacrifices aimed at deflecting the malice of Mars and Saturn, leaving them to Pico, who would not have wanted them. Although Copenhaver merely lists this text without discussing it, I think it bears out one conclusion he draws from his analysis of the ambivalent final chapter of *De vita*: "The ambitions of a perfected theurgy were, for Iamblichus, necessarily hypercosmic. If the Platonist in Ficino was perhaps tempted to follow this sublime path in his magic, the Christian in him must have trembled to aim so high" ("Iamblichus," forthcoming). In the preceding chapter (3.21) Ficino three times disavows worship of one or another entity: "it is better to skip incantations"; "be warned beforehand not to think we are speaking here of worshiping the stars"; "For we are not now speaking of worshiping divinities but of a natural power" (see also the disclaimers in 3.26 similarly interpreted by Copenhaver). Again, as with daemons, but more intensely, the guilt or danger Ficino feared must have centered not in the agent himself, not even in his polytheistic plurality, but in the specified means of contacting him, worship. Since no one has hitherto noticed the frequency of the favorable references to daemons, no one has undertaken to explain why the danger of the supercelestials seemed to him greater than that of the daemons.

The attraction and repulsion which the supercelestial gods exercised on Ficino can be seen elsewhere, along with an explanation. They are mentioned as

"numina quaedam a materiis penitus segregata" and as possible agents alternative to daemons by Ficino in the first and last chapters of *De vita* 3.[30] He prudently renounces using them directly, maintaining in 3.1 that they are by nature immaterial, impassive, and thus incapable of responding, though even in these renunciations he affirms that the Ideas (their equivalents) can be induced to reform things which have gone awry through the natural channel of assembled objects and the seminal reasons. The renunciation (except for the daemons) is Christian, but the language is pagan. Instead of his term *numina* ("divinities"), he as a Christian Platonist should have called them either Ideas in the mind of the One God or *substantiae separatae*, a scholastic term which would roughly equate them with higher angels; elsewhere, especially in his apologetic works, he frequently throws in such a loose equation with angels to sanctify one or another of his non-Christian agents, as in the equation of the personal daemon or genius with the guardian angel (3.23). He is here keeping within the terms his Neoplatonist author would have used, as befits a commentary. He announces that he will use the World-soul, star-souls, and daemons. These representatives of Soul, as Ficino and Pletho had explained, are "segregata" but not "penitus segregata" — separable from matter in theory but in fact always found animating a body. They are thus accessible, Ficino adds, to allurement by magical objects, which he lists enthusiastically at the end of the first chapter. Significantly for my thesis, the renunciation is a distorted echo of Iamblichus and a straightforward one of Synesius. Iamblichus had said, in Ficino's epitome, that because they are "immaterialia," those "numina" who are "Deo coniuncta" descend to the priest not coerced by some celestial figure he may have had in his horoscope, the sort of magic *De vita* usually directs at its agents, but voluntarily won over by "invocatio" and "operatio sacra" (*Op.*, p. 1888,2), the sort of magic *De vita* here disavows and elsewhere only momentarily slips into, as in 3.22. Ficino's language is the same but his evaluation is reversed. Iamblichus was of course attempting to bring back pagan worship in deliberate opposition to Christianity. Synesius, in Ficino's epitome, confirms the inaccessibility to the "illecebrae" of natural magic of "quantum extra mundum extat divinum." Synesius also renounces one kind of worship, though not that of supercelestials, a kind which Ficino translates as "expiationes . . . solennitatesque." To be exact, Synesius protests that "nihil in praesentia sermo moveat civili tantum legi fidem adhibens" about the "expiationes . . . solennitatesque." I propose that the "lex civilis" is Christianity, which has its own "expiationes . . . solennitatesque." *De insomniis* was written in 405–406, before Synesius made his profession of Christianity by becoming a bishop (410); it is precisely as the current "lex civilis" that Synesius the Platonist would have described Christianity—like all religions, a Platonic lie necessary to keep the lower classes in order.[31] Thus, Iamblichus taught Ficino that supercelestial gods could be contacted by worship, and Synesius showed him that a Christian

Platonist has to renounce some, but not all, traffic with the supernatural. Like Synesius, but even more so in proportion to the depth of his religious belief, Ficino wanted to avoid any magic which might compete with Christianity. Pletho and his troubles had taught him that the real competition lay not in natural magic — not even, it seems to me, in that questionable borderline between lower and higher magic, statue-magic, and its portable counterpart, figurate talismans, which he does endorse more frequently than he does the supercelestial gods — but in Iamblichan and Chaldean higher theurgy. In this context, I propose, daemons seemed to his own religious conscience to be preferable as agents because their relative corporeality (as Neoplatonists defined them) allowed them to be allured by mere sympathy with natural objects into a business relationship.

Not only pressure from his own Christianity and that of others but Ficino's own Neoplatonism led him to stress his use of daemons. For again in the very last chapter he issues a caution, which could not have earned him any credit with the Curia, that it may have been only the aery daemons, not the celestial, let alone anything higher, that were attracted into the statues, and that Iamblichus says daemons should be used not as objects of worship but as steps toward contacting the supercelestials (3.26.84-95, *Op.*, p. 571). This parallels at a lower ontological level Ficino's tendency, noted by Allen, to depart from Proclus and other commentators in demoting to the visible heavens gods whom they had put in the supercelestial place (*Platonism*, pp. 252-53). Ficino is as sincerely anxious to invoke and multiply the lower rungs of the ladder as is Proclus to invoke and multiply the higher ones. Ficino's brand of Neoplatonism advises the suppliant to work through channels. Indeed, the whole drift of *De vita* is to reduce celestial influence to the least common denominator, to sympathies, life, power, spirit, or failing that, to the next higher rung, daemons.

The supercelestial gods could not have been expected to involve themselves directly in Ficino's present concern, medicine. This preservation of the higher gods' transcendence is another reason for Ficino's otherwise imprudent substitution of the daemons. The penchant for working through channels also motivated his similar rewriting of *Picatrix*. The Arabic author had experienced a similar dilemma and taken the course which Ficino rejected. An effort to avoid the use of daemons had led him to "draw the power of the stellar spirits directly into the talisman along rays linking the celestial with the terrestrial" (Pingree, "Sources," p. 14). These stellar spirits (in the normal not the Ficinian sense of that word) are of course only celestial, not supercelestial, seemingly equivalent to the Olympian star-souls whom Ficino boldly invokes. While utilizing the stellar rays (e.g., 3.18, 3.22-3, 3.25-6), Ficino preferred what Pingree contrastingly describes as the other and more consistently Neoplatonic course of working through "demons who are subordinate beings in the chains descending from the planets" (p. 14). Indeed, Ficino glosses the "spiritus stellarum"

which the magicians of *Picatrix* enclose in their statues and images as either "mirabiles coelestium vires" or "daemonas etiam stellae huius illiusve pedissequos" (3.20.21-24, *Op.*, p. 561), thus bringing them down a peg or two. He must have rejected the Arabic author's individualized stellar spirits as unorthodox even from a Neoplatonic point of view because they were too exalted to traffic in medicine as *Picatrix* expected them to do. Plotinus in *Ennead* 2.9.14 had castigated magicians who invoke the highest gods and thus debase them, without, of course, obtaining their materialistic goals. It must be partly to dissociate himself from this debasement of high-ranking souls in *Picatrix* that he denies that "celestial, let alone any higher" beings animated the statues and acknowledges only their respective bands of attendants, the daemons (3.26).

Whether or not they were so closely connected as Walker, citing Aquinas, maintains, both daemons and images are prominent in *De vita* and were felt by Ficino's hypothetical critics to derogate from the worship of God. We have seen that Ficino probably succeeded in defending himself from one of the charges which he anticipated, but not from the other, where his belief was indeed at odds with Christianity as then defined. In regard to daemons, I would say that he does not vacillate; he is only being evasive in order to save his own skin. Particularly in the Apologia, he pretends that by avoiding worship he is avoiding them entirely and that, in any case, he is only paraphrasing Plotinus, whereas elsewhere, far from rejecting a business relationship with a good or neutral daemon, he even substitutes them for the supercelestials. But while Ficino never seems to have doubted the existence and usefulness of entities like the World-soul (though he told "the severe prelate of religion" he would on command replace it with "life," 3.25), star-souls, and the better sort of daemons, while he managed to reconcile the astrology of *De vita* with free will, in the internalized Curia of his own mind he did have real doubts and tergiversations about the value and legitimacy of theurgy and of some types of astrology: the particular, the causalistic, and that which employs images. Ficino's vacillation and evasions are not unnatural, as a friend assured him, in a basically honest man who lived a long time and was subject to pressures both from the Church and from a large and lively intellectual circle.[32] Contradictions, vacillations, and evasions are not just impediments to the researcher's understanding but interesting data in their own right. It is more interesting to know what Renaissance man vacillated about than what he was certain of. In the writing of Ficino's mind with regard to images, faithfully and sympathetically traced by Walker (pp. 42-44, 53) and Zanier (pp. 29-31), in his Platonically humble but theologically imprudent preference for daemons over supercelestial gods, badly concealed under a denial of worship and a denial of authorship, we have a dramatization of what it felt like to be both a devout Christian and a thinker devoted, however mistakenly, not just to refining human knowledge, but to enlarging it.

Notes

Importance of "De vita"

1. Andrea Corsini, "Il 'De vita' di Marsilio Ficino," *Rivista di storia critica delle scienze mediche e naturali* 10 (1919), p. 5.
2. Eugenio Garin, *Medioevo e Rinascimento* (Bari, 1954), "Immagini e simboli in Marsilio Ficino," p. 294.
3. Martin Plessner, ed., *Marsilius Ficinus: De vita libri tres*, edited from the manuscript by Felix Klein-Franke (Hildesheim, 1978), p. 245.
4. G. Sarton, "The Scientific Literature transmitted through the Incunabula," *Osiris* 5 (1938): 185. Although Sarton unfortunately counted only authors, not titles, these two titles represent the bulk of Ficino's scientific work. Some idea of the diffusion of *De vita* can be gleaned from the no less than 36 printed copies possessed by the Bayerische Staatsbibliothek alone, *Librorum impressorum Bibliothecae Regiae Monacensis Catalogus nominalis*, 16: 332.
5. R. Klibansky, E. Panofsky, and F. Saxl (London, 1964), first published by the two last in a shorter version as *Dürers 'Melencolia. I.' Eine quellen- und typengeschichtliche Untersuchung* (Leipzig, 1923), Part 3, chap. 2.2, hereafter cited as KP&S by page number in the text. D. P. Walker (London, 1958), hereafter cited by page number in text. Frances Yates (London, 1964), chap. 4, hereafter cited by page number in text. Shumaker (Berkeley, 1972), chap. 3.3, pp. 120–33, hereafter cited by page or chapter number in text. P. O. Kristeller's *Philosophy of Marsilio Ficino* (New York, 1943), hereafter cited as *Phil MF*, while essential for the understanding of Ficino's thought as a whole, devotes only a few pages to *De vita* as such.
6. Marielene Putscher, *Pneuma, Spiritus, Geist: Vorstellung vom Lebensantrieb in ihren geschichtlichen Wandlungen* (Wiesbaden, 1973), p. 187.
7. Review of Ficino, *Letters*, 2 (London, 1978), *Times Literary Supplement*, 28 July 1978, p. 864d.
8. *The Platonism of Marsilio Ficino: A Study of His 'Phaedrus' Commentary, Its Sources and Genesis* (Berkeley, 1984), pp. x–xi.

Summary of Contents

1. 1.1.23–29 (*Op.*, p. 495); see note ad loc. Wilhelm Kahl, "Die älteste Hygiene der geistigen Arbeit: Die Schrift des Marsilius Ficinus *De vita sana sive de cura valetu-*

dinis eorum, qui incumbunt studio litterarum (1482)," *Neue Jahrbücher für das klassische Altertum, Geschichte und deutsche Literatur und für Pedagogik* N. S. 18, no. 9 (1906): 482-91; 525-46; 599-619; Andrea Corsini, op. cit., p. 5. In his otherwise valuable study, *La medicina astrologica . . . Marsilio Ficino e i suoi contemporanei* (Rome, 1977), p. 21, n. 34, Giancarlo Zanier quibbles that the claim is exaggerated inasmuch as only Book 1 mentions intellectuals in the title; but Book 2 is sometimes referred to by Ficino as *De vita ingeniosis producenda/studiosis proroganda* (see "Editorial Introduction," n. 2); furthermore occasional references such as the title and beginning of 3.24, the "Ad lectorem" of Book 3, and the pervasive topic of Saturn as planet of the old and the intellectual do loosely bind the ensuing books to the first.

2. The special sense in which Ficino employs this term will be discussed in "Translation" and "Habits of Mind."

3. D. C. Allen, *The Star-Crossed Renaissance* (Durham, N. C., 1941), chap. 1.

Our Precursors

1. Wilhelm Kahl envisioned an edition, but died before completing it (see Plessner, p. 246); the late Raymond Marcel, in *Marsile Ficin* (Paris, 1958), pp. 29-30, forecast an edition of this work along with Ficino's *Contra iudicium astrologorum*; and Klibansky, Panofsky and Saxl (p. 255, n. 42), announced in 1964 that before the war a Prof. E. Weil of Paris had been planning an edition—but it has apparently not materialized either, Plessner, p. 246. An Italian ed. announced in *Studies in Philology* in 1964 has apparently turned out to be nothing but a reprint of Lucio Fauno's incomplete Italian translation of 1548. Charles Trinkaus reported in 1970 that Garin had announced an edition (*In Our Image and Likeness* [Chicago, 1970] 2:499), but this seems to have gone the way of the other three.

2. Plessner, p. 258: "Die Anmerkungen zum Text stellen keinen Kommentar zu dem Werk dar, sondern wollen nur Materialien für ihn bieten." For our similar disclaimer, see below, "Notes."

3. Charles Boer, trans., *Marsilio Ficino: The Book of Life* (Irving, Texas, 1980).

4. Michael J. B. Allen, in *Renaissance Quarterly* 35 (1982): 72.

Editorial Introduction

1. The title *De triplici vita* first appears in the verses of Amerigo Corsini appended to the end of *De vita* in the Florence 1489 *editio princeps* and subsequently in Laurenziana MS 73,39, fol. 174v, and in many later editions of the work. Although *De triplici vita* has often been cited as the title, Ficino himself simply refers to his work as *Liber* or *Libri de vita* (*Op.*, pp. 841,1; 904-10 *passim*; 929,4; 935,4; 955,3; 958,1). See Paul Oskar Kristeller, ed., *Supplementum Ficinianum*, 2 vols. (1937; reprinted Florence, 1973), 1: LXXXIII (hereafter cited as Kristeller *SF*). Martin Plessner, in his edition of *De vita* (see above, "Precursors"), p. 260, n.1, suggested, rather dubiously, that the title *De triplici vita* may have arisen from a confusion with another work by Ficino, "De triplici vita et fine triplici." This work, which has sur-

vived in only three manuscripts, seems to have been part of an appendix to Ficino's *Philebus Commentary*. See Kristeller *SF* 1: 80-81 and Michael J. B. Allen, ed., *Marsilio Ficino: The Philebus Commentary* (Berkeley, 1975), pp. 446-50.

2. The title of this treatise varies. *De cura valetudinis eorum qui incumbunt studio litterarum* is the title used in the early manuscripts. Ficino refers to this work elsewhere as *De curanda litteratorum valetudine* (*Op.*, pp. 836,2; 899,2; 901,2; 1506). The Basel *Opera omnia* of 1576 has *De studiosorum sanitate tuenda*. The shorter title, *De vita sana*, was used in the early editions of Florence 1489, Basel c. 1497, and Venice 1498.

3. In his *Epistolae*, Ficino refers to this work variously as *De vita ingeniosis producenda* (*Op.*, p. 901,2), *De vita studiosis proroganda* (*Op.*, p. 901,2), and *De differendo senio* (*Op.*, p. 901,1).

4. The evidence for the date of late 1480 is from the sixth book of Ficino's *Epistolae*, his letter to Bernardo Oricellario (Rucellai) (*Op.*, p. 836,2), in which he states that the work was recently composed. The letter itself is undated but is preceded and followed by letters dated November 1480 (*Op.*, p. 833,2) and December 1480 (*Op.*, p. 839,1). The treatise is also mentioned as complete in Ficino's argument to the seventh book of Plato's *Laws* (*Op.*, p. 1506), dated to 1484. A later date of 1482 for the composition of the work is suggested by Ficino's letter to Martinus Uranius (Martin Preninger), which is dated 29 August 1489 (*Op.*, p. 901,2), but the evidence is contradictory. Ficino says that this work was "compositum septimo aetatis septenario nostro, quo libros Platonis edidimus," that is, by October 1482. The Plato, however, was not printed till 1484. Raymond Marcel, *Marsile Ficin (1433-1499)* (Paris, 1958), pp. 462-66, suggested that Ficino had in mind the date of 1482 when the Plato was complete and in manuscript form; and Marcel has accordingly chosen the later date of 1482 for the composition of *De vita sana*. See also Kristeller *SF* 1: LXXXIII.

5. "Liber Epistolarum nostrarum septimus caput habet epistolam De curanda litteratorum valetudine disputantem. . . ."

6. "Promittebam modo, lector, huic libro septimo caput epistolam de valetudine litteratorum disputaturam, haec vero deinceps adeo nobis excrevit, ut non iam caput tam exigui corporis, sed ipsa seorsum totum aliquod corpus fore velit. Itaque secessit iam consilio meliore et in librum De vita feliciter adolevit" (*Op.*, p. 841,2).

7. See Ficino's two epistles to Pico della Mirandola (*Op.*, p. 900,3 and 901,1), dated 8 and 23 August 1489 respectively, and Kristeller *SF* 1: LXXXIV. In "Roger Bacon and the Composition of Marsilio Ficino's *De vita longa*," *JWCI* 49 (1986): 230-33, I argue that it was Bacon's *De retardatione accidentium senectutis* which Ficino had read and mistaken for the work of Arnald of Villanova. For Ficino's borrowings from Bacon, see below among the notes to *De vita* 2.

8. D. P. Walker, p. 3, n. 2, in response to Kristeller *SF* 1: LXXXIV, suggested that *De vita* 3 was a commentary on *Enneads* 4.4, especially chapters 30-42 which "deal with astral influence in much greater detail." For a fuller discussion of this controversy, see below, "*De vita* in the Canon" and among the notes to Book 3.

9. See his epistle to Pico, dated 8 August 1489, "quo die hinc abisti [i.e., 1 August 1489] libellum de vita coelitus comparanda peregi" (*Op.*, p. 900,3). See Kristeller *SF* 1: LXXXIV.

10. See John R. Clark, "The Manuscript Tradition of Marsilio Ficino's *De vita libri tres*," *Manuscripta* 27 (1983): 158-64.

11. *Ibid.* In the article cited, pp. 162-64, I isolate these particular readings.

12. See Albert Derolez, *The Library of Raphael de Marcatellis, Abbot of St. Bavon's, Ghent, 1437-1508* (Ghent, 1979), p. 217.

13. Cf. John R. Clark, "Marsilio Ficino among the Alchemists," *Classical Bulletin* 59 (1983): 50-54.

14. See John R. Clark, "Two Ghost Editions of Marsilio Ficino's *De vita*," *Papers of the Bibliographical Society of America* 73 (1979): 75-77; and the *Gesamtkatalog der Wiegendrucke*, Band VIII (Stuttgart and Berlin, 1978), p. 413. Kristeller *SF* 1: LXVII lists a Venice 1503 edition of Ficino's *De sole et lumine*, whose title page also lists *De vita*. Professor Kristeller informs me that this *De vita* edition too is a ghost. Alessandra Tarabochia Canavero, "Il *De Triplici Vita* di Marsilio Ficino: una strana vicenda ermeneutica," *Rivista di filosofia neo-scolastica* 69.4 (1977): 699-702, prints a long, detailed list of *De vita* editions, but the list is marred by the inclusion of a number of ghost editions.

15. Clark, "Two Ghost Editions," 77-79; *Gesamtkatalog*, 416-17.

16. *Gesamtkatalog*, 412; Hugh William Davies, *Devices of the Early Printers, 1457-1560: Their History and Development* (London, 1935), p. 374.

17. *Gesamtkatalog*, 413-15.

18. For a fuller discussion of the role played by Andreas Leenius in this textual recension, see Martin Plessner, *op. cit.*, pp. 252-54.

19. The Venice 1498 edition is now available in Plessner's 1978 reprint, but provided with a rather eclectic *apparatus criticus*. Plessner's *apparatus* includes no manuscripts and several later editions. See also above, "Precursors."

20. The marginal numbers in the present edition refer to the *Opera omnia* pagination.

21. For a description of this manuscript, although not of the various hands, see Csaba Csapodi, Klára Csapodi-Gardonyi, and Tibor Szántó, *Bibliotheca Corviniana: The Library of King Matthias Corvinus of Hungary*, translated by Zsuzsanna Horn, translation revised by Alick West (New York, 1969), pp. 53, 124, and Plate XVII. The authors have identified the coat of arms of Matthias painted over with that of the Medici in the manuscript and suggest that the volume was originally meant for Matthias, but was completed after his death and presented to Lorenzo de' Medici.

22. For a fuller description of this manuscript, especially of the illuminations and border decorations of the opening pages, see Csapodi *et al.*, *Bibliotheca Corviniana*, pp. 76, 350, 352, and Plates CXXX and CXXXI.

23. The text of *De vita* 1.26 was edited in Kristeller *SF* 1: 64-65.

24. For a full description of this manuscript, see Derolez, *The Library of Raphael de Marcatellis*, pp. 213-18.

25. According to the description of this edition in Marie Pellechet, *Catalogue général des incunables des bibliothèques publiques de France*, Vol. 3 (Paris, 1909), p. 394 No. 4799, and repeated in *Gesamtkatalog*, p. 412 No.9882, the first leaf contains verses by Jacques Paul Spifame (1502-1566) and Cornelius Duplicius de Scepper or De Schepper (1500-1550). I have learned through private correspondence with Professor Kristeller of the discovery by Ursula Baurmeister, Librarian in the Réserve

of Printed Books at the Bibliothèque Nationale in Paris that the first leaf in the Paris copy of the Florence 1489 edition (Res. Fol. Tc[11].14C) should properly belong at the end of a Paris 1521 edition by Simon de Colines of Boethius' *Arithmetica* (Res. V.146). See Philippe Renouard, *Bibliographie des éditions de Simon de Colines, 1520-1546* (Paris, 1894), pp. 15-16. I would like to thank Prof. Kristeller for this information and for his many other kindnesses.

26. Wilhelm Kahl, "Die älteste Hygiene," p. 531; Dieter Benesch, *Marsilio Ficino's 'De triplici vita' (Florenz 1489) in deutschen Bearbeitungen und Übersetzungen* (Frankfurt am Main, 1977), p. 114.

27. Kahl, p. 529.

28. See Benesch (above, note 26), pp. 126-29, for his manuscript descriptions. P. O. Kristeller, *Iter Italicum*, Vol. 3 (Leiden, 1983), p. 552, noted a fragmentary translation of Book 3 into Low Saxonian in a sixteenth-century manuscript at Hamburg, cod. Alchim. 191, fols. 282r-348v.

29. Kristeller *SF* 1: LXXXV and Canavero, "Il *De Triplici Vita*," p. 703, credit Beaufilz with a translation of only Book 1. He did in fact translate Books 1 and 2.

30. Canavero, pp. 704-5. Lucio Fauno is the pseudonym for Giovanni Tarcagnota (Canavero, p. 703).

31. See P. O. Kristeller, *Iter Italicum*, Vol. 1 (Leiden, 1963), pp. 390-91.

32. Allen in *Renaissance Quarterly* 35 (1982) 69-72. See above, "Precursors."

Principles of Translation, Scope of the Notes, and Indices

1. Apuleius uses them interchangeably; see James Tatum, "The Tales in Apuleius's *Metamorphoses*," *TAPA* 100 (1969): 509, n. 54. Lucretius makes the distinction, *De rerum natura* 1.31 and several times in 3; e.g., 3.94 ff.; see Cyril Bailey, ed., *Titi Lucreti Cari De Rerum Natura Libri Sex* (Oxford, 1950), ad loc., pp. 1005-6; and A.-M. Lathiére, "Lucréce traducteur d'Epicure: *Animus, anima* dans les livres 3 et 4 du *De rerum natura*," *Phoenix* 26 (1972): 123-33.

2. Garin, *Medioevo e Rinascimento*, p. 154, n. 4, trans. Peter Munz in *Science and Civic Life in the Italian Renaissance* (New York, 1969), p. 150, n.4.

3. "The Scholastic Background of Marsilio Ficino," in *Studies in Renaissance Thought and Letters* (Rome, 1956), p. 41.

4. It is also doubtful, however, that Ficino knew that he was using Bacon and not Arnald of Villanova. See above, Editorial Introduction, n.7.

5. Democritus in *De vita* 1.5, p. 497, is mediated by *De div*. 1.7.80 and/or *De oratore* 2.46.194. Similarly in the *Platonic Theology*, 15.2, *Op.*, p. 330, Dikearchus (Ficino's spelling) is mediated by Cicero, *Tusc. Disp.* 1.10.21; 11.24; 18.41; 22.51, as Marcel has noted in his ed. (Paris, 1970)3: 16 and n. 2.

The Author in the Work

1. Proem to *Comm. Plot.*, addressing Lorenzo de' Medici, *Op.*, p. 1537. Professor Katharine Park of Wellesley College informs me that, in actuality, Cosimo's

house doctor was a Mariotto di Nicolò. External documents confirm that Diotifeci was not only a surgeon ("chirurgicus Florentiae suo saeculo singularis," *Epistolae*, Book 1, Letter of 11 September 1474 to Francesco Marescalchi, *Letters* 1: 126, *Op.*, p. 644), but a "scholare di medicina"—see description in S. Gentile, S. Niccoli, and P. Viti, compilers, *Catalogo* of Mostra di Manoscritti, Biblioteca Medicea Laurenziana, *Marsilio Ficino e il ritorno di Platone* (Florence, 1984), no. 126 of MS Firenze, Archivio di Stato, Catasto 495 (entry dated 1433), fols. 130v-131r; an "egregius artis et medicine doctor"—see description in *Catalogo*, no. 131 of MS Firenze, Archivio di Stato, Notarile antecosimiano G 616/3, fols. 143r-145v (entry dated 30 April 1460); and "medicho di chasa" of the Hospital of Santa Maria Nuova—see quotation in *Catalogo*, no. 130 of the record of the payment of his stipend (entry dated 14 December 1454, one of several) in MS Firenze, Archivio di Stato, Ospedale di Santa Maria Nuova 4497, fol. 90r.

2. See Kristeller, "Philosophy and Medicine in Medieval and Renaissance Italy," in Stuart F. Spicker, ed., *Organism, Medicine, and Metaphysics: Essays in Honor of Hans Jonas* (Dordrecht, 1978), p. 34.

3. Reported in 1530 by Piero Caponsachi, *Sommario della vita di Marsilio Ficino*, and generally accepted, e.g., by Della Torre, pp. 496-97; by Marcel, p. 174; and by Garin, *Prosatori latini del Quattrocento* (Milan, 1952), p. 929. Marcel gives full information on Tignosi and explores his possible influence on Ficino, pp. 174-84. Ficino invokes Tignosi in an early letter to Cosimo, *Op.*, p. 615. For editions of bits of his work and comments upon the rest, under the name of Niccolò da Foligno, see Lynn Thorndike, *Science and Thought in the Fifteenth Century* (New York, 1929), pp. 161 ff. and 308 ff. For other possible teachers, see Kristeller, "The Scholastic Background of Marsilio Ficino," in *Studies in Renaissance Thought*, p. 42 and n. 40. On the Italian connection of philosophy and medicine, and consequent bypassing of the theology which dominated the universities of other nations, see Kristeller, "Humanism and Scholasticism in the Italian Renaissance," in *Studies in Renaissance Thought*, p. 575 and n. 62; also his "Philosophy and Medicine," pp. 29-40; and Nancy Siraisi, *Taddeo Alderotti and His Pupils: Two Generations of Italian Medical Learning* (Princeton, 1981), chap. 6.

4. Kristeller, "Un nuovo trattatello inedito di Marsilio Ficino," *Studies in Renaissance Thought and Letters*, p. 141, return address in text of Letter of 13 September 1454, to Antonio da San Miniato, p. 150; Marcel, p. 182; the eds. of the *Catalogo*, however, feel we can only infer "that Ficino made his home there, along with his father, in the neighborhood of the hospital" (trans. mine, no. 135). The father's place on the staff is now well established, see n. 1.

5. See Kristeller, "Il Ficino studente a Bologna," pp. 195-96, in "Per la biografia di Marsilio Ficino," in *Studies in Renaissance Thought and Letters*, correcting the tradition repeated even by Garin, *Prosatori latini*, p. 929. As to his practice, he is listed among the doctors of Florence in a chronicle entry of 1470, Della Torre, p. 777.

6. P. 48, n. 89.

7. P. 471; see *Op.*, pp. 794, 812, 821, 829, 865, 951, 1465; on him and other doctors of Ficino's circle, see also Della Torre, pp. 779-80.

8. So reads the Riccardiana manuscript, according to the London School of Economic Science translators, *Letters*, 1: 129; Basel, 1576, reads *Galienum nostrum*, which

sounds like a *lectio facilior*. "Our Galileo" Prof. Dyer identifies as Galileo di Giovanni Galilei, a prominent Florentine physician, a Medici partisan, and an ancestor of the famous Galileo.

9. *Contra* Marcel, p. 125. Prof. David Pingree has kindly plotted for me the precise hour of Ficino's birth and the exact positions then occupied by all the planets. Most interesting for our purposes, Saturn was in the twelfth degree of Aquarius, Mars in its zero degree, Jupiter in the nineteenth of Leo, and Venus in the twenty-first of Virgo.

10. Letter to Cavalcanti, *Op.*, p. 733. I have adapted my trans. from the trans. of the London School of Economic Science, *Letters*, 2: 33-34.

11. For Ficino's at least quondam endorsement of this negative view, see "Saturni Martisque natura," Letter to Cardinal John of Aragon, *Op.*, p. 819.

12. The text of the horoscope sent to Preninger as quoted by Marcel, p. 125, n. 3, is garbled. On planetary houses or domiciles, see *De vita* 3.9, *Op.*, p. 542; on the Part of Fortune, 3.23, *Op.*, p. 567, and on both, "Traditions."

13. *Marsilio Ficino e la filosofia dell' umanesimo* (Bologna, 1954), p. 9.

14. Letter to John of Hungary, *Op.*, p. 872. D. C. Allen, *Star-Crossed Renaissance*, p. 14, totally misunderstands their dispute.

15. See *De vita* 3.9.2, *Op.*, p. 542.

16. *De vita* 3.6.170-71, *Op.*, p. 539, on Jupiter's tempering of Saturn; see also 3.12.50-51, p. 547; 3.22.41-42, p. 565; and Letter to Rinaldo Orsini, Archbishop of Florence, *Op.*, p. 726.

17. 1 Proem 1.37-38, p. 494; Ptolemy, *Tetrabiblos* 4.4, p. 389.

18. Cf. *De vita* 3.24.1-2, *Op.*, p. 568; and Letter to Pico of 23 August 1489, p. 901,1.

19. *De vita* 1.8.18-19, *Op.*, p. 501; 3.23.80, *Op.*, p. 567.

20. *The Survival of the Pagan Gods*, trans. Barbara Sessions (New York, 1953), p. 61; see also Zanier, p. 46. On the "close and fundamental connection between melancholy and Saturn," see KP&S, pp. 127-28.

21. *Letters* 2: 33, *Op.*, p. 733, prescribed in *De vita* on the basis of Ficino's own experience, 1.10, p. 502; 2.15, p. 523.

22. KP&S, p. 271, citing *De vita* 2.15, p. 522; and 3.22, pp. 564 ff.

23. Cavalcanti, p. 732; Ficino's letters to John of Hungary, p. 872; and to Filippo Valori, 7 November 1492, p. 948.

24. For their faint survivals in medieval poetics, see E. R. Curtius, *European Literature and the Latin Middle Ages,* trans. Willard Trask (London, 1953), pp. 474-75. Ficino translated, mostly for the first time, those Platonic works which deal with them; and he dwelt on them in his other works. Leonardo Bruni had previously translated the relevant part of the *Phaedrus* (he had gotten as far as 257c, says M. J. B. Allen, ed. and trans., *Marsilio Ficino and the Phaedran Charioteer* [Berkeley, 1981], p. 5 and n. 15), and had alluded favorably to *furor* in his letter to the poet Marrasio (KP&S, p. 249); but these works of Bruni enjoyed only a limited influence. The Byzantines Pletho, George of Trebizond, and Cardinal Bessarion, who of course read it in the original, had disseminated some knowledge of it (see Allen, p. 5), but Ficino basically relied on the text and ancient authorities, whom he was among the first to read, see also M. J. B. Allen, *The Platonism of Marsilio Ficino: A Study*

of His 'Phaedrus' Commentary, Its Sources and Genesis (Berkeley, 1984), p. 230, nn. 5 and 6.

25. For intellectual causes, see, for the Arabic, *Libri duo de melancolia*, ed. Karl Garbers (Hamburg, 1977), pp. 104-7; and *Della melancholia*, trans. from the Latin and ed. M. T. Malato and U. de Martini (Rome, 1959), p. 54 (Latin) and p. 99 (Italian); see KP&S, pp. 82 ff. For Pietro, mentioned above, see *Expositio in Problematis Aristotelis*, ed. Hier. Faventinus (Mantua, 1475); no p. or sig. numbers, but the problem can be easily located by its number, 30.1.

26. *Practica* (Venice, 1517), fol. 23v. Guaineri flourished 1413-1448.

27. KP&S, p. 265; André Chastel, *Marsile Ficin et l'art* (Geneva, 1954), pp. 168-69 and n. 5; E. Gombrich, *Symbolic Images* (London, 1972), "Ficino and Art," pp. 46-78; for references to *De vita* in particular, see p. 58, nn. 89, 90. On this general subject, see also R. and M. Wittkower, *Born under Saturn, the Character and Conduct of Artists: A Documented History from Antiquity to the French Revolution* (London, 1963), especially chapter 5.

28. KP&S, Part 4, esp. pp. 284-397, the heart of their entire book. I use the term "intellectual" in their sense.

29. Sears Jayne, "Ficino and the Platonism of the English Renaissance," *Comparative Literature* 4 (1952): 220-21, esp. n. 37. The content of *De vita* 3 would probably have reached England in the frequent plagiarisms from it in Cornelius Agrippa's *De occulta philosophia*, on which see Walker, pp. 91-2.

30. "Ficino and Platonism," pp. 216 ff. The thrust of Jayne's article is that in England Ficino was more often the ultimate than the proximate source for knowledge of Plato, whereas on the Continent it was the other way around.

31. Floyd Dell and Paul Jordan-Smith, eds. (New York, 1927), Index, s.v. "Ficinus." Their account of *De vita* appended to this entry is mostly incorrect.

32. The lyrical and more psychological love-melancholy of the *Comm. Symp.* is absent; see "Place."

33. Cf. the lists of Lawrence Babb, *The Elizabethan Malady: A Study of Melancholia in English Literature* . . . (East Lansing, Mich., 1951); Bridget Gellert Lyons, *Voices of Melancholy: Studies in Literary Treatments of Melancholy in Renaissance England* (London, 1971); and Hellmut Flashar, *Melancholie und Melancholiker in den medizinischen Theorien der Antike* (Berlin, 1966), esp. p. 138. Babb pays considerable and accurate attention to *De vita*; neither of the latter works mentions it, though both mention KP&S.

The Place of "De vita" in the Canon

1. Letter grouped with those of 1480 to Bernardo Rucellai, p. 836.2; Letter of 29 August 1489, cited above, p. 901,2; and Proem dedicating the entire work to Lorenzo de' Medici, p. 493, though the chronology of composition therein claimed for Book 2 is false. The date of *De vita sana* seems to be 1480, see "Editorial Introduction."

2. *De vita* 2.20.34-35, p. 528; 3 Proem.25, p. 529; 3 "Ad lectorem," 34, p. 530; 3.26.1, p. 570; Apologia, 57, p. 573.

3. The MS is Florence, Biblioteca Laurenziana 82, 11 (Kristeller's L 15 and our *P*) finished on 12 Nov. 1490 by an amanuensis of Ficino. *Enn.* 4.3.11 has always been accepted as Ficino's lemma by Garin, "Le 'elezioni' e il problema dell'astrologia," first pub. in *Umanesimo e esoterismo*, ed. E. Castelli (Padua, 1960), p. 18 = p. 425 in the reprint, *L'età nuova: Ricerche di storia della cultura dal XII al XVI secolo* (Naples, 1969), with slight additions, principally to the notes. See "Editorial Introduction" on that MS. In the respective commentary sections of the printed editions, whether of the separate translations or of the *Opera omnia*, the subsequent withdrawal of the commentary on chap. 11 to make *De vita* 3 has left nothing on chap. 11, which throws off such chapter numbers as have been inserted, giving the impression that the commentary on chap. 12 is on chap. 11, etc., see for example *Op.*, p. 1737. Although needlessly confusing, the lacuna attests to his honesty about the origin of *De vita* 3.

4. The above is my translation of Ficino's Latin translation of it: "Atqui mihi videntur veteres sapientes quicunque optabant sibi adesse deos, sacra statuasque fabricantibus in ipsam universi naturam mentis aciem direxisse, atque inde animadvertisse naturam animae ubique ductu facilem admodum pronamque esse, omniumque facillime posse capi, siquis fabricaverit aliquid, quod facile ab ipsa pati possit, patiendoque portionem aliquam ab ipsa sortiri," *Plotini . . . Enneades* (1st ed. Florence, 1492), sig. bb iii, fol. 252, and for a more accessible ed., (Basel, 1580), pp. 380-81. Garin, "Le 'elezioni,' " p. 19 = 425. Although these scholars were not using Ficino's translation, their parallels hold good for it.

5. See for example *De vita* 3.1 ad init. and *Enn.* 4.4.42 ad fin.; 3.1 and 4.4.35, our n. 3; 3.2 and 4.4.32, our n. 9; and 3.26 and 4.4.40, our nn. 2 and 6. For Ficino's actual citations of Plotinus, see Index of Proper Names. Copenhaver's various articles, especially "Renaissance Magic," explore the contribution of Plotinian magic. Along with *Enn.* 4.4.30-44, 2.3 was suggested as the lemma by KP&S (p. 263, n. 67); 2.3 is indeed relevant, but since it contains Plotinus's attack on astrology, *De vita* would have to be not so much commenting on it as refuting or conspicuously ignoring it.

6. *Marsilio Ficino: The Philebus Commentary*, ed. and trans. Michael J. B. Allen (Berkeley, 1975), Introduction, p. 24.

7. Marian Heitzmann, "La libertà e il fato . . . Ficino," *Rivista di filosofia neoscolastica* 28 (1936): 355. Garin too is uneasy about Ficino's characterization "commentary," p. 18 = 425.

8. Zanier, *La medicina*, pp. 24 and 28-29. He is skeptical of Ficino's claim. On genethlialogy as Plotinus's target rather than astrology as a whole, see Thorndike, 1: 302. Yet *Enn.* 4.3.12 even endorses genethlialogy, as Garin observes, "Le 'elezioni,' " p. 26 = 434. On the basis of *Enn.* 2.3, KP&S assert more sweepingly that Plotinus never entertains except hypothetically the validity of any astrology, p. 263, n. 67.

9. Zanier, *La medicina*, pp. 28-29. P. Merlan, "Plotinus and Magic," *Isis* 44 (1953): 341-42. E. R. Dodds says, "Magic. . . .did not interest him. He saw in it merely an application to mean personal ends of [that sympathy which holds the universe together]," *The Greeks and the Irrational* (Berkeley, 1951), Appendix 2, p. 285. In general, says Kristeller, Ficino's understanding of Plotinus was excellent, *Phil MF*, Index, s.v. "Plotinus, . . . Ficino an outstanding commentator on."

10. See Sleeman and Pollet, *Lexicon Plotinianum* (Leiden, 1980), s.v. πνεῦμα. Plotinus cared even less about spirit in the technical sense than he did about magic and astrology. Most of his references consist of attacks on the Stoics' original formulation of it, see *Enn.* 4.7. (2) 4 and 5 and A. Graeser, *Plotinus and the Stoics* (Leiden, 1972), p. 44, also 4.7.7, ad init., and 4.7.8, passim. Plotinus once mentioned favorably a human πνεῦμα which is the astral body (3.6.5 ad fin.) and elsewhere one which seems distinct from the soul and may be synonymous with the astral body (2.2.2.21); but in general he avoids the word because of its associations of Stoic materialistic monism; on all of the above, see Verbeke, *L'Évolution de la doctrine du pneuma*, pp. 352-63. *Enn.* 4.4.26 attributes a πνεῦμα in what seems to be the normal theological sense of the word to the earth; and Ficino's commentary on this and succeeding chapters up through 32 (*Op.*, pp. 1744-45, see also p. 1736 on *Enn.* 4.3.8) takes this occasion to expound his own unusual theory of the medical and the cosmic spirit; but even Ficino does not pretend it is in his lemma. In 4.4.26-44, some of the functions of Ficino's world-spirit are performed by the general life of the universe and especially that lower and vegetative power of Soul common to the earth, animals, and the universe. The source of Ficino's doctrine of spirit lies elsewhere. Ficino's commentary on 4.4.26-44 bears little resemblance, aside from the spirits, to *De vita* 3 and was not withdrawn as was that on 4.3.11 but still appears as such in the final version, thus confirming that however much Ficino drew from this Plotinian passage, it did not constitute the lemma of *De vita* 3.

11. Garin cites it as one of Ficino's models, "Le 'elezioni,' " p. 20 = 426. The Greek original was rediscovered by J. Bidez and published by him in *Catalogue des manuscrits alchimiques grecs*, vol. 6, *Michel Psellus* (Brussels, 1928), Appendix, "Proclus sur l'art hiératique," pp. 148 ff. The French trans. of this given by A.-J. Festugière in *La révélation d'Hermès Trismégiste*, vol. 1, *L'astrologie et les sciences occultes* (Paris, 1949), pp. 134-36, omits from the original the material on θρυαλλίς (Ficino's *cannabis*) and on solar daemons with lion faces. For an ed. and English trans. of the Greek, see Copenhaver, Appendix to "Hermes Trismegistus, Proclus," forthcoming.

12. Festugière, *Révélation* 1: 134; E. R. Dodds, *The Greeks and the Irrational*, p. 291. Whether or not their guiding spirit Plotinus himself advocated and/or practiced theurgy is a debate which has little relevance to my case, see P. Merlan, "Plotinus and Magic" on the positive side, and A. H. Armstrong on the negative, "Was Plotinus a Magician?" *Plotinian and Christian Studies* (London, 1979), pp. 73-79, who does not, however, mention the first sentence of 4.3.11, which seems to me to portray a textbook example of theurgy.

13. 3.26, p. 571; Walker, pp. 40-41; Yates, p. 66; Garin, "Neoplatonismo ed ermetismo," *Lo zodiaco della vita: la polemica sull'astrologia dal Trecento al Cinquecento* (Bari, 1976), pp. 73-75, adding further "Hermetic" subtexts for Ficino's beliefs in astrology and in daemons—good, bad, and indifferent. Copenhaver in a forthcoming article will downgrade the influence of the Hermetic texts on *De vita* in favor of the more intellectually coherent "Platonici," "Hermes Trismegistus, Proclus," forthcoming. Copenhaver also assesses what in Ficino's thought appears also in the Hermetic texts (especially the *Asclepius*), and what in the Hermetic texts (especially the *logia* first trans. by Ficino) does not particularly contribute to *De vita*.

14. Ed. Marcel, p. 220. On this as the basis of Ficino's magic, see Paola Zam-

belli, "Platone, Ficino, e la magia," in *Studia Humanitatis . . . Ernesto Grassi . . .* ed. E. Hora and E. Kessler (Munich, 1973), pp. 121-42, esp., in the present instance, p. 130. On Ficino's doctrine of cosmic love in general, see also *Comm. Symp.* 3 and its lemma the speech of Eryximachus, *Symp.* 186a-188e, and Kristeller, *Phil MF*, pp. 111 ff.

15. See Samuel Sambursky, *Physics of the Stoics* (London, 1959), pp. 9-10; and *Enn.* 4.4.27.

16. *Marsile Ficin*, pp. 200-202. Although Prof. Kristeller does not date it this early, explaining Marcel's data as references to the lost but necessarily Timaeic *Institutiones Platonicae* of 1456 (*SF* 1: CXX; CLIV; CLXIV), the fact remains that something on the *Timaeus* is said by Ficino and others to be one of his earliest works. Even by Kristeller, the *Commentary* on the *Timaeus* is listed as relatively "early," "Marsilio Ficino as a Beginning Student of Plato," *Scriptorium* 20 (1966): 47.

17. On the World-soul as a concept encouraging to medieval science, see Winthrop Wetherbee, *Platonism and Poetry . . . The Literary Influence of the School of Chartres* (Princeton, 1972) chap. 1.3, p. 33.

18. For Ficino's own accounts of the place of *De vita* in his canon, see not only its own first Proem, pp. 493-94, and the letter to Preninger discussed above (*Op.*, p. 901,2), but the Dedicatory Epistle to the translation of Plotinus, pp. 1537 ff., and in general his three Catalogues of his works, ed. *SF*, 1: 1-3.

19. Ed. Kristeller, *SF*, 2: 11-76; beginning also duplicated in *Comm. Plot.*, p. 1609. See also above on Ficino's use of *Contra iudicium astrologorum* for the anti-astrological parts of his Plotinus commentary. For a redating of this *Disputatio* which collapses Ficino's two anti-astrological phases into a single late one under the influence of Savonarola, see D. P. Walker, "Ficino and Astrology," in *Marsilio Ficino e il ritorno di Platone* (Florence, 1986), pp. 342-43. Although the word sometimes specifies "interrogations" (see "Traditions"), Keith Thomas explains that "judicial" in such titles is generic, not restrictive, *Religion and the Decline of Magic* (New York, 1971), p. 286; hence we cannot resolve the contradiction by limiting the scope of Ficino's attack to one kind of astrology. For examples of such letters, see *Op.*, pp. 781 ff., 958.

Traditional Material and Innovations

1. "Ad lectorem," p. 530; Apologia, p. 573; Aristotle, *Metaphysics* 12.6-8, (1071b-1074b). On Galen's two treatises on astrological medicine, see Thorndike 1: 178-80; for the major treatise, see "Prognostica de decubitu ex mathematica scientia," ed. Kühn, 19: 529-31. The accepted theoretical connection of these two subjects had been well stated by John of Burgundy: "Since the heavenly or firmamental bodies are the first and primitive causes [of disease], it is necessary to have knowledge of them; for if the first or primitive causes be unknown, we may not come to know the causes secondary." The secondary causes are known by "physic," based, of course, on the four humors, *De pestilentia liber*, B. L., MS Sloane 3449, fol. 6, quoted by Walter Clyde Curry, *Chaucer and the Medieval Sciences*, 2nd ed. (New York, 1960), pp. 7, n. 5, and 9. Because of this connection, for example, Aristo-

tle's *De caelo* was a required text in the medical curriculum at Bologna; see Nancy Siraisi, *Taddeo Alderotti*, p. 152.

2. *The Discarded Image* (Cambridge, 1964), p. 94.

3. For further information, see KP&S, esp. pp. 10-12, and Lewis, *Discarded Image*, pp. 169 ff.; and, more specialized and relevant in different ways to our treatise, Walter Clyde Curry, *Chaucer and the Medieval Sciences*, and the various works on melancholy cited under the subsection "Value and Influence of Ficino's Doctrine of Melancholy," above.

4. Cf. KP&S, pp. 127-28, with Ptolemy, *Tetrabiblos*, 1.4; *De vita* 3.6.54, *Op.*, p. 538, slightly warm; 3.12, p. 546 bis, slightly cold.

5. See, for example, Firmicus Maternus, *Mathesis* 4.21; Ficino, *De vita* 3.24, p. 568; and Letter to Pico of 23 August 1489, p. 901, 1.

6. See 3.9, p. 542, on houses, terms, and exaltations.

7. See 3.23.51 f., p. 567, cf. Firmicus Maternus, *Mathesis* 4.17-18.

8. Ernst Cassirer, *The Individual and the Cosmos in Renaissance Philosophy*, trans. Mario Domandi (Philadelphia, 1972), p. 113.

9. For further background on this section, see A. Bouché-Leclercq, *L'astrologie grecque* (Paris, 1899), the definitive scholarly history of astrology; F. Boll, C. Bezold, and W. Gundel, *Sternglaube und Sterndeutung*, 5th ed. (Stuttgart, 1966); the articles entitled "Astrology" by David Pingree in *Encyclopedia Britannica* (1974) 2: 219, and in the *Dictionary of the History of Ideas* 1: 118-26; and, less technical and closer to our author and his time, KP&S on the history of interpretations of Saturn; the sections on astrology in the works by Wayne Shumaker, C. S. Lewis, and Walter Clyde Curry cited above; Robert Ackerman, *Backgrounds to Medieval English Literature*, which excels Lewis both in detail and by including diagrams; for the thinkers of the Italian Renaissance, E. Garin, *Lo zodiaco della vita*, trans. (rather poorly) as *Astrology in the Renaissance: the Zodiac of Life* by Carolyn Jackson, June Allen and Clare Robertson (London, 1983); S. K. Heninger, *The Cosmographical Glass: Renaissance Diagrams of the Universe* (San Marino, Calif., 1977); and for the actual practice of astrology in late-Renaissance England, Keith Thomas, *Religion and the Decline of Magic*, chaps. 10-12.

Habits of Mind

1. On the above and their relations, see *Theol. Plat.* 4.1, ed. 1: 165, *Op.*, p. 131, and *Comm. Symp.* 6.3, Marcel ed. 1: 203.

2. Zanier, pp. 6-7, esp. n. 7; Putscher, *Pneuma*, p. 194.

3. Fritz Saxl, "Il rinascimento dell'antichità," Sec. 3, "Die antike Astrologie als dämonisch-bewegende Macht in der Kultur der Frührenaissance," in *Repertorium für Kunstwissenschaft* 43 (1922): 232 ff. Garin, "Le favole antiche," in *Medioevo*, 1.3, pp. 82-87. Jean Seznec, *The Survival of the Pagan Gods*, trans. Barbara Sessions (New York, 1953), pp. 37-83. Plessner, ed., *De vita*, p. 248 and n. 14. Carol V. Kaske, "Marsilio Ficino and the Twelve Gods of the Zodiac," *JWCI* 45 (1982): 195-202.

4. An interesting exception is that passage which he prefaces with "ut peripatetice loquar," 3.19. 60-61, *Op.*, p. 560, a peripatetic answer to a query raised by Plotinus, *Enn.* 4.4.31.

5. Cf. Kristeller, *Phil MF*, pp. 137-38.
6. "Le 'elezioni,' " p. 29 = 437, my translation.
7. Garin, "Le 'elezioni,' " p. 29 = 438, citing *Enn.* 4.4.40.
8. See James Hutton, "Some English Poems in Praise of Music," *English Miscellany* 2 (1951): 17; and Leo Spitzer, *Classical and Christian Ideas of World Harmony: Prolegomena to the Interpretation of the Word 'Stimmung'* (Baltimore, 1963), pp. 7 ff., passim.
9. 4.3.12; 4.4.41; Synesius, *De insomniis*, trans. Ficino, *Op.*, p. 1969; *De vita* 3.17, *Op.*, p. 555, quoted by Walker, p. 14.
10. 3.21, *Op.*, p. 563-64, quoted by Walker, pp. 15-16; see also his "Orpheus the Theologian and Renaissance Platonists," *JWCI* 16 (1953): 100, 102. As I show in "Magic," this notion was probably inspired most directly by Al-Kindi.
11. Kristeller, *Phil MF*, pp. 101-2, quoting *Op.*, p. 1233. A. O. Lovejoy, *The Great Chain of Being* (Baltimore, 1961), pp. 60-62. See also Garin, *L'umanesimo italiano* (Bari, 1965), p. 115. On the chains, see Festugière, *La révélation*, p. 134. H. O. Taylor, *The Medieval Mind* (4th ed., Cambridge, Mass., 1949), draws comparisons between the "mediatorial system" of Neoplatonists and that of early Christians, 1: 54, though he sees both as equally personal and hence for him equally irrational.
12. "Le ciel de Platon [in the *Timaeus*] est couvert des modeles copiés elles-memes sur les idées divines," and such Platonism "est prêt à se convertir en astrologie," Bouché-Leclercq, p. 25; see also *Corpus Hermeticum*, Tr. 17, ed. Nock and Festugière, 2: 244.9-11; and KP&S, p. 151.
13. The seminal reasons or seeds which figure so largely in 3.1 were invented by the Stoics and reached Ficino chiefly through Plotinus, who gives them an even larger role. Conceived on analogy with the seeds and sperm of organic life, they all reside without extension in the World-soul (*Enn.* 2.3.14; 4.3.10). For Plotinus, they correspond in number to and respectively inhere in the individual beings which they form (4.3.10, though they are of course variously conditioned by matter; 4.9.15). For Ficino, however, they correspond to and generate only the species, not the individuals, since other necessary causes, contingent causes, and free will all go into the makeup of the latter, *Comm. Plot.*, "De fato," = *Enn.* 2, *Op.*, p. 1676. For Plotinus, they are the cause of the motion of Soul (4.3.15) and of the sensory in bodies (6.3.16), connections which Ficino does not express in *De vita*. See F. E. Peters, *Greek Philosophical Terms: A Historical Lexicon* (New York, 1967), s.v. "logoi spermatikoi."
14. Allen, *Phaedran Charioteer*, Intro., p. 19 and pp. 66-69.
15. I owe this phrasing to the advice of D. P. Walker, cf. Zanier, p. 24.
16. "The Astral Body in Renaissance Medicine," *JWCI* 21, 1-2 (1958): 120, with extensive discussion and bibliography; see also, for Ficino, KP&S, pp. 264-65, though they incorrectly describe it as a fluid, and pp. 372-73; for the history of the concept, G. Verbeke, *L'évolution de la doctrine du pneuma du stoïcisme à S. Augustin* Paris, 1945); E. Ruth Harvey, *The Inward Wits*, Warburg Institute Surveys, 6 London, 1975), pp. 16-18; Marielene Putscher, *Pneuma, Spiritus, Geist*; on the Stoic origins specifically, Michael Lapidge, "Stoic Cosmology," in *The Stoics*, ed. John M. Rist (Berkeley, 1978), pp. 168-76, hereafter "Lapidge" in text; and Owsei Temkin, "On Galen's Pneumatology," *Gesnerus* 8 (1951): 180-89, esp. 188-89. Besides

1.2, another long discussion of spirit in *De vita* is 3.2-6, *Op.*, pp. 534 ff. Antonio Guaineri of Pavia (fl. 1412-1448), in his *Practica*, Tr. 15.2, similarly employs the medical spirit in his discussion of melancholy.

17. *Timaeus* 38e-39e, 40a-c, 44; *Laws* 10 (886d-898d; 903b-c); 12 (966d-967d); Plotinus, *Enn.* 3.2.3; see also 4.3.7, citing Plato.

18. Garin, "Magia ed astrologia nella cultura del Rinascimento," *Medioevo*, p. 154; trans. Peter Munz, *Science and Civic Life in the Italian Renaissance* (New York, 1969), p. 149. *Asclepius* 1-3, *Corpus Hermeticum* 21. It is also shared by the then newly rediscovered Roman Stoic poet Manilius, as Ficino points out in *Theol. Plat.* 15.5, ed. 3:37, *Op.*, p. 339, citing his *Astronomica* 1.10-30; 2.60-66; 115-29, and also in *Op.*, pp. 851 and 1610. The cited visible and created mundane gods are "gods" only in the sense of "spiritus aliquos super homines" (*De vita* 3.26.91, p. 571).

19. *Theol. Plat.*, 4.1, ad fin., ed., 1: 165, *Op.*, p. 131, quoting Plato, *Epinomis* 983b-c.

20. Ficino, Apologia, injunction to Piero Soderini, lines 92-97, pp. 573-74.

21. Plotinus, *Enn.* 2.9.5; cf. his *Theol. Plat.*, 4.1, ed., 1: 165, *Op.*, p. 131, and references in n. 17, above.

22. 3.11.5, p. 544. see also his *Comm. Plot.* at 4.4.27, p. 1744; cf. Plotinus, *Enn.* 4.4.36.

Magic

1. The *editio princeps* of the Arabic text was produced by Hellmut Ritter, ed., Pseudo-Maǧriṭī, *Das Ziel des Weisen*, Studien der Bibliothek Warburg 12 (Berlin, 1933). The German trans. we have employed is by H. Ritter and M. Plessner, *Picatrix. Das Ziel des Weisen . . .* , Studies of the Warburg Institute, vol. 27 (London, 1962); on the work in general, see Thorndike, 5: 811-24. A. Warburg, *Gesammelte Schriften: Die Erneuerung der Heidnischen Antike* 2 (Leipzig, 1932), p. 527 *et passim*; Fritz Saxl, "Rinascimento," Section 3, "Die antike Astrologie als dämonischbewegende Macht in der Kultur der Frührenaissance," pp. 227 ff. Ritter, "Picatrix, ein arabisches Handbuch hellenistischer Magie," *Vorträge der Bibliothek Warburg* 1921-22 (1923), pp. 94-124; Yates, pp. 49-57, 69-72; Seznec, *Survival*, pp. 53 ff.; E. Garin, "Considerazioni sulla magia," in *Medioevo*, pp. 170-91; and more generally, "Magia ed astrologia nella cultura del Rinascimento," in the same vol., pp. 150-69, which last was trans. by Peter Munz, *Science and Civic Life*, pp. 145-65; "La diffusione di un manuale di magia," in *La cultura filosofica del Rinascimento italiano* (Florence, 1961), pp. 159-65; "Un manuale di magia: Picatrix," in *L'età nuova: Ricerche . . .* (Naples, 1969), pp. 389-419; and "Astrologia e magia: *Picatrix*," *Lo zodiaco della vita*, pp. 49-60; Paola Zambelli, "Platone, Ficino e la magia," pp. 121-42, esp., on *De vita* and *Picatrix*, p. 137, n. 32; Vittoria Perrone Compagni, "Picatrix latinus. Concezioni filosofico-religiose e prassi magica," *Medioevo. Rivista di storia della filosofia medievale* 1 (1975): 237-337 inclusive, text of article, pp. 278-85, Appendix on MSS, pp. 286-337, transcribed extracts from one MS; pages specifically on *De vita* (260-61) summarized below with refs. in text; see also her "La magia ceremoniale del *Picatrix* nel Rinascimento," *Atti dell'Accademia di' Scienze Morale e*

Politiche 88 (1977): 279-330; and articles of Pingree, namely, "Between the *Ghaya* and *Picatrix*, I: The Spanish Version," *JWCI* 44 (1981): 27-56; and especially the article cited in n. 4, below. Plessner's posthumous ed. of *De vita* undertakes to assess Ficino's debt to *Picatrix*, and he found no extensive verbatim translations but detailed indebtedness in 3.18 and a few other places; with the help of Compagni and Pingree, we have located a few more, as shown in our notes.

2. In response to Filippo Valori's request to borrow the MS of *Picatrix*, Acciari writes that Ficino, being ill, has asked him to reply on his behalf that "he has already returned that book of this person Picatrix which now for a long time George the doctor has let him use. He has taken a long time and read it straight through and devoted much effort and study to reflecting on it and to detailed reading of it, but he found much that seemed like show-tricks [perhaps thinking of the recipe to make a house seem to be full of serpents] having no practical use to speak of. But whatever in it was useful and worth reading, he transferred it to those books he himself composed, *De vita*; but the rest he left out as being frivolous, ineffectual, or even condemned by the Christian religion. Therefore Ficino himself warns you against reading it, because in so doing you will find much work but little of any practical use—especially since whatever is in any way useful or important in that work, may be read point for point perhaps better and certainly more fully and clearly in his own book *De vita*. If you reflectively and carefully read the latter, you won't miss a thing from . . . the famous Picatrix." Since the Latin is relatively inaccessible, I quote it as well: " . . . huiusmodi Picatricis librum quem iam diu a Georgio Medico sibi commodatum iam reddidisse, se quidem diu et multum perlegisse multamque in eo versando operam et acute legendo studium posuisse, sed invenisse plurima nullius fere momenti nugisque simillima; quae vero utilia inerant et lectione digna, ea in libros quos ipse de vita composuit [MS composita] transtulisse, reliqua vero aut frivola et vana aut et christiana religione damnata reliquisse. Dehortatur itaque te Ficinus ipse ab eiusmodi lectione in qua plurimum laboris, utilitatis vero parum invenitur, quum praesertim quae in eo ipso opere alicuius usus [vel] ponderis sunt eadem singula fortasse melius, compendiosius certe lucidiusque, legantur in illo ipso libro quem *De vita* inscripsit quem [MS que] quidem si diligentissime volveris, nihil . . . a Picatrice illo . . . desiderabis," MS Florence, Nazionale, Filza Rinuccini 17, Insert 6, fols. 8v-9v, Letter II in a hand which she finds characteristic of the late sixteenth or early seventeenth century, though Kristeller has dated the entire MS to no later than the beginning of the sixteenth (*Iter Italicum* 1: 167); Daniela Delcorno Branca, "Un discepulo del Poliziano: Michele Acciari," *Lettere italiane* 28 (1976): 464-81, esp. 470-71; Garin, "Postille sul ermetismo del Rinascimento," *Rinascimento*, Ser. 2, vol. 16 (1976), esp. pp. 245-46. This letter treats Picatrix as the author (the name may be a corruption of Hippocrates), but it also passed as its title.

3. Pingree's edition of the Latin *Picatrix* appeared too late to be incorporated in the present study.

4. My comparisons and contrasts between these works are influenced by David Pingree, "Some of the Sources of the Ghāyat Al-Ḥakīm" (the latter being the name of the *Picatrix* in the original Arabic, meaning *The Aim of the Sage*), *JWCI* 43 (1980): 1-15, hereafter cited by parentheses in text.

5. *Asclepius*, sec. 13. 37-38, *Corpus Hermeticum*, ed. A. D. Nock and A. J. Festugière (Paris, 1945), 2: 347-49; translated and discussed by Walker, pp. 40 and n. 3 and 41-42. Ficino never translated the *Asclepius*, though his citations show he knew the existing translation well; the commentary on it and on his version of the *Pimander* wrongly inserted as his in the Basel, 1576, *Opera omnia* is really by Lefèvre d'Étaples; see Kristeller, *SF*, 1: CXXX-CXXXI and 97-98. Copenhaver, "Hermes Trismegistus, Proclus," forthcoming. The "Platonici" are probably more important than the *Hermetica*, as Copenhaver argues; but the *Picatrix* is equally important because its heterogeneous contents include a magic equally Neoplatonic but materialistic in its ends like *De vita*.

6. Walker, p. 82; see, for example, 3.8, pp. 540, 541; 3.20, p. 560.

7. "Le 'elezioni,' " p. 437, trans. mine.

8. For Plotinus's rejection of the world-spirit from his system, see "Place," n. 10.

9. Garin, "Le 'elezioni,' " p. 437; he gives no reference, but see Proclus, *ET*, Props. nos. 196, 205-10, on which see E. R. Dodds's commentaries and his Appendix II, "The Astral Body in Neoplatonism" (2nd ed., Oxford, 1963), pp. 313 ff. There is no spirit, however, in Proclus's *De sacrificio*, *Op.*, pp. 1928-29, which therefore rates as only a partial analogue.

10. *Pneuma*, p. 43.

11. Walker, pp. 55-56, citing Pico, *Disputationes*, ed. Garin, 3.4, p. 206, p. 208; 3.6, p. 218.

12. Al-Kindi, *De radiis: Incipit theorica artium magicarum*, ed. M.-T. d'Alverny and F. Hudry, *Archives d'histoire doctrinale et littéraire du moyen âge* 41 (1974): 139-260.

13. Garin, "Postille," p. 246.

14. Garin, *Medioevo e Rinascimento*, p. 153, trans. Peter Munz, p. 148.

15. Yates, pp. 155-56; quoted and qualified in part by Charles Trinkaus, *In Our Image and Likeness* (Chicago, 1970), pp. 499-500; see for an example of this traditional preference in Ficino himself, the letter to Jacopo Antiquario or Antiquari, quoted above.

16. Even in the so-called Hippocratic Oath, the doctor forswears surgery. Quotation from anonymous article, "The College of General Practitioners," *British Medical Journal*, 20 Dec. 1952, p. 1344. Huling E. Ussery, *Chaucer's Physician: Medicine and Literature in Fourteenth-century England*, Tulane Studies in English 19 (New Orleans, 1971), pp. 29-30. Nancy Siraisi has recently questioned though not definitely refuted the presence of this division of labor in Italy from about the time of Taddeo Alderotti (d. 1295), *Taddeo Alderotti*, pp. 296-300. Kristeller documents the general split between theory and practice in medicine in Italy down to the eleventh century; but he credits the structure of the universities there, not magicians, with healing it, "Philosophy and Medicine in Medieval and Renaissance Italy," p. 31.

17. Garin, "Magia ed astrologia," p. 152; trans. Munz, pp. 147-48.

18. Joseph A. Mazzeo, *Renaissance and Revolution* (New York, 1965), p. 13.

19. Its specified prayers involving named deities make it more personal than is *De vita*; see the one which Pingree has edited in Spanish and Latin and translated from Arabic into English, "Between *Ghāya* and *Picatrix*," pp. 36, 55-56. Except for the crucial point about depersonalization, which derives from Walker, my conclu-

sion on the thematic importance of the *Picatrix* to *De vita* agrees with the recent thought of Garin, *Lo zodiaco*, pp. 49-59.

Repercussions

1. Kristeller, *Studies in Renaissance Thought*, "Per la biografia di Marsilio Ficino: Crisi spirituale e conversione," pp. 202 ff.; Marcel—while taking more seriously than does Kristeller Zanobi Acciaiuoli's story that St. Antoninus ordered Ficino to replace Plato with Aquinas—still reminds us that Ficino was very young then (1456) and that while he seems to have absorbed *verbatim* large chunks of Aquinas, he also went right on with Plato and the Platonists (*MF*, pp. 204-11); on pages 335-55, he denies the crisis of conscience alleged by Corsi (*Vita*, 8, ed. Marcel, Appendix 1, p. 683). They do not deny, of course, that Ficino was of two minds on certain issues, such as intellectualism vs. voluntarism, or that he felt an occasional conflict within or from without. But as Cassirer says, "In Ficino's life, generally so orderly and balanced, there is a moment of unrest and of constant inner tension as a result of his ambiguous intellectual and moral position towards astrology." He instinctively feels the power of the stars; see *The Individual and the Cosmos in Renaissance Philosophy*, trans. Mario Domandi, pp. 100-101. Garin adds that in Ficino's life there is "Non . . . un progressivo rifiuto dell'astrologia, ma se mai, il contrario; o per esser più esatti, una oscillazione continua," "Introduzione," to Pico, *Disputationes*, p. 11.

2. On the troubles in general and these letters in particular, see *SF*, 1: 85; Walker, pp. 52-53; Marcel, pp. 500-3; D. C. Allen, pp. 12 ff.

3. *Op.*, p. 958. On the contradictions between *De vita* and the Letter to Poliziano, and other works as well, see my "Ficino's Shifting Attitude Towards Astrology," in *Marsilio Ficino e il ritorno di Platone*, ed. G. Garfagnini (Florence, 1986), pp. 371-80.

4. Zambelli suggests, for example, that Pico and his trouble had highlighted the "dangerous conceptual and ceremonial alternative which magic represented to orthodox religion" and had associated Platonism with magic (p. 134); see also Yates, pp. 111 ff.; D. C. Allen; and Marcel, cited above.

5. Ed. pr. Bologna, 1496 (posthumous). Garin, "Introduzione" to Pico, *Disputationes*, pp. 3-6; and, in more definite terms, in their recent ed. of Savonarola's "Contra li astrologi" in vol. 1, *Scritti filosofici*, of the "Edizione Nazionale delle Opere di Girolamo Savonarola," (Rome, 1982), pp. 402-4, Garin and Garfagnini conclude that Savonarola exercised a general moral influence over the production of Pico's *Disputationes*.

6. In the *Heptaplus* (written 1488-1489), twice cited, albeit inaccurately, in *De vita* 3, commenting on the function of the stars as "signs," he guardedly allows for various opinions as to the nature of their influence; and he accepts not only the constellations as operative units, which he was later to reject, but even one of the least credible shifts of astrology, namely the hypothesis that the "more powerful" constellations are not the visible ones (which have in any case precessed from their places) but those permanently inscribed on the crystalline sphere, 2.4-5. Later,

however, he adds to his own guarded view the fact that both Christians and pagans condemned astrology, 5.4. See Garin, "Neoplatonismo ed Ermetismo," *Lo zodiaco*, pp. 87-88; *contra* Yates, pp. 88, 90, and cf. Walker, pp. 56-59. For Pico's slighting reference to talismans, see below.

7. Thorndike, 4: 495, see also below and D. C. Allen, p. 19.

8. 3.12, last sentence, p. 548; and 3.22, ad fin., p. 566, to be discussed below.

9. Borrowing from Firmicus Maternus, see our note ad loc., and from his own epitome of Iamblichus, *De mysteriis*, "De iudiciis astrologorum, et daemone," and "Unde proprius daemon veniat, quidve agat, et utrum sit unicus," pp. 1905-6.

10. "Le 'elezioni,'" rebutting Cassirer, pp. 423-24. The influence of the heavens, if not its predictability or control, was universally recognized, says Keith Thomas, upon the weather and the areas involved in agriculture and medicine, p. 286.

11. D. C. Allen felt that Ficino was unable to reconcile astrology with free will, pp. 6, 9, 18; so did Cassirer, pp. 112-15; see Hans Baron, "Willensfreiheit und Astrologie bei . . . Ficino," *Kultur- und Universalgeschichte: Festschrift für Walter Goetz* (Leipzig, 1927), pp. 145 ff.; Marian Heitzmann, "La libertà e il fato . . . Ficino," *Rivista di filosofia neo-scolastica* 28 (1936): 350-71; 29 (1937): 59-82; Zanier, p. 46. See for example his Letters in *Epist.* 12, to Filippo Valori, 7 Nov. 1482, "Saturnus, significator . . . ne dixerim ductor," p. 948,2; to Filippo Carducci, "siquid in negotiis eiusmodi coelestia valent. . . . Mercurio Saturnum . . . sive comitem, sive ducem," p. 948,3.

12. Ed. *SF,* 2: 11-76; D. C. Allen, pp. 12-13; while Allen is correct in his overall statement, he is incorrect to restrict the definition of "judicial" to "predictive." The semiological survived such condemnations in Plotinus's thought; indeed, Plotinus may have succeeded in reconciling some astrology with his Neoplatonism, Thorndike, 1: 302, cf. *Enn.* 2.3 with 4.4.26-44.

13. Garin, "Recenti interpretazioni di Marsilio Ficino," *Giornale critico della filosofia italiana*, 2nd s., 8 (1940): 306. On Ficino's avoidance of astrological determinism, see *Lo zodiaco*, "Neoplatonismo ed Ermetismo," pp. 76-77. Kristeller, *Phil MF*, p. 311.

14. E.g., 3.21. 54-56 and 148-49, pp. 562 and 564; 3.26.95, p. 571.

15. *Heptaplus* 2.7. Since the *Heptaplus* was written at Florence in 1488-1489, Walker suggests (p. 57) that this disparagement of images may be addressed to Ficino and the readers of a draft of *De vita* 3.

16. Huling E. Ussery, *Chaucer's Physician*, pp. 112-13. If Ussery is wrong and this detail is unfavorable, it is so in a subtle rather than an obvious way, for it is presented, "between two favorable comments," and hence still serves as an example of what Ficino could have gotten away with.

17. Thorndike on Pietro, chap. 70, 2: 881-82; 899-901; 938-47. On Gerson and the golden lion of the Montpellier physician, an incident which had small resonance at the time but perhaps set a precedent, chap. 43, 4: 122-23.

18. *SCG* 3.92; 104-7, quoted unenthusiastically by Ficino, 3.18 ad fin.; Walker, p. 48. This statement had been used by Gerson against the image of the golden lion, Thorndike, 4: 122-23.

19. *SCG* 3.105, ad fin. Copenhaver, "Scholastic Philosophy," pp. 533, 537.

20. Walker, pp. 44, 46; Ficino says the same thing, 3.18.157-160, p. 558, citing Iamblichus, but as a counsel of prudence not as a definition of heresy.

21. Ficino, *De vita*, 3.23, cited above, see also *Comm. Symp.* 6.3, Marcel, p. 203, n. 2. Aquinas, "Responsio ad 42 Art.," Art. 10, ed. Frettè and Marè 27: 250. Gerson had allowed prayers to the planetary angels but not observation of the constellations, Thorndike, 4: 116—almost the exact reverse of what Ficino allowed himself, see below.

22. Rev. 12: 3-4. *Comm. Phaedr.*, chap. 2, *Op.*, p. 1364, ed. Allen, *Phaedran Charioteer*, pp. 76-77; Letter from *Epistolae*, Book 8, to Braccio Martelli, *Op.*, pp. 875-79, esp. p. 876. Although the letter is not perfectly clear on this point, even John Colet, who was more orthodox than Ficino, interpreted it as I do, i.e., that freedom of choice "est in demonibus ut in hominibus," ed. Sears Jayne in *John Colet and Marsilio Ficino* (Oxford, 1963), pp. 123-24. On Ficino's demonology as regards the *Phaedrus* commentary, see Allen, *Platonism*, pp. 8-28; note especially, for present purposes, that it is rather inconsistent; that his daemons necessarily possess bodies of some sort; that Ficino acknowledges that some daemons fell and became the devils as Scripture teaches but expresses no interest in this group; and that his good daemons who remain cannot entirely be assimilated to angels, the alternative group in Christian demonology, because, for one thing, the former group have bodies while the latter group includes the Neoplatonic supercelestials or scholastic *substantiae separatae* who have no regular connection with bodies at all. Compare Aquinas's assimilation of classical, metaphysical, and astrological entities to angels, see Joseph McAllister, ed., *The Letter of St. Thomas Aquinas De occultis operibus naturae* (Washington, D. C., 1939), pp. 173 ff.

23. E.g., *Enn.* 3.4, "On Our Allotted Guardian Spirit"; and the important *Enn.* 4.4.43. On Plotinus's attitude towards magic and astrology see refs. in "Place" and n. 9 ad loc.

24. "Deos, id est spiritus aliquos super homines," 3.26.91, *Op.*, p. 571; see also *Comm.* on Plato's *Cratylus*, *Op.*, p. 1310. On subordination to the One God, see *Comm. Symp.* 4.5, ed. Marcel, pp. 174-75.

25. On the various attacks, see for example François Masai, *Pléthon et la platonisme de Mistra* (Paris, 1956), pp. 59 and 299-305. On Pletho's religion see also John Monfasani, *George of Trebizond* (Leiden, 1976), p. 160, nn. 124, 125; and Milton V. Anastos, *Pletho's Calendar and Liturgy*, Dumbarton Oaks Papers 4 (Cambridge, Mass., 1948), pp. 185-269. George of Trebizond (1395-1472 or 1473) charged that Pletho was more dangerous to Christianity than was Mahomet, Anastos, *Calendar*, p. 279.

26. Ficino in his preface to his translation and commentary on Plotinus (1490), credits Pletho with the idea of reviving the Platonic Academy and the idea of a tradition of the *prisca theologia*, *Op.*, p. 1537. Another and less-known link between Pletho and *De vita* in particular is their common (though by no means unique in Platonic circles) respect for the *Chaldean Oracles* ascribed to Zoroaster or his disciples; see Anastos, *Calendar*, p. 279 ff., our Index, and Copenhaver, "Iamblichus, Synesius, and the Chaldean Oracles," forthcoming. Pletho commented on the *Chaldean Oracles* in terms that would have appealed to Ficino, some of which will be mentioned below, *Oracula magica Zoroastris cum scoliis* [sic] *Plethonis et Pselli . . .* ed. Johannes Opsopoeus (Paris, 1607), which represents the longer of the two versions of the commentary hereafter cited parenthetically in text. For a survey of Ficino's

knowledge of Pletho, see Kristeller, *Studies in Renaissance Thought*, p. 36; and Walker, pp. 60-63.

27. On supercelestial gods, see Masai, *Pléthon*, pp. 208-14, esp. 209-10 and 213-14. Good daemons, too, were "métaphysiquement nécessaire" as "l'intermédiaire" for Pletho as for Ficino, p. 225, n. 5.

28. See Ardis Collins, *The Secular is Sacred* (The Hague, 1974), p. 39, citing *Theol. Plat.* 2.11, Marcel ed., 1: 109; and Kristeller, *Phil MF*, pp. 309 ff.

29. For a useful map of Ficino's cosmology and definitions of his levels of gods, see Allen, *Phaedran Charioteer*, pp. 66-69, and *Platonism*, p. 120. The simpler, non-Phaedran scheme is the one he used in *De vita*, so simple that he does not even quite distinguish supercelestials into intellectuals and intelligibles; he demotes the intellectuals into the mind of the World-soul, the next lower level, to preserve the gap which Christianity demands between its transcendent God and His creation; see for example 3.1, nn. 5 and 11, and on this gap, Allen, "The Absent Angel in Ficino's Philosophy," pp. 219-40, esp. p. 224. Allen refers frequently to Proclus and sometimes to the possible heresy of subdividing God's mind or diluting His transcendence, but never, understandably, do either Allen or Copenhaver mention the danger of being associated with Pletho; Walker mentions it in regard to Ficino's Orphic singing, pp. 60-63.

30. 3.1.24, p. 531, so also at the end, 3.26.80-86, p. 571, "numina penitus a materia segregata . . . sublimiores." Compare the atypical (Allen, *Platonism*, pp. 121-23) polytheistic statement in *Comm. Symp.* 5.10, that Ideas "dii dicuntur" (ed. Marcel, p. 195, *Op.*, p. 1340).

31. *De insomniis*, *Op.*, p. 1969,4. English trans. A. Fitzgerald, *Essays and Hymns of Synesius of Cyrene* (Oxford, 1930), 2 vols.; *Letters* (Oxford, 1926), Letter 105. Jay Bregman, *Synesius of Cyrene* (Berkeley, 1982), pp. 145, 155-57, 161.

32. To his letter claiming he had never believed in astrology Poliziano replied: "To change one's mind is not shameful in a philosopher who daily sees more," *Opera* (Basel, 1553), facs. ed. 1971, 1: 135.

DE VITA
TEXT AND TRANSLATION

Prooemium Marsilii Ficini Florentini in librum *De vita* ad magnanimum Laurentium Medicem patriae servatorem.*

CAPITULA PRIMI LIBRI QUI TRACTAT DE VITA SANA

Prooemium in quo etiam agitur sanitatem mentis sanitati corporis anteponendam.
Novem studiosorum duces. Cap. I.
Quam diligens habenda cura sit cerebri, cordis, stomachi, spiritus. Cap. II.
Litterati pituitae et atrae bili obnoxii sunt. Cap. III.
Quot sint causae quibus litterati melancholici sint vel fiant. Cap. IV.
Cur melancholici ingeniosi sint et quales melancholici sint eiusmodi, quales contra. Cap. V.
Quo pacto atra bilis conducat ingenio. Cap. VI.
Quinque sunt praecipui studiosorum hostes: pituita, atra bilis, coitus, satietas, matutinus somnus. Cap. VII.
Quae sit hora incohandis studiis opportunior, quisve continuandi modus. Cap. VIII.
Quomodo sit vitanda pituita. Cap. IX.
Qua ratione vitanda sit atra bilis. Cap. X.
Cura stomachi. Cap. XI.
De his quae fovent membra praecipua, vires, spiritus. Cap. XII.
Medicinae contra pituitam. Cap. XIII.
Destillatio atque eius cura. Cap. XIV.
Dolor capitis et cura eius. Cap. XV.
De cura visus. Cap. XVI.
De gustu instaurando. Cap. XVII.
De exacta atrae bilis cura. Cap. XVIII.
De syrupis. Cap. XIX.

1489 Table of Chapter Headings

Proem by Marsilio Ficino the Florentine of His Book "On Life" to the Magnanimous Lorenzo de' Medici, Preserver of His Country.

THE CHAPTERS OF THE FIRST BOOK WHICH TREATS OF A HEALTHY LIFE

Proem in Which Also Is Discussed the Priority of Mental over Physical Health.*
The Nine Guides of Scholars. Chap. I.
What Diligent Care We Should Take of the Brain, the Heart, the Stomach, and the Spirit. Chap. II.
Learned People Are Subject to Phlegm and Black Bile. Chap. III.
How Many Things Cause Learned People Either to Be Melancholy or to Eventually Become So. Chap. IV.
Why Melancholics Are Intelligent, and Which Melancholics Are So and Which Are Not. Chap. V.
How Black Bile Makes People Intelligent. Chap. VI.
The Special Enemies of Scholars Are Five: Phlegm, Black Bile, Sexual Intercourse, Gluttony, and Sleeping in the Morning. Chap. VII.
What Hour Is the Better Time to Begin Our Studies and How We Should Continue Them. Chap. VIII.
How to Avoid Phlegm. Chap. IX.
How to Avoid Black Bile. Chap. X.
The Care of the Stomach. Chap. XI.
On Those Things Which Support Special Parts, the Powers and the Spirits. Chap. XII.
Drugs Against Phlegm. Chap. XIII.
Rheum and Its Cure.* Chap. XIV.
Headache and Its Cure.* Chap. XV.
On the Care of the Sight. Chap. XVI.
On Restoring the Taste. Chap. XVII.
On the Special Cure of Black Bile Alone. Chap. XVIII.
On Syrups. Chap. XIX.

De pilulis. Cap. XX.
De medicina liquida. Cap. XXI.
De sanguinis missione. Cap. XXII.
De electuariis. Cap. XXIII.
De nimia vigilia. Cap. XXIV.
De hebetudine atque oblivione. Cap. XXV.
Corporeum quidem spiritum cura; incorporeum vero cole; veritatem denique venerare. Primum medicina praestat, secundum disciplina moralis, tertium vero religio. Cap. XXVI.

Prooemium in librum secundum *De vita longa*.

CAPITULA EIUSDEM LIBRI

Ad perfectionem scientiae necessaria est vita longa, quam etiam diligentia praestat. Cap. I.
Vitalis calor nutritur humore, quo deficiente fit resolutio, quo excedente fit suffocatio. Cap. II.
Quomodo temperandus calor ad humorem atque vicissim quodam Minervae consilio. Cap. III.
Quibus de causis arescit humor naturalis vel peregrinus exundat, et quam necessaria sit ad vitam perfecta digestio. Cap. IV.
Sanguis et humor accommodatus vitae aerius esse debet, qualitate temperatus, substantia medius atque tenax. Cap. V.
Communis comedendi bibendique regula et qualitas epularum. Cap. VI.
Ne utaris alimentis quae cito putrescunt, nec in eiusmodi regionibus habites. Vinum et triticum prae ceteris elige; putrefactionem et resolutionem fuge. Cap. VII.
Diaeta, victus, medicina senum. Cap. VIII.
Naturae aromatum et cordialium necessariae; et rursum qualis senum victus. Cap. IX.
De auro et aureis alimentis et recreatione senum. Cap. X.
De usu lactis sanguinisque humani pro vita senum. Cap. XI.
Diaeta, habitatio, consuetudo senum. Cap. XII.
Quae adminicula senes a planetis accipiant ad omnia membra fovenda. Ubi memento passulas uvas pinguefacere iecur atque corroborare, quod maximum est vitae subsidium. Cap. XIII.
Confabulatio senum sub Venere per virentia prata. Cap. XIV.
Mercurius alloquitur senes et consulit eis circa voluptatem, odores, cantus, medicinas. Cap. XV.

On Pills. Chap. XX.
On Liquid Medicine. Chap. XXI.
On Blood-Letting. Chap. XXII.
On Electuaries. Chap. XXIII.
On Excessive Sleeplessness. Chap. XXIV.
On Dullness and Forgetfulness. Chap. XXV.
Care for the Corporeal Spirit; Cultivate the Incorporeal; and Lastly Venerate the Truth. Medicine Takes Care of the First, Moral Discipline, the Second, but Religion, the Third. Chap. XXVI.

Proem to the Second Book, "On a Long Life."

THE CHAPTERS OF THIS BOOK

To Perfect Your Knowledge, You Need a Long Life; One Way to Procure It Is by Effort. Chap. I.
The Vital Heat Is Nourished by Radical Moisture; Too Little of It Causes Resolution, Too Much, Suffocation. Chap. II.
How Radical Heat and Moisture Must Be Proportioned to One Another by a Plan of Minerva's. Chap. III.
The Causes of the Drying up of the Natural Moisture or the Overabundance of Moisture from Outside, and How Necessary to Life Is a Perfect Digestion. Chap. IV.
To Be Suitable for Life, Blood and Moisture Must Be Airy, Tempered in Quality, Moderate and Firm in Substance. Chap. V.
The Ordinary Regimen for Eating and Drinking, and the Quality Your Foods Should Have. Chap. VI.
Do Not Use Foods Which Quickly Putrefy, nor Dwell in Regions Where Many Foods Do. Be Most Selective about Wine and Wheat-flour; and Avoid Putrefaction and Resolution. Chap. VII.
The Diet, Mode of Life, and Medicine of the Elderly. Chap. VIII.
The Natures the Elderly Must Have in Spices and Cordials and More about the Quality of the Mode of Life They Should Follow. Chap. IX.
On Gold, Foods Made of Gold, and the Revitalization of Old People. Chap. X.
On the Use of Human Milk and Blood for the Life of Old People. Chap. XI.
The Diet, Dwelling, and Customs of Old People. Chap. XII.
What Means of Fomenting All the Parts of the Body the Elderly May Receive from the Planets. In which place remember that raisins fatten and strengthen the liver, which is the greatest support to life.* Chap. XIII.
The Conversation of the Old People Traversing the Green Fields under the Leadership of Venus. Chap. XIV.
Mercury Addresses the Elderly and Counsels Them about Pleasure, Odors, Song, and Medicines. Chap. XV.

Confirmatio superiorum; et quod devitare debemus assiduam cogitationem et coitum. Cap. XVI.
De medicinis senum et de habitatione iterum atque diaeta. Cap. XVII.
De nutrimento spiritus et conservatione vitae per odores. Ubi in hoc capitulo de usu mellis dicitur. Memento rosaceum mel solidum et liquidum senibus conservandis accommodatissimum. Cap. XVIII.
Magorum medicina pro senibus. Cap. XIX.
De periculis evitandis ex quolibet vitae septenario imminentibus. Cap. XX.

Prooemium in librum tertium *De vita coelitus*.
Verba Marsilii Ficini ad lectorem sequentis libri.*

CAPITULA EIUSDEM LIBRI

In quo consistat secundum Plotinum virtus favorem coelitus attrahens, scilicet in eo quod anima mundi et stellarum daemonumque animae facile alliciuntur corporum formis accommodatis. Cap. I.
De concordia mundi. De natura hominis secundum stellas. Quomodo fiat attractus ab unaquaque stella. Cap. II.
Inter animam mundi et corpus eius manifestum est spiritus eius, in cuius virtute sunt quattuor elementa. Nos vero per spiritum nostrum hunc possumus haurire. Cap. III.
Spiritus noster haurit mundi spiritum per radios Solis et Iovis, quatenus ipse fit Solaris et Iovialis. Cap. IV.
Tres Gratiae sunt Iuppiter et Sol et Venus. Iuppiter est Gratia geminarum media et maxime nobis accommodata. Cap. V.
De virtute in nobis naturali, vitali, animali, et per quos planetas adiuventur, et quomodo per aspectum Lunae ad Solem et Venerem, maxime vero ad Iovem. Cap. VI.
Quomodo membra foveantur in nobis per comparationem Lunae ad signa et ad stellas fixas. Cap. VII.
De virtutibus et usu stellarum fixarum. Cap. VIII.
Dignitates planetarum in signis ad usum medicinarum observandae. Cap. IX.
Quomodo planetis uti debeamus in medicinis. Cap. X.
Quibus modis spiritus noster haurire plurimum potest de spiritu vitaque mundi; et qui planetae spiritum procreant atque recreant; et qualia ad unumquemque planetam pertinent. Cap. XI.
Res naturales atque etiam artificiosae habent virtutes a stellis occultas, per quas spiritum nostrum stellis eisdem exponunt. Cap XII.

A Confimation of the Aforesaid, and That We Should Avoid both Continual Thinking and Sexual Intercourse. Chap. XVI.
On Medicines for the Elderly and More about Their Dwellings and Their Diet. Chap. XVII.
On Nourishing the Spirit and Conserving Life through Odors. In which place in this chapter the use of honey is enunciated. Remember solid and liquid rose-honey is most suited for the preservation of old people.* Chap. XVIII.
The Medicine of the Magi for Old People. Chap. XIX.
On Avoiding Those Dangers Which Are Imminent in Any Septenary of Life. Chap. XX.

Proem to the Third Book "On Obtaining Life from the Heavens."
The Words of Marsilio Ficino to the Reader of the Following Book.

THE CHAPTERS OF THIS BOOK

In What, according to Plotinus, the Power of Attracting Favor from the Heavens Consists, Namely, That Well-adapted Physical Forms Can Easily Allure the World-soul and the Souls of the Stars and the Daemons. Chap. I.
On the Harmony of the World. On the Nature of Man according to the Stars. How to Attract Something from Some One Particular Star. Chap. II.
Between the Anima Mundi and Its Manifest Body Is Its Spirit, in Whose Power Are the Four Elements. We Are Able to Absorb This Spirit through Our Own Spirit. Chap. III.
Our Spirit Absorbs the Spirit of the World through the Rays of the Sun and of Jupiter, Insofar as It Becomes Solar and Jovial Itself. Chap. IV.
The Three Graces Are Jupiter and the Sun and Venus. Jupiter Is the Grace Which Is the Mean between the Two and Is Especially Accommodated to Us. Chap. V.
Concerning Our Natural Power, Our Vital, and Our Animal, and Which Planets Give Them Aid, and How They Do So through the Aspect of the Moon to the Sun, to Venus, and Especially to Jupiter. Chap. VI.
How Parts of Our Body Are Fostered through Relating the Moon to Signs and to Fixed Stars. Chap. VII.
Concerning the Powers and the Use of the Fixed Stars. Chap. VIII.
The Dignities of Planets in the Signs Which Must Be Observed for the Use of Medicines. Chap. IX.
How We Should Use the Planets in Medicines. Chap. X.
The Ways in Which Our Spirit Can Draw the Most from the Spirit and Life of the World; Which Planets Generate and Restore Spirit; and What Things Pertain to Each Planet. Chap. XI.
Natural and Even Artificial Things Have Occult Powers from the Stars, through Which they Expose Our Spirit to the Same Stars. Chap. XII.

De virtute imaginum secundum antiquos atque medicinarum coelitus acquisita. Cap. XIII.

Ordines rerum a stellis pendentium, ut Solarium atque similium; et quomodo spiritus fiat Solaris. Cap. XIV.

De virtute imaginum secundum antiquos atque medicinarum; et quomodo medicinae sint longe validiores quam imagines. Cap. XV.

De potestate coeli. De viribus radiorum, unde vim sortiri putentur imagines. Cap. XVI.

Quam vim habent figurae in coelo atque sub coelo. Cap. XVII.

Quales coelestium figuras antiqui imaginibus imprimebant; ac de usu imaginum. Cap. XVIII.

De fabricanda universi figura. Cap. XIX.

Quantam imagines vim habere putentur in spiritum, et spiritus in eas. Et de affectu utentis et operantis. Cap. XX.

De virtute verborum atque cantus ad beneficium coeleste captandum, ac de septem gradibus perducentibus ad coelestia. Cap. XXI.

Quomodo septem modis nos coelestibus accommodare possumus, et quibus Saturnus sit maleficus, quibus propitius; quos Iuppiter a Saturno defendat. Quomodo coelum agat in spiritum et corpus et animam. Cap. XXII.

Ut prospere vivas agasque, imprimis cognosce ingenium, sidus, genium tuum et locum eisdem convenientem. Hic habita. Professionem sequere naturalem. Cap. XXIII.

Qua ratione litterati cognoscant ingenium suum, sequanturque victum spiritui consentaneum. Cap. XXIV.

Astronomica diligentia in liberis procreandis, in praeparandis epulis, in aedificiis et habitatione atque vestibus; et quantum curare talia liceat. Cap. XXV.

Quomodo per inferiora superioribus exposita deducantur superiora, et per mundanas materias mundana potissimum dona. Cap. XXVI.

Apologia quaedam, in qua de medicina, astrologia, vita mundi; item de Magis qui Christum statim natum salutaverunt.

Quod necessaria sit ad vitam securitas et tranquillitas animi.*

Versus Amerigi Corsini.*

**Tutuli desunt. Addidi*

On the Power Acquired from the Heavens both in Images, according to the Ancients, and in Medicines. Chap. XIII.

The Orders of Things Depending on the Stars, as of Solar Things, and So Forth; and How Our Spirit May Be Made Solar. Chap. XIV.

On the Power Which, according to the Ancients, both Images and Medicines Possess; and on the Factors Which Make Medicines Far More Powerful than Images. Chap. XX.

On the Power of the Heavens. On the Powers of the Rays from Which Images Are Thought to Obtain Their Force. Chap. XVI.

What Power Is in Figures—Those in the Sky and Those beneath the Sky. Chap. XVII.

What Sorts of Figures of the Celestials the Ancients Engraved in Images. And concerning the Use of Images. Chap. XVIII.

How to Construct a Figure of the Universe. Chap. XIX.

What Great Power Images Are Thought to Have Over Spirit, and Spirit over Images. And concerning the Emotional State of the User and Operator. Chap. XX.

On the Power of Words and Song for Capturing Celestial Benefits and on the Seven Steps That Lead to Celestial Things. Chap. XXI.

Seven Ways in Which We Can Accommodate Ourselves to Celestial Things. The Sort of People to Whom Saturn is Malign, to Whom Propitious, and Whom Jupiter Defends from Saturn. How the Heavens Act on the Spirit, the Body, and the Soul. Chap. XXII.

To Live Well and Prosper, First Know Your Natural Bent, Your Star, Your Genius, and the Place Suitable to These; Here Live. Follow Your Natural Profession. Chap. XXIII.

By What System People Dedicated to Learning May Recognize Their Natural Bent and Follow a Manner of Life Suitable to Their Guardian Spirit. Chap. XXIV.

Astronomical Precautions to Be Taken in Procreating Children, in Preparing Meals, in Buildings, and in One's Dwelling-place and Clothing; and How Much It Is Permissible to Care about Such Things. Chap. XXV.

How by Exposing Lower Things to Higher Things, You Can Bring Down the Higher, and Cosmic Gifts Especially through Cosmic Materials. Chap. XXVI.

An Apologia Dealing with Medicine, Astrology, the Life of the World, and the Magi Who Greeted the Christ Child at His Birth.

That Freedom from Care and Tranquillity of Mind Are Necessary for Life. Poem by Amerigo Corsini.

*Chapter titles marked with an asterisk in the 1489 Table of Contents differ significantly from their counterparts in the body of the work.

Sigla

CODICES

De vita libri tres
  L   Laurentianus 73,39; saec. XV

De vita I
  A   Laurentianus Ashburnhamensis 917; saec. XV
  B   Berolinensis lat. fol. 374; saec. XV
  D   Laurentianus 90, sup. 43; saec. XV
  G   Guelferbytanus 2706 73 Aug. 2°; saec. XV
  R   Riccardianus 797; saec. XV
  e   ABDGR codicum consensus

De vita III
  P   Laurentianus 82,11; saec. XV

Excerpta
  M   Monacensis (Clm) 10781; saec. XV

EDITIONES

  w   Florentiae 1489 (Antonius Miscominus), editio princeps
  x   Venetiis 1498
  y   Basileae 1497 (Joannes de Amerbach)
  z   Basileae 1576 (Henricus Petri), Opera omnia

L^{ac}, A^{ac}, etc. LA, etc. ante corectionem
L^1, A^1, etc. LA, etc. a prima manu correcti
L^2 L a secunda manu correctus

Prooemium Marsilii Ficini Florentini in Librum De Vita Ad Magnanimum Laurentium Medicem Patriae Servatorem

Bacchum poetae, summum antistitem sacerdotum, bis natum canunt, forte significantes vel futurum sacerdotem statim initiatum oportere renasci, vel perfecti tandem sacerdotis mentem Deo penitus ebriam iam videri renatam; aut forsan humiliore sensu vinum, Bacchi germen, generari semel in vite quasi Semele maturis sub Phoebo racemis, regenerari rursum post 5 ipsum vindemiae fulmen in suo vase vinum velut in Iovis femore merum. Sed de sacris impraesentia mysteriis non est loquendum, ubi mox physica potius ope languentibus opitulaturi sumus. Nec agendum stilo gravitatis servo, sed libero potius et iocoso, postquam a Libero patre nescio quomodo statim exorsi sumus. Et recte, inquam, nescio quomodo, nam forte prudentior 10 aliquis a Phoebo, medicorum primo, potius quam a Baccho medicinam auspicatus esset. Quid vero, si quod non vanum omen sit in ore nunc sorte quadam proferente Bacchum? Hic enim almo quodam vino securitateque laetissima salubrius forte medetur, quam herbis ille suis carminibusque Phoebus.

Quocunque vero sensu vel illa vel haec acceperis, dux ille sacerdotum Bac- 15 chus geminas quasi matres habuisse fertur. Melchisedech autem, summus ille sacerdos, unam vix matrem, unum vix patrem habuit. Ego sacerdos minimus patres habui duos: Ficinum medicum, Cosmum Medicem. Ex illo natus sum, ex isto renatus. Ille quidem me Galieno tum medico tum Platonico commendavit; hic autem divino consecravit me Platoni. Et hic similiter atque ille 20 Marsilium medico destinavit: Galienus quidem corporum, Plato vero medicus animorum. Iamdiu igitur sub Platone salutarem animorum exercui medicinam, quando post librorum omnium eius interpretationem, mox decem atque octo De animorum immortalitate libros et aeterna felicitate composui, ita pro viribus patri meo Medici satisfaciens. Medico vero patri satis deinceps fa- 25

Totum prooemium deest in e; titulus prooemii deest in M   Prooemium *om. yz*   *post* Florentini *add.* Medici atque Philosophi *z*   *post* Servatorem *add.* Prologus *y; add.* Epistola dedicatoria *z*   1 sacerdotem *z*   5 racemus *M*   13 quondam *x*   14 carnibusque *x*

Proem by Marsilio Ficino the Florentine of his Book "On Life" To the Magnanimous Lorenzo de' Medici Preserver of his Country

The poets sing that Bacchus, the supreme prelate of priests,[1] was born twice — signifying perhaps either that one who is going to be a priest should be reborn at the moment of his initiation or else that when one is at length a perfected priest, his mind, deeply drunken with God, seems now to have been reborn. Or perhaps, in a less exalted sense, they mean that wine (the seed of Bacchus) is born once on the vine (Semele) when the clusters are ripe beneath Phoebus, and born again after the thunderbolt of the vintage as pure wine in its proper vessel (the thigh of Jupiter).[2] But our task is not at present to speak of sacred mysteries, when we are presently about to bring help to the sick by natural means. Nor ought we to proceed in a style that expresses gravity — after just beginning somehow or other with Father Liber — but rather in a style that is free [pun on "Liber"] and jocose. And rightly I say "somehow or other," for perhaps a more prudent author might have begun a work of medicine under the auspices of Phoebus the first of doctors rather than under those of Bacchus. But what if there might be a sign not without meaning in my mouth just now happening to utter "Bacchus"? For he perhaps heals more salubriously with his nourishing wine and his carefree jollity than that Phoebus with his herbs and songs.

But whichever interpretation you accept, Bacchus, that leader of priests, is said to have had, as it were, two mothers. Melchisidech, moreover, that highest of priests, had scarcely one mother, scarcely one father.[3] I, the least of priests, had two fathers — Ficino the doctor and Cosimo de' Medici.[4] From the former I was born, from the latter reborn. The former commended me to Galen as both a doctor and a Platonist;[5] the latter consecrated me to the divine Plato[6] And both the one and the other alike dedicated Marsilio to a doctor — Galen, doctor of the body, Plato, doctor of the soul. Therefore, for a long time now I have practiced the medicine salutary to souls under Plato: after translating all his books, I straightway composed eighteen books concerning the immortality of souls and eternal happiness, so to the best of my ability repaying my Medici father.[7] Thinking I ought next to repay my medical father, I have

ciendum putans, librum *De litteratorum valetudine curanda* composui. Desiderabant praeterea post haec homines litterati non tantum bene quandoque valere, sed etiam bene valentes diu vivere. His ergo deinde librum *De vita longa* dedi. Diffidebant autem medicinis atque remediis in re tanta terrenis. Adiunxi librum *De vita tum valida tum longa coelitus comparanda,* ut ex ipso mundi corpore vivo vita quaedam vegetior in corpus nostrum, quasi quoddam mundi membrum, velut ex vite propagaretur.

His vero tu medicinae libris ignosce, precor, indulgentissime Laurenti, si dum medicus esse volo, nescio quomodo etiam nolens sum, et si non bonus saepe poeta. Nam et Phoebus idem est medicinae repertor poesisque magister, vitamque ille suam nobis non tam per herbas quam per citharam cantumque largitur. Ipsa quinetiam Venus apud astrologos musicum aeque parit et medicum. Sed hactenus dum litteratorum civiumque similium vitae curiosius consulo, librorum meorum salutem negligo, quamdiu inter se patior esse seiunctos. Quamobrem in eos nunc primum pius in corpus unum copulo. Cuius artubus in unam formam iam compactis, vita protinus adsit. Non potest autem hoc opus physicum, id quasi corpus meum, vitam accipere nisi meam. Eiusmodi vero vita ex mea duntaxat pendet anima. Haec autem iamdiu penes te, magnanime Laurenti, mi patrone, vivit in ea praesertim amplissimarum aedium tuarum parte, ubi una cum Platone nostrum illud *De animorum immortalitate* servatur opus, tuo iampridem nomini dedicatum. At animus iste meus, etsi in beata quadam quasi patria penes te vitam agit, verumtamen, quod et theologi volunt, inquietus est interea, donec opus id physicum tanquam suum corpus accipiat. Accipe igitur, optime Laurenti, post illos de anima hos etiam de corpore libros, eodemque afflatu quo et illis dudum feliciter his aspira. Ita enim et corpus hoc sub tuo spiritu per suam vivet animam, et anima vicissim nostra cum hoc iam suo corpore in tuis laribus conquiescet.

---

34 et si] etsi *z*   38 civium *M*   39 curiosius *om. M*   45 nostro *M*   46 nomine *z*   51 his *om. M*   52 hoc *om. z*

composed a book *On Caring for the Health of Learned People.* In addition, after this, learned people desired not only to be healthy for a while, but also, being in good health, to live a long time. And so I then gave them a book *On a Long Life.* But they distrusted terrestrial medicines and remedies in a matter of such importance; and so I added[8] a book *On Obtaining a Life Both Healthy and Long from Heaven,* so that from the very living body of the world, a more vigorous life might be propagated as if from a vine into our own body, which is in a way a part of the world's body.

But I beg you, good-natured Lorenzo, to pardon these books of medicine, if while trying to be a doctor, I am, somehow or other, willy-nilly a poet, and often not a good one. For one and the same Phoebus is the discoverer of medicine and the master of poesy, and he gives us of his life not only by herbs but through the lute and music. And even Venus herself according to astrologers gives birth equally to the musician and the doctor.[9] But up to now, while I take assiduous care of the life of learned people and citizens of similar occupations, I neglect the welfare of my own books, so long as I allow them to be disjoined from each other. Accordingly, recognizing my duty to them for the first time, I am joining them in one body. Since their limbs have now been compacted into one form, let life be present forthwith. This work of natural science, this my body, so to speak, cannot receive any life but mine; but such life depends entirely on my soul. This soul, however, lives now this long time with you, Lorenzo, my patron, especially in that part of your spacious palace wherein together with Plato [meaning his translation] my work *On the Immortality of Souls* is kept, long since dedicated to your name. But that soul[10] of mine, even if it leads its life with you as in a blessed homeland, nevertheless, as the theologians say, it is still "unquiet" until it receives this work of natural science as its body.[11] Accept, therefore, O excellent Lorenzo, after those books on the soul these also on the body, and favor these with the same inspiration with which you long ago propitiously favored the others. For so also this body under your spirit[12] will live through having its own soul; and our soul in turn, being now together with this its body, will be at rest in your house.

Universalis Inscriptio

Liber De Vita in Tres Libros Divisus: Primus De Vita Sana, Secundus De Vita Longa, Tertius De Vita Coelitus Comparanda

De cura valetudinis eorum qui incumbunt studio litterarum

Marsilius Ficinus Florentinus Georgio Antonio Vespuccio et Ioanni Baptistae Boninsegnio, viris probitate doctrinaque insignibus, S.D. Multa vobiscum his temporibus Peripateticorum more deambulando confabulati sumus de curanda eorum valetudine qui assidue incumbunt studio litterarum, quae quidem brevi perstricta compendio vobis potissimum commendare decrevi. Neque prius id opusculum vel ipse probabo, quam a vobis praecipue viris amicisque probatissimis probatum esse rescivero, vel elegantissimum Laurentii Medicis nostri iudicium subire permittam, cuius quidem prosperae valetudini est imprimis, si opus fuerit, consulturum. Vix enim praesentibus litteratis praesertim nostris prospiciet unquam, nisi prius eorum patrono Maecenati prospexerit. Legite igitur diligenter atque curate valetudinem diligentissime. Sublata enim sanitate sublimes Musarum fores, nisi Deus omnipotens mira quadam virtute et ducat et patefaciat, aut non tanguntur a nobis unquam aut certe frustra pulsantur. Physicam vero hanc disputationem nostram eo potissimum tanquam argumentum quoddam spectare volumus, videlicet si consequendae sapientiae gratia corporis sanitas tantopere quaerenda est, multo magis sanitatem mentis, qua sola potest sapientia comprehendi, esse quaerendam. Alioquin inscite omnino scientiam quaerunt quicunque insana mente sapientiam capere moliuntur. Sanitatem quidem corporis Hippocrates, animi vero Socrates pollicetur. Sed veram utriusque sanitatem solus ille praestat, qui sic exclamat: "Venite ad me omnes qui laboratis et onerati estis, atque ego vos reficiam. Ego sum via veritasque et vita."

Universalis Inscriptio — De Vita Coelitus (Comparanda addidi) w; y habet Liber iste De vita in tres libros divisus est. Primus de vita sana sive de cura valetudinis eorum qui incumbunt studio litterarum, secundus de vita longa, tertius de vita coelitus comparanda; *deest in cett.   Titulus et secundum prooemium desunt in z   De Cura — Litterarum]* Marsilii Ficini Florentini liber primus de vita sana sive de cura valitudinis eorum qui incumbunt studio litterarum *habet x*; Marsilii Ficini Florentini in librum primum de vita sana ad Georgium Antonium Vespuccium et Ioannem Baptistam Boninsegnium Epistolare prooemium *habet y; Litterarum Studio Incumbunt transp. G   2 post* viris *add.* probatissimis *A   *S.D.] S. *B;* S.P.D. *G   5* commendare] dedicare *e   6* vel *om. e   * probavero *G   7-11* vel elegantissimum — prospexerit *desunt in e   11 post* patrono *add.* et *Krist. Sup. Fic. I.21   13* tangantur *D   22* honerati *Ɩ;* honorati *x   22 post* vita *add.* Valete *y*

General Title
A Book on Life Divided into Three Books:
Book One, On a Healthy Life,
Book Two, On a Long Life,
Book Three, On Obtaining Life from the Heavens

On Caring for the Health of Those
Who Devote Themselves to Literary Studies.

Marsilio Ficino the Florentine sends greetings to Giorgio Antonio Vespucci and Giovanni-Battista Buoninsegni, men who excel in probity and learning.[1] We have talked much with you recently, strolling like Peripatetics, about caring for the health of those who devote themselves fulltime to literary studies. These matters, condensed in a brief compendium, I decided to entrust to you above all. Nor will I myself approve this little piece before I either ascertain that you approve it—you whom I have put to a more thorough proof than any, both as men and as friends—or else permit it to undergo the refined judgment of our dear Lorenzo de' Medici, whose good health indeed is my special concern if ever there is need. For one will hardly be taking any care at all of the intellectuals of today, especially those of our own city, if he does not first take care of their patron, their Maecenas. Read carefully, then, and take care of your health still more carefully. For if health suffers, we either never even reach the high doors of the Muses or at least knock at them in vain—unless God who is omnipotent lead us and open them by miraculous power. We intend this medical disquisition of ours to have in view particularly as a theme, that if for the attainment of wisdom, health of body is so greatly to be sought, much more so is health of mind, by which alone wisdom can be comprehended; if it is not, they will seek knowledge but ignorantly who undertake to grasp wisdom with an unsound mind. Hippocrates promises health of body, Socrates, of soul. But the true health of both is furnished only by Him who cries: "Come unto me, all ye that labor and are heavy-laden, and I will refresh you. I am the way, the truth, and the life."[2]

Novem studiosorum duces.

Cap. I.

Quicunque iter illud asperum arduumque et longum ingrediuntur, quod quidem vix tandem ad excelsum novem Musarum templum assiduo labore perducit, novem omnino itineris huius ducibus indigere videntur. Quorum primi quidem tres in coelo, tres sequentes in animo, postremi tres in terra nos ducunt. Principio in coelo Mercurius, ut investigando Musarum iter aggrediamur, vel impellit vel adhortatur, siquidem Mercurio tributum est investigationis omnis officium. Deinde Phoebus ipse et quaerentes animos et res quaesitas splendore uberrimo sic illustrat, ut perspicue quod quaerebatur, a nobis inveniatur. Accedit gratiosissima Venus, Gratiarum mater, atque almis omnino laetisque radiis suis rem omnem adeo condit et ornat, ut quicquid et instigante Mercurio quaesitum fuit, et monstrante Phoebo iam erat inventum, mirifica quadam et salutari venustate Veneris circumfusum delectet semper et prosit. Sequuntur tres itineris huius duces in animo: videlicet voluntas ardens et stabilis, acumen ingenii, memoria tenax. Tres in terra postremi sunt: prudentissimus paterfamilias, probatissimus praeceptor, medicus peritissimus. Absque his novem ducibus nemo ad ipsum novem Musarum templum pervenire vel potuit vel poterit unquam. Ceteros quidem duces ab initio nobis praecipue Deus omnipotens naturaque tribuit, tres vero postremos nostra adhibet diligentia. Sed praecepta officiaque quae ad patremfamilias et quae ad praeceptorem circa litterarum studia pertinent, antiqui plures sapientesque tractaverunt, praecipue Plato noster et saepe alias et in libris *De republica* ac *De legibus* diligentissime, deinde Aristoteles in *Politicis,* Plutarchus quoque et Quintilianus egregie. Solus autem litterarum studiosis hactenus deest medicus aliquis, qui manum euntibus porrigat, salutaribusque consiliis atque medicinis adiuvet eos, quos neque coelum neque animus neque paterfamilias praeceptorve destituit. Ego igitur sortem eorum laboriosissimam miseratus, qui difficile Minervae minuentis nervos iter agunt, primus tanquam medicus debilibus et valetudinariis adsum, sed utinam facultate tam integra quam propitia voluntate. Surgite iam adolescentes Deo duce alacres. Surgite iuvenes atque viri, quos ardentius Minervae studium nimis enervat. Accedite libenter ad medicum qui vobis ad instituti vestri perfectionem, monstrante Deo atque favente, consilia remediaque salutaria largietur.

Ante capitulum primum y hunc titulum habet: Marsilii Ficini Florentini primus liber de vita sana sive de cura valetudinis eorum qui incumbunt studio litterarum incipit; *z habet:* Marsilii Ficini Florentini Medici atque Philosophi celeberrimi de studiosorum sanitate tuenda sive eorum qui literis operam navant bona valetudine conservanda. Liber I. *Capitula libri primi non numerantur in Lew   Novem studiosorum duces]* De novem studiosorum ducibus *yz*   1 arduum *G*   5 ducant *e*   10 atque] aut *x*   18 tribuerunt *z*   22 libro *D*   26 Ego] Ergo *D*   27 misertus *z*   29 alacres *om. e*   30 nimium *z*   32 largitur *z*

The Nine Guides of Scholars.

Chap. I

anyone who enters upon that rough, arduous, and long journey which barely, at the last, by continual hardship leads through to the high temple of the nine Muses, seems to need exactly nine guides in this journey. The first three lead us in the heavens, the next three in the soul, the last three on earth. To begin with, in the heavens, Mercury either impels or exhorts us that we should undertake the journey in search of the Muses, since to Mercury is attributed the charge of every investigation. Next is Phoebus, who so illuminates the seeking souls and the things sought with copious light, that we find clearly what we sought. Gracious Venus is added, the mother of the graces; and with her all-bountiful and joyful rays she so enhances and adorns the material, that whatever both by Mercury's instigation has been sought and by Phoebus's showing has been found, is invested with Venus's wonderful and health-giving charm and always delights and profits.[1] There follow three guides of this journey in the soul — that is, a fierce and firm will, sharpness of intelligence, and a tenacious memory. The last three are on earth — a prudent father, a thoroughly accredited teacher, and a thoroughly experienced physician. And without these nine guides, no man either has been or ever will be able to get all the way to the temple of the nine Muses. God omnipotent and nature, indeed, assigned the other guides to us from the beginning; the last three, however, our own effort summons.[2] But the precepts and duties appertaining to the father and the teacher in literary studies have been treated by many wise authors of antiquity, especially my author Plato, often elsewhere but most exhaustively in his books on the *Republic* and on the *Laws*,[3] then Aristotle in his *Politics*[4], Plutarch also,[5] and Quintilian[6] unusually well. Only a physician is as yet a desideratum for literary scholars[7] — one who might reach a hand to them as they go, and help with salutary counsels and medicines those who already have the heavens, the mind, the father, and the teacher. Since I pity the burdensome lot of those who make the difficult journey of Minerva who shrinks the sinews,[8] I am the first to attend as a physician sick and invalid scholars; but would that my ability were as sound as my will is dedicated! Rise up, now, God leading, those of you who are still lively adolescents! Rise up, young people and mature people enervated by too fierce pursuit of Minerva! Gladly approach the physician who will dispense to you (God revealing and helping) salutary counsels and remedies for the accomplishment of your purpose!

*Quam diligens habenda cura sit cerebri,
cordis, stomachi, spiritus.*

Cap. II.

Principio quantam cursores crurium, athletae bracchiorum, musici vocis curam habere solent, tantam saltem litterarum studiosos cerebri et cordis iecorisque et stomachi oportet habere; immo vero tanto maiorem, quanto et membra haec praestantiora quam illa sunt, et ii frequentius atque ad potiora his membris quam illi illis utuntur. Praeterea solers quilibet artifex instrumenta sua diligentissime curat: penicillos pictor, malleos incudesque faber aerarius, miles equos et arma, venator canes et aves, citharam citharoedus, et sua quisque similiter. Soli vero Musarum sacerdotes, soli summi boni veritatisque venatores tam negligentes, pro nefas, tamque infortunati sunt, ut instrumentum illud, quo mundum universum metiri quodammodo et capere possunt, negligere penitus videantur. Instrumentum eiusmodi spiritus ipse est, qui apud medicos vapor quidam sanguinis purus, subtilis, calidus et lucidus definitur. Atque ab ipso cordis calore ex subtiliori sanguine procreatus volat ad cerebrum; ibique animus ipso ad sensus tam interiores quam exteriores exercendos assidue utitur. Quamobrem sanguis spiritui servit, spiritus sensibus, sensus denique rationi. Sanguis autem a virtute naturali, quae in iecore stomachoque viget, efficitur. Tenuissima sanguinis pars fluit in cordis fontem, ubi vitalis viget virtus. Inde creati spiritus cerebri et (ut ita dixerim) Palladis arces ascendunt, in quibus animalis, id est sentiendi movendique vis, dominatur. Itaque talis plurimum ferme contemplatio est, quale sensus ipsius obsequium; talis autem sensus, qualis et spiritus; spiritus vero talis, qualis et sanguis et tres illae vires quas diximus: naturalis scilicet, vitalis et animalis, a quibus, per quas, in quibus spiritus ipsi concipiuntur, nascuntur atque foventur.

---

sit ante cura transp. D^1GR post stomachi add. et z   3 post habere add. rationem z   8 similem D   11 videntur z   12 et lucidus om. DR   13 post ipso add. spiritu D^1GR^1 16 sensus om. L   20 post talis add. ut e   22 scilicet om. G; et add. A^{ac} 23 post animalis add. tales ut sunt z

*What Diligent Care We Should Take of the Brain,
the Heart, the Stomach, and the Spirit.*

Chap. II

In the first place, as much care as runners habitually take of their legs, athletes of their arms, musicians of their voice, even so it behooves literary scholars to have at least as much concern for their brain and heart, their liver and stomach — and indeed so much the more, in proportion as the latter parts are more excellent than are the former and literary scholars use their parts more frequently and for more important things than the former people do theirs. Moreover, an expert craftsman takes most diligent care of his instruments — a painter his pencils, a coppersmith his hammers and anvils, a soldier his horses and arms, a hunter his dogs and birds, a lute-player his lute, and the same goes for anyone and the tools of his trade. But only the priests of the Muses, only the hunters after the highest good and truth, are so negligent (oh shame!) and so unfortunate, that they seem wholly to neglect that instrument with which they are able in a way to measure and grasp the whole world. This instrument is the spirit, which is defined by doctors as a vapor of blood — pure, subtle, hot, and clear.[1] After being generated by the heat of the heart out of the more subtle blood, it flies to the brain; and there the soul uses it continually for the exercise of the interior[2] as well as the exterior senses. This is why the blood subserves the spirit; the spirit, the senses; and finally, the senses, reason. Now the blood is made by that natural power which flourishes in the liver and the stomach. The lightest part of the blood flows into the fountain of the heart, where flourishes the vital power. The spirits generated from this ascend to the citadels of the brain and (as I might say) of Pallas;[3] in these [citadels, i.e., the brain] the animal force, that is, the power of sense and motion, dominates. Thus, undoubtedly the contemplation is usually as good as is the compliance of the sense; the sense is as good as is the spirit; the spirit is as good as is both the blood and those three forces which we mentioned — i.e., the natural, vital, and animal, by which, through which, and in which the spirits themselves are conceived, born, and nourished.

Litterati pituitae et atrae bili obnoxii sunt.

Cap. III.

Non solum vero membra illa viresque et spiritus homines litterarum cupidi curare diligentissime debent, verum etiam pituitam semper et atram bilem, non aliter quam navigantes Scyllam atque Charybdim, cautissime devitare iubentur. Quantum enim reliquo corpore otiosi sunt, tantum cerebro ac mente negotiosi. Inde pituitam, quod Graeci phlegma, hinc atram 5 bilem, quam iidem melancholiam vocant, gignere compelluntur. Illa quidem ingenium saepe obtundit et suffocat, haec vero, si nimium abundaverit flagraveritque, assidua cura crebrisque deliramentis vexat animum iudiciumque perturbat, ut non immerito dici possit, litteratos fore et praecipue sanos, nisi cum pituita molesta est, et laetissimos sapientissimosque omnium, nisi bilis 10 atrae vitio vel maerere saepe vel interdum desipere compellantur.

Quot sint causae quibus litterati melancholici sint vel fiant.

Cap. IV.

Ut autem litterati sint melancholici, tres potissimum causarum species faciunt: prima coelestis, secunda naturalis, tertia est humana. Coelestis quoniam Mercurius, qui ut doctrinas investigemus invitat, et Saturnus qui efficit ut in doctrinis investigandis perseveremus inventasque servemus, frigidi quodammodo siccique ab astronomis esse dicuntur — vel si forte Mer- 5 curius non sit frigidus, fit tamen saepe Solis propinquitate siccissimus — qualis est natura apud medicos melancholica; eandemque naturam Mercurius ipse Saturnusque litterarum studiosis eorum sectatoribus impartiunt ab initio ac servant augentque quotidie.

    Naturalis autem causa esse videtur, quod ad scientias praesertim difficiles 10 consequendas necesse est animum ab externis ad interna tanquam a circumferentia quadam ad centrum sese recipere, atque dum speculatur in ipso (ut ita dixerim) hominis centro stabilissime permanere. Ad centrum vero a circumferentia se colligere figique in centro maxime terrae ipsius est proprium, cui quidem atra bilis persimilis est. Igitur atra bilis animum, ut se et colli- 15

Quod litterati ... obnoxii sint *y*; Literatos ... esse *z*   4 evitare *z*   enim] vero *D*   6 idem *G*
9 et *om. z*   10 cum *om. z*   esset *z*   11 moerore *z*   compelluntur *D*; cogerentur *z*
    Cap. III. z   5—6 vel si—siccissimus *desunt in e*   8 et Saturnus *z*

Learned People Are Subject to Phlegm and Black Bile.

Chap. III

not only should learned people take very diligent care of those members and of the powers and of the spirits, but also they are told always scrupulously to avoid phlegm and black bile, even as sailors do Scylla and Charybdis. For just as they are inactive in the rest of the body, so they are busy in the brain and the mind. From the former circumstance they are compelled to secrete pituita, which the Greeks call phlegm, and from the latter, black bile, which they call melancholy. Phlegm dulls and suffocates the intelligence, while melancholy, if it is too abundant or vehement, vexes the mind with continual care and frequent absurdities and unsettles the judgment. Hence it can justly be said that learned people would even be unusually healthy, were they not burdened by phlegm, and the happiest and wisest of mortals, were they not driven by the bad effects of black bile to depression and even sometimes to folly.[1]

How Many Things Cause Learned People Either To Be Melancholy or To Eventually Become So.

Chap. IV

In the main, three kinds of causes make learned people melancholics. The first is celestial, the second natural, and the third human. The celestial: because both Mercury, who invites us to investigate doctrines, and Saturn, who makes us persevere in investigating doctrines and retain them when discovered, are said by astronomers to be somewhat cold and dry (or if it should happen to be true that Mercury is not cold, he is nonetheless often very dry by virtue of his nearness to the Sun), just like the melancholic nature, according to physicians. And this same nature Mercury and Saturn impart from birth to their followers, learned people, and preserve and augment it day by day.[1]

The natural cause seems to be that for the pursuit of the sciences, especially the difficult ones, the soul must draw in upon itself from external things to internal as from the circumference to the center, and while it speculates, it must stay immovably at the very center (as I might say) of man. Now to collect oneself from the circumference to the center, and to be fixed in the center, is above all the property of the Earth itself, to which black bile is analogous.

gat in unum et sistat in uno contempleturque, assidue provocat. Atque ipsa mundi centro similis ad centrum rerum singularum cogit investigandum, evehitque ad altissima quaeque comprehendenda, quandoquidem cum Saturno maxime congruit altissimo planetarum. Contemplatio quoque ipsa vicissim assidua quadam collectione et quasi compressione naturam atrae bili persimilem contrahit.

Humana vero, id est ex nobis, causa est: quoniam frequens agitatio mentis cerebrum vehementer exsiccat, igitur humore magna ex parte consumpto, quod caloris naturalis pabulum est, calor quoque plurimum solet extingui, unde natura cerebri sicca frigidaque evadit, quae quidem terrestris et melancholica qualitas nominatur. Praeterea ob frequentissimum inquisitionis motum spiritus quoque moti continue resolvuntur. Resolutos autem spiritus ex subtiliori sanguine instaurari necessarium est. Quapropter subtilioribus clarioribusque sanguinis partibus saepe consumptis, reliquus sanguis necessario densus redditur et siccus et ater. Accedit ad haec quod natura, in contemplatione cerebro prorsus cordique intenta, stomachum heparque destituit. Quare alimentis praesertim vel uberioribus vel durioribus male concoctis, sanguis inde frigidus crassusque et niger efficitur. Postremo nimio membrorum otio neque superflua excernuntur, neque crassi fuscique vapores exhalant. Haec omnia melancholicum spiritum maestumque et pavidum animum efficere solent, siquidem interiores tenebrae multo magis quam exteriores maerore occupant animum atque terrent. Maxime vero litteratorum omnium hi atra bile premuntur, qui sedulo philosophiae studio dediti mentem a corpore rebusque corporeis sevocant, incorporeisque coniungunt, tum quia difficilius admodum opus maiori quoque indiget mentis intentione, tum quia quatenus mentem incorporeae veritati coniungunt, eatenus a corpore disiungere compelluntur. Hinc corpus eorum nonnunquam quasi semianimum redditur atque melancholicum. Quod quidem Plato noster in *Timaeo* significat, dicens animum divina saepissime et intentissime contemplantem alimentis eiusmodi adeo adolescere potentemque evadere, ut corpus suum supra quam natura corporis patiatur exsuperet, ipsumque vehementioribus agitationibus suis aliquando vel effugiat quodammodo, vel nonnunquam quasi dissolvere videatur.

---

22 id est] ea *z*   agitatio] Sagittario *z*   28 subtiliore *y;* subtilione *z*   subtilibus *z*   33 Postremo] Demum *z*   34 crassi] glutinosi tenaces *z*   37 terent *z*   42 non unquam *L*   47 non unquam *L*

Therefore black bile continually incites the soul both to collect itself together into one and to dwell on itself and to contemplate itself. And being analogous to the world's center, it forces the investigation to the center of individual subjects, and it carries one to the contemplation of whatever is highest, since, indeed, it is most congruent with Saturn, the highest of planets. Contemplation itself, in its turn, by a continual recollection and compression, as it were, brings on a nature similar to black bile.

The human cause, that which comes from ourselves, is as follows: Because frequent agitation of the mind greatly dries up the brain, therefore, when the moisture has been mostly consumed—moisture being the support of the natural heat—the heat also is usually extinguished; and from this chain of events, the nature of the brain becomes dry and cold, which is known as the earthy and melancholic quality. Moreover, on account of the repeated movements of inquiry, the spirits continually move and get dispersed. But when the spirits are dispersed, they have to be restored out of the more subtle blood. And hence, when the more subtle and clear parts of the blood frequently get used up, the rest of the blood is necessarily rendered dense, dry and black. On top of this, nature in contemplation is directed wholly to the brain and heart and deserts the stomach and liver. For this reason foods, especially the more fatty or harsh foods, are poorly digested, and as a result the blood is rendered cold, thick, and black. Finally, with too little physical exercise, superfluities are not carried off and the thick, dense, clinging, dusky vapors do not exhale. All these things characteristically make the spirit melancholy and the soul sad and fearful—since, indeed, interior darkness much more than exterior overcomes the soul with sadness and terrifies it. But of all learned people, those especially are oppressed by black bile, who, being sedulously devoted to the study of philosophy, recall their mind from the body and corporeal things and apply it to incorporeal things. The cause is, first, that the more difficult the work, the greater concentration of mind it requires; and second, that the more they apply their mind to incorporeal truth, the more they are compelled to disjoin it from the body. Hence their body is often rendered as if it were half-alive and often melancholic. My author Plato signified this in the *Timaeus*; he said that the soul contemplating divine things assiduously and intently grows up so much on food of this kind and becomes so powerful, that it overreaches its body above what the corporeal nature can endure;[2] and sometimes in its too vehement agitation, it either in a way flies out of it or sometimes seems as if to disintegrate it.[3]

Cur melancholici ingeniosi sint et quales melancholici sint eiusmodi, quales contra.

Cap. V.

Hactenus quam ob causam Musarum sacerdotes melancholici vel sint ab initio vel studio fiant, rationibus primo coelestibus, secundo naturalibus, tertio humanis ostendisse sufficiat. Quod quidem confirmat in libro *Problematum* Aristoteles, omnes enim inquit viros in quavis facultate praestantes melancholicos extitisse. Qua in re Platonicum illud quod in libro *De scientia* scribitur confirmavit, ingeniosos videlicet plurimum concitatos furiososque esse solere. Democritus quoque nullos inquit viros ingenio magnos, praeter illos qui furore quodam perciti sunt, esse unquam posse. Quod quidem Plato noster in *Phaedro* probare videtur, dicens poeticas fores frustra absque furore pulsari. Etsi divinum furorem hic forte intelligi vult, tamen neque furor eiusmodi apud physicos aliis unquam ullis praeterquam melancholicis incitatur.

Deinceps vero assignandae a nobis rationes sunt, quare Democritus et Plato et Aristoteles asserant melancholicos nonnullos interdum adeo ingenio cunctos excellere, ut non humani sed divini potius videantur. Asseverant id Democritus et Plato et Aristoteles absque dubio, rationem vero tantae rei haud satis explicare videntur. Audendum tamen monstrante Deo causas indagare. Melancholia, id est atra bilis, est duplex: altera quidem naturalis a medicis appellatur, altera vero adustione contingit. Naturalis illa nihil est aliud quam densior quaedam sicciorque pars sanguinis. Adusta vero in species quattuor distribuitur: aut enim naturalis melancholiae aut sanguinis purioris aut bilis aut salsae pituitae combustione concipitur. Quaecunque adustione nascitur iudicio et sapientiae nocet. Nempe dum humor ille accenditur atque ardet, concitatos furentesque facere solet, quam Graeci maniam nuncupant, nos vero furorem. At quando iam extinguitur, subtilioribus clarioribusque partibus resolutis solaque restante fuligine tetra, stolidos reddit et stupidos. Quem habitum melancholiam proprie et amentiam vecordiamque appellant.

Sola igitur atra bilis illa quam diximus naturalem ad iudicium nobis sapientiamque conducit, neque tamen semper. Sane si sola sit, atra nimium densaque mole obfuscat spiritus, terret animum, obtundit ingenium. Si vero pituitae simplici misceatur, cum frigidus obstiterit circum praecordia sanguis,

---

Cur melancholici ... quales melancholici ... quales contra] melancholia ... qui horum ... aut secus *z*   3 sufficiat] sit satis *z*   6 *post* videlicet *add.* ut *e*   9 fore *x*   frustra *om. D*   13-17 Deinceps vero — indagare *desunt in B*   24 nos] nostri *B*

Why Melancholics Are Intelligent, and Which Melancholics Are So and Which Are Not.

Chap. V

So far, let it suffice that we have shown why the priests of the Muses either are from the beginning or are made by study into melancholics, owing to causes first celestial, second natural, and third human. This Aristotle confirms in his book of *Problems*, saying that all those who are renowned in whatever faculty you please have been melancholics.[1] In this he has confirmed that Platonic notion expressed in the book *De scientia*, that most intelligent people are prone to excitability and madness.[2] Democritus too says no one can ever be intellectually outstanding except those who are deeply excited by some sort of madness.[3] My author Plato in the *Phaedrus* seems to approve this, saying that without madness one knocks at the doors of poetry in vain.[4] Even if he perhaps intends divine madness to be understood here,[5] nevertheless, according to the physicians, madness of this kind is never incited in anyone else but melancholics.[6]

After this, reasons must be assigned why Democritus, Plato and Aristotle assert that not a few melancholics sometimes so excel everyone in intelligence that they seem to be not human but rather divine. Democritus, Plato, and Aristotle affirm it unhesitatingly, but they do not seem to give a sufficient explanation for so important a fact.[7] One must have the courage, however, God showing the way, to search out causes.[8] Melancholy or black bile is of two kinds: the one is called natural by doctors, the other comes about by adustion. The natural is nothing but a more dense and dry part of the blood. The adust, however, is divided into four kinds: it originates from the combustion either of natural melancholy, or of the purer blood [as opposed to "the more dense... part of the blood"], or of bile [meaning yellow or red bile, better known as choler], or of salty phlegm.[9] Any melancholy which arises from adustion, harms the wisdom and the judgment,[10] because when that humor is kindled and burns, it characteristically makes people excited and frenzied, which melancholy the Greeks call mania and we madness. But as soon as it is extinguished, when the more subtle and clearer parts have been dispersed and only a foul black soot remains, it makes people stolid and stupid; they properly call this disposition melancholy and also being out of one's wits and senselessness.[11]

Only that black bile which we call natural, therefore, leads us to judgment and wisdom — but not always. If it is alone, it beclouds the spirit with a mass that is black and dense, terrifies the soul, and dulls the intelligence. Moreover if it is mixed simply with phlegm, when "cold blood" stands in the way "around the heart" [*Georg.* 2.484; *Aen.* 10.452] it brings on sluggishness and torpor by

crassa quadam frigiditate segnitiem adducit atque torporem; atque ut densissimae cuiusque materiae natura est, quando eiusmodi melancholia frigescit, ad summum frigiditatis intenditur. Quo in statu nihil speratur, timentur omnia, taedet coeli convexa tueri. Si bilis atra vel simplex vel mixta putrescit, quartanam gignit febrem, lienis tumores et multa generis eiusdem. Ubi nimis exuberat, sive sola sit sive coniuncta pituitae, spiritus crassiores facit atque frigidiores, continuo animum afficit taedio, mentis aciem hebetat, neque salit Arcadico circum praecordia sanguis. Oportet autem atram bilem neque tam paucam esse, ut sanguis, bilis, spiritus quasi freno careant, unde instabile ingenium labilemque memoriam esse contingat; neque tam multam, ut nimio pondere praegravati dormitare atque egere calcaribus videamur. Proinde necessarium est omnino eam esse, quoad eius natura patitur, subtilissimam. Si enim tenuata pro natura sua maxime fuerit, poterit forsitan absque noxa etiam esse multa, atque etiam tanta ut aequare bilem saltem pondere videatur.

    Abundet igitur atra bilis, sed tenuissima. Non careat humore subtilioris pituitae circumfuso, ne arescat prorsus durissimaque evadat. Non tamen misceatur omnino pituitae, praesertim vel frigidiori vel multae, ne frigescat. Sed bili sanguinique adeo misceatur, ut corpus unum conficiatur ex tribus, dupla sanguinis ad reliqua duo proportione compositum; ubi octo sanguinis partes, duae bilis, duae iterum atrae bilis portiones existant. Accendatur aliquantum a duobus illis atra bilis, accensaque fulgeat, non uratur, ne quemadmodum solet materia durior, dum fervet nimium, vehementius urat et concitet; dum vero refrigescit, similiter frigescat ad summum. Bilis enim atra ferri instar, quando multum ad frigus intenditur, friget ad summum; quando contra ad calidum valde declinat, calet ad summum. Neque mirum videri debet atram bilem accendi posse facile atque accensam vehementius urere, siquidem videmus calcem illi similem aqua perfusam fervere statim atque exurere. Tantam ad utrumque extremum melancholia vim habet unitate quadam stabilis fixaeque naturae. Quae quidem extremitas ceteris humoribus non contingit. Summe quidem calens summam praestat audaciam, immo ferocitatem; extremo vero frigens timorem ignaviamque extremam. Mediis vero inter frigus caloremque gradibus affecta varie, affectus producit varios, non aliter quam merum praecipue potens bibentibus ad ebrietatem vel etiam paulo liberius affectus inferre varios soleat.

    Igitur opportune temperata sit atra bilis oportet. Quae cum ita moderata est, ut diximus, et bili sanguinique permixta, quia et natura sicca est et con-

---

36 et *om.* z   38 nec z   40 *post* bilis *add.* et z   41 multa *L*   51 sanguinis[1]] sanguis *G*
52 aliquantulum z   59 Tanta *G*   60 melancoliam *D*   62 summam] summa *D* ferocitati z   63 Medii *DR*   64 infecta z   65 bibenti *ex* bibentis *corr. G*   etiam] eam z
66 solet z

its heavy frigidity; and as is the nature of any very dense material, when melancholy of this kind gets cold, it gets cold in the extreme. When we are in this state, we hope for nothing, we fear everything, and "it is weariness to look at the dome of the sky" [*Aen.* 4.451]. If black bile—either simple or mixed—putrefies, it produces quartan fever, swellings of the spleen, and many infirmities of the same kind. When it is too abundant, whether alone or joined with phlegm, it makes the spirits heavier and colder, afflicts the mind continually with weariness, dulls the sharpness of the intellect, and keeps the blood from leaping "around the Arcadian's heart" [*Aen.* 10.452]. But the black bile should not be so small in quantity, that blood, bile, and spirit, as it were, lack a rein, from which will arise an unstable wit and a short memory; it should not be so great in quantity that, burdened with too much weight, we seem to sleep and to need spurs. Therefore it must be every bit as subtle as its nature allows; for if it were rarefied very greatly, to the extent of its nature, perhaps there could even be much of it without harm, and even so much that it should seem to equal the [yellow] bile, at least in weight.

Therefore let black bile abound, but very rarefied; make sure it has the moisture of the more subtle phlegm surrounding it, so that it doesn't become hard and completely dried up. But let it not be mixed only with phlegm, especially the more frigid sort, or much of it, lest it get cold. But let it be so mixed with bile and with blood, that one body is made of the three humors, compounded in a double proportion of blood to the [sum of the] two others; where there are eight parts blood let there be two portions bile and two again of black bile.[12] Let the black bile be kindled a bit from these two others, and having been kindled let it shine, but not burn, lest, as harder material characteristically does, when it boils too strongly, it should burn too intensely and become agitated, but when it cools off, it similarly should become cold in the extreme. For black bile is like iron; when it starts to get cold, it gets cold in the extreme; and on the contrary, once it tends towards hot, it gets hot in the extreme. Nor should it seem surprising that black bile can be kindled easily and when kindled burn with great intensity, for we see something similar in lime, in that when sprinkled with water it begins at once to boil and burn. Melancholy has a similarly great tendency towards either extreme, in the unity of its fixed and stable nature. This extremism does not occur in the other humors. Extremely hot, it produces the extremest boldness, even to ferocity; extremely cold, however, fear and extreme cowardice. Variously imbued with the intermediate grades between cold and heat, however, it produces various dispositions, just as wine, especially strong wine, characteristically induces various dispositions in those who have imbibed to the point of drunkenness, or even just a little too freely.[13]

Therefore it behooves you to temper black bile in an appropriate manner. When it is moderated as we specified and mixed with bile and blood, because

ditione quantum ipsius natura patitur tenuissima, facile ab illis accenditur; quia solida est atque tenacissima, accensa semel diutissime flagrat; quia tenacissimae siccitatis unitate potentissima est, vehementius incalescit. Quemadmodum lignum paleis si utraque accendantur, magis diutiusque calet et lucet. Atqui a diuturno vehementique calore fulgor ingens motusque vehemens et diuturnus proficiscuntur. Huc tendit illud Heracliti: "Lux sicca, anima sapientissima."

Quo pacto atra bilis conducat ingenio.

Cap. VI.

Quaeret forte quispiam, quale sit corpus illud humoris eiusmodi ex tribus illis humoribus ea qua diximus proportione conflatum. Tale est ferme colore quale aurum esse videmus, sed aliquantum vergit ad purpuram. Et quando tam naturali calore quam vel corporis vel animi motu accenditur, ferme non aliter quam ignitum rubensque aurum purpureo mixtum calet et lucet, atque velut Iris trahit varios flagrante corde colores.

Quaeret aliquis iterum, quonam pacto humor eiusmodi conducat ingenio. Nempe spiritus ex hoc humore creati primo quidem subtiles sunt, non aliter quam aqua illa quam et vitae seu vitis aquam nominant et ardentem, quotiens ex crassiori mero quadam ad ignem destillatione, ut fieri solet, exprimitur. Spiritus enim sub angustioribus atrae bilis eiusmodi compressi meatibus vehementiore ob unitatem calore maxime tenuantur, perque arctiores meatus expressi subtiliores erumpunt; deinde calidiores similiter atque eadem ratione lucidiores; tertio motu agiles, actione vehementissimi; quarto solido stabilique humore iugiter emanantes actioni diutissime serviunt. Tali autem animus noster obsequio fretus indagat vehementer, perseverat investigando diutius. Facilius quaecunque investigaverit, invenit, clare perspicit, sincere diiudicat, ac diu retinet iudicata.

Adde quod, quemadmodum in superioribus significavimus, animus instrumento sive incitamento eiusmodi quod centro mundi quodammodo congruit, atque (ut ita dixerim) in suum centrum animum colligit, semper rerum omnium et centra petit, et penetralia penetrat. Congruit insuper cum Mercurio atque Saturno, quorum alter, altissimus omnium planetarum, investigantem evehit ad altissima. Hinc philosophi singulares evadunt, praesertim cum ani-

---

72 *post* lignum *add.* in *z* calent *z* lucent *z* 74 sicca] sic *x*
conducat ingenio] ingeniosos efficiat *z* 1 ex] ea *x* 2 ea] ex *x* propositione *B* ferme *ante* est *transp. z* 4 acceditur *z* 5 ignotum *DR* 9 seu vitis *om. e* 14 quanto *B* 18 diu *om. z*
23 alter] alter (autem *D*) investigationem praestat alter *ABDR* altissimus *post* planetarum *transp. z*

it is dry by nature and in a condition rarefied insofar as its nature admits, it is easily kindled by them; because it is solid and tenacious, once kindled, it burns longer; because it is very powerful in the concentration of its very tenacious dryness, it burns vehemently. Like wood in straw when both are kindled, it burns and shines more and longer. But certainly by means of long-lasting and vehement heat, there arises huge radiance and vehement and long-lasting motion. This is what Heraclitus meant when he said, "A dry light, a soul most wise."[14]

How Black Bile Makes People Intelligent.

Chap. VI

One might perhaps ask what it is like—that humoral body composed out of those three humors in the aforementioned proportion. In color, it has much the appearance of gold, but somewhat inclining towards purple. And when it is heated, as much by natural heat as by motion of the body or of the mind, it burns and shines much like red-hot gold tinged with purple; and it takes on in the burning heart various colors like a rainbow [*Aen.* 4.700–701].

One might ask, again, how a humor of this kind conduces to intelligence. Well, in the first place, the spirits born of this humor have the subtlety of that water which is called *aqua vitae* or *vitis* and *aqua ardens*, when this liquor is extracted by the usual process from thicker wine by distillation at the fire. For the spirits of this kind of black bile are in the highest degree rarefied under pressure in the narrower passages by the heat that is intenser because of its concentration; and having been squeezed through these narrower passages, when they emerge they are more subtle. Second, they are correspondingly hotter and by the same token brighter; third, being quick in motion they are most vigorous in action; fourth, pouring forth continually from a solid and stable humor they can support an action for a very long time. Supported by such compliance, our mind explores eagerly and perseveres in the investigation longer. Whatever it is tracking, it easily finds it, perceives it clearly, soundly judges it, and retains the judgment long.

Add to this that, as we said above [1.5], the soul with an instrument or incitement of this kind—which is congruent in a way with the center of the cosmos, and, as I might say, collects the soul into its own center—always seeks the center of all subjects and penetrates to their innermost core. It is congruent, moreover, with Mercury and Saturn, of whom the second, the highest of planets, carries the investigator to the highest subjects. From this come origi-

mus sic ab externis motibus atque corpore proprio sevocatus, et quam proximus divinis et divinorum instrumentum efficiatur. Unde divinis influxibus oraculisque ex alto repletus, nova quaedam inusitataque semper excogitat et futura praedicit. Quod non solum Democritus atque Plato affirmant, sed etiam Aristoteles in *Problematum* libro et Avicenna in libro *Divinorum* et in libro *De anima* confitentur.

Quorsum haec de atrae bilis humore tam multa? Ut meminerimus quantum atra bilis, immo candida bilis eiusmodi, quaerenda et nutrienda est tanquam optima, tantum illam quae contra se habet (ut diximus) tanquam pessimam esse vitandam. Adeo enim dira res est, ut a malo daemone eius impetus instigari Serapio dixerit, et Avicenna sapiens non negaverit.

Quinque sunt praecipui studiosorum hostes: pituita,
atra bilis, coitus, satietas, matutinus somnus.

Cap. VII.

Ut autem redeamus illuc inde iam longius digressi sumus, longissima via est quae ad veritatem sapientiamque perducit, gravibus terraeque marisque plena laboribus. Quicunque igitur hoc iter aggrediuntur, ut poeta quispiam diceret, saepe terra marique periclitantur. Sive enim mare navigent continue inter fluctus, id est humores duos, pituitam scilicet et noxiam illam melancholiam, quasi inter Scyllam Charybdimque iactantur. Sive terra (ut ita dixerim) iter agant, tria monstra protinus sese illis obiciunt. Primum terrena Venus Priapusque nutrit, secundum Bacchus et Ceres, tertium nocturna Hecate frequenter opponit. Ergo et Apollo ab aethere et Neptunus ab aequore et a terra Hercules saepe vocandus, ut monstra eiusmodi Palladis inimica iaculis Apollo transfigat, Neptunus tridente domet, clava Hercules contundat et laceret.

Primum quidem monstrum est Venereus coitus, praesertim si vel paulum vires excesserit; subito namque exhaurit spiritus praesertim subtiliores, cerebrumque debilitat, labefactat stomachum atque praecordia. Quo malo nihil ingenio adversius esse potest. Cur nam Hippocrates coitum comitiali morbo similem iudicavit, nisi quia mentem, quae sacra est, percutit; tantumque obest, ut Avicenna in libro *De animalibus* dixerit: "Si quid spermatis, supra quam na-

---

25 montibus *x*   proprie *BD*   26 et *om. z*   27 inusita *D;* invisitataque *x*   28 affirmat *x*
35 negavit *A*
  Quinque sunt praecipui] Quod quinque sint praecipui *y;* Quinque praecipue *z*   2 marisque *ex* maris
*corr. L*²   8 Priapusque nutrit *om. z*   10 et *om. B*   vocandi *z*   Palladi *z*   10-11 *post* inimica
add. et *DR*   11 tridenti *e*   17 percellit *z*

nal philosophers, especially when their soul, hereby called away from external movements and from its own body, is made in the highest degree both a neighbor to the divine and an instrument of the divine. As a result, it is filled from above with divine influences and oracles, and it always invents new and unaccustomed things and predicts the future. Not only Democritus[1] and Plato[2] affirm this but also Aristotle confesses it in his book of *Problems*,[3] and Avicenna in his *Liber divinorum*[4] and in his *De anima*.[5]

What is the purpose of so much information about the humor black bile? That we may remember that just as much as black bile—or rather, I should call bile of this kind white—is to be sought and nourished as the best, just so that which is contrary to it, as we said, is to be avoided as the worst. For it is so pernicious a thing that Serapion says its onset is instigated by a bad daemon,[6] and the wise Avicenna does not deny it.[7]

The Special Enemies of Scholars Are Five: Phlegm, Black Bile, Sexual Intercourse, Gluttony, and Sleeping in the Morning.

Chap. VII

But to return from where we have been digressing now for quite a while, the road is very long which leads to truth and wisdom, full of heavy labors on land and sea. Hence people who undertake this journey are often at danger, as some poet might say, on land and sea. For if they sail on the sea, they are constantly tossed among the waves, that is, the two humors, namely phlegm and that noxious form of melancholy, as if between Scylla and Charybdis. Or if they journey on land, so to speak, three monsters immediately oppose them. The first monster is nourished by the earthly Venus and Priapus; the second, by Bacchus and Ceres; and the third, nocturnal Hecate often positions against us. Therefore Apollo must often be summoned from the heavens, Neptune from the sea, and Hercules from the land in order that Apollo may pierce such monsters, enemies of Pallas, with his shafts, Neptune may subdue them with his trident, and Hercules may crush and mangle them with his club.

The first monster is sexual intercourse, especially if it proceeds even a little beyond one's strength; for indeed it suddenly drains the spirits, especially the more subtle ones, it weakens the brain, and it ruins the stomach and the heart—no evil can be worse for one's intelligence. For why did Hippocrates judge sexual intercourse to be like epilepsy, if not because it strikes the mind, which is sacred;[1] and it is so harmful that Avicenna has said in his book *De animalibus*: "If any sperm should flow away through intercourse beyond that which

tura toleret, coitu profluat, obesse magis quam si quadragies tantundem sanguinis emanarit;" ut non iniuria prisci Musas atque Minervam virgines esse voluerint. Huc Platonicum illud spectat: cum Venus Musis minitaretur, nisi sacra Venerea colerent, se contra illas suum filium armaturam, responderunt Musae: "Marti, O Venus, Marti talia minitare; tuus enim inter nos Cupido non volat." Denique natura nullum sensum longius quam tactum ab intelligentia segregavit.

Secundum monstrum est vini cibique satietas. Quippe si vinum vel nimium vel nimis calidum vehemensque fuerit, caput ipsum humoribus pessimisque fumis implebit. Mitto quod insanos facit ebrietas. Cibus vero nimius primum quidem ad stomachum in ipso coquendo omnem naturae vim revocat; quo fit ut capiti simul speculationique intendere nequeat. Deinde inepte coctus multis et crassis vaporibus humoribusque aciem mentis obtundit. Quinetiam si satis coquatur, tamen, ut Galienus ait: "animus adipe et sanguine suffocatus coeleste aliquid pervidere non potest."

Tertium denique monstrum est ad multam noctem, praesertim post coenam, frequentius vigilare, unde etiam post ortum solis dormire cogaris. Quoniam vero in hoc errant falluntur que studiosi permulti, idcirco quantum ingenio noceat, latius explicabo, atque rationes septem praecipuas afferam: primam ab ipso coelo, secundam ab elementis, tertiam ab humoribus, quartam ab ordine rerum, quintam a natura stomachi, sextam a spiritibus, septimam a phantasia deductam.

Principio tres planetae, quemadmodum in superioribus dicebamus, contemplationi et eloquentiae maxime favent: Sol, Venus atque Mercurius. Hi vero paribus ferme passibus concurrentes adventante nocte nos fugiunt, die vero vel propinquante vel iam surgente resurgunt nosque revisunt. Post vero Solis ortum in plagam coeli duodecimam, quae carceri tenebrisque ab astronomis assignatur, repente trudantur. Ergo non qui vel nocte, quando nos fugiunt, vel die post Solis ortum, quando carceris tenebrarumque domum intrant, sed qui vel propemodum petentibus ortum, vel iam surgentibus ad contemplandum scribendumque ipsi quoque consurgunt, ii soli acutissime speculantur, et eloquentissime inventa sua scribunt atque componunt.

Ratio secunda, scilicet ab elementis, est talis: oriente sole movetur aer tenuaturque et claret, occidente vero contra. Sanguis autem et spiritus motum qualitatemque aeris circumfusi naturaque similis sequi necessario compelluntur.

Tertia ratio, quae ab humoribus ducitur, est eiusmodi: in aurora movetur sanguis et regnat motuque tenuatur et calescit et claret; spiritus vero sanguinem sequi imitarique solent. Verum accedente nocte melancholia illa crassior

---

19 tolleret *z*   23 nos *om. D*   35 etiam] et *G*   39 ab] ad *x*   41 deductas *z*   43 paribus] partibus *x*   44 surgente] fugiente *G*   46 traduntur $L^{ac}Bw^{ac}z$ 50 component *z*   57 *post* nocte *add.* vel *z*

nature tolerates, it is more harmful than if forty times as much blood should pour forth."[2] So it was with good reason that the ancients held the Muses and Minerva to be virgins. That Platonic saying has relevance here: When Venus threatened the Muses that, unless they celebrated the rites of love, she would send her son armed against them, "the Muses answered, 'O Venus, threaten Mars with such things, your Cupid does not fly among us.' "[3] Finally, nature has placed no sense farther from intelligence than touch.

The second monster is satiety in wine and food. For if wine is excessive or too hot and strong, it will fill the head with humors and very bad fumes. I pass over the fact that drunkenness makes men insane. And excessive food recalls all the power of nature first of all to the stomach to digest it. This renders nature unable to exert itself at the same time in the head and for reflection. In the next place, food badly digested dulls the sharpness of the mind with many dense vapors and with humors. But even if the food is sufficiently digested, nevertheless, as Galen says, "the mind that is choked up with fat and blood cannot perceive anything heavenly."[4]

Finally, the third monster is to stay awake too often for much of the night, especially after dinner, with the result that you are forced to sleep even after sunrise. Since many scholars err in this and are deceived, therefore I will explain further how much it hurts the intelligence and I will give seven main reasons. The first reason is drawn from the heavens themselves, the second from the elements, the third from the humors, the fourth from the order of things, the fifth from the nature of the stomach, the sixth from the spirits, and the seventh from the phantasy.

First of all, three planets, as we said above [1.1], especially favor reflection and eloquence: the Sun, Venus, and Mercury. Since they run almost in step together, at the approach of night these planets flee from us, but with day approaching or now rising they arise again and revisit us. But after sunrise, they are immediately thrust into the twelfth house of heaven, which is assigned by astronomers to prison and darkness.[5] Therefore it is not people who rise either at night, when they flee from us, or during the day after sunrise, when they enter the house of prison and darkness, who explore things most acutely and write and compose their findings most eloquently, but those people alone who, when they are either about to rise or now rising, themselves rise up with them to reflect and write.

The second reason, which is from the elements, is this: at sunrise the air is stirred, rarefied, and clear; but just the opposite happens at sunset. The blood and the spirits are compelled by necessity to imitate the motion and quality of the air because it surrounds them and is similar in nature.[6]

The third reason, which is drawn from the humors, is this: at dawn the blood moves and rules; it is rarefied by motion and grows warm and clear; and the spirits characteristically imitate and follow the blood. But at the approach of

et frigidior atque pituita dominantur, quae spiritus ad speculandum ineptissimos proculdubio reddunt.

Quarta ratio, quae trahitur ab ordine rerum, haec erit: dies vigiliae, nox somno tributa est, quoniam cum Sol vel ad hemisphaerium nostrum accedit vel super ipsum incedit, radiis suis meatus corporis aperit, atque a centro ad circumferentiam humores spiritusque dilatat, quod quidem ad vigiliam actionesque excitat atque conducit. Contra vero, quando recedit, omnia coartantur, quod naturali quodam ordine invitat ad somnum, maxime post tertiam aut quartam noctis partem. Quisquis igitur mane quidem dormitat, quando Sol mundusque excitat, ad multam vero noctem vigilat, quando natura dormire iam et a laboribus quiescere iubet, hic absque dubio cum ordini universi tum sibi ipsi repugnat, dum contrariis simul motibus perturbatur atque distrahitur. Sane dum ab universo movetur ad extima, ipse sese movet ad intima; atque contra, dum ab universo ad intima trahitur, ipse se interim retrahit ad externa. Ergo perverso ordine motibusque contrariis tum corpus totum, tum spiritus ingeniumque prorsus labefactatur.

Quinto loco a natura stomachi in hunc modum argumentamur: stomachus diuturna diurni aeris actione apertis poris admodum dilatatur, evolantibusque spiritibus tandem valde debilitatur. Igitur subeunte nocte novam spirituum copiam exigit, qua foveatur. Quapropter quicunque eo tempore contemplationes longas et difficiles incohat, ipsos ad caput spiritus retrahere nititur. Hi vero distracti neque stomacho satis neque capiti faciunt. Maxime vero nocet, si post coenam lucubrantes diu eiusmodi studiis attentius incumbamus, pluribus enim tunc ad concoquendum cibum spiritibus multoque calore stomachus indiget. Haec vero duo lucubratione studioque tali divertuntur ad caput; quo fit ut neque cerebro neque stomacho suppetant. Adde quod caput ob eiusmodi motum crassioribus cibi repletur vaporibus, atque cibus in stomacho a calore et spiritu destitutus crudescit et putret, unde rursus caput opplet et laedit. Denique matutinis horis quando surgendum est, ut excrementis omnibus somno retentis singula membra purgentur, tunc, id quod pessimum est, qui nocte lucubrando concoctionem penitus interruperat, idem dormiendo mane excrementorum expulsionem diutius impedire compellitur. Quod quidem tam ingenio quam corpori medici omnes obesse quam plurimum arbitrantur. Merito ergo qui nocte contra naturam pro die, atque converso die rursus pro nocte utuntur tanquam noctuae, ii etiam in hoc vel in-

---

60 traditur *x*   63 vigilias *G*   68 a *add.* L^2 conquiescere *ABDR*   69 repugnant *Lw*   70 externa *A*   ipsa *D*   72 extrema *Lw*^{ac}; extima *x*   73 tum *om. BDR*   75 diurni] diuturni *A; om. DR*   81 coquendum *A*^{ac}*B*   85 et]^1 *om. DR*   86 et] atque *z*   87 purgantur *D*   88 interrumpat *B*

night, that more dense and cold type of melancholy dominates, and phlegm, both of which without doubt render the spirits totally unfit for reflection.

The fourth reason, which is drawn from the order of things, will be this: day is assigned to wakefulness, night to sleep, since, when the sun either approaches our hemisphere or advances over it, it opens with its rays the passages of the body and spreads the humors and spirits from the center to the circumference, a thing which excites and leads to wakefulness and actions. But on the contrary, when the sun sets, all things are contracted, which by a certain natural order of things induces sleep, especially after the third or fourth part of the night. Therefore he who sleeps in the morning, when the sun and the world get up, and who is awake much of the night, when nature now commands us to sleep and to rest from labors — this man without doubt fights both with the order of the universe and especially with himself, while he is disturbed and distracted by contrary motions at the same time. Indeed, while there is movement on the part of the universe to the outer limits, he moves himself to the innermost. And, on the contrary, while there is attraction on the part of the universe to the most inward parts, he, meanwhile, draws himself back to externals. Such perverse order and contrary motions make both the entire body and the spirits and intelligence very unsteady.

In the fifth place, we argue from the nature of the stomach in this way: the stomach by the long action of daily air is quite dilated through open pores; when the spirits fly forth, it becomes at last exceedingly weak. Therefore, at the approach of night, it demands a new supply of spirits to sustain itself. This is why a person who begins long and difficult reflections at this time, has to strain to draw those spirits back to the head. When so divided, however, these spirits are not sufficient for either the stomach or the head. Indeed it is especially harmful, if, working at night after dinner, we concentrate too attentively for a long time on studies of this sort. For then the stomach needs many spirits for digesting food, as well as much heat. But these two by such work and study are diverted to the head; it happens as a result that they are sufficient for neither the brain nor the stomach. Add the fact that because of motion of this sort the head is filled with too-dense vapors coming from food; and food in the stomach without heat and spirit accumulates undigested and grows rotten, which again blocks up and injures the head. Finally, in the morning hours you must rise in order that each of your bodily parts may be purged of all the excrement retained during sleep. Then, worst of all, the person who had utterly interrupted his digestion by studying at night and likewise by sleeping in the morning is compelled to hinder the expulsion of excrement for a longer time — which, indeed, all physicians think is most harmful for the intelligence as well as the body. Rightly, therefore, those who against nature use night as day and, conversely again, day as night, like owls — these people also unwillingly imitate owls in this: that, just as the eyes of the owls grow weak

viti noctuas imitantur, ut quemadmodum illis sub solis lumine caligant oculi, ita et iis mentis acies sub veritatis splendore caliget.

Sexto loco a spiritus idem ita probatur: spiritibus fatigatione diurna praesertim subtilissimi quique denique resolvuntur. Nocte igitur pauci crassique supersunt litterarum studiis ineptissimi, ut non aliter mancis horum fretum alis ingenium volare possit quam vespertiliones atque bubones. Contra vero post somnum mane spiritibus recreatis membrisque adeo corroboratis, ut minimo spirituum adminiculo egeant, multi subtilesque spiritus adsunt, qui cerebro serviant, atque expeditius obsequi possunt, in membris fovendis regendisque parum admodum occupati.

Postremo septima ratio sic a phantasiae natura deducitur: phantasia sive imaginatio sive cogitatio seu quovis alio nomine nuncupanda videtur, multis, longis, contrariis invigilando imaginibus, cogitationibus curisque distrahitur atque turbatur. Quae quidem distractio perturbatioque sequenti contemplationi tranquillam serenamque mentem penitus postulanti nimium contraria est. Sola vero nocturna quiete agitatio illa sedatur tandem atque pacatur. Igitur accedente quidem nocte semper turbata mente, recedente vero ut plurimum mente tranquilla ad studia nos conferimus. Quicunque vero mente nimium agitata res ipsas iudicare conantur, ii non aliter quam illi qui vertiginem patiuntur, omnia verti putant (ut Plato inquit), cum ipsi vertantur. Quamobrem scite Aristoteles in *Oeconomicis* iubet ante lucem surgere, asseritque id et ad corporis sanitatem et ad philosophiae studia prodesse quam plurimum. Sed hoc ita accipiendum est, ut cita et modica coena matutinam cruditatem diligentissime devitemus. Denique sacer ille vates David, omnipotentis tuba Dei, nunquam dicit vespere, sed mane semper atque diluculo in Deum suum canendum se cithara psalmisque surgere. Surgere quidem mente ea hora omnino debemus, mox etiam corpore, si modo id commode fieri possit.

Quae sit hora incohandis studiis opportunior,
quisve continuandi modus.

Cap. VIII.

Ex iis quae in superioribus disputata sunt, ferme iam satis constat opportune nostra nos studia exordiri vel statim oriente sole, vel hora una saltem vel duabus ad summum ante solis exortum. Sed antequam e lecto surgas,

---

93 ut] vel *B*   94 ii *z*   97 fretum] fletus *L*   99 nimio *D*   101 fovendis] faciendis *D*   104 nuncupata *B*   113 scire *L*   118 sex *x*   119 potest *D*
1 *post* iis *add.* autem *G*

under the light of the sun, so too the mental sharpness of these people grows weak beneath the splendor of truth.[7]

In the sixth place, the same thing is proved from the spirits as follows: the spirits, especially all the most subtle ones, are eventually dispersed by daily fatigue. At night, therefore, few spirits are left, and they are dense and most unsuitable for literary studies, so that the intelligence, relying on these crippled wings, can fly only as do bats and owls. But, on the contrary, in the morning after sleep, with the spirits refreshed and with the bodily parts thus strengthened, so that they need the least help from the spirits, many subtle spirits are present; they serve the brain, and they are able to comply with it, since they are very little occupied with fostering and ruling the bodily parts.

Finally, the seventh reason is drawn from the nature of the phantasy as follows: Phantasy or imagination or apprehension ("cogitatio") or whatever other name it seems it ought to be called, is distracted and upset by many long and contrary imaginations, cogitations, and cares while it is awake. This distraction and confusion are too contrary to someone pursuing contemplation and requiring a completely tranquil and serene mind. Only during the quiet of night is that agitation finally calmed and put to rest. Therefore, at the approach of night we study with the mind always disturbed, but when night withdraws for the most part we give ourselves to study with a tranquil mind. A person who tries to judge truth with the mind too upset, is just like those people who suffer from dizziness and think everything is turning, as Plato said, when they themselves are turning.[8] This is why Aristotle in his *Economics* sensibly commands us to rise before dawn and asserts that it is most useful both for the health of the body and for the study of philosophy.[9] But this precept must be taken in such a way that we carefully avoid early morning indigestion by taking a quick and moderate dinner. Finally, that holy prophet David, the trumpet of the almighty God, never says that he rises to sing to his God with lyre and psalms in the evening, but always in the morning and at dawn.[10] Indeed we certainly ought to arise at that hour with our mind, and soon after also with our body, provided it can conveniently be done.

What Hour Is the Better Time to Begin Our Studies and How We Should Continue Them.

Chap. VIII

From what has been argued above, it is now almost sufficiently certain that the better time to begin our studies is either right at sunrise, or at least one hour, and at most two hours, before sunrise. But before you get out of

perfrica parumper suaviterque palmis corpus totum primo, deinde caput unguibus, sed id paulo levius. Hac in re te Hippocrates admoneat. Nam frictione, inquit, si vehemens sit, durari corpus; si levis, molliri; si multa, minui; si modica, impleri. Cum e lecto surrexeris, noli subitae lectioni meditationique prorsus incumbere, sed saltem horae dimidium cuilibet expurgationi concedito; mox meditationi accingere diligenter, quam ad horam circiter unam pro viribus prorogabis. Deinde remittes parumper mentis intentionem, atque interim eburneo pectine diligenter et moderate pectes caput a fronte cervicem versus quadragies pectine ducto; tum cervicem panno asperiori perfrica. Demum reversus ad meditandum, duas insuper horas aut saltem horam unam studio dedicato. Produci vero nonnunquam studia possunt, sed aliquanta interdum intermissione facta ad horam usque meridianam; quinetiam interdum, quamvis raro, nisi cibum interim cogamur assumere, post meridiem circiter horas duas. Sol enim circa ortum potens est, potens et in medio coelo; in plaga quoque illa coeli quae medium proxime sequitur, quam nonam astronomi vocant et sapientiae domum, Sol maxime gaudet. Quoniam vero poetae omnes Phoebum Musarum scientiarumque ducem esse volunt, merito si quid altius excogitandum est, his horis potissimum cogitent. Si Musae quaerendae, horis eisdem Phoebo duce quaerantur. Reliquae enim horae veteribus alienisque legendis potius quam novis propriisque excogitandis accommodatae videntur. Semper autem meminisse debemus qualibet hora semel saltem paulisper remittendam esse mentis intentionem. Cum enim ob intentionem eiusmodi spiritus resolvantur, merito si nunquam cesses tendere, lentus eris. Dum laboras animo, interim corpore conquiesce. Mala est defatigatio corporis, peior animi, utriusque simul pessima, oppositis hominem motibus simul distrahens, vitamque disperdens. Denique haud ulterius meditatio procedat quam voluptas, potius vero citra.

Quomodo sit vitanda pituita.

Cap. IX.

Operae pretium fore videtur, quae noxia litteratis esse diximus, repetere breviter, atque remedia singulis adhibere. Ergo ne pituita nimis augeatur, exercitatione quotidie stomacho ferme vacuo bis utendum, nunquam ta-

---

5 te *om. z* 6 lenis *DR* 7-9 Cum e lecto—concedito *desunt in e* 9-10 horam circiter unam] horas circiter duas *e* 14 non umquam *L; om. e* 16 quamvis raro *om. e* interim *om. B* summere *D;* sumere *R* 17 duas *om.₂ D* 18 quam] quaquam *D;* quamquam *R* 19 Quoniam] quando *B* 22 enim] vero *ex* enim *corr. L²* 24 huiusmodi *z* 27 lentus] mollis *G'* 27-30 Dum laboras—citra *desunt in e*
Quomodo sit vitanda pituita] Vitandae pituitae praecepta *z*

bed, first massage all your body for a while pleasantly with your palms, then massage your head with your nails, but a little more lightly. Let Hippocrates be your adviser in this matter. For he says that strong rubbing hardens the body; light, softens the body; much rubbing makes the body smaller; a moderate amount fills it out.[1] When you get out of bed, do not apply yourself wholly and suddenly to reading and meditation, but give over at least half an hour for expurgation; right after this, prepare yourself carefully for meditation, which you will continue for about one hour if you are able. Then relax for a little while your mind's intentness, and meantime, comb your head carefully and moderately with an ivory comb, drawing the comb back from forehead to neck about forty times. Then rub your neck with a rather rough cloth.[2] Finally, having returned to meditation, devote two more hours, or at least one hour, to study. Oftentimes studies can be extended with an occasional short intermission to the midday hour — why, sometimes even about two hours after noon, although rarely and if we are not forced meanwhile to take food. For the Sun is powerful around the time of rising, and powerful also at mid-heaven. The Sun also especially rejoices in that region of heaven which immediately follows the middle and which the astronomers call the ninth and the Place of Wisdom.[3] And since all poets would have it that Phoebus is the leader of the Muses and sciences, if you want to think out higher things, you will most rightly consider them during these hours. If you want to seek the Muses, you should seek them under Phoebus' leadership during the same hours. For the remaining hours seem suitable for reading the ancients and the work of other scholars rather than for thinking new thoughts of one's own. We ought always to remember, however, that in any hour, once at least, the mind's intentness should be relaxed for a little while. For when, on account of this intentness, the spirits are dispersed, if you keep on striving, you will deservedly be sluggish. While you work with your mind, in the meantime rest your body. Fatigue of the body is bad, that of the mind is worse, and the worst is fatigue of both at the same time, distracting the person by opposite but simultaneous motions and ruining life. Finally, do not let the meditation proceed for longer than it is pleasant, but rather stop while it is still pleasant.

How to Avoid Phlegm.

Chap. IX

It seems worthwhile to repeat briefly the things we said were harmful to learned people and to supply remedies for each. Therefore, to keep phlegm from increasing too much, exercise twice daily on an almost empty stomach,

men laboriosa; ne acuti spiritus dissolvantur, excrementa diligentissime ab omnibus meatibus expurganda. Sordes a corporis totius cute, capitis praecipue, tum lotione tum frictione penitus abstergendae. Vitanda alimenta frigida nimium atque, nisi obstiterit atra bilis, etiam humida et omnino quae pinguia, virulenta, viscosa, uncta glutinosaque sint, vel quae facile putrescere soleant. Si stomachus vel natura vel aetate sit frigidus, aut dimittendus omnino aut certe minuendus aquae potus. Moderatus cibus sit oportet, sed potio moderatior. Habitatio alta a gravi nubiloque aere remotissima. Tum ignis, tum calidi odoris usu humiditas expellenda. Prohibendum frigus a capite, maxime vero cervice atque pedibus, multum enim obest ingenio. Prodest moderatus usus aromatum in frigidioribus epulis: nucis muscatae praesertim et cinnamomi et croci, zinziberis quoque conditi mane stomacho vacuo, quod sensibus etiam et memoriae maxime prodest.

Qua ratione vitanda sit atra bilis.

Cap. X.

Pessimam vero illam, quam in superioribus detestabamur, atram bilem haec augent: crassum turbidumque vinum, praecipue nigrum; cibi duri, sicci, salsi, acres, acuti, veteres, usti, assi, fricti; carnes bovis et leporis, caseus vetus, salsamenta, legumina: praecipue faba, lenticula, melongia, eruca, brassica, sinapis, radicula, allium, cepa, porrum, mora, cariotae, et quaecunque calefaciunt vel frigefaciunt simul atque desiccant, et omnia nigra; ira, timor, misericordia, dolor, otium, solitudo, et quaecunque visum et olfactum auditumque offendunt, omnium vero maxime tenebrae; praeterea exsiccatio corporis nimia, sive longis nata vigiliis, sive multa mentis agitatione, vel cura, seu frequenti coitu usuque rerum calidarum multum atque siccarum, seu immoderata quadam deiectione atque purgatione, vel exercitatione laboriosa, vel inedia, siti, calore, vel sicciore vento, vel frigore. Cum vero bilis atra semper siccissima sit, frigida quoque, licet non aeque, huic certe resistendum est rebus quidem modice calidis, humidis vero quam maxime, cibis elixis assidue, qui coquantur facile et subtilem gignant sanguinem atque clarissimum.

Sed interim ut stomachi et pituitae ratio habeatur, perinde atque bilis atrae, epulae cinnamomo et croco et sandalis condiantur. Conferunt semina

---

10 aquae *ex* atque *corr.* L^2 11 Tum] Cum *x* 15 gignat *z*

but never strenuously; and to keep the sharp spirits from being destroyed, purge the excrements carefully from all passages. Completely wipe the dirt from the skin of the entire body, especially the head, both by washing and by rubbing. Avoid excessively cold foods and also, unless black bile precludes it, the excessively moist, and, most of all, those which are fatty, full of poison, sticky, oily and glutinous or which have a strong tendency to rot. If the stomach is cold by nature or by age, give up drinking water completely or certainly reduce it. Eating should be moderate but drinking still more moderate. The dwelling should be high and far away from heavy and cloudy air.[1] Expel humidity by the use of fire and warm odor. Keep coldness away from the head and especially from the neck and feet, for it is very harmful for the intelligence. A moderate use of spices is of advantage in colder meals: especially nutmeg, cinnamon, saffron, and also preserved ginger early in the morning on an empty stomach; it is also useful for the senses and especially for the memory.

How to Avoid Black Bile.

Chap. X

The following things increase that most awful kind of black bile which we denounced above: heavy and thick wine, especially if it is dark; food which is hard, dry, salted, bitter, sharp, stale, burnt, roasted, or fried; beef and the meat of the hare, old cheese, foods pickled in brine, vegetables (especially the broad-bean, the lentil, the eggplant ["melongia"], the colewort, cabbage, mustard, the radish, the garlic, the onion, the leek, the black medic, and carrots), and whatever causes warmth or cold, and likewise dryness and everything that is black; anger, fear, pity, sorrow, idleness, solitude, and whatever offends the sight, smell, and hearing, and most of all, darkness. Moreover, excessive dryness of the body increases black bile, whether it be the result of long wakefulness or much agitation of the mind, or worry, or frequent sexual intercourse and the use of things which are very hot and dry, or the result of any immoderate flux and purgation, or strenuous exercise, or fasting, or thirst, or heat, or a too dry wind, or cold. Since, indeed, black bile is always very dry and also cold — although not equally so — it must certainly be resisted with things which are moderately hot but as moist as possible, and with foods that have been thoroughly boiled, since they are easily digested and produce blood which is subtle and very clear.[1]

But in order that you might have a plan that works for the stomach and phlegm at the same time as black bile, let meals be seasoned with cinnamon,

peponis atque cucumeris et pinei nuclei abluti. Conveniunt lacticinia omnia: lac, caseus recens, amygdalae dulces. Conveniunt carnes avium et pullorum gallinaceorum quadrupedumve lactentium, ova sorbilia maxime, et ex membris animalium cerebellum, dulcia mala, pyra, Persica, pepones, pruna Damascena atque similia, cucurbita rite cocta, herbae humidae, non viscosae. Cerasia vero, ficus, uvas minime laudo. Nauseam vero et satietatem valde detestor. Nihil autem adversus hanc pestem valentius est quam vinum leve, clarum, suave, odorum, ad spiritus prae ceteris perspicuos generandos aptissimum. Nam, ut Platoni et Aristoteli placet, hic humor hoc vino non aliter mollitur atque dulcescit et claret quam vel lupini aqua perfusi vel ferrum flammis accensum. Verum quantum eius usus spiritibus et ingenio prodest, tantum nocet abusus. Praeterea infundere aurum vel argentum maxime ignitum eorumque folia in poculis vel in ipso iure prodesse consentaneum est, atque aureo vel argenteo vasculo bibere cibosque sumere. Item perutile est, si saepe stomacho vacuo liquiritiae succus deglutiatur, succus quoque Punici pomi dulcis atque dulcis arancei.

Conducunt non mediocriter suaves odores, temperati maxime, at si regnat frigus, ad calidum declinantes; sin dominetur calor, vergentes ad frigidum. Temperandi sunt igitur ex rosis, violis, myrto, camphora, sandalis, aqua rosacea, quae frigida sunt; rursus ex cinnamomo, citro, aranceo, gariophylis, menta, melissa, croco, ligno aloe, ambra, musco, quae calida. Verni flores prosunt imprimis et folia citri sive arancei odoraque poma, sed maxime vinum. Odores eiusmodi, prout cuique convenit, et naribus hauriendi sunt, et pectori atque stomacho admovendi. Odores vero calidos multum siccosque, si soli fuerint et continui, non probamus. Tenendus ore hyacinthus, qui animum vehementer exhilarat. Hierobotanum quoque, id est sclarea silvestris, tum cibo tum odore confert; buglossa rursus, borago, melissa, horumque trium aqua. Rursus lactuca, endivia, uva passula, lac amygdalinum mensae familiarissima esse debent. Fugiendus aer aut fervens aut glacialis nimium aut nubilus, sed aer temperatus serenusque liberrime admittendus.

Mercurius, Pythagoras, Plato iubent dissonantem animum vel maerentem cithara cantuque tam constanti quam concinno componere simul atque erigere. David autem, poeta sacer, psalterio psalmisque Saulem ab insania liberabat. Ego etiam, si modo infima licet componere summis, quantum adversus atrae bilis amaritudinem dulcedo lyrae cantusque valeat, domi frequenter experior.

Laudamus frequentem aspectum aquae nitidae, viridis rubeive coloris, hortorum nemorumque usum, deambulationem secus flumina perque amoena prata suavem; equitationem quoque, gestationem navigationemque lenem

---

19-20 Conveniunt—dulces *om.* z   22 cerebrum *DR*   32 auro z   argenteo *ex* argento *corr.* L^2
34 arancei *ante* dulcis *transp. L*   38 ex] et *DR*   39 Verni] Verum *D*   40 sed] si z   41 et[1] *om. D*
42 multos *DR*   43 fuerunt *A*   44 Hierobatana z   47 aut[1]] ut z   52 adversum *L*

saffron, and sandal. The seeds of the melon and the cucumber and washed pine-nuts are good. Of advantage are all milky foods: milk, fresh cheese, sweet almonds. Also of advantage are the meat of birds and young cocks or of four-footed sucklings, and especially raw eggs, and among the bodily parts of animals, their brains; also good are sweet apples, pears, peaches, melons, damson plums, and similar fruits, gourds properly cooked and herbs which are moist but not slimy. Cherries, however, and figs and grapes I do not advocate in the least. And I thoroughly detest nausea and gluttony. Nothing, however, is better against this pest than wine which is light, clear, pleasant, fragrant — the best adapted to generate spirits clearer than any others. For, as Plato and Aristotle believe, by means of this wine, black bile is softened and grows sweet and clear just as do lupines soaked in water or iron burnt with fire.[2] But just as the use of wine helps the spirits and the intelligence, so the abuse harms them. Moreover, infusing gold or silver, especially red-hot, and their leaves, in drinks or even in soup is likely to be helpful, and also to drink and consume food in a gold or silver vessel. Likewise it is very useful if one often swallows on an empty stomach the juice of licorice and also the juice of a sweet pomegranate and of a sweet orange.

Also of no little use are pleasant smells,[3] especially tempered ones, those verging toward warmth if coldness prevails end those tending toward cold if warmth dominates. Therefore smells must be tempered from roses, violets, myrtle, camphor, sandal, and rose water, which are cold; and again from cinnamon, citron, orange, cloves, mint, melissa, saffron, aloe wood, amber, and musk, which are warm. Spring flowers are especially useful and the leaves of the citron or of the orange, and fragrant fruits, but especially wine. Smells of this sort should be absorbed through the nose and applied to the breast and stomach as convenient for the individual. We do not, however, approve of smells which are too warm and dry, especially if they are constantly only so. The hyacinth, which greatly freshens the mind, must be held in the mouth. The holy herb also, that is *scariole* [Fr. translation has "the wild celandine"], is useful both for food and smell, and, again, bugloss, borage, melissa, and the water of these three. And again, lettuce, endive, raisins, and almond milk ought to be very familiar on the dinner-table. Avoid air which is hot or too icy or cloudy, but let in freely air which is temperate and clear. Hermes Trismegistus, Pythagoras, and Plato tell us to calm and to cheer the dissonant and the sorrowful mind with constant and harmonious lyre and song.[4] Moreover, David, the sacred poet, used to free Saul from madness with psaltery and psalms.[5] I, too (if I may now compare the lowliest person with the greatest), frequently prove in myself how much the sweetness of the lyre and song avail against the bitterness of black bile.

I advocate the frequent viewing of shining water and of green or red color, the haunting of gardens and groves and pleasant walks along rivers and through lovely meadows;[6] and I also strongly approve of horseback riding, driving, and

valde probamus, sed varietatem imprimis facilesque occupationes diversaque negotia non molesta, assiduam hominum gratiosorum consuetudinem.

Cura stomachi.
Cap. XI.

Sequitur ut curam stomachi diligentissimam habeamus, ne nauseam cruditatemve adducat unquam satietas, caputque offendat. Bis cibus quotidie sumendus est, et modicus atque levis, cinnamomo, mace, nuce muscata moderate conditus. Semper tamen siccus cibus pondere alimenta mollia potumque exsuperet, nisi forte atrae bilis siccitatem admodum vereamur. Famem (si commode fieri potest) cibus, sitim potus expectet. Aviditas utriusque supersit mensae; fastidium et saturitas procul absint. Abstinendum ab iis quae ob nimiam humiditatem vel virulentam et unctam viscosamque materiam stomachum relaxando debilitant, vel etiam frigida aut calidissima sunt, aut propter duritiam aegre coquuntur; et quae talia sunt, ut diu post mensam palato saporem reddant molestiorem, sive inflent, sive caput multis vaporibus impleant; ab omnibus imprimis quae facile vel extra alvum vel in alvo putrescant. Dulces sapores aut acres, si soli sint, nullo pacto probamus, sed dulces acri quodam vel acuto vel sicco volumus temperari.

Mastix et menta sicca, salvia recens, uvae passulae, cydonia poma cocta, condita saccharo, cichorea, rosa, corallus, lotus capparis et aceto conditus stomacho amicissima sunt. Mala praeterea Punica sapore inter acidum dulcemque medio, et omnino quaecunque moderate acida sunt et aliquantulum austera, quae medici styptica vocant, sive quae aliquantum acuta sunt vel salsa vel aromatica. Myrobalani autem omnia superant. Vinum quoque rubeum potius quam album sapore quasi paululum subamaro, ac nisi caliditas vel destillatio aliter postulaverit, optimum erit merum bibitum paulatim. Omnino autem liquidores epulae prius sumendae quam duriores. Sumpto vero cibo, convenit coriandrum pomumque cydonium conditum saccharo, mala Punica et pyra austera, mespila quoque et Persica sicca atque similia; mandere oportet, antequam deglutiantur, singula exactissime. Fovendus stomachus, si oportet extrinsecus, mastice, rosa, menta, corallo.

Cavendum ne post cibum duabus aut tribus proximis horis vel cogitationi difficili vel lectioni sedulo incumbamus. Necessariae forsan erunt horae vaca-

---

58 sed] et *z*
    Cura] De curatione *yz*   *Cap.XI]* Cap.X *z*   1 ut *om. B*   diligentissimam] quam diligenter *z*
4 moderata *L*   4–5 mollia potumque] mollita motumque *z*   8 et *om. z*   10 duritiem *e*   16 capparus *B*   18 acida *yz*; arida *Lewx*   aliquantum *BD*   19 sint *z*   20 Myrobalani—superant *desunt in e*   22 paululum *z*   23 sumendum *z*   25 mespila *xz*; nespile *LDGw;* nespilae *ABRy*
8 aut] et *z*   aut tribus *om. e*   29–33 Necessariae—concoxeris *desunt in e*   29 forsitan *z*

smooth sailing, but above all, of variety, easy occupations, diversified unburdensome business, and the constant company of agreeable people.

The Care of the Stomach.

Chap. XI

It follows that we should take diligent care of the stomach to keep fullness from leading to nausea or indigestion and injuring the head. Twice a day, eat food that is both moderate and light, and that is seasoned with cinnamon, mace, and nutmeg. But always let the dry food exceed the soft food and the drink in weight — unless the dryness of black bile should be a threat. Let food wait for hunger, if it can conveniently be done, and drink for thirst. Stop eating and drinking while you still want them, and stay far away from distaste and fullness. Abstain from those things which, on account of their excessive moisture or poisonous, oily, and slimy matter, weaken the stomach by loosening it, and also from those things which are cold or very hot, or which are difficult to digest because of their hardness. And those things must be avoided which for a long time after the meal make a very bad taste in the mouth, or puff up or fill the head with many vapors, and, above all, those things which easily decay either outside or within the stomach. Sweet or sharp tastes, if they are only so, I do not approve of at all, but I want the sweet to be tempered with something sharp or keen or dry.

Mastic and dry mint, fresh sage, raisins, quinces cooked and preserved with sugar, chicory, rose, coral, and caper washed and pickled in vinegar, are most friendly to the stomach. Then, too, so are pomegranates with a taste halfway between sour and sweet, as well as all things which are moderately sour and a little tart, which doctors call astringent, or those which are a little sharp, salty, or spicy. Myrobalan, however, surpasses all these.[1] Wine also, red rather than white, with a taste, as it were, a little bitter; and it will be best, unless heat or sweating precludes it, if unmixed and drunk a little at a time. Dishes which are more liquid should certainly be consumed before harder ones. But when the food has been consumed, coriander is appropriate, quince seasoned with sugar, pomegranates, sour pears, medlars, dried peaches, and similar things. But each one must be chewed most precisely before it is swallowed. The stomach must be fomented if necessary from the outside with mastic, rose, mint, and coral.

Take care that for two or three hours following a meal we do not devote ourselves to difficult thinking or careful reading. Perhaps four hours of relaxa-

tionis quattuor, si cibus potusve uberior fuerit, aut cibus durior. Malum est 30
cibo potuve ventrem extendere; pessimum stomacho sic extento difficilia cogitare. Aut igitur nutrimentum sume levissimum, aut sumpto, vaca donec quasi concoxeris. Neque dormiendum post cibum meridie, nisi maxima cogat necessitas, atque id quidem non prius quam horas duas vigilaverimus. Nocte tamen sumpta coena, hora (ut videtur) una vigiliae sufficit. Coitus stomacho 35
pestilens, praesertim si vel saturo statim vel esuriente concumbas. Otio maeret stomachus, exercitatione gaudet, nisi dum cibo sit plenus. Sumpto cibo statim modice deambulandum, mox vero sedendum.

De his quae fovent membra praecipua, vires, spiritus.

Cap. XII.

Sed iam praestare videtur ut nonnulla ex medicorum officina in medium producamus, quae stomachi, cordis, cerebri, spirituum, ingenii vires vel servent integras vel restituant; ac si vel pituita vel atra bilis excrescat vel immineat nausea, longe propellant. Omnes sine controversia medici consenserunt, nihil esse salutarius theriaca fovendis confirmandisque tum singulis 5
membris et viribus, tum spiritibus atque ingenio. Huius igitur imprimis utemur drachma dimidia aut saltem drachmae tertia parte bis qualibet hebdomada hieme atque autumno, sed aestate atque vere semel, vel sola vel, si placet, frigidis humidisque temporibus cum pauculo mero claro, suavi; temporibus vero calidis siccisque, praesertim si natura vel aetas sit calidior, cum 10
aquae rosaceae duabus unciis aut tribus stomacho scilicet vacuo sex aut septem horis ante cibum. Si theriaca desit, dabimus mithridatum. Sed ubi theriacam mithridatumve sumimus, eo die ab omni re calida penitus abstinendum; ac si aestas aut ver fuerit, frigidis est utendum.

Secundo vero loco eadem in causa probatur ab omnibus aloe rite electa 15
atque lota. Sume myrobalanorum chebularum drachmas duas, rosarum purpurearum, sandali rubei, emblicarum, cinnamomi, croci, corticis pomi citri, been, melissae, id est citrariae, singulorum drachmam unam, aloes electae riteque ablutae drachmas duodecim. Ex his confice pilulas optimo mero, qui-

---

32-33 Aut igitur—concoxeris *om. z*   33 dormiamus *e*   35 sufficit] sat est *z*
   post vires add. et z   1 praestare videtur] operaeprecium facturus *z*   14 ac] et *z*   16 myrobalanorum chebularum drachmas duas] karabe (car- *G*; kr- *R*) id est succinci coralli rubri *e*   18 *post* unam *add.* et *B*   19 duodecim] decem *e*   mero *ante* optimo *transp. ABD*

BOOK ONE   CHAP. XII   139

tion will be necessary, if the food and drink was too rich, or the food too hard. It is bad to strain the stomach with food and drink, and worst of all, with the stomach so strained, to think difficult thoughts. Therefore, either take the lightest nourishment, or having taken it, relax until you shall have digested somewhat. No sleeping after taking food at midday without the greatest necessity and then, indeed, not before we have stayed awake for two hours! Still, at night, after dinner has been eaten, one hour seems to be enough to stay awake. Sexual intercourse is very bad for the stomach, especially if you have intercourse immediately on a full stomach or while hungry. The stomach grieves in idleness and rejoices in exercise, except when it is full of food. After eating, one should immediately take a little walk but sit down right after that.

On Those Things Which Support Special Parts, the Powers, and the Spirits.

Chap. XII

Now it seems an excellent idea that we should bring forth to public view some things from the doctors' shop which either keep whole or restore the forces of the stomach, heart, brain, spirits, and intelligence, and which, if phlegm or black bile becomes excessive or nausea threatens, drive them far away. All doctors unanimously agree that nothing is more beneficial than theriac[1] for supporting and strengthening both particular parts and powers and also the spirits and the intelligence. Therefore, we will use, principally, half a dram of theriac, or at least a third of a dram, twice a week during winter and fall, but once a week during summer and spring, taken either by itself or with a little clear, pleasant, unmixed wine, if you like, during cold and wet times; but during hot and dry times, especially if the patient's nature or age is rather hot, taken with two or three ounces of rose water on an empty stomach and six or seven hours before eating. If we have no theriac, we will give mithridate. But when we take theriac or mithridate, on that day we must abstain completely from everything hot, and, if it is summer or spring, we must use cold things.

But in the second place, aloe rightly chosen and washed is approved by all for the same motives. Take two drams of chebule myrobalan, one dram each of purple roses, red sandal, emblic myrobalan, cinnamon, saffron, citron peel, ben, and melissa, that is, citraria, and twelve drams of aloe, select and properly washed. From these ingredients make pills of a weight which befits your nature with the best unmixed wine and use them once a week at dawn — dur-

bus hebdomada qualibet semel utaris diluculo, eo scilicet pondere quod naturae tuae conveniat; aestate quidem cum aqua rosacea, alias vero cum vino. Quibus autem diebus neque theriacam neque pilulas assumes, utere confectione eiusmodi mane atque vespere duabus aut tribus ante cibum horis. Sume cinnami electissimi drachmas quattuor, chebularum myrobalanorum duas et totidem emblicarum, croci, rosarum purpurearum drachmam dimidiam, sandalorum rubrorum drachmas duas, corallorumque similium drachmam unam, sacchari albissimi quantum satis est. Funde saccharum aqua rosacea atque succo citri vel limonum, aequalibus videlicet portionibus; coque suaviter. Deinde adde musci tertiam drachmae partem atque ambrae tantundem. Demum confice bolos solidos, quos morsulos vulgo nominant, auroque involve.

Tria haec ipsi eo usu quo praescripsimus experti sumus, theriacam et aloem ita (ut diximus) temperatam confectionemque illam singulis conferre membris et viribus et spiritibus, acuere sensus atque ingenium, memoriam confirmare; pituitam quoque et bilem atque atram bilem illis pilulis facile vel educi vel emendari. Praeterea aetati cuilibet et naturae tria quae diximus familiarissima iudicantur.

Medicinae contra pituitam.

Cap. XIII.

Si adversus exundantem pituitam acrius pugnandum fuerit, pilulas aurora ex hierapicra Galieni, vel quas Mesues elephanginas nominat, dabimus, scilicet quot et quotiens oportuerit; vel etiam in robustiore natura pilulas ex hiera atque trochiscis agarici pari portione compositas, semper vero cum melle rosaceo liquido atque oxymelle aquaque marathri, id est feniculi. Qui certe syrupus in pituita digerenda etiam ante pilulas atque post eas maxime prodest. Si una cum pituita ceteri quoque humores turbent, pilulis ex reubarbaro Mesues, vel pilulis quae Sine quibus a posterioribus nuncupantur, opportune purgabimus. Omnem vero vehementem repentinamque deiectionem purgationemque penitus detestamur, nam stomachum corque debilitat, spiritus multos exhaurit, confundit humores, spiritus fumis humorum fuscis obtenebrat.

---

20 diluculo *om. A*   22 assumens *B*   24-25 chebularum — emblicarum] corticis citri *e*   25 purpurearum *om. z;* singulorum *add. e*   26 corallorum *D*   28 coquas *z*   29-30 Deinde—tantundem *desunt in e*   34 et¹ *om. z*   sensum *G*
   Medicinae] De medicinis *y*   *Medicinae contra pituitam. Cap.XIII]* Pharmaca pituitae repressiva atque eductiva Cap. XXIII *z*   2 nominat *om. DR;* nominant *x*   4 *post* vero *add.* una *A*   6 *ante* ante etiam *transp. L*   atque] et *z*   7 quaeque *z*   pilulas *DGR*   11 contundit *z*   humorum] humorem *z*

ing the summer, with rose water, but at other times with wine. But on the days when you take neither theriac nor pills, use the following confection in the morning and in the evening two or three hours before eating: take four drams of the best cinnamon, two of chebule myrobalan and two of emblic myrobalan and of saffron, half a dram of purple roses, two drams of red sandal, and one dram of red coral and as much as you need of the whitest sugar. Moisten the sugar with rose water and the juice of a citron or of lemons in equal proportions, and cook it gently. Then add one-third dram of musk and the same amount of amber. Finally, make solid balls, which are commonly called morsels, and gild them with gold.

We have tested by experience that these three—theriac, aloe properly mixed as specified, and that other confection—are good in the very use which we have described above for particular parts, powers, and spirits, that they sharpen the senses and intelligence, and strengthen the memory. We also know that phlegm, bile, and black bile are easily either eliminated or corrected by those pills. Moreover, these three which we have mentioned are judged to be most friendly to any age and nature.

Drugs against Phlegm.

Chap. XIII

If we must put up quite a strong fight against an excess of phlegm, we will give pills at dawn consisting of the hierapicra of Galen,[1] or those which Mesue calls "Elephangine,"[2] as much and as often as necessary, or even, if the patient has quite a strong nature, both pills composed of hiera and, in equal proportion, trochees of agaric; but we will always administer these with liquid rose-honey, oxymel, and water of marathrum, that is, of fennel, which syrup in truth is also good for breaking up the phlegm both before the pills and especially after them. If along with phlegm all the other humors are acting up, it will be fitting to purge them with the rhubarb-pills of Mesue,[3] or with pills which are called by moderns "Sine quibus." But we altogether denounce all strong and sudden flux and purgation, for it weakens the stomach and the heart, it drains away many spirits, and it brings the humors into confusion and with the black fumes of the humors darkens those spirits which remain.

Destillatio.
Cap. XIV.

Ubi caput propter pituitam destillationibus fluctuat, quandoque hora somni aliquot ex pilulis quas modo descripsimus dabimus. Iubebimus praeterea ea hora et aliis thus saepe mandere, nam mirifice destillationibus et sensibus omnibus memoriaeque succurrit. Rursus muscata nux et theriaca ore retenta probatur; maiorana quoque, quam amaracum nominant, vel 5 eius aqua admota naribus vel infusa. Post cibum vero alimentorum fumos coriandro cydoneisque coercebimus.

Dolor capitis.
Cap. XV.

Si caput saepe doleat humore gravatum frigido, praeter illa quae narravimus, confectionem illam quam diambram nominant vel diacori vel plisarchoticon tenere ore iubebimus. Quinetiam masticem saepe mandere. Praeterea linire frontem, tempora, cervicem maioranae, feniculi, rutae foliis una cum oleo rosaceo tunsis, similiter aloe, aceto, oleo aquaque rosaceis per- 5 fecte diluta.

De cura visus.
Cap. XVI.

Ubi oculi caligant neque rubent, tamen neque aliud praebent ullum caloris indicium, tunc sane collyrium ex aqua feniculi, maioranae, chelidoniae, rutae, adhibito croco et antimonio, confert; sed aqua eiusmodi prius densior panno est exprimenda. Nihil tamen admoveas oculis, nisi antea pilulis lucis saepe purgaveris. At si caligantes oculi rubeant, subito pilulis ex 5

Destillatio atque eius cura *x*; De destillatione *y*; Catarrhi et destillationis communis studiosorum pestis remedia *z*   3 thus] olibanum *BR;* olibanum id est thus *ADGR*[1]
    Dolor capitis] et cura eius *add. x*; De dolore capitis *yz*   2 vel[1] *om. DR*   3 plirisarcoticon *z*   5 rosaceo—oleo *om. z*   tunsis] fusis *BR*[ac]
    De cura visus] Visus caligantis medelae *z*

Rheum.

Chap. XIV

When the head is swimming with rheums ["destillationibus," a word Ficino also uses to mean "sweat"] because of phlegm, we will sometimes give at bedtime some of those pills which I have just described. We will also give the order to chew frankincense often at this hour and at other times, since it is of great help against rheums and for all the senses and the memory. Nutmeg and theriac held in the mouth are also approved, as well as marjoram, which they call amaracum, or its water either applied to the nostrils or given to drink. And after eating, we will control the fumes of the food with coriander and quinces.

Headache.

Chap. XV

If the head often aches because it is burdened with a cold humor, besides those things which we have related, we will order the patient to hold in the mouth that confection which they call "diambra," "diacori," or "plisarchoticon"; to chew mastic often; and also to besmear the forehead, temples, and neck with the leaves of marjoram, fennel, and rue, beaten together with rose-oil, and do the same with aloe and vinegar completely diluted with rose-oil and rose-water.

On the Care of the Sight.

Chap. XVI

When the eyes are dim, but not inflamed, and offer no other indication of heat, then indeed a salve is useful, one made out of water of fennel, marjoram, swallow-wort, and rue, with saffron and antimony added. But water of this sort must first be filtered through a rather thick cloth. Still, you should not apply anything to the eyes before you clean them repeatedly with

fumo terrae compositis purga. Mox collyrium ex aqua rosacea et saccharo prodest, nonnunquam vero albumine ovi, tutia, lacte adiectis quam primum opitulatur. Omnino autem quotidianus usus marathri visum servat et acuit. Semen quidem eius frequenter ore tenere oportet, folia vero comedere. Triphera minor a Mesue descripta optima est. Optimum quotidie vacuo stomacho myrobalanum chebulam conditam sumere, atque cum ea nonnihil panis ex saccharo marathroque in pulverem ducto compositi, quod insuper ingenio mirum in modum ac producendae vitae prodest. Eufrasiae quinetiam usus oculis est singulare praesidium. In omni vel dolore capitis vel caligine oculorum divertendi sunt retro vapores frictionibus cucurbitulisque. Ac si calor in causa sit sanguisque abundet, hirudines cervici et humeris adhibebimus.

De gustu instaurando.
Cap. XVII.

Stomachus saepe litterarum studiosis gustum fere omnem amittit. Si id pituitae vitio incidit, quod acidus oris sapor vel saliva multa et glutinosior indicat, postquam alvum subduxeris medicinis quas supra narravimus, aromatico rosaceo utere, scilicet saccharo rosaceo mixto, melle quoque rosaceo, cum cinnamo; solo etiam vel zinzibere condito vel mentae syrupo, sed imprimis theriaca. Sin autem bilis copia forte contingit, quod quidem os amarum ostendere solet, similiter post purgationem ex aloe, sicut diximus, praeparata vel reubarbaro, assume vel triasandalum vel oxysaccharum et saccharo aceto albo et vino acrioris Punici mali compositam; vel Persica pyrave sive condita sive syrupo confecta, sicut Mesues docet; vel nostram eiusmodi confectionem gustui saluberrimam. Sume sacchari rosacei uncias quattuor, diamarenati uncias duas, diacitoniten tantundem, scilicet uncias duas, myrobalanorum chebularum semunciam, emblicarum tantundem, sandali rubei, coralli rubri, utrorunque aeque drachmam dimidiam. Funde insuper iuleb ex succo citri vel limonis tres uncias aut duas. Quod si stomachus debilis est et frigidus, adiice duas cinnami drachmas. His ante cibum duabus horis utendum. Nauseam semper ab utroque natam humore tollit diacitoniten et usus capparis cum aceto; item potus modicus ieiuno stomacho albi aceti rosacei, si duplo sacchari pondere misceatur; rursus mentae syrupus atque absinthii; item menta vel aceto condita vel acido mali Punici succo diluta.

9–14 Triphera—praesidium *desunt in* e   13 Eufragiae *Lwxy*   16 sanguinisque *z*   hirundines *DRz*
De gustu instaurando] De sensorio gustus instaurando *z*   8 oxysaccharum *z*; oxysaccharam *Lewxy* et *om.* z   8–9 saccharo aceto albo] saccharo, aceto albo *z*   12 diacytoniles *z*   12–13 scilicet—tantundem *om. Le;* scilicet uncias duas *habent* AD^1R^1; Mirobalanorum citrinarum semunciam emblicarum tantundem *add. in marg.* L   14 rubri] rubei GR^{ac} aequa *z*   15 uncias *ante* treis *transp.* z   16 duas cinnami drachmas] unam cinnami drachmam *e*   17 diacytonites *z*   18 rosati *B*   19 duplo] aequali *e*   20 *post* diluta *add.* atque rigata *z*

pills of light. But if the dim eyes are inflamed, clean them at once with pills made out of fumitory. Right after that, a salve of rose water and sugar is useful, and sometimes it is helpful to add as soon as possible an egg-white, tutty, and milk. At all events, the daily use of fennel preserves and sharpens the vision. One should frequently hold a fennel seed in one's mouth and eat the leaves. The lesser theriac, described by Mesue, is the best.[1] It is best to take daily, on an empty stomach, a preserved chebule myrobalan, and to take with it some bread made of sugar and of powdered fennel, which is especially good for the intelligence and for wonderfully prolonging life. The use of euphrasia is also a special help for the eyes. In every headache or dimness of the eyes, turn back the vapors by rubbing and cupping-glasses. But if heat is the cause and blood is in abundance, we will apply leeches to the neck and shoulders.

On Restoring the Taste.

Chap. XVII

The stomach of learned people often loses almost all sense of taste. If it happens through the fault of phlegm—as is indicated by a sour taste in the mouth or an abundance of rather glutinous saliva—after you have purged the bowels with the medicines which we related above, use a rose-spice (which means rose-sugar, rose-honey also, mixed with cinnamon) either alone or seasoned with ginger or mint-syrup, but especially use theriac. If, however, an abundance of bile should occur, which a bitter mouth usually shows, similarly after a purge of aloe prepared as we have said or of rhubarb, take either triasandalum or oxysaccharum (composed of both white vinegar-sugar and the wine of a rather tart pomegranate). Or take peaches or pears preserved or prepared with a syrup, as Mesue teaches.[1] Or take our own confection which is most beneficial for the sense of taste: take four ounces of rose-sugar, two ounces of diamarenat and diacitonite, one-half ounce of chebule myrobalans and one-half ounce of emblic myrobalans, one-half dram apiece of red sandal and red coral. Pour in two or three ounces of a julep made out of citron- or lemon-juice. But if the stomach is weak and cold, add two drams of cinnamon. These things should be used two hours before eating. Diacitonite and the use of capers with vinegar always relieve the nausea which is produced by either of the two humors. So does a moderate drink of white rose-vinegar on an empty stomach, if it is mixed with twice its weight in sugar; and so do a mint- and absinthe-syrup, as well as mint either seasoned with vinegar or diluted with the tart juice of the pomegranate.

De exacta atrae bilis cura.

Cap. XVIII.

Verum missa haec tanquam leviora iam faciamus, atque ad id quod periculosissimum est revertamur, scilicet ad atram bilem quae, quotiens abundat et furit, cum corpus totum tum vel maxime spiritum, quasi quoddam instrumentum ingenii, ipsumque ingenium et iudicium labefactat. Primum in ea curanda praeceptum sit, ut docuit Galienus, ne repente illam educere contendamus, ne forte parte eius liquidiore subtilioreque subducta residuum densius admodum sicciusque resideat, sed paulatim molliatur digeraturque pariter atque educatur. Secundum et interim tam cibis humidioribus quam lavacris dulcibus et modicis unguentisque similibus caput et corpus totum ad summum pro viribus humectetur, ea tamen cautione ne vel destillatio irritetur, vel destruatur stomachus aut iecur, vel meatus corporis obstruantur. Tertium vero, et id quidem maxime necessarium, ut continue cor foveatur roboreturque rebus congruis partim intus acceptis, partim extra pectori naribusve adhibitis. Aspiciantur quoque et audiantur, odorentur et cogitentur assidue quae oblectent, contraria vero longius arceantur.

De syrupis.

Cap. XIX.

Multa quidem a multis adversus hunc humorem composita sunt. Ego autem impraesentia tria quaedam remediorum genera e plurimis afferam electissima omnium atque tutissima, accepta primum a priscis, deinde a recentioribus confirmata, interdum etiam a nobis ad usum nostrum accommodata. In primo est syrupi optimi compositio, in secundo pilulae probatissimae, in tertio electuaria saluberrima. His tribus opportune adhibitis, melancholicus humor mollitur et digeritur atque solvitur, spiritus acuuntur et illustrantur, fovetur ingenium, memoria confirmatur.

Syrupus est huiusmodi: sume boraginis, buglossae, florumque utriusque, melissae, capillorum Veneris, endiviae, violarum, cuscutae, polypodii, senae, epithymi, singulorum quantum manu capitur, pruna Damascena numero viginti, odora poma numero decem, passularum unciam unam, liquiritiae un-

---

De exacta atrae bilis cura] Exquisitissima atrae bilis remedia *z*   1 ad id quod] id quidem *D*   2 ad atram bilem *ante* scilicet *transp. z*   6 eius *ante* parte *transp. z*   9 et[1] *om. G*   11 destruantur *G*   11–12 stomachus—obstruantur *om. G*   14 naribusve] manibusve *D*
De syrupis] De syrupo *A*; Syrupi melancholicis maximo futuri commodo *z*

On the Special Cure of Black Bile Alone.

Chap. XVIII

Let us pass over these former things as less important, however, and return to that most dangerous thing, black bile, which as often as it becomes excessive and rages, disturbs not only the whole body but especially also the spirit — which is, as it were, an instrument of the intelligence — as well as the intelligence itself and the judgment. This should be the first rule in curing it, as Galen taught: not to strive to draw it out suddenly, lest by chance after its more fluid and subtle part has been removed, the much denser residue and the dryer residue still remain; but to soften it gradually, separate it, and so draw it out.[1] The second rule should be that in the meantime the head and the entire body, if possible, be moistened to the utmost with foods which are rather moist, with baths which are sweet and moderate, and with similar ointments — but take care not to provoke rheum, ruin the stomach or the liver, or block the pores of the body. The third and most necessary rule should be to warm the heart continuously and strengthen it with substances that are of like nature, in part taken internally and in part applied externally to the breast or nostrils. Similarly, to continually look at, hear, smell, and think about things which are pleasing, and to keep at a distance things which are not.

On Syrups.

Chap. XIX

Against this humor, many things have been composed by many people. For now I, however, will put forth just three types of remedies, the choicest and safest of all, which were first accepted by the ancients, then confirmed by the moderns, and sometimes even adapted by me for my own use. I give you the composition, in the first place, of the best syrup, second, the most approved pills, and third, the most wholesome electuaries.[1] When these three are fittingly brought to bear, the melancholic humor is softened, separated, and dissolved, the spirits are sharpened and illumined, the intelligence is supported, and the memory is strengthened.

The syrup is of this sort: take a handful of each of the following: borage and bugloss as well as their flowers, melissa, maidenhair, endive, violets, cuscuta, polypody, senna, and epithyme; take twenty Damson plums, ten fragrant

ciam dimidiam, cinnami, sandali rubri, corticum citri, singulorum drachmas tres, croci drachmam dimidiam. Coquantur in aqua omnia praeter epithymum et aromata, donec pars tertia consumatur. Decoctio expressa post cum saccharo iterum et epithymo moderate coquatur. Postremo infundantur aromata, scilicet cinnamum atque crocus. Huius syrupi aurora calefacti unciae tres bibantur, simulque unciae duae aut tres aquae buglossae, atque una cum his ex sequentibus pilulis accipi debent duae saltem ac plures, prout cuique convenit, eo scilicet pacto ut alvus quotidie paulum moveatur.

De pilulis.
Cap. XX.

Pilularum vero, quantum ad propositum spectat, duo sunt genera: aliae delicatis congruunt, robustioribus aliae. Primae aureae sive magicae nominari possunt, partim Magorum imitatione, partim nostra inventione sub ipso Iovis Venerisque influxu compositae, quae pituitam, bilem, atram bilem educunt absque molestia, singula membra corroborant, spiritus acuunt et illuminant. Ita eos dilatant, ne constricti maestitiam pariant, sed dilatatione et lumine gaudeant; ita rursus stabiliunt, ne extensione nimia evanescant. Sume igitur auri grana duodecim, maxime foliorum eius si pura sint, thuris, myrrhae, croci, ligni aloes, cinnami, corticis citri, melissae, serici crudi coccinei, mentae, been albi, been rubei, singulorum drachmam dimidiam, rosarum purpurearum, sandali rubri, coralli rubri, myrobalanorum trium, scilicet emblicarum, chebularum, Indarum, singulorum drachmam unam, aloes rite ablutae tantundem quantum cunctorum pondus. Confice pilulas mero quam electissimo.

Sequuntur pilulae ad solvendam melancholiam aliquanto validiores, verumtamen minime violentae. Sume paeoniae, myrrhae, stichados Arabici, melissae, thuris, croci, myrobalanorum trium, scilicet emblicarum, chebularum, Indarum, rosarum, singulorum drachmam unam, trochiscorum agarici, polypodii, epithymi, senae, lapidis lazuli loti rite et praeparati, lapidis Armeni affecti similiter, drachmas tres singulorum, aloes lotae uncias duas; vino perfecto pilulas confla. Si cum melancholia manifesta caliditas dominetur, quae in hac compositione sunt frigida, ad tertiam insuper ponderis sui partem augenda erunt. Has pilulas, ut litterarum studiosis convenit, Graecorum, Latinorumque Arabumque imitatione composui. Nolui vero fortiora miscere, quale

---

15 consumetur *B*   19 ac] aut *z*
  De pilulis] Pilulae ad humores vitiosos molliendos et expurgandos *z*   2 dedicatis *R*   4 fluxu *yz*   6 dilatatione] dilatione *x*   11 *post* rubri² *add.* karabe (car- *G;* kr- *B*) id est succini *e*   12 *post* Indarum *add.* myrthi spodii terre sigillate *e*   13 ritae *L*   15 *post* validiores *add.* sed *DR*   17 *post* melissae *add.* ligni aloes *e*   18 *post* rosarum *add.* sandali karabe (char- *G;* kr- *R;* karabi *B*) *e*   19 loti rite *om. D;* rite *ante* loti *transp. z*   20 effecti *z*   23 ut] prout *e*   24 arabum *D*

fruits, one ounce of raisins, one-half ounce of licorice, three drams apiece of cinnamon, red sandal, and citron peel, and one-half dram of saffron. Boil them all in water, except the epithyme and spices, until reduced by a third. After the decoction has been squeezed out, boil it afterwards a second time with the sugar and epithyme. Then pour in the spices, i.e., the cinnamon and saffron. At dawn, drink three ounces of this syrup warm as well as two or three ounces of bugloss-water; and together with these things, take two at least of the following pills, and even more as it suits each person, in order that the bowels may be moved a little every day.

On Pills.
Chap. XX

For this purpose, there are two types of pills: some which are suited for delicate people and others for the more robust. The first pills can be called golden or magical, composed partly in imitation of the Magi,[1] and partly through my own invention under the influence of Jupiter and Venus; they draw out phlegm, choler, and black bile without difficulty, strengthen the individual bodily parts, and sharpen and illumine the spirits. They expand the spirits so that they may not, being contracted, engender sadness, but may rejoice in their expansion and light; and in turn they stabilize these spirits so that they do not vanish through being too extended. Take, therefore, twelve grains of gold, especially its leaves if they are pure; one-half dram apiece of frankincense, myrrh, saffron, aloe-wood, cinnamon, citron-peel, melissa, raw scarlet silk, white ben and red; one dram apiece of purple roses, of red sandal, of red coral, and of the three sorts of myrobalans (emblic, chebule, and Indic), with an amount of properly washed aloe equal to the weight of all the rest. Make pills with pure wine of the best possible quality.

Secondly, there are pills to dissolve melancholy which are somewhat stronger, but not at all violent. Take one dram apiece of peony, myrrh, Arabian stechados, melissa, frankincense, saffron, the three sorts of myrobalans (emblic, chebule, and Indic), and roses; take three drams apiece of trochees of agaric, polipody, epithyme, senna, lapis lazuli properly washed and prepared, and the Armenian stone similarly treated;[2] and two ounces of washed aloe; make pills with excellent wine. If, along with melancholy, heat obviously dominates, the ingredients in this mixture which are cold will have to be increased by one third of their weight. In imitation of the Greeks, Latins, and Arabs, I have composed these pills as is fitting for learned people. I did not wish to mix

veratrum, quo Carneades phanaticus utebatur. Viris enim litteratis tantum
vel paulo firmioribus consulo, quibus nihil pestilentius est quam
violentia. Ideo praetermisi pilulas Indas lapidisque lazuli vel Armeni notas et
quam compositionem hieralogodion appellant.

Si denique decet simpliciorem compositionem inserere qua ego familiarius
utor, sume aloes lotae unciam unam, myrobalanorum emblicarum atque chebularum, utriusque pariter drachmas duas, masticis drachmas duas, duas
quoque rosarum, praesertim purpurearum; confice pilulas vino. Proinde pilulis aut iis aut illis, ex iis scilicet quas probavimus, nemo unquam solis uti
debet, ne forte nimium exsiccetur, quod quidem in melancholia pessimum
est; immo vel una cum syrupo quem secuti partim Mesuem, partim Gentilem Fulginatem supra descripsimus, vel cum vini odori levisque uncia una
sive duabus sive tribus, ut cuique convenit, aut cum aqua mellis et passularum atque liquiritiae aut, sicubi caliditas dominatur, cum iuleb violaceo
aquaque violacea.

Omnino autem consulo litteratis, quicunque ad atram bilem sunt proniores, ut hac purgatione bis quolibet anno, vere scilicet autumnoque utantur
diebus quindecim continuis vel viginti, pilulis scilicet cum syrupo atque similibus. Quicunque vero paulo minus huic morbo obnoxii sunt, sat habebunt si pilulas primas aut ultimas toto anno sumant semel hebdomada qualibet, aestate quidem cum iuleb, ut diximus, alias vero cum vino.

De medicina liquida.

Cap. XXI.

Meminisse vero oportet, ubi maximum in exsiccatione periculum imminet, purgare tamen necessitas cogit, operae pretium esse pilulas
intermittere, atque in ipso syrupo vel simili quadam decoctione facta in aqua
buglossae, quando purgandum est, interdum infundere diasenae vel diacatholiconis vel tripherae Persicae unciam unam aut saltem dimidiam. Quod si
vel corpus robustius sit, vel astrictior et durior alvus, addere electuarii hamech drachmam unam aut duas. Utilis quoque hic est confecta cassia, utilior
manna. Haec omni melancholiae speciei conveniunt, sed illi maxime quae
adustione creatur. Sin autem melancholia naturalis sit, conveniunt quidem,
verum praecipue si in syrupo addatur polypodii portio dupla vel tripla similiter liquiritiae crocique et passularum; item medicinae addantur mellis ro-

28 ieraglodion z   29-32 Si denique—vino *desunt in e, sed add. in marg.* A^1 29 *post* decet *add.* his A^1
quam y   familiaribus z   30-31 atque chebularum—duas^1] unciae dimidium A^1 35 vel *om.* z
sicuti *DG*   Gentilem] Galienum *D*   39 violacea] rosacea z   44 aut ultimas *om. e*   45 quidem
om. z   *De medicina liquida]* A liquidarum medicinarum usus medelae z   1-2 in exsiccatione periculum imminet] imminet *ante* in *transp. A;* imminet periculum in exsiccatione *transp. D;* immineat in periculum (in *add.* R^1) exsiccatione *R*   6 hamer *B*   8 Haec $L^{ac}e$] Nec L^1wxyz

stronger things, such as hellebore, which Carneades used to use when he was mad.[3] For I am counseling only learned people or people a little stronger, for whom nothing is more harmful than violence. Therefore I have left out Indian pills and the well-known pills of lapis lazuli or the Armenian stone and the mixture which they call hieralogodion.

Finally, if it is fitting to include a simpler mixture, which I use more commonly — take one ounce of washed aloe, two drams apiece of emblic and chebule myrobalans, two drams of mastic, two drams of roses, especially purple ones, and make into pills with wine. No one should ever take these pills without accompaniment, or those from the materials I have recommended earlier, lest by chance he get excessively dry, which indeed is very bad in the case of melancholy. But rather take the pills either with the syrup which we described above, partly following Mesue and partly Gentile da Foligno;[4] or with one, two, or three ounces of a fragrant, light wine, as is fitting for each person; or with the water of honey, raisins, and licorice; or, whenever heat dominates, with a violet julep and violet-water.

I am expressly counseling learned people and others who are rather prone to black bile, that they should use this purgation — pills with syrup and similar things — twice a year in spring and autumn for fifteen or twenty days in a row. But those who are a little less subject to this disease will have enough if, during the entire year, once a week they take the first or last pills, in the summer with a julep, as we said, or at other times with wine.

On Liquid Medicine.

Chap. XXI

When a very great danger of dryness threatens, but necessity demands a purgation, one must remember that it is worthwhile to stop the pills and sometimes, when purgations must be made, to infuse in the syrup itself or in a similar decoction made with bugloss-water an ounce or at least a half-ounce of diasenna, diacatholicon or Persian triphera. But if the patient's body is stronger or the bowels rather tight and hard, add one or two drams of the electuary hamech. A confection of cassia is also useful here, and manna even more so. These are good for every kind of melancholy, but especially for the kind which is generated by adustion. If the melancholy is a natural one, they are still good, but especially if a double or triple portion of polypody, licorice, saffron, and raisins is added in the syrup; likewise if to the medicine are added

sacei liquidi unciae duae. Quotiens vero syrupus sumendus sit, in superioribus diximus, sed medicina cum ipso ter viginti diebus sumenda erit.

Verum si melancholicus nullus humor appareat, tantum vero complexio melancholica, scilicet frigida membrorum qualitas atque sicca, memento ducere alvum vel mittere sanguinem minime expedire; sed reliqua duntaxat facere quae vel diximus vel dicemus, praesertim quaecunque ad corpus pertinent mediocriter calefaciendum atque magnopere humectandum, spiritusque, quoad fieri potest, illuminandos, fovendaque membra. Ubi vero ipse atrae bilis humor exundat, non madefacimus tantum corpus atque humorem, sed etiam solvimus alvum ea cautione qua diximus, nunquam vero vehementer. Siquidem Plato in *Timaeo* nos monet diuturnum morbum, qualis est melancholicus, non esse nimis valentibus medicamentis atque molestis pharmacis irritandum.

De sanguinis missione.

Cap. XXII.

Sunt nonnulli in sanguine mittendo audaciores, quos medici sapientes admodum detestantur, nam sanguis est atrae bilis temperamentum, spiritus fomes, vitae thesaurus. Solum vero ubi abundantiam sanguinis indicat vel profusior risus audaciaque et confidentia multa vel color rubens venarumque tumor, mittere sanguinem litteratis, quando res postulat, debemus e vena lienis sinistri bracchii lata quadam incisione, quattuor uncias mane, vespere totidem. Deinde paucos post dies, saltem septem, ad summum quattuordecim, tum frictione quadam asperiore, tum admotis hirudinibus, quas sanguisugas nominant, mariscas irritare, ut sanguinis unciae tres aut quattuor inde destillent. Haec ambo robustioribus tantum facienda videntur; debilioribus vero, si necessitas postulat, mariscas solum, sicut docuimus, irritare. Sed neque ventrem medicinis solvere, neque mittere sanguinem licet, nisi prius clysteribus pinguibus mollibusque lenieris. Atque hoc sit in melancholica natura commune praeceptum, dandam esse operam ut, si oportuerit, eiusmodi clysteribus frequentatis venter inferior lubricus semper sit atque purgatus.

---

21 quam *B*   22 admonet *B*
  De sanguinis missione] Sanguinis mittendi canones *z*   1 nonnulli *ante* sunt *transp. z*   4 calor *D* rubeus $R^{ac}z$ 5 postulat] exigit *A*   5-6 lineis *z*   6 quidem *z*   8 hirudinibus *z*   10 *post* ambo add. in *BDR*   12 mittere *om. z*   sanguinem] saniem *BDR*

two ounces of liquid rose-honey. How often the syrup must be taken, we have mentioned above, but the medicine will have to be taken with it thrice every twenty days.

If no melancholic humor appears, but only a melancholic complexion, i.e., a cold and dry quality in the bodily parts, remember that it does no good at all to discharge the bowels or to bleed. But at least remember to do the other things which we have mentioned, or will mention, especially those things which pertain to warming the body moderately and moistening it greatly, to illuminating the spirits insofar as possible, and to fomenting the bodily parts. When the humor of black bile becomes excessive, however, we not only moisten the body and the humor, but we also loosen the bowels, being careful, as we said, never to do it violently. For indeed Plato in the *Timaeus* warns us that a long-lasting disease, such as melancholy, must not be irritated by too-strong remedies and annoying drugs.[1]

On Blood-Letting.
Chap. XXII

There are some people who are too bold in bleeding, but wise doctors strongly denounce them, for blood is the proper temperer of black bile,[1] the tinder of the spirit,[2] the repository of the life.[3] Only when rather excessive laughter and much boldness and confidence or a ruddy complexion and a swelling of the veins indicates an abundance of blood, should we bleed learned people, when the situation demands it, from the spleen-vein of the left arm with a wide incision — four ounces of blood in the morning and four ounces in the evening. Then a few days afterwards — seven at the least, fourteen at the most — irritate the welts with a rather harsh rubbing and the application of leeches, which they call blood-suckers, in order that three or four ounces of blood may drip out. These two things should be done only to the stronger patients; but for the weaker, if necessity demands it, we ought only to irritate the welts as we have taught. It is permitted neither to loosen the bowels nor to let blood unless you first soften the bowels with oily and mild clysters. And let this be a general rule in the case of a melancholic nature: to see to it, if it be necessary, that the lower belly be always lubricated and purged by frequent clysters of this sort.

De electuariis.
Cap. XXIII.

Sequuntur electuaria, ex quibus laudo equidem quod Rasis exhilarans appellavit, praeterea quae in libro *De viribus cordis* Avicenna componit, sed multo magis quod Mesues ita conscribit. Sume crudum sericum colore coccineo nuper tinctum, pondere libram unam; id merge succo pomorum dulcium et suaviter redolentium atque succo buglossae aquaque rosacea, singulorum libra una; post quattuor et viginti horas totum id coque suaviter, donec aqua rubeat. Deinde extrahe sericum atque insuper exprime diligenter. Infunde mox sacchari candidissimi centum et quinquaginta drachmas; coque rursus donec quasi mel spissetur. Amove tunc ab igne atque infunde, dum calet, ambrae crudae diligenter concisae drachmas sex, et ut liquescat ambra permitte. Postremo adde his pulverem eiusmodi: sume ligni aloes crudi, cinnami, utriusque aeque sex drachmas, lapidis lazuli rite abluti drachmas tredecim, unionum, id est albarum margaritarum, drachmas duas, auri veri drachmam unam, musci electi partem drachmae dimidiam. Dantur ex eo cum vino drachmae duae vel una mane ac vespere ante cibum tribus aut quattuor horis. Id mihi prae ceteris valde placet.

Verumtamen probo etiam diamuscum Mesues dulcem compositionemque gemmarum, modo cum aqua rosacea assumantur. Laudarem quoque mirifice quod est a Petro Aponensi, philosopho summo, conflatum, nisi ipsemet ex eius immodico usu dilatationem exhalationemque spirituum nimiam formidaret. Quamobrem duo quaedam insuper excogitavi tutissima, atque ob temperationem suam cuilibet tempori, aetati, naturae convenientissima, in quibus miscetur utile dulci. Quae tantum nutriunt, quantum fovent et roborant; praeterea spiritui et ingenio tantum stabiliendo, quantum acuendo et illustrando conveniunt. Sume sacchari rosacei uncias quattuor, sacchari una cum floribus buglossae concocti uncias duas, corticis pomi citri saccharo conditi unciam unam, chebulae conditae uncias duas, cinnami electi drachmam unam, sandali, coralli, scilicet utriusque rubri, item serici coccinei crudi concisi, croci, margaritarum, singulorum drachmam dimidiam, auri, argenti, singulorum tertiam drachmae partem, ambrae, musci, utriusque grana duo. Funde omnia simul succo citri vel limonis saccharo cocti.

Sequitur confectio altera, aliquanto salubrior, certe multo suavior: sume amygdalarum dulcium quattuor uncias, nucleorum pineorum scilicet ablutorum diei unius spatio, seminum cucumeris, utrorunque pariter uncias duas, sacchari duri quod candum, id est candidum, vocant quattuor uncias, sacchari alterius, sed albissimi, libram unam atque dimidiam. Funde cuncta

---

post electuaribus add. et confectis z   2 componit] composuit *G*   8 coque *ex* quoque *corr.* L^2 9 dissipetur *B*   10 conscissae *yz*   11 eiuscemodi ABR^1 12 aequae *x*   17 Mesues] cum Mesue *DR*, *sed* cum *expunxit D*   18 adsumuntur *z*   19 est *om. D*   Aponensi *scripsi ex* Ebanensi; Apo- *add. supra* Eba- *in L*   20 exaltationemque L^{ac}; exhilationemque *z*   22 suam *om. B*   24 spiritu *G*   25 rosacei—sacchari *om. z*   27 unciam unam *om. e*   unam *om. z*   chebulae *z*] chebuli *Lewxy* chebulae—duas] Chebuli (Chebu *G*) conditi utriusque pariter unciam unam *e*   28 corallis $Lw^{ac}x$ 28 *post* crudi *add.* et *z*   conscissi *yz*   31 cocti] conditi *G*   34 duas *om. z*   36 *post* sed

On Electuaries.

Chap. XXIII

Electuaries are next: I, for my part, advocate that one which Rhazes called "exhilarating";[1] those which Avicenna composes in his book, *On the Powers of the Heart*;[2] but much more the one which Mesue prescribes as follows. Take one pound of raw silk, recently dyed scarlet, submerge it in one pound apiece of the juice of sweet and pleasant-smelling fruits, bugloss-juice, and rose-water; after twenty-four hours, boil it all gently until the water is red. Then remove the silk and squeeze it out carefully. Next pour in 150 drams of the whitest sugar; boil it again until it thickens like honey; then remove it from the fire and, while it is hot, pour in six drams of raw amber, carefully broken up, and let the amber liquefy. Then add to these things the following powder: take six drams apiece of raw aloe-wood and cinnamon, thirteen drams of properly washed lapis lazuli, two drams of unions, i.e., white pearls, one dram of pure gold, and one-half dram of choice musk. One or two drams of it are given with wine, morning and evening, three or four hours before eating.[3] I like this a lot, more than all the rest.

Nevertheless, I also approve of the sweet diamusk of Mesue[4] and his compound of precious stones,[5] provided they be taken with rose-water. I would also advocate strongly the electuary compounded by the excellent philosopher Pietro d'Abano, except that he himself is afraid that an excessive expansion and exhalation of the spirits may result from using it too much.[6] Accordingly I have invented two electuaries—most safe, and because of their tempering in which the useful is mixed with the sweet, most appropriate for any time, age, and nature. They nourish as much as they warm and strengthen, and are as suitable for stabilizing the spirit and the intelligence as they are for sharpening and illuminating them. Take four ounces of rose-sugar, two ounces of sugar cooked with bugloss-flowers, one ounce of citron-peel preserved with sugar, two ounces of preserved chebule myrobalans, one dram of choice cinnamon, one-half dram apiece of red sandal, red coral, chopped up raw scarlet silk, saffron, and pearls, one-third dram apiece of gold and silver, and two grains apiece of amber and musk. Moisten them all at the same time with citron or lemon juice boiled with sugar.

Next comes the second confection, somewhat more wholesome and certainly much more pleasant. Take four ounces of sweet almonds, two ounces apiece of pine-nuts which have been washed for a day and cucumber seeds, four ounces of that hard sugar which they call "candy," i.e., "white" ("candidum"), and one and one-half pounds of the other kind of sugar, but very white. Infuse all these

haec aqua rosacea atque limonis et citri, in qua extinctum fuerit ignitum aurum et argentum; simul coque suaviter. Demum adde cinnami, been rubri, sandali rubri, coralli similis, singulorum drachmam unam, margaritarum nitidissimarum, croci, serici crudi coccinei minuissime attriti, singulorum 40 drachmam dimidiam, auri, argenti, utriusque grana duodecim, hyacinthi, smaragdi, sapphyri, carbunculi, singulorum tertiam drachmae partem. Si cui vero desunt aurum, argentum, ambra, muscus, pretiosi lapilli, confectiones illae etiam prodesse multum sine his poterunt.

Quarum tres potissimum eligo, unam scilicet Mesues quam recensui, duas 45 vero nostras quas modo descripsimus. Quo vero pacto iis utendum sit, superius satis exposuimus. Si quis autem simplicius aliquid appetat, omnibus tamen accommodatum, hic citri pomum perfecte maturum, integrum perfecte contundat; multoque saccharo et multo rosarum succo adhibito coquat. Coctum vero modico cinnamo crocoque condiat, aut aromatico rosaceo uta- 50 tur sic temperato: sume aromatici rosacei unciam unam, sacchari rosacei, sacchari diabuglossati, utriusque uncias duas; aut similiter misceat diamuscum. Quanquam enim duo haec non sint simplicia, tamen facile satis habentur. Ac si caliditas timeatur, diaprunis et saccharum violaceum adiungantur.

De nimia vigilia.

Cap. XXIV.

Saepe melancholicis praesertim litteratis accidere solet, ut nimium exsiccato cerebro vigiliis longis extenuentur. Quoniam vero nihil atrae bilis mala magis auget quam longa vigilia, tanto malo omni studio succurrendum. Ideo lactucas post cibos alios edant una cum pane modico, pauculo croco, vinumque purum sorbeant post lactucam, neque ultra horam lucubrent. Cum- 5 que se dormitum conferunt, confectionem eiusmodi sumant, in qua seminis papaveris albi unciae duae sint, seminis lactucae uncia una, amomi, croci, scilicet utriusque pars drachmae dimidia, sacchari unciae sex. Dilue et coque omnia simul syrupo papaveris. Edant huius drachmas duas, simulque nonnihil syrupi papaveris gustent aut vini. Illinias eis frontem temporaque oleo 10 ex violis et ex nenufare, adiecta camphora, item lacte oleoque amygdalino atque violaceo. Odorem croci et camphorae putaminumque dulcis mali naribus admovebis, aceti insuper modici, sed aquae rosaceae plurimae. Sternes quoque lectum plantarum foliis frigidarum. Aures gravibus cantibus sonisque de-

---

add. et z   39 sandali] coandali z   44 multam z   49 rosarum] citri rosarumque *e*   53 Quamvis ex Quanquam *corr.* L²   hab tur x   54 Ac] At *ABDRz*   timeatur] teneatur G   violaceam z
  De nimia vigilia] Emaciantis vigiliae remedia z   4-5 una cum—lactucam *desunt in e*   5 Cumque] Cum x   7 sunt B   scilicet *om.* B   11 neufare x   13 admovebimus *DR*   Sternes] Senes z   14 *post* lectum *add.* herba B   gravibus] suavibus z

things in rose-, lemon-, and citron-water in which red-hot gold and silver have been extinguished; boil it all gently. Finally, add one dram apiece of cinnamon, red ben, red sandal, and red coral, one-half dram apiece of the brightest pearls, saffron, and raw scarlet silk which has been pounded up very fine, twelve grains apiece of gold and silver, and one-third dram apiece of jacinth, emerald, sapphire, and carbuncle. But if anyone does not have gold, silver, amber, musk, and precious stones, these confections can be of much help even without them.

Of these confections I single out three in particular: the one of Mesue which I have listed and the two of our own which we have just described. We have sufficiently expounded above how they should be used. But if anyone should desire something simpler, though still suitable for all, he should pound a completely ripe, completely intact citron and boil it with a large application of sugar and rose-juice. He should either season it, when boiled, with a moderate amount of cinnamon and saffron; or use an aromatic rose-spice tempered in the following way: take one ounce of aromatic rose-spice and two ounces apiece of rose-sugar and diabugloss-sugar; or let him similarly mix in diamusk. Although these two electuaries are not simple, they can still be obtained easily enough. But if you are worried about heat, add diaprunes and violet-sugar.

On Excessive Sleeplessness.

Chap. XXIV

It often happens to melancholics, especially to those who are learned, that when their brain has been dried out with long bouts of sleeplessness, they become thin. Since nothing increases the evils of black bile more than long bouts of sleeplessness, every effort must be made against this great evil. Therefore they should eat lettuce after other foods, together with a moderate amount of bread and a little saffron, drink pure wine after the lettuce and not study late. Whenever they are ready to sleep, let them take the following confection, in which there are two ounces of white poppy seed, one ounce of lettuce seed, one-half dram apiece of amomum and saffron, and six ounces of sugar. Dilute and boil them all in poppy-syrup. Let them eat two drams of it and at the same time drink some poppy-syrup or wine. You should smear their brows and temples with the oil of violets and of water-lilies ["nenufare"] (having added to them camphor, likewise milk and the oil of almonds and of violets). You will apply to their noses the scent of saffron, camphor, and the peel of a sweet apple, some vinegar in addition, but much rose-water. Strew their beds with the leaves of cold plants. Soothe their ears with low songs and sounds. Often moisten

linies. Humectabis saepe caput eiusmodi lavacris, scilicet aqua in qua cocta
sint frusta papaveris, lactuca, portulaca, malva, rosarum, vitis, salicis arundinumque folia, addita camomilla. Balneis quoque dulcibus ex rebus eiusmodi saepe tibia bracchiaque, saepe totum corpus est humectandum. Lac insuper bibere mixtum saccharo scilicet stomacho vacuo, si modo stomachus optime toleraverit, maxime prodest. Humida haec melancholicis etiam, si satis dormiant, mirifice conferunt. Memento lac amygdalinum mensae familiarissimum esse debere.

De hebetudine atque oblivione.

Cap. XXV.

Accidit vero nonnunquam ut studiosis, vel quia sedulo inclinato capite legant scribantve, vel quia otio nimio torpeant, pituita quaedam viscosior una cum frigida nimis melancholia caput occupans gravet, atque hebetes obliviososque efficiat. His ergo caput exonerandum est iis remediis, quae alias diximus pituitae convenire. Sin minus illa suffecerint, ad pilulas Indas et cocchias hieralogodionque confugito; praeterea ad hieram diacoloquintidos vel Archigenis vel Andromachi vel Theodotionis aut ad pilulas Iudaei, quas Mesues in capitulo De capitis dolore describit. Quod si natura aetasve frigidior sit, nec aestas obstiterit, post purgationem utere confectione illa anacardina quam Mesues sapientium confectionem nominat in *Antidotario;* rursus anacardina illa quam in capitulo De oblivione ex sententia filii Zachariae recenset. Da summo mane drachmam unam, sed qui eam sumit, ab ira, coitu, ebrietate, labore rebusque calidis eo die prorsus abstineat. Haec quidem adversus hebetudinem oblivionemque valentissima sunt.

At vero si familiaria magis optes, da zinziber saccharo conditum, sed modico thure mixtum, quod sensibus et memoriae magnopere prodest, praesertim his adiectis: scilicet melle anacardi, melle chebularum, acoris, ciperis, ambra, musco. Prodest etiam diambra, plisarchoticon, diacori, sed haec ore diutius retinenda, naribus etiam et auribus infundenda. Odor quoque thuris, amaraci, marathri, nucis muscatae, rutae, gariophylorum prodest non mediocriter. Memento tamen theriacam in his atque similibus, quemadmodum ab initio diximus, nulli unquam remedio postponendam. Praeterea hebetibus obliviosisque tempora et cervicem unctione eiusmodi unge: sume olei sambu-

---

16 frustra *BDGR*　　lactuca portulaca malva] lactucae portulacae malvae *z*
　　De hebetudine atque oblivione] Memoriae hebetis atque oblivionis remedia *z*　　1 vero *om. D*　　3 frigidae *z*　　melancholica *x*　　6 hieram] iaram *z*　　7 theodonis *DR*　　8 frigior *z*　　15 optet *z*　　saccharo *om. z*　　modico *om. e*　　17 anachardino *x*　　18 pliris sarcoticon *z*

their heads with these baths, namely water in which the following have been boiled: bits of poppy; lettuce; purslain; mallows; and leaves of roses, of grapevine, of willow, and of reeds; with the addition of camomile. The legs, the arms, and the entire body should often be moistened by sweet baths composed of such things. It is especially good to drink milk mixed with sugar on an empty stomach, provided that the stomach can tolerate it. These moist things are of great advantage to melancholics, even if they get enough sleep. Remember that almond milk ought to be most familiar on the dining-table.

On Dullness and Forgetfulness.

Chap. XXV

It sometimes happens to learned people (either because they read or write continually with their heads bowed, or because they are sluggish through excessive inactivity) that a rather viscous phlegm, together with a very cold melancholy, fills up and weighs down their heads, making them dull and forgetful. Therefore their heads must be relieved by those remedies which we said elsewhere are good against phlegm. But if they are not sufficient, resort to Indian pills, pills of cochee, and hieralogodion, moreover to the hiera of diacoloquintida, of Archigenes, of Andromachus, or of Theodotion[1]; or resort to the pills of the Jew[2] which Mesue describes in his chapter on headaches.[3] But if the patient's nature or age is rather cold, and summer does not preclude it, use after purgation that confection anacardina which Mesue in his book *On Antidotes* calls the confection of the wise,[4] or that anacardina which he recounts in his chapter on forgetfulness according to the opinion of the son of Zacharias.[5] Give one dram of it very early in the morning, but let the person who takes it altogether abstain that day from anger, coitus, drunkenness, labor, and hot things. These remedies are very good against dullness and forgetfulness.

But if you desire ingredients more familiar, give ginger seasoned with sugar and mixed with a little frankincense. This is very good for the senses and memory, especially if you add honey of cashews, honey of chebule myrobalans, sweet flags, galingales ["cyperos," possibly, as Fr. glosses, *herbe Indianne*], amber and musk. Diambra, plisarchoticon, and diacoron are also good, but they must be held rather long in the mouth and poured into the nose and ears. The smell of incense, marjoram, fennel, nutmeg, rue, and clove is also quite good. Nevertheless, remember that in these and similar matters, as we have said from the first, theriac should never take second place to any remedy. Moreover, anoint the temples and neck of dull and forgetful men with the fol-

cini unciam unam, olei de been uncias duas, euphorbii unciam dimidiam, castorei quoque tantundem. Perfricabis bracchia, crura cervicemque vehe- 25 menter, ac si opus fuerit, cervici cucurbitulas admovebis. Verticem praeterea capitis amaraco, thure, nuce muscata tunsis operies atque fovebis.

Corporeum quidem spiritum cura; incorporeum vero cole;
veritatem denique venerare.
Primum medicina praestat, secundum disciplina
moralis, tertium vero religio.

Cap. XXVI.

Si homines veritatis cupidi tanta medicorum diligentia corporeum spiritum curare debent, ne forte omnino neglectus vel impedimento sit, vel inepte serviat quaerentibus veritatem, multo proculdubio diligentius incorporeum spiritum, id est intellectum ipsum, disciplinae moralis institutis colere decet, quo solo veritas ipsa, cum sit incorporea, capitur. Nefas enim est so- 5 lum animi servum, id est corpus, colere, animum vero, corporis dominum regemque, negligere, praesertim cum Magorum Platonisque sententia sit, corpus totum ab animo ita pendere ut, nisi animus bene valuerit, corpus bene valere non possit. Quapropter medicinae auctor Apollo non Hippocratem, quamvis ex sua stirpe genitum, sed Socratem sapientissimum iudicavit, 10 quippe cum quantum Hippocrates corpori, tantum Socrates animo sanando studuerit, quanquam quod tentaverant illi, solus Christus effecit.

Proinde si mentem nostram optimis colere moribus a Socrate idcirco iubemur, ut lucem veritatemque a nobis naturae instinctu quaesitam serena mente facilius assequamur, quanto magis veritatem ipsam divinam imprimis 15 religione sancta fas est venerari? Ad quam quaerendam capiendamque non aliter creata mens est quam oculus ad lumen solis perspiciendum. Atque ut Plato noster inquit, quemadmodum visus nihil usquam visibile perspicit, nisi in ipso summi visibilis, id est solis ipsius splendore, ita neque intellectus humanus intelligibile quicquam apprehendit, nisi in ipso intelligibilis summi, 20 hoc est Dei lumine nobis semper et ubique praesente—in lumine, inquam, quod illuminat omnem hominem venientem in hunc mundum; in lumine de quo canit David: "In lumine tuo videbimus lumen."

---

24 de been *z*; deben *LDGwxy*; debem *ABR*
    Corporeum ... cura ... cole ... venerare] Quod corporeum ... curare debemus (debeamus *y*) ... colere ... venerari *xy*   *Corporeum—religio]* Spirituum custodiae nos intentos esse debere *z*   *Corporeum— Cap.XXVI]* Exhortatio ad moralem et contemplativam religiosamque vitam *M; Marsilius Ficinus amicis suis s. d. add. in marg. M*   3 servias *z*   5 Nefas enim] Neque enim fas *z*   6 animi *x*   12 temptaverant *BDR*   illi *om. A* efficit *D*   13 si *om. z*   21 in lumine inquam *om. A*

lowing ointment: take one ounce of elder-oil, two ounces of ben-oil, one-half ounce of oil of euphorbea and castor-oil. Rub the arms, legs, and neck strongly, and, if necessary, apply cupping-glasses to the neck. Cover and foment the top of the head with brayed marjoram, frankincense, and nutmeg.

Care for the Corporeal Spirit; Cultivate the Incorporeal; and Lastly, Venerate the Truth. Medicine Takes Care of the First, Moral Discipline, the Second, but Religion, the Third.

Chap. XXVI

If lovers of truth ought to care for the corporeal spirit with such great efforts of doctors lest it either, if entirely neglected, prove a hindrance in their pursuit of truth, or else serve them inadequately, then no doubt they must try still harder to cultivate with the teachings of moral philosophy the incorporeal spirit, i.e., the intellect, by which alone truth, being itself incorporeal, is apprehended. For it is wrong to cherish only the slave of the soul, the body, and to neglect the soul, the lord and ruler of the body, especially since the Magi and Plato[1] assert that the entire body depends upon the soul in such a way that if the soul is not well, the body cannot be well. This is why Apollo, the founder of medicine, decided the wisest man was not Hippocrates, though born of his own race, but Socrates, since, while Hippocrates strove to heal the body, Socrates strove to heal the soul.[2] But Christ alone accomplished what those men attempted.

Thus, if we are enjoined by Socrates to cultivate our mind by behaving in the best way to the end that with a serene mind we may the more easily acquire the light and truth which we sought by the instinct of nature,[3] how much more is it right to venerate above all that divine truth by holy religion? The mind was created for seeking and receiving it no less than the eye was created for beholding the light of the Sun. And as my author Plato says, just as the eyesight nowhere sees anything visible except in the radiance of the highest thing visible, that is, the Sun itself, so the human intellect apprehends nothing intelligible, except in the light of the highest thing intelligible,[4] that is, in the light of God, which is always and everywhere present for us — in the light, I say, which lights every man coming into this world, in the light of which David sings, "in your light shall we see light."[5]

Profecto quemadmodum purgatis oculis inque lumen ipsum aspicientibus subito splendor eius infunditur, coloribus figurisque rerum abunde refulgens, ita cum primum ab omnibus corporis perturbationibus per moralem disciplinam purgata mens est, atque in divinam veritatem, id est Deum ipsum, religioso quodam flagrantissimoque amore directa, subito, ut divinus inquit Plato, divina menti veritas influit, rationesque rerum veras, quae in ipsa continentur quibusve omnia constant, feliciter explicat; quantoque mentem circumfundit lumine, tanto simul et voluntatem gaudio beate perfundit.

FINIS

---

29 rerum *om. z*   31 quanto *M*
FINIS] om. BDRM; primi libri *add. y; LIBRI I. FINIS z*

Just as when the eyes have been purged and are looking at the light itself, suddenly its radiance pours in, reflecting abundantly from colors and shapes of things, so, as soon as the mind is purged of all fleshly perturbations through moral discipline and is directed towards divine truth (i.e., God himself) through a religious and burning love, suddenly (as the divine Plato says) truth from the divine mind flows in and productively unfolds the true reasons of things — reasons which are contained in it [i.e., in the divine mind, see 3.1] and by which all things remain in existence. And the more it surrounds the mind with light, the more it also blessedly fills the will with joy.[6]

THE END

Prooemium in Librum De Vita Longa

Marsilius Ficinus Florentinus Philippo Valori, civi optimo atque nobilissimo, S.D. Quanquam Plato noster genio suo vivit, et victurus est (ut arbitror) dum mundus ipse vivet, meus me tamen genius huc semper impellit, ut post divinum cultum ante omnia Platonis vitae prospiciam. Ad hoc ipsum iamdiu nobis aspirat prae ceteris Medica domus. Ad idem conspiras et tu, mi Valor, Medicum amicissimus et Platonicae gloriae atque disciplinae admodum studiosus. Quam ergo vitam Platoni semper exopto, eandem opto Medicibus similemque Valori. Quamobrem hortor et obsecro te, mi Valor, ut quanta semper opera gloriae Platonicae faves, tanta aliquando diligentia praecepta haec nostra de vita producenda legas atque serves. Quibus diu vivens resurgenti nuper disciplinae Platonis diutius una cum magnanimo Laurentio Medice patrocinari possis. Vale.

Prooemium—Longa] Marsili Ficini Florentini in librum secundum De vita longa (producenda *z*) ad Philippum Valorem Epistolare prooemium *xyz*   1-2 Marsilius—S.D. *desunt in z*

Proem to the Book "On a Long Life."

Marsilio Ficino of Florence sends greetings to Filippo Valori, her most upright and her noblest citizen.[1] Although my author Plato lives through his own genius, and will live, I judge, so long as this world lives, nevertheless my genius always impels me, after the honor of God, to take his life under my care. To this very purpose the house of the Medici above all others has long bestowed its favor on me. You also, my Valori, have likewise joined your favor to theirs, being yourself a close friend of the Medici and completely devoted to the glory of Plato and to his philosophy. This is why the life that I always covet for Plato, I desire also for the Medici and for Valori. Hence I urge and beseech you, dear Valori, that with the great pains with which you always promote Plato's glory, you should someday with equal zeal read and heed these precepts of mine on prolonging life. I urge you to live long through these precepts so that you may join with the magnanimous Lorenzo de' Medici [see Gen. Proem] in supporting for a longer time the now resurgent philosophy of Plato. Farewell.

Marsilii Ficini Florentini Liber De Vita Longa

Ad perfectionem scientiae necessaria est vita longa,
quam etiam diligentia praestat.

Cap. I.

Ad artem scientiamque perfectam non tam vel docilitas ingenii vel memoriae firmitas quam prudentis iudicii perspicacia nos perducit. Iudicium vero propter ambiguitatem ex coniecturarum diversitate conceptam adeo difficile est, ut experimento sit necessario confirmandum. Experimentum quoque fallax tum propter iudicii ipsius difficultatem, tum propter fugacem opportuni in experimento captando temporis brevitatem. Quibus sane de causis artem esse longam una cum Hippocrate recte concludimus, nec posse nos eam nisi vitae longitudine consequi. Vitam vero longam non solum ab initio semel fata promittunt, sed nostra etiam diligentia praestat. Quod et astrologi confitentur, ubi de electionibus et imaginibus agunt, et medicorum cura diligens experientiaque confirmat. Qua quidem providentia non solum homines natura validi saepissime, sed etiam valetudinarii vitam longam aliquando consequuntur, ut non mirum sit Herodicum quendam litterarum studiosum, omnium sui temporis infirmissimum (ut Plato Aristotelesque testantur), eiusmodi providentia annum fere centesimum implevisse. Plutarchus praeterea narrat multos, corpore alioquin parum firmo, vitam sola diligentia longam consecutos. Mitto impraesentia quot imbecillos ipse noverim prudentiae munere robustissimorum annos superavisse. Neque igitur inutile fuerit, neque vanum, post librum *De curanda valetudine litteratorum* a nobis compositum, praecepta quaedam insuper ingeniis scientiae cupidis ad vitam longam conducentia tradere. Instituta vero haec nec inertibus ignavisque communicari volumus. Quid enim cupiamus istos diu vivere, qui nec vivunt quidem, quasi fucos nutriamus, non apes? Nec hominibus divulgari perdita voluptatum libidine dissolutis, qui brevem quotidie voluptatem longe stulti praeponunt; nec improbis iniquisque patefieri, quorum vita mors est bonorum; sed viris duntaxat prudentibus atque temperatis, solertis ingenii viribus humano generi vel privatim vel publice profuturis.

Liber De Vita Longa] Medici atque Philosophi insignis De vita producenda sive longa, Liber II. *z* post *Longa* add. incipit *y*
    Ad] Quod ad *y*   sit *y*   *etiam om. z*   2 indicii *L*   7 recte *add. L^2*   14 et Aristoteles *z*   15 fere *om.* Lw^{ac}; *add. L^2*   15-18 Plutarchus—superavisse *add. L^2*   16 vita *z*   17 imbecilles *z*   20 ingenii *z*   21 inertibus] in itineribus *z*   22 cupiamus] conemur *L*   23-25 Nec hominibus—praeponunt *add. in marg. L^2*   24 longe] longae vitae *z*   25 iniquisque *om. L*   26 prudentibus—viribus *om. L*

The Book of Marsilio Ficino the Florentine "On a Long Life."

To Perfect Your Knowledge, You Need a Long Life; One Way to Procure It Is by Effort.
Chap. I

Neither a teachable intelligence nor firmness of memory leads us to perfect skill and knowledge so much as does the discrimination of a prudent judgment. But judgment, because of the ambiguity created by the diversity of conjectures, is so difficult that it must be confirmed by the requisite experience. Experience is also deceptive both because of the difficulty of judgment itself and because of the fleeting brevity of the opportune time for apprehending the experience. This is why we are certainly right to conclude with Hippocrates that art is long and we can only attain it by a long life.[1] But a long life is not just something the fates promise once for all from the beginning, but something that is procured by our effort. This is both acknowledged by astrologers, when they deal with elections and images, and confirmed by the careful concern and the experience of physicians. Through this foresight not only do people who are strong by nature very often attain a long life but also sometimes the weakest, so that it is not surprising that a man named Herodicus, as Plato and Aristotle declare, a scholar and the feeblest of all the men of his age, by foresight of this sort lived to be almost a hundred.[2] Plutarch reports that many people who were otherwise physically infirm have attained a long life just by taking care of themselves.[3] I pass over for now the many sickly people I myself know of who have lived longer than the strongest people by the gift of prudence. It would therefore be profitable and fruitful, after the book I composed *On Caring for the Health of Learned People,* to put forward besides, for minds that are yearning for knowledge, some precepts conducive to a long life. But I have no wish to impart these instructions to indolent and lazy people. For why should we wish those people to live long who do not even live, as if we were nourishing drones and not bees? Nor do I wish them to be divulged to people who are dissolute through their corrupt passion for pleasures, fools who far prefer the brief pleasure that lasts only a day; nor disclosed to the wicked and unjust whose life is the death of good men; but only to prudent and temperate people of sophisticated intelligence who will benefit mankind, whether in the private or the public sphere.

Vitalis calor nutritur humore, quo deficiente fit resolutio,
quo excedente fit suffocatio.

Cap. II.

Vita quidem tanquam lumen in naturali calore consistit, caloris vero pabulum est humor aerius atque pinguis quasi oleum. Sive igitur humor eiusmodi forte deficiat, sive prorsus excedat vel inquinetur, calor statim debilitatur et tandem debilitatus extinguitur. Si humoris defectu calor debilitatur et perditur, mors resolutione contingit; si potius obruitur humoris excessu 5
vel vitio, vita suffocatione perit. Suffocatio vero humoris cuiuslibet exundantia vel putrefactione contingit, praesertim pituita vel excrescente vel quomodolibet putrefacta, ut non immerito pituita petens vitam fuerit nominata. Praecepta igitur ad producendam vitam maxime necessaria, hinc quidem resolutionem, inde vero suffocationem putrefactionemque aeque devitant—aeque, 10
inquam, ratione communi. Nam si calidiorem siccioremve hominem forte curant, et cui meatus quidem aperti sunt, humores autem spiritusque subtiles resolutioni magis occurrunt. Sin autem contraria ratione corpus affectum tractant, potius suffocationi subveniunt. Maxime vero in alterutro student, si ad alterutrum locus tempusve declinet. At ubi ingeniosis studiosisque consu- 15
lit, utrunque praeceptum ferme est pariter necessarium, in utroque similiter laboratur. His enim acutum quidem calidumque ingenium et imaginationis motus assiduus resolutionem, otium vero corporis atque cruditas suffocationem minitari videtur. Nusquam igitur medici vehementius quam in eiusmodi hominum curatione laborant. Etsi tota libri superioris disputatio ad 20
prorogandam vitam maxime confert, propriam tamen quandam res tanta curam, qualem deinceps quoad potero paucis comprehendam, postulare videtur.

Quomodo temperandus calor ad humorem
atque vicissim quodam Minervae consilio.

Cap. III.

Ceterum dum oleum istud pingue, igneo huic vigori nostro necessarium, pingui Minerva tractamus, Minerva interim olivifera, olei vitalis origo,

---

Vitalis calor nutritur] Quod vitalis calor nutriatur *y*   *Vitalis — suffocatio]* Vitalem calorem nutriri humore, citius ultra citraque excessu fieri corruptionem dissolutionemque *z*   1 tanquam lumen *add. L²*   2 quasi oleum *add. L²*   3-4 statim debilitatur et tandem] naturalis statim *z*   7 quodlibet *L;* corr. *L²*
11 forte *add. L²*

Totum tertium capitulum deest in L   *Quomodo — vicissim]* Quomodo sunt temperandi calor et humor *z*

*The Vital Heat Is Nourished by Radical Moisture;
Too Little of It Causes Resolution, Too Much, Suffocation.*

Chap. II

Life, just like light, consists of natural heat, but the sustenance of heat is an airy and rich moisture, like oil. If, then, this radical moisture should give out, become excessive, or acquire impurities, the heat is immediately weakened and finally, being weakened, is extinguished. If the heat is weakened by a lack of radical moisture and is lost, death by resolution results; but if it is overwhelmed by an excess of, or fault in, the radical moisture, life perishes by suffocation. Suffocation is something that results from the overabundance or putrefaction of any humor, especially from the immoderate increase or putrefaction in some way of phlegm, so that phlegm has not without cause been called "the attacker of life" ["petens vitam"]. This is why precepts which are very necessary for prolonging life avoid equally both resolution on the one hand and suffocation and putrefaction on the other—equally, I say, meaning by a common method. For if they happen to attend a person who is hotter and drier, whose passages are open, the humors and subtle spirits run a greater risk of resolution. But if they treat a sick body by an opposite method, they increase the likelihood of suffocation. They are most careful about either danger if the place or time is tending to it. But when one is caring for the intellectual and learned, one precept is just as necessary as the other; pains are taken similarly for both. For their sharp and hot intelligence and the constant activity of their imagination seem to threaten them with resolution, but their body's inactivity and indigestion seem to threaten them with suffocation. Hence there is no case in which physicians labor harder than in the care of such people. Although the entire argument of the preceding book is very helpful for preserving life, nevertheless, such an important topic seems to demand special attention, which I will now express in a few words to the best of my ability.

*How Radical Heat and Moisture Must be Proportioned
to One Another by a Plan of Minerva's.*

Chap. III

But while we are discussing clumsily [lit. "with a fat Minerva," idiom] that rich oil which is necessary for this fiery vigor of ours, in the meantime Minerva—bearing an olive, the source of vital oil, and born, of course, from

almi videlicet Iovis capite nata, ridet quod sui muneris quantitatem plane cernentes, interea non satis vidimus qualitatem. Ridens ergo, "vobis," inquit, "oleum non modo quantum sat flammae nutriendae foret, abunde dedi, sed etiam sine amurca sincerum infundi lucernae." Haec illa. Nos autem inter loquendum errantes offendimus, quoniam lucerna pedibus nostris verbum suum nondum nobis auditum. Ex hac ergo lucerna discamus, oleum iugiter flammae subministrandum ea scilicet diligentia, ut nec repentina quadam lumen obruamus illuvione, nec rursum differamus sitibundo potum. Sed haec quidem duo satis in superioribus tractata putamus. Reliqua nobis duo sunt, quorum alterum leviter tetigisse, alterum vix attigisse videmur, tangentes interim ita Palladem, ut ridere nunquam solita nos rideret. Quid ergo? Primo quidem considerabimus flammam vel pauculam esse prorsus edacem, ideoque lucernam illam lucere diutius, in qua sic flammula est ad ellychnium, id est lucinium, temperata, ut non ebibat oleum, sed pitisset. Itaque et nos in omni diaeta cavebimus, ne quando, praesertim in iuventute, nimium invalescat insitus ignis suapte natura vorax. Sat vero fuerit tum humorem inundantem, tum penetrabile frigus hinc arcere. Deinde lucernam cogitabimus frequenter extingui, quando non sincerum oleum instillaverit, sed (ut ita dixerim) amurcosum. Unde paulo post concrescunt ex amurca fungi, lumenque extinguunt. Iam vero nos almum a Pallade suscepimus oleum, scilicet aerium quam plurimum purumque, et nativo quodam lentore tenax atque firmum. Quod ergo huic paulatim absumpto subgeritur, non solum huic aequale debet esse, sed simile. Ut vero sit simile, non tantum aerium esse debet et pingue, sed penitus ab amurca secretum, id est a faece quadam ex terra et aqua crassiore congesta. Hanc ergo congestionem faecemque vitaturi, alimenta eiusmodi fugiamus et otium et cruditatem atque sordes. Interea vero Minervam ea moderatione colamus, ut caput quidem, de quo nata est ipsa, nobis augeat, nervos autem stomachumque non minuat.

---

6 infudi *z*   10 illivione *wy*   rursus *z*   11 tactata *z*   22 alumnum *z*

BOOK TWO   CHAP. III   **171**

father Jupiter's head — is laughing because, although we clearly see the quantity of her gift, we do not sufficiently see its quality. And so she laughs and says, "To you I have given oil not only in an abundance sufficient to feed a flame, but also I have poured it into your lamp pure without dregs." So she speaks. But I, in my wandering speech, have bumped into something because the "lamp unto our feet" is her "word"[1] which I have not yet heard. From this lamp therefore let us learn that oil must be given to the flame always with careful attention in order neither to overwhelm the light by a sudden gush, nor, on the other hand, to put off giving drink to the wick when it is thirsty. But these two considerations have, I believe, been sufficiently discussed in the foregoing. Two considerations remain to me, the first of which I seem to have touched upon lightly, the other scarcely touched at all, while touching Pallas in such a way that she who never used to laugh, laughed at me. Well then, I will first consider that even a very small flame is truly voracious and, therefore, that that lamp will shine longer, in which a little flame is so limited to the wick like a glowworm that it does not drink up the oil but tastes it sputteringly.[2] Therefore we will take care in every diet at any time, especially in youth, to keep the inborn fire, voracious by its own nature, from becoming too strong. It would be sufficient to ward off now the superabundant moisture, now the penetrating cold. Secondly, we will consider that the lamp is often extinguished when an oil which is not pure, but, so to speak, full of dregs, has dripped in. And consequently a little later the snuff grows from the dregs and quenches the light. But now we have already [i.e., from our birth] received an oil which is the foster-child of Pallas, as airy as possible, pure, and by a natural viscosity steadfast and firm. Therefore whatever we add to this when it has been consumed little by little must be not only equal to it in amount but similar in quality. But in order to be similar, it must be not only airy and rich, but completely devoid of dregs, that is, of an impurity which collects from earth and a too-dense water. Therefore, in order to avoid this congestion and impurity, let us avoid foods of this sort, and idleness, indigestion, and filth. But meanwhile let us serve Minerva with such moderation that she may enlarge our head, the part of the body from which she herself was born, but that she may not diminish our sinews[3] and our stomach.

*Quibus de causis arescit humor naturalis,
vel peregrinus exundat, et quam
necessaria sit ad vitam perfecta digestio.*

Cap. IV.

Naturalem humorem velociter haec exsiccant: sanguinis fluxus uberior, violenta solutio ventris, diu lubricus alvus, profusus sudor, latius patefacti meatus, coitus ad debilitatem factus, sitis anhela, fames crucians, vigilia longa, usus calidarum rerum simul atque siccarum, laboriosus animi corporisque motus, anxietas, ira, dolor, siccior simul atque ferventior aer, praesertim igne calescens, ventus aridior et violentus atque diuturnus. Humorem supra modum augent his contraria. Ebrietas frequens utrunque facit, nimio enim tum calore siccat, tum humore suffocat ebriosum. Nihil autem magis quam cruditas ad utrunque nocet, ubi enim non concoquitur alimentum, hinc quidem deest quo naturalem irriges humorem, inde vero putrefactum superest, quod exundans calorem obruat naturalem. Quamobrem Avicenna corrumpi sanguinem inquit, ubi digestio ipsa corrumpitur, secutusque Galienum appellat digestionem vitae radicem. Optima igitur est et quasi unica haec regula Galieni: concoctionem cibi prae ceteris ubique curare. Nam quod maximum videtur esse praeceptum, salubribus videlicet uti, nihil proderit, nisi coquas, siquidem ex his ferme sicut ex contrariis noxius humor profluit, si cruda membris influxerint. Ex cibis autem etiam minus arte laudatis, saepe minus malum accipitur nutrimentum, si vehementius concoquantur. Cruditatem igitur tanquam gravem resolutionis simul et suffocationis causam diligentissime devitemus, quantitate videlicet cibi potusque nobis accommodata, qualitate, simplicitate, praeparatione, contritione, ieiunio revocante famem ac, si opus fuerit, stomachi etiam exteriore fomento, rebusque quibusdam stypticis post epulas intus assumptis. Caveamusque diligenter ne cibum potus exsuperet, neu cibus sit liquidior aut durior, aut hic vel ille valde sit actu frigidus, aut alimenta sint longe diversa, aut crudum addamus crudo; haec enim concoctionem magnopere prohibent. Caveamus insuper diligentissime ne vel coitu statim post cibum, vel somno meridiano saepius non necessario, vel nocturna vigilia, vel labore animi ullo sive corporis importuno, vel alio quopiam pacto digestionem impediamus. Digestionem dico equidem non primam tantum,

---

Quibus — exundat] Arescentis humidi naturalis et alieni exuberantis causae *z*   arescat *y*   *et om. x*
2 lubrica *z*,   4 praecalidarum *z*   6 diurnus *z*   10 irriget *xz*   11–13 Quamobrem — radicem *add.*
*in marg. L*²   14 cibi] sibi *z*   17 etiam] et *L*   19 resolutioni *L*   24 neve *z*

*The Causes of the Drying up of the Natural Moisture
or the Overabundance of Moisture from Outside,
and How Necessary to Life Is a Perfect Digestion.*
Chap. IV

The things which quickly dry up the natural moisture are as follows: a too plentiful flow of blood, a violent loosening of the bowels, a long bout of diarrhea, excessive perspiration, passages too widely opened, intercourse to the point of weakness, panting thirst, grievous hunger, long periods of wakefulness, the combined use of hot things and dry things, the laborious movement of mind and body, anxiety, anger, sorrow, air which is too dry as well as too hot (especially one heated with a fire), and a dry and blustery wind of long duration. The opposite things immoderately increase the moisture. Frequent drunkenness does both, for it dries up the inebriate with too much heat and suffocates him with moisture. But nothing is so harmful in both directions as indigestion, since, when food is not digested, that material disappears with which you should nourish the natural moisture, and on the other hand the putrefied food remains in abundance and overwhelms the natural heat. This is why Avicenna says that the blood is corrupted when the digestion itself is corrupted;[1] and, following Galen, he calls digestion the root of life. This rule of Galen, therefore, is the best and practically unparalleled: to care for the digestion of food before everything else.[2] For that precept which seems to be the greatest — to take wholesome food — will do no good unless you digest it, since indeed a noxious moisture pours forth from these almost as much as from foods which are unwholesome, if they flow into the members undigested. But even from those foods which are less praised by my profession, often good nourishment is received if they are digested very actively. Let us then most carefully avoid indigestion as a serious cause of both resolution and suffocation, namely, by a quantity of food and drink which is suitable for us, by its quality, simplicity, preparation, grinding, by fasting which restrains hunger, and, if necessary, even by an exterior fomentation of the stomach and by certain astringent things taken internally after foods. And let us take great care that the drink does not exceed the food and that the food is not too moist or hard, that neither food nor drink is very conducive to cold, that the foods are not very diverse or that we do not add undigested food onto undigested food, for these things greatly impede digestion. Let us also be very careful not to hinder digestion by having intercourse immediately after eating, by too frequent unnecessary midday naps, by staying awake at night, by any unsuitable labor of mind or body, or by any other means. By digestion I mean not only the first stage,

quae fit in stomacho, sed secundam etiam quae fit in iecore, tertiam insuper 30
quae in venis, quartam denique quae in membris efficitur. Quae longo quodam indigent intervallo, et quavis impedita pabulum non suppeditatur humori.
   Proinde sicut digestionem, sic excrementorum purgationem adiuvare imprimis necessarium est ad vitam. Necessarium sordes etiam a cute detergere.
Necessarius est motus corporis tam continuus, tam temperatus, tam varius 35
quam coelestium aerisque motus et ignis et aquae, servata duntaxat concoctionis et somni necessitate, defatigatione vero et resolutione vitata. Praeterea
sub umbra situm cariemque obducimus. Sub divo, sub lumine vivimus, quod
pater meus Ficinus, insignis medicus, frequenter habebat in ore. Sed ad haec
feliciter peragenda operae pretium foret, non tam urbanis negotiis quam rus- 40
ticis quibusdam exercitationibus a tenera statim aetate corpus assuefecisse, et
quodammodo similibus, interdum etiam nutrimentis, et vitae genus quodammodo varium tenuisse; quod me saepe prudens ille monebat. Qui enim in
omni aetate lautissima quadam curiositate vivunt, saepe minus tuti vivunt;
qui vero adolescentes se minus assuefecerint, adulti saltem assuefaciant, cau- 45
tioribus tamen gradibus id tentantes.

*Sanguis et humor accommodatus vitae aerius esse debet,
qualitate temperatus, substantia medius atque tenax.*

Cap. V.

Graeci omnes inter praecepta ad diuturnam vitam maxime necessaria
mandant ut euchimis alamur. Euchima vocamus alimenta salubria,
quae bonum afferunt nutrimentum, id est, sanguinem bonum. Bonum vero
sanguinem appellamus non frigidum, non siccum, non turbulentum, sed
calidum et humidum atque clarum — calidum quidem calore non acri, humi- 5
dum vero humore non aqueo, clarum quoque, nec tamen interea tenuissimum. Iam vero ferventior sanguis naturalem tum calorem exacuit, tum
exsiccat humorem, et quem ipse humorem infert vel calorem resolubilem
praestat atque fugacem. Sanguis praeterea humidior proniorque ad aquam
naturalem obtundit calorem, humorem quoque naturalem vel hebetat, vel 10
impellit sub calore liquescere, vel suffocat humiditate calorem; et omnino si
qua portio naturalis humoris ex aqueo sanguine trahitur, tum putrescit facile, tum cito diffluit atque dissolvitur. Hinc efficitur ut qui molliores fructus
herbasque comedunt, nisi raro forsan et pro medicina tunc ventrem leniente

---

32 indiget *x*   suppeditat *x*   34 *post* etiam *add.* est *L*   43 saepe prudens ille monebat] saepius ille prudens manebat *z*   44 aetati *z*   46 gradibus] et paulatim *z*
   Quod sanguis ... debeat *y*   6 nec *add.* L^2 13–17 Hinc efficitur — miscentur *add. in marg.* L^2

which takes place in the stomach, but also the second, which takes place in the liver, the third, in the veins, and the fourth, in the bodily parts. These processes require a long interval and when any one of them is interrupted, nourishment is not supplied to the radical moisture.

Just as this moisture was vitally necessary to help digestion, so it is to help the purgation of excrement. It is also necessary to cleanse filth from the skin. Another thing that we need is motion of the body, as continuous, moderate, and varied as the motion of the heavenly bodies, and of air, fire, and water, provided that we preserve the necessity of digestion and sleep and avoid fatigue and resolution. Moreover, we conceal filth and decay beneath the shade; under the light and the sky we live; so my father Ficino the distinguished doctor always used to say. But in order to accomplish these things successfully, it would be worthwhile to accustom the body right from youth not so much to urban occupations as to rustic exercises and similar things, and meanwhile to maintain a somewhat varied kind of nourishment and life-style, as my father prudently used to advise me. For people who live all their lives in elegant fastidiousness often live less safely. But those who as young men have not accustomed themselves to them, at least let them do so when older, but by trying it in cautious steps.

To Be Suitable for Life, Blood and Moisture Must Be Airy, Tempered in Quality, Moderate and Firm in Substance.
Chap. V

Among their precepts which are particularly necessary for long life, all the Greeks order us to live on *euchima*.[1] We call *euchima* wholesome foods that impart good nourishment, which is to say, good blood. We call that blood good which is neither cold, dry, nor turbid but rather hot, moist, and clear—hot, but not with a stinging heat, moist but not with a watery moisture, and clear but nevertheless not very thin. For blood which is too hot both aggravates the natural heat and dries up the moisture and furnishes the moisture or heat which it does carry, in a readily dispersed and volatile state. Blood which is too moist, moreover, and too much like water, dulls the natural heat and also either makes the natural moisture sluggish, or forces it to liquefy under the natural heat, or suffocates the heat with moisture; and if any portion at all of the natural moisture is derived from watery blood, it not only putrefies easily but also quickly flows away and is dispersed. Hence it comes about that people who eat fruits and green vegetables which are too soft, except perhaps on the rare occasion

sumant, brevi venas succo crudo putrefactionique obnoxio penitus impleant. Ac ne id accidat, tutius pro alimento vel coquuntur, vel saltem cum pane miscentur. Sanguis ergo nec igneus esto, nec aqueus, sed aerius—non aeri crassiori similis, ne proclivior sit ad aquam; non aeri subtilissimo, ne facile incalescat in ignem; sed substantiam teneat mediocrem, in qua medius aer dominatum habeat plurimum. Cetera elementa insint quatenus aeris accommodantur imperio.

Non sit eius substantia subtilissima, ne humorem instabilem generet, spiritumque volatilem et dissolutioni subiectum. Non sit crassissima, alioquin et ingenio minime ministrabit, et vix in naturalem humorem ac spiritum permutabitur, meatus obstruet, suffocationi dabit occasionem; et spiritus qui vix tandem crassus inde creatur, densitate sua et ipse parum idoneus est ad vitam, et calorem naturalem ita suffocat, sicut fumus densior flammam comprimit protinus et extinguit. Mitto quod saltem adeo tenebrosus est, ut vitam efficiat maestam, morte deteriorem. Imprimis autem, ut mihi videtur, ad vitam expedit diuturnam, sanguinem una cum substantia quidem aeria valde, nec admodum crassa, habere glutinosum aliquem in se humorem atque tenacem, qualem ferme cum subtilitate habet oleum olivarum, et humor anguillae pinguis simul atque tenuis, et oleum ex terebentina quadam sublimatione tractum. Tu igitur alimenta ceteraque omnia quae sanguinem pro viribus humoremque talem efficiant, diligenter eligito. Sanguis enim humorque talis, sicut oleum flammae, ita vitali calori pabulum est, et una cum subtilitate habet etiam firmitatem. Praeceptum enim Rasis est pro iuventute servanda, rebus uti sanguinem ad praecordia traducentibus, ibique condensantibus, corque foventibus. Quod Avicenna probat, aquosum labilemque sanguinem praecipiens evitandum.

Differens autem in hoc pro differentia corporum ratio est habenda; nam ubi densius corpus est, ad subtilitatem sanguinis; ubi rarius, ad crassitudinem eiusdem omnibus est remediis declinandum. Ubi media corporis habitudo, via similiter media tutius imus. Nunquam tamen naturalem corporis habitudinem extirpare conabimur, alioquin vitam ipsam extirparemus. Expedit insuper meminisse, ubi subtilitatem sanguinis valde veremur, et stomachus interea non sit admodum natura validus, minutioribus ad crassitudinem gradibus accedendum esse, dum gracilem hominem crassioribus alimentis nutrire contendimus; et fovendum interim stomachum, producendum somnum, exercitationem corporis pro viribus augendam, animi minuendam, quae plurimis saepissime nocet. Ac si minus ferat alimenta viscosa nimium duraque vel admodum frigida, usu saltem corallorum, sandalorum, rosarum, corian-

---

19 incalescant z in *om. z*   23 et dissolutioni subiectum *om. L*   25-29 et spiritus—deteriorem *add.* in *marg. L*^{2} 28 vitam] utinam z 29 more z 37-40 Praeceptum—evitandum *add.* in *marg. L*^{2} 38 condensantibus] conducentibus z 39 aquosam z 44 imus] proficiscimur *L*   49 *post* stomachum *add. et z*   somnium z 50-51 quae plurimis saepissime nocet *om. L*   50 At z

when they take them as a soothing remedy for the stomach, fill up their veins with a perishable juice undigested and subject to putrefaction. And to keep this from happening, in order to eat them more safely, cook them or at least mix them with bread. Let not the blood be fiery either, nor watery, but airy — not airy like a too-dense air, lest it be too much like water, nor like a very subtle air, for fear it may easily kindle into fire; but let it maintain moderation in its substance; let the middle sort of air greatly predominate. Let the other elements be present, provided they are not so plentiful as to interfere with the dominance of the air.

Its substance should not be very subtle lest it give rise to a moisture which is unstable and a spirit which is volatile and easily dissolved. It should not be very dense either, or it will not serve the intelligence at all and will scarcely be changed into natural moisture and spirit; it will block the passages and give occasion for suffocation; and the dense spirit which at last with difficulty is created from it, by its density is itself not sufficiently fit for life and suffocates the natural heat just as a too dense smoke immediately oppresses and puts out the flame. I pass over the fact that at the very least it is so dark that it makes life sad, worse than death. To my way of thinking, it is especially good for a long life that the blood should have, along with this quite airy and not-too-dense substance, some glutinous and firm moisture in itself. Olive oil has this as well as the subtlety; so has the fatty as well as fine moisture extracted from an eel, and the oil extracted by sublimation from the turpentine-tree. Therefore, if you can, carefully choose foods and all other things which produce such a blood and moisture. For such blood and moisture, like oil to the flame, thus acts as the sustenance of the vital heat and has firmness as well as fineness. For Rhazes teaches that to preserve youth you should use things which lead blood to the heart, condense there, and warm the heart.[2] Avicenna approves this, warning us to avoid watery and perishable blood.[3]

But in this matter, different methods must be employed for different bodies; for when the body is more dense, all the remedies must serve to make the blood thin; but when the body is thinner, to make the blood thick. When the condition of the body is in between, we proceed more safely by a way that is similarly in between. Nevertheless, we will never try to root out the natural condition of the body lest we root out the very life. Moreover, while we are striving to nourish a slender man with denser foods, it is of advantage to remember that when we fear that the blood is thin and meanwhile the stomach is not very strong by nature, the patient's blood must ascend to thickness by smaller steps; and in the meantime his stomach must be fomented and his sleep prolonged; bodily exercise must be increased as far as possible and that of the mind must be lessened, because it is very often harmful to many people. But if he cannot bear foods which are too viscous and hard or very cold, we will eventually attain that strength of blood and of moisture which we are unable to attain safe-

drorum, myrobalanorum, cydoniorum et diacydonion, saccharique rosacei stypticarumque rerum eam sanguinis humorisque firmitatem denique consequemur, quam rebus nimium glutinosis hic tuto consequi non valemus. 55 Commodissime vero ex nucleis pineis pistaciisque et glycyrrhizae succo et amido, additis amygdalis dulcibus, earumque oleo et cydoniorum semine atque oleo sesamino una cum saccharo candidissimo aquaque rosacea nutrientur, qui viscosa grandiorum animalium membra concoquere nequeant. Concedemus his praeterea extrema gallinarum vel haedorum et testudines et 60 limaces atque testiculos. Vina dabimus non alba, sed rubra stypticaque et quodammodo subamara, aqua vinum ferrea vel masticea temperantes. Oleo quoque masticis cydoniorumque cutem leviter leniemus, et vetabimus interim quae sanguinem subtilem faciunt vel ferventem, nisi forsan nonnihil croci vel cinnamomi tenacioribus epulis infundamus, ut et facilius concoquantur, et 65 cocta per meatus angustos transferantur ad membra. Difficile namque est viscosa vel alimenta paulo firmiora ex stomacho non admodum valido usque ad digestionem tertiam quartamque perducere, nisi eiusmodi vehiculis perferantur atque insuper frictionibus levibus provocentur. Quas quidem cum facies, manibus eas mollioribus facito, ac memento madefacere manus odo- 70 rifero quodam vino, in quo camomillam myrtumque coxeris atque rosas.

Communis comedendi bibendique regula, et qualitas epularum.

Cap. VI.

Sed missa impraesentia faciamus obtusissima hominum corpora vel tenuissima, ad communem vivendi rationem perveniamus, communi mediaeque corporis habitudini prorsus accommodatam. Cave ne ulla ratione meatus corporis vel supra modum pateant vel nimium obstruantur; ibi enim resolutione et iniuria extrinsecus inferenda discrimen, hic autem in putre- 5 factione et suffocatione periculum. Etsi non artissimo regulae freno, quod Hippocrates damnat, te cohibeo, non tamen habenas tibi ad licentiam usque relaxo. Herbas et fructus humidiores accipe parce, parcius lac et pisces et utrunque cum melle, parcissime fungos atque cum aromaticis ac semine pyri; similiter purum aquae potum atque una cum parcitate. Quae humidiora sunt 10 vel pinguia, aromaticis acribusque condito, alioquin et humorem alienum membris plurimum inferunt atque putridum, et si quem necessarium naturae

---

56 glycyrrhizae *ex* liquiritie *corr.* L^2 61 atque testiculos *add. in marg.* L^2 63 levitur L liniemus L vitabimus z 69 finctionibus L lenibus L
Communis comedendi] De communi edendi (comedendi *y*) *yz* qualitate *yz* 8-9 et utrunque cum melle *add. in marg.* L^2 9 atque cum—pyri *om.* L 10-11 Quae—pinguia *add. in marg.* L^2

ly with things which are too glutinous by the use of coral, sandal, roses, corianders, myrobalans, quinces, diaquinces, rose-sugar, and astringents. But people who are unable to digest viscous cuts of meat from larger animals will be properly nourished with pine and pistachio nuts, with licorice juice, with starch[4] to which sweet almonds have been added, and with almond-oil, with quince-seeds, with sesame oil, as well as with the whitest sugar and rose water. In addition we will allow these patients to eat the extremities of hens and young goats; tortoises; snails; and testicles. We will give wine—not the white but the red which is astringent and somewhat bitter, tempering the wine with water of iron or of mastic. We will also soften the skin gently with oil of mastic and of quince. We will forbid those things which make the blood thin or hot— except perhaps some saffron and cinnamon which we should infuse in the more firm dishes so that they may be easily digested and, when digested, carried through the narrow passages to the bodily parts. For it is difficult to conduct foods which are viscous or a little too firm from a stomach which is not very sound to the third and fourth stages of digestion [stages which occur, respectively, in the blood vessels and in the bodily parts] unless they are carried by such vehicles and, moreover, are stimulated by gentle rubbings. When you do rub, do it gently, and remember to wet your hands with a fragrant wine in which you have cooked camomile, myrtle, and roses.

The Ordinary Regimen for Eating and Drinking, and the Quality Your Foods Should Have.

Chap. VI

But having dispatched for now the bodies of men which are very weak or thin, let us come to an ordinary way of life designed for the ordinary, middling physical condition. Beware of any method that might immoderately open the passages of the body or too much block them up; for with the first there is risk of causing resolution or injury from outside, but with the second there is danger of putrefaction and suffocation. Although I do not restrain you with the very tight rein of a regimen, which Hippocrates condemns,[1] nevertheless I do not relax your reins to the point of license. Eat sparingly those green vegetables and fruits which are rather moist, eat even more sparingly milk and fish, and eat both with honey; eat mushrooms most sparingly, and do so with spices and a pear seed; likewise drink pure water, and sparingly. Those foods which are rather moist or rich, season with sharp spices, otherwise they produce a moisture which is very alien to the members and putrid;

humorem suggerunt, hunc praestant citae admodum corruptioni subiectum, quod non aliter quam aquosum vinum conturbatur celeriter et corrumpitur. Hinc cita canities et pallor rugositasque senilis. Carnes quoque si quotidie comedantur, ac etiam si pondere pani propinquent, citam putrefactionem inferunt. Unde Porphyrius, Pythagoreorum antiquiorumque auctoritate fretus, esum animalium detestatur. Nonne homines accepimus ante diluvium longaevos animalibus pepercisse? Quanquam medici non tam carnium usum vetant quam abusum.

Denique humida tanquam putrefactioni obnoxia fuge, memoria tenens humidos et pingues senescere citius atque mori, quod et Hippocrates ait et res ipsa declarat. Siccissima rursum accipe moderate, vel saltem liberiore tempera potu. Media tutus eligito. Tametsi Avicenna formam cibi paulo sicciorem molli praeponit ad canitiem evitandam. Ad frigida nimium aut calida cautissimus esto; calida simul et humida sequere. Si fervet aer, epularum humor calorem superet; si friget, calor humorem; utrobique vero modicus sit excessus. Ubique calor et humor nonnihil glutinosum habeat atque stypticum, ut illinc membris irrigatus humor inhaereat firmius ac diu sub calore perduret. Electum triticum et panis electus hoc imprimis habet, deinde rubrum stypticumque vinum parumque dulce, tertio pinei nuclei resque his temperie et lentore persimiles, quarto carnes non humidae simul atque laxae, ut suillae et agninae lactentes. Medici tamen veteres, maxime Galienus, suis carnes et sanguinem propter quandam cum corpore nostro similitudinem valde commendant. Optimae sunt igitur similibus corporibus, ut rusticis et robustis corpusque multum exercitantibus, praesertim si quatriduum gariophylis, coriandris praeparatis, sale conditae serventur. Et sanguis forsan utilis si cum saccharo coquatur, defecatusque ad summum fuerit atque liquens.

Sed ut ad numerum revertamur: non probantur carnes humidiores, quales diximus, non durae simul atque siccae, quales vetustioris leporis atque bovis, sed mediae quaedam, ut gallinaceorum pullorum, caponum, pavonum, phasianarum, perdicum, forte etiam pullorum columbinorum, praesertim domesticorum. Tales quoque sunt capreoli vitulique iuvenes et anniculi verveces pariter atque apri. Haedos non sperno lactentes caseumque recentem. Aviculas equidem praetermisi, frequens enim subtiliorum alimentorum usus stomacho solum convenit crassiora minime toleranti; qui vero validior est, fugacem ex his fumum reportat vel humorem. Ova tamen gallinarum non praetermitto, si vitellus una cum albo comedatur; vitellus namque solus de-

---

15-23 Carnes quoque—declarat *desunt in L*   22 mori] moveri *z*   24-25 Tametsi—evitandam *add. in marg.* L^2 26 castitissimus *z*   fervet *ex* fruet *corr.* L^2 28 glutinosum] viscidos *ex* viscidum *corr.* L^2 33 lactantes *z*   33-40 Medici—diximus *desunt in L*   34 commendat *wxy*   42 fasianorum $L^{ac}w^{ac}x$ perdicium L pullorum columbinorum *ex* pippionum *corr.* L^2 43-44 anniculi verveces] annui (verveces *add.* L^2) castrati L 48 albo] albumine L^{ac}

and if they supply any of the moisture which is necessary to nature, they present it in a condition subject to very quick corruption, just as a watery wine is quickly disturbed and corrupted. The results are early gray hair, pallor, and the wrinkles of old age. Meat also, if it is eaten daily, even if it is about the same as the bread in weight [see below], quickly causes putrefaction. For this reason Porphyry, relying on the authority of the Pythagoreans and the ancients, denounces the eating of animals.[2] Surely we have heard that people before the flood lived a long time and left their animals alone? Yet physicians do not forbid the use of animals so much as their abuse.

Finally, avoid moist things, since they are subject to putrefaction, keeping in mind that moist and fat men grow old and die more quickly — which Hippocrates also says[3] and the facts themselves makes clear. On the other hand, take very dry things in moderation or at least temper them quite liberally with drink. Choose the mean and be safe. And yet, in order to avoid gray hairs, Avicenna prefers the kind of food which is a little drier to that which is soft.[4] Be very wary of things which are either too cold or too hot; strive for things that are at the same time cold as well as hot [e.g., some wines, licorice, and rose-oil; see 2.7] If the air is hot, let the moisture of the food exceed the heat; if cold, let the heat exceed the moisture; but in either case let the overplus be small. Always let the heat and moisture contain something glutinous and astringent so that the moisture diffused in the bodily parts may cling there more firmly and endure for a long time under the heat. High-quality wheat and bread especially have this combination; almost as good is a red, astringent, and not-too-sweet wine; third would be pine nuts and things very similar to them in temperedness and viscosity; fourth, meats which are not moist and loose as are pork and suckling lambs. Nevertheless the ancient physicians, especially Galen, strongly recommend the meat and blood of a pig because of a certain similarity with our body.[5] Pork is best, therefore, for bodies which are piglike, as are those of rustics and hardy men and those which get a lot of physical exercise, especially if the pork is preserved with salt and with cloves and dried coriander-seeds for four days. And the blood perhaps is useful if cooked with sugar and thoroughly purified and fluid.

But to return to our account: meat which is rather moist is not approved, as we have said, nor that which is hard or dry as that of hares or beef-cattle that have gotten too old, but a moderate sort of meat is approved, as that of barnyard cocks, capons, peacocks, pheasants, partridges, perhaps even of young doves, especially if domesticated. Such also are young roebucks and bull-calves, yearling wethers and likewise wild boars. Nor do I reject the suckling kid and fresh cheese. I have indeed omitted small birds, for the frequent use of foods which are too fine is suitable only to the stomach which has no tolerance at all for denser food; but a healthier stomach acquires a fleeting smoke or moisture from these foods. Nevertheless, I do not omit hen eggs, if the yolk is eaten

licatorum est nutrimentum. Nam Avicenna probat nutrimentum nullum expedire magis in diminutione sanguinis et dissolutione spiritus cardiaci, quam vitellum ovi gallinae vel perdicis vel phasianae. Neque forte ab re fuerit anseres nutrire spelta aquave nitida, ac post necem carnes, sale et coriandris aceto praeparatis conditas, dies septem servare prius quam edas; cervumque similiter, si stomachus fuerit validissimus. Probabile namque est longaeva quaedam animalia ad vitam conferre longaevam, si tamen huiusmodi carnes iuvenes comedantur; similiterque aliae carnes vicissim sunto tum assae tum elixae.

Cibus esto duplus ad potum, panis duplus et sesquialter ad ova, triplus ad carnes, quadruplus ad pisces, herbas, fructus humidiores. Ne incipiat a potu mensa, neque potus sit semel uberior. Semper stypticum aliquid absque potu vel modico sequatur mensam. Ubi complexio, aetas, locus, tempus ad calidum siccumve labitur, tu quoque paulisper ad opposita declinato; ubi ad frigidum aut humidum, similiter ad opposita vergito; ubi temperies, servato temperiem. Eatenus autem exercitationi quidem corporis est addendum, et animi detrahendum, quatenus epulis vescimur durioribus, ad diuturnitatem vitae aliquando forsitan necessariis. Mensae tibi sint in novem diei horis duae et utrobique parcae, parcior vero coena. Exercitationes corporis duae ferme post digestionem primam ad sudorem quasi productae. Somnus quidem nocturnus, quia semper est necessarius, semper bonus; diurnus autem, nisi admodum necessarius, nunquam bonus.

Ne utaris alimentis quae cito putrescunt,
nec in eiusmodi regionibus habites.
Vinum et triticum prae ceteris elige;
putrefactionem et resolutionem fuge.

Cap. VII.

animalia vero, quaecunque in nostram custodiam veniunt, mundis electisque alimentis nutrienda sunt antequam vescamur; atque haec et alia omnia ex pascuis altioribus et odoriferis eligenda sunt. Inter haec regulam

---

49-51 Nam Avicenna—phasianae *desunt in* L   53 septem *ex* septimum *corr.* L^2 55-56 si tamen—aliae *add. in marg.* L^2 56 comedantur similiterque] comedant similiter z   sunto] sumpto L; sunt z   tum^1] totum z   56-57 tum elixae] melisse L   59-60 Ne incipiat—uberior *add. in marg.* L^2
61 mensa x   aetas *add.* L^2 65-66 ad diuturnitatem—necessariis *add. in marg.* L^2 67-70 Exercitationes—nunquam bonus *add.* L^2

Ne utaris] Quod non sit utendum *y*; Non esse utendum *z*   putrescant *y*   habitandum *y*   Vivum *w* elige—*fuge]* eligenda (sunt *add. y*) putrefactio et resolutio fugienda *yz*

together with the white; for indeed the yolk alone is nourishment enough for weak men. Avicenna indeed proves that no nourishment is more useful in the case of lessening blood and dissolution of the cardiac spirit than the yolk of a hen's egg or of a partridge or pheasant egg.[6] Nor perhaps would it be wrong to nourish geese with spelt and clear water and, after butchering, to keep the meat for seven days seasoned with salt and dried coriander-seed pickled with vinegar before eating; and to do likewise with a deer if your stomach is very healthy. For indeed it is likely that certain long-lived animals contribute to longevity, provided, however, that one eats meat of this kind when one is young, and likewise, in turn, that other meat be sometimes roasted, sometimes boiled.

There should be twice as much food as drink; the proportion of bread to drink should be two to one; of bread to eggs, one and one-half to one; of bread to meat three to one; and of bread to the moister fish, green vegetables, and fruits, four to one. The meal should not begin with drinking, nor should the drink be too abundant at any time. Something astringent and with no drink, or a small one, should always follow the meal. When your constitution, age, place, or time leans to hot or dry, then you also should turn to the opposite things for a while; when they become cold or moist, turn likewise to their opposites; when they are temperate, maintain a balance. But we must add to the exercise of the body and withdraw from that of the mind whenever we eat that drier meal which is perhaps sometimes necessary for a long life. You should take two meals during the nine hours of the day — both sparse, but dinner the sparser — and both times, soon after the first digestion, physical exercise prolonged almost to the point of sweating. Take sleep at night, because it is always necessary and good; but sleep during the day, unless very necessary, is never good.[7]

Do Not Use Foods Which Quickly Putrefy,
nor Dwell in Regions Where Many Foods Do.
Be Most Selective about Wine and Wheat-flour;
and Avoid Putrefaction and Resolution.

Chap. VII

All the animals which come under our keeping must be nourished with fine and choice foods before we eat them; these, like other foods [see below], must be chosen from the higher and more fragrant pastures. Always keep in mind the rule about these matters which has been confirmed before all others

ante omnes ab Arnaldo philosopho comprobatam memori semper mente teneto: animantes, herbas, poma, fruges, vina ex altis odoriferisque (ut diximus) regionibus eligere oportere, quas venti temperati serenant, suaves solis radii fovent, ubi aquae nullae stagnant, culta sterquilinio non pinguescunt, sed humore nativo, ubi etiam quaecunque nascuntur, diu permanent incorrupta. Hic duntaxat habitandum est, his quoque vescendum. Neque confidendum est ex alimentis, quae brevi putrescunt, humorem nos comparaturos diuturnum et a putrefactione remotum; neque sperandum facile nos diu victuros, ubi terrae fructus incorrupti diu non conservantur, ubi rari admodum homines sunt longaevi. Quantum vero sit in loco victuque discrimen, pomum declarat Persicum: in Persia quidem venenum, in Aegypto cordis amicum; et helleborus in Anticyra impune sumptus, alibi vero venenum. Aristoteles habitationem eligit altam ad meridiem orientemque spectantem, sub aere subtili, nec humido, nec frigido; et Plato longaevos in editissimis atque temperatis repperit regionibus. Deterrimum vero est stercorare agros, vel aquas stagnantes ex agris minime derivare; omnia enim illic citae corruptioni subiecta nascuntur. Quamobrem eos non vituperare non possum, qui sapientem Hesiodum idcirco vituperant, quod in re rustica sterquilinium praetermiserit. Sed ille prudens salubritati potius quam fertilitati consuluit; satis autem ex lupinorum fabarumque foliis tempestive subversis agrum pinguefieri posse putavit. At vero si regiones humidiores immundasque colere et alimenta minime duratura sumere compellamur, eum quasi servemus victum quem sub aere pestilenti medici mandaverunt. Qua de re in libro *Contra pestilentiam* satis egimus.

Summatim vero suavibus et quodammodo calidis utemur odoribus. Aloe rite praeparata saepe leviterque purgabimur — rite vero praeparatam dicimus, si lota fuerit aqua rosacea vel succo rosarum, aut si cum rosis recentibus contritisque fuerit perfecte commixta; deinde addatur ei myrobalanus atque mastix et forte rosa. Medicina haec extra controversiam mirabilis est ad conservandam diu mentem sanam in corpore sano. Praeterea corpus exercitabimus; opportuno utemur foco. Hoc pulvere epulas condiemus: myrobalanorum emblicarum sit pars unciae quarta, sandalorum vero dimidia, cinnamomi integra, octava croci. Hoc itaque pulvere rebusque simul acribus imminentem ex putridis alimentis et locis corruptionem forsitan inhibere poterimus. Meminerimus autem, ubi multo plures putrefactione suffocationeque quam resolutione pereunt, ibi putrefactioni et suffocationi maxime resistendum. Ubi vero contra, vicissim uti condimentis aromaticis et quodammodo austeris (ut

---

5 oporiferisque *z*   9-10 his quoque — est] hi*c* quoque nascentibus vescendum est *z*   12 raro *z*
13-18 Quantum vero — regionibus *add. in marg.* L^2 14 Persia] Persica *z*   18 reperit *z*   22 salubritatem *z*   24 si *om. z*   26 pestem *L*   29-33 rite vero — Praeterea *add. in marg.* L^2 33 exercitabimur *L*, *corr.* L^2; excitabimus *z*   34 opportuno *add.* L^2 35 sit pars *add. in marg.* L^2 unciae quarta] uncia sit dimidia *L*; unciae *corr.* L^2 vero] quoque *L*   36 acribusque *z*   37 ex] et *z*   38 multo *om. z*

by Arnald [of Villanova] the philosopher: that you should select animals, green vegetables, fruits, field-produce, and wines from regions that are high and fragrant, as we have said, kept clear by temperate winds, warmed by the pleasant rays of the sun—places where no waters are stagnant and the cultivated land grows rich not with dung-pits but with a natural moisture, where also the crops, whatever they may be, remain for a long time uncorrupted.[1] Here only one must dwell; these things also one must eat. We should not assume that we are going to obtain from foods which grow rotten in a short time a moisture lasting and free from decay; nor should we hope that we can easily live a long time where the fruits of the earth are not preserved uncorrupted for very long, where it is quite rare for people to live long lives. The peach shows how much depends on location and mode of life: in Persia, indeed, it is a poison; in Egypt, a friend of the heart.[2] And hellebore is taken with impunity in Anticyra but elsewhere is a poison. Aristotle prefers a high dwelling-place which looks toward the south and east under a fine air, neither moist nor cold;[3] and Plato found long-lived men in lofty and temperate regions.[4] But it is very bad to manure fields or not to drain the stagnant water off them; for all things grown there are subject to quick corruption. Therefore I have to blame those who blame the wise Hesiod in this matter because in his *(De) re rustica* he left out the dung-pit. But that prudent man cared for health rather than fertility; he thought that a field could be sufficiently enriched by leaves of lupines and of beans turned over at the proper time.[5] But if we should indeed be forced to inhabit regions which are rather moist and impure and to eat foods which will not last, let us observe virtually that mode of life which physicians have laid down for those who live in the air of the pestilence—a mode of life which I have sufficiently discussed in my book *Consiglio contro la Pestilenza*.[6]

To put it briefly [he expands upon this later], we should use odors which are pleasant and somewhat hot. We should purge ourselves often, but lightly, by means of aloe rightly prepared—I call it rightly prepared if it has been washed with rose water or rose juice or if it has been thoroughly mixed with pounded fresh roses, and then are added to it myrobalans and mastic and perhaps a rose. This medicine is unquestionably marvelous for preserving for a long time a sound mind in a sound body. Moreover, we will get physical exercise; we will use fire at the proper time. We will season our foods with this powder: one-fourth ounce of emblic myrobalan, one-half ounce of sandal, an ounce of cinnamon, and one-eighth of an ounce of saffron. And so with this powder and with things which are also acrid we shall perhaps be able to ward off the decay which threatens from rotten foods and places. But we will remember that where many more perish by decay and suffocation than by resolution, there we principally have to resist decay and suffocation. But where the opposite situation prevails, the use in turn of spicy condiments which are somewhat

diximus) odoribusque similibus quovis tempore putrefactionem prohibet; ungi oleo frigoris iniuriam; uti lavacris ex aqua et oleo resolutionem ex labore vel calidis temporibus imminentem. Similiter os aqua saepe colluere; succum glycyrrhizae vel saccharum crystallinum ore tenere; aqua rosacea multa paucoque aceto rosaceo manus faciemque perfundere, similibusque odoribus uti; septima quaque hora alimentis modicis recreari; corpore simul et animo conquiescere, calore vitato.

   Plurimum vero interest quale sit vinum et triticum quibus assidue vescimur. Haec ergo sint talia ut ultra annum et potius ad triennium integra perseverent, si modo incorruptibilem ex his alimoniam sperare debemus. Vinum sive album sive rubrum sit, esto clarum, suave, stypticum, odoriferum, et quod indigeat aqua, nisi forte vinum reppereris leve simul atque durabile, quod rarissimum esse solet. Quod vero validius est, philosophus Isaach vinum dicit esse vinosum coctum sole ventisque purgatum, quod aqua fontis puri temperari iubet aliquamdiu antea quam bibamus, ut perfectius misceatur. Aquosum vero vinum atque debile vel acerbum fugiendum monet, utpote quod intra venas et membra acidum cito fiat aut aliter putrefiat. Vinum quidem aquosum putrefactioni subiectum, si conservata eius substantia coctum fuerit, hoc saltem erit utile, alioquin non laudatum, quod humorem corruptibilem non creabit, sed acumen eius aqua electa temperandum erit. Vinum vero quale probavimus, Isaach ex antiquorum sententia theriacis magnis inquit esse persimile. Quod (ut diximus) temperatum habitudinem corporis frigidam calefacit, refrigerat calefactam, humefacit siccam, humidiorem vero desiccat, atque (ut Galienus ait) naturalem humorem recreat, calorem fovet, utrunque contemperat. Miscere vero vinum eiusmodi magis necessarium est iuvenibus, minus senibus, frigidis vero senibus minime. Frigida namque duraque senectus (ut inquit Plato) ita mero fervet atque mollitur, sicut vel igne ferrum vel aqua lupini. Quod diximus per vinum opposita fieri atque diffidentia temperari, scito etiam per glycyrrhizam fieri, sed debilius, fieri etiam per oleum rosaceum, sed extrinsecus. Haec ergo tibi familiaria sunto. Neque diffidas quicquid et qualitate temperatum est et virtute potens, posse reliqua temperare, sicut frigus alia frigefacere; id imprimis habere temperamento Iovis, quo etiam saluberrima sunt. Sed de his alibi disputandum.

---

44 glycyrrhizae] liquiritiae *L*   46 quaque] que *L*, *corr. L*² ; qua quae *z*   48 vinum et triticum] triticum atque vinum *Lw*ᵃᶜ*x*   52–53 nisi forte−est *add. in marg. L*²   52 reperis *yz*   57–60 Vinum quidem−erit *add. in marg. L*²   61 Isaach *add. L*²   ex *om. x*   sententiam *x*   inquit *om. L*   67 molitur *z*   69 glycyrrhizam *ex* liquiritiam *corr. L*²

harsh (as we said) and similar odors wards off decay in any season; and to daub with oil wards off an injury due to the cold; and to take a bath with water and oil wards off the resolution which threatens from labor or seasons which are hot. It is similarly beneficial to rinse the mouth frequently with water; to hold in the mouth licorice juice or a crystal of sugar; to moisten your hands and face with lots of rose water and a little rose vinegar; to use odors of rose; to refresh ourselves every seven hours with moderate food; likewise to rest our body and mind, away from the heat.

It makes a big difference what sort of wine and wheat-flour we regularly eat. They should be such that they stay fresh for more than a year, preferably up to three years, since indeed we must rely on them for an incorruptible sustenance. Wine, whether it be white or red, should be clear, pleasant, astringent, fragrant, and the kind that needs tempering with water—unless perchance you find a wine which is both light and durable, which is very rare. But that which is rather strong, Isaac the philosopher calls winey wine, cooked by the sun and cleansed by the winds; he commands us to temper it with the water of a pure spring for a while before we drink it so that it may be more thoroughly diluted. But he warns that a watery wine, weak and bitter, should be avoided, seeing that it quickly turns to acid in the veins and bodily parts or in some other way putrefies.[7] A watery wine, indeed, which has already gone sour, if it has been digested with its essence preserved, though worthy of no other praise, will at least be useful in this way: that it will not create a corruptible moisture; but its sharpness will have to be tempered with the best water. But the wine which we have approved, Isaac says is very similar to the great theriacs compiled from the opinions of the ancients.[8] This wine, when tempered as we said, warms a cold condition of the body, cools a warm, moistens a dry, dries a moist, and, as Galen says, recreates the natural moisture, supports the natural heat, and tempers them both together.[9] But to dilute a wine of this sort is more necessary for young people, less so for old people, and least of all for cold old people. For indeed a cold and hard old age (as Plato says) is warmed and softened by unmixed wine just as iron with fire, or lupines with water.[10] Just as we have said that opposite things take place [1.5] and discordant things are tempered through wine, so you should know that this also takes place through licorice, but more weakly; it also takes place through rose oil, but externally. Let these things then be familiar to you. Do not doubt that whatever is both suitably mixed in quality and powerful can temper the rest, just as cold chills other things, and that this ability is obtained especially through the tempering of Jupiter, who also makes all things most healthy. But these matters must be discussed elsewhere.[11]

Diaeta, victus, medicina senum.
Cap. VIII.

Qui septimum iam septenarium impleverunt, quinquagesimum attingentes annum, cogitent Venerem quidem significare iuvenes, Saturnum vero senes, atque has apud astronomos stellas inter se maxime omnium inimicas existere. Rem ergo Veneream Saturnii fugiant, quae iuvenibus etiam vitae plurimum detrahit. Non enim natis consulit, sed nascituris, ipsasque etiam herbas statim producto semine siccat. Praeterea frigus aeremque nocturnum letiferum sibi putent, atque eum omnino victum servent, ex quo sanguinem plurimum sperent spiritumque quam plurimum: ex vitellis videlicet ovorum recentibus, vino aliquantum quidem dulci, odorifero quam plurimum. Nam hic vitellus proprie cordis sanguinem, vinum praecipue spiritum recreat. Carnibus electissimis coctuque facillimis omni summatim utantur diaeta calidum pariter et humidum augente. Spiritum odoribus praesertim vini assidue recreent. Vigiliam et inediam sitimque devitent, laborem rursus corporis atque animi et solitudinem et maerorem. Musicam repetant, si forte intermiserint, nunquam intermittendam. Ludos quosdam et mores, quoad decet, olim ante actae pueritiae revocent; difficillimum namque est (ut ita dixerim) reiuvenescere corpore, nisi ingenio prius repuerescas. Itaque in omni etiam aetate magnopere conducit ad vitam nonnihil pueritiae retinere et oblectamenta varia semper aucupari—longum vero profusumque risum minime, spiritum namque nimis ad exteriora dilatat.

Sed redeamus ad senes. Hi praeterea si frigeant, fomenta petant aromatica et calida simul atque humida. Meminerint puerile non esse puerile illud Avicennae fomentum, factum quidem a Davide, sed tardius forte factum. Fomentum seni mirificum: medulla recentis adhuc calentis panis, infuso malvatico vino cum pulvere mentae, apposita stomacho et saepe ad olfactum adhibita. Nam et medulla eiusmodi etiam sola Democrito iamiam expiraturo retinuit spiritum quoad placuit fugitivum. Praeterea frictionibus utantur levibus, seu quandoque lavacris nutrimentum provocantibus ad extrema. Nucleos ante omnia pineos videlicet ablutos familiares habeant. Hoc enim nutrimentum medici veteres senibus aptissimum probaverunt; calidum enim et humidum est et pingue, et omnem lenit asperitatem, atque simul (quod mi-

---

Diaeta victus] De dieta victu *y*   *post victus add.* et *z*   4 Saturno *z*   12 et] atque *z*   26 medullas *z* iamiam] iam *z*

The Diet, Mode of Life, and Medicine of the Elderly.

Chap. VIII

Those who have already completed their forty-ninth year and are nearing their fiftieth, should reflect that young people are signified by Venus, while old people are signified by Saturn, and that according to astronomers these stars are the most hostile of all to each other. Therefore those Saturnine people should avoid the Venereal act, which takes away most of the life even of people who are young. For she takes no thought for things already born, but for those about to be born, and even dries up the green plants as soon as they have produced seed. Furthermore, they should consider that cold night air is fatal for them, and they should observe that mode of life from which they may hope for the greatest possible amount of blood and spirit. This is, first, from fresh egg-yolks and from wine that is somewhat sweet and as fragrant as possible; for this yolk particularly refreshes the blood of the heart, and wine especially refreshes the spirit. They should make use of the choicest meats, the easiest to digest, of every diet, in short, which increases warmth as well as moisture. They should constantly refresh their spirit with fragrances, especially that of wine. They should avoid wakefulness, fasting, and thirst, fatigue of body and mind, solitude, and grief. They should take up music again, if perchance they have neglected it, which should never happen. Insofar as it is fitting, they should resume some of the games and customs in which they once previously spent their youth; for indeed it is very difficult, so to speak, to rejuvenate the body if you do not first become young again in spirit. And so at every age it is especially conducive to life to retain something of your childhood and always to strive for a variety of pleasures — but not a long, immoderate laughter, for it extends the spirit too much to the extremities.

But let us return to old people. In the next place, if they grow cold, they should seek aromatic fomentations which are warm and at the same time moist. They should remember that that "puerile fomentation" of Avicenna[1] — one which was made indeed by David, but perhaps made too late — is not for the young.[2] A marvelous fomentation for the old is the inside of fresh bread which is still warm on which has been poured malmsey wine with mint powder, applied to the stomach and often to the sense of smell. For indeed just the plain inside of bread of this sort held back the departing spirit of Democritus when he was at the point of death for as long as he pleased.[3] Furthermore, they should make use of light massages or sometimes baths which call forth nourishment to the extremities. They should frequently eat nuts, especially pine-nuts which are well washed. For the ancient physicians recommended this nourishment as most fitting for old people, since it is hot, moist, and rich, and softens

rum est) dum naturalem humorem auget, interea superfluum desiccat putridumque expurgat humorem. Sunt qui nucleorum eiusmodi drachmam unam quotidie post cibos exhibent senibus comedendam. Ego drachmam quoque alteram ieiuno stomacho senibus exhiberem, vel recens, calens, auratum, pinucleatum. 35

Componerem quoque electuarium hoc pacto: sume amygdalarum dulcium mundarum uncias quattuor, tantundem eiusmodi nucleorum, pistaciorum duas, unam seminum cucumeris, unam nucum avellanarum mundarum; contunde, coque una cum candidissimo saccharo, cui tamen addideris unam 40 zinziberis recentis conditi drachman, croci dimidiam, musci tertiam, ambrae tantundem. Saccharum aqua melissae, id est citrariae, rosarumque fundito; multa auri folia his adhibito. Huius enim usu quotidiano vitam senes validiorem longioremque consequentur. Possunt et in mensa hoc accipere, et pluribus horis ante mensam. Utilius autem tunc erit, si quid albi odorique vini 45 una cum confectione eiusmodi biberint. Temporibus vero calidioribus saccharum rosaceum una cum auri foliis et conditae myrobalani vitam senibus prorogabunt. Theriacam nemo dubitat ad idem humidis convenire personis atque temporibus; de cuius usu satis in libro superiore dictum. Nemo etiam negabit his prodesse admodum radices inulae beeniasque radices, albas simi- 50 liter atque rubeas, maxime vero recentes — illam quidem pro nutrimento, has etiam pro aromate — et omnia simpliciter calida humidaque et aromatica simul et styptica simulque pinguia. Certum est senes electo glycyrrhizae succo familiariter uti debere. Tradunt enim glycyrrhizam esse humani corporis calori pariter et humori persimilem, praeterea variis senum morbis opitulari. 55 Lac quoque amygdalinum et amidus cibus familiaris esto, et saccharum atque passulae.

Rasis tripheram ex myrobalanis Indis, emblicis, belliricis confectam, item myrobalanos Indas conditas saccharo, non solum ad retinendam, sed etiam ad retardandam senectutem valde probat. Avicenna laudat tripheram myro- 60 balanorum maiorem atque minorem, rursus confectionem de squama ferri, maxime vero auri. Iubet quotidie mandere myrobalanos praecipue chebulas rite conditas ad differenda senectutis incommoda.

---

32 superfluum] humorem L; corr. L²   40 post addideris add. duas been utriusque dragmas L^ac
42 tantundem] quartam L   id est citrariae om. L   43 adhibeto xz   50 enulae z   51 rubras x
54 familiares z   59 retinendum z

all harshness; and at the same time, which is remarkable, while it increases the natural moisture, it meanwhile dries up any superfluous moisture and purges it when putrid. There are those who present one dram of nuts of this sort for the elderly to eat daily after food. I would present to the elderly on an empty stomach a second dram also of a nut which is fresh, warm, golden, and just taken out of the pine cone ["pinucleatum"].

I would also compound an electuary in this way: take four ounces of clean, sweet almonds, four ounces of pine-nuts, two ounces of pistachio-nuts, one ounce of cucumber seeds, one ounce of clean filbert nuts, grind them up, cook them together with very white sugar, to which nevertheless you will have added one dram of freshly preserved ginger ["zinziberis recentis conditi," cf. "zinziber. . . recens et conditum" in 2.9.20–21], one-half dram of saffron, one-third dram of musk, and one-third dram of amber. Moisten this sugar with water of melissa (that is, citraria) and of roses; apply to these [presumably as a coating for individual doses of it] many leaves of gold. For by the daily use of this electuary old people will attain a stronger and longer life. They can take it both during the meal and several hours before, but at that time it will do more good if together with this confection they drink some fragrant white wine. During warmer seasons, rose-sugar together with leaves of gold and preserved myrobalan will extend the lives of old people. No one doubts that theriac is likewise fitting for moist people and seasons; enough has been said about its use in the preceding book. No one will deny that for these people also the roots of elecampane are very useful and the roots of ben, both white and red, but especially if they are fresh (the former are good for nourishment, but the latter are also good for a spice), as are all things which are simply hot and moist and at the same time aromatic, astringent, and rich. Certainly old people must frequently use the select juice of licorice; for they say that licorice is very similar to the heat and moisture of the human body, and besides, that it is good against the various diseases of the elderly. Let almond-milk, starch, sugar, and raisins be familiar food.

Rhazes strongly recommends trifera which is made of myrobalan—Indic, emblic, and belliric—likewise Indic myrobalan preserved with sugar not only for keeping alive the old but for slowing the aging process.[4] Avicenna praises the greater and lesser triphera of myrobalan and, on the other hand, a confection made from iron scales, but especially from scales of gold. He orders us to eat myrobalans daily, especially properly preserved chebule myrobalans, to put off the troubles of old age.[5]

Naturae aromatum et cordialium necessariae;
et rursum qualis senum victus.

Cap. VIIII.

Scito myrobalanis varias inesse virtutes: unam quae mirabiliter superfluum exsiccat humorem, unde canitiem prohibet; secundam quae humorem colligit naturalem, et a corruptione simul et inflammatione tuetur, unde vitam producit in longum; tertiam quae styptica aromaticaque potentia virtutem et spiritum naturalem et animalem congregat et fovet et roborat. Hinc aliquis vitae lignum in paradiso myrobalanum forte fuisse putabit. Simile quiddam ferme faciunt aurum et argentum, corallus spodiumque et pretiosi lapilli, quamvis pro aromatica virtute facultatem afferant illustrandi. Tu vero memento aromatica tunc maxime prodesse nobis ad vitam, ut supra significavimus, quando cum vigore quodam aromatico humida sunt pariter atque calida, lentoremque pinguem habent, commodum augmento. Quales sunt imprimis radices beeniae, albae similiter atque rubentes, praesertim recentes; aut saltem quando cum virtute quadam subtili odorifera et acuta substantiam densam habeant, et stypticam valde proprietatem. Qualis utique compositio inter cordialia frigida primum myrobalanis inesse videtur et succino, deinde rosis et succo et semini citri, tertio sandalis et coriandris atque myrto certerisque similibus; inter calida vero cordialia zedoariae, ligno aloes, citri cortici et gariophylis, nuci muscatae, maci, olibano, mastici atque doronico, qualem etiam salviae experimur inesse.

Tradunt ambram et muscum stypticam habere virtutem. Zinziber autem ob quandam eius humiditatem, praesertim recens et conditum, senibus saepe prodest. Sed hoc et gariophylus propter caloris vehementiam caute videtur accipiendum; zedoaria quoque caute, tametsi theriacae similis iudicatur, et stypticam simul atque pinguem naturam habet, senibus commodissimam. Ambra propter calorem quasi temperatum tuto ferme sumitur, ac propter lentorem cum styptica subtilitate mixtum praerogativam habet ad vitam in membris et spiritibus confirmandam. Tum vero si ex ea fiat aqua cutisque lavetur, digestionem quartam restituit, ac morbos eius defectu contingentes expellit. Aromatica vero quae subtilem admodum substantiam habent, qualem cinnamomum atque crocus, cordialibus frigidis et durioribus sunt miscenda. Nam aromatica si tantum calida subtiliaque sunt et sola sumantur, naturalem calorem nimis excitant humoremque dissolvunt. Necessaria tamen sunt tum frigidioribus et humidioribus epulis concoquendis, tum cordialibus duris ad praecordia transferendis.

Naturae ... necessariae] De naturis ... necessariis *yz*   4 viam *z*   5 animalium *z*   9 vero] mero *z*   15 myrobalanus *z*

The Natures the Elderly Must Have in Spices and Cordials and More about the Quality of the Mode of Life They Should Follow.
Chap. IX

You should know that myrobalans contain various virtues: one, which wondrously dries up superfluous moisture and thus precludes grey hair; a second which gathers together the natural moisture and protects it from decay and inflammation, thereby leading to a long life; a third which by its astringent and aromatic power collects, warms, and strengthens the natural and animal power and spirit. This will lead someone to think that perhaps the tree of life in Paradise was a myrobalan.[1] Gold and silver, coral, iron slag, and precious stones do something similar, although in place of the aromatic power, they carry the power of illumination. But remember that spices do our life the most good when, as I have shown above, along with a certain aromatic strength, they are both moist and hot and have a rich viscosity suitable for growth, as do in particular ben roots, both white and red, especially fresh ones; or at least when, along with a certain subtle, fragrant, and sharp power, they have a dense substance and very astringent properties. This combination of properties seems to inhere in, among the cold cordials, myrobalans and *succinum*[2] first of all; almost as good are roses and the juice and seed of the citron; the third choice would be sandal, corianders, myrtle, and other similar things; but among hot cordials, it inheres in zedoary, aloe-wood, the rind of the citron, clove, nutmeg, mace, frankincense [*olibanum*], mastic, and doronicum; this combination I have found to be present also in sage.

They say that amber and musk have an astringent power. Ginger, on account of its moisture, especially the fresh and the preserved, is often advantageous for old people; but this and the clove, because of the strength of their heat, apparently must be taken cautiously — zedoary also cautiously, although it is judged to be similar to theriac and has an astringent and rich nature most proper for old people. Amber, because of its heat which seems already to have been tempered, is for the most part safe to take, and because of its viscosity mixed with an astringent fineness, is preferred for strengthening life in the bodily parts and spirits. Then, too, if you compose a water from it with which you wash the skin, it reactivates the fourth stage of digestion and expels those diseases which are caused by the failure thereof. But spices which have a very fine substance, as do cinnamon and saffron, must be mixed with the cold and the rather hard cordials. For if spices which are only hot and fine are taken by themselves, they excessively stimulate the natural heat and dissolve the moisture. Nevertheless, they are called for both when rather cold and moist foods must be digested and when hard cordials must be conveyed to the heart.

Te namque latere non debet, humorem ipsum vitae necessarium primas in 35
corde sedes habere et arteriis venisque eiusdem, quod Isaach perspicue docet;
atque ut Avicenna probat, hic humor naturali ceterorum membrorum humore frequenter irrigatur atque fovetur. Quapropter cavendum est ne membri ullius humor casu quopiam arefiat, multoque magis ne praecordiorum
humor comminuatur. Atque ut nutrimenta vel fomenta et cordialia omnia 40
per angustos meatus ad praecordia latissime perferantur, his insere crocum;
ut vero sistantur ibi, myrobalanos adhibe; ut autem consequaris utrunque,
accipe inter calida muscum atque ambram, inter frigida rosas atque myrtum.
Memento dulce marathrum senibus profuturum, nam et nutrimentum per
membra diffundit, et qua facultate lac, eadem humorem auget naturalem. 45
Unde Dioscorides marathro serpentes ait annuam exuere senectutem. Probamus et salviam, haec enim naturae virtutem temperate calefacit et firmat,
paralysim propulsat. Probamus et moderatum conditi zinziberis usum, habet
enim cum calore pinguedinem.

De auro et aureis alimentis et recreatione senum.

Cap. X.

Aurum omnes ante omnia probant, tanquam omnium rerum temperatissimum et a corruptione tutissimum; Soli quidem propter splendorem,
Iovi autem propter temperantiam consecratum; ideoque posse calorem naturalem cum humore mirifice temperare, humores a corruptione servare, Solarem et Iovialem spiritibus et membris inferre virtutem. Verumtamen optant 5
durissimam auri substantiam subtiliorem facere, penetratuque facillimam.
Noverunt enim cordialia tunc maxime latentem cordis recreare virtutem,
quando in eis attrahendis minime natura laborat. Ut autem minime fatigetur,
vel subtilissima iam effecta vel cum subtillissimis sunt exhibenda. Optimum
fore putant, si absque aliena permixtione aurum potabile fiat; sin minus pos- 10
sit, contusum et in folia redactum accipi volunt.

Aurum ferme potabile habebis (ut dicam): collige flores boraginis, buglossae, melissae, quam citrariam nominamus; et quando Luna Leonem subit vel
Arietem vel Sagittarium aspicitque Solem aut Iovem, coque cum candido
saccharo aqua rosacea liquefacto, et pro qualibet uncia insere diligenter auri 15
folia tria. Ieiunus cum vino quodam aureo sume. Item aquam ex capone des-

---

recreatione] refocillatione *z*   2 Soli quidem] Siquidem *z*   3 temperaturam *z*   5 optant] oportet
z   6 sacere *z*   9 subtilissima *ex* subtilissime *corr.* L²

And indeed you ought to know that the moisture necessary for life has its first seat in the heart and in its arteries and veins, as Isaac clearly teaches.[3] Avicenna shows that this moisture is frequently made moister and fomented by the natural moisture of the rest of the bodily parts.[4] Accordingly, beware lest the moisture of any bodily part be dried up by any accident, and even more lest the moisture of the heart be diminished. And in order that nourishment, fomentations, and all cordials be conveyed most widely through the narrow passages to the heart, mix them with saffron; in order that they may stay there, bring to bear myrobalans; but in order to accomplish both, take among hot things, musk and amber, among cold, roses and myrtle. Remember that sweet fennel will be good for old people, for it spreads nourishment through the bodily parts, and just as it increases milk, with the same faculty it increases the natural moisture. Wherefore Dioscorides says that with fennel snakes annually strip off their old age.[5] We approve also of sage, for it moderately warms and strengthens the power of nature and wards off paralysis. I approve also the moderate use of preserved ginger, for it has richness as well as heat.

On Gold, Foods Made of Gold, and the Revitalization of Old Men.

Chap. X

All writers place gold before everything else, as the most suitably mixed of all things and the most safe from decay — consecrated to the Sun because of its splendor and to Jupiter because of its temperedness; it can therefore marvelously temper the natural heat with moisture, save the humors from corruption, and bring a Solar and a Jovial power to the spirits and the bodily parts.[1] But nevertheless, they want to make the very hard substance of gold more fine and most quick to penetrate. For they know that cordials then especially refresh the hidden power of the heart, when nature incurs least work in attracting them. But in order that nature be fatigued as little as possible, they want the gold to be already in the finest form or to be used with the finest things. They think it would be best if the gold be made potable without mixing it with anything foreign; but if this cannot be done, they want it taken ground and reduced to leaves.

Here is how you will have the gold almost potable, I would say. Gather the flowers of borage, bugloss, and the melissa which we call "citraria," and when the Moon enters Leo, Aries or Sagittarius and aspects the Sun or Jupiter, cook it with the whitest sugar dissolved in rose-water and carefully add three gold leaves per ounce. Take it on an empty stomach with a golden wine. Likewise

tillantem foco vel aliter consumpto una cum iuleb sume rosaceo, in quo auri
folia quaedam ante contuderis. Praeterea in nitidissimam fontis aquam aurum extingues ignitum; cum eadem auri contundito folia. Eadem vinum aureum temperato, et una cum eiusmodi potu comedito recentem ovi vitellum.   20

Facile vero in tota corporis arbore servabis humorem, si in radicibus conservaveris. Accipe igitur gallinarum et pullorum eiusmodi atque caponum cor, iecur, stomachum, testiculos, cerebellum; coque aqua modica, minimo sale. Cocta contunde ex tota carne et toto iure et saccharo, addito recentis ovi vitello; fac placentam modico cinnamomo crocoque conditam et auratam. Hac vesceris esuriens semel saltem quarto quoque die, et tunc quidem sola, claro tamen ad potum addito vino.   25

De usu lactis sanguinisque humani pro vita senum.

Cap. XI.

Saepe post decimum statim et nonnunquam post nonum septennarium arbor humana arefacto paulatim humore tabescit. Tunc primum humano iuvenilique liquore irriganda est haec arbor humana, quo revirescat. Eliges ergo puellam sanam, formosam, hilarem, temperatam, et famellicus lac eius sugito crescente luna, statimque comedito marathri dulcis modicum   5
pulverem saccharo rite confectum. Saccharum quidem lac in ventre cogi vel putrefieri non permittet; maratrum vero, cum et subtile sit et lactis amicum, dilatabit ad membra.

Quos hectica senilis exedit, medici diligentes liquore humani sanguinis, qui arte sublimi destillavit ad ignem reficere moliuntur. Quid ergo prohibet quo-   10
minus senio iam quasi confectos interdum hoc etiam potu reficiamus? Communis quaedam est et vetus opinio, aniculas quasdam sagas, quae et stringes vulgari nomine nuncupantur, infantium sugere sanguinem, quo pro viribus iuvenescant. Cur non et nostri senes omni videlicet auxilio destituti sanguinem adolescentis sugant? — volentis, inquam, adolescentis, sani, laeti, tempe-   15
rati, cui sanguis quidem sit optimus, sed forte nimius. Sugent igitur more hirudinum ex bracchii sinistri vena vix aperta unciam unam aut duas; mox vero sacchari vinique tantundem sument, idque esurientes et sitibundi facient cres-

---

19 eadem¹] eodem z   23 *post* testiculos *add.* atque z   26 vescere z   quarto] quanto z
  1 novum z   7 permittit z   16 Sugant z   iridinum L^{ac}; hirundinum z

take the moisture dripping from a capon which you have set over a fire or from which you have extracted it in some other way, together with a rose julep into which you have previously beaten some gold leaves. In addition, extinguish red-hot gold in very clear spring-water and beat some gold leaves into this water. Temper golden wine with it, and with a drink of this sort eat a fresh egg yolk.

You will easily maintain the moisture in the entire tree of the body if you preserve it in the roots. Therefore take the heart, the liver, the stomach, the testicles, and the brain of hens, chickens, and capons; cook them with a little water and a pinch of salt. When cooked, grind them out of all their flesh, and with all the broth, and sugar, add a fresh egg-yolk; make a cake seasoned with a little cinnamon and saffron, and coated with gold. Eat this, when hungry, at least once every four days and by itself, though with a clear wine added for a drink.

On the Use of Human Milk and Blood for the Life of Old People.

Chap. XI

Immediately after the age of seventy and sometimes after sixty-three, since the moisture has gradually dried up, the tree of the human body often decays. Then for the first time this human tree must be moistened by a human, youthful liquid in order that it may revive. Therefore choose a young girl who is healthy, beautiful, cheerful, and temperate, and when you are hungry and the Moon is waxing, suck her milk; immediately eat a little powder of sweet fennel properly mixed with sugar. The sugar will prevent the milk from curdling and putrefying in the stomach; and the fennel, since it is fine and a friend of the milk, will spread the milk to the bodily parts.

Careful physicians strive to cure those whom a long bout of hectic fever has consumed, with the liquid of human blood which has distilled at the fire in the practice of sublimation. What then prevents us from sometimes also refreshing by this drink those who have already been in a way consumed by old age? There is a common and ancient opinion that certain prophetic old women who are popularly called "screech-owls" suck the blood of infants as a means, insofar as they can, of growing young again.[1] Why shouldn't our old people, namely those who have no [other] recourse, likewise suck the blood of a youth? — a youth, I say, who is willing, healthy, happy, and temperate, whose blood is of the best but perhaps too abundant. They will suck, therefore, like leeches, an ounce or two from a scarcely-opened vein of the left arm; they will immediately take an equal amount of sugar and wine; they will do this when

cente luna. Si crudus aegre concoquitur, coquatur prius una cum saccharo, vel ad aquam calidam moderate destillet saccharo mixtus; deinde bibatur. Fovere quoque stomachum tunc sanguine suillo praesens auxilium est. Quem utique sanguinem e vena suilla fluentem spongia calente vino madefacta combibat, et stomacho statim calens admoveatur.

Galienus atque Serapio morsum rabidi canis sanguinis canini potu curari dicunt, rationem vero illis assignare non placuit. Ego igitur biduum eam quaeritans, opinor denique salivam canis rabidi venenosam, impresssam hominis pedi laeso, per venas paulatim ad cor ascendere more veneni, nisi quid interea distrahat. Si igitur interim canis alterius sanguinem ille biberit, sanguis ille crudus ad multas horas natat in stomacho, eum denique velut peregrinum deiecturo per alvum. Interea caninus sanguis iste salivam caninam superiora membra prensantem, priusquam ad praecordia veniat, derivat ad stomachum; nam et in canino sanguine virtus est ad salivam canis attrahendam, et in saliva vicissim virtus ad similem sanguinem prosequendum. Venenum igitur a corde semotum, sanguinique imbibitum in alvo natanti, una cum sanguine per inferiora deducitur, hominemque ita relinquit incolumem. Quorsum haec? Primo quidem ut rei tam occultae succurrentem inter disserendum causam aperuerim; deinde ut moneam, sanguinem potari posse et quidem salubriter, atque in sanguine humano virtutem esse, qua humanum sanguinem attrahat et mutuo prosequatur. Ne forte diffidas iuvenilem sanguinem a sene bibitum trahi ad venas membraque posse, ibique prodesse quam plurimum.

Diaeta, habitatio, consuetudo senum.

Cap. XII.

Meminisse decrepitos expedit, naturam debilem non esse nutrimentorum pondere fatigandam vel etiam epularum diversitate nimia distrahendam; nam et iuvenilis aetas hoc vitio fit cito senilis. Dividant ergo mensas, nec tam multa naturam alimonia quam frequenti reficiant, intervallo interim ad digestionem dato; nam saepe etiam postquam stomachus ipse concoxerit, nisi et iecur quasi digesserit, sumere nutrimentum naturam distrahit atque fatigat, qua quidem lassitudine saepius frequentata advolat intem-

---

19 crudas *z*   35 relinquit *xz*; reliquit *Lwy*   39 Nec *z*
  Diaeta habitatio consuetudo] De diaeta habitatione (et *add. z*) consuetudine *yz*   7 quae *z*

hungry and thirsty and when the Moon is waxing.[2] If they have difficulty digesting raw blood, let it first be cooked together with sugar; or let it be mixed with sugar and moderately distilled over hot water and then drunk. At that time, the blood of a pig is also an effective aid in warming the stomach. A sponge soaked with hot wine should absorb this blood flowing from the pig's vein and, while hot, should immediately be applied to the stomach.

Galen and Serapion say the bite of a mad dog is cured by drinking dog's blood, but it did not please them to assign a reason.[3] I, therefore, after investigating this for two days, am finally of the opinion that the poisonous saliva of a mad dog, pressed into the bite on a person's foot, climbs little by little through the veins to the heart like poison unless something draws it away in the meantime. If, therefore, that person has drunk the blood of another dog in the meantime, that undigested blood swims for many hours in the stomach, which finally drives it out through the bowels as something foreign. Meanwhile, that dog's blood diverts to the stomach the saliva which is taking hold of the upper bodily parts before it reaches the heart; for there is a power in canine blood to attract canine saliva and in saliva, in turn, to follow blood of a similar nature. Therefore the poison, put aside from the heart and absorbed by the blood swimming in the bowels, is drawn out together with the blood through the lower bodily parts and thus leaves the person safe. Why have I gone into all this? First of all, in order that I might reveal, within the material I have to discuss, the underlying cause for such an obscure fact; second, to point out that it is possible and indeed beneficial to drink blood, and that there is a power in human blood both to attract and, in turn, to follow human blood; and to reassure you that the blood of a youth drunk by an old person can be drawn to the veins and the bodily parts and can do a lot of good there.

The Diet, Dwelling, and Customs of Old People.

Chap. XII

If the patients are decrepit, they should remember that a weak nature ought not to be wearied with the weight of nourishment and distracted by too great diversity of foods; for by this bad habit even youth quickly turns into old age. Let them therefore split up their meals; let them refresh nature by food not so much abundant as frequent — provided, however, they afford an interval between for digestion; for often, even after the stomach itself has digested, unless the liver too has almost digested, it distracts and wearies nature to consume the nourishment; and when Old Age has been visited too often by occasion

pestiva senectus. Senes hieme velut oves aprica petant, aestate velut aves amoena rivosque revisant. Frequenter inter virentes versentur plantas et suaviter redolentes, hae namque viventes spirantesque conspirant ad spiritum hominis augendum. Ad loca vero communiter apibus amica confugiant, mellaque hieme degustent, mel enim cibus est senibus imprimis amicus, nisi ubi bilis timetur incendium. Amicus caseus recentissimus; amici dactyli, ficus, passulae, cappares, dulcia Punica, zizipha, hysopus, scabiosa, betonica, sed pistacia multo magis, pinei vero nuclei maxime omnium, sicut diximus. Ex quibus plurimum referent adiumentum, si eos horas duodecim in aqua paulum calida teneant, priusquam edant, sic enim stomacho non nocebunt; ac praeterea si, dum his utuntur, etiam inter pineta et oliveta vitesque versentur, aut saltem pini vaporem accipiant et odorem. Item gummi lachrymaeque pini cum oleo vel vino corpus saepe deliniant; probabile enim est arbores longa naturaliter vita dotatas, praesertim si etiam hieme virescant, ad longam tibi vitam umbra, vapore, novo fructu, ligno, et tempestivo quolibet usu prodesse. De animalibus autem longaevis supra diximus. Iam vero ad idem tibi forte conducet, si vivas plurimum penes eos qui sani tibi sano natura sint similes et amici, ac magis forsan si paulo iuniores. Utrum vero et quomodo frequens adolescentum consuetudo parumper senium retardare valeat, pudicus Socrates consulendus.

Quae adminicula senes a planetis accipiant ad omnia membra fovenda.

Cap. XIII.

Verum consulite potius solliciti senes Apollinem, qui Socratem Graecorum sapientissimum iudicavit. Consulite Iovem insuper atque Venerem. Phoebus ipse, artis medicinae repertor, nucem muscatam vobis fovendo stomacho dabit; Iuppiter cum Phoebo masticem atque mentam; Venus vero corallum. Fovendo rursum capiti Phoebus paeoniam, thus, amaracum et cum Saturno myrrham; spicam nardi macemque Iuppiter; Venus denique dulce marathrum atque myrtum. Ad cor vero fovendum accipietis a Phoebo quidem citrariam, crocum, lignum aloes, thus, ambram, muscum, doronicum, modicum gariophylum, citri corticem, cinnamomum; ab Iove lilium, buglos-

---

14 zizipha z; zinziba Lwxy 19 lachrimoque $w^{pc}y$; lachrimaque z 21 sic z
6 saturo $L^{ac}wy$

of this fatigue, he flies up prematurely. In winter, let old people like sheep seek places exposed to the sun; in summer, let them like birds revisit the pleasant places and rivers. Let them dwell continually among green and sweet-smelling plants; for these living and breathing things conspire [pun] to augment the human spirit. Let them habitually withdraw to places frequented by bees; in winter let them taste honey; for honey is a food especially friendly to old people, except when we are afraid of kindling choler. Also friendly are the following: the freshest cheese, dates, figs, raisins, capers, sweet pomegranates, jujubes, hyssop, scabious, betony; more friendly are pistachio-nuts. But best of all, as we have said, are pine nuts, from which they will get the most good if before they eat them they keep them twelve hours in tepid water, for this way they will not harm the stomach, and if besides, while they use them, they will also dwell among the pine-groves, olive-groves, and vines, or at least inhale the vapor of the pines and the smell. Likewise let gum and the gum-drops of the pine, with oil or wine, often besmear their bodies; for it is probable that trees endowed by nature with long life, especially if they stay green even in winter, will help you live long by their shade, their vapor, their fruit when new, their wood, and any timely use. Of long-lived animals, we have spoken above [2.6]. But now it will perhaps lead you to the same end if you dwell chiefly with people who are healthy, whose nature is similar to yours when you are healthy, and who are your friends; and perhaps it is preferable if they are a little younger. But as to whether and how the frequent companionship of youths avails for a while to hold back old age, consult the chaste Socrates.[1]

What Means of Fomenting All the Parts of the Body the Elderly May Receive from the Planets.

Chap. XIII

But rather [than Socrates], you old people who care about these things, consult Apollo, who judged Socrates to be the wisest of the Greeks.[1] Consult Jupiter besides, and Venus. Phoebus himself, the discoverer of the art of medicine, will give you the nutmeg for a fomentation to your stomach; Jupiter with Apollo, the mastic and the mint; and Venus, coral. Again, for fomenting your head, Phoebus will give you peony, frankincense, marjoram, and, in cooperation with Saturn, myrrh; Jupiter will give spikenard and mace; then Venus, sweet fennel and myrtle. For fomenting the heart, you receive from Phoebus citraria, saffron, aloe-wood, frankincense, amber, musk, doronicum, a little clove, citron-peel, and cinnamon. From Jupiter, the lily, bugloss,

sam, ocimum et mentam beeniasque radices, et candidas pariter et rubentes; a Venere sola quidem myrtum et sandalum atque rosam, una cum Saturno coriandrum. Haec vos contundite diligenter; et quae stomachi sunt, cydoniorum oleo in formam ceroti conficite. Quae vero capitis, oleo spicae perfundite, ac illinite cervicem, tempora, frontem. Quae denique cordis, aureo vino spargite aquaque rosacea, eaque foris praecordiis admovete. At iecur imprimis creando sanguini necessarium nescio quomodo praetermisimus. Huic ergo semper eupatorio et opobalsamo Phoebus opitulabitur; pistaciis Iuppiter atque passulis; Venus autem hepatica, endivia, spodio, cichorea. Lieni tandem fovendo Saturnus ille vester una cum Iove capparim dabit vobis, scolopendriam, tamariscum. Sicut vesicam Iuppiter cum Venere pina, glycyrrhiza, amido, cucumeris seminibus, malva, althaea, manna, cassia curat.

 Saturnum vero verendum pluribus ne adeo vos fugite senes. Hic enim quam peregrinus est iuvenibus tam vobis domesticus erit. Ut igitur totum ipse quoque vobis corpus vegetet pro viribus atque confirmet, accipietis nonnunquam ab eo regnante pariterque a Phoebo mumiam simul et anseris assi pulpam. Haec anseris adipe modico delinite; contundite diligenter; myrobalanorum chebularum atque Indarum melle concoquite; ambra, musco, croco condite. Ante omnia vero haec vobis profutura confidite, credentes medicinarum ad vitam conferentium vitam esse fidem. Qua speretis et Deum supplicantibus vobis adspiraturum, et res ab eo creatas, praesertim coelestes, mirificam proculdubio ad augendam vel conservandam vitam habere potentiam.

Confabulatio senum sub Venere per virentia prata.

Cap. XIV.

Sed a gravioribus his numinibus ad Venerem parumper vos per hortos et prata senes virentia revoco. Ad almam Venerem vos omnes advoco, non ludentem quidem vobiscum, sed iocantem. Haec et vobis, inquam, et mihi iam seni primo quidem iocosum hoc fundit oraculum: "Ego, filii, si nescitis, voluptate motuque vobis vitam dedi. Ego igitur voluptate quadam mo-

---

11 quidem *ante* sola *transp. z*   12 condite *z*   sunt cydoniorum] sint cydonicum *z*   19 unam *L*
23 ipsi *z*   25 muniam *z*   28 Ante omnia—confidite *om. z*   29 vitam²] veram *z*
   De confabulatione *yz*

basil, mint, and roots of ben, both white and red. From Venus alone you receive myrtle, sandal, and the rose; and from Venus along with Saturn, coriander. Grind these up carefully. What pertains to the stomach, prepare it with oil of quince in the form of a wax-salve. But what pertains to the head, moisten it with oil of spikenard and besmear the back of the neck, the temples, and the forehead. Then what pertains to the heart, sprinkle it with golden wine and rose-water and apply it externally to the region of the heart. But we have somehow forgotten the liver, the prime necessity for the creation of the blood. To it, Phoebus will always administer agrimony and balm [*opobalsamum*]; Jupiter, pistachio-nuts and raisins;[2] Venus, hepatica, endive, slag, and chicory. Finally, for fomenting the spleen, Saturn, your own planet, along with Jupiter, gives capers, scolopendrium, and tamarisk. Just so, Jupiter along with Venus cures the urinary bladder by pine, licorice, starch, cucumber seeds, mallows, wild mallows, manna, and cassia.

But you old people, do not flee so far from Saturn, though he is to be feared by the multitude. For to the same degree that he is foreign to young people, so he will be right at home with you. Therefore, that he too may enliven all your body as much as possible and make it strong, receive sometimes from him while he is reigning, and likewise from Phoebus at the same time, mummy[3] and the flesh of a roast goose. Soften these things with a little of the goose-fat, pound them carefully, cook them with honey of both chebule and Indic myrobalan; season them with amber, musk, and saffron. But above all, trust that these things are going to help you, believing that faith is the life of medicines [for another application of the expression, see "Quod Necessaria Sit" ad fin.] that conduce to life. Hope thou in this, and that God is going to favor you when you supplicate him, and that the things created by him, especially the celestial things, have without a doubt a marvelous power to lengthen or preserve life.

The Conversation of the Old People Traversing the Green Fields under the Leadership of Venus.

Chap. XIV

But I recall you, old people, from these graver powers for a little while, through the gardens and green fields to Venus. To our nursing-mother Venus I call all of you; she is not tricking you but jesting. For you and for me who am myself already old, first she utters this mock-oracle: "I, my children, gave life to you (in case you didn't know) by pleasure and by motion.

tuque, etsi non simili, vobis servabo vitam. Eandem quoque servabit libertate
Liber, vitis sator, propagator vitae. Liber ipse semper odit servos et, quam
vino promittit vitam, solis liberis implet longam. Meae quidem vitae simul
atque menti quondam profuit regnante Saturno diminuta menta, placetque
quotidie. Vobis autem maior menta menti vitaeque prodest, diminuta nocet.
Risum ex meis hortis legite, neglegite ficum. Has vero violas quando carpitis,
carpere vos existimate lilia; prehendentes lilium, comprehendere crocum.
Crocum a Phoebo Iuppiter ipse nactus propagavit in lilium. Lilium ego a
Iove suscipiens, in has quas hic videtis violas transformavi. Denique rosa
quidem vobis esto Lucifer, Hesperus vero myrtus."

Post oraculum nobis cogitandum mandat rerum viridium naturam, quatenus virent, non solum esse vivam, sed etiam iuvenilem, humoreque prorsus salubri et vivido quodam spiritu redundantem. Quapropter odore, visu, usu, habitatione frequenti iuvenilem inde spiritum nobis influere. Inter virentia vero deambulantes interim causam perquiremus, ob quam color viridis visum prae ceteris foveat salubriterque delectet. Inveniemus tandem naturam visus esse lucidam ac lucis amicam, volatilem tamen ac facile dissipabilem. Idcirco dum per lucem se dilatat, velut amicam, interdum nimio lucis excessu rapi prorsus, et vehementi dilatatione dissolvi; tenebras autem naturaliter velut inimicas fugere, ideoque radios in angustum inde retrahere. Optat vero visus ita perfrui lumine, ut per amicum hoc suum amplificetur quidem, nec tamen interim dissipetur. Iam vero in quocunque colore plus admodum tenebrarum sive nigredinis est quam lucis, non dilatatur, nec ideo delectatur radius visus ad votum. Ubi vicissim plus admodum splendidi coloris est quam nigri, spargitur latius, noxia quadam voluptate distractus. Quamobrem color viridis maxime omnium nigrum cum candido temperans, praestat utrunque, delectans pariter atque conservans; et molli insuper et adhuc tenera qualitate, sicut et aqua, radiis oculorum absque offensione resistit, ne abeuntes longius disperdantur. Quae enim dura sunt simul et aspera, frangunt quodammodo radios; quae vero rarissima sunt, dissolutioni aditum patefaciunt. Sed quae soliditatem aliquam habent lenemque simul aequalitatem, sicut specularia corpora, nec ipsa quidem frangunt, neque longius disperdi permittunt. Quae denique praeter haec beneficia tenera quoque sunt et mollia, sicut aqua resque virides, liquidis oculorum radiis mollitia blandiuntur. Denique visus radius quidam est in quadam oculorum aqua naturaliter nobis accensus, ac temperatum lumen in aqua quodammodo resistente requirit. Itaque

10 menti] mente *z*   12 prehendetes *x*   17 solam *z*   23 velut *om. z*   26 visus] usus *z*   28 delectatur] dilatatur *z*   33 radii *z*   34 enim] non *L*

BOOK TWO   CHAP. XIV   205

I therefore will preserve your life by a certain pleasure and a certain motion—
although not the same kind. And Liber, too, planter of the vine, propagator
of life, will preserve it too in liberty. Liber himself always hates slaves, and
that life which he promises by wine, he gives it for long only to the free. For
my sort of life and mind, indeed, the smaller kind of mint was good once when
Saturn reigned, and it pleases me daily. For your sort of mind and life, however,
the larger mint is good, whereas the smaller harms it. Select from my garden
rice ["risum"], but let the fig alone. But when you pluck these violets, think
that you are plucking lilies; taking the lilies, take with them the crocus.[1]
Jupiter himself, acquiring the crocus from Phoebus, sowed it as the lily; I,
receiving the lily from Jupiter, transformed it into these violets which you see.
Finally, let the rose be your morning star, the myrtle your evening star."

After the oracle, she gives us this to meditate on: that the nature of green
things, for so long as they stay green, is not only alive but even youthful and
abounding with very salubrious humor and a lively spirit; and because of this
a certain youthful spirit flows to us through the odor, sight, use, and frequent
habitation of and in them. While we are walking among the green things, let
us figure out why the color green more than others foments the sight and healthfully delights it. We will discover at last that the nature of sight is bright and
friendly to light but volatile and easily dissipated. And on this account, while
it dilates itself through light as through a friend, at the same time through excess of too much light it is absolutely carried off and dissolved by great dila-
tion. Darkness, however, it flees as an enemy and therefore draws in its rays
to a narrow angle. The sight wants to use light in such a way that through
its friend it may be amplified, indeed, but not at the same time dissipated.
Now in whatever sort of color there is more of darkness or blackness than of
light, the visual ray is not dilated, and therefore not delighted as it would like.
Conversely, where there is more of a shining color than a black, it is scattered
more widely, distracted by a harmful pleasure. On which account the color
green tempering most of all black with white, furnishes the one effect and the
other, equally delighting and conserving the sight. Besides, by its soft and withal
tender quality, just like water, it opposes the visual rays without striking against
them, lest departing too far they should be destroyed. For things that are hard
and at the same time rough somehow break the rays; but things which are
very rarefied open the way to dissolution. But things that have some solidity
and at the same time a smooth equality, such as mirror-like bodies, neither
themselves break the rays nor permit them to be dispersed too far. Finally,
things which besides this benefit are also tender and soft, like water and green
things, with their softness soothe the liquid rays of the eyes.[2] And then, sight
is a certain ray kindled by nature in the water of the eyes [meaning, as Fr.
points out, the aqueous humor] and it requires a tempered light in water somehow opposing it. And so it rejoices in water; it is delighted by mirrors similar

gaudet aqua, delectatur speculis aquae similibus, viridibus oblectatur. In quibus sane viridibus solis lumen insitum adhuc vernum secum habet humorem aquamque subtilem occulto quodam lumine plenam. Ex quo fit etiam ut color viridis cum tenuatur, in croceum resolvatur.

Quorsum haec? Ut intelligamus frequentem viridium usum, siquidem visus spiritum recreat, qui in animali spiritu quodammodo praecipuus est, animalem quoque reficere. Atque etiam meminerimus, si color viridis, quia inter colorum gradus medius atque temperatissimus est, tantum animali spiritui prodest, multo magis quae per qualitates temperatissima sunt, naturalem et vitalem spiritum iuvatura, atque admodum profutura nobis ad vitam. Nihil in mundo temperatius est quam coelum, nihil sub coelo ferme temperatius est quam corpus humanum, nihil in hoc corpore temperatius est quam spiritus. Per res igitur temperatas vita permanens in spiritu recreatur. Spiritus per temperata coelestibus conformatur.

Denique discamus ex temperie viridis (quae illuminando aeque congregat animalem spiritum atque dilatat ideoque maxime iuvat) nos quoque in cordialibus eligendis, componendis, utendis aromatica subtilia et acuta, quae spiritum extendere vel etiam illuminare solent, quod facit crocus atque cinnamomum, cum aromaticis semper stypticis congregantibusque, ceu myrobalanis et similibus, commiscere, atque vicissim. Neque praetermittere quae absque acumine etiam aromatico simul utrunque conficiunt, aliquantum videlicet dilatant atque admodum congregant multumque illuminant, quae et alias narravimus—quod efficit aurum, argentum, spodium, corallus, electrum, sericum, pretiosi lapilli, inter quos hyacinthus vel ore detentus ob Iovialem temperiem plurimum comprobatur. Cum enim sub terra nequeant speciosissima et quasi coelestia procreari absque summo quodam beneficio coeli, probabile est rebus eiusmodi mirificas coelitus inesse virtutes. Compositio vero eiusmodi, quae dilatando et illuminando spiritum aeque congregat, ita delectat eum intrinsecus atque recreat, sicut foris viriditas oculos, atque ipsum etiam apud senes in naturali quadam viriditate diutissime servat, quasi laurum, olivam, pinum, etiam hieme virentem. Tantoque magis id efficit, quo efficit et interius, atque maxime si compositio talis aromatico flagret odore alliciatque sapore. Profecto sicut corpus ex crassioribus humorum partibus compositum in quintam redigitur formam, ita spiritus ex subtilissimis eorundem portionibus constitutus formam habet quintam naturaliter temperatissimam atque lucidam ideoque coelestem. Atque in hac ipsa forma conservandus est, ut subtilis quidem sit et interea firmus, sicut diximus. Sit omnino

---

42 aquae *om.* z   46 visus] usus z   49 spiritu L   51 iuvatura] in natura z   nobis *ante* profutura *transp.* z   56 ex *add.* L²   59 sacit y   60 seu z   61 praemittere z   62 aliquanto z   66 comprobantur z

to water and by green things. The light of the Sun which is incorporated in these green things certainly is accompanied by a still-vernal moisture and a subtle water full of a hidden light. This is why the color green, when it is thinned out, is resolved into yellow.

Why have I gone into all this? That you may understand that the frequent use of green, since it recreates the spirit of sight, which is in a way the principal part of the animal spirit, refreshes also the animal spirit itself. And we will also remember that if the color green, which among the colors is the middle grade and the most tempered, is so good for the animal spirit, much more will those things which through their qualities are the most temperate help the natural and vital spirits and conduce greatly towards our life. Now nothing in the world is more tempered than the heavens; virtually nothing under the heavens, more tempered than the human body [one sublunary thing that is more so, is gold, see 2.10.1-2]; nothing in this body more tempered than the spirit. Through tempered things, therefore, the life which resides in the spirit is recreated; through tempered things the spirit is conformed to celestial things.

Finally, let us learn through the temperateness of green — which in illuminating at once collects the animal spirit and dilates it and therefore most of all helps it — that we also, in choosing, compounding, and using cordials, should mix the subtle and sharp spices, which characteristically dilate or even illuminate the spirit (e.g., saffron and cinnamon), with the styptic and congregating spices (e.g., myrobalans and so on) and vice versa. Let us learn not to omit those materials which even without an aromatic sharpness accomplish both at the same time — namely, they dilate a little, they congregate a lot and illuminate a great deal — which things we have listed elsewhere. Gold has this power, as do silver, slag, coral, electrum [meaning a mixture of gold and silver], silk, and precious stones, among which the jacinth, held in the mouth, if you will, is most highly esteemed on account of its Jovial temperateness [cf. 1.10, 1.23, 2.15, etc.]. For since these most beautiful and almost celestial things could not be created under the earth without the greatest gift from the heavens, it is probable that in things of this kind wonderful powers from the heavens inhere. A compound of this kind — which in dilating and illuminating the spirit equally collects it — so delights it inwardly and refreshes it as greenness does externally to the eyes, and so preserves it in old people in a state of natural greenness for a very long time as if it were a laurel, olive, or pine, green even in winter. It does this the more insofar as it does it internally, and most of all if such a composition is redolent with a spicy odor and attracts by its taste. Precisely as the body, which is composed from the thicker parts of the humors, is reduced into a fifth form, so the spirit, which is constituted from the subtler portions of the humors, has naturally a fifth form most tempered and bright and therefore celestial [like the stars which are made of quintessence]. And it must be kept in this very form in order that, as we said, it might be subtle indeed and

lucidus, sed etiam quodammodo solidus. Ac praeterea rebus odoriferis, firmis, lucidis assidue foveatur, si vitam cupimus conservare, quae viget in spiritu, 80 et vendicare nobis coelestia dona. Haec hactenus iussu Veneris contemplati, Venerem ipsam audivisse putemus.

Mercurius alloquitur senes et consulit eis circa voluptatem, odores, cantus, medicinas.

Cap. XV.

Interea dum inter senes ipsa quasi Venus confabularetur, forte quidem hactenus satis belle, deinceps vero prolixius forsan fabulatura foret. Sermonem hunc his Mercurius vocibus, sermonum auctor, interpellat: "Quidnam vobis est cum Venere istac semper puella, senes? Quid rursum Veneri cum sermonibus? Nonne mei simul atque vestri sunt sermones? Mea ratio pariter 5 atque vestra? Audite me igitur eadem nunc attentione qua illam, et multo maiore insuper attentione quam Venerem. Quinque scitis esse sensus: visum, auditum, olfactum, gustum, tactum. Esse rursum quinque (ut ita dixerim) discite rationes. Dum enim per quinque sensus quotidie imbuitur vobis animus, rationesque inde rerum ipse concipit, interea notiones habitusque ad res 10 iudicandas quinque, tanquam rationes quinque, resultant. Praeterea sicut quinque hinc quidem sunt sensus, inde vero quodammodo rationes, ita vitae tenor quinque gradibus circa sensum rationemque disponitur. Unde quinque numerantur aetates: prima quidem sensu tantum trahitur, secunda sensu magis admodum allicitur quam ratione ducatur, tertia post haec alternis pariter 15 rationis et sensus persuasionibus agitur, quarta ratione potius quam sensu ducitur, quinta tandem ratione tantum regi debet. Prima igitur aetas atque secunda, tanquam subiecta Veneri, Venerem, si placet, loquentem audiat; reliquae vero Mercurium. Ego igitur reliquos vos omnes alloquor non pro me quidem tantum, sed pro Diana etiam hac, quam ad sinistram meam cernitis. 20 Nempe cum haec elinguis sit, ego vero bilinguis, iure pro hac ipsa cuius ego linguam habeo loquor.

Unam profecto noxiamque Venus vobis indidit voluptatem, qua noceret quidem vobis, prodesset vero futuris, exhauriens paulatim vos per latentem quandam quasi fistulam, aliudque vestris liquoribus implens atque procre- 25

Mercurius—consulit eis] Quod Mercurius alloquatur senes et consulat eis *y*; Prosopopoeia Mercurii senibus consulentis *z*   *post cantus add.* et *z*   *Cap.XV om. L*   15 alterius *x*   25 liquoribus] coloribus *z*

at the same time firm, that it might by all means be bright but also somewhat solid. And besides, let it be continually fomented with odoriferous, firm, bright things if we want to preserve life, which flourishes in the spirit, and to claim for ourselves celestial gifts. Having reflected on these things thus far by the command of Venus, let us consider that we have listened to Venus herself.

Mercury Addresses the Elderly and Counsels Them about Pleasure, Odors, Song, and Medicines.
Chap. XV

During the time that Venus herself, as it were, chatted among the old people — perhaps prettily enough up to now — she might have still gone on chatting at greater length. This speech Mercury, the author of speech, interrupted with these words: "What have you to do with Venus, that perpetual girl, you old people? Again, what has Venus to do with speeches? Don't speeches belong to me and also at the same time to you? Doesn't reason belong to me and likewise also to you? Hear me, therefore, with the same attention with which you heard her, and with much more attention besides. You know there are five senses: sight, hearing, smell, taste, touch. Learn also that there are in turn, so to speak, five reasons. For while your mind is daily instructed through the five senses, and itself conceives therefrom the reasons of things, meanwhile there arise five notions and habits for the judgment of things[1] constituting the five reasons. Besides, just as from this side [i.e., the body] the senses are five, but from that side [i.e., the mind] in a way the reasons are five, so one's course of life is disposed into five stages with regard to the senses and reason. That is why they enumerate five ages of man: The first age is attracted by sense alone; the second is allured by sense much more than led by reason; after this the third is driven equally by the alternate persuasions of reason and the senses; the fourth is led by reason more than by the senses; and finally, the fifth ought to be ruled by reason alone. Let the first and second ages, as subject to Venus, hear Venus speaking if they want to, but let the remaining ages hear Mercury. I therefore address all the rest of you, not indeed for myself alone, but also for Diana here whom you discern at my left. Especially since she has no tongue while I have a double tongue [punning on Mercury's characterization as a deceiver], I have a right to speak for her since I have her tongue.

Venus endowed you with only one pleasure, and that harmful, with which she harms you but profits those to come, little by little draining you as it were through a secret pipe, filling and procreating another thing with your fluid,

ans, vos tandem quasi vetustum quoddam spolium cicadarum iam exhaustum humi relinquens, cicadae interim teneriori prospiciens. Nonne videtis quod Venus de materia vestra generat esse recens quiddam et vivum sensuque praeditum? Surripit ergo vobis iuventutem et vitam atque sensum ex toto, inquam, corpore per totius voluptatem, ut efficiat inde totum. Ego interim materiae illius quae quartae digestioni superest qualitate monitus, vos commoneo alimenta similiter quarta digestione cocta plurimum vitae vestrae succurrere: ovum recens videlicet, integrum et sorbile una cum saccharo exiguoque croco, lac humanum vel suillum vel caprinum cum pauculo melle sumptum. Atque haec duo tunc salubriora sunt, quando nativo adhuc calore flagrant. Et si ovum aliam mox cocturam desiderare videtur, praesertim in stomacho minus valido, sed leviter est coquendum.

Verum ut parumper ad Venerem redeamus, si quando vidistis Venerem, iuvenilem admodum vidistis et quasi meretriciis fucis et ornatibus expolitam. Haec ergo, quae nova semper est, nova semper affectat, odit vetera. Facta destruit, unde construat facienda. Haec rursum, si dictu fas est, quasi meretrix non uno quovis est contenta viro, vulgus amat et, ut dialectice loquar, speciei passim potius quam individuo suffragatur. Iam vero neque tactu tantum vos praecipitat, sed etiam gustu, fallit quotidie perditque deceptos. Quos enim vos in rebus sapores percipitis, mediocri quadam temperie gratos, hos Diana haec Apollinis Iovisque munere tradidit. Illecebras vero saporum miras, quibus quotidie velut hamo capti clam miseri vitam perditis, Venus insidiosa fabricat. Quid igitur Martem incusatis? Quid Saturnum? Mars quidem raro admodum vobis palamque nocet. Saturnus quoque saepius vultu se profitetur hostem, nocet tardius, tempusque remediis nulli negat. Sola Venus palam ut amica venit, clam inimica venit. Hanc igitur incusate potius, si quem inter superos incusare licet. Ad multiplices huius insidias tum oculis Argivos ipsos instruite, tum Palladis clipeo vos munite. Aures autem ad blandas pollicitationes eius tanquam ad letales Syrenum cantus obstruite. Hunc denique providentiae florem a me accipite, quo Circes huius veneficia devitetis. Haec vobis duas vix tandem et has quidem letiferas pollicetur voluptates, potius quam largitur; ego vero beneficio patris atque fratris quinque promitto vobis, quinque praesto puras, perpetuas, salutares, quarum infima est in olfactu, superior in auditu, sublimior in aspectu, eminentior in imaginatione, in ratione excelsior atque divinior. Quo maior delectatio in tangendo percipitur atque gustando, eo vitae gravius frequenter accidit detrimentum. Contra vero quanto maiorem in olfactu voluptatem et auditu atque visu, item imaginatione et saepe ratione quotidie reportatis, tanto fila vitae longiora producitis.

---

47 amo L^{ac}; homo *z*   51 igitur *om. z*   60 Quae *z*

and leaving you finally as if you were an old skin of a cicada drained upon the ground,[2] while she looks after the fresh cicada. Don't you see that Venus generates a fresh being, living and endowed with sense, from your own matter? She steals from you, therefore, the youth, life, and sense, from your whole body, I say, through pleasure of the whole body, that she may from thence make a whole body. Meanwhile, warned by the quality of that material which remains after the fourth digestion, I admonish you to assist your life greatly with food similarly digested in the fourth digestion, namely, a fresh, whole, raw egg along with sugar and a little saffron, human milk or that of a pig or goat taken with a little honey.[3] And both of these are more healthful when they still glow with their original heat. And if it seems that the egg is going to require another digestion right away, especially in a weak stomach, it should be cooked, but lightly.

But to return for a bit to Venus, if at any time you see Venus, you see her looking juvenile and embellished like a prostitute with rouge and ornaments. Because she is ever new, therefore she always likes new things and hates old things. She destroys what has been made in order to construct from them what is still to be made. Again like a whore (if I may say so), not content with one man, she loves the crowd and (to speak like a dialectician) favors the species generally rather than the individual. But now she not only overthrows you by touch but also deceives daily by taste, and dooms those she has deceived. For those flavors you perceive in things which are pleasing because of their moderate temperedness, those Diana gave you by the gift of Apollo and of Jupiter. But those wonderful allurements of taste by which daily you, secretly miserable, lose your life like people caught on a hook—these are the ones that insidious Venus fashions. Therefore, why do you blame Mars? Why Saturn?[4] Mars indeed harms you very rarely, and face to face. Saturn also more often declares himself an enemy to your face; he harms more slowly, and leaves everyone enough time for remedies. Only Venus comes before your face as a friend, secretly as an enemy. Rather blame her, therefore—if one can blame any among the powers above. Against her multiple deceptions equip yourselves with the eyes of Argus; fortify yourselves with the shield of Pallas; and stop your ears to her flattering promises as to the lethal songs of the Sirens; finally, accept from me this flower of prudence with which you may avoid the sorcery of this Circe. She promises (rather than gives) you at last barely two pleasures, and these indeed lethal; but I promise you with the kindness of a father and a brother five pleasures, and five I give, pure, perpetual, and wholesome, of which the lowest is in smelling; the higher, in hearing; the more sublime, in seeing; the more eminent, in the imagination; the higher and more divine in the reason. The greater the delight experienced in touching and tasting, the graver damage frequently befalls. But, on the contrary, the greater pleasure you gain daily in smelling, hearing, and seeing, likewise in imagination and often in reason, the longer you extend the thread of life.

Verum sicut in blandimentis tangendi atque gustandi cavendam vobis subdolam admonui Venerem, sic in ipsa secretiore nimisque assidua contemplativae mentis delectatione cavete Saturnum, illic enim frequenter filios ipse suos devorat. Nam quos sublimiorum contemplationum suarum rapit illecebris et illic agnoscit ut suos, hos interim, si modo diutius gradum ibi sistant, falce quadam e terris amputat, terrenamque incautis vitam saepe surripit. Hoc saltem Venere interim indulgentior, quod Venus quidem vitam, quam tibi detrahit, donat alteri, nihil tibi pro detrimento restituens; Saturnus autem pro vita terrena, a qua separatus ipse te denique separat, coelestem vitam reddit atque sempiternam. Hoc ipso similes esse videntur inter se Venus atque Saturnus, qui sane quam Aquario gaudet tam regnat in Libra, quod homines et hic et illa generandi libidine vexat, nocetque vexatis, ut inde posteritati prosit. Sed haec quidem fecundat corpus stimulatque fecundum; ille mentem suo semine gravidam urget ad partum. Vos igitur proverbii memores, ne quid nimis, assiduis prudentiae frenis parturientis utriusque libidinem cohibete. Tametsi multo citius graviusque ille laedit quos taedio, torpore, maerore, curis, superstitione premit, quam quos supra vires corporis moresque mortalium elevat ad excelsa. Omnino vero servate, moneo, quod aequus Iuppiter Pythagoram docuit et Platonem: humanam vitam in quadam aequali animae ipsius cum corpore proportione servari; utrunque suis quibusdam alimentis et exercitationibus ali ac similiter augeri. Si quis alterutrum educatione praecipue sua multo robustius altero tandem efficit, non mediocrem facit vitae iacturam. Propterea quicunque inter res medicorum arte laudatas potissimum eas eligit, quae corpori simul et ingenio prosunt, maximum vitae sibi vendicat adiumentum. In earum vero numero vinum, mentam, myrobalanum, muscum, ambram, zinziber recens, thus, aloem, hyacinthum, similesque lapillos herbasve consimiles esse putate, et quae ad utriusque utilitatem a medicis pariter componuntur.

Sed longioribus his quandoque interceptis ambagibus, ego quoque medicus huc accessi. Si sapores ex rebus accepti non ultra viventibus, item odores ex aromatis iam siccis vitaque vacuis multum ad vitam conferre censentur, quidnam dubitatis odores ex plantis radicibus adhuc suis haerentibus viventibusque mirum in modum vitae vires accumulaturos? Denique si vapores exhalantes ex vita duntaxat vegetali magnopere vitae vestrae prosunt, quantum profuturos existimatis cantus aerios quidem spiritui prorsus aerio, harmoni-

---

67 delectationi *z*   69 hos *om. z*   76 ut *add. L*²   79 assiduis *rep. z*   80 cohibite *z*   85 auderi *z*
94 acceptis *z*   95 aromatibus *z*   99 spiritu *z*

But just as I have admonished you to shun deceitful Venus in her blandishments of touching and tasting, so you should shun Saturn in that secret and too constant pleasure of the contemplative mind; for there he frequently devours his own children. For those whom he carries away with the allurements of their own sublimer contemplation and there acknowledges as his own (provided that they stay too long there on that level)—while they are doing this, he amputates them from earth with his sickle and often steals from imprudent followers their earthly life. At the same time, in this he is at least more indulgent than Venus, because Venus gives to another the life she extracts from you, repaying you nothing for the damage; Saturn, however, for the earthly life from which he himself is separate and finally separates you, repays you with a life celestial and everlasting. In this very thing Venus and Saturn seem to resemble each other (Saturn who, just as he rejoices in Aquarius, so he reigns [i.e., has his exaltation] in Libra [one of the two houses of Venus]) that both he and she vex mankind with the lust for procreation, and harm those they vex, in order that they may thereby profit posterity. But she makes the body fertile and stimulates it when fertile; he urges to birth the mind pregnant with his seed. You, therefore, be mindful of the proverb "Nothing to excess" and restrain with the continual reins of prudence the lust of either god for procreation. But even so, he wounds much more quickly and seriously those whom he pushes down with world-weariness, torpor, sadness, cares, and superstitions than those whom he elevates to the heights above their physical strength and the customs of mortals. But by all means I advise you to observe what Jupiter the even-handed taught Pythagoras and Plato: to keep human life in a certain equal proportion of soul to body and to nourish and augment each of the two with its own proper foods and exercises. If anyone eventually renders one of the two much more robust than the other, especially by training, it will do considerable damage to life[5]. On this account, whoever chooses among the things praised by the art of doctors those especially which profit both the body and the intelligence, he will win for himself the greatest aid to life. Reckon in the list of these: wine, mint, myrobalan, musk, amber, fresh ginger, frankincense, aloes, jacinth and similar stones, or similar herbs, [j/hyacinth is the name of both a stone and an herb, and is so used in this work], and things which are compounded by doctors for the use of both body and mind.

But now that I have intercepted a rather long digression [that of Venus], I also have stepped forward as a doctor. If the savors from collected things that are no longer living and odors from spices now dried up and void of life are regarded as very conducive to life, how can you doubt that odors from plants still retaining their roots and living are going to multiply the powers of life in a wonderful way? And then, if vapors exhaling from a merely vegetable life are greatly beneficial to your life, how much more beneficial do you think will be songs which are made of air to a spirit wholly aerial, songs

cos harmonico, calentes adhuc vivosque vivo, sensu praeditos sensuali, ratione conceptos rationali. Hanc ergo vobis a me fabricatam trado lyram cantumque cum ipsa Phoebeum, solamen laborum, diuturnae vitae pignus. Sicut enim res qualitate temperatissimae simulque aromaticae tum humores inter se, tum spiritum naturalem secum ipso contemperant, sic odores eiusmodi vitalem spiritum, sic rursum similes quoque concentus spiritum animalem. Dum igitur fides in lyra sonosque, dum tonos temperatis in voce, similiter spiritum vestrum intus contemperari putate. Ac ne ipse Venere sim avarior quae sine Baccho friget, ab hoc ipso Libero patre per me nectar hoc accipite. Qui praecipue inter vos frigent, temporibus similibus bis septimo quoque die uncias vernacei vel malvatici dulcis meri duas sumant cum una panis uncia tribus ante mensam horis; semel autem drachmam unam sublimis aquae destillantis ex vino cum iuleb rosacei semuncia. Quo quidem liquore illinire etiam cutem et ad olfactum uti commodissime possunt. Atque ut post eiusmodi nectar ambrosiam quoque vobis afferam, hanc insuper acceptam ab Iove largior medicinam: quattuor myrobalanorum uncias accipite chebularum, tres rosacei sacchari, conditi zinziberis hieme quidem unciam, aestate vero semunciam. Tria haec cum emblicarum melle concoquite suaviter septemque auri foliis exornate. Ieiuni bolum ante prandium quattuor horis accipite. Anno saltem integro quotidie id assumite, ut inde 'velut aquilae renovetur vestra iuventus.'" Hactenus quasi Mercurium locutum existimemus.

Confirmatio superiorum; et quod devitare debemus assiduam cogitationem et coitum.

Cap. XVI.

astrologi Venerem et Saturnum inimicos invicem esse ferunt. Cum vero in coelo, ubi omnia amore moventur, ubi defectus est nullus, odium esse nequeat, inimicos, id est effectu diversos, interpretamur. Mittamus impraesentia reliqua. Ecce nunc Saturnus quidem nobis in centro, Venus autem in circumferentia posuit voluptatem. Voluptas vero spirituum esca quaedam est. Igitur ex opposito Venus atque Saturnus spiritus nostri volatum aucupantur. Illa per voluptatem suam allicit ad externa, hic interim per suam ad intima revocat. Distrahunt itaque spiritum, si ferme eodem tempore moveant, atque

---

110 panis] pacis z
    De confirmatione ... debeamus y   quod devitare—coitum] vitandi coitus assiduaeque cogitationis praecepta z

which are harmonic to a spirit which is harmonic, warm and still living to the living, endowed with sense [i.e., meaning] to the sensitive [i.e., capable of sensation], songs conceived by reason to a spirit that is rational? Therefore I pass on to you this lyre which I made, and with it a Phoebean song, a consolation of travail, a pledge of long life. For just as things which are most tempered in quality, and at the same time aromatic, temper both the humors among themselves and the natural spirit with itself, so odors of this kind do for the vital spirit; so again harmonies of this kind do for the animal spirit. While therefore you temper the strings and the sounds in the lyre and the tones in your voice, consider your spirit to be tempered similarly within[6]. And lest I should be more stingy than Venus, who gets cold without Bacchus, receive this nectar through me from Father Liber himself: Those of you who get very cold, let them take at cold seasons twice every week two ounces of sweet wine (vernage or malmsey), with one ounce of bread, three hours before a meal; once a week only, however, let them take one dram of potable spirits [lit., sublimed water distilling from wine] with a half-ounce of rose-julep. They can conveniently also smear this liquor on their skin and sniff it. So that I may after this nectar also bring you ambrosia, I give besides a medicine received from Jupiter: Take four ounces of chebule myrobalans, three of rose-sugar, in winter one ounce of preserved ginger, in summer half an ounce. Cook these three gently with emblic honey and coat it with seven leaves of gold. Take a morsel of it four hours before dinner on an empty stomach. Take it daily for at least a whole year and 'thy youth shall be renewed like the eagle's.' "[7] Let us consider that Mercury spoke this much to us.

A Confirmation of the Aforesaid, and That We Should Avoid Both Continual Thinking and Sexual Intercourse.

Chap. XVI

astrologers say that Venus and Saturn are inimical to each other. But since there can be no hate in the heavens, where all things are moved by love, where there is no lack, let us interpret "inimical" as "diverse in effect." Let us omit the rest [of the heavenly bodies] for the present. Behold now Saturn has placed his pleasure in our center, Venus hers, however, in our circumference. But pleasure is a sort of food for the spirits. Therefore from opposite sides Venus and Saturn ensnare the flight of our spirit. She through her pleasure lures to external things, while he through his, recalls us to the internal. If they move the spirit at about the same time, they distract and dissipate it. For this reason

dissipant. Quamobrem nihil contemplatori vel curioso pestilentius quam Venereus actus, nihil vicissim hunc sectanti alienius quam cura et contemplatio   10
esse potest. Contemplatorem vero physicum religiosumque eodem in gradu
connumeramus, et gradu simili quemlibet in negotiis suis valde cogitabun-
dum gravibusque curis obnoxium. Hinc rursus efficitur, ut si quem Saturnia
vel contemplatione nimium occupatum vel cura pressum levare interim et aliter consolari velimus, per Venereos actus, ludos, iocos id tentantes, tanquam   15
per remedia longe distantia, frustra atque etiam cum iactura conemur; atque
vicissim, si quem Venereo vel opere perditum vel ludo iocoque solutum mo-
derari velimus, per Saturniam severitatem emendare non facile valeamus.
Optima vero disciplina est per quaedam Phoebi Iovisque, qui inter Saturnum
Veneremque sunt medii, studia similiaque remedia homines ad alterutrum   20
declinantes ad medium revocare.

 Sed ut tandem simus medici, sicut flamma duobus communiter modis vio-
lentis extinguitur—aut velut difflata ventis, aut contra quasi compressa cine-
ribus—sic spiritum vel celeriter effectu Venereo dissipamus vel sensim Saturnio suffocamus, ac saepe exprimimus comprimendo pariterque resolvimus.   25
Spiritus utique frequenter ad extima volans, intima reddit vel vacua vel aliena
vitae, sed ad intima saepe coactus, cetera circum membra praestat vitae minus idonea. Citam igitur senectutem tum Venus interioribus nostris, tum Saturnus exterioribus infert—Venus quidem praecipue, ubi ex quovis eius motu
facile corpus debilitatur atque labascit; Saturnus quoque potissimum, quando   30
ex quocunque contemplationis officio vel curae labore ingenii corporisque vires labefactantur. Et si vel qui ad contemplationem vel qui ad libidinem natus est, plerunque ad suum uterque officium est natura fortissimus. Natura
enim saepe coniungit cum voluptate simul et facilitate potentiam. Unusquisque
igitur se cognoscat, suique ipsius moderator ac medicus esto. Coitum quidem   35
frequentaturi ceteros consulant. Ego vero exercitaturis ingenium libro etiam
superiore consului. Denique omni diaeta omnibus remediis uti debent, quibus membra, spiritus, sensus, ingenium, memoria confirmentur; cogitationes
per intervalla repetere, nec expectare vel minimum ex cogitatione laborem;
maxime vero cum primum canescunt, quamvis nonnulli sint qui non tam de-   40
bilitate naturae, videlicet adhuc iuvenes, canos emittunt quam vel aegritudine
vel aegrotatione aliqua praecedente, aut etiam parentum similitudine, a quibus scilicet iam canescentibus fuerint generati.

---

15 id *om. z*   18 vellimus *x*   Saturnum *z*   28 *post* Venus *add.* in *x*   31 cura *z*   32 Et si] etsi *z*   34 coniungito *z*   40 debilitatae *wx*   42 a *om. x*

nothing can be more noxious to the contemplator or the investigator than the Venereal act; nothing more alien, in turn, to those pursuing the latter, than care and contemplation. (Let us count the scientific and the religious contemplator as being on the same level, and on a similar level the person who is full of cogitations about his business affairs and subject to heavy responsibilities.) Hence again it comes about that if we should wish to uplift awhile and otherwise to console a person who is too occupied by Saturnine contemplation or oppressed with cares, and should attempt it by the Venereal act, games, and jokes, as a cure through opposites, our effort would be futile and even harmful; and conversely if we should wish to rein in anyone abandoned to the works of Venus or relaxed in gaming or joking, we will not easily prevail to amend him through Saturnine severity. No, the best discipline is to recall to the mean those declining to either side through certain pursuits and remedies of Phoebus and of Jupiter, who are the middle planets between Saturn and Venus.

But finally, to be medical: just as there are two violent means whereby a flame can generally be extinguished—either being blown out as it were by wind or, contrariwise, being compressed by ashes—so we either quickly dissipate the spirit by the Venereal effect or gradually suffocate it by the Saturnian, and often by this repression we force it out and so by the same means we resolve it. Indeed the spirit frequently flying to the outside renders the inside either empty or alien to life; but when forced often to the inside, it leaves the rest of the surrounding bodily parts less suitable for life. Therefore sometimes Venus brings old age to the interior parts, sometimes Saturn to the exterior— Venus especially when by reason of any Venereal motion the body is easily weakened and totters; Saturn especially when by reason of some duty of contemplation or labor of responsibility he causes the powers of mind and body to totter. And yet if a given person is born for contemplation, or another one is born for lust, either is usually very strong by nature toward performing his own vocation. For nature often accompanies power with simultaneous pleasure and facility. Therefore let everyone know himself; each of you be the ruler and doctor of himself. Let those who are going to have an active sex life consult other doctors. But in the preceding book I have counseled those who are going to exercise their intelligence. Next, they ought to use every diet, all the remedies by which the bodily parts, the spirit, the senses, the intelligence, and the memory may be strengthened; they ought to return to their cogitations with breaks and not wait for a break until they derive even a little fatigue from them. This is especially important, moreover, as soon as they start to get gray— although there are not a few who put forth white hairs while still young, not so much from debility of nature as from either sorrow or some past sickness or even likeness to their parents from whom they were generated when the latter were already getting gray.

*De medicinis senum
et de habitatione iterum atque diaeta.*

Cap. XVII.

Chaldaeorum regula est forte probanda ad iuventutem recuperandam: peregrinos humores imbibitos corpori expurgare gradatim, tum interiores competentibus medicinis, tum exteriores frictionibus et lavacris provocationibusque sudoris; intereaque salubribus duraturisque alimentis paulatim corpus implere. Sunt autem qui trochiscis quibusdam ex vipera factis vel helleboro praeparato promittunt humores omnes veteres putridosque prorsus educere; quibus expurgatis et humore rursum saluberrimo alimentis salutaribus recreato, restituere iuventutem. Et qui cautiores sunt, helleboro gallinas pascunt, hominem vero gallinis. Eiusmodi vero curationem tanquam periculosam in iuventute arbitror potius quam in senectute tentandam, ne forte iuventutem illam a Medea Peliae seni promissam experiamur. Nam et iuvenes medicinis exquisite purgantibus cito senescere Hippocrates asserit. Sed ubi diaeta non sufficit, clystere vel manna vel aloe praesertim lota securus uteris; si tibi sit alvus astricitor, manna cum iure caponis myrobalanique virtute. Sin minus, hac te iuvenem etiam in senectute purgatione servabis: sume unciam lotae aloes unam, myrobalanorum emblicarum drachmas duas, chebularum quoque tantundem, duas item rosarum purpurearum, masticis quoque tantundem; malvatico vino confice pilulas, quando Luna feliciter collocata propitio fruitur Iovis aspectu, praesertim si domicilia fixa possederit vel ipsa vel Iuppiter. Haec enim ad diuturnitatem vitae magnopere conferunt. Potes etiam utiliter reubarbarum hic cum aloe componere, scilicet dimidiam aloes partem, dimidiam reubarbari; et quotiens opus fuerit, unam mane sumere pilulam ad tres usque vel quinque, modicumque insuper vinum bibere. Ubi vero pituitam magis times, potes commode in his pilulis trochiscorum agarici tertiam partem accipere una cum tertiis aloes duabus, dimisso reubarbaro. Sed primam illam ego iam multis annis pilularum compositionem omni aetati experior esse tutissimam.

    Eadem hora confectionem eiusmodi facito: sume myrobalanorum emblicarum, belliricarum, Indarum, chebularum, unciam uniuscuiusque unam, cinnamomi vero duas, unam quoque doronici, rosarum purpurearum unam, sandalarum rubeorum duas, unam croci drachmam, tertiam drachmae partem musci, ambrae tantundem. Candidum post haec cum aqua rosacea succoque citri fundito saccharum; coque, fac bolos, auroque involve. Hoc ante prandium quattuor horis sumentes atque dantes, utiliter experti sumus ad virtutem corroborandam, ad illustrandum spiritum atque firmandum. Ma-

---

De medicinis] Medicinae *z*   5 trochisaeis *z*   25 omisso *z*   33 fac] ac *z*

*On Medicines for the Elderly
and More about Their Dwellings and Their Diet.*
Chap. XVII

To recover youth, we should probably endorse the rule of the Chaldeans: gradually to purge out foreign humors which the body has incurred, both the more internal by the appropriate medicines and the more external by rubbings and baths and provocations to sweat; and during that time to fill the body little by little with healthy and long-lasting food.[1] There are those, however, who promise to eliminate right away all old or putrid humors with certain trochees prepared from a viper or from hellebore; they promise that when they have purged these and restored very healthy moisture by wholesome foods, they will restore youth. Those who are more cautious feed chickens with the hellebore, and the patient with the chickens. But I think that a cure of this kind, being somewhat dangerous, should be attempted in youth rather than in old age, lest perchance we experience that youth which was promised by Medea to the old Pelias.[2] For according to Hippocrates even the young quickly grow old if they take medicines which purge totally. But where diet does not suffice [to maintain regularity], you are safe using a clyster, manna, or aloes, especially if washed; or, if you have a belly that is too bound up, manna with the juice of a capon and extract of myrobalan. But if it is not too bound up, you will be kept young even in old age by the following purgation: one ounce of washed aloes, two drams of emblic myrobalan, the same amount of chebule myrobalan, the same amount of purple roses, the same amount of mastic; make into pills with malmsey wine, when the Moon, fortunately located, enjoys a favorable aspect with Jupiter, especially if either she or Jupiter occupy their fixed houses. For these things contribute very greatly to length of life. You can also usefully compound rhubarb with aloes, that is, half aloes, half rhubarb; and in the morning, as often as needed, take one, three, or even up to five pills of it, and drink besides a little wine. But when you are more fearful of phlegm, you can conveniently put in these pills a third part of agaric trochees in place of the rhubarb along with two thirds of aloes. But after many years I now find the first composition of pills to be the safest for every age-group.

In the same astrological hour, make an electuary of this kind: Take of myrobalans one ounce each of the emblic, the belleric, the Indic, and the chebule, but two ounces of cinnamon, also one ounce of doronicum, one ounce of purple roses, two of red sandal, one dram of saffron, one-third dram of musk, the same amount of amber. After this, pour in white sugar with rose-water and citron-juice, cook, make morsels, and roll them with gold. For strengthening a power, for illuminating the spirit and firming it up, we have found

xime vero proderit, si paulum quid insuper vini aurei biberis. Proderit et saepe calefactum panem aureo mero et rosacea aqua perfundere, ac modico insuper cinnamomo saccharoque uberiore condire; frequenter etiam duo haec cum lacte amygdalino et modico pane miscere, nam eiusmodi mixtiones naturam referunt Iovialem.

Praeter omnia quae in superioribus explicavimus vel saltem significavimus, ab his omnes urbani diligenter cavere debent: aestu, gelu, quolibet vel post calorem frigore vel nocturno, nebulis, ventis vel ex palude flantibus vel irrumpentibus ex angusto, locis item ubi aer vel movetur violentius vel nullo modo movetur, habitatione quavis humidiore, fetore, torpore, maerore — diligentius autem Mercurii sectatores, diligentissime senes. Qui praeterea postquam mane corpus totum leviter perfricuerint, delinient ipsum adversum aeris et laboris incommoda calente oleo vel vino quopiam subamaro, cui prius infuderint myrrham et rosam atque myrtum. Salviam frequenter ore ferant, nervis ac dentibus amicissimam; et quando dentium vitio liquida velut infantes alimenta repetere compelluntur, mollissima caveant. Lac quidem vino referant moderato. Utantur igne duntaxat ut medicina, quantum videlicet expellendi frigoris et suscitandi caloris innati necessitas postulat, alioquin tanquam edace humorem naturalem exsiccaturo. Solem vero, quoad delectat, sequantur ut alimentum, destillatione vitata et aestu similiter declinato. Faciles quidem motus diligant, excitando calori admodum necessarios. Labores autem corporis oderint, et multo magis animi; nec minus longam sitim et inediam atque vigiliam.

De nutrimento spiritus et conservatione vitae per odores.

Cap. XVIII.

Legimus in calidis quibusdam regionibus ac plurimo passim odore flagrantibus multos gracili corpore et imbecillo stomacho quasi solis odoribus ali, forte quoniam ipsa natura loci tum herbarum et frugum atque pomorum succos ferme totos redigit in odores, tum corporum humanorum humores illic resolvit in spiritum. Cum igitur uterque videlicet odor et spiritus sit vapor quidam, et simile simili nutriatur, nimirum et spiritus et spiritalis homo plu-

---

45 maerore *ante* torpore *transp. z*   48 calentem $L^{ac}w^{ac}$ 51 compelluntur] cogantur *z*   56 quidam *z*
   Cap. XVIII. om. L   1 fragrantibus *z*

it useful to take and administer this four hours before dinner. It would do the most good if you would drink it with a little bit of golden wine. Often it would also be good to moisten hot bread with golden, unmixed wine and rose-water, and besides to season it with a little cinnamon and considerably more sugar. The latter two should frequently also be mixed with almond-milk and a little bread, for mixtures of this kind restore a Jovial nature.

Besides all those things which we have explained, or at least indicated, in the foregoing, all city-dwellers ought carefully to avoid the following: namely, heat of summer; cold of winter, or indeed any cold that's after heat or nocturnal; clouds; winds that come from a swamp; drafts; likewise places where the air moves violently or does not move at all; also any habitation that is too damp; stench; torpor; and sadness; the followers of Mercury should do this more carefully, old people most carefully of all. Besides, in the morning they should also rub their whole body lightly; let them anoint it against adverse effects of air and occupation with warm oil or slightly bitter wine in which they have previously infused myrrh, rose, and myrtle. In their mouth they should often carry sage, which is very kind to sinews and teeth; and when through lack of teeth they are forced to seek again liquid food like infants, they should avoid foods which are extremely soft. Let them even go back to milk, keeping the wine in due measure. Let them use fire only like a medicine, insofar, that is, as necessity demands for expelling cold and arousing the natural heat; used otherwise, it will voraciously dry out the natural moisture. But let them seek the sun like food, insofar as it pleases them, while avoiding sprinkly weather and shunning summer heat. They should delight in easy movements, which are very necessary to stimulate heat. But they should abhor exertion of the body and much more that of the mind, no less long thirst, fasting, and sleeplessness.

On Nourishing the Spirit and Conserving Life through Odors.

Chap. XVIII

We read that in certain regions that are hot and redolent throughout with many odors, many people of delicate body and weak stomach are nourished almost on odors alone[1] — perhaps because the very nature of the place reduces as it were all the juices of the green vegetables, field-produce, and fruits into odor, and in consequence there it resolves the humors of human bodies into spirit. Since each of them — that is, odor and spirit — is a certain vapor, and like is nourished by like, no doubt the spirit and the person

rimum ab odoribus accipit alimentum. Nutrimentum vero, qualecunque id sit, per odores sive fomentum apprime senibus et gracilibus necessarium est, quo defectum alimenti solidioris atque verioris utcunque compensare possimus. Ambigere tamen nonnulli solent, utrum spiritus odoribus nutriatur. Ego autem opinor solis forsan ita nutriri, ut nisi alimenta quae crassa sunt digestione tandem in vapores extenuentur, spiritus ipse, quem diximus vaporem esse, nullum illinc suscipiat nutrimentum. Itaque vinum odore plenum spiritum subito recreat, quem cetera vix tandem reficere possunt. Vaporem vero illum, in quem cibi cocti denique transferuntur, ideo appellamus odorem, quoniam et odor ubique vapor quidam est, et hic tractus intus ex alimentis vapor, nisi spiritui quodam odore placeat, vix ullum spiritui exhibet alimentum. Quamobrem Avicennam nostrum valde probamus dicentem, corpus quidem dulcedine, spiritum vero quadam (ut eius verbis utar) aromaticitate nutriri — quoniam crassitudo corporis non nisi crassa natura, qualis est in dulcedine, coalescere valeat; tenuitas vero spiritus non alio quam fumo quodam atque vapore, in quo aromaticitas ipsa viget, refici possit. Aromaticam vero qualitatem dicimus odoram et acutam et quodammodo stypticam. Proinde quoniam iecur quidem corpori per sanguinem alimentum praestat, dulcedine plurimum augetur; cor autem, quia et creat spiritum, et spiritui procreat alimentum, merito desiderat aromatica. Expedit tamen et aromatica pro corde condiri dulcedine, et dulcia pro iecore aromaticis commisceri, dulcedinemque interea nimiam evitare.

Quid plura? Galienus ipse secutus Hippocratem spiritum non solum odore putat nutriri, sed aere — aere, inquam, non simplici, sed potius opportune permixto. Quibus quidem si fidem habebimus, nec alimentorum nec rei ullius delectum magis ad vitam necessarium quam aeris nobis accommodati esse censebimus. Aer enim et inferiorum et coelestium qualitatibus facillime semperque affectus, et immensa (ut ita dixerim) amplitudine circumfusus, perpetuoque motu nos undique penetrans, ad suam nos mirabiliter redigit qualitatem — praesertim spiritum, praecipue vitalem in corde vigentem, in cuius penetralia tum assidue influit, tum repente; sic protinus afficiens spiritum, ut est affectus, perque spiritum vitalem, qui et materia et origo est spiritus animalis, pariter afficiens animalem. Cuius quidem qualitas maximi momenti est ingeniosis eiusmodi spiritu plurimum laborantibus, itaque ad nullos potius quam ad eos attinet puri luminosique aeris odorumque delectus atque musicae. Haec enim tria spiritus animalis fomenta praecipua iudicantur. Potissimus vero ad vitam est aer electus. Nam octavo mense nati in

---

9 utrunque Lw^{ac} 39 efficiens z

with a lot of spirit receive great nourishment from odors. But this nourishment, whatever it is, or this fomentation through odors is especially necessary to people who are old or delicate; by this we can compensate, in one way or another, for their lack of more solid and genuine food. But some people frequently question whether the spirit can be nourished by odors. I think, though, that perhaps it is never nourished by anything else, in that if foods, which are dense, are not finally attenuated by digestion into vapors, the spirit, which itself is a vapor, as we have said, will receive no nourishment therefrom. For that reason wine full of odor renews instantly a spirit which other things can scarcely restore in a long time. But we call an odor that vapor into which digested food is subsequently transformed on these grounds: because odor is always a vapor, and this vapor extracted from foods inside us scarcely affords any nourishment to the spirit unless it pleases the spirit by an odor. For this reason I heartily approve my favorite authority Avicenna saying that the body is nourished by sweetness, the spirit, however, by a certain (to use his term) aromaticity[2] — since the density of the body cannot coalesce without a dense nature such as inheres in sweetness; while the fineness of the spirit cannot be restored otherwise than by a certain smoke and vapor in which that aromaticity flourishes. We call aromatic a quality that is odorous and sharp and somewhat styptic. Accordingly the liver, because it furnishes food to the body through the blood, is much augmented by sweetness; the heart, moreover, because it both creates the spirit and generates food for it, rightly desires spices ["aromatica"]. Notwithstanding, it is expedient that spices for the heart be seasoned with sweetness, and that the sweet things for the liver be mixed with spices, all the while avoiding excessive sweetness.

What more shall I say? Galen himself, following Hippocrates, thinks the spirit is nourished not only by odor but by air[3] — by air, I say, that is not simple but rather suitably mixed. If we believe them, we will judge that it is not more necessary to life to select either foods or any other thing than it is to select air adapted to us. For air, affected easily and always by qualities of things both sublunary and celestial, poured around us with a sort of immeasurable amplitude, and with its perpetual motion penetrating us on all sides, reduces us wonderfully to its quality — especially our spirit, especially the vital spirit, which flourishes in the heart, into whose chambers it [the air] flows now steadily, now suddenly; thus straightway affecting the spirit according as it is itself disposed, and through the vital spirit — which is the matter and origin of the animal spirit — equally affecting the animal spirit. For intellectuals, the quality of the animal spirit is of the highest concern because they mostly work by means of this spirit; and so they, more than anyone, have to select pure and luminous air, odors, and music. For these three are judged to be the principal fomentations of the animal spirit. Most important to life, however, is choice air. For in Egypt, many babies born in the eighth month survive, and also many in

Aegypto plurimi vivunt, et nonnulli in plagis Graeciae temperatis saluberrimi aeris beneficio, quod Aristoteles narrat et Avicenna confirmat. Sed profecto sicut corpus ex variis compositum variis (quamvis non eadem mensa) nutriendum est alimentis, ita spiritus similiter compositus varietate quadam aeris semper electi oblectandus est atque fovendus; simili quoque electorum odorum varietate quotidie recreandus, nam aer et odor quasi spiritus quidam esse videntur.

Iam vero Alexander et Nicolaus Peripatetici una cum Galieno concludunt spiritum vitalem et animalem ideo nutriri tum odore, tum aere, quoniam uterque mixtus est atque conformis, et utrunque haustum in praecordia penetrare, ibi coqui temperarique ad vitam, perque arterias diffundi. Ubi uterque coctus iterum, nutrit spiritum (ut aiunt) utrunque, praecipue animalem. Aiunt etiam spiratum aerem non solum refrigerando calori prodesse, sed etiam nutriendo, nam et animalia etiam valde frigida spirant. Addunt aerem crassiorem spiritui naturali tanquam magis corporeo convenire, subtilem vero, purum, lucidum spiritui potius vitali, potissimum animali. Neque mirum videri debet spiritum adeo tenuem rebus quoque tenuibus ali, siquidem et pisciculi multi aqua nitidissima nutriuntur, et ocimum in aqua simili vivit, crescit, floret, redolet. Mitto quibus elementis chameleontem et salamandram nutriri nonnulli ferant.

Redeamus ad nostra. Interest certe quam plurimum, qualem spiremus aerem, quales hauriamus odores; talis enim et spiritus in nobis evadit. Eatenus vero nos anima per vitam vegetat, quatenus spiritus harmoniam servat cum anima concinentem. Spiritus quidem in nobis primus vivit et maxime et quasi vivit solus. Nonne repentino quodam saepe casu vel affectu vita, sensus, motus subito membra deserunt, regresso videlicet ad cordis penetralia spiritu; et saepe statim revertuntur ad membra per frictiones et odores illuc spiritu redeunte, quasi vita in ipso spiritu videlicet re volatili potius insit quam humoribus aut membris? Alioquin propter horum crassam tenacitatem tardius admodum accederet vita membris atque recederet. Quicunque igitur vitam in corpore producere cupitis, spiritum imprimis excolite: hunc augete nutrimentis sanguinem augentibus, temperatum videlicet atque clarum; hunc aere semper electo fovete; hunc quotidie suavibus odoribus alite; hunc sonis et cantibus oblectate. Sed interea odores cavete calidiores, frigidiores fugite, capescite temperatos; frigidos calidis, siccos humidis temperate. Odorem vero omnem, quia pars corporis subtilissima est, scitote nonnihil habere caloris; atque ex rebus quae ipsae nutriunt, odores sperate potius nutrituros, ut ex

---

46 mensa] immensa *z*   49 odorum *om. z*   54 ibi *yz*; ubi *Lux*   56 spiritum *x*   63 nonnulli *om.* *z*   67 concinientem *x;* continentem *z*   in *om. x*   68 effectu *x*   71 ipso] eo *z*   72 tenuitatem $L^{ac}w^{ac}$ 80 sperate] separate *x*   potius *ante* sperate *transp. z*   nutritos *z*

the temperate regions of Greece, thanks to the very salubrious air—which Aristotle recounts and Avicenna confirms.[4] But assuredly just as the body composed of various things must be nourished by various foods (albeit not at the same meal), so the spirit similarly composed must be delighted and fomented by a variety of air, always well selected; it should also be refreshed daily by a similar variety of choice odors; for air and odor themselves seem to be things resembling spirits.

Now the Peripatetics Alexander and Nicolas along with Galen conclude that the vital and the animal spirits are nourished with odor and with air for this reason: because both of the latter are mixed and are of like form and both having been absorbed penetrate into the heart and there are digested and tempered to the use of life and poured through the arteries. In the arteries, as they say, both having been digested, again nourish both of these spirits and especially the animal spirit. Moreover, they say that the air we breathe is good not only for cooling our heat but also for nourishment, on the grounds that even animals who are very cold [e.g., reptiles] breathe. They add that the thicker air is more suitable for the natural spirits, these being the more corporeal; the thin air, pure and clear, suitable rather for the vital and, most of all, for the animal spirit.[5] Nor should it be any surprise that the spirit being so tenuous is nourished by things that are also tenuous, since indeed many small fishes are nourished by the clearest water, and in such water basil lives, grows, flourishes, and gives forth its odor—not to mention those elements which the chameleon and the salamander are frequently said to subsist on.[6]

Let us go back to our own concerns. It is as important as possible what sort of air we breathe, what sort of odors we inhale; for the spirit in us also becomes like them. For just as the soul quickens us with life, just so the spirit preserves complete harmony with the soul. The spirit indeed is what lives in us first, and most of all, and as if it alone lived. Do not life, sense, and motion often in a certain sudden accident or passion suddenly desert the bodily parts, the spirit having retreated suddenly to the chambers of the heart; and often do they not return right away to the bodily parts through rubbings and odors when the spirit returns to them, as if life indeed inhered rather in that volatile spirit than in the humors or the bodily parts? Otherwise, on account of the thick viscosity of the humors, life would come to and recede from the bodily parts much more slowly. Therefore people who wish to lengthen their life in the body, should especially cultivate the spirit: augment it with nutriments which augment blood, that blood which is tempered and clear; foment it always with choice air; feed it daily with sweet odors; and delight it with sound and song. But meanwhile beware the hotter odors, flee the colder ones, seize on the temperate ones; temper the cold with the hot, the dry with the moist. But beware that every odor because it is the most subtle part of the given body, has some heat; and expect that those odors are going to be more nourishing which come

aromatico pyro pomoque Persico similique pomo, magis autem recente pane calente, maxime carnibus assis, quam maxime vino. Atque sicut sapor, qui mirifice placet, plurimi velocisque nutrimenti causa est vel occasio corpori, sic odorem ad spiritum se habere putate. Commemorare vobis iterum placet Democritum iamiam expiraturum, ut obsequeretur amicis, spiritum ad quatriduum usque olfactu calentium panum retinuisse, ulterius etiam, si modo placuisset, spiritum servaturum. Sunt et qui dicunt id mellis odore fecisse. Ego, si modo usus est melle, existimo illum mel vino liquefactum albo calentibus panibus infudisse, neque enim spernendus est mellis odor. Flos namque florum mel existit, nec parum nutrit ipsa dulcedine, ac diu qualitate sua res integras a putrefactione tuetur. Itaque si quis noverit hoc etiam ad cibum ita vesci, ut nec dulcedine nimia meatus oppleat, nec tali quodam calore bilem exaugeat, certum habebit longioris vitae subsidium. Saltem igitur condimentum hoc frigidis et humidis adhibete.

Verum ut vos revocem ad odores. Ubicunque suffocationem compressionemque spirituum nimiam extimescitis, quod maeror frequens torporque portendit, odores circumfusos amate. Ubi vero fugam exhalantium spirituum expavescitis, odores potius infusos nutrimentis accipite. Et si quid odorum praeterea foris sumitis, velut clypeum costis duntaxat admovete sinistris. Nonne videtis quam repente sursum vel deorsum ad odores se matrix ipsa praecipitet? Quam velociter ad os, ad nares spiritus advolet, suavis odoris esca pellectus? Ubi igitur spiritus vel exiguus vel fugacissimus esse deprehenditur, quod pusillanimitas saepe declarat corporisque debilitas vel parva de causa multa contingens, odoribus non tam extrinsecus obiectis quam intrinsecus iniectis allicite, immo potius pascite, retinete. Odorem vero vini ante omnes eligite, multum namque nutrit spiritum odor exhalans ex natura, tum plurimum et velociter nutriente corpus, tum voluptate sensum afficiente. Tale vero vinum est prae ceteris calidum, humidum et odorum atque clarum. Tale etiam saccharum esse dicerem, si sumat odorem; cinnamomum quoque simile, et doronicum anisumque et dulce marathrum, si acumini suo ad exiguam dulcedinem adderent ampliorem. Sed quam temperiem natura non fecit, vobis ipsi conficite. Et quotiens distractionem spirituum formidatis, calidioribus acutioribusque et subtilissimis adhibete, quae cohibere parumper volatum spiritus ac sistere valeant, ceu croco, gariophylis, cinnamomo adustum panem, rosaceam aquam acetumque rosaceum, rosam, myrtum, violam, sandalum, coriandrum, cydonium pomum atque citrum. Horreo vero camphoram, ubi contra canitiem est agendum. Recentem vero semper mentam diligo, menti etiam salutarem spirituique tutissimam.

Denique mementote res omnes veneno contrarias esse vitae admodum sa-

---

82 sicut] si ut z   87 servaturus Lw^{ac} 92 tali *post* bilem *transp.* x   96 extimescetis z   97 spiritum Lw 98 expavescetis z   106 ex] et $L^{ac}w^{ac}$ 109 dicitur z   114 seu z   116 Hordeo z

from things which are themselves nourishing, as for example from the aromatic pear, the peach, and similar kinds of fruit—more, however, from fresh, hot bread; most from roasted meat; most of all from wine. And consider that just as taste, which wondrously pleases, is the cause or occasion of the most and quickest nourishment to the body, so odors behave toward the spirit. It is pleasant to remind you again how Democritus, when he was at the point of death, to gratify the wishes of his friends retained his spirit for four days by the smell of hot loaves; he would have kept his spirit even longer if only it had pleased him to do so.[7] There are also those who say that he did this by the smell of honey. I think that if he used honey at all, he poured it, liquefied with white wine, into the hot loaves. For the odor of honey is not to be scorned; for it is the flower of the flowers; it nourishes considerably by its very sweetness; moreover, by its quality things are kept for a long time whole from putrefaction. And so if anyone knows how to eat honey, even as a food, so as not to fill up his passages with too much sweetness nor to augment choler with its heat, he will possess a sure support for a longer life. Present this, therefore, at least as a condiment to the cold and moist foods.

But let us get back to odors. When you get very worried about too much suffocation and compression of the spirit, which portends frequent sadness and torpor, tell people to scatter odors around the patient. But when you get worried about the escape of exhaled spirit, take the odors infused in the nourishment instead. If besides you take any odor externally, apply it as a shield only to the left ribs. Don't you see how quickly the very matrix flings itself upwards or downwards towards odors?—how swiftly the spirit flies to the mouth, to the nostrils, allured with the bait of a sweet odor? Therefore where the spirit is found either meager or prone to escape, of which the signs are pusillanimity or great weakness of body arising even from a small cause, allure it with odors not so much offered externally as inserted internally—indeed, feed it and keep it. But choose the odor of wine before all others, for its odor exhaling from its nature nourishes the spirit much; while most of all and quickly it nourishes the body and affects the sense with pleasure. Such wine is particularly hot, moist, odorous, and clear. I would say sugar is like this, if it assumes an odor; cinnamon is also similar, and doronicum, anise, and sweet fennel, if, with their sharpness, people add more sweetness to the little that they have. Thus make for yourselves that balance which nature did not make. And as often as you fear dispersion of the spirit, bring to bear the hotter, sharper, and very subtle things, which inhibit a little the volatile spirit and prevail upon it to stand still, as you do by saffron, cloves, and cinnamon, namely: toast, rose-water, rose-vinegar, a rose, myrtle, violet, sandal, coriander, quince, and citron. But I abhor camphor when we have to counteract gray hair. But I always like fresh mint, salutary also to the mind and very safe for the spirit.

Finally, remember that all things which are contrary to poison are very salu-

lutares, non gustu tantum, sed etiam odoratu, maxime theriacam. Has vero in libro *Contra pestilentiam* enarravimus, narrabimus et in libro sequenti. Inter eas autem ne quid vos lateat, numeramus et vinum; nam sicut homini venenum est cicuta, ita cicutae vinum, non simul quidem, sed paulo post ebibitum. Ac ne solis vos odoribus hic alliciam, componendum vobis mando electuarium, quotidie mane gustandum, olfactu gustuque suave et vitae admodum salutare. Accipite tres chebularum uncias, unam emblicarum et Indarum unam unamque belliricarum, semunciam vero doronici, cinnamomi uncias duas, croci drachmam unam, ambrae partem drachmae tertiam, musci quoque tantundem. Contundite diligenter. Tantum rosacei sacchari adhibete, quantum gustui satis facit, sandalorum rubentium quantum sat est colori, mellis item emblicarum vel chebularum quantum molli expedit electuarii formae, auri folia totidem quot praedictae sunt unciae. Ubi vero difficilior est compositio multiplex, experti sumus simplicem hanc optimam esse, scilicet ex chebulis, marathro dulci, saccharo aqua rosacea liquefacto, sumptam vero tum ieiuno stomacho, tum post coenam. Memineritis autem myrobalanos conditas meliores esse; siccas vero saltem diem integrum oleo amygdalarum dulcium vel butyro vaccino prius infundite quam confletis. Probat et Avicenna vobis confectionem ex emblicis atque Indis cum melle anacardorum coctoque butyro, item chebulas cum zinzibere et squama ferri et potius auri. Probat item Petrus Aponensis compositionem ex croco, mace, castoreo, per partes aequales acceptis atque contusis et vino commixtis; unde affirmat vitam etiam propemodum moribundis produci consuevisse. Denique Haly astrologus medicusque excellens asserit usu tripherae similiumque rerum vitam effici longiorem. In omni vero triphera myrobalanus fundamentum est; sed hanc temperant subtilibus quibusdam atque mollibus, praesertim ubi siccior est myrobalanus, ut et penetret, nec meatus obstruat, nec alvum exsiccet nimium vel astringat. Cum vino praeterea commodissime utimur, sed modico, ne forte diluat. Compositionem vero Petri, quam modo narrabam, si modo utilis est, arbitror olfactu potius quam potu utilem fore.

Magorum medicina pro senibus.

Cap. XIX.

Magi, stellarum observatores, ad Christum, vitae ducem, stella duce venerunt, pretiosum vitae thesaurum offerentes, aurum, thus et myrrham, tria dona pro tribus planetarum dominis stellarum Domino dedi-

---

128 croci] coci *z*   129 adhibite *yz*   141 aequales *om. z*   145 temperant] superant *z*
    De magorum *y*   Cap. XVIII. *Lw*

tary to life, by means not only of taste but of smell, and especially theriac. But we have recounted these in our book *Consiglio contro la pestilenza*, and we will recount them in the next book.[8] So that you will know them all, among these antidotes, moreover, we number also wine; for just as hemlock is poison to man, so wine is to hemlock, when drunk not at the same time but a little after. And lest I should allure you here only with odors, I entrust to you the makings of an electuary, to be tasted every morning, sweet to smell and taste and very salutary to life. Take three ounces of chebule myrobalans, one of emblic, one of Indic, one of belleric, but one-half ounce of doronicum, two ounces of cinnamon, one dram of saffron, one-third dram of amber, and the same amount of musk. Grind it thoroughly and add as much rose-sugar as will satisfy the taste, as much red sandal as is sufficient for color, likewise as much of emblic or chebule honey as needed to make the electuary soft, and as many leaves of gold as there are ounces aforesaid. But when a multiple compound is too difficult, we have found that this simple one is the best, namely, of chebule myrobalan, sweet fennel, and sugar dissolved in rose-water, taken sometimes on an empty stomach, sometimes after supper. Remember that preserved myrobalans are the best; moisten the dry ones at least a whole day in sweet almond-oil or cow-butter before you mix them with anything. Also, Avicenna endorses for you a confection made of emblic and Indic myrobalans with cashew-honey and melted butter, likewise chebule myrobalans with ginger and scales of iron and preferably of gold.[9] Likewise Pietro d'Abano approves a compound made from equal parts of saffron, mace, and castor, and ground and mixed with wine with which he affirms that he often extended even a life which was practically moribund.[10] In conclusion, Haly, the astrologer and excellent physician, asserts that life is made longer by the use of triphera and similar things.[11] In every triphera, myrobalan is the foundation; but this one they temper with subtle and soft things, especially when the myrobalan is somewhat dry, so that it penetrates yet does not obstruct the passages or dry up the belly too much or constrict it. I use it most conveniently with wine alongside, but just a little, so as not to dilute it. But Pietro's composition which I recounted just now, if it is useful, I think it will be useful rather to smell than to drink.

The Medicine of the Magi for Old People.

Chap. XIX

The Magi, observers of the stars, came to Christ, the guide of life, under the guidance of a star; they offered a precious treasury of life—gold, frankincense, and myrrh; they dedicated three gifts representing the lords of

cantes: aurum quidem pro temperamento Iovis maxime omnium temperatum, thus autem pro Sole praecipue Phoebeo calore simul odoreque flagrans, myrrham denique firmantem corpus atque conservantem pro Saturno omnium firmissimo planetarum. Huc igitur omnes ad sapientes Magos venite senes, munera vobis quoque vitam productura ferentes, quibus auctorem vitae quondam venerati traduntur. Venite senes, inquam, senectutem graviter tolerantes. Venite et vos praeterea quoscunque senectutis propemodum adventantis formido sollicitat. Accipite, precor, alacres vitalia dona: sumite uncias quidem thuris duas, unam vero myrrhae, auri rursum in folia ducti dimidiam drachmae partem; contundite tria simul, conflate, confundite in pilulas aureo quodam mero, idque tunc opportune conficite, quando Diana propitio Phoebi vel Iovis gaudet aspectu. Sumite posthac thesauri tanti aurora qualibet portiunculam, ac exiguo perfundite meri potu, nisi forsan incaluerit aestas, tunc enim aquam rosaceam bibere praestat. Si quis autem inter vos calorem quovis tempore magis metuat, is myrobalanum chebulam aut emblicam aequalem ad thuris myrrhaeque et auri simul pondus adiiciat. Hoc humorem proculdubio naturalem a putrefactione tuebitur, hoc humoris resolutionem longius propulsabit, hoc tres in vobis spiritus — naturalem, vitalem, animalem — fovebit, confirmabit, corroborabit; hoc rursum vegetabit sensum, acuet ingenium, memoriam conservabit.

De periculis evitandis ex quolibet vitae septenario imminentibus.

Cap. XX.

Cum astronomi singulas deinceps diei horas planetis ordine singulis distribuerint similiterque septem hebdomadae dies, atque in ipso foetu per menses digesserint officia planetarum, cur non etiam per annos eadem disponamus? Ut quemadmodum infantem in alvo latentem rexit primo mense Saturnus, ultimo Luna, sic statim natum ordine iam converso primo ipsius anno ducat Luna, secundo (si vis) Mercurius, tertio Venus, quarto Sol, quinto Mars, sexto Iuppiter, septimo vero Saturnus; atque deinceps ordo per vitam similis repetatur. Itaque in septimo quolibet vitae anno fit in corpore mutatio maxima ideoque periculosissima, quandoquidem et Saturnus nobis

---

6 conservantem] confirmantem *z*   19 aequalem] a qualem *z*   addiciat *Lw*   20 resolutione *z*
  vitandis *z*   Cap. XVIIII. *Lwx*

the planets to the Lord of the stars: gold, that is, representing the temperedness of Jupiter, because gold is the most tempered substance of all; frankincense for the Sun, because it especially glows with Phoebean heat as well as odor; and finally myrrh, which firms up the body and preserves it, for Saturn the most stable of all planets. Therefore all you old people, come here to the wise Magi who are bearing gifts for you too — gifts that are going to lengthen your life, gifts with which they are said to have once worshipped the author of life. Come, old people, I say, who are taking old age hard. Come too, you who are just troubled by the fear that old age is quickly approaching. Please receive gladly these gifts: Take two ounces of frankincense, one of myrrh, again one-half dram of gold formed into leaves; grind the three together, mingle them, mix them with a golden wine to form pills, and perform this at the lucky hour when Diana enjoys the favorable aspect of Phoebus or of Jove. Thereafter take a small portion of this great treasure any day at dawn, and wash it down with a little drink of wine — except if it be in the heat of summer, for then it is better to drink rose-water. Moreover, if at any time any of you especially fears heat, let him add a myrobalan, either chebule or emblic, equal to the combined weight of the frankincense, myrrh, and gold. Beyond any question, this will guard your natural moisture from putrefaction, this will ward off for a longer time the resolution of the moisture, this will foment, confirm, and strengthen in you the three spirits — natural, vital, and animal; again, this will quicken your senses, it will sharpen your intelligence, it will conserve your memory.[1]

On Avoiding Those Dangers Which Are Imminent in Any Septenary of Life.

Chap. XX

Since astronomers have distributed the respective hours of the day in succession to the respective planets in order; and in similar order the seven days of the week; and have in the very unborn babe organized by months the functions of the planets, why should we not also arrange the same functions by years? Just as Saturn rules the babe hidden in the womb for the first month and the Moon for the last, so, as soon as he is born, now in reverse order the Moon should rule in his first year; in his second, if you will, Mercury; in the third, Venus; in the fourth, the Sun; in the fifth, Mars; in the sixth, Jupiter; and in the seventh, Saturn; and afterwards the order should be repeated throughout life. And so in any seventh year of life there occurs a very great and therefore very dangerous change in the body, both because Saturn is alien

communiter est peregrinus, et ab eo tunc planetarum summo ad Lunam e vestigio planetarum infimam gubernatio redit. Hos annos astronomi Graeci climactericos nominant; nos scalares vel gradarios vel decretorios appellamus. Forte vero in morbis ipsum humoris vel naturae motum planetes per dies eodem ordine regunt, unde et septimus quisque eadem ratione iudiciarius appellatur, quartus quoque quoniam medium in septenario tenet. Tu igitur si vitam producere cupis ad senectutem nullis eiusmodi gradibus interruptam, quotiens septimo cuilibet propinquas anno, consule diligenter astrologum. Unde immineat tibi discrimen ediscito, deinde vel adito medicum, vel prudentiam et temperantiam accersito. His namque remediis prohiberi minas astrorum Ptolemaeus etiam confitetur. Addit quinetiam astrorum promissa sic augeri posse, ut agrorum cultor auget terrae virtutem.

Probat Petrus Aponensis argumentationibus multis et testimonio Aristotelis, Galieni, Haly naturalem vitae finem non esse ab initio ad unguem determinatum, sed ultra citraque moveri posse; idque asserit tum ex astris, tum etiam ex materia. Concludit his auctoribus rationibusque obitum etiam naturalem differri posse cum astrologiae machinis, tum praesidiis medicorum. Igitur neque nos temere in his praeceptis elaboramus, neque te pigeat perquirere a medicis quae naturaliter tua sit diaeta, et ab astrologis quae stella vitae faveat. Et quando haec bene se habet, et ad eam Luna, compone quae prodesse didiceris. Neque pudeat saepe illos auscultare, qui non tam fortuna quam virtute senectutem prosperam consecuti videntur. Praeterea Ptolemaeus et ceteri professores astronomiae imaginibus quibusdam ex certis lapidibus et metallis sub certo sidere fabricatis vitam prosperam pollicentur atque longaevam. Verum de imaginibus quidem ex parte ac plurimum de reliquo favore coelesti commentarium componimus in Plotinum, quem librum huic operi deinceps subiciendum existimamus, quemadmodum hoc post librum scribi volumus, quem *De curanda litteratorum valetudine* composuimus.

Favorem vero coelestem, quem modo dicebam, pro iuventute longa nunc, quantum quasi poetae cuidam licet loqui, quantum rursus medico licet facere, a Phoebo Bacchoque petemus.

> Solis aeterna est Phoebo Bacchoque iuventus,
> Nam decet intonsus crinis utrunque deum.

Phoebus et Bacchus semper individui fratres sunt; ambo fere sunt idem. Phoebus quidem est ipsa sphaerae illius anima, sphaera vero Bacchus. Immo et Phoebus est totus ipse sphaerae circus, Bacchus autem est flammeus ille

---

17 propinques Lw^{ac} 31 virtutem z 39 tunc z

to man in general and because then the governance returns abruptly from him, the highest of the planets, to the Moon, the lowest of the planets. These years the Greek astronomers call climacterics; we call them scalary or gradary years or decretorial years.[1] Indeed, in diseases the planets largely rule the very motion of the moisture or of nature day by day in the same order, which is why on the same principle any seventh day, too, is called critical—the fourth also, since it occupies the middle in the septenary. Therefore, if you want to prolong your life unbroken by any of these steps into old age, as often as you attain to any seventh year, earnestly consult an astrologer. Learn from what direction the crisis threatens you, and then either go to a physician or summon prudence and temperance. For even Ptolemy confesses that by these remedies one can ward off the threats of the stars. Moreover, he adds that the promises of the stars are able to be increased by this means, as the cultivator of a field increases the fertility of the soil.[2]

Pietro d'Abano proves by many arguments and by the testimony of Aristotle, Galen, and Haly, that the end of one's natural life-span is not predetermined from the beginning in every detail, but is able to be moved farther or nearer (he asserts) both by the stars and by material things. He concludes from these authors and arguments that even natural [not to mention violent] death can be postponed not only by the schemes of astrologers but by the protection of doctors.[3] Hence we have not labored inconsiderately in these precepts. Do not consider it too much trouble to inquire from doctors what diet is natural to you and to learn from astrologers what star favors your life. And when that star is well situated, and the Moon in relation to it, compound those things which you have learned are good. Do not be ashamed to listen often to those who seem to have arrived at a prosperous old age not so much by fortune as by vigor. Besides all this, Ptolemy and the other professors of astronomy promise a life prosperous and long from certain images contrived from specific stones and metals under specific stars.[4] But indeed on the subject of images in part and especially of the other kinds of celestial favor, we are composing a commentary on Plotinus, which book we think ought afterwards to be subjoined to this work in the same way that we want this one to be inscribed after the one we composed *On the Care of the Health of Learned People*.[5]

We will now request that celestial favor for a long youth of which I just spoke—this much a would-be poet is permitted to say, this much in turn a doctor is permitted to do—from Phoebus and Bacchus:

Phoebus and Bacchus alone have youth eternal,
For uncut hair befits both gods.[6]

Phoebus and Bacchus are always inseparable brothers; the two are practically identical. Phoebus indeed is the very soul of that sphere, Bacchus assuredly is the sphere itself. Phoebus is the whole circle of the sphere [i.e., the circuit of the planet Sol]; Bacchus is that flaming little circle [i.e., the visible sun]

in hoc circo circulus. Immo vero Phoebus est almum in hoc flammeo globo lumen, Bacchus autem existit ibidem salutaris ex lumine calor. Semper ergo fratres comitesque sunt, fere semper alter et idem. Quid vero? Si Sol in vere quidem Phoebus est, cantu suo tunc avium cantus excitans, cithara rursum 50 tempora temperans, in autumno vero Sol idem, auctor vini, Bacchus existit. Tria nobis ad servandam iuventutem pater ille Liber, qui amat colles, Bacchus affert: hos quidem apricos primum colles, in his autem collibus suavissimum praecipue vinum, perpetuam in vino securitatem. Tria quoque Phoebus, Bacchi frater, pari benignitate largitur: diurnum primo lumen, sub 55 fomento luminis herbas suaviter redolentes, ad luminis huius umbram citharam cantumque perennem. His ergo pensis potissimum, his staminibus Clotho nobis iam non parca longa vitae fila producet. Tres Parcas fere omnes poetae canunt. Tres quoque nos non poetae canimus: prudens quidem in omni victu parcitas vitam nobis longam incohat; constans quoque in curis 60 subeundis parcitas producit vitam; parcitas vero in coelo fruendo negligens vitam occat. Tres Pythagoras temperantias ante omnia celebrat, tres etiam nos impraesentia celebramus: temperantiam in affectibus conservato, temperantiam in omni victu servato, temperiem aeris observato. Hac enim providentia humorum intemperiem, quae citae senectutis et intempestivae mortis 65 causa est, aspirante Deo procul admodum propulsabis. Aspirabit autem auctor ille vitae, si ea tantum conditione vitam optaveris diuturnam, ut diutius cum generi humano vivas, tum maxime vivas illi, quo mundus totus inspirante vivit.

FINIS

---

53 Nos *x*   62 temperantias] temperantius *z*   64 observato] conservato *L*   Haec *x*   65 tempestivae *x*   68 genere *z*   tum maxime vivas *om. z*
Finitur secundus liber *y*; De vita studiosorum producenda libri finis *z*

in this circle. In that flaming globe Phoebus is the fostering light; in the same place Bacchus is the salutary heat from that light. Therefore they are always brothers and comrades and practically always second selves ["alter idem," a clichè for the ideal friend]. How is this? If the Sun in spring is Phoebus — then exciting by his singing the song of the birds, with his lyre in turn tempering the weather — in autumn, the same Sun as the creator of wine is Bacchus. Bacchus, that Father Liber who loves hills, gives us three things to preserve youth: first, those hills exposed to the Sun; on these hills, moreover, the sweetest wine; and in wine perpetual freedom from care.[7] With equal kindness, Phoebus the brother of Bacchus also gives three things to preserve youth: in the first place, daylight; then herbs sweetly smelling with the warmth of daylight; and in the shade of this light, the lyre and perennial song. With this wool above all, with these fibers, Clotho, no longer stingy [pun on "Parca" and "parca"] toward us will draw out a long thread of life. Practically all poets sing of the three Fates.[8] I also who am not a poet sing of three: a prudent frugality [parcitas] in every necessity of life begins a long life for us [like Clotho]; a constant frugality also in assuming responsibilities extends life [like Lachesis]; but a negligent frugality in availing oneself of the heavens breaks it up [like Atropos]. Pythagoras celebrated three temperances before all,[9] and I also at present celebrate three: preserve temperance in emotions; keep temperance in every necessity of life; pay attention to the proper mixture of the air. For by this foresight you will keep far off, with God's help, that imbalance of humors which is the cause of quick old age and untimely death. But He who is the author of life will favor ["aspirabit"; a pun on "spiro" begins here] you only if you pray for long life on these terms, that you may live longer both for the human race and especially for Him by whose inspiration the whole universe lives.

THE END

A diagram of the Ptolemaic universe which corresponds to Ficino's cosmology. Sherburne's caption reads in part: "In this System the Terraqueous Globe is seated in the midst or Centre; about it, the Elementary Region; next above that, the *Moon*; then *Mercury*; next above him, *Venus*; the Sun, as Moderator of all, being placed, as in a Throne in the midst of the Planets, environed not only by the three foregoing, called the Inferiour, but by *Mars* likewise, *Jupiter,* and *Saturn*, called the Superiour Planets. Above Saturn is the Sphere of the Fixed Stars, called 'Απλάνη, i.e. *Aplane*, or Unerring; by some, the Firmament. . . . And this was the first *Pythagorean* System, embraced by *Archimedes,* the *Chaldeans, Aristotle, Cicero, Livy, Ptolemy, Alphonsus, Purbachius,* and the greatest part of Astronomers, until the time of *Maginus* and *Clavius.*"
Manilius, *The Sphere*, translated by Edward Sherburne (London, 1675), Part II, p. 130. Reproduced with permission from the original in the Huntington Library.

Prooemium in Librum
De Vita Coelitus Comparanda

Marsilius Ficinus Florentinus Serenissimo Pannoniae Regi Semper Invicto. Philosophi veteres, rex omnium felicissime, coelestium vires inferiorumque naturas diligentissime perscrutati, cum existimarent hominem frustra sapere qui non sibi sapit, totam merito perscrutationem suam imprimis ad vitam sibi coelitus comparandam retulisse videntur; iudicantes (ut arbitror) tum elementa et quae ex his componuntur frustra sibi cognita fore, tum motus coelestium et influxus temere nimium observatos, nisi haec una cum illis cognita simul atque coniuncta aliquando sibi ad vitam felicitatemque conducerent. Profluit autem illis, ut videtur, eiusmodi contemplatio ad vitam primo praesentem. Nam Pythagoras et Democritus Apolloniusque Theaneus et quicunque ad id potissimum studuerunt, rerum sibi cognitarum usu prosperam valetudinem consecuti sunt vitamque longaevam. Contulit insuper ad futuram vitam, tum per gloriam apud posteros propagandam, tum apud Deum in aeternitate fruendam, siquidem ex mirabili mundi totius ordine eius tandem cognovere rectorem et ante omnia cognitum amaverunt. Tibi vero gloriam per saecula cuncta futuram magnanimitas, magnificentia, victoria perpetua pollicentur. Vitam quoque apud Deum in aevo beatam divina clementia insigni pietati tuae iustitiaeque promittit. Vitam denique prosperam inter mortales satisque longam, quantum ex indiciis quibusdam mihi licuit coniectare, felicia tibi sidera decreverunt. Ut autem quod pollicentur, id et praestent firmissima fide et cumulo insuper prorogent pleniore, diligentia tua et medicorum astrologorumque cura efficere proculdubio potest. Iam vero id posse scientia et prudentia fieri doctissimi quique astrologi ac medici confitentur. Cum igitur inter Plotini libros magno Laurentio Medici destinatos in librum Plotini de favore coelitus hauriendo tractantem nuper

post Prooemium add. Marsilii Ficini Florentini *L; ante Prooemium add.* Marsilii Ficini *x   Comparanda deest in Lw   Prooemium—*Invicto] Marsilii Ficini Florentini in librum tertium de Vita coelitus comparanda ad Serenissimum Pannoniae regem epistolare Prooemium *yz   Coelitus—*Invicto] Celitus Comparanda ad Serenissimum Panoniae Regem Mathiam Semper Invictum *L   *1 Semper Invicto] Mathie semper invicto suppliciter se commendat *M   *3 perscrutari *z   *10–11 Apolloniusque Theaneus *om. LM   *15 cognatum *z   *17 *post* beatam *add.* a *L   *18 prosperam] proximam *M   *19 satisque] atque *L   *21 id *om. L   post* praestent *add.* et *M*

Proemium to the Book
"On Obtaining Life from the Heavens"

Marsilio Ficino the Florentine to the serene and never-conquered King of Hungary.[1] The ancient philosophers, O king blessed above all men, once they had diligently and thoroughly examined the powers of the heavens and the natures of things below, thinking that a man has wisdom in vain who has it not for his own good, seem rightly to have narrowed their whole examination first and foremost to the end of obtaining life for themselves from heaven. They judged, as I suppose, that the elements and all that is composed therefrom would be known by them in vain, and that the motions and influences of the heavens would be too aimlessly observed, if the knowledge of both, taken jointly together, did not eventually lead to life and happiness for themselves. Thoughts of this kind profited them, as it seems, first of all for this present life; for Pythagoras and Democritus and Apollonius of Tyana[2] and all who have made this their special study have by using the things they knew attained good health and long life. Such thinking was also of advantage for their future life, both to prolong it by spreading their fame among posterity and to enjoy it in eternity with God, since from the wondrous order of the whole universe they ultimately came to know its Helmsman[3] and once they knew Him, they loved Him above all things. As for you, your magnanimity, magnificence, and continual victories promise glory through all the generations to come. Also, divine clemency promises a blessed life everlasting in the presence of God in return for your outstanding piety and justice. Lastly, your lucky stars have decreed for you a life among mortals which is prosperous and fairly long (insofar as I have been able to infer from certain indications).[4] Without a doubt, your own careful attention and the care of doctors and astrologers can so arrange things that the stars both give faithfully what they promise and even extend it further with a fuller increase. All the learned astrologers and doctors now testify that this can be done by science and common sense. Now among the books of Plotinus destined for the great Lorenzo de' Medici I had recently composed a commentary (numbered among the rest of our commentaries on him) on the book of Plotinus which discusses drawing favor down from the

commentarium composuissem, inter cetera in eum nostra commentaria numeratum, id quidem seligere nunc, Laurentio quidem ipso probante, atque maiestati tuae potissimum dedicare decrevi. Spero equidem dum vitae tuae prosperitatique consulam, vitae interim et splendori saeculi nostri et humani generis consulturum. Atque ut valetudini prosperitatique regiae validius haec 30 nostra prodessent, per Valorem ipsum mittenda putavi. Hunc tu igitur Valorem nostrum, clementissime rex, complectere, precor. Tantum enim natura, virtus, auctoritas tua valet, ut absque te nequeat vel Valor ipse valere. X. Iulii, MCCCCLXXXIX Florentiae.

Verba Marsilii Ficini ad lectorem sequentis libri

Salve, hospes ingeniose. Salve iterum, quisquis es salutis avidus qui nostra ad limina tendis. Vide, precor, hospes cupide, primum quam hospitalis sim. Intrantis erat certe salutem statim hospitio dicere, ego vero salute praeveniens mox prospectum salvere te iussi. Intrantem et adhuc ignotum perlibenter excepi. Trahentem apud me moras promissa, si Deus aspiraverit, 5 salute donabo. Hospitium ergo nactus es amicum quidem omnibus et amoris nunc erga te plenum. Si quid forte fers tecum amori contrarium, si quid habes odii, prius ponito, precor, quam medicinas hic vitales attingas. Vitam enim tibi dedit amor voluptasque parentum. Vitam vicissim demit odium atque dolor. Quem igitur odiosus vexat dolor, huic nullus usquam medicinae 10 vitali relictus est locus. Quamobrem deinceps te non ut hospitem tantum iam alloquor, sed amicum.

Officina Marsilii tui aliquanto est amplior, quam his cancellis duntaxat quos hic vides coerceatur. Non enim solo hoc libro sequente, sed duobus etiam praecedentibus circumscribitur. Tota vero summatim medicina quae- 15 dam est pro viribus opitulatura vitae, ut valida tibi vita sit, ut longa; idque ubique medicorum ope coelitus adiuta molitur. Varia sane pro diversis hominum ingeniis atque naturis nostra haec officina antidota, pharmaca, fomenta, unguenta, remedia profert. Si qua tibi fortasse minus placeant, mittito quidem ista; cetera propterea ne respuito. Denique si non probas imagines as- 20 tronomicas, alioquin pro valetudine mortalium adinventas, quas et ego non tam probo quam narro, has utique me concedente ac etiam (si vis) consulente dimittito. Medicinas saltem coelesti quodam adminiculo confirmatas,

27 id quidem] id equidem *M*   29-30 prosperatique — valetudini *om. M*   34 MCCCLXXXVIII *M* Florentiae *om. M*   X. Iulii MCCCCLXXXIX Florentiae *deest in L;* Marsilii Ficini Florentini Liber de vita celitus ad Serenissimum Regem Panoniae Mathiam semper invictum *add. L*   Verba ad lectorem desunt in *L; M* tantum habet Salve hospes etc.
Verba *om. xyz*   Libri *om. z;* Exhortatio *add. xyz*   5 aspiravit *z*   7 erga te *ante* nunc *transp. z*   7-8 odii *ante* habes *transp. z*   11 iam *om. z*   19 mitto *x*

heavens.[5] With all this in mind, I have just decided to extract that one (with the approval of Lorenzo himself) and dedicate it especially to your Majesty. For my part, while I am taking care of your life and prosperity, I hope that I will indeed at the same time be taking care of the life and glory of our generation and of the human race. And so that this work of ours might be more strongly ["validius"] beneficial to the king's health ["valetudo"] and prosperity, I judged that they ought to be sent by Valor itself. I beg you, gentle King, to embrace this our friend Valori.[6] For your natural disposition, virtue, and authority are so strong, that without you even Valor itself can have no strength. The 10th of July, 1489, at Florence.

The Words of Marsilio Ficino to the Reader of the Following Book

Hail, intellectual guest! Hail to you, too, whosoever you are who approaches our threshold desiring health! See, eager guest, first of all, how hospitable I am. For certainly it was the role of the visitor, to first salute the hostelry; but I, before you could salute me, have saluted you as soon as I saw you. I have gladly welcomed you while you were entering and as yet unknown. And if you stay with me awhile, I will give you, please God, the health [*salute*] I promised you. You have gained a lodging friendly to all and now full of love towards you. If by chance you bring with you anything contrary to love, if you have any hate, please dispose of it first, before you approach the life-giving medicines here. For it was the love and pleasure of your parents that gave you life. Conversely, hate and displeasure take away life. Therefore the person who harbors disagreeable resentment, has no share in life-giving medicine. So from now on I address you not only as my guest but as my friend.

The shop of your friend Marsilio is a bit larger than what you see here, enclosed only in these boundaries. For it is defined not only by the book to come, but also by the two preceding. The whole forms an epitome of Medicine which will assist your life as much as possible, that it may be both healthy and long; and it employs at every point the resources of doctors, aided by the heavens. This shop of ours displays various antidotes, drugs, fomentations, ointments, and remedies, according to the differing mental capacities and natures of men. If in some way they happen to displease you, pass over these, by all means, but do not for that reason repudiate the rest. Finally, if you do not approve of astronomical images, albeit invented for the health of mortals—which even I do not so much approve of as report—dismiss them with my complete permission and even, if you will, by my advice.[1] At least do not neglect medi-

nisi forte vitam neglexeris, ne negligito. Ego enim frequenti iamdiu experientia compertum habeo tantum interesse inter medicinas eiusmodi atque alias 25 absque delectu astrologico factas, quantum inter merum atque aquam, ut etiam infans octavo a conceptione mense natus Florentiae mense Martio, nocte ascendente Saturno retrogrado, semivivus eiusmodi diligentia videatur a nobis, immo a Deo, quasi vitae redditus potius quam servatus; trienniumque validus ferme iam impleverit. Iam vero si praeter ea generis eiusdem 30 plura narravero, vera loquar, nec gloriabundus (quod est a philosopho penitus alienum), sed exhortabundus potius afferam. Verum satis iam partim quidem conciliantes, partim etiam exhortantes allocuti te sumus. Deinceps igitur cum Plotino loquamur, ita demum tibi diligentius consulturi.

In omnibus quae hic aut alibi a me tractantur, tantum assertum esse volo, quantum ab ecclesia comprobatur.

24 ne] haud *z*   25 inter *om. z*   huiusmodi *yz*   26 delicto astrologo *z*   atque] et *z*   *ante* In *xy habent* Protestatio catholici auctoris   In omnibus—comprobatur *desunt in Lz*   *post* comprobatur *add.* Capitulorum tertii libri De vita coelitus comparanda Annotatio etc. *y*

cines which have been strengthened by some sort of heavenly aid, unless perhaps you would neglect life itself. For I have found by long and repeated experience that medicines of this kind are as different from other medicines made without astrological election as wine is from water. For example, there was an infant who was born half dead in the eighth month from conception[2] at Florence in the month of March, at night when Saturn, retrograde, was ascending; by this sort of care the child seemed almost to be brought back to life rather than preserved by me, or rather, by God; and he has lived in good health now for nearly three years. Moreover, if I told you more cases of this sort besides, I would be speaking the truth, and I would report them, not to boast, which is totally out of place in a philosopher, but to persuade. But we have addressed you enough already, partly to gain your good will, partly also to persuade you. From now on, then, let us speak with Plotinus, but in such a way that we will still be taking even greater care of you.

In all things which I discuss here or elsewhere, I intend to assert only so much as is approved by the Church.

Marsilii Ficini Florentini
Liber De Vita Coelitus Comparanda compositus
ab eo inter Commentaria eiusdem in Plotinum

In quo consistat secundum Plotinum virtus favorem coelitus attrahens, scilicet in eo quod anima mundi et stellarum daemonumque animae facile alliciuntur corporum formis accommodatis.

Cap. I.

Si tantum haec duo sint in mundo, hinc quidem intellectus, inde vero corpus, sed absit anima, tunc neque intellectus trahetur ad corpus — immobilis enim est omnino caretque affectu, motionis principio, tanquam a corpore longissime distans — neque corpus trahetur ad intellectum, velut ad motum per se inefficax et ineptum longeque ab intellectu remotum. Verum si interponatur anima utrique conformis, facile utrinque et ad utraque fiet attractus. Primo quidem ipsa omnium facillime ducitur, quoniam primum mobile est et ex se et sponte mobile. Praeterea cum sit (ut dixi) media rerum, omnia suo in se modo continet et utrinque ratione propinqua; ideoque conciliatur et omnibus, etiam aequaliter illis quae inter se distant, ab ea videlicet non distantibus. Praeter enim id quod hinc quidem conformis est divinis, inde vero caducis, et ad utraque vergit affectu, tota interim est simul ubique.

Accedit ad haec quod anima mundi totidem saltem rationes rerum seminales divinitus habet, quot ideae sunt in mente divina, quibus ipsa rationibus totidem fabricat species in materia. Unde unaquaeque species per propriam rationem seminalem propriae respondet ideae, facileque potest per hanc saepe aliquid illinc accipere, quandoquidem per hanc illinc est effecta. Ideoque si quando a propria forma degeneret, potest hoc medio sibi proximo formari rursum perque id medium inde facile reformari. Ac si certe cuidam rerum speciei vel individuo eius rite adhibeas multa quae sparsa sunt, sed eidem ideae conformia, mox in materiam hanc ita opportune paratam singulare munus ab idea trahes per rationem videlicet animae seminalem; non enim intellectus ipse proprie, sed anima ducitur. Nemo itaque putet certis mundi materiis trahi numina quaedam a materiis penitus segregata, sed dae-

---

Marsilii—Plotinum desunt in L   *compositum z*   *eo*] eodem *yz*   post *Plotinum* add. incipit *y secundum Plotinum—attrahens*] virtus magici operis et imaginum *P*   Cap. XI. *P*   5 ab intellectu *om. LP*   6 animam *P*   conformem *P*   7 ducimur *z*   8 sit ut] sicut *z*   12 ad *om. z*   21 eidem] etiam *z*

The Book "On Obtaining Life from the Heavens" by Marsilio Ficino of Florence, Which He Composed among His Commentaries on Plotinus[1]

In What, According to Plotinus, the Power of Attracting Favor from the Heavens Consists, Namely, That Well-adapted Physical Forms Can Easily Allure the World-soul and the Souls of the Stars and the Daemons.

Chap. I

If there were only these two things in the universe—on one side the Intellect, on the other the Body—but no Soul, then neither would the Intellect be attracted to the Body (for Intellect is absolutely motionless, without affect, which is the principle of motion, and very far away from the Body), nor would the Body be drawn to the Intellect (for Body is in itself powerless, unsuited for motion, and far removed from the Intellect). But if a Soul which conforms to both were placed between them, an attraction will easily occur to each one on either side. In the first place, Soul is led most easily of all, since she is the Primum Mobile and movable of herself, of her own accord. Moreover, since, as I have said,[2] she is the mean of things, in her own fashion she contains all things and is proportionally [Intellect: Soul:: Soul: Body] near to both. Therefore she is equally connected with everything, even with those things which are at a distance from one other, because they are not at a distance from her. For besides the fact that on the one side she conforms to the divine and on the other side to the transient, and even turns to each by desire, at the same time she is wholly and simultaneously everywhere.[3]

In addition, the World-soul possesses by divine power precisely as many seminal reasons of things as there are Ideas in the Divine Mind. By these seminal reasons she fashions the same number of species in matter. That is why every single species corresponds through its own seminal reason to its own Idea and oftentimes through this reason it can easily receive something from the Idea—since indeed it was made through the reason from the Idea. This is why, if at any time the species degenerates from its proper form, it can be formed again with the reason as the proximate intermediary and, through the Idea as intermediary, can then be easily reformed. And if in the proper manner you bring to bear on a species, or on some individual in it, many things which are dispersed but which conform to the same Idea, into this material thus suitably adapted you will soon draw a particular gift from the Idea, through the seminal reason of the Soul:[4] for, properly speaking, it is not Intellect itself which is led, but Soul. And so let no one think that any divinities wholly separate from matter are being attracted by any given mundane materials, but that dae-

mones potius animatique mundi munera stellarumque viventium. Nemo rursum miretur per materiales formas animam quasi allici posse, siquidem escas eiusmodi sibi congruas ipsamet, quibus alliceretur, effecit, et semper libenterque habitat in eisdem. Neque in mundo vivente toto quicquam reperitur tam deforme, cui non adsit anima, cui non insit et animae munus. Congruitates igitur eiusmodi formarum ad rationes animae mundi Zoroaster divinas illices appellavit, quas et Synesius magicas esse illecebras confirmavit.

Nemo denique credat ad propriam quandam materiae speciem et tempore certo hauriri omnia prorsus ex anima dona, sed pro opportunitate dona duntaxat seminis, quo talis species pullulavit, seminumque conformium. Itaque hic homo, humanis tantum adhibitis, non proprias piscium vel avium dotes inde sibi vendicat, sed humanas atque consimiles. Adhibitis autem quae ad stellam talem pertinent atque daemonem, stellae daemonisque huius proprium subit influxum, velut lignum per sulphur paratum ad flammam ubique praesentem. Atque hunc non modo per ipsos stellae daemonisque radios, sed etiam per ipsam mundi animam ubique praesentem, in qua et cuiuslibet stellae daemonisque ratio viget, partim quidem seminalis ad generandum, partim etiam exemplaris ad cognoscendum. Haec enim secundum Platonicos antiquiores rationibus suis aedificavit ultra stellas in coelo figuras partesque ipsarum tales, ut ipsae quoque figurae quaedam sint; impressitque his omnibus proprietates. In stellis autem, figuris, partibus, proprietatibus, omnes rerum inferiorum species continentur et proprietates earum. Universales vero figuras octo posuit atque quadraginta, scilicet in zodiaco duodecim, extra vero sex atque triginta; item in zodiaco triginta sex ad numerum facierum; rursus ibidem ter centum atque sexaginta ad numerum graduum, in quovis enim gradu sunt stellae plures, ex quibus ibi conficiuntur imagines. Similiter imagines extra zodiacum in plures divisit figuras pro facierum ibidem graduumque suorum numero. Constituit denique ab imaginibus his universalibus ad universales imagines habitudines et proportiones quasdam, quae ipsae quoque imagines illic existunt. Eiusmodi vero figurae continuitatem quaeque suam habent ex radiis stellarum suarum in se invicem peculiari quadam proprietate coniectis. A quibus formis ordinatissimis dependent inferiorum formae, illinc videlicet ordinatae. Sed et coelestes illae tanquam et inter se disiunctae procedunt a rationibus animae coniunctis invicem, et quodammodo mutabiles a stabilibus. Sed hae quatenus se ipsas non comprehendunt, referuntur ad formas in mente vel animali vel eminentiore sese comprehendentes,

---

32 Nemo] Nempe z   speciem] spem P   33 haurire z   37-39 proprium subit—ubique praesentem] velut paratum vas proprium subit influxum LP   44 siet z   46 Universale z   50-51 Similiter imagines om. L   51 divisis P   56 coniecturis z   57 Sed om. z   et² om. L^{ac}P   59 quatenus post ras. L; quia P   60 vel animali vel eminentiore add. in marg. L; om. P

mons rather are being attracted and gifts from the ensouled world and from the living stars.[5] Again, let no man wonder that Soul can be allured as it were by material forms, since indeed she herself has created baits of this kind suitable to herself, to be allured thereby, and she always and willingly dwells in them. There is nothing to be found in this whole living world so deformed that Soul does not attend it, that a gift of the Soul is not in it. Therefore Zoroaster called such correspondences of forms to the reasons existing in the World-soul "divine lures" and Synesius corroborated that they are magical baits.[6]

Finally, let no one believe that absolutely all gifts are drawn from the Soul to any one particular species of matter at a specific time, but rather at the right moment only those gifts of that one seed from which such a species has grown, and of seeds that are similar to it. Accordingly, the person who has employed only human things, will thence claim for himself not the gifts proper to fish or to birds but the human gifts and similar ones. But if he employs things which pertain to such and such a star and daemon, he undergoes the peculiar influence of this star and daemon, like a piece of wood treated with sulfur for a flame that is everywhere present. And he undergoes this influence not only through the rays of the star and the daemon themselves, but also through the very Soul of the World everywhere present. For the reason of any star and daemon flourishes in her. It is partly a seminal reason so that she can generate, and partly an exemplary reason so that she can know.[7] For according to the more ancient Platonists, from her reasons, the World-soul constructed in the heavens besides the stars, figures[8] and such parts of them as are also themselves figures of a sort;[9] and she impressed properties on all these. In the stars, moreover—in their figures, parts and properties—are contained all the species of things below and their properties. She arranged 48 universal figures: 12 in the zodiac and 36 outside it; likewise she placed 36 more figures in the zodiac according to the number of its faces.[10] Again she arranged in the Zodiac 360 more figures according to the number of its degrees—for in each degree whatsoever there are many stars that make up images there. Similarly the images [constellations] outside the zodiac she divided into many figures [paranatellonta] according to the number of the Zodiacal faces and degrees. Finally, she established certain relations and proportions of the latter universal images to the former universal images—relations and proportions which themselves are also images out there. Figures of this kind each have their own coherence from the rays of their stars directed toward each other by their own special property. On these well-ordered forms the forms of lower things depend; they are ordered by them. But even those celestial forms, being [spatially] set apart from each other, proceed from reasons of the Soul that are joined together; and being forms somewhat changeable, they proceed from the reasons which are stable. But the reasons, insofar as they do not make up a unity, are traced back to the Forms in the Intellect—the intellect in Soul and the higher Intellect—

quae tanquam multiplices rediguntur ad simplicissimum unum atque bonum, sicut figurae coelestes ad polum.

Sed redeamus ad animam. Quando igitur anima gignit speciales inferiorum formas viresque, eas per rationes efficit proprias sub stellarum formarumque coelestium adminiculo. Singulares vero individuorum dotes, quae saepe nonnullis insunt tam mirabiles quam in speciebus esse solent, exhibet per seminales similiter rationes, non tam sub adminiculo formarum figurarumque coelestium quam situ stellarum et habitu motionum aspectuumque planetarum, tum inter se, tum ad stellas planetis sublimiores. Anima quidem nostra ultra vires membrorum proprias communem ubique promit in nobis vitae virtutem, maxime vero per cor, tanquam ignis animae proximi fontem. Similiter anima mundi ubique vigens per Solem praecipue suam passim explicat communis vitae virtutem. Unde quidam animam et in nobis et in mundo in quolibet membro totam potissimum in corde collocant atque Sole.

Semper vero memento sicut animae nostrae virtus per spiritum adhibetur membris, sic virtutem animae mundi per quintam essentiam, quae ubique viget tanquam spiritus intra corpus mundanum, sub anima mundi dilatari per omnia, maxime vero illis virtutem hanc infundi, quae eiusmodi spiritus plurimum hauserunt. Potest autem quinta haec essentia nobis intus magis magisque assumi, si quis sciverit eam aliis elementis immixtam plurimum segregare, vel saltem his rebus frequenter uti, quae hac abundant puriore praesertim; ceu electum vinum et saccharum et balsamum atque aurum pretiosique lapilli myrobalanique et quae suavissime redolent et quae lucent, maxime vero quae in subtili substantia qualitatem habent calidam humidamque et claram; quale praeter vinum est albissimum saccharum, praesertim si huic adhibueris aurum odoremque cinnami atque rosarum. Praeterea sicut alimenta rite in nobis assumpta per se non viva rediguntur per spiritum nostrum ad vitae nostrae formam, sic et corpora nostra rite accommodata corpori spirituique mundano, videlicet per res mundanas et per nostrum spiritum, hauriunt ex vita mundana quam plurimum.

Si volueris ut alimentum rapiat prae ceteris formam cerebri tui vel iecoris atque stomachi, simile quantum potes accipe alimentum, id est, cerebrum et iecur et stomachum animalium ab humana natura non longe distantium. Si optas corpus tuum atque spiritum ex aliquo mundi membro, videlicet ex Sole, virtutem accipere, quaere quae ante alia sunt Solaria inter metalla lapillosque, magis autem inter plantas, sed inter animalia magis, maxime inter

---

61 *ante* rediguntur *transp.* ad simplicissimum z   unum atque *om. LP*   67 rationales z   77 viget] *post ras. L;* latet P   79 *post* essentia *add.* a yz   82 atque] et P   88 ritae z   corpore z   91 ut *om. L*

which do make up a unity; and these Forms, being multiples, are reduced to the perfectly simple One and Good, just as the celestial figures diminish to a point at the Pole.[11]

But let us return to the Soul. When, therefore, the Soul gives birth to the specific forms and the powers pertaining to the species of things below, she makes them through their respective reasons with the aid of the stars and the celestial forms. But she produces the endowments peculiar to individuals (which are often in some individuals as marvelous as they habitually are in the species themselves) likewise through the seminal reasons, but not so much with the aid of celestial forms and figures as by the location of the individual stars and the relation of the motions and aspects of the planets both among themselves and with respect to the stars which are above the planets. Now our own soul beyond the particular forces of our members puts forth a general force of life everywhere within us—especially through the heart as the source of the fire which is the nearest thing to the soul. In the same way the World-soul, which is active everywhere, unfolds in every place its power of universal life principally through the Sun. Accordingly, some thinkers say the entire Soul, both in us and in the universe, dwells in any member but most of all in the heart and in the Sun.[12]

Always remember, though, that just as the power of our soul is brought to bear on our members through the spirit, so the force of the World-soul is spread under the World-soul through all things through the quintessence, which is active everywhere, as the spirit inside the World's Body, but that this power is instilled especially into those things which have absorbed the most of this kind of spirit.[13] This quintessence can be ingested by us more and more if a person knows how best to separate it, mixed in as it is with other elements, or at least how to use those things often which are filled with it, especially in its purer form. Such things are: choice wine, sugar, balsam, gold, precious stones, myrobalans, and things which smell most sweet and which shine, and especially things which have in a subtle substance a quality hot, moist, and clear; such, besides wine, is the whitest sugar, especially if you add to it gold and the odor of cinnamon and roses. Then too, just as foods we eat in the right way, although not themselves alive, are converted through our spirit to the form of our life, so also our bodies rightly accommodated to the body and spirit of the world (that is through cosmic things and through our spirit) drink in as much as possible from the life of the world.

If you want your food to take the form of your brain above all, or of your liver, or of your stomach, eat as much as you can of like food, that is, of the brain, liver, and stomach of animals which are not far removed from the nature of man. If you want your body and spirit to receive power from some member of the cosmos, say from the Sun, seek the things which above all are most Solar among metals and gems, still more among plants, and more yet

homines; similiora enim tibi magis proculdubio conferunt. Haec et extra sunt adhibenda et intus pro viribus assumenda, praesertim in die et hora Solis et Sole in figura coeli regnante. Solaria vero sunt omnia ex lapillis et floribus quae heliotropia nominantur, quia vertuntur ad Solem; item aurum et auripigmentum aureique colores, chrysolitus, carbunculus, myrrha, thus, muscus, ambra, balsamum, mel flavum, calamus aromaticus, crocus, spica nardi, cinnamomum, lignum aloes, ceteraque aromata; aries, astur, gallus, olor, leo, cantharis, crocodillus, homines flavi, crispi, saepe calvi, magnanimi. Superiora partim cibariis, partim unguentis suffumigationibusque, partim usui accommodari possunt. Haec sentienda et cogitanda frequenter et imprimis amanda; et luminis plurimum est quaerendum.

Si dubites ventrem ab iecoris fomento destitui, trahe ad ventrem iecoris facultatem tum frictionibus, tum fomentis per ea quae iecori congruunt: per cichoream, endiviam, spodium et eupatorium et hepaticam atque hepata. Similiter ne destituatur tuum corpus ab Iove, move corpus in die horaque et regno Iovis, et utere interim Iovialibus: argento, hyacintho, topazio, corallo, crystallo, berillo, spodio, sapphyro, viridibus aeriisque coloribus, vino, saccharo, albo melle, et cogitationibus affectibusque plurimum Iovialibus, id est, constantibus, aequis, religiosis atque legiferis; et inter homines eiusmodi sanguineosque et pulchros venerabilesque versabere. Sed memento primis illis rebus frigidis inserendum esse aurum et vinum mentamque et crocum et cinnamomum atque doronicum; animalia vero Iovialia esse agnum pavonemque et aquilam et iuvencum.

Quomodo vero virtus Veneris attrahatur turturibus, columbis et motacillis et reliquis, non permittit pudor ostendere.

De concordia mundi.
De natura hominis secundum stellas.
Quomodo fiat attractus ab unaquaque stella.

Cap. II.

Neque vero diffidere debet quisquam nos atque omnia quae circa nos sunt praeparamentis quibusdam posse sibi vendicare coelestia. Nam coelitus haec facta sunt assidueque reguntur et illinc imprimis praeparata

---

98 exhibenda z   101 aurique x   *post* chrysolitus *add.* et P   103 aromata] arbuta P   austur x   104 cantharis yz; cantharus LPωx   104-105 *post* partim *transp.* superiora P   105 suffumigationibus z   108 destrui x   110 spodium *add. in marg.* L; *om.* P   hepaticum z   111 tuum] tum x et] in z   112 topazio *add. in marg.* L; *om.* P   113 viridibus aeriisque *post ras. add.* L² aeriisque] celestibusque P   113-114 saccharo, albo melle] saccharo albo, melle z   116 versantos z   117 mentamque *add. in marg.* L; *om.* P   117-118 et cinnamomum atque doronicum *om.* z   atque doronicum] *add. in marg.* L; *om.* P   118 pavonemque *post ras.* L²; *om.* P   119 iuvencam P   120 attrahitur x   *post* turturibus *add.* et L^{ac}P   *post* mundi *add.* et z

among animals, especially human beings; for surely things which are more similar to you confer more of it. These must both be brought to bear externally and, so far as possible, taken internally, especially in the day and the hour of the Sun and while the Sun is dominant in a theme of the heavens.[14] Solar things are: all those gems and flowers which are called heliotrope because they turn towards the Sun, likewise gold, orpiment and golden colors, chrysolite, carbuncle, myrrh, frankincense, musk, amber, balsam, yellow honey, sweet calamus, saffron, spikenard, cinnamon, aloe-wood and the rest of the spices; the ram, the hawk, the cock, the swan, the lion, the scarab beetle,[15] the crocodile, and people who are blond, curly-haired, prone to baldness, and magnanimous. The above-mentioned things can be adapted partly to foods, partly to ointments and fumigations, partly to usages and habits. You should frequently perceive and think about these things and love them above all; you should also get a lot of light.

If you suspect that your belly is being deprived of the heat of the liver, draw the power of the liver to the belly both by rubbing and by fomentations made from things which agree with the liver, namely from chicory, endive, spodium, agrimony, hepatica, and livers. In the same way, so that your body may not be deprived of Jupiter, take physical exercise in Jupiter's day and hour and when he is reigning; and in the meantime use Jovial things such as silver, jacinth, topaz, coral, crystal, beryl, spodium, sapphire, green and aery colors, wine, sugar, white honey; and entertain thoughts and feelings which are especially Jovial, that is, steadfast, composed, religious, and law-abiding; and you will keep company with men of the same kind—men who are sanguine, handsome, and venerable. But remember to mix those first things on my list, since they are cold, with gold, wine, mint, saffron, cinnamon and doronicum; remember too that the lamb, the peacock, the eagle, and the young bullock are Jovial animals.

But how the power of Venus may be attracted by turtle-doves, pigeons, white water wag-tails, and the rest, modesty forbids me to reveal.[16]

On the Harmony of the World.
On the Nature of Man according to the Stars.
How to Attract Something from Some One Particular Star.

Chap. II

No one should doubt that we ourselves and all things which are around us can, by way of certain preparations, lay claim to celestial things. For these lower things were made by the heavens, are ruled continually by them,

sunt ad illa. Et quod maximum est, mundus animal in se magis unum est
quam quodvis aliud animal, si modo est animal perfectissimum. Ergo sicut
in nobis membri cuiuslibet, praesertim principalis, qualitas motusque ad alia
pertinet, ita membrorum principalium actus in mundo commovent omnia,
et membra inferiora facile capiunt a supremis ultro dare paratis. Quo enim
potentior causa est, eo est promptior ad agendum, eo igitur propensior est ad
dandum. Exigua igitur praeparatio nobis insuper adhibita sufficit coelestium
muneribus capiendis, si modo quisque ad id praecipue se accommodet, cui
est praecipue subditus.

Sed ante uniuscuiusque nostrum proprietatem, humanae speciei proprietatem considerare debemus. Hanc igitur esse Solarem astrologi Arabes consenserunt. Quod ego e statura hominis erecta pulchraque humoribusque subtilibus et spiritus claritate imaginationisque perspicuitate studioque veritatis
et gloriae verum esse coniecto. Addo quinetiam proprietatem huic Mercurialem ob strenuum versatilis ingenii motum; et quoniam humanum genus natum nudum, inerme, omnium egenum, haec omnia propria industria sibi
comparat—quod est Mercurii proprium. Addo etiam Iovialem ob complexionem corporis temperatam atque leges, et quoniam secundo mense, quo
Iuppiter dominatur, vitam accipimus, atque nascimur nono, quo iterum recipit dominatum. Itaque humana species ab his tribus potissimum dotes insuper ampliores ita demum sibi poterit vendicare, si per Solaria Mercurialiaque
et Iovia se ipsam eis magis indies atque magis accommodabit. De reliquis
autem quid? Saturnus non facile communem significat humani generis qualitatem atque sortem, sed hominem ab aliis segregatum, divinum aut brutum, beatum aut extrema miseria pressum. Mars, Luna, Venus affectus et
actus homini cum ceteris animantibus aeque communes.

Ad Solem igitur et Iovem atque Mercurium revertamur. Solaria quidem
nonnulla et Iovia diximus, Mercurialia vero nescio quomodo praetermisimus.
Sunt autem eiusmodi: stannum, argentum, praesertim vivum, marcassita
argentea, lapis achates, vitrum porphyriticum et quae croceum cum viridi
misceant, smaragdum atque lacca, animalia sagacia et ingeniosa simul et
strenua: simiae, canes, homines eloquentes, acuti, versatiles, oblonga facie
manibusque non pingues.

Sunt autem quaerenda et exercenda quae ad aliquem planetam attinent,
eo videlicet dominante (ut diximus) in die et hora eius, si fieri potest, etiam
quando ipse sit in domicilio vel exaltatione vel saltem triplicitate sua et ter

---

4 unum] vinum *z*   7 commovet *LP*   9 *post* promptior *transp.* est *z*   augendum *x*   14 igitur]
ergo potissimum *LP*   15 ego] ergo *P*   humoribus *L*   18 humanam *z*   19 nudum] mundum
L   haec] enim *add. L*   27 bruta *z*   32 stannum *yz*; stamnum *LPwx*   33 lapis achates *om. LP*
33-34 *ante* et quae *transp.* smaragdum *LP*   34 sagacia et *om. LP*   35 simiae canes *om. LP*

and were prepared from up there for celestial things in the first place. Most important, the cosmos is itself an animal more unified than any other animal, the most perfect animal, provided that it is an animal.[1] Therefore, just as in us the quality and motion of any member, in particular a principal member, extend to our other members, so in the cosmos the acts of the principal members move all the rest, and the inferior members easily receive from the highest, which are ready of their own accord to give. For the more powerful the cause, the more ready it is to act and therefore the more inclined to give. A little additional preparation, therefore, on our part suffices to capture the gifts of the celestials, provided each accommodates himself to that gift in particular to which he is particularly subject.

But before we consider what is the astrological property of every one of us as individuals, we ought to consider the property of the human species. And this, the Arab astrologers have agreed, is Solar.[2] I infer this to be true from the stature of man, erect and beautiful, from his subtle humors and the clearness of his spirit, from the perspicuity of his imagination and his pursuit of truth and honor. But I also add to this a Mercurial property on account of the nimble motion of his versatile intelligence. And since man is born naked, defenseless, in need of everything, he obtains all these things for himself by his own industry—which is a property of Mercury. I add also a Jovial property on account of the temperate complexion of his body and his laws and because we receive life in the second month of gestation, which Jupiter rules, and we are born in the ninth, in which he again resumes his authority. And so the human species will be able to appropriate from these three in particular endowments greater still, if and only if it will accommodate itself to them daily more and more through Solar, Mercurial and Jovial things. But what of the other planets? Saturn cannot easily signify the common quality and lot of the human race, but he signifies an individual set apart from others, divine or brutish, blessed or bowed down with the extreme of misery. Mars, the Moon, and Venus signify affects and actions common equally to man and to the other animals.

Let us return, therefore, to the Sun and Jupiter and Mercury. We have spoken of quite a few Solarian and Jovial things, but somehow we have omitted the Mercurial things, which include: tin, silver, especially quicksilver, silver marcasite,[3] agate, glass—both porphyritic and those kinds which mix yellow with green—emerald, lac, animals which are sagacious and clever and at the same time active such as monkeys and dogs, and people who are eloquent, sharp, and versatile, and who have oblong faces and hands which are not fat.

But those things which pertain to any planet should be sought and performed precisely when it has dignities as I have previously specified: in its day and hour if possible, also when it is in its own house or in its exaltation or at least

mino et angulo coeli, extra combustionem directus ac saepius orientalis, si 40
Sole sit superior, item in Auge, et aspiciatur a Luna. Si quis autem ab ipsa
Luna beneficium et a Venere poscat, tempora similia observare debebit. A
Venere quidem per animalia sua, quae diximus, et per corneolam et sapphyrum lapidemque lazuli, aes croceum atque rubeum et corallum omnesque
pulchros variosque vel virides colores et flores atque concentus suavesque 45
odores atque sapores. A Luna per alba et humida et viridia, per argentum
atque crystallum et uniones et argenteam marcassitam. Quoniam vero Saturnus quidem statui et perseverantiae dominatur, Mars autem efficaciae motus,
cogimur nonnunquam horum quoque gratia ab eis patrocinia postulare, temporibus videlicet similiter observatis. Ab illo quidem per materias quasdam 50
quodammodo terreas et fuscas atque plumbeas et fuscam iaspidem et magnetem et camoinum atque chalcidonium et ex parte quadam per aurum et auream marcassitam. A Marte vero per ignea, rubea, aes rubeum, sulphurea
omnia, ferrum lapidemque sanguineum. Neque diffidas Saturnum habere
nonnihil in auro; nam propter pondus id putatur habere. Quinetiam Soli au- 55
rum simile sic omnibus metallis inest, sicut Sol in planetis omnibus atque
stellis. Iam vero si quis convicerit Saturnum et Martem natura noxios esse,
quod equidem nunquam crediderim, tamen his quoque utendum, quemadmodum venenis nonnunquam utuntur et medici, quod Ptolemaeus in *Centiloquio* probat. Proderit ergo quandoque vis Saturni caute sumpta, sicut apud 60
medicos quae adstringunt atque continent, immo et quae stupefaciunt, sicut
opium et mandragora; Martis quoque sicut euphorbium et helleborus. Cautissimi vero hac in re fuisse videntur Magi, Brachmanes, Pythagorici, qui
cum ob sedulum philosophandi studium Saturni tyrannidem formidarent,
vestibus albis amiciebantur, Iovialibusque sive Phoebeis quotidie sonis et can- 65
tibus utebantur, plurimumque sub divo vivebant.

Ubique vero memento per affectum studiumque animi et per ipsam spiritus qualitatem nos facillime subitoque exponi planetis eundem affectum ac
eiusmodi studium et qualitatem significantibus. Per separationem igitur a
rebus humanis, per otium, solitudinem, firmitatem, per theologiam secre- 70
tioremque philosophiam, superstitionem, magiam, agriculturam, per maerorem Saturno subicimur. Per civilia et ambitiosa negotia, per philosophiam
naturalem communemque, per religionem civilem perque leges Iovi; Marti
per iram atque certamina; Soli Mercurioque per studium eloquentiae cantus-

---

40-41 si Sole sit superior item *om. L*   42 et *om. P*   44 aes] et *LP*   45 vel virides *om. LP*   et flores *om. LP*   46 et viridia *om. LP*   per² *om. P*   50 observabis *z*   51 et¹ *om. P*   fucas *z* fuscam *yz*; fuscum *LPwy*   54 sanguinem *z*   diffidas] diffusas *z*   58 tamen] tum *P*   60 quandoque] quenque *L*   62-66 Cautissimi vero — vivebant *desunt in LP*   66 dio *z*   67 ipsum *z* 69 eiusmodi *om. LP*ᵃᶜ   Per separationem] Persaepe rationem *xyz*   a *om. P*   70 solitudinem] et *L; om. P*   70-71 per theologiam — agriculturam *desunt in L*   71 superstitionem magiam agriculturam *om. P*   72-73 per philosophiam — civilem *om. L*   73 communemque per religionem civilem] per regionem *P*   perque] quique *L*   74-75 eloquentiae cantusque et *om. LP*

in its triplicity, in its term, or in a cardine of heaven, while it is direct in motion, when it is outside of the burned path,[4] and preferably when it is east of the Sun, if it is above the Sun, if it is in apogee, and if it is aspected by the Moon. If anyone begs a favor from the Moon herself and Venus, he will be obliged to do it when they are in similar periods. One obtains things from Venus through her animals which we have mentioned[5] and through carnelian, sapphire, lapis lazuli, brass (yellow or red), coral, and all pretty, multicolored or green colors and flowers, musical harmony, and pleasant odors and tastes. From the Moon, through things that are white, moist, and green and through silver and crystal and pearls and silver marcasite. But since Saturn governs stability and perseverance, and Mars, effective motion, for the sake of these qualities we are often forced to beg favor from them too, doing it when they are in periods similar to those described above. To get something from Saturn, we use any materials that are somewhat earthy, dusky and leaden; we use smoky jasper, lodestone, cameo [?camoinum], and chalcedony; gold and golden marcasite are partly useful for this. From Mars, materials which are fiery or red, red brass, all sulphurous things, iron, and bloodstone. Do not doubt that Saturn has quite a bit to do with gold. His weight leads people to believe so; furthermore, gold, being similar to the Sun, is by the same token in all metals in the way that the Sun is in all the planets and stars [because, as they thought, all their light is but reflected from the Sun]. But now if anyone wishes to convict Saturn and Mars of being harmful by nature, which I never would believe,[6] still they also are to be used just as doctors sometimes use poisons; Ptolemy endorses this in his *Centiloquium*.[7] The force of Saturn, therefore, cautiously taken, will sometimes profit, just as doctors say those things do which are astringent and constrictive, even those things which stupefy, as opium and mandrake, and among the Martial substances, euphorbium [a plant-juice which has emetic or purgative qualities] and hellebore [whose drastic effects are discussed at length in Book 2 and beneficial ones mentioned in 3.20]. The Magi, Brahmans, and Pythagoreans seem to have been most prudent in this, in that when they feared that Saturn would oppress them on account of their sedulous zeal for philosophizing, they would wear white clothes, use Jovial or Phoebean sounds and songs every day, and live continually in the open air.[8]

Always remember that through a given affect and pursuit of our mind and through the very quality of our spirit we are easily and quickly exposed to those planets which signify the same affect, quality, and pursuit. Hence, by withdrawal from human affairs, by leisure, solitude, constancy, by theology, the more esoteric philosophy, superstition, magic, agriculture, and by sorrow, we come under the influence of Saturn. We come under the influence of Jupiter by civic occupations, by those occupations which strive for honor, by natural philosophy, by the kind of philosophy which most people can understand, by civil religion, and by laws; of Mars, by anger and contests; of the Sun and

que et veritatis et gloriae atque solertiam; Veneri per laetitiam et musicam 75
et festiva; Lunae per victum plantis similem. Sed hanc inter hos differentiam
mente teneto, exercitationem ingenii magis publicam atque amplam ad Solem spectare, privatam vero et artificio mancipatam potius ad Mercurium;
tum vero musicam gravem quidem Iovis Solisque esse, levem Veneris, mediam vero Mercurii. Similis quoque de stellis fixis ratio est. Haec quidem 80
communis humanae speciei regula.

Propria vero unicuique regula fuerit explorare quae stella quid boni cuique
in genitura promiserit, atque ab ea potius quam ab alia reposcere gratiam,
et ab unaquaque non quodlibet donum et quod aliarum est, sed eius proprium expectare, nisi forte tum a Sole communia multa reportes, tanquam 85
communi quodam duce coelestium, et ab Iove ferme similiter, tum mundana
pariter omnia ab anima spirituque mundi. Quem sicut et quodvis animal
multoque efficacius animatum esse, non solum Platonicae rationes, sed etiam
astrologorum Arabum testimonia comprobant. Ubi etiam probant ex applicatione quadam spiritus nostri ad spiritum mundi per artem physicam affec- 90
tumque facta, traiici ad animam corpusque nostrum bona coelestia. Hinc
quidem per spiritum nostrum in nobis medium et tunc a mundi spiritu roboratum, inde vero per radios stellarum feliciter agentes in spiritum nostrum, et radiis natura similem et tunc se ipsum coelestibus coaptantem.

Inter animam mundi et corpus eius manifestum est spiritus eius,
in cuius virtute sunt quattuor elementa.
Nos vero per spiritum nostrum hunc possumus haurire.

Cap. III.

Profecto mundanum corpus, quantum ex motu generationeque apparet,
est ubique vivum, quod Indorum philosophi probant ex eo quod passim
ex se viventia generet. Ergo per animam vivit ubique sibi praesentem ac
prorsus accommodatam. Igitur inter mundi corpus tractabile et ex parte caducum atque ipsam eius animam, cuius natura nimium ab eiusmodi corpore 5
distat, inest ubique spiritus, sicut inter animam et corpus in nobis, si modo
ubique vita est communicata semper ab anima corpori crassiori. Talis nam-

---

75 et musicam *om. LP*   76-80 Sed hanc—Mercurii *desunt in LP*   76 hos] hoc *z*   80 *post* est *add.*
Nam a stella Algol que est in Tauri gradu xviii. adamas et artemisia ad nos virtutem trahicit, que spiritum reddit audacem; et habet ipsa Saturni Iovisque naturam. Prope hanc sidus et Pleides Martium et
Lunare, a quo cristallus et herba diacedos semenque feniculi vim mutuatur ad acuendum visum. In
Leone quinetiam Cor Leonis in gradu xxi. (et in *P*) Leonis per lapidem granatum et celidoniam atque
masticem reprimit atram bilem, spiritumque ad gratiam temperat; vimque ipsa Iovis habet et Martis.
Item Cor Scorpionis in tertio Sagiptarii gradu Martium atque Iovium est, et colorem tibi bonum efficiet
spiritumque (spiritum *P*) letum et sapientiae aptum securumque prestabit, si adhibueris sardium lapidem et ametistum, herbam aristologiam longam atque crocum (et *add. L*); haec enim naturam huius
stelle sequntur. Que numeravi vel extra vel intus assummenda vel gestanda sunt anulo; idque faciendum quando Luna aut subit stellam aut aspicit aspectu sextili vel trino, et stella (*om. L*) in medio celo
habenda vel adscendente. Haec gratia exempli pauca de multis multarum stellarum viribus nunc numeravisse sufficiat. *LP [cf. infra, Cap. VIII, ll. 3-46*   80 Haec] Que *LP*   81 *post* regula *add.* est *LP*
82 regula *om. L*   quid] qui *z*   84 non *om. P*   85 *post* tum *add.* et *L*   86 ab Iove ferme similiter
tum *om. L*   87 Quem] Que *L*   91 traiici ad] trahiciat *P*   94 naturalem *P*   captantem *P*
Inter ... est] Quod inter ... sit *yz*   mundi *om. P*   *Nos vero ... possumus]* Et quod nos ... possimus *yz*
2-3 quod Indorum—generet *desunt in LP*   3 vivit *om. LP*   4 ex parte caducum] oculis manifestum *L*
7 crassiori] manifesto *L*

of Mercury, by the pursuit of eloquence, of song, of truth, and of glory, and by skill; of Venus, by gaiety and music and festivity; of the Moon, by a vegetable existence. But keep in mind this difference between them: the more public and grand exercise of one's wits pertains to the Sun, the more private and that given over to skill and ingenuity rather to Mercury. Likewise, solemn music belongs to Jupiter and the Sun, merry music to Venus, the middle sort to Mercury. There is a similar system with regard to the fixed stars. This is the rule common to the human species.

The specific rule for an individual would be to investigate which star promised what good to the individual at his nativity, to beg grace from that star rather than from another, and to await from any given star not just any gift and what belongs to other stars, but a gift proper to that one. Of course you can gain much that is common to all planets from the Sun as general leader of the celestials, or from Jupiter for much the same reason, or all mundane things equally from the soul and spirit of the cosmos. That the cosmos is animate just like any animate thing, and more effectively so, not only Platonic arguments[9] but also the testimony of Arabic astrologers thoroughly proves. In the same works, the Arabic writers also prove that by an application of our spirit to the spirit of the cosmos, achieved by physical science and our affect, celestial goods pass to our soul and body.[10] This happens from down here through our spirit within us which is a mediator, strengthened then by the spirit of the cosmos, and from above by way of the rays of the stars acting favorably on our spirit, which not only is similar to the rays by nature but also then makes itself more like celestial things.

Between the Anima Mundi and Its Manifest Body Is Its Spirit, in Whose Power Are the Four Elements. We Are Able to Absorb This Spirit through Our Own Spirit.

Chap. III

Assuredly, the world's body is living in every part, as is evident from motion and generation. The philosophers of India deduce its life from the fact that it everywhere generates living things out of itself.[1] It lives, therefore, through a soul which everywhere attends it and which is entirely accommodated to it. Therefore, between the tangible and partly transient body of the world and its very soul, whose nature is very far from its body, there exists everywhere a spirit, just as there is between the soul and body in us, assuming that life everywhere is always communicated by a soul to a grosser body. For

que spiritus necessario requiritur tanquam medium, quo anima divina et adsit corpori crassiori et vitam eidem penitus largiatur. Corpus autem omne facile tibi sensibile, tanquam sensibus tuis accommodatum, crassius est et ab anima divinissima longe degenerans. Opus est igitur excellentioris corporis adminiculo, quasi non corporis. Proinde scimus viventia omnia, tam plantas quam animalia, per quendam spiritum huic similem vivere atque generare, atque inter elementa, quod maxime spirituale est, velocissime generare perpetuoque moveri quasi vivens. Sed quaeres interea, si elementa atque animantes generant aliquid sibi simile suo quodam spiritu, cur lapides et metalla non generant, quae inter elementa et animantes media sunt. Quia videlicet spiritus in eis crassiori materia cohibetur. Qui si quando rite secernatur secretusque conservetur, tanquam seminaria virtus poterit sibi simile generare, si modo materiae cuidam adhibeatur generis eiusdem. Qualem spiritum physici diligentes sublimatione quadam ad ignem ex auro secernentes, cuivis metallorum adhibebunt aurumque efficient. Talem utique spiritum ex auro vel ex alio rite tractum atque servatum, elixir Arabes astrologi nominant.

Sed ad mundi spiritum redeamus, per quem mundus generat omnia, quandoquidem et per spiritum proprium omnia generant, quem tum coelum, tum quintam essentiam possumus appellare. Qui talis ferme est in corpore mundi, qualis in nostro noster, hoc imprimis excepto, quod anima mundi hunc non trahit ex quattuor elementis, tanquam humoribus suis, sicut ex nostris nostra, immo hunc proxime (ut Platonice sive Plotinice loquar) ex virtute sua procreat genitali, quasi tumens, et simul cum eo stellas, statimque per eum parit quattuor elementa, quasi in illius spiritus virtute sint omnia. Ipse vero est corpus tenuissimum, quasi non corpus et quasi iam anima, item quasi non anima et quasi iam corpus. In eius virtute minimum est naturae terrenae, plus autem aqueae, plus item aeriae, rursus igneae stellarisque quam plurimum. Ad horum graduum mensuras ipsae quantitates stellarum elementorumque prodierunt. Ipse vero ubique viget in omnibus generationis omnis proximus auctor atque motus, de quo ille: "Spiritus intus alit." Totus est suapte natura lucidus calidusque et humidus atque vivificus, ex dotibus animae superioribus dotes eiusmodi nactus. Quem plurimum hausisse Apollonium Theaneum testificatus est Indus Hiarchas, dicens: "Mirari nemo debet, O Apolloni, te divinandi scientiam consecutum, cum tantum aetheris in anima geras."

9-10 facile tibi *om. L*   11 excellentioris] insensibilis *L*   13 simile *z*   16 sibi *om. z*   17 et animantes *om. L*   18 Qui si] Quasi *z*   20 spiritum *om. LP*   21 diligenter *z*   22 *post* efficient *add.* Quod fecisse Arnaldum physicum ex argento vivo, testis est Iohannis Andreas, doctor legum, coetaneus eius, qui hoc asserit se vidisse *LP*   25 genera *L*   *post* coelum *add.* occultum *L*   26 Qui] Quis *z*   29 hunc *om. z*   ut Platonice sive Plotinice loquar *om. L*   sive Plotinice *om. P*   30 et simul cum eo stellas *om. L*   31 *post* parit *add.* stellas et *L*   32 tenuissimum] quintum *L*   35 stellarisque] plurimum stellaris postremo *L*   36 ipsae *L*   elementorumque] et elementorum quatuor *L*   38 de quo—alit *om. LP*   Totusque *LP*   39-42 Quem plurimum—geras *add. in marg. L; om. P*

BOOK THREE   CHAP. III   257

such a spirit is necessarily required as a medium by which the divine soul may both be present to the grosser body and bestow life throughout it. But every body easily perceivable by you, being accommodated to your senses, is grosser than and far degenerated from the completely divine soul. Therefore the aid of a more excellent body—a body not a body, as it were—is needed. We know that just as all living things, plants as well as animals, live and generate through a spirit like this, so among the elements, those which are most full of spirit generate very quickly and move perpetually as if alive.[2] But you ask meanwhile, "If elements and living things generate something like themselves by a spirit of their own, why don't gems and metals, which act as means between the elements and living things, generate?" Well, because the spirit in them is inhibited by the grosser material. When this spirit is rightly separated and, once separated, is conserved, it is able like the power of seed to generate a thing like itself, if only it is employed on a material of the same kind. Diligent natural philosophers, when they separate this sort of spirit from gold by sublimation over fire, will employ it on any of the metals and will make it gold. This spirit rightly drawn from gold or something else and preserved, the Arab astrologers call Elixir.[3]

But let us return to the spirit of the world. The world generates everything through it (since, indeed, all things generate through their own spirit); and we can call it both "the heavens" and "quintessence." It is practically the same thing in the world's body as in our body, with this primary exception, that the World-soul does not draw this spirit out of the four elements serving as her humors the way our soul does from our humors, but she procreates this spirit in the first instance (to speak Platonically, or rather Plotinically)[4] as if pregnant by her own generative power, and the stars along with it. Immediately through the spirit the World-soul gives birth to the four elements, as though everything were contained in the power of that spirit. Spirit is a very tenuous body, as if now it were soul and not body, and now body and not soul. In its power there is very little of the earthy nature, but more of the watery, more likewise of the airy, and again the greatest proportion of the stellar fire.[5] The very quantities of the stars and elements have come into being according to the measures of these degrees.[6] This spirit assuredly lives in all as the proximate cause of all generation and motion, concerning which the poet said, "A Spirit nourishes within."[7] It is wholly clear and hot by its own nature, moist, and life-giving, having acquired these gifts from the higher gifts of Soul. Hiarchas the Indian testified that Apollonius of Tyana drank of this spirit in great abundance, saying, "No one should wonder, O Apollonius, that you have acquired the knowledge of divination, since you bear in your soul so much ether."[8]

*Spiritus noster haurit mundi spiritum
per radios Solis et Iovis,
quatenus ipse fit Solaris et Iovialis.*

Cap. IV.

Nunc tu igitur studebis tibi imprimis insinuare, hoc enim medio naturalia quaedam beneficia reportabis, tum corporis mundani, tum animae, tum etiam stellarum atque daemonum. Nam ipse inter crassum mundi corpus et animam medius est, et in ipso stellae sunt et daemones atque per ipsum. Sive enim mundi corpus atque mundana sint ab anima mundi proxime, sicut Plotino placet atque Porphyrio, sive mundanum corpus, sicut et anima, proxime sit a deo, ut nostris placet et forte Timaeo Pythagorico, omnino vivit mundus atque spirat, spiritumque eius nobis haurire licet. Hauritur autem proprie ab homine per suum spiritum illi suapte natura conformem, maxime si reddatur etiam arte cognatior, id est, si maxime coelestis evadat. Evadit vero coelestis, si expurgetur a sordibus et omnino ab eis quae inhaerent sibi dissimilia coelo. Quae quidem sordes non solum intra viscera si fuerint, verum etiam si in animo, si in cute, si in vestibus, si in habitatione et aere, spiritum frequenter inficiunt. Efficietur tandem coelestis, si ad orbicularem animi corporisque motum ipse quoque orbes efficiat; si ad aspectum cogitationemque lucis frequentiorem etiam ipse subrutilet; si adhibeantur ei similia coelo ea communiter diligentia qua Avicenna in libro *De viribus cordis* spiritum curat, et nos in libro *De curanda litteratorum valetudine* curare contendimus. Ubi primum segregantur ab eo vapores obnubilantes medicinis ita purgantibus, secundo rebus lucentibus illustratur, tertio ita colitur ut et tenuetur simul et confirmetur. Fiet denique coelestis maxime, quantum dictat ratio praesens, si applicentur ei potissimum radii influxusque Solis inter coelestia dominantis. Atque ita ex hoc spiritu tanquam in nobis medio coelestia bona imprimis insita sibi in nostrum tum corpus, tum animum exundabunt — bona, inquam, coelestia cuncta, in Sole enim omnia continentur. Conferet autem Sol ad spiritum Solarem efficiendum proprie, quando sub Ariete fuerit vel Leone, ipsum aspiciente Luna, maxime in Leone, ubi

---

Spiritus ... haurit ... Iovis ...fit] Quod spiritus ... hauriat ... Iovis (et *add. z*) ... fiat *yz*   *Cap. IIII*
om. LP   7 Pythagorico *om. P*   9 ille *z*   conforme *P*   13 in[1] *om. z*   16 etiam] est *P*   19 segregant *P*   20 ita] etiam *z*   21 et[1] *om. P*   22 dicat *L*[ac]*P*   23 spiritum *z*

Our Spirit Absorbs the Spirit of the World through the Rays of the Sun and of Jupiter, Insofar as It becomes Solar and Jovial Itself.

Chap. IV

You will bend your efforts to insinuate into yourself this spirit of the world above all, for by this as an intermediary you will gain certain natural benefits not only from the world's body but from its soul, and even from the stars and the daemons. For this spirit is an intermediary between the gross body of the world and its soul; and the stars and daemons exist in it and by means of it. For whether the world's body and mundane things have their being directly from the World-soul (as Plotinus and Porphyry think) or whether the world's body just like its soul has its being directly from God, as is the opinion of our theologians and perhaps Timaeus the Pythagorean,[1] the world does wholly live and breathe, and we are permitted to absorb its spirit. This is absorbed by man in particular through his own spirit which is by its own nature similar to it, especially if it is made more akin to it by art, that is, if it becomes in the highest degree celestial. Now it becomes celestial if it is purged of filth, and anything at all inhering in it which is unlike the heavens. If there are impurities, not only in the bowels but in the mind, if on the skin, if on the clothing, if in the dwelling and the air, they frequently infect the spirit. The spirit will be made celestial, finally, if according to the circular motion of the soul and body of the world it too makes circles,[2] if when you frequently behold and think about light it too glows a little; and if things similar to the heavens are frequently brought to bear on it with that care which Avicenna in his book *On the Powers of the Heart* prescribes for the spirit and which we attempt in our book *On Caring for the Health of Learned People*. In our book, first, the beclouding vapors are separated from the spirit by medicines that purge them. Second, the spirit is made luminous by luminous things. Third, it is so cared for that it may be at the same time rarefied and strengthened.[3] Finally, it will be made celestial to the highest degree, so far as that system dictates which we are now outlining, if the rays and influences chiefly of the Sun, when he is dominant among the celestial bodies, are applied to it. And so from this spirit, acting as a mediator in us, the celestial gifts located mainly in it will overflow not only to our body but also to our mind—I say all the celestial goods, because they are all contained in the Sun. Now the Sun will conduce in particular to making the spirit Solar when he is under Aries or Leo and the Moon aspects him, especially in Leo; then he so enlivens our spirit that he can fortify it to

adeo spiritum nostrum vegetat, ut ipsum muniat contra venenum epidemiae repellendum. Quod perspicue apparet in Babylonia et Aegypto et regionibus spectantibus ad Leonem, ubi Sol Leonem intrans, epidemiam sedat ea duntaxat ratione qua diximus.

Tunc ergo et tu Solaria passim exquisita compone. Tunc incipe Solaribus uti, ea tamen cautione qua sub aestu exsiccationem diligenter evites. Non poterit autem facile spiritus Solaris evadere, nisi sit quam plurimus; ad Solem enim maxime pertinet amplitudo. Quam plurimum vero faciet tum diligentia, cor rebus cordialibus intus et extra fovens, tum etiam victus ex alimentis quidem subtilibus, multum tamen et facile et salubriter nutrientibus. Motus quoque frequens atque lenis et opportuna quies aerque tenuis atque serenus et ab aestu geluque remotus, praecipue laetus animus. Rursum nec Solaris erit, nisi calidus fuerit et subtilis et clarus. Subtilem clarumque facies, si tristia et crassa devitabis et fusca; uteris lucidis laetisque intus et extra; luminis multum die nocteque excipies; sordes expelles et otium et torporem; imprimis tenebras devitabis. Perducturus autem spiritum ad calorem Soli naturalem, cave ne ad tertium caloris gradum siccitatemque deducas. Calor enim ipse Solis naturaliter non exsiccat — alioquin non esset Sol vitae generationisque dominus et auctor augmenti — siccare vero contingit radiis eius in concavis materiae siccae conclusis. Humorem itaque calori subtilem, qualis est Solaris et maxime Iovius, adhibebis, et conservabis in spiritu rerum eiusmodi usu, si Solarem sis effecturus, ne alioquin ad Martium potius quam ad Solarem forte deducas.

Martem quidem Soli esse similem in paucis et his quidem manifestis, nec admodum excellentibus, et interim inimicum esse ferunt. Iovem vero Soli simillimum in plurimis excellentibusque muneribus, quamvis occultioribus, et amicissimum esse scimus. Unde Ptolemaeus, ubi de consonantia disputat, Iovem ait cum Sole prae ceteris perfectissime consonare, Veneremque cum Luna. Omnesque astrologi universalem beneficentiam Soli tribuunt similiter atque Iovi, quamvis Sol eadem efficacius agat et Iuppiter sub virtute Solis efficiat. In utroque calor viget superatque humorem, sed in Iove superat modice, in Sole superat excellenter, utrobique benefice. Cum igitur adeo consonent, facile poteris spiritum Solarem efficere pariter atque Iovium, ac res Solares et Ioviales rite poteris invicem commiscere, praesertim si et has invicem componas et spiritui adhibeas, quando Iuppiter Solem trino aspicit vel sextili, vel saltem quando Luna ab aspectu alterius ad alterum procedit aspiciendum, maxime quando ab aspectu Solis ad coitum cum Iove progreditur. Seorsum vero Solarem pro-

---

30 sedet *P*   33 tamen] tum *P*   39 praecipue laetus animus] animusque laetus *P*   42 torporem imprimis *om. P*   48 sis] sic *P*   53 *post* Unde *add.* et *z*   59 atque *P*   60 spiritu *L*   61 sextile *z*

repel the poison of the Plague. This clearly appears in Babylon and Egypt and regions pertaining to Leo, where the Sun stops the Plague when he enters Leo for precisely the reason we have said [see also 3.9 and "Traditions"].

You, therefore, collect under Leo Solar things which you have sought out far and wide; then begin to use Solar things — with this caution, however, that you should carefully avoid drying yourself out under the summer's heat. The spirit, however, can not easily become Solar, unless there is as much of it as possible; for amplitude belongs especially to the Sun. What will make it as ample as possible is not only taking care to warm the heart with cordial things inside and out, but also eating a diet of foods that are subtle but also very nourishing and easily and healthfully so. The same goes for frequent and gentle exercise, timely rest, fine and serene air far from heat or cold, and most of all a joyful mood. Again, the spirit will not be Solar unless it is hot and fine and clear. You will make it fine and clear if you avoid sad, gross, and dusky things, if you use lucid and joyful things within and without, if you take in a lot of light day and night, and drive out impurities, inactivity, and insensibility and above all if you avoid darkness. But if you intend to lead your spirit into the natural heat of the Sun, beware lest you lead it on to the third degree of heat and dryness. For although the heat of the Sun does not itself dry things up — otherwise the Sun would not be the Lord of life and generation and author of increase — nevertheless his rays dry accidentally when they are confined in the hollows of a dry material. And so you should add to the heat subtle moisture, such as is Solar and especially Jovial, and you should conserve it in your spirit by the use of such Solar and Jovial things if you intend to make your spirit Solar; otherwise you might lead it rather to be Martian than Solar.

They say that in a few properties which are manifest and not entirely excellent, Mars is similar to the Sun, and at the same time that they are enemies. We know that Jupiter, on the other hand, is most similar to the Sun in gifts that are many and excellent, albeit more occult, and that they are the best of friends. That is why Ptolemy, where he discusses consonance,[4] says Jupiter is the most perfectly consonant with the Sun above all, and Venus with the Moon. And all astrologers attribute universal beneficence to the Sun and Jupiter alike — although the Sun does the same things more efficaciously and Jupiter acts under the power of the Sun. In both, heat flourishes and outweighs moisture, but in Jupiter it outweighs it slightly, in the Sun, it outweighs it by far, in both, benignly. Since, therefore, they are so harmonious, you will easily be able to make your spirit not only Jovial but even Solar too; and you will be able rightly to mix Solar and Jovial things, especially if you also compound them together and bring them to bear on your spirit when Jupiter looks upon the Sun with a trine or sextile aspect, or at least when the Moon proceeds from an aspect with one to an aspect with the other, especially when she proceeds from an aspect with the Sun to a conjunction with Jupiter. You will make your

prie facies vel Iovialem, quando aspectum Lunae ad Solem observaveris vel
ad Iovem. Tametsi consecutus naturam huius, naturam mox illius facile con- 65
sequeris. Sextilem vero aspectum intellige, quando planetae duo inter se signorum duorum spatio distant; trinum autem, quando quattuor signorum discrepant intervallo. Coniunctionem vero vel aspectum Lunae ad alios duodecim
gradibus citra totidemque ultra metimur.

Tres Gratiae sunt Iuppiter et Sol et Venus.
Iuppiter est Gratia geminarum media
et maxime nobis accommodata.

Cap. V.

Compositiones quidem et curationes Iovias simul atque Solares invenies
in libro nostro *De vita longa* et in libro *De litteratorum cura*, ubi etiam mis-
cuimus pleraque Venerea, nam et nos in studiosis timemus exsiccationem,
cui resistit Venus. Et haec ipsa Venus est amicissima Iovi, sicut et Soli Iuppiter, quasi Gratiae tres inter se concordes atque coniunctae. Ab his quidem 5
tribus coeli Gratiis et a stellis eiusdem generis astrologi gratias et sperant et
diligenter exquirunt, easque per Mercurium atque Lunam quasi nuntios
transmitti putant atque curant, facile vero communiterque per Lunam. Lunam quidem cum Iove coniunctam aut Venere feliciorem esse putant, quam
si per sextilem aspexerit aut trinum. Verumtamen si per trinum aspiciens 10
etiam suscipiatur ab illis, quasi existimant esse coniunctam. Similiter si a
Sole perspecta fuerit simulque recepta.

Nos autem si horum trium stellarumque similium vires effectusque omnes
percurrere singulatim velimus, longum opus aggrediemur, exquisitu difficile,
difficillimum observatu. Si ad Venerem nos proprie conferamus, non facile 15
Solem habemus; si ad Solem proprie, non facile Venerem. Ut igitur tres
simul in uno Gratias complectamur, ad Iovem tandem confugiemus, inter
Solem Veneremque natura effectuque medium, qualitate admodum temperatum, et quaecunque sperantur a Venere vel a Sole suo quodam pacto traden-
tem, magnificentius quidem honestiusque quam Venus, temperatius quoque 20

66–69 Sextilem — metimur *desunt in* P   69 metiuntur *z*
   Tres ... sunt ... Iuppiter est] Quod tres ... sint ... et quod Iuppiter sit *yz*   2 De vita — libro *desunt in* P
3 et *om. z*   8 communiter *P*   9 Venerem *P*   12 cepta *z*   14 aggrederemur *z*   16 habebimus *z*
18 Venerem *P*

spirit separately Solar or Jovial in particular when you observe an aspect of
the Moon either to the Sun or to Jupiter. Though to be sure when you have
attained the nature of Jupiter, you will then easily attain the nature of the Sun.
Now understand that the sextile aspect is when two planets are two signs away
from each other, but the trine, when they are four signs away from each other.
However, we measure a conjunction with, or an aspect of, the Moon towards
the others if they are within twelve degrees on either this or that side of the
point in question.[5]

*The Three Graces Are Jupiter and the Sun and Venus.
Jupiter Is the Grace Which Is the Mean Between the Two
and Is Especially Accommodated to Us.*

Chap. V

You will find the Jovial and Solar compounds and cures in our book *On a Long Life* [2.10] and in the book *On the Care of Learned People* [1.22]. We intermingled also several Venereal ones, because studious patients are in danger of drying out, which Venus prevents. And this same Venus is most friendly to Jupiter, just as Jupiter is to the Sun — three Graces, as it were, concordant and conjoined among themselves.[1] From these three Graces of the heavens, and from stars of the same kind, astrologers hope for and diligently seek out favors [pun on *gratia*]. These favors they believe to be transmitted through Mercury and the Moon as if through messengers, and they take care that this happens often, but most easily and generally through the Moon. And they believe the Moon is more fortunate when conjoined with Jupiter or Venus than if she is in an aspect sextile or trine. Nevertheless, in a trine aspect, if she is also received by them, they consider her as if she were conjoined with them. So also if she is aspected and at the same time received by the Sun.

If we wanted to run through, one by one, all the powers and effects of these three and of stars that are similar to them, we would undertake a long work, difficult to research, most difficult to comply with. If we betake ourselves strictly to Venus, we do not easily get the Sun; if strictly to the Sun, we do not easily get Venus. Therefore, in order that we may at one time embrace three Graces in one, we will flee at last to Jupiter, who is the mediator between the Sun and Venus by nature and effect. For he is very temperate in quality, giving whatever is hoped for from Venus or the Sun in a way of his own, more magnificently and honorably than Venus, more temperately too than the Sun; and

quam Sol, et in omnibus cum humana natura maxime congruentem. Utemur itaque Ioviis, quando et ipse et Luna dignitatem tum naturalem, tum accidentalem habuerint, sintque simul, vel feliciter se aspiciant. Si quando id fieri omnino non possit, misce Solaria in unum simul atque Venerea, faciesque sic Ioviale ex utrisque compositum, quando videlicet Luna a coitu Veneris eat ad sextilem Solis aspectum, vel econverso. Memento vero in rebus componendis quae cor spiritumque foveant et corroborent, Lunam conferre potissimum, si una cum his muneribus hoc etiam habuerit, ut per aeria signa discurrat — maxime per Aquarium, quod esse maxime putant aerium — vel si in suo domicilio sit aut exaltatione sua vel domo Iovis aut Solis, et ubicunque sit, si mansionem ex viginti illis et octo teneat, tum sibi, tum etiam operi competentem.

De virtute in nobis naturali, vitali, animali,
et per quos planetas adiuventur,
et quomodo per aspectum Lunae ad Solem
et Venerem, maxime vero ad Iovem.

Cap. VI.

Praecipua vero disciplina est recte tenere quem spiritum, quam vim, quam rem potissimum hi planetae significant. Luna ergo Venusque vim et spiritum naturalem atque genitalem et quae hunc augent. Iuppiter eadem, sed efficacius heparque et stomachum, habetque non mediocrem partem in corde et spiritu virtuteque vitali, quatenus suapte natura cum Sole consentit — immo et per se ipsum, alioquin cor vitalem spiritum non proprie in mense Iovis acciperet. Unde Iovem Graeci appellant vitam et per quem vita. Habere quoque in animali spiritu potestatem testantur astrologi, dicentes Iovem ad philosophiam et veritatem inveniendam religionemque conferre. Et Plato ubi ait ab Iove philosophos proficisci. Quod etiam significavit Homerus antiquorum opinione dicens: "Talis est mens hominibus, qualem indies adducit pater hominum atque deorum." Nusquam vero numen aliquod ita cognominat praeter Iovem. Sol spiritum vitalem praecipue corque significat, et habet nonnihil, immo non parum, in capite propter sensum atque motum, cuius est ipse dominus; neque vim deserit naturalem. Mercurius cerebrum et instrumenta sensuum ideoque spiritum animalem.

---

25 Venereis z   30 suo *om. P*   31 mansionem] stationem *P*
   De virtute — Iovem] De virtutibus naturalibus, vitalibus et animalibus, et qui planetarum singulis aut commodent incommodentve, idque maxime per aspectus *z*   10-13 Quod etiam — praeter Iovem *desunt in P*   13 ita] itaque *z*

he is in everything most like human nature. And so we will use Jovial things, when he and the Moon have dignity both natural and accidental and are together or aspecting each other felicitously. If at times this is absolutely impossible, mix into one both Solar and Venereal things, and you will thereby make of the two a Jovial compound; do this when the Moon goes from conjunction with Venus to a sextile aspect of the Sun or vice versa. But remember, in compounding things that warm and strengthen the heart and spirit, the Moon is most effective if she has along with the above gifts this also, that she runs through an airy sign — especially through Aquarius, because that sign is thought to be the most airy — or if she is in her own house, or her exaltation, or the house of Jupiter or the Sun, and wherever she is, if she holds the mansion of the 28 which is compatible both with herself and with the work.[2]

Concerning Our Natural Power, Our Vital, and Our Animal, and Which Planets Give Them Aid, and How They Do So through the Aspect of the Moon to the Sun, to Venus, and Especially to Jupiter.

Chap. VI

It is truly a discipline of special importance to grasp correctly which spirit, which force, which thing these planets especially signify. The Moon, then, and Venus signify the natural and procreative force and spirit as well as whatever increases the latter. Jupiter signifies the same, but more efficaciously, also the liver and stomach; and he plays no mean role in the heart, the spirit, and the vital power insofar as he agrees with the Sun in his own nature — and indeed he plays this role in and of himself, otherwise the heart would not properly receive the vital spirit in the month of Jupiter. This is why the Greeks call Jupiter life [referring to the etymology of "Zeus"] and the cause of life.[1] The astrologers declare that he also has power over the animal spirit, saying that Jupiter is useful for philosophy and discovering truth, and for religion. So also Plato, when he says that philosophers spring from Jupiter.[2] Homer has also signified this, when he said, expressing the opinion of the ancients, "The mind in men is of such a quality as the father of gods and men brings upon them from day to day."[3] He nowhere names any other divinity in this way except Jupiter. The Sun signifies principally the vital spirit and the heart, and has some power, indeed quite a lot, in the head, on account of sense and motion, whose master he is; and he has some connection with the natural force. Mercury signifies the brain and the sense-organs and thus the animal spirit.

Proinde tutissima via erit nihil sine Lunae beneficio facere, quandoquidem coelestia communiter et frequenter atque facile ad inferiora demittit. Quam alterum Solem nominant, quolibet mense quattuor anni tempora facientem. In prima enim sui quarta Peripatetici putant esse calidam atque humidam, in secunda calidam et siccam, in tertia frigidam atque siccam, in quarta frigidam atque humidam. Lumenque eius proculdubio Solis esse lumen; humores generationemque regere, omnesque mutationes foetus ipsius in alvo conversionibus suis metiri; et quotiens Soli iungitur, vivificam ab eo virtutem recipere, quam infundat humori, atque ibidem a Mercurio vim humores commiscentem. Quam vim Mercurius et transformatione in omnes sua et gyris multiplicibus affert. Ibidem mox a Venere vim, quae conducat ad formas geniturae convenientes.

Operae pretium vero fuerit meminisse diurnum Lunae cursum in quattuor distribui quartas. In prima quidem ab oriente ad medium ascendit coelum, atque interim humorem et spiritum auget naturalem. In secunda a coeli medio petit occasum, efficitque in nobis oppositum. Tertia ab occasu coelum subter medium adit, iterumque spiritum illum auget et humorem. Quarta cadit inde versus ortum, minuitque vicissim. Quod maxime in Oceani ripis apparet, ubi ad hunc cursum mare manifestius accedit atque recedit, eodemque ordine vigor in aegrotantibus. Probabile etiam est Solem per easdem sui quartas calorem naturalem et spiritum vitalem augere vel diminuere; animalem quoque, quatenus Mercurium habet comitem. His cognitis poterit medicus pro humore et calore naturali et quolibet spiritu recreando tempora opportuniora servare. Sed nunc de Luna satis.

Neque dimittere decet Iovem in cuius mense altero quidem vitam accepimus, altero autem communiter et felicius nati sumus. Et qui inter Solem atque Venerem, item inter Solem atque Lunam est qualitate effectuque medius, ideoque complectitur omnia. Solem vero ipsum praetermittere coeli dominum nefas atque periculosum existimamus, nisi forte quis dixerit eum, qui Iovem habet, in Iove Solem iam habere, illic potissimum ad homines temperatum. In Sole certe omnes coelestium esse virtutes, non solum Iamblichus Iulianusque, sed omnes affirmant. Et Proculus ait ad Solis aspectum omnes omnium coelestium virtutes congregari in unum atque colligi. Iovem vero esse Solem quendam ad nos temperatum nemo negabit. Lunam quoque temperatam ad Venerem ne neglexeris. Multum enim ad validam prosperamque

---

17 Lunae *om. P* 20 *post* quarta *add.* ut Lw^{ac} Peripatetici putant *om. P* 25 recipere quam] accipere quum *z* 26 et transformatione in omnes sua et *om. P* 29–40 Operae pretium — satis *desunt in P* 37 *post* quartas *add.* ad *z* 41 docet *z* 51 ne] haud *z*

Therefore the safest way will be to do nothing without the favor of the Moon, since she conveys heavenly things generally, frequently, and easily to things below. They call her a second Sun because she creates in any month [the equivalent of] four seasons of the year. For in her first quarter the Peripatetics think the Moon is hot and moist; in the second, hot and dry; in the third, cold and dry; and in the fourth, cold and moist. They believe that her light is indubitably the light of the Sun; that she rules moisture and generation and measures out all the changes of the foetus in the womb by her own changes [i.e., by months], and that as often as the Moon is in conjunction with the Sun, she receives a life-giving power from him which she infuses in her moisture; and she receives from Mercury in the same place [Mercury is always near the Sun] a force which blends her moistures. Mercury has this force both by virtue of his own transformation into all other planets and by virtue of his many revolutions.[4] Likewise at the same time and place she receives a force from Venus [she too is always near the Sun] which conduces to forms suitable for generation.

It would be worthwhile to remember that the daily course of the Moon is also divided into four quarter-circles. In the first quarter, then, she ascends from the East to the mid-heaven, and during this time she increases moisture and the natural spirit. In the second quarter, from mid-heaven she comes to the West and effects the opposite in us. In her third quarter, from the West she approaches the mid-heaven underneath and again increases that spirit and moisture. In the fourth quarter, she sinks thence towards her rising and in turn diminishes them. This is especially apparent on the shores of the Ocean, where the sea quite clearly flows and ebbs according to this pattern, and in the same way strength flows and ebbs in sick men. It is probable that the Sun too, by the same quarter-circles of his own, increases or lessens the natural heat and the vital spirit. He similarly affects the animal spirit insofar as he has Mercury for his companion. Knowing these things, the physician will be able to keep to the more opportune times to refresh natural heat or moisture or any spirit at all. But now that's enough about the Moon.

Do not disregard Jupiter, in one of whose months [the second] we have received life and in the other [the ninth] most of us, the luckier ones, were born. And in quality and effect he is the mediator between the Sun and Venus, and likewise between the Sun and the Moon, and therefore he embraces all things. We consider it criminal and dangerous to neglect the Sun, the Lord of heaven himself, unless perhaps you could say that he who has Jupiter, already has in him the Sun, and that there the Sun is best tempered for human beings. That all the powers of the heavens are assuredly in the Sun, not only Iamblichus and Julian but all men affirm, and Proclus says that all the powers of all the celestials are gathered and collected into one in the presence of the visible Sun.[5] That Jupiter indeed is a Sun tempered for us no one will deny. Do not overlook the fact that the Moon also is tempered to Venus. For Venus

quae fit in stomacho, sed secundam etiam quae fit in iecore, tertiam insuper 30
quae in venis, quartam denique quae in membris efficitur. Quae longo quodam indigent intervallo, et quavis impedita pabulum non suppeditatur humori.
  Proinde sicut digestionem, sic excrementorum purgationem adiuvare imprimis necessarium est ad vitam. Necessarium sordes etiam a cute detergere. Necessarius est motus corporis tam continuus, tam temperatus, tam varius 35 quam coelestium aerisque motus et ignis et aquae, servata duntaxat concoctionis et somni necessitate, defatigatione vero et resolutione vitata. Praeterea sub umbra situm cariemque obducimus. Sub divo, sub lumine vivimus, quod pater meus Ficinus, insignis medicus, frequenter habebat in ore. Sed ad haec feliciter peragenda operae pretium foret, non tam urbanis negotiis quam rus- 40 ticis quibusdam exercitationibus a tenera statim aetate corpus assuefecisse, et quodammodo similibus, interdum etiam nutrimentis, et vitae genus quodammodo varium tenuisse; quod me saepe prudens ille monebat. Qui enim in omni aetate lautissima quadam curiositate vivunt, saepe minus tuti vivunt; qui vero adolescentes se minus assuefecerint, adulti saltem assuefaciant, cau- 45 tioribus tamen gradibus id tentantes.

Sanguis et humor accommodatus vitae aerius esse debet,
qualitate temperatus, substantia medius atque tenax.

Cap. V.

Graeci omnes inter praecepta ad diuturnam vitam maxime necessaria mandant ut euchimis alamur. Euchima vocamus alimenta salubria, quae bonum afferunt nutrimentum, id est, sanguinem bonum. Bonum vero sanguinem appellamus non frigidum, non siccum, non turbulentum, sed calidum et humidum atque clarum — calidum quidem calore non acri, humi- 5 dum vero humore non aqueo, clarum quoque, nec tamen interea tenuissimum. Iam vero ferventior sanguis naturalem tum calorem exacuit, tum exsiccat humorem, et quem ipse humorem infert vel calorem resolubilem praestat atque fugacem. Sanguis praeterea humidior proniorque ad aquam naturalem obtundit calorem, humorem quoque naturalem vel hebetat, vel 10 impellit sub calore liquescere, vel suffocat humiditate calorem; et omnino si qua portio naturalis humoris ex aqueo sanguine trahitur, tum putrescit facile, tum cito diffluit atque dissolvitur. Hinc efficitur ut qui molliores fructus herbasque comedunt, nisi raro forsan et pro medicina tunc ventrem leniente

---

32 indiget *x*   suppeditat *x*   34 *post* etiam *add.* est *L*   43 saepe prudens ille monebat] saepius ille prudens manebat *z*   44 aetati *z*   46 gradibus] et paulatim *z*
   Quod sanguis ... debeat *y*   6 nec *add.* L^2 13–17 Hinc efficitur — miscentur *add. in marg.* L^2

is very good for a healthy and prosperous life, since she makes a man fruitful and happy; therefore you will observe her. And yet if you should properly combine the Moon, similar to Venus, absolutely equal in moisture and scarcely less hot, with Jupiter or the Sun, you would almost now have a Venus.

Well, then, in order to proceed by the safest and also the most convenient way, observe the Moon when she aspects the Sun and is coming together with Jupiter, or at least when she aspects Jupiter and the Sun at the same time, or certainly when, soon after an aspect with the Sun, she is moving to a conjunction or aspect with Jupiter. And at one and the same time, combine with each other Solar and Jovial things together with Venereal and apply them to yourself. If necessity or business should force you to have recourse to only one out of the great ones, have recourse to Jupiter himself or preferably to both the Moon and Jupiter. For no star supports and strengthens the natural forces in us — indeed all the forces — more than does Jupiter, nor does any star offer more or more prosperous things. And to receive him is beneficial in all circumstances, but to receive the Sun is perhaps not in all circumstances safe. For Jupiter is always beneficial, the Sun often seems to harm. Venus, in and of herself, is as if she were weak. Therefore only Jupiter is called "helping father" [etymology].[6] Ptolemy too confirms this when he says that a drug has hardly any effect at all upon nature when the Moon comes together with Jupiter.[7] And he even thinks that the whole nature of the body of the universe is strengthened especially from that conjunction. Furthermore, I know by experience that when the Moon is in conjunction with Venus, medicine has hardly any effect. Yet when phlegm is a danger, we should observe the Moon in relation rather to the Sun, and only when we fear bile and drying-out, in relation to Venus; nevertheless, if you direct the Moon to Jupiter, it is somewhat useful for all these things and especially for the expulsion of black bile and for the renewal and strengthening of the complexion common to all human beings. For just as licorice and rose-oil make colder things warm and hotter things cool, and the same goes for wine (which in addition moistens the dry and dries the moist), so Jupiter is similar to human heat, like wine, rose oil, camomile, and licorice. When, therefore, you hear Albumasar saying: "There is no life for the living, aside from God, except through the Sun and Moon,"[8] understand this insofar as it concerns the influence common to all living things. More proper to man and most accommodated to him is the influence from Jupiter.

There are in the nature of the body forces of attraction, retention, digestion, and expulsion.[9] All these therefore are aided by Jupiter himself, but especially that power of concocting or digesting and of generating, nourishing, and growing, because of his airy and abundant moisture and his ample heat which moderately dominates the moisture. Indeed, the rays of Jupiter, always and everywhere diffused, greatly temper the light of the Sun for the particular welfare of man, while the rays of Venus contribute continuously to the same

Luna. Radii quidem Veneris atque Lunae tanquam humidiores quodam indigent temperante, sicut et Solis radii tanquam calidiores humidioris cuiusdam temperiem exigunt. Radii autem Iovis temperamentum nullum desiderant. Quid enim aliud Iuppiter est, nisi Sol quidam ad salutem rerum praecipue humanarum ab initio temperatus? Quid rursus aliud, nisi Luna Venusque facta tamen calidior atque potentior? Ideo astrologi ab Iove auspicantur annum fertilem, serenum, salubrem, et ab eo imminentium morborum remedia sperant. Atque Empedocles ubi propria unicuique planetarum munera tribuit, Iovem solum generationis principem nominat, Orpheum imitatus.

Praeter Iovem praecipiunt Lunam diligenter in omnibus operibus observandam tanquam medium inter coelestia competens atque terrena. Sit ergo Luna in gradu situque et aspectu ad opus optatum conveniente. Non sit in eclyptica, nec sub radiis Solis per gradus duodecim ultra citraque, nisi forte sit in eodem minuto cum Sole. Plerique vero volunt omnes planetas fore fortes, quando in unitate Solis extiterint; unitatem vero metiuntur minutis duobus atque triginta, ut xvi. quidem citra, xvi. vero ultra connumerentur. Non impediatur a Saturno vel Marte. Non descendat in latitudine meridionali, quando duodecim dictos gradus egreditur. Non sit opposita Soli, nec lumine minuatur, nec tarda cursu, quando scilicet die uno duodecim non peragit gradus. Non sit in via combusta a gradu Librae xxviii. ad tertium Scorpionis, nec in octava, nec in ascendente, nec in finibus Martis vel Saturni. Quidam vero nec in sexta, duodecima, nona, quarta Lunam volunt. In ceteris vero coeli plagis approbant. Ubi haec omnia complecti non potes, Iovem saltem expecta vel Venerem in ascendente vel decima, sic enim subveniunt detrimentis Lunae. Nec ab re fuerit recordari quatenus Luna lumine augetur, eatenus et nobis non solum humorem, sed spiritum etiam virtutemque augeri, atque haec ad circumferentiam dilatari, maxime in secunda eius quarta. Quando vero minuitur, contra contingere, praesertim in ultima quarta. Primum eius ad Solem trinum praeesse secundo; hunc sextili primo; hunc sextili secundo. Lunam quatenus lumine, eatenus repleri calore. Videntur ergo quidam non tam observare quomodo aspiciat Luna Solem (semper enim aspicit) quam ut plurimum lumen habeat, praesertim dum augetur. Aspiciat vero interim trino vel sextili Iovem aut Venerem.

Proinde virtutem attractivam ignea iuvant, retentivam terrea, digestivam

---

90 *post* humidiores *add.* calore P   quaedam z   96 serenum] ferreum z   98 munere z   104–106 Plerique—connumerentur *desunt in* P   110 xxviii.] 18. P   111–112 Quidam—approbant *desunt in* P   115–123 Nec ab re—Venerem *desunt in* P

end, and the Moon contributes likewise when she transmits it. The rays of Venus and the Moon, as they are rather moist, need some tempering factor, just as the rays of the Sun, being rather hot, demand the tempering of something rather moist. But the rays of Jupiter need no tempering. For what else is Jupiter but a Sun tempered from the start especially for the welfare of human things? What else is he but a Moon and a Venus, made, however, more hot and powerful? Accordingly, from the position of Jupiter, astrologers predict that a year will be fertile, fair, and healthful, and hope he will remedy whatever diseases are impending.[10] And when Empedocles assigned to each of the planets its proper functions, following Orpheus, he named Jupiter alone the ruler of generation.[11]

Besides Jupiter, they advise that the Moon be carefully observed in all works as a suitable mediator between heavenly and earthly things. Accordingly, let the Moon be in the degree, position, and aspect fitting for the desired work. Let her not be in the ecliptic [i.e., on her ascending or descending node], nor under the rays of the Sun within the space of twelve degrees on this side or that, unless she happens to be in the very same minute with the Sun. Indeed, many authorities would have it that all planets are strong when they are in conjunction with the Sun; they measure conjunction moreover by thirty-two minutes [his apparent diameter], since they count sixteen on this side and sixteen on that. Do not let the Moon be impeded by Saturn or Mars; do not let her be down in a southern latitude when she traverses those twelve degrees surrounding the Sun. Let her not be in opposition to the Sun nor diminished in light, nor slow in her course, that is, when in one day she does not move twelve degrees. Let her not be in the burned path from the 28th degree of Libra to the third of Scorpio, nor in the eighth [place], nor in the ascendant, nor in the terms of Mars or Saturn. Some authorities do not even wish the Moon to be in the sixth, twelfth, ninth, or fourth [place]. In the other regions of heaven they approve her. In cases where you are not able to manage all these caveats, at least look for Jupiter or Venus either in the ascendant or in the tenth place, for so they compensate for the debilities of the Moon. In this connection, remember that insofar as the Moon is increasing in light, so far also not only moisture is increased in us but also spirit and power; and these dilate to the circumference, especially in her second quarter. But when she is decreasing in light, the opposite happens, especially in her last quarter. Her first trine aspect to the Sun takes precedence over her second, her second trine over her first sextile, and her first sextile over her second. Insofar as the Moon is refilled with light, so also is she refilled with heat. Some authorities seem therefore to observe not so much how the Moon aspects the Sun (for she always aspects him) as that she have as much light as possible, especially when she is waxing. And meanwhile she should be in a trine or sextile aspect with Jupiter or Venus.

Now fiery things aid the attractive power, earthy things the retentive power,

aeria, expulsivam aquea. Si tu has omnes in te adiuvare volueris, attractivam quidem per ignea maxime roborabis, quando Luna in signis vel stationibus igneis constituta Iovem aspicit, scilicet Ariete, Leone, Sagittario. Retentivam per terrea, potissimum quando intuetur eundem in signis vel stationibus terreis collocata, Tauro, Virgine, Capricorno. Digestivam generativamque per aeria, scilicet Geminis, Libram, Aquarium, quotiens sub aeriis Iovem suspicit aut subit. Expulsivam per aquea, Cancrum, Pisces, Scorpium, quando sub aqueis ipsa posita Iovis radiis illustratur. Maxime vero in his omnibus consequeris optata, si Iuppiter eadem vel similia vel saltem non dissimillima signa mansionesve possederit. Citaturus alvum solidis medicinis, accipe Pisces; liquidis Scorpionem; mediis vero Cancrum. Per inferiora purgaturus, Pisces et Scorpium; per superiora Cancrum. Malum Saturni vel Martis ad Lunam devitabis aspectum, ille enim vexat stomachum, hic intestina dissolvit. Capricornum evitabis et Taurum, nauseam enim afferunt. Scis membrum irritandum non esse, quando Luna signum occupat membro praefectum (humores namque movet), sed potius esse fovendum.

Haec vero de virtute et spiritu naturali in iecore praecipue dominantibus, quae in quattuor officia quae narravimus dividuntur, dicta sufficiant. De virtute vero spirituque vitali in corde vigente quidnam monemus? Satis id ferme significatum est. Nam per res imprimis igneas et quodammodo simul aerias haec adiuvantur, quando Luna in domiciliis mansionibusve consimilibus suspicit Iovem, praecipue si Iovem complectatur et Solem. Virtutem quoque animalem per sensum et motum in capite dominantem confirmare potes per aeria imprimis, subiunctis igneis, quando Luna in domiciliis vel sedibus consimilibus Iovem suspicit, praesertim si Iovem propemodum Mercuriumque complectitur.

Hic vero te moneo, ne Mercurium putes aqueum esse vel terreum (quod et ego aliquando suspicatus sum), alioquin motibus celeritatique ingenii non conferret, sed quodammodo aerium esse scias. Nam et ob eandem causam tam mobilis est, tam facile convertibilis, tantum ingenio confert, praesertim in Aquario plurimum aerio constitutus. Humor quidem in eo temperatus est; calor exiguus. Sub Sole positus dicitur exsiccare; longior autem a Sole factus humectare putatur. Ibi quidem calefacere multum ex natura Solis; hic vero calefacere parum admodum et humefacere magis suapte natura. Calore forsan non cedit Veneri, Lunam superat; humore vero cedit utrisque. Haly

---

125 *post* expulsivam *add.* per *yz*   127 scilicet—Sagittario *om. P*   Retentiva *z*   129 Tauro Virgine Capricorno *om. P*   131 aquea *Pwx*; aqueam *Lw*^(ac)*yz*   Cancrum Pisces Scorpium *om. P*   132 aquis *z*   133 dissimilia *z*   134 mansionesve] stationesve *P*   134–140 Citaturus—fovendum *desunt in P*   135 Scorpionum *z*   135–136 Per inferiora—Cancrum *om. L*   139 profectum *z*   142 quae *om. z*   143 vero *om. z*   quid *P*   145 mansionibusve] stationibusve *P*   151 terrenum *P*   153 quodammodo *om. z*   155 in¹ *om. z*   plurimum aerio *om. P*   156 longios *z*   157 humectate *z*   159 forsan non] quidem *P*   159–166 Haly—posse *desunt in P*

airy the digestive, and watery the expulsive. If you want to help all these in yourself, strengthen especially the attractive power through fiery things, when the Moon is set in fiery signs or positions (namely in Aries, Leo, and Sagittarius) and aspects Jupiter. Aid the retentive through earthy things especially when the Moon is located in earthy signs or positions (Taurus, Virgo, and Capricorn) and aspects him. The digestive and generative virtue is aided through airy things, as often as the Moon under airy signs (Gemini, Libra, and Aquarius) aspects or approaches Jupiter. The expulsive virtue is aided through the watery, that is, when the Moon placed under watery signs (that is, Cancer, Pisces, and Scorpio) is illuminated by the rays of Jupiter. But especially will you attain that which you desire in all these areas if Jupiter occupies the same, similar, or at least not very different signs or positions [as the Moon]. If you are going to stimulate the bowels with solid medicines, look to Pisces; with liquid medicines, Scorpio; and with something in between, Cancer. If you are going to purge through the lower part, look to Pisces and Scorpio; if through the upper part, Cancer. Avoid the malefic aspect of Saturn and Mars towards the Moon, for the former disturbs the stomach, the latter loosens the intestines. Avoid Capricorn and Taurus, for they bring nausea. You know not to irritate a part of the body when the Moon occupies the sign ruling it (for indeed she moves the fluids)[12] but rather to foster that part.

These recommendations are sufficient for the natural power and spirit dominating particularly in the liver, which are divided into the four functions which we have related. But what are we to advise concerning the vital power and spirit flourishing in the heart? Almost enough has been said of them. For these are aided especially through fiery and also somewhat through airy things, when the Moon aspects Jupiter in houses or seats similar to his, especially if she includes Jupiter and the Sun. You can also strengthen the animal spirit, which rules in the head because it rules sense and motion, through airy things in particular, with fiery ones subjoined, when the Moon aspects Jupiter in houses or seats similar to his, especially if she similarly includes not only Jupiter but Mercury.

Here, indeed, I warn you lest you think Mercury watery or earthy (which I also once suspected) for if he were, he would not be useful for motion or quickness of intelligence; on the contrary, you should know that he is somewhat airy. For this is the reason that he is so mobile, so easily changeable, and that he is so good for the intelligence, especially when situated in Aquarius which is quite airy. Moisture, indeed, is tempered in him; heat is slight. Positioned under the Sun's rays, he is said to dry. At his elongation from the Sun, however, he is thought to moisten. Under the Sun's rays, he is thought to heat a lot according to the nature of the Sun, but away from him, to heat very slightly and to moisten more in accordance with his own nature. In heat, perhaps, he does not yield place to Venus, he surpasses the Moon, but he yields to both

probat Mercurium qualitates coelestium commiscere, quoniam facillime permutetur tum in qualitatem termini quem subit, tum in naturam stellae quam aspicit. Ego igitur hunc tam facile permutari puto, quia nec excellentem potestatem quam Iuppiter habet, nec excedentem qualitatem quam pleraque coelestia, per quam alterationi resistat. Denique probabile est Mercurium, assiduum Solis Achatem, multas illius vires habere, ideoque sperari Solaria quaedam a Mercurio posse.

Aliquando vero et Martem tradunt Solem in quibusdam muneribus imitari, ac Venerem quae ad Lunam pertinent elargiri. Haec igitur in agendo memineris. Neque negligas unquam terminos. Aiunt enim planetas in diversis terminis ceu lucidis atque tenebrosis opposita facere. Denique ubi Martem times, oppone Venerem. Ubi Saturnum, adhibe Iovem. Ac da operam ut in perpetuo quodam pro viribus motu verseris, tantum defatigatione vitata, ut et proprium motum externis motibus clam nocituris opponas, et coelestem actum pro viribus imiteris. Quod si poteris spatia motibus ampliora peragere, sic et coelum potius imitaberis, et plures coelestium vires passim diffusas attinges.

Quomodo membra foveantur in nobis per comparationem Lunae ad signa et ad stellas fixas.

Cap. VII.

Totum, quemadmodum diximus, corpus fovere poteris, caput vero potissimum, si planetas observaveris in Ariete, vel in suo quemque domicilio primo. Praecordia, si in Leone; stomachum iecurque, si in Cancro atque Sagittario aut saltem in Virgine. Et acceperis ea quae proprie membrum petunt. Expedit quoque nosse quae quisque planeta membra in signo quolibet habeat. Potes etiam proprie pro aetatis discrimine consulere unicuique per quattuor aetates Lunae. Haec enim a novilunio usque ad quadraturam primam iuvenis est. Deinde ad plenilunium est iuvenis atque virilis. Hinc ad quadraturam alteram virilis simul atque senilis. Inde usque ad coniunctionem est senilis. Aetatem itaque Lunae feliciter aetati curandi corporis adhi-

---

162 tamen *x*   173 opponas *om. P;* opponis *z*   176 diffusus *z*
2 quemque] quisque in *P*

in moisture. Haly shows that Mercury mixes together the qualities of the celestials, since he is so easily changed both into the quality of the term which he enters and the nature of the star he aspects.[13] I think that this planet is so easily changed because he does not have the superior power which Jupiter has, nor a pre-eminent quality as most celestials have, through which he might resist change. Finally it is probable that Mercury, the constant Achates of the Sun, has many of the Sun's forces and hence that you can hope to get Solar things from Mercury.[14]

But sometimes they say that Mars too imitates the Sun in certain benefits and that Venus bestows those things which pertain to the Moon. Remember these counsels, then, in your operations. Nor should you ever neglect terms. For they say that the planets, when they are in terms as different from each other as light and dark, do opposite things. Finally, when you fear Mars, set Venus opposite. When you fear Saturn, use Jupiter. And see to it that you engage in some continual motion so far as possible, just so you avoid weariness; and make sure that your own motion is the opposite of the external motions which are secretly going to harm you, and that you imitate so far as possible the action of the heavens. But if you can pass through larger spaces in your motion, you will thereby imitate the heavens all the more and will get in contact with more of the strengths of the celestials which are diffused everywhere.[15]

How Parts of Our Body Are Fostered through Relating the Moon to Signs and to Fixed Stars.

Chap. VII

You will be able to foster the entire body, as we have said, and especially the head, if you will wait to act until the planets are in Aries or each one in his own first house. The same goes for the heart, if they are in Leo; the stomach and the liver, if in Cancer and Sagittarius, or at least in Virgo. You will act when those combinations occur which especially relate to the part in question. It is also useful to know which part of the body each planet rules in any sign whatever. You can also properly take care of each patient according to his particular age through the four ages of the Moon. For from the new moon to the first quarter she is youthful. Then to the full moon she is youthful and manly. From here to the other quarter she is both manly and old. Then to her conjunction she is old. And you will thus apply the age of the Moon profitably to the age of the body you are treating, if you also wait until she

bebis, si tunc aspectum eius ad aliquam trium Gratiarum acceperis. Qui sane aspectus Lunae semper et cito gratiosa largitur. Neque tamen facile admodum diuturna vel maxima, nisi praeter intuitum Lunae etiam ipsae Gratiae mutuo se conspiciant iam, vel propemodum conspecturae sint, aut tres ipsae aut duae. Imprimis vero diuturna praebent signa fixa: Leo scilicet, Aquarius, Taurus, Scorpius. Si forte non possis impraesentia Lunam ad planetas gratiosos opportune dirigere, stellas elige fixas Gratiarum naturam, id est Iovis aut Veneris aut Solis, habentes, et ad eas directam Lunam elige. Tutius tamen est Lunam interea Iovem propemodum adire vel Venerem. Stellae namque fixae si solae spectent, proportionem humanam, id est unius hominis, nimis exsuperant; proportionem vero cum civitatibus moderatiorem habent.

De virtutibus et usu stellarum fixarum.

Cap. VIII.

Tradunt astrologi maiores quasdam stellas a Mercurio compertas auctoritatem habere quam plurimam. Qualis est in Arietis gradu xxii. Umbilicus Andromedae Mercurialis atque Venereus. Item in Tauri xviii. Caput Algol naturam Saturni possidens atque Iovis, cui subesse volunt adamantem et artemisiam, et audaciam victoriamque praestare. In eiusdem gradu xxii. Pleiades, Lunare sidus et Martium, cui subiciunt crystallum, herbam diacedon, semen feniculi. Conferre putant ad acuendum visum. Quod autem nonnulli dicunt conducere ad daemonas convocandos, figmentum esse iudico. Aldeboran primo vel tertio Geminorum gradu Martium atque Venereum. Hircus gradu eorundem xiii. Iovius atque Saturnius. Huic subiciunt sapphyrum, prassium, mentam, artemisiam, mandragoram. Ad dignitatem et principum gratiam adiuvare confidunt, nisi forte eos opinio fallat. Illi subesse volunt rubinum, titimallum, matrisilvam; divitias et gloriam augere. In Cancri vi. vel vii. Canis Maior Venereus; praeest berillo, savinae, artemisiae, draconteae; praestat gratiam. Item in xvii. eiusdem Canis Minor Mercurialis et Martius, cui subesse volunt lapidem achatem, herbam solsequium et pule-

---

11 aspectu *z*   aliquantum *z*   14 sint *om. P*   21 moderationem *L*
  Cap.XIII *z*   12 principium *P*   16 solsequium *z*; solsequiam *Lwxy*; obsequiam *P*

is in an aspect with one of the three Graces. Such an aspect of the Moon always bestows agreeable things, and it does it quickly. Nevertheless, it will not very easily bestow lasting things, or the greatest things, unless, besides aspecting the Moon, the Graces themselves should also aspect one another already, or be about to do so, either all three or two of them. The fixed signs in particular—that is, Leo, Aquarius, Taurus, and Scorpio—furnish things that last. So if you should happen not to be able just then to wait until the Moon fittingly approaches[1] the "gracious" planets, choose fixed stars which share the nature of the Graces (that is, of Jupiter, Venus, or the Sun [for what these are, see 3.8]) and wait until the Moon is directed to these instead. Nevertheless, it is safer that the Moon at the same time should be on the verge of approaching Jupiter or Venus. For indeed if the fixed stars alone are in the aspect with her, they excessively overcome the human proportion, I mean, that of one individual; but fixed stars are more commensurate with cities.

Concerning the Powers and the Use of the Fixed Stars.

Chap. VIII

Astrologers say that certain major stars discovered by Mercurius[1] have the greatest power possible, such as: the Mercurial and Venereal Navel of Andromeda in the twenty-second degree of Aries. Likewise, in the eighteenth degree of Taurus the head called Algol, which possesses the nature of Saturn and of Jupiter. They would have it that diamond and mugwort are under this star and that it promotes boldness and victory.[2] In the twenty-second degree of Taurus, there are the Pleiades, a constellation that is Lunar and Martial, under which they place crystal, the herb diacedon, and fennel-seed.[3] They think it is useful for sharpening the sense of vision. The belief of some, however, that it is good for calling together daemons, I consider to be a fiction. Aldebaran in the first or third degree of Gemini is Martial and Venereal.[4] The Goat in the thirteenth degree of Gemini is Jovial and Saturnine.[5] Under the Goat they place sapphire, horehound, mint, mugwort, and mandrake. They believe it helps one towards honor and the favor of princes, unless perhaps their imagination deceives them [see Ficino's own less transitive version of this magic, below, and "Magic"]. They would have it that ruby, spurge, and woodruff are under Aldebaran and that it increases riches and glory. In the sixth or seventh degree of Cancer, the Venereal Canis Major; it rules beryl, savine, mugwort, and dracontea; it proffers favor.[6] Likewise in the seventeenth of the same, the Mercurial and Martial Canis Minor; they think that under it the agate, helio-

gium; atque gratiam elargiri. In Leonis xxi. Cor Leonis, stella regia, Iovialis et Martia. Huic subici putant lapidem granatum, chelidoniam, masticem; melancholiam reprimere, temperatum gratiosumque efficere.

In Virginis xviiii. Cauda Ursae Maioris Venerea et Lunaris. Lapidem eius magnetem putant, herbam cichoream et artemisiam, a raptoribus veneficiisque tueri. In Librae vii. Ala Corvi dextra, item in eiusdem xii. et forte xiii. Ala sinistra Saturnia simul et Martia. Eius herbam lapathium et iusquiamum esse aiunt cum lingua ranae, audaciam augere, fore noxiam. In eiusdem xv. vel xvi. Spica Venerea Mercurialisque, quam sequatur smaragdus, salvia, trifolium, promarulla, artemisia, mandragora; divitias augeat et victoriam, et ab angustia vindicet. Denique in eiusdem xvii. vel xviii. Alchameth. Huic subdunt iaspidem et plantaginem. Firmare sanguinem sperant, febres omnes expellere. In Scorpionis quarto Elpheia Venerea Martiaque. Secundum vero computationem aliam in gradu eiusdem quinto est Cornea, forsan eadem, praesidens topazio, rorimarino, trifolio, hederae. Augere gratiam, castitatem, gloriam putant. In Sagittarii tertio Cor Scorpionis Martium atque Iovium, praesidens sardonio, amethisto, aristolochiae longae, croco. Opinantur colorem bonum efficere, animum laetum sapientemque reddere, daemonia propulsare. In Capricorni gradu septimo Vultur Cadens. Hanc sequitur chrysolitus, satureia, fumus terrae. Stella est Mercurialis atque Venerea, temperata. In ascendente medioque coelo prodest. Quod autem excantandi auctoritatem afferre dicant, nihilipendo. In Aquarii xvi. Cauda Capricorni Saturnia Mercurialisque, quam sequitur chalcidonius, maiorana, nepita, artemisia, mandragora. Praestare in causis gratiam opinantur, divitias augere, hominem ac domum incolumem reddere. In Piscium tertio Humerus Equi Iovialis et Martius.

Thebit philosophus docet ad captandam alicuius stellae modo dictae virtutem lapidem eius accipere herbamque eiusdem, anulumque aureum facere vel argenteum, in quo lapillum inseras herba subiecta gerasque tangentem. Id autem efficias, quando Luna subit stellam aut aspicit aspectu trino vel sextili, et stella in medio percurrit coelo vel ascendente. Ego vero quae ad eiusmodi stellas attinent in formam potius medicinae quam anuli componerem, intrinsecus vel extrinsecus adhibendae, opportunitate videlicet praedicti temporis observata. Tametsi prisci anulos magnifecerint. Nam Damis et Philostratus

---

21 et artemisiam *om. z*   23 iusquiamum] hyoscyamum *z*   26 prorulla *z*   29 Elpheia *om. z*   34 sapientumque *L*^ac; sapientem *P*   35 satureia *z*; sauregia *LPwxy*   40 opinatur *L*   42 capiendam *P*

trope (the herb), and pennyroyal are placed and that it bestows favor.[7] In the twenty-first degree of Leo, the Heart of the Lion, a royal Jovial and Martial star, under which they think are placed the garnet, swallowwort, and mastic. They think that it represses melancholy and makes a man temperate and agreeable.[8]

In the nineteenth degree of Virgo is the Venereal and Lunar Tail of Ursa Major.[9] They think that its stone is the magnet, its herbs, chicory and mugwort, and that it provides protection from robbers and poisonings.[10] In the seventh degree of Libra, the Right Wing of the Raven, likewise in the twelfth or perhaps the thirteenth degree of Libra, the Saturnine and Martial Left Wing of the Raven. They say [or rather, Ficino alone says] that its herbs are sorrel and henbane along with frog's tongue; that it increases boldness, and that it will be noxious. In the fifteenth or sixteenth degree of Libra, the Venereal and Mercurial Spica, which emerald, sage, trefoil, *promarulla*, mugwort, and mandrake follow; that it increases riches and victory and releases from poverty.[11] Then, in the seventeenth or eighteenth degree of Libra, Alchameth. To this they subject jasper and plantain. They hope that it strengthens the blood and expels all fevers.[12] In the fourth degree of Scorpio, the Venereal and Martial Elpheia. But according to another computation in the fifth degree of Scorpio is Cornea, perhaps it is the same star, presiding over topaz, rosemary, trefoil, and ivy. They think it increases grace, chastity, and glory.[13] In the third degree of Sagittarius the Martial and Jovial Heart of the Scorpion presiding over sardonyx, amethyst, long birthwort, and saffron. They think that it makes the color good, the mind happy and wise, and that it drives out daemons.[14] In the seventh degree of Capricorn, the Falling Vulture, which chrysolite, savory, and fumitory follow. This star is Mercurial, Venereal, and temperate. It is beneficial when in the Ascendant and mid-heaven. But as for their belief that it confers the authority to exorcize, I discount it.[15] In the sixteenth degree of Aquarius, the Saturnine and Mercurial Tail of Capricorn, which chalcedony follows, and marjoram, catnip, mugwort, and mandrake. They think it furnishes favor in lawsuits, increases wealth, and makes men and their homes safe. In the third degree of Pisces, the Jovial and Martial Shoulder of the Horse.[16]

Thebit the philosopher teaches that, in order to capture the power of any of the stars just mentioned, one should take its stone and herb and make a gold or silver ring and should insert the stone with the herb underneath it and wear it touching [your flesh].[17] Do this when the Moon passes the star or looks at it with a trine or sextile aspect, and when the star itself is passing the midheaven or the Ascendant. But I, indeed, would compound the things which pertain to stars of this sort in the form of a medicine rather than of a ring, applied internally or externally, waiting, of course, for the aforesaid proper time. And yet the ancients thought highly of rings. For Damis and Philostra-

narrant Hiarcham, sapientum Indorum principem, simili quadam ratione
septem anulos confecisse, stellarum septem nominibus appellatos, eosque
Apollonio Theano dedisse, qui deinde singulos diebus singulis gestaverit, iuxta dierum nomina hos distinguens. Dixisse vero Hiarcham Apollonio avum
suum philosophum annos centum atque triginta vixisse, eiusmodi forsan coelesti munere fretum. Quo et Apollonius deinde usus centesimo etiam anno,
ut aiunt, iuvenem praeferebat. Denique si quid eiusmodi anuli virtutis habent ex alto, id quidem non tam ad animam vel ad crassum corpus pertinere
arbitror quam ad spiritum, calefacto paulatim anulo, sic inde vel sic affectum, ut firmior efficiatur aut clarior, vehementior aut mitior, severior aut
laetior. Quae quidem affectiones in corpus quidem omnino et in animam sensualem quodammodo, plerunque indulgentem corpori, transeunt. Quod autem adversum daemonas aut hostes aut ad principum gratiam profuturos
anulos pollicentur, vel fictum est, vel inde deductum quod spiritum interritum firmumque efficiant, vel etiam mansuetum obsequioque amabilem atque
gratiosum.

Iam vero si quid coelestia praeter corpoream valetudinem conferre ad ingenium, artem, fortunam dicerem, ab Aquinate Thomma nostro non dissiderem, qui in libro *Contra gentiles* tertio probat a corporibus coelestibus imprimi nonnihil in corpore nostro, cuius munere disponamur ad eligendum
saepe quod melius est, etiam si rationem finemque nesciamus. Qua quidem
in re bene fortunatos appellat atque consentiente Aristotele bene natos. Addit
etiam virtute coelesti fieri nonnullos in quibusdam artium effectibus efficaces
(ut eius verbis utar), sicut miles in vincendo, agricola in plantando, medicus
in sanando felices. Ait enim sicut herbae lapidesque mirabiles quasdam ultra
naturam elementalem vires coelitus habent, sic homines quoque in artibus
nonnullos habere. Mihi vero satis fuerit factum, si coelestia quomodocunque,
quasi per medicinas sive interiores sive exteriores, ad prosperam conferant
valetudinem, dummodo interea salutem corporis perquirentes iacturam nullam salutis animae faciamus. Nihil omnino tentemus a sancta religione prohibitum. Praeterea in opere quovis conficiendo fructum operis ab eo speremus
atque petamus imprimis, qui et coelestia et quae continentur coelo fecit et
virtute donavit movetque semper atque conservat.

---

57 crassam *z*   62 principium *z*   63 interritum] intentum *z*   64 efficiat *P*   74 Ait] At *z*   75 elementarem *P*; elementa rem *z*   76 *post* quomodocunque *add.* vel *Lw*^{ac}

tus relate that Hiarchas, the chief of the Indian wise men, made seven rings in a similar way, named after the seven stars, and gave them to Apollonius of Tyana, who afterwards wore one of them each day, distributing them according to the names of the days [of the week].[18] Hiarchas told Apollonius that his grandfather, a philosopher, had lived for one hundred thirty years, perhaps because of his reliance upon a celestial gift of this sort. Apollonius, then, used this and looked young, so they say, until he was a hundred.[19] But in brief, if rings of this sort have any power from on high, I do not think that it pertains so much to the soul or to our gross body as to the spirit, which is affected in this way or that as the ring is heated little by little, so that it is made firmer or clearer, stronger or milder, more austere or more joyful. These influences pass over completely into the body and somewhat into the sensual part of the soul which quite often gives in to the body. But insofar as they promise that the rings are useful against daemons or to acquire the favor of rulers, this is either a fiction or deduced from the fact that they make the spirit fearless and firm, or in the other case gentle, amiable in serving, and complaisant.

But now if I were to say that celestial things confer something beyond physical health to one's intelligence, skill, and fortune, I would not be at variance with our Thomas Aquinas, who in his third book *Against the Gentiles* proves that something is impressed on our body by celestial bodies, by whose gift we are disposed often to choose what is better, even if we do not know the reason or the outcome. He indeed calls such men "favored by fortune" in this regard, and, with Aristotle's support, "favored by birth." He also adds that by celestial power some men are made successful in the execution of certain arts, to use his words, as, a soldier lucky in conquering, a farmer in planting, a physician in healing. For he says that just as herbs and stones have certain wondrous powers from the heavens beyond their elemental nature, so also do some men in the arts.[20] It would satisfy me, if the celestials were able somehow or other, as if through medicines internal or external, to contribute to good health — provided that while seeking the health of our bodies, we do not throw overboard the salvation [pun on "salus" as both "health" and "salvation"] of our souls. Let us by no means ever attempt anything forbidden by holy religion. Moreover, in performing any work let us hope for and seek the fruit of the work principally from Him who made both the celestials and those things which are contained in the heavens, who gave them their power, and who always moves and preserves them.

Dignitates planetarum in signis
ad usum medicinarum observandae.

Cap. IX.

Saturni domus Aquarius et Capricornus; exaltatio Libra. Iovis domus Sagittarius atque Pisces; exaltatio sive regnum Cancer. Martis domicilium Scorpius et Aries; exaltatio Capricornus. Solis sedes quidem est Leo; regnum Aries. Veneris habitaculum Taurus atque Libra; exaltatio Pisces. Mercurii aedes Virgo atque Gemini; regnum Virgo. Lunae domus Cancer; exaltatio Taurus. Saturnus et Iuppiter triplicitatem habent in igneis aeriisque signis; Sol in igneis tantum; Mercurius in aeriis solum; Mars, Venus, Luna in aqueis atque terreis.

Planetae quilibet praeter Solem ac Lunam in quolibet signo fines quosdam suos possident, quos et terminos appellamus. Igitur in Ariete Iuppiter sex ibi primos terminos obtinent, Venus sex inde sequentes, Mercurius posteriores octo, Mars quinque deinceps, postremos quinque Saturnus. In Tauro ordine deinceps simili Venus fines habet octo, Mercurius sex, Iuppiter octo, Saturnus quinque, Mars denique tres. In Geminis Mercurius sex, Iuppiter sex, Venus quinque, Mars septem, Saturnus sex. In Cancro Mars septem, Venus sex, Mercurius totidem, Iuppiter septem, Saturnus quattuor. In Leone Iuppiter sex, Venus quinque, Saturnus septem, Mercurius sex, Mars totidem. In Virgine Mercurius septem, Venus decem, Iuppiter quattuor, Mars septem, Saturnus duos. In Libra Saturnus sex, Mercurius octo, Iuppiter septem, Venus totidem, Mars duos. In Scorpione Mars septem, Venus quattuor, Mercurius octo, Iuppiter quinque, Saturnus sex. In Sagittario Iuppiter duodecim, Venus quinque, Mercurius quattuor, Saturnus quinque, Mars quattuor. In Capricorno Mercurius septem, Iuppiter septem, Venus octo, Saturnus quattuor, Mars totidem. In Aquario Mercurius septem, Venus sex, Iuppiter septem, Mars quinque, Saturnus totidem. In Piscibus Venus duodecim, Iuppiter quattuor, Mercurius tres, Mars novem, Saturnus denique duos. Sol autem et Luna alia ratione fines suos habent. Nam Sol quidem signa sex pro finibus habet: Leonem, Virginem, Libram, Scorpium, Sagittarium, Capricornum. Luna vero reliquos: Aquarium, Pisces, Arietem, Taurum, Geminos, Cancrum. Solem igitur atque Lunam in his signis eum principatum effectumque quem reliqui planetae in suis finibus habere putant.

Praeter fines habent in signis suas planetae facies, quas Graeci decanos nominant, decem occupantes signi gradus. In Ariete facies prima Martis, secunda Solis, qui Martem in coelo sequitur. Ordine Chaldaeorum tertia Veneris, quae Soli succedit in coelo. In Tauro prima facies Mercurii, sequen-

---

Dignitates ... observandae] De dignitatibus ... observandis *yz* 7 in[1] *om. z* 15 Saturnus—septem[1] *om. P* 23-24 Iuppiter—Mercurius septem *om. P*

The Dignities of Planets in the Signs Which Must Be Observed for the Use of Medicines.

Chap. IX

The house of Saturn is Aquarius and Capricorn; his exaltation, Libra. The house of Jupiter is Sagittarius and Pisces; his exaltation or kingdom, Cancer. The house of Mars is Scorpio and Aries; his exaltation, Capricorn. The house of the Sun is Leo; his exaltation, Aries. The house of Venus is Taurus and Libra; her exaltation, Pisces. The house of Mercury is Virgo and Gemini; his exaltation, Virgo. The house of the Moon is Cancer; her exaltation, Taurus. Saturn and Jupiter have their triplicity in fiery and watery signs; the Sun only in fiery signs; Mercury only in airy signs; Mars, Venus, and the Moon in watery and earthy signs.

Each of the planets, except for the Sun and Moon, possess in each sign certain borders of their own, which we call "terms." Accordingly, in Aries, Jupiter there has the first six [degrees as its] terms, Venus the next six, Mercury the next eight, Mars the next five, and Saturn the last five. In Taurus, then, in a similar order, Venus has eight terms, Mercury six, Jupiter eight, Saturn five, and finally Mars three. In Gemini, Mercury has six, Jupiter six, Venus five, Mars seven, and Saturn six. In Cancer, Mars has seven, Venus six, Mercury six, Jupiter seven, and Saturn four. In Leo, Jupiter has six, Venus five, Saturn seven, Mercury six, and Mars six. In Virgo, Mercury has seven, Venus ten, Jupiter four, Mars seven, and Saturn two. In Libra, Saturn has six, Mercury eight, Jupiter seven, Venus seven, and Mars two. In Scorpio, Mars has seven, Venus four, Mercury eight, Jupiter five, and Saturn six. In Sagittarius, Jupiter has twelve, Venus five, Mercury four, Saturn five, and Mars four. In Capricorn, Mercury has seven, Jupiter seven, Venus eight, Saturn four, and Mars four. In Aquarius, Mercury has seven, Venus six, Jupiter seven, Mars five, and Saturn five. In Pisces, Venus has twelve, Jupiter four, Mercury three, Mars nine, and Saturn two. The Sun and the Moon, however, have their own terms by another rule. For the Sun has six signs for its terms: Leo, Virgo, Libra, Scorpio, Sagittarius, and Capricorn. The Moon has the rest: Aquarius, Pisces, Aries, Taurus, Gemini, and Cancer. They therefore think that the Sun and the Moon in these signs have that dominion and effect which the rest of the planets have in their terms.

In the signs, besides their terms, the planets have faces, which the Greeks call decans, each occupying ten degrees of the sign. In Aries, the first face is that of Mars, the second is that of the Sun, who follows Mars in the sky. In the order of the Chaldeans,[1] the third face would be that of Venus, because she follows the Sun in the sky. In Taurus, the first face is that of Mercury,

tis Venerem; secunda Lunae, quae Mercurio succedit; tertia Saturni. Ad hunc enim redeundum est, impleto iam numero planetarum. In Geminis prima Iovis, sequentis videlicet Saturnum; secunda Martis, tertia Solis eodem ordine similiterque deinceps.

Quomodo planetis uti debeamus in medicinis.
Cap. X.

Commemoravimus autem quas in signis planetae dignitates habent ut quotiens facturi compositurique sumus quae ad planetam aliquem attinent, sciamus eum in suis dignitatibus collocare; praesertim quando habuerit in nostra revolutione in genesi principatum, ut etiam Saturnus atque Mars, alioquin deprimendi nobis, tamen sint erigendi si geniturae nostrae significatores extiterint. Maxime vero operae pretium ex hac commemoratione fecerimus, si quando usuri in medicinis conficiendis beneficio Lunae et Veneris atque Iovis, cavebimus ne in finibus Saturni vel Martis existant; nisi forte ubi cogimur vel per Saturnum cohibere dissolutionem aestumque reprimere, vel per Martem frigidissima calefacere, torpentia suscitare — alioquin fines Iovis et Veneris eligemus. Accipiemus quoque Mercurii fines, Mercurialibus imprimis hominibus profuturi. Neque latere nos debet homines valde Mercuriales, quales sunt qui ingenio, artificio, eloquio pollent, non mediocriter esse Solares. Mercurius enim semper est Apolline plenus.

Ut autem quivis intelligat quomodo figuras in coelo describamus in oras, signum quod ab oriente surgit primam appellamus vitaeque domum. Quod succedit in ortum secundam tertiamque deinceps aliasque similiter, ita ut septima domus sit signum quod in occidente iam descendens opponitur ascendenti. Huic octava succedit. Nona vero e medio cadit coelo, quod decimam domum efficit. Huic succedit undecima, sed duodecima cadit ab ascendente.

Ut igitur planetae sint potentes, habendi sunt in angulis vel orientis vel occidentis vel medii utrinque coeli, maxime vero in angulo ascendentis aut decimae medium supra caput obtinentis coelum, aut saltem in plagis quae an-

---

39 similiter *z*
    4 revolutione] redutione *Lw*^{ac} 17 ut] in *z*   18 quo *z*   19 Hic *z*   succepit *z*   vero *om.* P

who follows Venus; the second face is that of the Moon who follows Mercury, the third is that of Saturn. For we must return to him, now that we have enumerated all the planets. In Gemini, the first face is that of Jupiter who follows Saturn; the second is that of Mars; the third is that of the Sun in the same order and similarly thereafter.

How We Should Use the Planets in Medicines.

Chap. X

We have recounted the dignities which the planets have in the signs so that, whenever we are about to make or compound those things which pertain to any planet, we may know how to place the planet in its dignities, especially when the planet held the first place in our anniversary and nativity. Accordingly, even Saturn and Mars, although otherwise we ought to place them in their debilities, must be placed in their dignities if they have been signifiers in our natal horoscope. But we will really have accomplished something worthwhile with this treatise if we become careful, when we are going to use the favor of the Moon, Venus, and Jupiter in making medicines, that they are not in the terms of Saturn or Mars; unless we happen to need either to check looseness and repress the heat of infection by means of Saturn, or to warm the very cold parts and arouse the torpid ones by means of Mars. In all other cases, we will choose the terms of Jupiter and Venus. We will also choose the terms of Mercury, when we mean to help people who are especially Mercurial. It ought not to escape our notice that people who are very Mercurial, such as those who are strong in intelligence, in professional skill, and in eloquence, are quite Solar. For Mercury is always full of Apollo.

But in order that anyone may understand how we distribute the figures in the sky into zones,[1] we call the sign which is rising from the eastern horizon [at a given time] the first place and the place of life. The sign which rises next we call the second place, then the third, and so on for the rest, so that the seventh place is the sign which is now descending in the West and is opposite to the ascending sign. The eighth place is succeedent to this one; the ninth, indeed, is cadent from mid-heaven, which forms the tenth place. The eleventh is succeedent to this one, but the twelfth is cadent from the Ascendant. In order, therefore, for the planets to be powerful, one must have them in the cardines either of the East or the West or of the mid-heaven on both sides [of the earth], but especially in the cardine of the Ascendant or of the tenth place which occupies the mid-heaven above our head, or at least in the places which are direct-

gulis mox succedunt. Tametsi Solem quidem in nona quae a medio cadit coelo, Lunam vero in tertia etiam cadente gaudere putant. Duas inter haec regulas mente teneri astrologi volunt: unam quidem aegrotantis ratione, alteram vero medici. Nempe ubi aegrotantis septima domus per Saturnum vel Martem infortunata est, vel dominus eius infelix, separa medicum ab aegroto, si Ptolemaeo credis. Praeterea medicum electurus Saturnium Martialemque declinare iubent, eumque perquirere in cuius genitura domus sexta per aspectum Solis vel per Venerem aut Iovem quomodocunque fuerit fortunata. Infortunatum vero dicimus signum vel planetam per Saturnum aut Martem, nisi propria domicilia sint vel regna, quando videlicet vel ibi sunt vel illuc aspiciunt opposito vel quadrato. Oppositum vero aspectum dicimus inter illa quae intervallo discrepant quam longissimo; quadratum vero ubi hoc ab illo quarta parte coeli, id est signorum trium spatio, distant. Minus tamen per coniunctionem, oppositum, quadratum Saturnus et Mars planetis aliis nocent, quando tanquam hospites eos domicilio vel regno suo terminove suscipiunt. Quemadmodum planetae felices magis prosunt, quando praeter sextilem trinumve aspectum atque coniunctionem etiam, ut diximus, sic excipiunt, Solis tamen coniunctionem planetae verentur, aspectu gaudent trino videlicet vel sextili.

Proinde necessarium est meminisse Arietem praeesse capiti atque faciei, Taurum collo, Geminos bracchiis atque humeris, Cancrum pectori, pulmonibus, stomacho, lacertis, Leonem cordi et stomacho atque iecori et dorso et costis posterioribus, Virginem intestinis et fundo stomachi, Libram renibus et femori atque natibus, Scorpionem genitalibus, vulvae, matrici, Sagittarium femori atque subinguinibus, Capricornum genibus, Aquarium cruribus tibiisque, Pisces pedibus. Huius enim ordinis memor cavebis membrum tangere ferro vel igne vel cucurbitulis, quando Luna sub eius signo discurrit. Tunc enim auget Luna humores in membro, quorum affluentia et consolidationem prohibet et gravat membri virtutem. Observabis autem tunc membrum remediis quibusdam amicis vel extra vel intus adhibitis opportune feliciterque fovere. Expedit vero nosse quod signum ascenderit tibi nascenti. Nam praeter Arietem hoc etiam tibi caput significat, atque in hoc Luna tibi caput aspicit. Praeterea quando Luna Arietem subit, opportune balnea tentas et lavacra. Quando Cancrum, feliciter minue sanguinem, medicinam accipe praesertim electuarii formam. Quando est in Leone, ne provoca vomitum. Cum in Libra, clysteribus apta est. In Scorpione balnea nec tentes. Sunt

24 in *om.* z   27 vel] et z   31 fortunatam z   37 Saturnum z   39 praeter] per z   48 super inquinibus P   59 acta L

ly succeedent to the cardines — although they think that the Sun even rejoices in the ninth place which is cadent from mid-heaven, the Moon in the third which also is cadent. Among these rules, astrologers want two to be kept in mind: one, with reference to the sick man; the other, to the doctor. When the seventh place of a sick person is unfortunate because of Saturn or Mars, or when the Lord of that place is unfortunate, separate the doctor from the sick person, if you believe Ptolemy.[2] In addition, if you are going to choose a doctor, they bid you to avoid a Saturnine or a Martial one [this caveat would put Ficino himself out of business!], and to seek out him in whose geniture the sixth place was fortunate in some way through an aspect of the Sun or because of Venus or Jupiter. Now we call a sign or planet unfortunate through Saturn or Mars (unfortunate, that is, unless the signs happen to be the houses or exaltations of Saturn or Mars) either when Saturn and Mars are there or when they look thither from opposition or a quartile aspect. We call the aspect "opposition" between those stars which are separated by the furthest distance possible; and quartile when this star is distant from that by a quarter of the sky, that is, by the space of three signs. Saturn and Mars, however, are less harmful to the other planets through conjunction, opposition, and the quartile aspect, when they [Saturn and Mars] also receive them as guests in their respective houses, exaltations, or terms. In the same way the fortunate planets are of greater usefulness, when, besides their sextile or trine aspect and their conjunction, they also thus receive the other planets into their houses. Nevertheless, planets fear conjunction with the Sun; they rejoice in his trine or sextile aspect.

Accordingly you must remember that Aries has power over the head and face; Taurus over the neck; Gemini, the forearms and shoulders; Cancer, the breast, lungs, stomach, and upper arms; Leo, the heart, stomach, liver, back, and back parts of the ribs; Virgo, the intestines and lower stomach; Libra, the kidneys, thighs,[3] and buttocks; Scorpio, the genitals, the vulva, and the womb; Sagittarius, the thighs and parts below the groin; Capricorn, the knees; Aquarius, the legs and shins; Pisces, the feet. Mindful of this order, you will take care not to touch a part of the body with iron or fire or cupping-glass when the Moon enters the part's sign. For then the Moon increases the fluids in the part, the flow of which both keeps it from knitting together and weighs down its power. But then you will take care to foster the part opportunely and fortunately with certain pleasing remedies applied either externally or internally. But it is useful to know what sign was in the ascendant when you were born. For besides Aries this sign also signifies your head; and the Moon, when in this sign, looks after your head. Moreover, when the Moon enters Aries, you may opportunely try baths and washings. When she enters Cancer, diminish the blood; it is the fortunate time for it; and take medicine specifically in the form of an electuary.[4] When the Moon is in Leo, do not induce vomiting. When she is in Libra, she is suitable for clysters. When she is in Scorpio,

qui medicinam soluturam dare nec prohibent neque iubent. In Capricorno 60
medicinam sumere nocet, similiter in Aquario; in Piscibus vero prodest.
Quae vero membra in quovis signo unusquisque habeat planetarum, etsi
scitu necessum est, tamen narratu prolixum.

Neque vero in purgatione alvi latere nos debet Ptolemaei praeceptum. Medicinam accipere purgatoriam, quando Luna est in Cancro, Piscibus, Scorpione, probamus, praesertim si dominus signi tunc ascendentis applicet se 65
planetae sub terra currenti. Sin autem ascendentis dominus coniungatur interea supra caput cum planeta medium tenente coelum, nausea statim et vomitus incitabitur. Denique concludamus cum Galieno astrologiam esse medico
necessariam, qui de criticis diebus disputans ait certam esse Aegyptiorum 70
sententiam, id est, Lunam significare affectionem indies aegrotantis atque
sani adeo ut si misceantur cum Luna radii Iovis et Veneris, bene afficiatur
uterque; sin autem Saturni vel Martis, contraria ratione se habeat. Sed latius
iam pervagati ad spiritum tandem et vitam atque Gratias revertamur.

*Quibus modis spiritus noster haurire plurimum potest de spiritu
vitaque mundi; et qui planetae spiritum procreant atque recreant;
et qualia ad unumquemque planetam pertinent.*

Cap. XI.

Huc vero tendunt haec omnia ut spiritus noster rite per naturalia praeparatus atque purgatus accipiat ab ipso vitae mundanae spiritu plurimum per radios stellarum opportune susceptos. Vita quidem mundi omnibus
insita propagatur evidenter in herbas et arbores, quasi pilos sui corporis
atque capillos. Tumet insuper in lapides et metalla, velut dentes et ossa. Pul- 5
lulat quoque in viventes conchas terrae et lapidibus adhaerentes. Haec enim
non tam propria quam ipsa communi totius vita vivunt. Quae sane communis vita multo etiam magis super terram in corporibus viget subtilioribus tanquam propinquioribus animae. Per cuius vigorem intimum aqua, aer, ignis
viventia sua possident atque moventur. Vita haec aerem ignemque etiam 10

---

63 necessarium *yz*   64 purificatione *z*   66 applicat *z*   71 id est] scilicet *P*
     possit *yz*   procreent *yz*   recreent *yz*   pertineant *yz*   Cap.IX *z*   7 ipsi *z*

do not try baths; there are those who neither prohibit nor prescribe giving a loosening medicine. When she is in Capricorn, it is harmful to take medicine, and likewise in Aquarius; but when in Pisces, it is good. Now as to which parts each one of the planets rules in any sign, even if it is necessary to know, nevertheless it is too lengthy to recount.

But we should notice Ptolemy's precept in purging the bowels: we approve of taking a purgative medicine when the Moon is in Cancer, Pisces, or Scorpio, especially if the Lord of the sign then ascending is approaching a planet which is passing under the earth. If, on the contrary, the Lord of the Ascendant is at the time in conjunction overhead with a planet which occupies the mid-heaven, you should immediately induce nausea and vomiting.[5] Finally, let us conclude with Galen that astrology is necessary for the physician. Discussing critical days, he says that what the Egyptians say is true: namely, that the Moon signifies the condition of both the sick and the healthy person day by day, so that if the rays of Jupiter and Venus are mixed with the Moon, each of them [the sick and the well] is influenced for the better. If, on the contrary, it is the rays of Saturn and Mars, each would find himself to be affected adversely.[6] But now, having digressed rather widely, let us return at last to the spirit, to life, and to the Graces.

The Ways in Which Our Spirit Can Draw the Most from the Spirit and Life of the World; Which Planets Generate and Restore Spirit; and What Things Pertain to Each Planet.

Chap. XI

All these discussions are for this purpose, that through the rays of the stars opportunely received, our spirit properly prepared and purged through natural things may receive the most from the very spirit of the life of the world. The life of the world, innate in everything, is clearly propagated into plants and trees, like the body-hair and tresses of its body. Moreover, the world is pregnant with stones and metals, like its bones and teeth. It sprouts also in shells which live clinging to the earth and to stones. For these things live not so much by their own life as by the common life of the universal whole itself. This universal life indeed flourishes much more above the earth in the subtler bodies, which are nearer to Soul. Through its inward power, water, air, and fire possess living things proper to them and partake of motion.[1] More than

magis quam terram et aquam fovet agitatque perpetuo motu. Et denique coelestia corpora quasi mundi caput vel cor vel oculos quam maxime vegetat. Unde per stellas velut oculos radios non visibiles solum, sed etiam visuales usquequaque diffundit. Quibus more struthi, ut diximus alibi, inferiora conspicit fovetque vivendo, immo etiam ita tangendo generat et format omnifariam atque movet. Igitur ad motum nitentis aquae, sereni quoque aeris ignisque moderate distantis atque coeli motum mundanae vitae suscipies, si ipse quoque leniter et ferme similiter movearis, quosdam pro viribus gyros agens, vertigine devitata, coelestia lustrans oculis, mente versans.

 Item frequenti quodam usu plantarum similiterque viventium potes e mundi spiritu plurimum haurire, praesertim si adhuc viventibus recentibusque et matri terrae quasi adhuc haerentibus nutriaris atque fovearis. Inter plantas suaviter redolentes vel saltem non male olentes verseris quam frequentissime. Omnes enim herbae, flores, arbores, poma redolent, quamvis saepe minus animadvertas. Quo quidem odore quasi flatu spirituque vitae mundanae te undique recreant atque vegetant. Spiritum inquam tuum odoribus eiusmodi natura simillimum, perque spiritum medium inter corpus et animam facile corpus quoque reficiunt et animae mirifice prosunt. Inter haec diutissime diurno tempore sub divo versaberis, quatenus tuto vel commode fieri potest, in regionibus altis et serenis atque temperatis. Sic enim Solis stellarumque radii expeditius puriusque undique te contingunt, spiritumque tuum complent mundi spiritu per radios uberius emicante. Praeterea naturalis ipse motus aeris qui perpetuus est in orbem, quamvis ob lenitatem suam consuetudinemque diuturnam vix percipiatur ab ullo, te die sub divo deambulantem habitantemque in patentibus editisque locis libere lambit penetratque pure; ac motum vigoremque spiritui tuo mundanum mirifice praestat. Dixi equidem die, compertum enim habemus nocturnum aerem esse spiritibus inimicum. Conferet autem diurni usus, praesertim si plurimum in aperto deambulans devites primo quidem nimiam aeris intemperiem. Deinde frequentius movearis in eo, quando praeter temperiem et serenitatem eius stellarum positio magis est hominibus salutaris. Item si loca eligas prae ceteris odorifera, per quae situm quotidie mutes et ipse quasi continue et leniter movearis. Mutare locum quamvis semper cum delectu praecepi, quoniam bona coelestium et universae naturae apud nos sunt rebus locisque aliis passim atque aliis distributa, quibus denique omnibus est fruendum. Mitto quod

---

13 visuales] visibiles *P*   15 videndo *P*   16 serenique *P*   18 ipsae *x*   20 planetarum *z*
22 planetas *Pz*   24 arbor *z*   redolet *z*   35 parentibus *z*   37 Dixit *z*   38 Confert *z*   43 quam *P*

it does earth and water, this life warms air and fire and drives them in perpetual motion. And finally it animates in the highest degree possible the celestial bodies which are like the head, heart, or eyes of the world. From there, through the stars as through eyes, it spreads everywhere not only its visible but also its visual rays. By these, like a sparrow, as we have said elsewhere,[2] it looks upon things below and fosters them by its look, and even thus generates them by its touch, shapes them variously, and moves them. While experiencing, therefore, the motion of shining water, of clear air, of a fire that is not too close, and of the sky, you will receive the motion of the life of the world, if you yourself also move lightly, and in almost the same way — executing as many gyrations as you can without dizziness, traversing the celestial bodies with your eyes, and revolving them in your mind.[3]

Likewise by a frequent use of plants and a similar use of living things, you can draw the most from the spirit of the world, especially if you nourish and foster yourself by things which are still living, fresh, and all but still clinging, as it were, to mother earth; and if you dwell as frequently as possible among plants which have a pleasant smell, or at least not a bad one. For all herbs, flowers, trees, and fruits have an odor, even though you often do not notice it. By this odor, they restore and invigorate you on all sides, as if by the breath and spirit of the life of the world. Your spirit, I say, is very similar by nature to odors of this sort; and through the spirit, a mediator between the body and the soul, the odors also easily refresh the body and are of wondrous advantage to the soul. Among these things you will dwell by day in the open air for the longest time that it can safely or conveniently be done, in lofty, clear, and temperate regions. For thus the rays of the Sun and the stars touch you more readily and purely on all sides; and they fill your spirit with the spirit of the world shining forth more richly through their rays. Moreover, even the natural motion of the air, which goes perpetually round and round, although it is scarcely perceived by anyone on account of its gentleness and its constant daily presence, laps you freely and penetrates you purely when you are walking about by day in the open air and dwelling in open and lofty places; and it wondrously furnishes your spirit with the motion and power of the world. Note I said "by day," for we have found by experience that night air is bad for the spirits. But the use of daytime air helps them, especially if in your frequent strolls in the open you first of all avoid excessively inclement air. Next you should move about in it more when, besides its temperateness and clearness, the position of the stars is more salutary to human beings. Likewise it is good if you select the most odoriferous places, through which you should change your dwelling daily and yourself move almost constantly and gently. I have advised changing your place — though always by your own choice — because the good things of the heavens and of all nature are distributed among us widely in this or that thing or place; and all of them indeed should be enjoyed. Not to mention

varietas taedium prohibet spiritibus inimicum propriumque Saturno. Voluptatem vero affert, per quam (ut ita dixerim) Venus ipsa voluptatis amica venit in spiritum atque, quod eius officium est, hunc statim ingressa propagat. Summatim vero si quis consideret paradisum et pomi vitae usum apud Mosem, item similem victum a Platone positum in *Phaedone* et quae Plinius de populis ait odore viventibus, intelliget esse vera quae dicimus.

    Sed ad naturam spiritus descendamus. Spiritus quidem qualitas est proculdubio Iovia, cuius tempore nobis infunditur. Est et Solaris, Iuppiter enim hunc infundit, quatenus ingentem Solis in se temperat potestatem. Item alia quoque ratione Iovia est, quoniam calida est et humida, et calore abundat potius quam humore, nasciturque sanguine, et vapor quidam sanguineus appellatur. Rursus quoniam fervet et subtilis est admodum atque lucens oriturque corde, Solaris proculdubio iudicatur. Habet et quodammodo Veneream in se virtutem, nam motu Venereo prorsus exundat, profluit, transfertur prolemque propagat, ad voluptatem cuiuslibet sensus se dilatat refugitque dolorem. Summatim vero spiritus, quatenus corpori ad vitam et motum propagationemque conducit, Iovius, Venereus, Solaris existimatur. Quatenus animo ad sensum imaginationemque ministrat, Solaris Mercurialisque censetur, et ubique Mercurialis existit, quando quidem adeo mobilis est et tam facile convertibilis atque formabilis. Saturni, Martis, Lunae sanus communiter spiritus non multum habet, alioquin ex illo saepe stupidus, ex hoc furiosus, ex hac obtusus quodammodo foret. Quamobrem Lunaria quidem velut crassiora simulque humidiora a subtili et volatili natura spiritus sunt admodum aliena. Quae vero Saturnalia multum atque nimium Martialia sunt quasi venena sunt spiritui naturaliter inimica: illa quidem ob extremam frigiditatem atque siccitatem, haec autem ob siccitatem caloremque edacem. Iovia igitur et Solaris imprimis, deinde Mercurialis et quodammodo Venerea spiritus natura censetur. Distinctione vero praecipua spiritus quidem naturalis Iovi proprie dedicatur, vitalis autem Soli, animalis vero Mercurio. Quando igitur res postulat aliquem e tribus spiritum adiuvare, patrono tunc suo infortunato vel debili, non facile clientulo succurrere poteris. Difficillime vero spiritui animali, dum Mercurius infeliciter est affectus, qui tantam in animali spiritu auctoritatem habet ut caduceo quodam suo animos tum consopire tum suscitare dicatur, id est, suo quodam aspectu sic aut aliter se habente obtundere ingenium vel acuere, debilitare sive corroborare, vexare vel sedare mirifice possit. Tu igitur quotiens spiritum aliquem studes excolere,

---

52 quidem *om. z*   56 quidem *z*   57 *post* oriturque *add.* a *z*   58 et *om. z*   69 Martialia] mortalia *P*   70 spiritu *L*

the fact that variety prevents boredom, which is hostile to the spirits and belongs to Saturn. Indeed, variety brings pleasure, through which, so to say, Venus herself the friend of pleasure comes into the spirit, and as soon as she has entered it she propagates it as is her function. In sum, if one considers Paradise and the use of the fruit of life written of by Moses, if he considers the similar mode of life posited by Plato in the *Phaedo* and what Pliny says about people whose subsistence is odors,[4] he will understand that what we say is true.

But let us proceed to the nature of the spirit. The quality of the spirit is undoubtedly Jovial, in whose time [i.e., the second or Jovial month of foetal development] it is infused into us. Its quality is also Solar; for Jupiter infuses this into us insofar as he tempers in himself the overwhelming power of the Sun. Likewise it is also Jovial in another way, since it is hot and moist, and abounds more in heat than in moisture, and is born of blood, and indeed is called a vapor of blood. Again, it is judged without a doubt to be Solar because it is hot and very subtle and shining and arises from the heart. It also has a somewhat Venereal virtue in it, for by the Venereal motion it rushes forth, flows along, is transferred [to the female], and propagates offspring; dilates to the pleasure of any sense; and flees pain. In sum, then, the spirit is considered Jovial, Venereal, and Solar insofar as it leads to the body's life, motion, or propagation. It is considered Solar or Mercurial insofar as it ministers sense and imagination to the mind — and in any case it is Mercurial since it is so mobile and so easily changeable and plastic. A healthy spirit does not have much in common with Saturn, Mars, or the Moon; otherwise it would be foolish as a result of the first, mad from the second, and insensitive from the last. In line with this, Lunar things, being too heavy and moist, are very foreign to the subtle and volatile nature of the spirit. Things which are very Saturnine and too Martial are like poisons, naturally hostile to the spirit, the former on account of Mars's extreme coldness and dryness, the latter on account of Saturn's dryness and consuming heat. Therefore the nature of the spirit is considered to be chiefly Jovial and Solar, in the next place Mercurial and in some measure Venereal; but with this important subdivision: that the natural spirit properly is assigned to Jupiter; the vital spirit, to the Sun; the animal, to Mercury. When, therefore, the case demands that you help some one of the three spirits, the poor "client" will be difficult to help at a time when its patron is unfortunate or debilitated. But most difficult of all will be helping the animal spirit while Mercury is unfortunately disposed, because he has such power over the animal spirit that he is said both to put minds to sleep and to wake them up with his caduceus, that is to say, by any aspect of his, disposed this way or that, he can miraculously either blunt the wits or sharpen them, weaken or strengthen them, agitate or calm them. Therefore, as often as you desire to cultivate any spirit, you will not only make sure that its patron

non modo patronum suum observabis fortunatum atque potentem, sed etiam Lunam eliges ad hunc opportune directam. Non creatur autem neque recreatur aliquando proprie per influxum Saturni solum substantia spiritus, sed semper ab externis ad intima et saepe ab imis revocatur ad summa. Unde ad secretiora et altiora contemplanda conducit. Potest tamen, etsi raro, vis Martis atque Saturni spiritui tanquam medicina prodesse vel calefaciendo, cum opus fuerit, et excitando atque dilatando, vel vicissim nimis volatilem coercendo.

Per ea vero potissimum quae quattuor illis planetis consentanea sunt, creatur natura spiritus atque recreatur. Verum si ad Solaria quaelibet valde et absque delectu declines, exacues illum et exsiccabis tandem atque dissolves. Si similiter ad Venerea, liquefacies paulatim vel obtundes. Si confidas tantum Mercurialibus, parum admodum inde proficies. Erit igitur operae pretium Iovialibus uti quam plurimum eisque reliqua mediocriter admiscere ac frequentius uti rebus quae vel his omnibus aeque sint communes vel propriae Iovi. Nam hae quoque omnibus quodammodo sunt communes. Communiter autem ad hos omnes attinent quae substantiam habent nec igneam nimis nec prorsus terream nec simpliciter aqueam, nec acutissimam nec obtusissimam qualitatem, sed mediocrem et tactu lenem et quodammodo mollem, vel saltem non duram sive asperam, item gustu quodammodo dulcem, olfactu suavem, visu gratam, auditu blandam atque iucundam, cogitatu laetam.

Dulcedo igitur quaedam saporis et gratia his omnibus est communis. Si dulcedo quasi aquea est et simul pinguis, ad Venerem magis attinet. Si quasi insipida vel aliquantum austera, potius ad Mercurium. Atque haec spiritui non multum prosunt, necessaria tamen sunt interdum ad hebetandum nimium eius acumen. Si dulcedo manifesta sit atque subtilis et paulum habeat styptici acutique saporis, Iovialis proprie iudicatur. Cui congruit substantia dulcis amygdalae, pinei nuclei, avellanae, pistacii, amidi, glycyrrhizae, passularum, vitelli ovi, carnium gallinacei pulli, phasianarum, pavonum, perdicum similiumque, item radicum been atque inulae, rursum vini odoriferi, clari, aliquantum dulcis et styptici, sacchari candidissimi, tritici albissimi. Ad Iovem pertinet etiam manna, si modo myrobalani infusa virtute firmetur; alioquin non minus ad Venerem attinet quam ad Iovem. Haec est utique substantia dulcedoque Iovis propria, quae sane spiritui creando et recreando ante omnia confert. Iovia vero plurimum sunt omnia quae in libro *De longa vita* diximus et servare iuventutem et senibus salubria fore. Sin autem dul-

---

83 direptam *L*   85 ab externis *om. P*   98 hos *add. L²*   attinent *Pz*; attinet *Lwxy*   100 levem *z*   110 fasianorum *z*

BOOK THREE CHAP. XI

is fortunate and powerful, but also elect a time when the Moon is directed opportunely toward this patron. Now through the influence of Saturn alone, the substance of spirit is properly neither created nor recreated at any time, but it is always recalled by him from the outer to the innermost faculties and subjects and often from the lowest to the highest. For this reason he helps one contemplate the more secret and the higher subjects. Nevertheless, although rarely, the power of Mars and of Saturn can be of advantage to the spirit as a medicine, either by warming it when necessary and by stimulating and dilating it, or, in Saturn's case, by repressing a spirit that is too volatile.

But the nature of the spirit is especially created and restored through those things which are in accord with the former four planets. But if you turn away intensively and unselectively to whatever is Solar, you will sharpen the spirit and then dry it up and eventually dissipate it. If similarly you should turn to Venereal things, you will soften it little by little, or blunt it. If you trust only in Mercurial things, then you will accomplish very little. Hence it will be worthwhile to use Jovial things as much as possible and to mingle the other kinds of things moderately with them, and to make a more frequent use of those which are either equally common to all the planets or proper to Jupiter. For things proper to Jupiter are also somewhat common to all. But in common to all the planets belong those things which have a substance neither too fiery, nor all earthy nor simply watery; and a quality not very sharp or dull but moderate; smooth and somewhat soft to touch, or at least not hard or rough; sweet to taste; agreeable to smell; pleasant to see; charming and delightful to hear; joyful to think about.

A certain sweetness of taste and pleasing quality, therefore, is common to all these planets. If the sweetness is, as it were, watery and at the same time rich, it pertains more to Venus. If it is, as it were, insipid and somewhat harsh, it pertains rather to Mercury. And these things are not of much use to the spirit; nevertheless, they are sometimes necessary for blunting its excessive sharpness. If the sweetness is palpable and subtle [as opposed to insipid and harsh], and has a somewhat astringent and sharp taste, it is properly judged to be Jovial. In this class belong the essential nature of sweet almond, the pine-nut, the hazel-nut, the pistachio-nut; of starch,[5] licorice, raisins, yolk of egg;of the meat of the barnyard chicken, of pheasants, of peacocks, of partridges, and of similar animals; likewise that of the roots of ben and elecampane; and likewise that of fragrant, sparkling wine, somewhat sweet and astringent; or of the most glistening-white sugar and the whitest wheat flour. To Jupiter also pertains manna, provided that it is strengthened with the infused power of myrobalan; otherwise it pertains no less to Venus than to Jupiter. This is in truth the substance and sweetness peculiar to Jupiter, which is above all truly useful for creating and restoring the spirit. In fact, all of the things which in the book *On a Long Life*, we called preservative of youth and healthful for the

cedo admodum pauca sit multumque acuti stypticique habeat vel etiam nonnihil amari, Solaris esse censetur.

Similis quaedam ratio est et distinctio de odoribus, hi enim saporum germani sunt. Similis etiam de coloribus. Colores sane aquei, albi, virides, aliquantum crocei, similes violarum, rosarum, liliorum coloribus, necnon odores eiusmodi Venerem referunt et Lunam atque Mercurium. Colores vero sapphyrii qui etiam dicuntur aerii, item purpurei pleniores aureique argento mixti et perpetuo virides Iovem. Ardentes autem crocei, aurei puri, purpurei clariores Solem. Quilibet vero colores si vivi sint vel saltem sericii magis stellares existunt. In metallis quoque et lapidibus atque vitris propter coelestem similitudinem sunt potentes.

Sed ut redeamus ad Iovem, sapor et odor eius quasi est qualis in aureo pomo Persico similique pyro vel aranceo et vino malvatico leviore levique vernaceo; qualis in viridi zinzibere vel cinnamomo vel dulci marathro vel doronico, si haec plurimo saccharo condita gustentur. Nam quattuor haec et nux muscata recens sola si sunt, potius Solaria sunt. Solaris et gariophylus et muscus, sed odoratu non gustu, non aspectu. Ambra Solaris plurimum atque Iovia. Crocus in omnibus est Solaris, tametsi color eius et odor apud astrologos omnibus Gratiis dedicatur; sapor autem ad Solem proprie pertinet. Denique omnia odorifera et aromatica, quatenus odorem gratum ferunt, ita ad Iovem Veneremque et Mercurium pertinent ut ad Solem; quamvis inter haec acutiora magis ad Solem, obtusiora ad Venerem Mercuriumque potius, ad Iovem proprie temperata olfactu, gustu, auditu, visu, tactu. Soni quinetiam cantusque grati blandique ad Gratias omnes spectant atque Mercurium; minaces autem admodum atque flebiles Martem praeferunt et Saturnum. Neque vero mireris nos multum coloribus, odoribus, vocibus attribuere. Nam sapores quidem ad spiritum praecipue pertinent naturalem, odores autem potius ad vitalem animalemque, colores, figurae, voces ad animalem. Motus quoque animi vel laetus vel maestus vel constans spiritum ad similitudinem suam agitat vehementer: animalem primo, per hunc vitalem, per hunc insuper naturalem. Spiritus tandem omnis quia ob naturam quodammodo igneam aeriamque omnino et lucidam atque mobilem similis est luminibus ideoque coloribus et vocibus aeriis et odoribus motibusque animi, ideo per haec subito in utramque partem movetur atque formatur. Et qualis evadit ipse, talem vicissim efficit quodammodo affectum animi et omnino corporis qualitatem. Denique cum primum per illa quae Gratiarum propria sunt opportune Gratiis est expositus, utpote qui et naturaliter illis consentaneus erat, statim per illarum radios tum ubique vigentes, tum ipsi germanos mirifica reportat munera Gratiarum.

---

120 hic *P*   124 aureique] aurei *z*   134 non²] aut *z*   136 ad *om. P*   137 et] etiam *P*   140 temperati *P*   144 pertinet *L*   155 radios tum *om. P*

elderly are very Jovial. But if, on the contrary, the sweetness is very slight and contains much sharpness and astringency, or even some bitterness, it is thought to be Solar.

There is a similar rationale and distinction about odors, for they are blood-brothers of tastes. A similar one also about colors. Colors which are very watery, white, green, a bit yellowish, similar to the colors of violets, roses, and lilies, and also odors of this sort, refer to Venus, the Moon, and Mercury. But the colors of sapphire, which also are said to be airy, and richer purple colors, golden mixed with silver, and greens, always refer to Jupiter. But blazing yellows, pure golds, and lighter purple colors refer to the Sun. Indeed, any colors, if they are fresh or at least pertain to silk, are more stellar; they are potent also in metals and stones and glass because of their resemblance to celestial things.

But to return to Jupiter, his taste and odor are, as it were, like that found in a golden peach, in a golden pear, or in an orange, and in a rather light malmsey wine and in a light vernage wine; such a taste and odor as in green ginger or in cinnamon, sweet fennel, or doronicum, if these things are tasted seasoned with plenty of sugar; for these last four, and fresh nutmeg, if they are alone, are Solar instead. Both clove and musk are Solar, but in respect of their smell, not their taste or appearance. Amber is very Solar and Jovial. Saffron is Solar in all respects, although its color and smell are assigned by astrologers to all the Graces, but its taste pertains properly to the Sun. And then all things which are odoriferous and aromatic, insofar as they bear a pleasant smell, pertain as much to Jupiter, Venus, and Mercury as to the Sun; although among these the sharper things pertain to the Sun; the duller, rather to Venus and Mercury; the properly tempered in smell, taste, sound, sight, and touch, to Jupiter. Furthermore, sounds and songs which are pleasing and agreeable pertain to all the Graces and to Mercury; sounds which are quite threatening and tearful, however, represent Mars and Saturn. Nor indeed should you be surprised that we attribute much to colors, odors, and sounds. For tastes especially pertain to the natural spirit; odors, however, rather to the vital and animal spirit; colors, shapes, and sounds to the animal. A motion of the mind too, whether happy, sad, or constant, violently drives the spirit to its likeness: first the animal, then through this the vital, and moreover through this the natural. Finally, every spirit—since on account of its somewhat fiery, completely airy, clear and mobile nature it is similar to lights and thus to colors and to voices, which are made of air, and to odors and to motions of the mind—every spirit is therefore instantly moved one way or the other and formed by these things. And however it turns out, such in turn in some degree it makes the mind, and absolutely such, the quality of the body. Then as soon as it is opportunely exposed to the Graces through things pertaining to them, being also naturally in accord with those things, it immediately gains wondrous gifts of the Graces through their rays, which both flourish everywhere and are akin to it.

Res naturales atque etiam artificiosae habent virtutes a stellis occultas, per quas spiritum nostrum stellis eisdem exponunt.

Cap. XII.

Cum vero dicimus spiritum exponi Gratiis per illa quae sunt Gratiarum, non solum per qualitates quae videntur, audiuntur, odorantur, gustantur, sed etiam per illas quae tanguntur accommodari putamus. Memento igitur calidum in primo gradu Iovis esse, in secundo Solis cum Iove, in tertio Martis cum Sole, in quarto Martis. Frigidum in primo Veneris, in secundo Lunae, in tertio Lunae cum Saturno, in quarto Saturni. Humidum in primo Mercurii cum Iove, in secundo Veneris cum Luna, in tertio Lunae cum Venere, in quarto Lunae quando Veneri Mercurioque coniungitur. Siccum in primo Iovis, in secundo Mercurii cum Sole, in tertio Solis cum Marte, in quarto Martis cum Saturno. Summatim ex qualitatibus planetarum quas Ptolemaeus describit in *Quadripartito*, colligimus harmoniam ex cunctis conflatam ad calorem humoremque declinare. Calor enim Martis ingens atque Solis et temperatus Iovis ingentem superat Saturni frigiditatem et Veneris Lunaeque exiguam, ita ut calor ibi frigus excedat. Item humiditas Lunae Venerisque plurima et propinqua nobis atque temperata Iovis siccitatem Saturni Martisque multam superat et temperatam Solis. Calor igitur humorque frigori siccoque dominantur, atque similiter calor humori. Quemadmodum in sani corporis homine ad coelestem consonantiam temperato ex calore et siccitate cordis, item calore et humore iecoris, rursum frigore et humore cerebri coalescit complexio quaedam ad calorem humoremque vergens mediocriter calore regnante. Calor enim cordis et iecoris frigus cerebri superat; item humor iecoris atque cerebri siccitatem cordis excedit. Neque vero praetermissum a nobis velim talem existere ex stellis fixis harmoniam cunctis communem, qualem diximus ex planetis, hos enim illis similes astrologi putant. Quorsum haec? Ut memineris spiritum corpusque nostrum per temperiem quandam ad calorem humoremque vergentem vel natura constantem vel arte quaesitam accommodari posse coelestibus, sibique coelestia vendicare.

Neque tamen dicimus spiritum nostrum coelestibus duntaxat per qualitates rerum notas sensibus praeparari, sed etiam multoque magis per proprietates

---

Quod res *yz* eisdem *om. P; eiusdem z* 11 scribit *z* 12 atque Solis *om. P* 16 Calor] Cum *z* 18 hominem *P* 26 arte *om. z* 27–28 vendicare Neque tamen dicimus *om. P*

Natural and Even Artificial Things Have Occult Powers from the Stars, through Which They Expose Our Spirit to the Same Stars.
Chap. XII

When we say the spirit is exposed to the Graces through those things which pertain to the Graces, we mean that it is accommodated not through those qualities alone which are seen, heard, smelled, and tasted, but also through those perceptible by touch. Remember, therefore, that the hot is in the first degree Jovial; in the second degree it pertains to the Sun along with Jupiter; in the third, to Mars along with the Sun; in the fourth, to Mars. The cold belongs in the first degree to Venus; in the second, to the Moon; in the third, to the Moon with Saturn; in the fourth, to Saturn. The moist in the first degree pertains to Mercury along with Jupiter; in the second, to Venus along with the Moon; in the third, to the Moon along with Venus; in the fourth, to the Moon when she is joined with Venus and Mercury. The dry is in the first degree Jupiter's; in the second, Mercury's along with the Sun; in the third, the Sun's along with Mars; in the fourth, Mars's along with Saturn. In brief, from the qualities of the planets which Ptolemy describes in his *Tetrabiblos*,[1] we gather that the harmony conflated from them all is weighted towards heat and moisture; for the great heat of Mars and the Sun plus the temperate heat of Jupiter outweighs the great coldness of Saturn plus the slight coldness of Venus and the Moon, so that there the heat exceeds the cold. Likewise the moisture of the Moon and Venus (much and near to us and temperate) plus that of Jupiter outweighs the great dryness of Saturn and Mars plus the temperate dryness of the Sun. Therefore the hot and moist dominate the cold and dry, and similarly the heat dominates the moisture. In the same way in a person having a healthy body tempered into harmony with the heavens, there coalesces out of the heat and dryness of the heart, the heat and moisture of the liver, and the cold and moisture of the brain, a complexion verging towards heat and moisture, with the heat moderately dominant. For the heat of the heart and liver outweighs the cold of the brain; likewise the moisture of the liver and brain exceeds the dryness of the heart. I wouldn't want us to overlook that there is the same sort of overall harmony from all the fixed stars as we have said there is from the planets; for astrologers think they are similar.[2] To what purpose is all this? That you may remember that by a temper verging towards heat and moisture, whether established by nature or acquired by art, our spirit and body can be accommodated to celestial things and lay claim to them.

At the same time, we do not say that our spirit is prepared for the celestials only through qualities of things known to the senses, but also and much more

quasdam rebus coelitus insitas et sensibus nostris occultas, rationi vix deni- 30
que notas. Nam cum proprietates eiusmodi earumque effectus elementali virtute constare non possint, consequens est a vita spirituque mundi per ipsos
stellarum radios singulariter proficisci, ideoque per eas spiritum affici quam
plurimum atque quam primum, coelestibusque influxibus vehementer exponi. Hac utique ratione smaragdus, hyacinthus, sapphyrus, topazius, rubi- 35
nus, unicorni cornu, praecipue vero lapis bezaar apud Arabes appellatus occultis Gratiarum proprietatibus praedita sunt. Et idcirco non solum intus
assumpta, sed etiam si carnem tangant ibique calefacta virtutem suam pro-
mant, vim inde coelestem spiritibus inserunt, qua se contra pestem tuentur
atque venena. Quod autem haec similiaque tale aliquid agant virtute coelesti, 40
id argumento est quia etiam exiguo pondere sumpta non exiguum habent in
agendo momentum. Quod elementari qualitati vix unquam est concessum,
igni videlicet valde coelesti. Materialis enim virtus ut agat multum, materiam desiderat multam; formalis autem etiam cum minima materia valet plurimum. 45

Simili virtute imprimis Phoebea paeonia carnem tangens contra caducum
morbum spiritus armat, vapore ad eos intus infuso. Simili corallus et chalcidonius adversum atrae bilis illusiones Iovis praecipue Venerisque virtute;
ceteraque similiter. Eiusmodi quadam proprietate myrobalani iuventutem
servant acuuntque sensus et ingenio prosunt atque memoriae propter Iovem 50
imprimis, Saturni temperatorem, atque Mercurium sensus amicum. Quam
quidem arborem forte aliquis in paradiso ad vitam prorogandam extitisse
putabit. Mercurio lapidem achatem consecrant, unde physici conveniunt ad
facundiam visumque et contra venena valere. Serapio scribit eum qui hyacinthum vel ex eo sigillum gestat, esse a fulgore tutum, atque hanc virtutem 55
eius esse latissime divulgatam. Quam si habet, ab Iove putamus habere. Lapis aetites vel aquilinus habet a Lucina, id est Venere atque Luna, ut admo-
tus vulvae partum mox et facillime citet. Quod Rasis confirmante Serapione
frequenter se dicit expertum. Forsan et a Phoebo, qui transfixit pythonem,
Cretaea dictamus habet, ut et venenosis obsistat et ferrum e vulnere trahat. 60
Solis virtute zinziber infusum epulis arcet syncopim. Gentiana canis rabiem
sedat fugatque serpentes. Verbena vaticinium praestare fertur laetitiamque
et expiationes et visum. Ruta et zedoaria contra venena theriacam agunt.
Thus vitalem et animalem spiritum adversus hebetudinem, oblivionem, timo-
rem fulcit. Salvia vero mentaque virtute Iovis: illa quidem paralysim fugat, 65
haec vel odore roborat animum. Eadem virtute pentaphyllon resistit venenis,

---

35 ratione *add. in marg.* P; *om.* z   38 calefactu z   39 inferunt z   43 Materialis] Martialis z
47 armas z   50 sensus] senes z   57 aetites] echites LPw^{ac} 59 transfixis z   61 arcetque z
Gentiana z; Sentiana LPwxy   62 Verbena Lz; Berbena L^{ac}Pwxy   64 et *om.* P   66 vel] vero z

through certain properties engrafted in things from the heavens and hidden from our senses, and hence only with difficulty known to our reason. For since properties of this kind and their effects could not come into being by elemental power, it follows that they proceed from the life and spirit of the cosmos, particularly through those very rays of the stars; and that therefore through them the spirit is affected as much and as soon as possible and exposed very much to celestial influences. It is for just this reason that emerald, jacinth, sapphire, topaz, ruby, unicorn's horn, but especially the stone which the Arabs call bezoar, are endowed with occult properties of the Graces.[3] And therefore, not only if they are taken internally, but even if they touch the flesh, and, warmed thereby, put forth their power, they introduce celestial force into the spirits by which the spirits preserve themselves from plague and poison. The fact that by celestial power these and similar things can achieve something like that, is an argument that even a slight weight taken internally can achieve no small thing. What is hardly ever granted to an elemental quality is granted to a fire that is very celestial; for a material power requires much matter if it is to achieve much; but a formal power even with a minimum of matter avails very much.

By a similar power the Phoebean peony touching the flesh arms the spirits against the falling sickness [epilepsy] by infusing vapor into them within.[4] By a similar power from Jupiter and Venus in particular, coral and chalcedony are good against the delusions of black bile;[5] and so with the rest. By a property of this kind from Jupiter, the moderator of Saturn, and from Mercury, the friend of the senses, myrobalans preserve youth, sharpen the senses, and benefit the intelligence and the memory. This tree one might well suppose was the tree for prolonging life which was in Paradise.[6] To Mercury they consecrate the stone called "agate" [by a pun, because Mercury is "the faithful Achates of the Sun," 3.6.165]; therefore physicians agree that it is good for eloquence and vision and against poison. Serapion writes that he who wears a jacinth, or a signet made from one, is safe from lightning; and that this power of it is very widely known;[7] if it has this power, I think it comes from Jupiter [as god of lightning]. The stone "aetites" or eagle-stone has from Lucina (that is, from Venus and the Moon) the power when applied to the womb to incite a quick and very easy child-birth; Rhazes, with Serapion confirming, says he has frequently proved this by experience.[8] Perhaps it is from Phoebus who stabbed the python that the Cretan dittany has its power both to resist poisonous things and to draw the spear-head from the wound. By the power of the Sun, ginger infused in foods prevents fainting; gentian allays rabies in a dog and puts serpents to flight; vervain, they say, promotes prophecy, joy, atonements, and sight; rue and zedoary act as a theriac against poison; frankincense supports the vital and the animal spirit against dullness, forgetfulness, and fear. By Jupiter's power, sage drives away paralysis and mint strengthens the mind with its odor. By the same power cinquefoil resists poisons; one of

eiusque folium bis quotidie unum vino bibitum curat ephimeram, tria tertianam, quattuor vero quartanam. Hac herba sacerdotes antiqui propter puritatem suam in purificationibus utebantur. Agnus castus potestate Saturni Venereum sistit motum; iaspis vero sanguinem. Mirabiles autem provenire solent effectus, ubi occultae proprietati proprietas servit elementalis, velut in myrobalano ad spiritum corpusque firmandum non solum virtus illa coelestis agit, sed etiam styptica multum nec parum aromatica virtus, quae putrefactionem dissolutionemque mirifice prohibet spiritumque corroborat. Iam vero ut crocus petat cor, spiritum dilatet, provocet risum, non solum occulta Solis virtus mirabiliter efficit, sed ad idem quoque conducit ipsa natura croci subtilis, amplificabilis, aromatica, lucida.

Quod autem de simplicibus dico, de compositis similiter dictum intelligi volo. Dic age theriaca quomodo contra venenum nobis opituletur. Non educit illa venenum, astringit enim alvum. Non mutat omnino tam subito veneni naturam, non enim haec adeo debilis est atque mutabilis. Sed spiritum vitalem potius valde tenuem et mutabilem subito conformi quadam ad ipsum proportione corroborat usque adeo, ut ipse iam validus tanquam agens una cum theriaca velut instrumento partim superet venenum, partim mutet, partim a praecordiis arceat. Sed quanam proportione sive virtute id efficit theriaca? Ioviali simul atque Phoebea, quam ex commixtione multarum rerum secundum certam proportionem invicem confusarum sibi vendicavisse videtur. Est autem in ea virtus triplex. Haec ipsa inquam coelestis, quam modo dicebam. Item coelestis alia prius in herbis aromatisque proprietas, quibus electis ipsa rite componitur, quae virtuti prius dictae subministrat ad idem. Est insuper alia virtus in plerisque partibus eius elementalis potius quam coelestis, verumtamen talis ut spiritui muniendo conducat. Stypticam dico et aromaticam qualitatem: illa quidem spiritum firmat, ista fovet. Mirabilem ergo theriaca vim nacta est contra properantem senectutem atque venenum, tribus videlicet in ea virtutibus ad idem pariter conspirantibus. Quarum una quidem est coelestis per artificiosam acquisita commixtionem, alia coelestis iterum sed partibus eius naturaliter insita, alia prorsus elementalis.

Sed illa quam prius dixi coelitus acquisita multo etiam foret admirabilior, si non solum proportione Iovia Solarique et ex rebus eiusmodi conflaretur, sed etiam opportunum ad hoc observatione coelestium tempus eligeretur. Nam quemadmodum corpus se habet ad locum atque tempus, ita motus et actio se habet ad tempus. Sicut ergo certa passim corpora eorumque formae certis et locis et temporibus coalescunt atque servantur, sic et proprie quaedam actiones ex propriis quibusdam temporibus efficaciam nanciscuntur;

---

75 dilatat *x*   85 sive] sine *z*   87 vendicasse *z*   88 eo *z*   103 propriae *z*

its leaves drunk twice daily in wine cures the one-day fever; three leaves, the tertian fever; four leaves, the quartan; this herb was used by the ancient priests in their purifications on account of its purity. By the power of Saturn, the "chaste tree" stops Venereal motions; and jasper, blood. But wonderful effects usually ensue where the elemental property subserves the occult property, as in myrobalan for firming up the spirit and the body; not only that celestial power is at work, but also much astringent power and enough aromatic power, which wonderfully prevents putrefaction and dissolution and strengthens the spirit. When saffron seeks the heart, dilates the spirit, and provokes laughter, it is not only the occult power of the Sun which is doing this in a wondrous way; but the very nature of saffron — subtle, diffusible, aromatic, and clear — also conduces to the same end.

What I say of simples I want to be understood similarly of compounds. Go on, say, how does theriac help us against poison? It does not bring out the poison, for it constricts the belly; it does not entirely change the nature of poison so quickly, for the nature of poison is not so weak and mutable as that. But instead it strengthens the vital spirit, which is very tenuous and mutable, and it does so quickly by a certain agreeable proportion which it has to the spirit, so that the spirit is so strong acting with the theriac as an instrument, as to partly overcome the poison, partly change it, partly repel it from the heart. But by what proportion or power does theriac do this? By Jovial power together with Phoebean, which it seems to acquire out of this mélange of many things mingled together [theriac had many ingredients] according to a definite proportion. There is in it a triple power: the celestial power itself of which I spoke just now; likewise another celestial property existing beforehand in the herbs and spices selected for its proper composition, which subserves the same end as the aforementioned power. There is besides another power in many parts of it that is rather elemental than celestial, but such as conduces to the fortifying of the spirit: I mean an astringent and aromatic quality; the former firms up the spirit, the latter foments it. Wonderful is the power, therefore, which theriac has acquired against poison and the onset of old age, having three powers in it conspiring equally to the same end, one of which is celestial acquired through artificial mixture, another again celestial but naturally inherent in its ingredients, another wholly elemental.

But that first-mentioned power acquired from the heavens would be even more wonderful if it were not only mixed in a Jovial and Solar proportion and out of Solar and Jovial ingredients, but also if an opportune time were elected for this by observation of the celestials. For just as the body is disposed according to the place and time, so motion and action are disposed according to the time. Therefore, just as in various places, certain bodies and their forms coalesce at certain places and times and are preserved; so also certain actions properly achieve efficacy in their own certain seasons; and this Socrates signifies in the

idque in *Alcibiade* significat Socrates et Proculus explicat. Quod sane Pytha- 105
goras animadvertens ipsum bonum perfectionemque rerum opportunitatem
cognominavit. Primum namque principium sic apud Pythagoram et Platonem omnium est mensura, ut aliis corporibus actionibusque alia loca distri-
buerit atque tempora. Unde sicut res quaedam non alibi quam hic nec alias
quam tunc proprie nascuntur feliciter et coalescunt atque servantur, sic et 110
materialis actio, motus, eventus talis aut talis non alias efficaciam sortitur
effectumque perfectum quam quando coelestium harmonia ad idem undique
consonat. Quae sane harmonia tantam habere potestatem existimatur, ut
non solum agricolarum laboribus atque medicorum artificiis per herbas aro-
mataque conflatis, sed etiam imaginibus quae apud astrologos ex metallis 115
lapidibusque fiunt, virtutem saepe mirificam largiatur.

 Sed imagines caput iam proprium exigunt. Quantum vero ad horas pro
actionibus et operibus eligendas pertinet, plurimum confirmatur a Ptolemaeo
ubi ait in *Centiloquio:* "Qui eligit quod melius est, nihilo differre videtur ab eo
qui habet hoc ex natura." Quibus in verbis tum coelestium tum arbitrii elec- 120
tionisque nostrae potestatem confirmare videtur. Albertus quoque Magnus
inquit in *Speculo:* "Non enim libertas arbitrii ex electione horae laudabilis coer-
cetur, sed potius in magnarum rerum inceptionibus electionem horae con-
temnere est arbitrii praecipitatio, non libertas."

De virtute imaginum secundum antiquos
atque medicinarum coelitus acquisita.

Cap. XIII.

Ptolemaeus ait in *Centiloquio* rerum inferiorum effigies vultibus coelestibus esse subiectas, antiquosque sapientes solitos certas tunc imagines
fabricare, quando planetae similes in coelo facies quasi exemplaria inferiorum
ingrediebantur. Quod quidem Haly comprobat, ibi dicens utilem serpentis
imaginem effici posse, quando Luna Serpentem coelestem subit aut feliciter 5
aspicit. Similiter scorpionis effigiem efficacem, quando Scorpii signum Luna
ingreditur ac signum hoc tenet angulum ex quattuor unum. Quod in Aegypto suis temporibus factum ait seque interfuisse, ubi ex sigillo scorpionis in
lapide bezaar ita facto imprimebatur thuri figura dabaturque in potum ei
quem scorpius ipse pupugerat, ac subito curabatur. Quod quidem utiliter ef- 10
fici Hahamed physicus affirmat, confirmante Serapione. Praeterea narrat

---

106 perfectionumque *L*   111 metus *z*   112 harmoniam *L*   113 consonant *x*   121 potestatum *z*
  5 affici *z*   11 Hahameth *z*

Alcibiades and Proclus explains it. And Pythagoras, considering this, rightly called the good itself and the perfection of things by the name of "timeliness."⁹ Thus the first principle of all things is measure, according to Pythagoras and Plato, that it might distribute divers places and times to divers bodies and actions.¹⁰ In consequence, just as a given thing is fortunately born and coalesces and is preserved not elsewhere than here nor at any other time but just then, so also such or such a material action, motion, or event does not obtain full or perfect efficacy except when the celestial harmony conduces to it from all sides. This harmony is thought to have such great power that it oftentimes bestows a wonderful power not only on the works of farmers and on artificial things composed by doctors from herbs and spices, but even on images which are made out of metals and stones by astrologers.

But images now require a chapter of their own. As much, however, as pertains to the election of hours for actions and works is completely confirmed by Ptolemy where he says in the *Centiloquium*, "He who elects what is better, he seems to be no different from him who has it by nature."¹¹ In these words, he seems to confirm the power both of the celestials and of our free will and election. Also Albertus Magnus says in his *Speculum*, "Freedom of will is not repressed by the election of an excellent hour; rather, to scorn to elect an hour for the beginnings of great enterprises is not freedom but reckless choice."¹²

On the Power Acquired from the Heavens Both in Images, according to the Ancients, and in Medicines.

Chap. XIII

Ptolemy says in the *Centiloquium* that images of things here below are subject to the celestial images; and that the ancient wise men used to manufacture certain images when the planets were entering similar faces of the heavens, the faces being as it were exemplars of things below.¹ Haly confirms this, saying in his commentary on this text that a useful image of a serpent can be formed when the Moon enters the celestial Serpent or aspects it favorably. Similarly an effective image of a scorpion can be formed when the Moon enters the sign Scorpio and this sign is occupying one of the four cardines. This he says was done in Egypt in his time, and he was present; in this case a figure was imprinted in frankincense from a signet of a scorpion made under these conditions from the stone bezoar; it was given in a drink to a person whom a real scorpion had stung, and right away he was cured.² Hahamed the physician affirms that this was effectively performed, and Serapion confirms

Haly notum illic sibi virum sapientem industria simili fecisse imagines quae moverentur, qualem effectam nescio quomodo legimus ab Archita. Quales et Trismegistus ait Aegyptios ex certis mundi materiis facere consuevisse, et in eas opportune animas daemonum inserere solitos, atque animam avi sui Mercurii, item Phoebi cuiusdam et Isidis Osyridisque sic in statuas descendisse profuturas hominibus vel etiam nocituras.

Huic illud simile: Prometheum figmento quodam luteo vitam rapuisse lucemque coelestem. Magi quinetiam, Zoroastris sectatores, ad evocandum ab Hecate spiritum utebantur aurea quadam pila characteribus insignita coelestium, cui et sapphyrus erat insertus, et scutica quadam facta tauri corio vertebatur, atque interim excantabant. Sed cantiones equidem libenter omitto, nam et Psellus Platonicus eas improbat atque deridet. Hebraei quoque in Aegypto nutriti struere vitulum aureum didicerunt, ut eorundem astrologi putant, ad aucupandum Veneris Lunaeque favorem contra Scorpionis atque Martis influxum Iudaeis infestum. Porphyrius quoque in *epistola ad Anebonem* imagines efficaces esse testatur, additque certis quibusdam vaporibus qui a propriis suffumigationibus exhalabant, aerios daemonas insinuari statim consuevisse. Iamblichus in materiis quae naturaliter superis consentaneae sint et opportune riteque collectae undique conflataeque fuerint, vires effectusque non solum coelestes, sed etiam daemonicos et divinos suscipi posse confirmat. Idem omnino Proculus atque Synesius.

Opera quidem ad salutem mira, quae a medicis in astrologia peritis per res ex multis compositas, id est pulveres, liquores, unguenta, electuaria fieri possunt, probabiliorem in se rationem et notiorem quam imagines habere videntur, tum quia pulveres, liquores, unguenta, electuaria opportune confecta coelestes influxus facilius citiusque suscipiunt quam materiae duriores ex quibus imagines fieri consueverunt; tum quia vel assumuntur intus affecta iam coelitus et in nos convertuntur, vel saltem admota foris inhaerent magis et denique penetrant; tum etiam quoniam ex uno quodam duntaxat aut perpaucis imagines construuntur, illa vero ex quam plurimis conflari pro arbitrio possunt. Ut si centum Solis Iovisve dotes per centum plantas et animalia similiaque sparsae fuerint, componere simul haec centum tibi comperta possis et in unum conficere formam, in qua Solem ferme Iovemque totum iam videaris habere. Scis profecto naturam inferiorem non posse uno quodam capere cunctas superioris naturae vires, ideoque illas per plures apud nos

---

18 Prometheo *P*   19 Zoroastri *z*   27 vaporibus] temporibus *z*   34-36 fieri possunt — electuaria om. *P*   39 fores *z*   41 constari *z*

BOOK THREE CHAP. XIII

it.³ Besides, Haly tells of a wise man who in a similar endeavor made images which moved; we read that this was also effected somehow by Architas.⁴ Trismegistus says the Egyptians also used to make such images of specific cosmic materials and used to insert into them at the right time the souls of daemons and the soul of his ancestor Mercury. Likewise the souls of a certain Phoebus and of Isis and Osiris thus descended into statues to help people or even to harm them.⁵

That myth is similar to this one: that Prometheus stole life and celestial light by means of a clay figure.⁶ Yes, and the magicians who were disciples of Zoroaster, when they wanted to summon a spirit [rare use of *spiritus* in normal sense] from Hecate, would use a golden ball on which characters of heavenly bodies were engraved and in which also a sapphire had been inserted: they would whirl it around in a strap made of bull's hide while they chanted.⁷ But the incantations I gladly omit; for even Psellus the Platonist disapproves of incantations and makes fun of them.⁸ The Hebrews, from having been brought up in Egypt, learned how to construct the golden calf, as their own astrologers think, in order to capture the favor of Venus and the Moon against the influence of Scorpio and Mars, which was inimical to the Jews. Porphyry also in his *Letter to Anebo* testifies that images are efficacious; and he adds that by certain vapors arising from fumigations proper to them, aerial daemons would instantly be insinuated into them.⁹ Iamblichus confirms that in materials which are naturally akin to the things above and have been both collected from their various places and compounded at the right time and in the proper manner, you can receive forces and effects which are not only celestial, but even daemonic and divine.¹⁰ Proclus and Synesius absolutely agree.¹¹

Certainly those wonderful therapies which doctors trained in astrology are able to perform through medicines composed of many things—i.e., powders, liquids, unguents, electuaries—seem to have in themselves a more probable and obvious explanation than do images: first, because powders, liquids, unguents, and electuaries, made at the right time, receive celestial influences more easily and quickly than the harder materials from which images usually are made; second, because once impregnated with celestial influences, they are either taken internally and converted into our very selves, or at least when applied externally they stick closer and finally penetrate; third, because images are constructed of only one or a very few materials, but medicines can be made of as many as you like. For instance, if a hundred gifts of the Sun or Jupiter were scattered throughout a hundred plants, animals, etc., and you discovered them and were able to compound them and work them up into one form, in this you would actually seem already to possess completely the Sun or Jupiter. Certainly you know that the lower nature cannot hold all the forces of the higher nature in one subject; and, therefore, that these forces are dispersed in our world through many natures; and that they can be collected more easily through

naturas esse dispersas, commodiusque per opera medicorum atque similia quam per imagines colligi posse.

Proinde imagines ex ligno confectae vim forte parvam habent. Nam lignum et forsan durius est ad coelestem influxum facile capiendum et minus tenax, si acceperit, retinendum; et omnino postquam ex matris terrae visceribus est evulsum, paulo post ferme totum amittit mundanae vitae vigorem et facile in qualitatem aliam transmutatur. Lapilli vero atque metalla etsi ad accipiendum coeleste munus duriora videntur, diutius tamen retinent (quod confirmat Iamblichus), si acceperint. Sua nempe duritia vestigia quoque donaque vitae mundanae post evulsionem diutissime continent, quae quondam haerentia terrae possederant. Quamobrem ob hoc saltem aptae materiae ad capienda tenendaque coelestia iudicantur. Est et probabile quod libro superiore dixi, res adeo speciosas non posse sub terra conflari, nisi maximo quodam conatu coeli, atque durare in eis impressam semel ex conatu virtutem. Nam in his coquendis cogendisque diutissime coelum elaboravit. Verum cum nequeas facile eiusmodi plura componere, cogeris diligenter exquirere quod metallum inter cetera in ordine sit alicuius stellae potissimum, quive lapis in ordine summus, ut saltem in uno quodam totius generis ordinisque supremo reliqua pro viribus comprehendas, atque eiusmodi susceptaculo coelestia huic consentanea mutueris; ceu si exempli causa in ordine Solari sub homine Phoebeo summum inter animalia teneat astur aut gallus, inter plantas balsamum aut laurus, inter metalla aurum, inter lapides carbunculus vel pantaura, inter elementa fervidus aer (nam ignis ipse Martius esse censetur). Quod autem diximus influxum Solis vel Iovis aut Veneris augendum, intelligimus ratione communi, non tamen illi in cuius genesi aliquis horum interfector appareat.

Ordines rerum a stellis pendentium, ut Solarium atque similium; et quomodo spiritus fiat Solaris.

Cap. XIV.

Dixi equidem alibi desuper ab unaquaque stella (ut Platonice loquar) seriem rerum illi propriam usque ad extrema pendere. Sub ipso Scorpionis Corde post eiusmodi daemonas atque homines scorpiumque animal collocare possumus etiam herbam asterion, id est stellarem, figura stellae similem, nocte fulgentem, quam medici tradunt qualitatem habere rosae vim-

---

53 etsi *om.* P   55 acceperit z   58 iudicatur P   63 quisve z   67 balsamus P
De ordinibus yz

medical procedures and the like than through images.

Similarly, images made of wood have little force. For wood is both perhaps too hard to take on celestial influence easily and less tenacious, if it does receive it, in retaining it; and it soon loses almost any vigor of cosmic life at all and is easily transmuted into another quality after it is rooted out of the bowels of its mother earth. But gems and metals, although they seem too hard for accepting a celestial influence, nevertheless retain it longer if they receive it, as Iamblichus confirms.[12] That is to say, by their hardness they also retain the vestiges and gifts of the life of the world, which they had once possessed while embedded in the earth, for a very long time after being rooted out. On this score, at least, they are judged to be apt materials for capturing and holding celestial things. Also it is probable, as I said in the preceding book,[13] that things so beautiful cannot be fused under the earth without a consummate effort of the heavens, and that the power impressed in them once and for all from that effort remains. For the heavens have labored an immense length of time in concocting and assembling these things. But since you cannot easily compound several things of this kind, you are forced to inquire diligently what metal among others is most powerful in the order of any given star, what stone is highest in that order, so that at least in some one thing, supreme in its entire genus and order, you may, insofar as possible, comprehend the rest, and that you may borrow in a receptacle of this kind celestial things that are in sympathy with it; as, for example, in the Solar order, below a Phoebean man, the hawk or the cock holds the highest place among the animals; among the plants, balsam or laurel; among metals, gold; among stones, carbuncle or pantaura;[14] among elements, hot air (for fire itself is agreed to belong to Mars). But our advice to increase the influence of the Sun, of Jupiter, or of Venus [3.5 ff.], we understand as a general rule, not, however, for that patient in whose horoscope one of these planets appeared as a Signifier of death.

The Orders of Things Depending on the Stars, as of Solar Things, and So Forth; and How Our Spirit May Be Made Solar.

Chap. XIV

I have said elsewhere that down from every single star (to speak Platonically) there hangs its own series of things down to the lowest.[1] Under the very Heart of the Scorpion, after daemons and men of its kind, and the scorpion, the animal, we can place also the aster, whose name means "stellar," similar in shape to a star shining at night, which doctors tell us has the quality of the

que contra morbos genitalium mirabilem possidere. Sub Serpente vel Serpentario coelesti Saturnum ponunt et quodammodo Iovem, postea daemonas qui saepe serpentum formas induunt, similes insuper homines, serpentes animantes, serpentariam herbam, lapidem draconitem capite draconis natum, item communi nomine serpentinum, et praeterea quae in sequentibus afferam. Sub stella Solari, id est Sirio, Solem primo, deinde daemonas quoque Phoebeos, quos aliquando sub leonum vel gallorum forma hominibus occurrisse testis est Proculus, homines subinde persimiles bestiasque Solares, Phoebeas inde plantas, metalla similiter et lapillos et vaporem aeremque ferventem. Simili ratione a qualibet firmamenti stella per aliquem planetam existimant contextum rerum gradatim sub illius proprietate descendere. Si igitur, ut dicebam, Solaria omnia per gradum eius ordinis quemlibet opportune comprehenderis: homines videlicet tales vel talis hominis aliquid, item bruta, plantas, metalla, lapillos et quae ad haec attinent, virtutem Solis usquequaque combibes et quodammodo naturalem Solarium daemonum facultatem. Similiterque de aliis dictum puta.

Solares quidem homines sunt quales antea dixi et qui ascendente Leone Soleque hunc vel tenente vel aspiciente nascuntur et qui sub Ariete similiter. Solaris est et sanguis e sinistro eorum bene valentium bracchio missus. Phoebeus crocodillus, astur, leo, gallus et cygnus et corvus. Nec alia ratione leo veretur gallum, nisi quoniam in ordine Phoebeo gallus est leone superior. Eadem ratione inquit Proculus Apollineum daemonem, qui nonnunquam apparuit sub figura leonis, statim obiecto gallo disparuisse. Maxime vero in his animalibus cor est Solare. Arbitror etiam marinum vitulum coelestis Leonis Cordi subesse, et hac ipsa ratione corium eius, quem cingit nudum fibula eiusdem osse confecta, a renum dolore redimere. Nam contra dolorem eiusmodi solent astrologi sideris illius influxibus uti. Eadem forte ratione fertur haec pellis a fulgure nos tueri. Inter plantas palma Phoebea est et imprimis laurus, qua virtute venenosa repellit et fulgur. Fraxinus quoque simili facultate venenosa longius arcet. Loton esse Phoebeam rotunda tum folia, tum poma testantur et explicatio foliorum eius die, replicatio nocte. Paeoniam Phoebeam esse non solum virtus indicat, sed et nomen. Ad idem attinent flores et herbae quae restringuntur abeunte Sole, redeunte protinus explicantur et ad Solem continue vergunt; aurum praeterea et lapis elitis radiis aureis Solem imitans; lapis item qui Solis oculus appellatur figuram habens pupil-

---

24 bene valentium] benevolentium *z*   28 his *om. x*   30 corium eius *om. LPw*^ac   31 *post* eiusdem *add.* esse *P*   35 tum folia *om. z*   36 *post* replicatio *add.* vero *z*   40 qui] quam *x*

rose and possesses a wonderful force against diseases of the genitals.[2] Under the celestial Serpent or the entire constellation of the Serpent-bearer, they place Saturn and sometimes Jupiter, afterwards daemons who often take on serpent's form, in addition men of this kind, serpents (the animals), the snake-weed [or snake's grass], the stone draconite which originates in the head of a dragon, and the stone commonly named serpentine, and besides, those which I will adduce in what follows. Under the Solar star, that is Sirius, they set the Sun first of all, and then Phoebean daemons, which sometimes have encountered people under the form of lions or cocks, as Proclus testifies,[3] then similar men and Solar beasts, Phoebean plants then, similarly metals and gems and vapor and hot air. By a similar system they think a chain of beings descends by levels from any star of the firmament through any planet under its dominion. If, therefore, as I said, you combine at the right time all the Solar things through any level of that order, i.e., men of Solar nature or something belonging to such a man, likewise animals, plants, metals, gems, and whatever pertains to these, you will drink in unconditionally the power of the Sun and to some extent the natural power of the Solar daemons. Consider that I have said similar things about the others.

Solar are those people of the sorts that I specified before [3.1 ad fin.], also those who are born when Leo is ascending and the Sun either is in it or aspects it, and similarly those who are born under Aries. Blood let from the left arms of healthy people is also Solar. Also Phoebean are the crocodile, the hawk, the lion, the cock, the swan, and the raven. It is for no other reason that the lion fears the cock but that in the Phoebean order he is superior to the lion. For the same reason, says Proclus, the Apollonian daemon who often appeared under the shape of a lion disappeared as soon as a cock was put in his way.[4] In these animals, the heart is especially Solar. I think that the seal too is subject to the Heart of the celestial Lion[5] and that it is for this very reason that he who girds its leather against his bare skin with a buckle made of its bone, is relieved of pains in the kidneys. For against such pain astrologers are accustomed to use the influences of this star. Perhaps for the same reason, its pelt is said to keep us safe from lightning. Among plants, the palm is Phoebean and most of all the laurel, by virtue of which it repels poisonous things and lightning. The ash-tree also by a similar faculty repels poisonous things far away. That the lotus is Phoebean, is testified by the roundness both of its leaves and of its fruit and by the unfolding of its leaves in the day and their folding back up at night.[6] That the peony is Phoebean, is indicated not only by its power but even by its name ["Paeonius" is an epithet of Phoebus]. To the Sun belong flowers and herbs which close up when the Sun is absent, unfold as soon as he returns, and continually turn towards the Sun; gold, too, and "lapis elitis," which imitates the Sun by its golden rays; likewise the stone which is called "eye of the Sun," having the shape of a pupil which radiates light; also

lae, ex qua lumen emicat; rursum carbunculus nocte rutilans vel pantaura omnes in se lapidum vires continens, ut aurum metallorum et Sol stellarum. Multa denique in superioribus nobis significata. Unde si modo liceat, sub imperio Solis ex illo sanguine et animalium illorum cordibus et foliis fructibusque arborum praedictarum, item floribus atque herbis et auri foliis, necnon pulveribus lapillorum electuarium vel unguentum conficere poteris, addito croco, balsamo, calamo aromatico, thure, musco, ambra, ligno aloes, zinzibere, mastice, spica nardi, cinnamomo, doronico, citri cortice, zedoaria, nuce muscata, mace, gariophylis cum melle flavo vel oleo balsamino, masticeo, laurino, nardino; ad cor et stomachum et caput intus aut extra fovendum, ut spiritus inde Solaris evadat. Ex his omnibus inquam aut saltem ex pluribus componendum dominante Sole aliquid. Quo etiam sub eiusdem dominatu incipias uti, dummodo et Solaria induas, habites, conspicias, audias, olfacias, imagineris, cogites, cupias. Item imiteris et vita dignitatem et munera Solis. Inter Solares homines plantasque verseris laurumque assidue tangas.

Tutius autem ad valetudinem fuerit Solaribus admiscere Iovialia simul atque Venerea — Veneream maxime humiditatem, Solaris caloris moderatricem, qualis est aqua succusque rosarum atque violarum. Sed medicinas eiusmodi in libro *De curandis litteratis* primum, deinde in libro *De vita longa* partim equidem composui, partim ab aliis compositas enarravi, partim etiam temperavi. Item quales herbae a Sole Ioveque miras contra epidemiam et venenum vires habeant, diximus in libro *Contra pestem,* inter quas perforata fuga daemon appellata est. Nec alia facultate quam coelestium Gratiarum noxios malorum daemonum vapores a nobis arcere putatur. Et si qua inter herbas alia vel lapillus ut corallus, idem videatur efficere. Herba profecto Lunaris a Mercurio tradita foliis caeruleis atque rotundis, crescente Luna unum quotidie producens folium, decrescente deponens, annos utenti promittit Lunares. Sed iam ad imagines altero quodam exordio redeamus.

---

41 Pantataura *z*   46 lapillorum] pupillarum *z*   48 bortice *z*   zedoario *z*   49 oleo] aureo *z*
54 obfacias *Lw*ᵃᶜ   55 plantasque] et plantas *P*   57 solarius *L*ᵃᶜ; Solaris *P*

the carbuncle which shines at night, or the pantaura which contains in itself the powers of all stones as gold does of metals, and the Sun of stars.[7] Many things, then, are indicated for us in the above lists, from which, provided you can manage it, you will be able to compound electuaries or unguents when the Sun is dignified for fostering either internally or externally the heart, the stomach, and the head, that the spirit may thence become Solar; I mean with that blood I mentioned and the hearts of those animals, and with the leaves and fruits of the aforesaid trees, likewise with flowers and herbs and gold-leaves and also powders of gems; to these, you should also add saffron, balsam, sweet calamus, frankincense, musk, amber, aloe-wood, ginger, mastic, spikenard, cinnamon, doronicum, rind of citron, zedoary, nutmeg, mace, cloves, with yellow honey or with the oil of balsam, of mastic, of laurel, of spikenard. From all these things, I say, or at least from many of them, you should compound something while the Sun is dignified. Begin to use it, too, under his domination, whilst you also put on Solar clothes and live in, look at, smell, imagine, think about, and desire Solar things. Likewise you should imitate both the dignity and the gifts of the Sun in your life. You should pass your time among Solar men and plants; you should touch laurel continually.

But it would be safer for your health if you would mix with the Solar, things that are Jovial and at the same time Venereal—Venereal moisture especially, such as the water and juice of roses and violets, because it moderates the Solar heat. But medicines of this kind I have already partly compounded, partly recounted as compounded by others, partly [taken from others but] also modified by blending, in the first book, *On Caring for Learned People*, and then in the book *On a Long Life*. Likewise, I have specified in the book *Against the Plague* which herbs have from the Sun and Jupiter a wonderful power against the plague and poison, among which the "Perforata" is called "Daemon-router."[8] It is thought to remove harmful vapors of evil daemons by a power none other than that of the celestial Graces. And if there is any other power among herbs or a gem such as coral, the same thing seems to produce it. Assuredly the lunar herb recounted by Mercurius with bluish, round leaves, which shoots forth one leaf per day when the Moon is waxing and drops one when she is waning,[9] promises lunar years to him who uses it. But now let us return to images and make a second beginning.

De virtute imaginum secundum antiquos
atque medicinarum; et quomodo medicinae
sint longe validiores quam imagines.

Cap. XV.

Si lapillos quos paulo ante Phoebeos narravimus nactus fueris, nihil opus erit imagines eis imprimere. Suspendes itaque collo comprehensos auro crocei serici filis, quando Sol sub Ariete vel Leone percurrit ascenditque, vel medium tenet coelum aspicitque Lunam. Multo vero potentiores in serie Lunae lapillos narrat Proculus: primum quidem selinitim, qui non modo figura Lunam imitetur, sed et motu, circumeatque cum Luna. Hunc si forte reppereris et argento circumdatum argenteo filo collo suspenderis, Luna Cancrum vel Taurum subeunte angulosque tenente sibi convenientes, spiritum inde tuum reddes postremo Lunarem; dum videlicet calefactus abs te lapillus ipse Lunaris virtutem suam tuis assidue spiritibus inserit. Alterum vero recenset lapillum helioselinon cognomento, qui Solis Lunaeque coniunctae Soli naturaliter habet imaginem. Hunc ergo quisquis argento inclusum deaurato similibusque collo filis admoverit, quando Luna in domicilio suo vel Solis in eodem minuto cum Sole congreditur suosque teneat angulos, Solarem simul atque Lunarem spiritum reportabit, aut saltem talem qualis evadit Luna per centrum copulata Soli. Hic vero tu vides dispersas Phoebi dotes velut Osyridis membra sororem eius Phoebem velut Isidem congregare.

Sed utinam Solarem alicubi lapidem facile reperiremus vel Lunarem adeo in eorum ordine praepotentem, quemadmodum sub serie septentrionalis poli magnetem habemus et ferrum. Solarem profecto ferunt invenisse apud Indos Apollonium Theaneum lapidem scilicet nomine pantauram, ignis instar micantem, sub terra passus quattuor nascentem, cui tantum spiritus insit, ut tumeat et plerunque scindatur terra, ubi eiusmodi lapis concipitur; ita ceteros ad se lapillos trahens, sicut magnes ferrum. Sed lapis hic Herculeus ad se contemplandum vehementius adhuc nos impraesentia rapit. Videmus in specula nautarum, indice poli, libratum acum affectum in extremitate magnete moveri ad Ursam, illuc videlicet trahente magnete, quoniam et in lapide hoc praevalet virtus Ursae et hinc transfertur in ferrum et ad Ursam trahit utrunque. Virtus autem eiusmodi tum ab initio infusa est, tum continue Ursae ra-

---

1 plebeos *Lw*^ac   2 auro] cum *P*   6 Luna *P*   9 reddet *z*   14 tenet *P*   16 *post* dotes *add.* et *x*   21 pantaurum *z*   29 Virtus *om. P*

*On the Power Which, according to the Ancients,
Both Images and Medicines Possess;
and on the Factors Which Make Medicines
Far More Powerful Than Images.*

Chap. XV

If you have acquired the gems which we listed as Phoebean a little while ago, there will be no need to imprint images on them. Accordingly, hang them set in gold from your neck on threads of yellow silk, when the Sun is in Aries or Leo and is ascending or else occupies the mid-heaven and aspects the Moon. But Proclus recounts that in their series the gems of the Moon are much more powerful. The first of these is selenite, which imitates the Moon not only in shape but even in motion, for it turns with the Moon. If by chance you should find one of these and suspend it from your neck set in silver by a silver thread when the Moon is entering Cancer or Taurus and occupies the cardines appropriate for her, from this you will eventually render your spirit Lunar, while the Lunar gem, being heated by your flesh, continually inserts its power into your spirit. But he lists another gem, helioselinon by name, which has on it by nature the image of the Sun and Moon in conjunction.[1] If therefore anyone applies it, set in gold-plated silver, by threads of similar material when the Moon comes together in the same minute with the Sun while she is in her house or in his and occupies her cardines, he will gain a spirit that is both Solar and Lunar, or at least such as the Moon becomes when she is conjoined to the Sun by their being centered on the same celestial longitude. When this happens, you see Phoebe the sister of Phoebus gathering up his scattered gifts just as Isis gathered the members of Osiris.

But O that somewhere we might easily find a Solar or Lunar stone so overpowering in its order, as we have in the lodestone and iron in the order of the Northern Pole-star! True, they do report that Apollonius of Tyana found among the Indians a Solar stone, pantaura by name, shining like fire, originating four paces under the earth, in which so much spirit inheres, that the earth swells and often bursts where it is conceived; and it attracts other gems to itself just as a lodestone does iron. But the latter Herculean stone, since it is at hand, more strongly snatches our attention yet again to itself.[2] In the lookouts of sailors, to tell them where the Pole is, we see that a balanced needle influenced on its end by a lodestone points towards the Bear; this happens because the lodestone draws it in that direction, since the power of the Bear prevails in this stone; and from there it is transferred into the iron and pulls both toward the Bear. Moreover this sort of power both was infused from the beginning

diis vegetatur. Forsitan ita se habet succinum ad polum alterum et ad paleas. 30
   Sed dic interea cur magnes trahat ubique ferrum—non quia simile, alioquin et magnetem magnes traheret multo magis ferrumque ferrum; non quia superior in ordine corporum, immo superius est lapillo metallum. Quid ergo? Ambo quidem ordine Ursam sequente clauduntur, sed superiorem in ipsa Ursae proprietate gradum tenet magnes, inferiorem vero ferrum. Superius 35 autem in eodem rerum contextu trahit quidem quod est inferius et ad se convertit, vel aliter quomodolibet agitat aut afficit virtute prius infusa. Inferius vicissim eadem ad superius infusione convertitur vel aliter agitatur vel prorsus afficitur. Sic in serie Solis inferior homo admiratur superiorem, in ordine Iovio veneratur, in Martio timet, in Venereo inferior ad superiorem 40 rapitur amoris ardore deseritque seipsum, in Mercuriali semper hic discit vel persuadetur ab illo, in Lunari motum hic ab illo saepius exorditur, in Saturnali quietem.
   Ego autem cum haec explorata hactenus habuissem, admodum gratulabar cogitabamque iuvenis adhuc magneti pro viribus insculpere coelestis Ursae 45 figuram, quando Luna melius illuc aspiciat, et ferreo tunc filo collo suspendere. Sperabam equidem ita demum virtutis me sideris illius compotem fore. Sed cum diutius explorassem, inveni tandem sideris illius influxus Saturnales esse plurimum atque Martiales. Accepi a Platonicis malos daemonas plurimum septentrionales existere. Quod etiam Hebraeorum astronomi confitentur, 50 noxios Martiosque daemonas in septentrione ponentes, propitios autem et Iovios in meridie. Didici a theologis et ab Iamblicho imaginum fictores a daemonibus malis occupari saepius atque falli. Vidi equidem lapillum Florentiam advectum ex India, ibi e capite draconis erutum, rotundum ad nummi figuram, punctis ordine quam plurimis quasi stellis naturaliter insignitum, 55 qui aceto profusus movebatur parumper in rectum, immo obliquum, mox ferebatur in gyrum, donec exhalaret vapor aceti. Existimavi equidem lapillum eiusmodi coelestis Draconis habere naturam atque quasi figuram, motum quoque illius accipere, quatenus per aceti seu vini valentioris spiritum Draconi illi sive firmamento familiarior redderetur. Hunc igitur qui gestaret et 60 aceto saepe perfunderet, vim aliquam forte Draconis illius acciperet, qui geminis anfractibus hinc quidem Ursam Maiorem implicat, inde Minorem. Extat et prope Scorpionem Serpentarius quasi homo serpente cinctus, manu dextra caput serpentis tenens, sinistra caudam, genibus quasi flexis, capite

---

31 trahet *y;* trahit *z*   51 proprios *x*   52 ab *om. z*   Zamblicho *Lw*^{ac}   56 perfusus *P*   61 saepe] semper *P*

and also grows continually by the rays of the Bear. Perhaps amber behaves in this way towards the other Pole even as it does towards straw.[3]

But tell me, while we are on this subject, why does the lodestone everywhere draw iron? — not because they are similar, otherwise lodestones would draw lodestones much more readily and iron, iron. Not because lodestones are superior in the order of bodies; on the contrary, metal is superior to gem. Why then? Both are comprised in the order depending on the Bear, but the lodestone holds the superior rank in the very property of the Bear; iron, however, the inferior. The superior draws what is inferior in the same chain of beings and turns it towards itself, or else otherwise agitates it in some way or other, or influences it by a power infused beforehand. The inferior in turn by the same infusion is turned towards the superior or otherwise agitated or deeply influenced. Thus in the series of the Sun the inferior person admires the superior; in the Jovial order he honors him; in that of Mars, he fears him; in the Venereal, the inferior is swept away with the ardor of love for the superior and abandons himself; in the Mercurial, he always learns of, or is persuaded by, him; in the Lunar he is frequently set in motion by him; in the Saturnine, put to rest.

As soon as I had explored these things thus far, while I was still a youth, I greatly rejoiced, and I planned to engrave a lodestone as best I could with the figure of the celestial Bear when the Moon was in one of her better aspects with it and then to suspend it from my neck with an iron thread. Then at last, I was hoping, I would share in the power of that constellation. But when I had explored further, I found in the end that the influence of that constellation is very Saturnine and Martial. I learned from the Platonists that evil demons are mostly Northern, which even the Hebrew Astronomers confess, placing harmful Martial daemons in the North, propitious and Jovial ones in the South.[4] I learned from the theologians and Iamblichus that makers of images are often possessed by evil daemons and deceived.[5] I personally have seen a gem at Florence imported from India, where it was dug out of the head of a dragon, round in the shape of a coin, inscribed by nature with very many points in a row like stars, which when doused with vinegar moved a little in a straight line, then at a slant, and soon began going around, until the vapor of the vinegar dispersed.[6] For my part, I thought a gem of this kind had the power of the celestial Dragon and almost its picture [in the points]; that it received also its motion, whenever through the spirit of vinegar or strong wine it was rendered more responsive to that Dragon or the heavens. Whoever wore this, therefore, and often doused it with vinegar would perhaps borrow some of the power of that Dragon which with his two coils enfolds on one side the Great Bear and on the other, the Little. There is also near Scorpio the Serpentarius [= Ophiucus], as it were a man girded with a serpent, holding the head of the serpent with his right hand, his tail with his left, with knees somewhat bent,

paulum resupino. Legi equidem Magos Persarum regi consuluisse, ut imagi- 65
nem hanc lapidi imprimeret haematiti, quem aureo clauderet anulo ita tamen, ut inter lapillum atque aurum serpentariae radicem insereret. Hoc
enim anulo gestantem contra venenum morbosque venenosos tutum fore, videlicet si Luna Serpentarium aspiciente feceris. Hanc imaginem Petrus Aponensis confirmavit. Ego vero, si hanc anulus ille vim habet, arbitror non tam 70
per figuram quam per materias eiusmodi et hoc pacto temporeque compositas sibi coelitus vendicare.

 Memento lapillos nascentes in animalibus, nec inde languentibus, ut in
dracone, gallo, hirundine ceterisque, efficaces existere ferme ut lapilli in terra
nascentes, atque ad easdem referri stellas, ad quas haec animalia pertinent. 75
Hinc alectorius ex ventriculo galli veteris tractus pollet potestate Solari, per
quam Dioscorides ait saepe compertum esse, eum pugnare invictum qui lapillum hunc ore gestaret. Idem ait chelidonium erutum ex hirundine rufum
curare melancholicum et amabilem idoneumque reddere. Quod quidem habet ex Iove per ea quae diximus: scilicet res ubique infra Lunam stellares ex- 80
istere. Confirmatur dictum illud valde Platonicum: hanc mundi machinam
ita secum esse connexam, ut et in terris coelestia sint conditione terrena et in
coelo vicissim terrestria dignitate coelesti, et in occulta mundi vita menteque
regina mundi coelestia insint, vitali tamen intellectualique proprietate simul
et excellentia. Per haec insuper confirmant nonnulli etiam illud magicum: 85
per inferiora videlicet superioribus consentanea posse ad homines temporibus
opportunis coelestia quodammodo trahi, atque etiam per coelestia supercoe-
lestia nobis conciliari vel forsan prorsus insinuari. Sed postremum hoc illi viderint.

 Verum illud arte quadam rite et opportune in unum plurima colligente fieri 90
posse probabile satis (ut diximus) esse videtur, tum rationibus quas in superioribus assignavimus, tum quia eiusmodi multa, quando apud medicum et
astrologum colliguntur, contunduntur, commiscentur, concoquuntur sub sidere certo, dum ipsa per se ratione concoctionis atque fermenti novam paulatim formam subeunt, hanc ipsam acquirunt certo quodam fomento coelesti, 95
radiis tunc intus agentibus, ideoque coelestem. Metallum vero vel lapillus
quando momento sculpitur, non videtur novam accipere qualitatem, sed figuram; neque motio illa per debitos digestionis gradus, quos alteratio naturalis atque generatio solet observare, progeditur. Cum vero natura coelestis
tanquam inferioris naturae regula soleat tenore quodam progredi naturali et 100

---

65 paulatim *P*   71 per² *om. P*   75 ad¹ *om. z*   77 quem *z*   86 per] pro *z*

his head bent back a bit. I have read, in fact, that the Magi counseled the Persian king that he should engrave this image on the stone haematite, and set it in a golden ring, but in such a way that between the gem and the gold they would insert the root of the snake-weed. For when wearing this ring you would be safe from poison and poisonous diseases, provided, of course, you make it when the Moon aspects Serpentarius. Pietro d'Abano has confirmed this image.[7] But I think that if that ring has such power, it is not so much through the figure as through the materials of this kind, composed by this method and at this time, that it claims for itself things from the heavens.

Remember that gems originating in animals, provided they are not sick from them, as in the dragon, the cock, the swallow, etc., are just as effective as those originating in the earth, and they refer to the same stars to which these animals pertain. Hence the cock-stone drawn from the gizzard of an old cock, operates with Solar power; Dioscorides says he often found that through this gem one could fight and not be conquered if he carried it in his mouth.[8] He also says the red swallow-stone dug out of the swallow, cures a melancholic and renders him lovable and capable.[9] It has this from Jupiter through the aforesaid connections, namely, that everywhere beneath the Moon stellar things exist. That Platonic saying is strongly confirmed, that the fabric of the universe is so connected with itself, that not only are there celestial things in earth in an earthly condition; and terrestrial things in turn in the heavens in celestial dignity; but also in the secret Life of the world and in the Mind, Queen of the world, there are celestial things in both a vital and an intellectual property and dignity.[10] Through this, moreover, many people confirm that magic doctrine that by means of lower things which are in accord with higher ones, people can in due season somehow draw to themselves celestial things, and that we can even through the celestials reconcile the super-celestials to us or perhaps wholly insinuate them into us—but this last matter I leave to them.

It seems sufficiently probable, however, as we said, that the former can be done by a certain art of collecting together rightly and at the right time many things in one. It seems probable, in the first place, for the reasons which we have assigned above; and in the second place, because many things of this kind—when they are collected by someone who is both a doctor and an astrologer, pounded up, mixed, and cooked under a certain star, while they gradually take on by the very reason of the concoction and by fermentation a new form—acquire this form by a certain celestial fomentation, the rays then acting within; and, finally, because the form is therefore celestial. But a metal or gem when it is engraved in a moment [as opposed to the lengthy processes described above] does not seem to receive a new quality, only a new shape; that motion does not proceed by those due degrees of arrangement which natural change and generation characteristically observe. Moreover, since the celestial nature usually proceeds as if by the rule of the lower nature at a natural

ita progredientibus aspirare, merito diffidunt plerique imagines eiusmodi coelestem aliquam virtutem habere. Ego quoque ambigo saepius ac, nisi et omnis antiquitas et omnes astrologi vim mirabilem habere putarent, habere negarem. Negarem equidem non omnino, opinor enim, nisi quis aliter persuaserit, ad prosperam valetudinem saltem aliquam habere virtutem, electae 105 praesertim ratione materiae; tametsi multo maiorem inesse pharmacis arbitror et unguentis sidereo favore conflatis. Quid vero voluerim, ubi modo dicebam electae ratione materiae, in sequentibus declarabo.

Quae vero ex Magorum vel astrologorum opinione ad Plotinum interpretandum pro imaginibus allegari possunt, deinceps breviter afferam, si te prius 110 hic admonuero, ne putes probare me usum imaginum, sed narrare. Ego enim medicinis ad coelum temperatis, non imaginibus utor, atque ita ceteris quotidie consulo. Tu vero si concedis Deum rebus infra Lunam mirabiles inseruisse virtutes, mirabiliores concede coelestibus. Praeterea si licere iudicas homini ad prosperam valetudinem inferioribus uti, iudica superioribus quo- 115 que licere, atque inferiora ad superiorum normam sic medicorum artificio temperare, sicut etiam a Deo sunt ab initio temperata.

De potestate coeli. De viribus radiorum,
unde vim sortiri putentur imagines.

Cap. XVI.

Immensa ferme coelestium magnitudo, virtus, motio facit, ut omnes omnium siderum radii terrae molem, quae quasi punctum est ad coelum, momento facillimeque usque ad centrum recti penetrent, quod omnes astronomi confitentur. Ibique, ut placet Pythagoreis atque Platonicis, fortissimi sunt, tum quia recti undique centrum tangunt, tum quia in angustum collecti sunt 5 cuncti. Quorum vehementia materia ibi terrae sicca, procul ab humore remota, prorsus accenditur accensaque extenuatur atque dispergitur per meatus undique et efflat incendia pariter atque sulphur. Sed ignem hunc putant valde caliginosum esse et quasi incendium quoddam luminis expers, sicut in coelo extat expers incendii lumen; ignis autem inter coelestem atque infer- 10

---

101 diffundunt *x*   113 consulto *z*   114 mirabiliore *P*
  1 ferme *post ras. P;* formae *Lw*ᵃᶜ   4 Ibi *z*   tum] cum *x*

pace and so approaches its goal step-by-step, many justly doubt whether images of this kind have any celestial power. I also often doubt it, and, were it not that all antiquity and all astrologers think they have a wonderful power, I would deny it. Of course I would not deny it categorically, for I am of the opinion, unless someone should persuade me otherwise, that especially by reason of the material selected they have at least some power towards good health, even though I think much more of it resides in drugs and unguents compounded with the favor of the stars. But what I meant when I said "by reason of the material selected," I will declare in the chapters that follow.

I will then briefly adduce what can be alleged from the opinion of magicians and astrologers in favor of images in order to interpret Plotinus — provided I will have warned you here at the outset that you must not think I approve the use of images, only recount it [see also "Ad Lectorem" and Apologia]. For as for me, I use medicines tempered in accordance with the heavens, not images, and I daily counsel others to do so. But as for you, if you [now meaning in particular his critics] concede that God has engrafted wonderful powers in things beneath the Moon, concede more wonderful ones to the celestial things. Moreover, if you judge it is lawful for a man to use lower things for good health, judge it is also lawful to use higher things, and even so to temper lower things according to the norm of higher things by the art of medicine as they have been tempered by God from the beginning.

On the Power of the Heavens. On the Powers of the Rays from Which Images Are Thought To Obtain Their Force.

Chap. XVI

Assuredly, as all astronomers confess, the immense size, power, and motion of celestial things brings it about that all the rays of all the stars penetrate in a moment the mass of the earth (which is as a point in relation to the sky) and with consummate ease straight to the center. In the center, as the Pythagoreans and Platonists would have it, the rays are the strongest, both because they touch the center perpendicularly on all sides and because they are all collected in a confined space. By the rays' intensity, the material of the earth there — being dry and far from any moisture — is immediately kindled and, once kindled, is vaporized and dispersed through channels in all directions and blows out both flames and sulfur. But they think that this fire is very dark and, as it were, a sort of flame without light, just as in the heavens light is without flame, whereas the fire between the celestial and the infernal combines light

num lumen cum fervore coniungit. Putant autem ignem e centro flantem ignem esse Vestalem, siquidem Vestam esse terrae vitam numenque putabant. Ideoque Vestae templum veteres in mediis urbibus construebant, ignemque in medio perpetuum collocabant.

Sed ne ulterius pervagemur, concludamus iam si stellarum radii totam mox terram penetrant, negari non facile posse metallum atque lapillum, quando caelantur imaginibus, subito penetrare, eisque miras vel saltem qualescunque imprimere dotes, quandoquidem et in alvis terrae pretiosissima generant. Sed quis neget per haec radios penetrare? Siquidem aer et qualitas eius et sonus minus efficax solida transit subito et sua quadam afficit qualitate. Iam vero si duritia radiis obsisteret penetrantibus, lumen multo citius aerem quam aquam pertransiret, et hanc ocius multo quam vitrum, et vitrum similiter quam crystallum. At cum eodem momento solida, quo liquida cuncta transverberet, perspicue constat duritiam radiis nullo modo resistere. Atque idcirco dicent non esse negandum metalla coelestium radios influxusque suscipere, atque etiam conservare ad tempus tunc sibi coelitus destinatum — conservare, inquam, virtutem quandam ex radiorum concurrentium contactu creatam. Quid vero, si materia durior hoc ipso, quod videtur obsistere causae praepotenti, magis ictibus se exponit? Sic ensis lignum sub lana incidit non incisa lana. Sic radius ille fulmineus corio quandoque non laeso dissolvit in eo metallum.

Cum vero natura coelestis nostro hoc igne incomparabiliter sit praestantior, non est putandum radii coelestis officium esse duntaxat quale opus ignei radii manifeste videmus — scilicet illuminare, calefacere, exsiccare, penetrare, extenuare, dissolvere, quae nostris sensibus notissima sunt — sed multo plures mirabilioresque vires et effectus habere. Alioquin et materia inferior et caducus sensus cum divinitate coeli penitus aequaretur. Sed quis nesciat virtutes rerum occultas, quae speciales a medicis nominantur, non ab elementali natura fieri, sed coelesti? Possunt itaque (ut aiunt) radii occultas et mirabiles ultra notas imaginibus imprimere vires, sicut et ceteris inserunt. Non enim inanimati sunt sicut lucernae radii, sed vivi sensualesque tanquam per oculos viventium corporum emicantes, dotesque mirificas secum ferunt ab imaginationibus mentibusque coelestium, vim quoque vehementissimam ex affectu illorum valido motuque corporum rapidissimo; ac proprie maximeque in spiritum agunt coelestibus radiis simillimum. Agunt insuper in corpora vel durissima, omnia enim haec ad coelum infirmissima sunt. Sunt autem in variis

18 dotes] potes *z*   22 et vitrum *om. z*   23 momenta *z*   26 etiam] et *x*   27 contractu *z*   36 caducis *z*   38–39 quae speciales — occultas *om.* P   45 simillum P

and heat. They believe the fire that breathes out of the center to be Vesta's, since indeed they thought Vesta was the life and patron deity of the earth. And therefore the ancients used to construct the temple of Vesta in the middle of the cities and place a perpetual fire in the middle of it.[1]

But lest we wander too far afield, let us now conclude that if the rays of the stars quickly penetrate the whole earth, it cannot easily be denied that they quickly penetrate metal and precious stone when they are engraved with images, and imprint in them wonderful gifts, or at least gifts of some kind, since indeed they generate supremely precious things in the womb of the earth. But who would deny that rays penetrate through these things? For indeed air and its quality and sound — a less powerful thing — passes right away through solid things and influences them with a quality of its own. Now if hardness stood in the way of penetrating rays, light would pass through air much more quickly than through water, water much more swiftly than glass, and glass much more swiftly than crystal. But since in the same moment it strikes through everything, solid as much as liquid, clearly it is established that hardness offers no resistance whatever to rays. And in this regard, they say, it is undeniable that metals take on rays and influences of the celestials, and even that they conserve them for the time destined for them then by heaven — conserve, I say, a power created by the contact of converging rays. What if, moreover, a harder material by this very fact that it seems to resist a more powerful cause, exposes itself to more impacts? Thus a sword cuts wood under a fleece and the fleece is not cut. Thus that ray which is lightning sometimes melts the metal in a piece of leather while leaving the leather unharmed.

But since celestial nature is incomparably more excellent than this our fire, it should not be supposed that the function of the celestial ray is only such work as we sensibly perceive a ray of fire doing — namely, to illuminate, warm, dry, penetrate, rarefy, melt, which are well known to our senses — but that it has much more and more wonderful powers and effects. Otherwise, inferior matter and transitory senses would be completely equated with the divinity of the heavens. But who does not know that the occult virtues of things, which are called "specific virtues" by natural philosophers, are made not by the elemental nature, but by the celestial? And so the rays can (as they say) imprint in images forces occult and wonderful beyond those we know, just as they introduce them into all things. For they are not inanimate like the rays of a lamp, but living and perceiving, since they shine forth through the eyes of a living body [see Apologia below and 3.11, ad init. and note ad loc.], and they bring with them marvelous gifts from the imaginations and minds of the celestials, also a very intense force from their strong mental disposition and from the very rapid motion of their bodies; and they act in particular and to the greatest extent on the spirit, which is most similar to the celestial rays. They act besides on even the hardest bodies, for all these things are very weak before the heavens.

stellis variae quoque vires, et idcirco in radiis earum inter se variae. Praeterea in radiorum ictibus aliter atque aliter incidentibus virtutes diversae nascuntur. Denique in concursibus radiorum mutuis aliter atque aliter, et hic aut ibi, et tunc aut alias effectis diversae subito vires suboriuntur, multo magis atque citius quam in aliis atque aliis elementorum qualitatumque elementalium mixtionibus, multo etiam citius quam in tonis et numeris apud musicum aliter et aliter concinentibus. Si haec diligenter consideraveris, forsitan non diffides, dicent, subito quodam radiorum iactu vires imaginibus imprimi atque ex diverso iactu diversas.

Numquid ergo tam cito? Mitto fascinationes repentino quodam intuitu factas et amores acerrimos statim accensos radiis oculorum, qui et ipsi sunt fascinamenta quaedam, quod in libro *De amore* probamus. Mitto quam cito rubens oculus inficiat intuentem, et speculum intuens femina menstruosa. Nonne et familiae quaedam apud Illyricos et Triballos iratae intuitu homines interemisse feruntur, et feminae quaedam in Scythia idem facere consuevisse? Et catoblepae regulique serpentes radiorum ex oculis iactu homines perimunt. Torpedo quoque marina tactu etiam procul per virgam manum subito stupefacit. Echinus praeterea pisciculus grandem solo tactu navem sistere fertur. Phalangia quinetiam in Apulia ictu quopiam vel occulto spiritum animumque repentino stupore permutant. Quid rabiosus canis facit vel non apparente morsu? Quid scopa? Deinde quid arbutus? Nonne levissimo tactu venenum concitant atque rabiem? An ergo negabis coelestia oculorum suorum radiis, quibus nostra contuentur simul atque contingunt, statim miranda perficere? Iam vero gravida mulier tactu statim signat membrum hominis nascituri rei desideratae nota. An vero dubitabis radios aliter aliterve tangentes diversa conficere? Cum et tu, helleborum herbam colligens, sive folium deorsum trahas sive sursum, hoc subito tactu causa sis helleboro, ut deorsum educat humores aut sursum. Nonne ab initio rei cuiusque generandae coelestes influxus concoctione materiae digestioneque perfecta non tam tempore quam momento dotes mirificas largiuntur? Nonne suffragante coeli vultu innumerabiles saepe ranae similesque animantes ex arenis momento prosiliunt? Tanta est in materiis praeparatis potentia coeli, tanta celeritas. Denique si ignis hoc habet, ut tempore quam brevissimo faciat quae cetera longo ob id praecipue quod est coelo simillimus, quisnam dubitet coelum magna quasi

---

47 in *om. L*   53 et] atque *z*   54 ictu *P*   55 ictu *P*   57 *post* statim *add. in marg.* et oportune *P* sunt *om. z*   58 quod] quae *z*   64 praeterea] quoque *z*   pisculus *z*   *post* solo *add.* praeterea *z* 71 dubitavit *z*   79 ignis] signis *P*

There are also in various stars various forces; and they differ among themselves in just this respect of their rays. Besides, from the impacts of the rays falling in one way and another, diverse powers arise. Finally, diverse powers come into being in the combinations of rays with each other of one sort or another, here and there, effected at this time or that; they arise right away much more and faster than in such and such mixtures of elements and elemental qualities, much faster even than in tones and rhythms in music combining in this way or in that. If you would diligently consider these things, perhaps you will not doubt, they will say, but that instantly with an emission of rays forces are imprinted in images, and divers forces from a different emission.

But is it so quick as all that? I pass over fascinations achieved by a sudden glance and very passionate loves instantly kindled by rays from the eyes, which also are fascinations of a sort, as I prove in the book *De amore*.[2] Nor will I mention how quickly an inflamed eye afflicts whoever looks at it and how a menstruous woman affects a mirror by looking in it.[3] Isn't it said that certain families among the Illyrians and Triballi, when they were angry, killed people by looking at them and that certain women in Scythia did this habitually?[4] And down-lookers and the serpents called reguli kill people by shooting rays from their eyes.[5] Also the marine torpedo-fish numbs instantly the hand that touches it even at a distance with a rod. In addition, the little fish echinus is said to stop a great ship, and only with a touch. Furthermore, by a bite, even if invisible, the phalangium-spiders in Puglia suddenly transmute the spirit and mind into a stupor.[6] What can a mad dog accomplish even without an apparent bite? What the broom? What the wild strawberry tree?[7] Doesn't their lightest touch excite poison and madness? In the light of all this, are you going to deny that the celestials with the rays of their eyes with which they both look at us and touch us, achieve wonders in an instant? But now a pregnant woman instantly by touch stamps a bodily part of the person who is about to be born with a mark of something she desires [alludes to a birthmark resembling a strawberry, a fruit pregnant women are said to crave]. Are you then going to doubt nevertheless that rays touching in this way or that accomplish diverse things? — since even you yourself, when in collecting the herb hellebore you pull the leaf either downwards or upwards, by this sudden touch are the cause determining whether the hellebore evacuates the humors downwards or upwards. From the beginning of any thing that is to be generated, do not celestial influences bestow wonderful gifts in the concoction of the matter and in its final coming together, not so much during a period of time as in an instant? Do not innumerable frogs and similar animals often, when the face of the heavens favors it, leap forth out of the sand in a moment? Such is the power of the heavens in well-disposed material, such the swiftness. Finally, if fire has this property, that it can do in the briefest time ever what other things do in a long time chiefly because it is most similar to the heavens, who would

momento perficere etiam in materia minus parata, sicut flamma solet ingentior? Quid ergo dubitas, inquiunt, in imagine construenda ferme similiter agere coelum?

Dices, opinor, sicut et ego dicebam, naturales hic alterationis gradus abesse. Qui sane defectus minuit quidem coeleste donum, nec tamen penitus auferre videtur. Nolunt enim physici ex quolibet metallo vel lapide imaginem fabricari, sed certo, in quo quidem natura coelestis virtutem olim ad hoc ipsum quod optatur naturaliter incohaverit, et quasi iamiam perfecerit, ut in sulphure flammam. Quam sane virtutem tunc demum perficiat, quando materia haec per artem sub simili quodam influxu coelesti vehementer agitatur, et agitata calescit. Itaque ars suscitat incohatam ibi virtutem, ac dum ad figuram redigit similem suae cuidam coelesti figurae, tunc suae illic ideae prorsus exponit, quam sic expositam coelum ea perficit virtute, qua coeperat, exhibens quasi sulphuri flammam. Sic potentia quaedam ad rapiendas paleas coelitus data succino, quodammodo debilis, saepe per frictionem calefactionemque facta validior, subito rapit. Similem virtutem Serapio scribit datam lapidi albugedi quasi hyacintho simili, sed non prius trahere paleas quam capilli hoc lapide perfricentur.

Sic item lapis ille Iovius bezaar, id est a morte liberans, quem descripsimus in libro *Contra pestem,* vim ab initio contra venenum accepit ab Iove, sed non usque adeo validam, ut eandem tradere possit materiis aliis exercendam. At vero cum primum sub Scorpionis coelestis influxu figuram superni illius acceperit, perfectam contra scorpiones subito vim reportare putatur, quam mastici communicare valeat aut thuri. Eadem quoque de hyacintho, topazio, smaragdo ceterisque ratio est habenda, ut fabrica figurarum non alibi efficaciam habeat, quam ubi materia cum stella congruit et effectu, a qua hunc faber exoptat accipere; ac praeterea ubi haec ipsa materia quasi iam talis est ab initio, qualem affectas reddere per figuram. Nullis ergo materiis ad imagines uti consulunt, nisi his ipsis quae tibi notae sunt hanc ipsam ferme iam vim habere quam cupis. Lapillorum itaque vires atque metallorum diligentissime perscrutari iubent, intereaque meminisse inter lapillos quidem carbunculum in tenebris coruscantem atque pantauram praecipue Soli subesse, sapphyrum Iovi, smaragdum Veneri, Mercurio, Lunae. Praeterea metalla praeter aurum et argentum vix ullam ad haec habere virtutem. Tutioremque in his rationem fore, si aurum quidem purum ad Solem referas atque Iovem: ad illum quidem propter colorem, ad hunc autem propter temperatam commixtionem, nihil enim Iove et auro temperatius. Purum vero argentum ad

---

85 subesse *z*   87 virtute *P*   107 est *om. z*   108 Nullius *z*   112 pantaurum *z*

doubt that the heavens can accomplish great things almost in a moment, even in unprepared material, such as a larger fire generally does? In the light of all this, why do you doubt, they say, that the heavens act in practically the same way during the construction of an image?

I suppose you will say, just as I too used to do, that here the natural steps of change are absent. Certainly this lack diminishes the celestial gift, but it seems not to take it away completely. For natural philosophers do not intend the image to be made of just any metal or stone, but of a certain one in which the celestial nature has initiated some time ago the power for what is desired and already almost perfected it, as it does the flame in the sulfur. It then finally perfects this power when this material is violently agitated by art under a similar celestial influence and begins to get warm from the agitation. And so art arouses inchoate power there, and when it has reduced it to a figure similar each to its own celestial figure, then forthwith it exposes it there to its own Idea [see 3.1]; when the material is thus exposed, the heavens perfect it by that power with which they had also begun it, tendering as it were the flame to the sulfur. Just so a somewhat weak power to snatch up straws, given to amber by the heavens, after it has been strengthened by friction and heating suddenly snatches them up. Serapion writes that a similar power is given to the stone albugedi, similar to a jacinth; but that it will not attract the straws until it has been rubbed over hair.[8]

So likewise, that Jovial stone bezoar (which means "liberating from death") which we have described in our book *Against the Plague*, initially got from Jupiter its power against poison, but a power not strong enough to be communicable to other materials.[9] But as soon as under the influence of the celestial Scorpion it receives the figure of that one above, it is said to obtain forthwith a perfect force against scorpions which it can communicate to mastic or to frankincense. The same rule holds also in the case of jacinth, topaz, emerald, and the rest, that the making of figures has no efficacy except in cases where it is similar in material and effect to some star from which the maker wants to receive this effect; and, in addition, where the material itself is already from the beginning of almost such a quality as you desire to render it through the figure. Hence they counsel you to use no materials for images but those which you know to possess already almost that very force which you desire. And so they order you to scrutinize most diligently the forces of gems and metals, and in the meantime to call to mind the following: that among gems, the carbuncle sparkles in darkness and pantaura particularly belongs to the Sun, the sapphire to Jupiter, the emerald to Venus, Mercury, and the Moon; in addition, that metals, aside from gold and silver, have scarcely any power for images. It will be a safer rule in these matters if you refer pure gold to the Sun and Jupiter — to the Sun on account of its color, to Jupiter on account of its temperate makeup, for nothing is more temperate than Jupiter and gold. Refer

Lunam, sed ad Iovem simul atque Venerem aurum argento permixtum. Praeterea imaginem efficaciorem fore, si virtus in materia eius elementalis conveniat cum speciali eiusdem virtute naturaliter insita, atque haec insuper cum virtute altera speciali per figuram coelitus capienda. Denique figuras inferiores et formas coelestibus conformari, inde perdisces (ut aiunt) quod Perseus truncato Medusae capite futuram nonnullis obtruncationem portendere consuevit multaque similiter, et Lunam aliosque planetas sub certis signis certa in nobis membra movere non dubitant.

Quam vim habeant figurae in coelo atque sub coelo.

Cap. XVII.

Sed ne figuris nimium forte diffidas, meminisse iubebunt in regione hac sub Luna elementali elementarem quoque qualitatem posse quam plurimum, in transmutatione videlicet ad aliquid elementale tendente: calorem scilicet et frigus et humorem atque siccitatem. Qualitates autem quae minus elementares materialesve sunt, scilicet lumina, id est colores, numeros quoque similiter et figuras ad talia forsitan minus posse, sed ad coelestia munera (ut putant) valere permultum. Nam et in coelo lumina et numeri et figurae sunt ferme omnium potentissima, praesertim si nulla sit ibi materia, quod Peripatetici plerique putant. Sic enim figurae, numeri, radii, cum non alia substineantur ibi materia, quasi substantiales esse videntur. Atque cum in ordine rerum mathematicae formae physicas antecedant, tanquam simplices quidem magis et minus egenae, merito in antecentibus mundi gradibus, id est coelestibus, auctoritatem sibi maximam vendicant, ut non minus inde fiat numero, figura, luce quam elementari quadam proprietate. Huius quidem auctoritatis habetur etiam sub Luna signum. Qualitates enim valde materiales plurimis rerum speciebus sunt communes, eisque quodammodo permutatis non usquequaque species commutantur. Figurae autem numerique partium naturalium proprietatem cum specie inseparabilem peculiaremque possident, utpote quae coelitus una cum speciebus destinata fuerunt. Immo et cum ideis maximam habent in mente mundi regina connexionem. Atque cum ipsae numerique species quaedam sint ideis ibi propriis designatae, ni-

---

125 memora *z*
2 Luna *yz*; Lunam *LPwx*   4 Qualitas *z*   8 si *om. z*   10 quali *z*   15 etiam *add. in marg. L*

pure silver to the Moon, but gold mixed with silver to Jupiter together with Venus. Besides this, the image will be more efficacious if the elemental power in its material agrees with the specific power naturally inherent in the same material, and this, in addition, with the other specific power to be seized from the heavens through the figure. Finally, they say that the lower figures and forms conform to the celestial ones; from this you will learn, so they say, that Perseus [the constellation] when he has cut off Medusa's head usually portends a beheading in store for some people, and so forth; and they do not doubt that the Moon and the other planets under certain signs move certain parts of our bodies.

What Power Is in Figures — Those in the Sky and Those beneath the Sky.
Chap. XVII

To keep you from distrusting figures too much, astrologers will order you to remember that in this elemental region beneath the Moon, a quality that is likewise elemental can do a great deal in a transmutation that is directed toward some end that is itself elemental. (Elemental qualities are, of course, heat, cold, moisture, and dryness.) Qualities, however, which are less elemental or material, such as lights (that is, colors), similarly also numbers and figures, are perhaps less powerful for such ends; but to obtain celestial gifts (as they think) they are very powerful. For in the heavens, lights, numbers, and figures are practically the most powerful of all, especially if, as many Peripatetics believe, there is no matter up there. For thus figures, numbers, and rays, since there they are sustained by no other material, seem practically to constitute what things are made of ["quasi substantiales"].[1] And since, in the order of being, mathematical forms precede physical ones, being more simple and less defective, then deservedly they claim the most dignity in the primary — that is, the celestial — levels of the cosmos, so that consequently as much comes about from number, figure, and light as from some elemental property.[2] Of this dignity there is evidence even here beneath the Moon. For the extremely material qualities are common to most species of things; and if you change these qualities somewhat, the species are not everywhere altered. But the figures and numbers of natural parts possess a property peculiar to a given species and inseparably linked to it; they have been appointed in the heavens along with the species. Indeed, they have the greatest affinity with the Ideas in Mind, the Queen of the world. And since figures themselves and numbers are species of a sort, represented in Mind by their own Ideas,[3] they indisputably get their

mirum vires inde proprias sortiuntur. Ideoque tum species naturalium certis figuris, tum motus et generationes et mutationes certis numeris astringuntur.
De lumine vero quid dicam? Est enim actus intelligentiae vel imago. Colores autem sunt lumina quaedam. Quamobrem ubi lumina, id est colores, figurasque et numeros astrologi dicunt in materiis nostris ad coelestia praeparandis posse quam plurimum, non temere (ut aiunt) debes ista negare.

Non ignoras concentus per numeros proportionesque suas vim habere mirabilem ad spiritum et animum et corpus sistendum, movendum, afficiendum. Proportiones autem ex numeris constitutae quasi figurae quaedam sunt, velut ex punctis lineisque factae, sed in motu. Similiter motu suo se habent ad agendum figurae coelestes. Hae namque harmonicis tum radiis, tum motibus suis omnia penetrantibus spiritum indies ita clam afficiunt, ut musica praepotens palam afficere consuevit. Nosti praeterea quam facile multis misericordiam moveat figura lugentis, et quantum oculos imaginationemque et spiritum et humores afficiat statim atque moveat amabilis personae figura. Nec minus viva est et efficax figura coelestis.

Nonne principis in urbe vultus quidem clemens et hilaris exhilarat omnes? Ferox vero vel tristis repente perterret? Quid ergo coelestium vultus, dominos omnium terrenorum, adversus haec efficere posse putas? Quippe cum etiam coeuntes ad prolem plerunque vultus, non solum quales ipsi tunc agunt, sed etiam quales imaginantur, soleant filiis diu postea nascituris imprimere, vultus eadem ratione coelestes materias confestim suis notis inficiunt, in quibus si quando diu latitare videntur, temporibus deinde suis emergunt.

Vultus autem coeli sunt figurae coelestes. Potes vero facies illic appellare figuras ceteris ibi stabiliores; vultus autem figuras quae magis ibi mutantur. Aspectus quoque inter se stellarum motu quotidiano confectos vultus appellare potes similiter et figuras, nam hexagoni, pentagoni, tetragoni nominantur.

Esto, dicet quispiam. Sint, ut placet, potentissimae ad efficiendum figurae coelestes. Verum quid hoc ad figuras imaginum artificio factas? Respondebunt non id potissimum contendere, ut potentissimae per se ad agendum sint nostrae figurae, sed ut paratissimae ad actiones et vires figurarum coelestium capiendas, quatenus opportune fiunt dominantibus illis atque examussim ad illas configurantur. Exigit enim figura illa figuram. Nonne sonante cithara quadam altera reboat? Ob id tantum, si et ipsa similem figuram habeat atque e conspectu sit posita, et fides in ea positae et intentae similiter. Quidnam hic efficit, ut cithara subito patiatur a cithara, nisi situs aliquis

---

29 *post* movendum *add.* et *z*   45–46 Vultus autem—stabiliores *om. P*   48 pentagoni *om. z*
57 subito *om. P*   patitur *z*

distinctive forces from up there. And therefore not only are natural species delimited by particular figures, but also natural motions, generations, and mutations are delimited by particular numbers.

What shall I say about light? For it is the action, or, if you will, the image, of the Intellect.[4] And colors are particular lights. On which account (so astrologers say), you should not rashly deny their statement that lights—that is, colors, figures, and numbers—can do a great deal towards preparing our materials for celestial things.[5]

You are not unaware that harmonious music through its numbers and proportions has a wonderful power to calm, move, and influence our spirit, mind, and body. Well, proportions constituted out of numbers are almost figures of a sort, made, as it were, out of points and lines, but in motion. And similarly celestial figures by their own motion dispose themselves for acting; for by their harmonious rays and motions penetrating everything, they daily influence our spirit secretly just as overpowering music generally does openly. Besides, you know how easily a mourning figure moves pity in many people, and how much a figure of a lovable person instantly affects and moves the eyes, imagination, spirit, and humors; no less living and efficacious is a celestial figure.

In a city, does not the countenance of a prince, if mild and cheerful, cheer everybody up, but if fierce or sad, instantly terrify them? What then do you think the countenances of the celestials, the lords of all earthly things, are able to effect in comparison to these?[6] I think that inasmuch as even people uniting to beget offspring often imprint on children to be born long afterwards not only the sort of countenances they then wear but even the sort of countenances they are merely imagining, in the same way the celestial countenances rapidly impart to materials their characteristics. If sometimes the characteristics seem to lie hidden there a long time, eventually in their season they emerge.

The countenances of the sky are the celestial figures. You may call "faces" those figures there which are more stable than the others; but "countenances" those up there which change more. You may also call the aspects composed by the daily motion of the stars in relation to each other, "countenances" and likewise "figures"; for aspects are called hexagons, pentagons, and tetragons.

"So be it," someone will say, "let celestial figures be as powerful in operation as you like, but what does this have to do with the figures of images made artificially?" Astrologers do not especially argue, they will respond, that our figures are the most powerful agents in themselves, but that they are the best prepared for catching the actions and forces of the celestial figures, insofar as they are made at the right time when the celestial ones are dominant and are made to conform exactly to them. For that figure perfects this figure. When one lute sounds, does not another echo it? It only does so if it has a similar figure, and is placed opposite, and the strings in it are similarly placed and tuned. What do you think causes lute to respond instantly to lute, but their

et quaedam figura conformis? Figura speculi lenis, concava, nitens, coelo congrua ob hoc ipsum proprie munus tantum coelitus accipit, ut radios Phoebi in se cumulatissime complectatur, et solidissimum quodque ad centrum suum e conspectu locatum repente comburat. Ergo ne dubites, dicent, quin materia quaedam imaginis faciendae, alioquin valde congrua coelo, per figuram coelo similem arte datam coeleste munus tum in se ipsa concipiat, tum reddat in proximum aliquem vel gestantem. Non solum vero figura, sed etiam dispositio pervia, quam diaphanam vocant, inefficax quiddam est et passivum suapte natura. Verumtamen quoniam pervia dispositio est in coelo proprium luminis susceptaculum, ideo ubicunque sub coelo haec vel est naturalis, vel modo aliquo comparatur, subito praesens coeleste lumen acquiritur; atque etiam conservatur, ubi una cum hac vel calor est igneus, ut in flamma, vel est aliquid aerium aqueumve simul et glutinosum, ut in noctilucis et nocticernis et carbunculis atque forsan quodammodo in camphora. Quid inde sequatur pro imaginibus ipse reputa.

Quales coelestium figuras antiqui imaginibus imprimebant;
ac de usu imaginum.

Cap. XVIII.

Aliquis autem quaeret, quas potissimum coeli figuras imaginibus imprimere soleant. Sunt enim ibi formae oculis valde conspicuae et a multis quales sunt quasi depictae, ut Aries, Taurus similesque figurae zodiaci et quae sunt extra zodiacum manifestae. Sunt ibi praeterea formae quam plurimae, non tam visibiles quam imaginabiles per signorum facies, ab Indis et Aegyptiis Chaldaeisque perspectae vel saltem excogitatae: velut in prima facie Virginis virgo pulchra sedens, geminas manu spicas habens, puerumque nutriens. Et reliquae quales describit Albumasar ceterique nonnulli. Sunt denique characteres quidam signorum et planetarum ab Aegyptiis designati. Volunt igitur imaginibus omnia haec insculpi. Ut si quis exspectet proprium a Mercurio beneficium, collocare eum in Virgine debeat vel saltem ibi Lunam cum aspectu Mercurii, et imaginem tunc ex stanno conficere vel argen-

---

58 figura¹] forma *z*   60 complectitur *z*   67 vel *om. z*   68 aliquando *x*   69 construatur Lw^{ac}
10 insculpsi *P*

placement and the fact that they share a like figure? The figure of a mirror — smooth, concave, shining, and shaped like the heavens — receives because of this in particular such a great gift from the heavens, that it gathers to itself most abundantly the rays of Phoebus and instantly burns a very solid thing which is located opposite its center.[7] Therefore you should not doubt, they say, that the material for making an image, if it is in other respects entirely consonant with the heavens, once it has received by art a figure similar to the heavens, both conceives in itself the celestial gift and gives it again to someone who is in the vicinity or wearing it. The same rule holds not only for figure but also for transparent, so-called diaphanous constitution. It is by its own nature something ineffectual and passive. Yet since a transparent constitution is in the heavens the proper receptacle of light, so wherever under the heavens it either exists naturally or is obtained by some means, the celestial light then available is instantly acquired, and also may be stored up,[8] in cases where there is along with this light either fiery heat as in flame, or where there is something airy or watery and at the same time glutinous, as in lanterns, lamps, carbuncles, and perhaps, in a way, in camphor. Ponder for yourself what consequence for images follows from that fact.

What Sorts of Figures of the Celestials the Ancients Engraved in Images; and concerning the Use of Images.

Chap. XVIII

Someone will ask, what figures of the heavens do astrologers usually engrave as images? For there are in the heavens forms which are very conspicuous to the eye, and some which really are just as they have been depicted by many people, as Aries, Taurus, and similar zodiacal figures, and there are those outside the zodiac which we can see. Besides these, up there very many forms exist which are not so much visible as imaginable — those perceived, or at least thought up, by the Indians, Egyptians, and Chaldeans as dwelling throughout all the faces of the signs,[1] for example: in the first face of Virgo, a beautiful girl, seated, holding two ears of grain in her hand and nursing a child. And the rest, as Albumasar and some others describe.[2] Then there are the particular written characters of the signs and planets as delineated by the Egyptians. They want all these, therefore, to be engraved on images. For example, if anyone looks for a special benefit from Mercury, he ought to locate him in Virgo, or at least locate the Moon there in an aspect with Mercury, and then make an image out of tin or silver; he should put on it the whole

to, in qua totum sit Virginis signum et character eius characterque Mercurii. Ac si prima Virginis facie sis usurus, addas etiam figuram quam in prima facie diximus observatam. Similiterque de ceteris.

Postremi quidem imaginum auctores universam earum formam ad coeli similitudinem accepere rotundam. Antiquiores autem, quemadmodum in quodam Arabum collegio legimus, figuram crucis cunctis anteponebant, quia corpora per virtutem agunt ad superficiem iam diffusam. Prima vero superficies cruce describitur, sic enim imprimis habet longitudinem atque latitudinem. Primaque haec figura est, et omnium recta quam maxime, et quattuor rectos angulos continet. Effectus vero coelestium maxime per rectitudinem radiorum angulorumque resultant. Tunc enim stellae magnopere sunt potentes, quando quattuor coeli tenent angulos, immo cardines: orientis videlicet occidentisque et medii utrinque coeli. Sic vero dispositae radios ita coniiciunt in se invicem, ut crucem inde constituant. Crucem ergo veteres figuram esse dicebant tum stellarum fortitudine factam, tum earundem fortitudinis susceptaculum; ideoque habere summam in imaginibus potestatem, ac vires et spiritus suscipere planetarum.

Haec autem opinio ab Aegyptiis vel inducta est vel maxime confirmata, inter quorum characteres crux unus erat insignis, vitam eorum more futuram significans, eamque figuram pectori Serapidis insculpebant. Ego vero quod de crucis excellentia fuit apud Aegyptios ante Christum non tam muneris stellarum testimonium fuisse arbitror, quam virtutis praesagium quam a Christo fuerat acceptura. Astrologos autem qui statim post Christum fuerunt, videntes a Christianis miranda per crucem fieri, nescientes autem vel nolentes in Iesum tanta referre, in coelestia retulisse, quanquam considerare debebant per crucem ipsam absque nomine Iesu miracula minime perpetrari. Convenire quidem imaginibus eam, quia referat fortitudinem planetarum omniumque stellarum, forsitan est probabile; non tamen ob hoc duntaxat ingentem habere potentiam. Posse vero nonnihil una cum ceteris quae necessaria sunt coniunctam ad prosperam forsan corporis valetudinem.

Sed ad narrandas aliorum opiniones, ut coepimus, revertamur. Saturni veteres imaginem ad vitae longitudinem faciebant in lapide de Feyrizech, id est sapphyro, hora Saturni, ipso ascendente atque feliciter constituto. Forma erat homo senex in altiore cathedra sedens vel dracone, caput tectus panno quodam lineo fusco, manus supra caput erigens, falcem manu tenens aut

---

16 eorum *x*   17 accipere *z*   18 qui *x*   25 coeli *om. z*   27 sortitudinis *z*   31 una *z*   35 fuerat] esset *z*   38 debeant *x*   40 omnium *P;* omnium quoque *x*   44 de *om. z*

sign of Virgo and its character and the character of Mercury. And if you are going to use the first face of Virgo, add also the figure which we said has been observed in the first face, and similarly with the rest.

The recent authorities on images have accepted as the general form for these a round shape in imitation of the heavens.[3] The more ancient authorities, however, as we have read in a certain Arabic miscellany, used to prefer above all other figures that of a cross, for the following reason. Bodies act through their power as soon as it has diffused to a plane. But this primary plane [prior to the sphere mentioned above, which represents a further diffusion from point to line to plane to solid] is marked out by a cross, since above all a cross, like a plane, possesses length and breadth. This figure of the cross is primary; also, of all the figures, it is rectilinear in the highest degree, and it has four right angles.[4] Now it is through the perpendicularity of rays and of the Angles that the effects of the celestials most strongly appear; for the stars are much more potent at the time when they occupy the four Angles, or rather cardines, of the sky: that of the East, that of the West, and the mid-heaven on either side. When so positioned, they cast their rays one upon another in such a way as to form a cross. The cross, therefore, said the ancients, is a figure which is made by the strength of the stars and serves as a receptacle of their strength; it therefore possesses the greatest power among images and receives the forces and spirits of the planets.[5]

This opinion was either introduced or principally confirmed by the Egyptians, among whose characters a prominent one was the cross, which signified in their usage the future life; and they would engrave this figure on the breast of Serapis.[6] But I think as follows: What the Egyptians before Christ thought about the excellence of the cross was not so much a testimony of the gifts of the stars as a prophecy of the power that it was going to receive from Christ. Astrologers who came right after Christ, seeing that wonderful things were done by Christians through the cross, but not knowing or not wanting to ascribe such great things to Jesus, ascribed them to the heavens; though they ought to have considered that through the cross itself without the name of Jesus no miracles at all were performed. That a cruciform figure is appropriate to images because it resembles the strength of the planets and all stars, is perhaps probable; but this is not a sufficient reason for it to have such tremendous power. But in concert with the other things which are necessary it is perhaps able to do something towards bodily health.

But let us go back to recounting the opinions of others as we began. To obtain long life, the ancients used to make an image of Saturn from the stone Feyrizech, that is, sapphire, in the hour of Saturn, when he was ascending and fortunately placed. The form was this: an old man sitting on a rather high throne or on a dragon, his head covered with a dark linen cloth, raising his hands above his head, holding in his hand a sickle or some fish, and clothed

pisces, fusca indutus veste. Ad longam vitam atque felicem Iovis imaginem in lapide claro vel albo. Erat homo sedens super aquilam vel draconem, coronatus, hora Iovis, ipso in exaltatione sua feliciter ascendente, croceam induto vestem. Contra timiditatem hora Martis imagines fabricabant prima Scorpionis facie oriente: Martem armatum et coronatum. Ad morbos curandos fingebant Solis imaginem in auro hora Solis, prima facie Leonis ascendente cum Sole: regem in throno, crocea veste, et corvum Solisque formam. Ad laetitiam roburque corporis Veneris imaginem puellarem, poma floresque manu tenentem, croceis et albis indutam, hora Veneris, facie Librae vel Piscium vel Tauri ascendente cum Venere. Imaginem Mercurii ad ingenium et memoriam prima facie Geminorum. Item contra febres sculpebatur Mercurius: homo tela manu tenens, hora Mercurii, surgente Mercurio. Sculpebant hanc in marmore, subinde materiae cuipiam imprimebant languentibus assumendae. Hinc omne genus febrium curari dicebant. Imaginem Lunae ascendente prima facie Cancri ad augmentum. Forma Mercurii: homo sedens in throno, galeratus cristatusque, pedibus aquilinis, sinistra gallum tenens aut ignem, alatus, aliquando super pavonem, dextra tenens calamum, veste varia. Luna: puella pulchra cornuto capite super draconem vel taurum, serpentes supra caput et sub pedibus habens. Ad curandum calculum genitaliumque dolores et ad sanguinem astringendum imaginem hora Saturni, surgente tertia facie Aquarii cum Saturno. Item leonem auro imprimebant, lapidem in formam Solis pedibus revolventem, hora Solis, primo gradu faciei secundae Leonis oriente. Hanc expellendis morbis profuturam existimabant. Ad renum morbos similem faciebant, quando Sol in Corde Leonis coelum medium obtineret, a Petro Aponensi comprobatam et experientia confirmatam, sed hac conditione, ut Iuppiter aut Venus medium aspiciat coelum, planetae vero noxii cadant infortunatique sint. Accepi a Mengo, physico praeclaro, eiusmodi imaginem factam Iove ibidem coniuncto cum Sole liberavisse Ioannem Marlianum, mathematicum nostro seculo singularem, a pavore quo sub tonitru affici consueverat.

Praeterea ad firmandam sanitatem et veneficia devitanda imaginem ex argento fingebant hora Veneris, Luna angulos obtinente ac Venerem feliciter intuente, dummodo dominus sextae domus Venerem aspiciat aut Iovem trino quodam intuitu vel opposito, Mercurius autem non sit infelix. Agebant haec hora diei Solis ultima, ita ut dominus horae decimam teneret coeli plagam. Petrus Aponensis inquit medicum per imaginem infirmum curare posse,

---

50 *post* feliciter *add.* secundae Lw^{ac} 58-59 sculpebatur—Mercurio *om.* z   64 calamum] calvum Lw^{ac} 65 pulchra *om.* z   67 ad *om.* L

in a dusky robe.⁷ For a long and happy life, they made an image of Jupiter in clear or white stone. It was a man crowned, sitting on an eagle or a dragon, wearing a yellow robe, made in the hour of Jupiter when he was fortunately ascending in his exaltation.⁸ Against timidity, in the hour of Mars, when the first face of Scorpio was rising, they fabricated images: Mars armed and crowned.⁹ For curing diseases they fashioned an image of the Sun in gold, in his hour, when the first face of Leo was ascending with him: a king on a throne in a yellow garment and a raven and the form of the Sun.¹⁰ For gaiety and strength of body, a young Venus holding apples and flowers in her hand, dressed in yellow and white, made in the hour of Venus, when the first face of Libra, or of Pisces, or of Taurus, was ascending with her.¹¹ They made the image of Mercury for intelligence and memory when the first face of Gemini was ascending. Likewise against fevers Mercury was engraved: a man holding a javelin in the hour of Mercury when Mercury was rising. They used to carve this image in marble; then they would impress it in some substance or other to be swallowed by those who were sick. They said it cured every kind of fever.¹² For growth, they made an image of the Moon when the first face of Cancer was rising.¹³ The form of Mercury: a man sitting on a throne in a crested cap, with eagle's feet, holding a cock or fire with his left hand, winged, sometimes on a peacock, holding a reed with his right hand, in a multicolored garment.¹⁴ The Moon: a beautiful girl with horns on her head, on a dragon or a bull, having serpents above her head and under her feet.¹⁵ For curing the stone, for pains in the genitals, and for drying up blood, they made an image in the hour of Saturn, when the third face of Aquarius was rising with him.¹⁶ Likewise they would imprint a lion in gold, rolling under his feet a stone in the form of the Sun, in the hour of the Sun, when the first degree of the second face of Leo was rising. They thought this was good for expelling diseases.¹⁷ They made a similar one for kidney diseases when the Sun had attained the mid-heaven in the Heart of the Lion — an image approved by Pietro d'Abano and confirmed by experience, but with this condition, that Jupiter or Venus should aspect the mid-heaven; and that the noxious planets should be cadent and in unfortunate positions.¹⁸ I have heard from Mengo the famous physician that an image of this kind, fashioned when Jupiter was in precise conjunction with the Sun, delivered Giovanni Marliani, the foremost mathematician of our time, from his former fear of thunder.¹⁹

Besides this, to confirm health and to keep from being bewitched, they fashioned an image of silver in the hour of Venus, when the Moon had attained a cardine of heaven and was in a fortunate aspect with Venus, provided that the lord of the sixth place looked at Venus or Jupiter from a trine or opposite aspect; and that Mercury too was not unfortunate. They would do this in the last hour of the Sun's day, in such a way that the lord of the hour occupied the tenth place. Pietro d'Abano says that a doctor can cure the sick by

modo in ea fabricanda observet, ut anguli ascendentis, medii coeli, occidentis sint fortunati, et ascendentis dominus et eadem ratione secunda, sed sexta et dominus eius sit infelix. Ait etiam sanitatem fore firmiorem vitamque longiorem quam ab initio fuerit instituta, si nativitate perspecta fiat imago, in qua haec fortunata ponantur: scilicet illius significator vitae, item vitae datores, tum signa, tum domini, praesertim ascendens eiusque dominus, item coeli medium, locus Solis, pars fortunae, dominus coniunctionis vel praeventionis ante nativitatem factae. Mali quinetiam infortunati cadant. Concludit astrologorum nullum dubitare, quin ad producendam vitam talia conferant.

Prolixum foret dictu, quas per quaelibet signa facies antiqui, et quas Lunae stationes tanquam necessarias in exprimendis imaginibus observabant. Nam in statione Lunae a gradu Virginis decimoseptimo ad finem eius faciebant imagines contra morbos et odia et ad iter felix. In statione a principio Capricorni ad gradum duodecimum contra morbos et discordias atque captivitatem. In statione a gradu duodecimo Capricorni ad gradum vigesimumquintum adversus languorem et carcerem. In statione a gradu quarto Piscium ad gradum eiusdem decimumseptimum ad curandos morbos, ad lucrum, societatem, ad augendas messes. Et in aliis similiter alias vana saepius curiositate machinabantur. Solas vero recensui quae non tam Magum quam medicum redolerent. Nam et medicinam eiusmodi vanam plurimum fore suspicor.

Pro aliis autem magis legitimis medicinarum confectionibus eiusmodi mansiones Lunae arbitror eligendas atque etiam in Ariete gradum sextum, rursus decimumnonum, minuta xxvi.; item in Geminis gradum decimum, minuta li.; in Cancro gradum decimumnonum, minuta xxvi.; in Libra gradum sextum, minuta xxxiiii.; in Capricorno gradum decimumnonum, minuta xxvi.; in Aquario gradum secundum, minuta xvii.; in eodem gradum decimumquintum, minuta viii. Praeterea sententiam Haly mente tenendam: quodlibet signum, quamdiu Sol est in eo, vivum fieri, ceteris dominari, effectum eius prae ceteris evenire, ut illuc Lunam dirigas ad donum inde proprium pro medicinis suscipiendum. Illuc, inquam, id est, ad signum et faciem et maxime gradum, ut si bona Iovis affectas, ad haec directam Lunam erigas vel unitam, quamdiu locum eiusmodi Sol illustrat, ubi proprietas Iovia viget. Similiterque de ceteris.

---

85 dominis *z*   86 sit *om. z*   88 ponatur *xz*   106 granum *z*   110 xvii] xvi *P;* xxvii *z*   111 gradu *z*
sententia *P*   113 illic *z*   115 afferas *P*

an image, provided that he fashions it at a time when the cardines of the Ascendant, the mid-heaven, and the Descendant are fortunate, and likewise the lord of the Ascendant and the second place; but let the sixth place and its lord be unfortunate. Pietro also says that health will be more lasting and life longer than was initially appointed, if after you investigate the person's nativity you make an image in which these fortunate things are inscribed: the significator of that life; likewise the givers of the life, both the signs and their lords, especially the ascendant sign and its lord; likewise the mid-heaven; the location of the Sun; the Part of Fortune; the lord of [the place of] the conjunction or syzygy [of the Sun and Moon, see Ptolemy, *Tetrabiblos*, 3.2] which occurred before the birth. Moreover, pick a time when the evil and unfortunate planets are cadent. No astrologer doubts, Pietro concludes, that such things contribute to a long life.[20]

It would be prolix to say what faces the ancients observed within every sign and what positions of the Moon they held to be necessary for the fashioning of images. For they made images against disease and hatred and for a prosperous journey when the Moon was positioned anywhere from the seventeenth degree of Virgo to its end.[21] They made images against disease, discord, and captivity when she was positioned from the beginning of Capricorn to its twelfth degree.[22] When she was positioned from the twelfth degree of Capricorn to its twenty-fifth degree, they made images against lassitude and prison.[23] In the position from the fourth degree of Pisces to its seventeenth degree, they made images for curing diseases, for profits, for companionship, for increasing the harvest.[24] And in other positions they very often used to contrive other images in their vain curiosity. I enumerate only the ones which savor not so much of magic as of medicine. For even the medicine I suspect to be mostly vain.

But I think such positions of the Moon should be chosen for the sake of other more legitimate preparations of medicine; and also when she is in Aries, the sixth degree, and in the same sign, the nineteenth degree and twenty-sixth minute; likewise in Gemini the tenth degree and fifty-first minute; in Cancer the nineteenth degree and twenty-sixth minute; in Libra the sixth degree and thirty-fourth minute; in Capricorn the nineteenth degree and twenty-sixth minute; in Aquarius the second degree and seventeenth minute; in the same, the fifteenth degree and eighth minute. In addition, you should keep in mind Haly's maxim: Whatever the sign, for so long as the Sun is in it, the sign is made active, it dominates the rest, its effects come to pass more readily than others, so that you should direct the Moon towards it in order to receive from it a gift proper to medicine.[25] Towards it, I say, meaning towards the sign and the face and especially the degree, so that if you want good things from Jupiter, you should erect the Moon, either moving directly towards or united with his signs, faces, and degrees, so long as the Sun is enhancing one of these places where the Jovial property is strong. And the same goes for the rest.

Curiosum vero narratu foret et forte noxium, quas imagines et quemadmodum associandos vel dissociandos inter se animos fabricabant ad afferendam felicitatem vel inferendam calamitatem vel uni cuidam vel domui vel civitati. Ego quidem fieri posse talia non affirmo. Astrologi autem fieri posse putant et quomodo docent, qualia ego narrare non audeo. Porphyrius ubi vitam Plotini magistri sui describit, talia fieri posse confirmat. Atque Olympium Magum et astrologum Aegyptium narrat contra Plotinum Romae talia tentavisse, dum conaretur per imagines vel res eiusmodi siderare Plotinum, sed conatus in auctorem suum ob excelsam Plotini animam fuisse retortos. Albertus quoque Magnus, astrologiae pariter atque theologiae professor, ait in *Speculo,* ubi a licitis discernere se inquit illicita, imagines rite ab astrologis constitutas virtutem effectumque acquirere a figura coelesti. Atque subinde narrat mirabiles earum effectus, quales Thebit Benthorad et Ptolemaeus ceterique astrologi pollicentur. Describitque imagines ad calamitatem alicui prosperitatemque afferendam, quas consilio praetermitto. Et interea confirmat effectum eas habere posse, quanquam et ut vir bonus artis damnat abusum, et ut legitimus theologus orationes suffumigationesque detestatur, quas impii quidam ad daemones imaginibus fabricandis adhibuerunt. Neque tamen reprobat figuras et litteras dictionesque imaginibus impressas ad hoc ipsum duntaxat ut donum aliquod accipiant a figura coelesti. Quod quidem posse per imagines comparari, Petrus Aponensis confirmavit. Immo et affirmavit regionem nescioquam fuisse destructam per imaginem illam, quam Thebit narrat a Phedice astrologo fabricatam.

Thomas Aquinas, dux in theologia noster, magis ista formidat et minus tribuit imaginibus. Tantum namque virtutis duntaxat per figuras coelitus putat acquirere, quantum conducat ad illos effectus, quos solet communiter coelum per herbas resque alias naturales efficere. Non tam quia figura talis sit in ea materia, quam quoniam compositum tale iam positum est in certa quadam artificii specie, qualis cum coelo consentiat. Haec ait in libro *Contra gentiles* tertio, ubi characteres et litteras figuris additas ridet, figuras vero non adeo, nisi pro signis quibusdam ad daemones adiungantur. In libro etiam *De fato* ait constellationes dare ordinem essendi atque perdurandi non solum rebus naturalibus, sed etiam artificiosis; ideo imagines sub certis constellationibus fabricari. At si quid mirabile per eas ultra consuetos naturalium effectus nobis eveniat, in daemonas reiicit hominum seductores. Quod in libro *Contra gentiles* perspicue patet; maxime vero in libello *De occultis naturae operibus,* ubi videtur ipsas etiam imagines parvipendere quocunque factas,

---

120 vel uni cuidam *rep. z*   129 figura] virtute *P*   133 ut *om. P*   135 ad *om. z*   144 figura talis] figuralis *z*   154 *post* videtur *add.* in *P*   etiam *ante* ipsas *transp. z*

BOOK THREE   CHAP. XVIII   341

It would be unduly curious and perhaps harmful to recite what images they fashioned and how, for the mutual meeting of minds or their alienation, for bringing felicity or inflicting calamity, either to some individual, or to a household, or to a city.[26] I do not affirm that such things can be done. Astrologers, however, think such things can be done, and they teach the method, but I dare not tell it. Porphyry in the book where he sketches the life of his master Plotinus confirms that such can be done. And he recounts that Olympius, an Egyptian magician and astrologer, attempted such a thing against Plotinus at Rome, seeking to planet-strike Plotinus through images or things of this kind. But because of the exalted soul of Plotinus, the attempt recoiled upon its author.[27] Also Albertus Magnus, professor both of theology and of magic, says in his *Speculum,* a work where he claims to be distinguishing what is permitted from what is forbidden, that images rightly constituted by astrologers acquire power and effect from a celestial figure.[28] And thereupon he narrates their marvelous effects as promised by Thebit Benthorad and Ptolemy[29] and the rest of the astrologers. And he describes images to bring calamity and prosperity to someone, which I deliberately pass over. At the same time, he confirms that they can have an effect, although he also, as a responsible man, condemns the abuse of the art and, as an orthodox theologian, detests the prayers and fumigations which certain impious people have offered to daemons when they are making images. Nevertheless, he does not disapprove of figures, letters, and sayings impressed upon images for the precise purpose of receiving some gift from a celestial figure, which Pietro d'Abano has confirmed can be obtained through images. Moreover, Pietro also affirms that some region or other was destroyed by that image which Thebit says was fashioned by Phedix the astrologer.[30]

Thomas Aquinas, our leader in theology, is more fearful of these practices and attributes less to images. For he thinks only so much power is acquired from the heavens through figures as conduces to those effects which the heavens ordinarily bring about through herbs and other natural things—and then that it harmonizes with the heavens not so much because a given figure is in that material as because it is composed of a given material and already set in such and such a species of artificial objects. This he says in the third book of the *Summa Contra Gentiles* where he derides characters and letters added to the figures, but figures not so much, unless they are added for the purpose of signs to daemons.[31] Also in his book *On Fate* he says the constellations give the order of existence and duration, not only to natural things but also to artificial; and that therefore images are fashioned under certain constellations. But if anything wonderful happens to us through them outside the accustomed effects of nature, he rejects it as the work of daemons out to seduce people.[32] This is clear in the book *Contra Gentiles,*[33] but especially clear in his letter *On the Occult Works of Nature,* where he seems to give little credit even to the images them-

quas et ego quatenus ipse iusserit nihilipendam. Referre autem mirabiles
quosdam effectus imaginum in daemonum falsitatem nec est a Platonicis
alienum. Nam et Iamblichus ait eos qui religione summa sanctimoniaque
posthabita, imaginibus duntaxat confisi, ab eis divina sperant munera, hac
in re a malis daemonibus saepissime falli sub praetextu bonorum numinum
occurrentibus. Contingere tamen ex imaginibus legitima astrologiae ratione
constructis naturalia quaedam bona non negat.

Denique tutius fore arbitror medicinis quam imaginibus se committere;
rationesque a nobis de potestate coelesti pro imaginibus assignatas in medicinis potius quam in figuris efficaciam habere posse. Probabile enim est, si
quam vim imagines habent, hanc non tam per figuram nuper acquirere,
quam per materiam possidere naturaliter sic affectam. Ac si quid denuo acquiritur dum insculpitur, non tam per figuram comparari quam per calefactionem contusione quadam provenientem. Quae quidem contusio calefactioque facta sub harmonia coelesti simili harmoniae, quae quondam materiae
virtutem infuderat, excitat virtutem ipsam atque corroborat, sicut flatus flammam; et manifestam efficit ante latentem, sicut calor ignis in aspectum producit litteras scriptas succo cepae delitescentes. Atque litterae hirci adipe inscriptae lapidi, prorsus occultae, si lapis submergatur aceto, prodeunt et
quasi sculptae eminentes extant. Immo vero sicut tactus scopae vel arbuti
suscitat rabiem consopitam, sic forte contusio quaedam et calefactio sola latentem in materia virtutem prodit, facta videlicet opportune. Qua quidem
coelesti opportunitate expedit in medicinis conficiendis uti. Aut si quis forte
tractare metalla lapidesque voluerit, praestat percutere solum atque calefacere quam figurare. Praeter enim id quod inanes esse figuras suspicor, haud
temere vel umbram idolatriae debemus admittere. Item nec temere uti stellis vel salutaribus ad morbos his simillimos expellendos. Hos enim saepe augent, sicut noxiae stellae dissimiles sibi morbos aliquando minuunt, quod
sane Ptolemaeus et Haly perspicue docent.

De fabricanda universi figura.

Cap. XIX.

Sed curnam universalem ipsam, id est, universi ipsius imaginem praetermittimus? Ex qua tamen beneficium ab universo sperare videntur. Sculpet ergo sectator illorum forte qui poterit formam quandam mundi totius

---

163 de *om.* z   171 calos z   174 quasi *om.* z   175 labentem z   178 percurrere *P*
1 permittimus z

selves, however they are made;³⁴ and insofar as he requires it, I give them no credit at all. Even the Platonists attribute certain wonderful effects of images to the deception of daemons. For Iamblichus too says that those who place their trust in images alone, caring less about the highest religion and holiness, and who hope for divine gifts from them, are very often deceived in this matter by evil daemons encountering them under the pretense of being good divinities.³⁵ Iamblichus does not deny, however, that certain natural goods come to pass from images constructed according to a legitimate astrological plan.³⁶

I think, therefore, that it would be safer to trust oneself to medicines than to images; and that the things we said cause celestial power in images can have their efficacy rather in medicines than in figures. For it is probable that, if images, have any power, they do not so much acquire it just at the moment of receiving a figure as possess it through a material naturally so disposed; but if an image eventually acquired something when it was engraved, it obtained it not so much through the figure as through the heating produced by hammering. This hammering and heating, if it happens under a harmony similar to that celestial harmony [cf. 3.2, p. 534] which had once infused power into the material, activates this power and strengthens it as blowing strengthens a flame and makes manifest what was latent before, as the heat of a fire brings to visibility letters previously hidden which were written with the juice of an onion; and as letters written with the fat of a goat on a stone, absolutely unseen, if the stone is submerged in vinegar, emerge and stick out as if they were sculptured. Yes, and just as the touch of the broom or the wild strawberry excites a dormant madness, thus perhaps hammering and heating alone brings out the power latent in the material, if it is done at the right time. It is a good idea to use the right celestial time in making up medicines. And if anyone should want to deal with metal or stones, it is better only to strike them and heat them rather than to engrave them. For besides the fact that I suspect the figures to be useless, we ought not rashly to allow even the shadow of idolatry. Likewise we ought not rashly to use stars, even salutary ones, to expel diseases that are like themselves. For they often augment the diseases, just as harmful stars sometimes mitigate diseases that are unlike themselves, as Ptolemy and Haly clearly teach.³⁷

How to Construct a Figure of the Universe.

Chap. XIX

But why, then, should we neglect a universal image, an image of the very universe itself?¹ Through it, they seem to hope for a benefit from the universe. The adherent of these things, if he can do it, should sculpt an ar-

archetypam, si placebit, in aere, quam deinde opportune in argenti lamina imprimat aurata. Sed quando potissimum imprimet? Quando Sol minutum primum Arietis attigerit. Hinc enim astrologi tanquam ex sui natalis revolutione fortunam mundi eo saltem anno imminentem auspicantur. Ille igitur in hoc ipso mundi natali totius imprimet mundi figuram. At videsne quam belle inter disserendum mundi aliquando nati nobis succurrerit argumentum? Siquidem quolibet anno renascitur. Nonne in ipsa hominis genesi metiuntur astrologi primum in quo signo, quo gradu, quo minuto Sol extiterit? Ibique totius figurae iaciunt fundamentum. Et quolibet deinceps anno, cum primum Sol minutum subierit idem, quasi renatum hominem arbitrantur, atque inde praesagiunt anni fortunam. Sicut igitur id in homine facere non valerent, nisi quasi renasceretur, atque hic non posset quasi renasci, nisi fuisset aliquando natus, sic et mundum coniicere licet aliquando genitum, Sole videlicet sub minuto Arietis primo tunc posito, quandoquidem per eundem quolibet anno situm sors quaedam quasi renascentis mundi revolvitur. Tunc igitur ille fabricabit mundi figuram.

    Cavebit autem ne Sabbato, Saturni die, figuram sculpat aut exprimat. Hoc enim die Deus mundi faber ab opere traditur quievisse, quod ab ideali die Solis inceperat. Quantum enim Sol generationi accommodatus est, tantum Saturnus ineptus. Perfecerat autem opus in Venere pulchritudinem operis absolutam significante. Sed de mundanae fabricae rationibus nihil ultra, Ioannes enim Picus noster Mirandula divina de genesi mundi mysteria Moseos divinitus his diebus expressit. Quamobrem ut redeamus ad institutum, et ille mundum suum primum die vel hora Saturni non sculpet, sed die potius vel hora Solis. Imprimet autem in anni natali, praesertim si tunc felices accedant Iuppiter atque Diana.

    Optimum vero fore putabunt praeter liniamenta opificio colores inserere. Sunt vero tres universales simul et singulares mundi colores: viridis, aureus, sapphyrinus, tribus coeli Gratiis dedicati. Viridis quidem Veneri simul atque Lunae: humidus videlicet humidis atque nascentium proprius, accommodatus et matribus. Aureum Solis esse colorem nemo dubitat, et ab Iove insuper atque Venere non alienum. Sapphyrinum denique Iovi maxime dedicamus, cui et sapphyrus ipse dicitur consecratus. Unde et lapis lazulus hoc

9 differundum *L*   19 ille *om. z*   fabricavit *z*   20 insculpat *P*   24 nihil *om. z*   27 die[2] *om. z*

chetypal form of the whole world, if he pleases, in bronze; he should imprint this subsequently at the right time in a thin gilded plate of silver.[2] But when exactly should he imprint it? When the Sun has reached the first minute of Aries. For astrologers customarily tell the fortune of the world—at least, what is going to happen in that year—from this moment, since it is the return of its birthday. He should therefore imprint this figure of the whole world on the very birthday of the world. But don't you see how beautifully the argument that the world was born at a particular time will help us in this discussion? For it is born in any and every year. In the horoscope of a person, don't astrologers measure first in what sign, in what degree, in what minute was the Sun? And then they lay the foundation of the whole figure. And in any year thereafter, as soon as the Sun enters the same minute, they think that the man is, as it were, reborn; and thence they prophesy his year's fortune. Therefore, just as in man it does no good to do this unless he is, so to speak, reborn, and he cannot be, as it were, reborn unless he had been born at some particular time, so it can be conjectured that the world, too, was born at some time, namely, when the Sun entered the first minute of Aries, because a particular Lot of the world being reborn, so to speak, is revolved through the same position in every year.[3] At this time, therefore, he should construct the figure of the world.

But he should be careful not to sculpt or imprint a figure on the Sabbath, the day of Saturn [Saturday]. For on this day it is held that God, the maker of the world, rested from the work which He had begun on the ideal day of the Sun. For by so much as the Sun is accommodated to generation, Saturn is unsuited to it. God had completed the work on the day of Venus [Friday], who signifies the perfect beauty of the work. But there is no need to say more about the reasons of the construction of the world, for recently our friend Giovanni Pico della Mirandola has divinely expressed the divine mysteries of Moses touching the genesis of the world.[4] Accordingly, to return to what we began, the adherent of these things likewise should first sculpt his world not in the day or hour of Saturn, but rather in the day or hour of the Sun. He should engrave it, moreover, on the birthday of the year, especially if then Jupiter and Diana [read "Venus"], the benefics, are present.

But they would like him to insert not only lines but colors into the work. There are, indeed, three colors of the world, at once universal and peculiar: green, gold, and sapphire-blue, dedicated to the three heavenly Graces [as in 3.5]. Green is the color of Venus and also of the Moon—moist for moist complexions, quite proper for newborns, accommodated also to mothers. Nobody questions but that gold is the color of the Sun, and besides not alien to Jupiter and Venus. Finally, sapphire-blue we especially dedicate to Jupiter, to whom also the sapphire itself is said to be consecrated. For this reason too, on account of its Jovial power, the lapis lazuli, richly endowed with this color, pos-

colore dotatus ob virtutem Ioviam contra bilem atram a Saturno profectam apud medicos praerogativam habet, nasciturque cum auro aureis distinctus notis, ita comes auri sicut Solis est Iuppiter. Similemque vim habet lapis Armenus, colorem similem cum viridi quodammodo possidens. Expedire igitur iudicabunt ad Gratiarum coelestium munera capessenda tres potissimum hos colores frequentissime contueri, atque in formula mundi quam fabricas sapphyrinum colorem mundi spheris inserere.

Operae pretium fore putabunt aurea spheris ad ipsam coeli similitudinem addere sidera, atque ipsam Vestam sive Cererem, id est terram, viridem induere vestem. Eiusmodi formulam sectator illorum vel ipse gestabit, vel oppositam intuebitur. Utile vero fore spectare spheram motibus suis praeditam, qualem Archimedes quondam et nuper Florentinus quidam noster, Laurentius nomine, fabricavit. Neque spectare solum, sed etiam animo reputare. Proinde in ipsis suae domus penetralibus cubiculum construet in fornicem actum, figuris eiusmodi et coloribus insignitum, ubi plurimum vigilet atque dormiat. Et egressus domo non tanta attentione singularum rerum spectacula, quanta universi figuram coloresque perspiciet. Sed haec imaginum fictores illi viderint. Tu vero praestantiorem in te finges imaginem. Nempe cum noveris nec quicquam ordinatius esse quam coelum, neque temperatius aliquid cogitari quam Iuppiter, sperabis ita demum beneficia coeli Iovisque consequi, si cogitationibus, affectibus, actionibus, victu te ipsum ordinatissimum temperatissimumque praestiteris.

At postquam in mentionem temperantiae coelestis incidimus, opportunum forte fuerit recordari nullum inesse coelo elementalis qualitatis excessum, ut peripatetice loquar; alioquin sive ita compositum sit, iam esset tot saeculis dissolutum, sive etiam simplex, tanta saltem magnitudine, potentia, motione cetera perdidisset. Sed profecto tanquam moderatissimum omnia moderatur, ac diversa commiscet in unum. Praeterea tum hac ipsa temperantia sua, tum excellentia formae divinitus vitam meruit. Nam et res compositas tunc demum vitam adipisci videmus, quando qualitatum perfecta commixtio priorem iam contrarietatem fregisse videtur, ut in plantis. Perfectiorem deinceps in animalibus vitam, quatenus inest eis complexio a contrarietate remotior quam in plantis. In hominibus rursum eadem ratione perfectiorem et quodammodo iam coelestem. Siquidem humana complexio ad coelestem temperantiam iam accessit, praesertim in spiritu, qui ultra substantiae suae sub-

---

46 ipse *om.* z   52 tantam z   58 temperantissimum x   59 temperaturae z   60 elementatis x
67 Perfectionem P   68 *post* inest *add.* in z

sesses according to doctors the prerogative of curing black bile, which comes from Saturn. Lapis lazuli comes into being along with gold and is decorated with golden marks; thus it is the companion of gold as Jupiter is of the Sun. The Armenian stone has a similar power, possessing a color somewhat similar to the above along with green [i.e., blue-green].[5] They therefore judge it useful to look at these particular colors above all, in order to capture the gifts of the celestial graces and, in the model of the world which you are making, to insert the blue color of the world in the spheres [doubtless represented by rings, since he could hardly be thinking of concentric, completely closed spheres].

They think it worthwhile to add to the spheres, for a true imitation of the heavens, golden stars, and to clothe Vesta herself or Ceres, that is, the earth, with a green garment. The adherent of those things should either carry about with him a model of this kind or should place it opposite him and gaze at it. But it will be useful to look at a sphere equipped with its own motions; Archimedes once constructed one and a Florentine friend of ours named Lorenzo did so just recently.[6] Nor should one simply look at it but reflect upon it in the mind. In like manner, in the very depth of his house, he should construct a chamber, vaulted and marked with these figures and colors, and he should spend most of his waking hours there and also sleep. And when he has emerged from his house, he will not note with so much attention the spectacle of individual things as the figure of the universe and its colors. But I leave this to those who make images. You, however, will fashion a better image within yourself when you know that nothing is more orderly than the heavens and that nothing can be thought of that is more temperate than Jupiter; you should hope at last to attain benefits from the heavens and from Jupiter if you have rendered yourself very orderly and temperate in your thoughts, emotions, and mode of life.

But after we have chanced to mention celestial temperateness, it would perhaps be a good time to recall that there is indeed no excess of an elemental quality in the heavens (to speak like the Peripatetics); otherwise, either being composite in this way, it would in so many ages by now have disintegrated, or else, being simple, it would in so great size, power, and motion at any rate have destroyed the other qualities. But in fact, as a most moderate thing, it governs all and mixes different things into one. Besides, both by this its very temperateness and also by the excellence of its form, it has merited life from the Divine. For we see composite things acquire life only then, when a perfect commixture of qualities seems to have broken up the initial contrariety, as in plants. Next, we see in animals a more perfect life, insofar as their complexion is farther from contrariety than it is in plants. In human beings, again, by the same principle, we see a life still more perfect and already somewhat celestial. For the human complexion indeed already approximates celestial temperateness, especially in its spirit which (in addition to its subtlety of substance

tilitatem qualitatumque temperantiam, quibus cum coelo consentit, coelestem quoque lucem est adeptus. Hic insuper ubi maxime talis est, potissimum est coelestis, vitamque coelestem divinitus prae ceteris est adeptus; et quatenus se talem in omni victu legeque vitae efficit atque servat, eatenus singularia coelestium dona reportat.

Quando vero dicimus non esse in coelo ullum elementaris qualitatis excessum, intelligimus vel nullam esse ibi eiusmodi qualitatem, sed virtutes potius effectrices qualitatum temperatas, vel si quae sunt illic quodammodo similes qualitates, quasi aeriam habere temperiem. Atque ubi quaedam illic frigida siccaque nominamus, Platonica haec accipimus ratione, id est, ut frigidum appelletur quod minimi caloris est causa, siccum vero quod humorem nobis exhibet minimum. Sic astrologus Abraham Saturnum inquit corpus nostrum quodammodo relinquere frigidum atque siccum, quia calorem et humorem affert nostro minorem. Eadem ratione carnes bovis et leporis in se quidem calidae atque humidae nobis frigidae sunt et siccae. Ex hac autem inductione duo haec accipe corollaria: primum quidem si corpora magis deinceps temperata magis vivunt, coelum maxime temperatum quam maxime vivere — immo vero vicissim ex eo quod coelum exactissime temperatum absolutissimam in se vitam possidet, coniectari ut quatenus reliqua ad temperiem vitamque illius accedunt, eatenus vitam sortiri praestantiorem. Alterum vero vitam esse formam in se perfectam perficientemque corpus motionisque principium exhibentem — principium, inquam, intimum motionis quoque tum intrinsecus actae, tum per omnem partem extrinsecus expeditae. Si igitur id ipsum vita est, mente captum existimato qui eiusmodi formam non cognoverit inesse coelo, corpore praestantissimo, circumeunte semper motione perfecta, cuncta vivificante magisque illa gradatim, quae vel ad ipsius similitudinem naturaliter propinquius accesserunt, vel quotidie huius influxibus aptius se exponunt.

Quantam imagines vim habere putentur
in spiritum, et spiritus in eas.
Et de affectu utentis et operantis.

Cap. XX.

Compertum habemus, si quis rite utatur helleboro feratque potenter, mutare quodammodo exquisita purgatione et occulta eius proprietate qua-

---

72 temperantium *z*   73 Hinc *P*   est ² *om. z*   77 qualitas *z*   80 *post* qualitates *add.* et *x*   aeriam] etiam *P*   84 et] atque *z*   87 haec *om. z*   88–89 maxime temperatum — coelum *om. z*

and temperateness of qualities whereby it agrees with the heavens) also has acquired celestial light. This spirit, moreover, when it is like this in the highest degree, is especially celestial and has acquired celestial life above the rest from the Divine; and so long as it renders itself and keeps itself like this in all its diet and regimen, to that extent it gains the singular gifts of the celestials.

But when we say that in the heavens there is not any excess of an elemental quality, we understand either, 1) that no such quality exists there, but rather temperate virtues that bring qualities into being, or 2) that if qualities somehow similar to those here below exist there, then we understand that they have a sort of airy tempering. And when we call some things up there cold or dry, we are taking it according to the Platonic explanation, i.e., that a thing may be called cold which is the cause of least heat, and dry which produces for us least moisture.[7] Thus Abraham the astrologer says that Saturn leaves our body somewhat dry and cold because it brings our body less heat and moisture.[8] For the same reason, the meat of cattle and of hares, which is in itself hot and moist, is to us cold and dry. From this induction, learn two corollaries: First, if bodies after further tempering live more, then the heavens, being as temperate as possible, live as much as possible — or rather, conversely, because the heavens are most exactly tempered and possess in themselves the most absolute life, it can be conjectured that insofar as other things approximate that temperance and life, so far they will be endowed with a more excellent degree of life. Second, life is a form perfect in itself, perfecting the body and giving it the principle of motion, the inward principle of a motion, I repeat, that both acts internally and is deployed externally through every part. If therefore all this itself constitutes life, consider him mentally deficient who does not know that such a form [as life] exists in the heavens — in the most perfect body that revolves always with perfect motion and gives life to all, and more and more life by degrees to those things which either have naturally become like it or which daily expose themselves more readily to its influences.

What Great Power Images Are Thought To Have over Spirit, and Spirit over Images. And concerning the Emotional State of the User and Operator.

Chap. XX

We have verified that if anyone uses hellebore according to medical rules and is strong enough to tolerate it, then, by the resulting purgation and by its occult property, he changes somehow the quality of his spirit, the

litatem spiritus corporisque naturam et ex parte motus animi, et quasi reiuvenescere, ut ferme videatur esse renatus. Unde Medeam Magosque tradunt herbis quibusdam reddere iuventutem consuevisse, quam non tam reddunt myrobalani quam conservant. Similem astrologi potestatem propitias habere imagines arbitrantur, per quam gestantis naturam et mores quodammodo mutent; in meliusque restituant, ut quasi iam alter evaserit; aut saltem prosperam valetudinem diutissime servent. Imagines vero noxias adversus gestantem habere vim hellebori praeter artem potentiamque assumpti, venenosam videlicet atque pestiferam. Adversus autem alium quendam, ad cuius calamitatem fabricatae intentaeque fuerint, vim aenei speculi concavique sic prorsus obiecti, ut collectis repercussisque in oppositum radiis comminus quidem comburant, eminus autem caligare compellant. Hinc orta est historia vel opinio, putans astrologorum machinis Magorumque veneficiis homines, bruta, plantas siderari atque tabescere posse. Ego autem imagines in rem distantem vim habere ullam non satis intelligo. Habere vero in gestantem nonnullam suspicor. Non tamen talem opinor, qualem plerique fingunt—et hanc ratione materiae potius quam figurae—atque (ut dixi) longo intervallo medicinas imaginibus antepono.

Quanquam Arabes et Aegyptii tantum statuis imaginibusque attribuunt arte astronomica et magica fabricatis, ut spiritus stellarum in eis includi putent. Spiritus autem stellarum intelligunt alii quidem mirabiles coelestium vires, alii vero daemonas etiam stellae huius illiusve pedissequos. Spiritus igitur stellarum qualescunque sint, inseri statuis et imaginibus arbitrantur, non aliter ac daemones soleant humana nonnunquam corpora occupare, perque illa loqui, moveri, movere, mirabilia perpetrare. Similia quaedam per imagines facere stellarum spiritus arbitrantur. Putant daemonas, mundani ignis habitatores, per igneos humores vel ignitos similiterque per ignitos spiritus et affectus eiusmodi nostris insinuari corporibus. Similiter stellarum spiritus per radios opportune susceptos suffumigationesque et lumina tonosque vehementes competentibus imaginum materiis inseri, mirabiliaque in gestantem vel propinquantem efficere posse. Quae quidem nos per daemonas fieri posse putamus, non tam materia certa cohibitos quam cultu gaudentes. Sed haec alibi diligentius.

Tradunt Arabes spiritum nostrum quando rite fabricamus imagines, si per imaginationem et affectum ad opus attentissimus fuerit et ad stellas, coniungi cum ipso mundi spiritu atque cum stellarum radiis, per quos mundi

---

5 tum z   13 percussisque z   14 comburat x   post autem add. saltem LPw[ac]   24 stellas z
29 humeros z   37 effectum z

nature of his body, and in part also the motions of his mind; and he is, as it were, rejuvenated so that he seems to be well-nigh reborn. Whence the story—Medea and the magicians used certain herbs to restore youth;[1] myrobalans do not so much restore as preserve it. Astrologers think that propitious images have a similar power, by which they somehow change the nature and behavior of the wearer; restore him to a better state, so that he becomes now almost another person; or at least preserve him in good health for a very long time. They say that harmful images, however, possess against the wearer the force of hellebore that has been taken in a measure exceeding medical rules and the patient's capacity—a poisonous and deadly force. Moreover, they say that images fashioned and directed for the ruin of some other person have the power of a bronze and concave mirror aimed directly at him, so that by collecting rays and reflecting them back, at close range they completely incinerate him, and even at long range they make him blind. From this has arisen the story or belief which supposed that by the machinations of astrologers and the witchcraft of magicians, people, animals, plants can be planet-stricken and waste away. I do not quite understand, however, how images have any force upon a distant target, but I suspect that they have some force on the wearer. Yet I do not think that they have the sort of force that many suppose—and what they do have is caused by the material rather than the figure—and (as I said) I prefer medicines to images by far.

Yet the Arabs and the Egyptians ascribe so much power to statues and images fashioned by astronomical and magical art that they believe the spirits of the stars are enclosed in them.[2] Now some regard the spirits of the stars as wonderful celestial forces, while others regard them as daemons attendant upon this or that star. They think the spirits of the stars—whatever they may be—are introduced into statues and talismans in the same way that daemons customarily use on the occasions when they take possession of human bodies and speak, move themselves or other things, and work wonders through them. They think the spirits of the stars do similar things through images. They believe that the daemons who inhabit the cosmic fire[3] are insinuated into our bodies through fiery or ignited humors, and likewise through ignited spirits and fiery emotions. Similarly they think that through rays caught at the right time and through fumigations, lights and loud tones, the spirits of the stars can be introduced into the compatible materials of images and can work wonders on the wearer or bystander. This could indeed be done, I believe, by daemons, but not so much because they have been constrained by a particular material as because they enjoy being worshipped. But I deal with these things more exhaustively elsewhere.[4]

The Arabs say that when we fashion images rightly, our spirit, if it has been intent upon the work and upon the stars through imagination and emotion, is joined together with the very spirit of the world and with the rays of the

spiritus agit; atque ita coniunctum esse ipsum quoque in causa, ut a spiritu
mundi per radios quidam stellae alicuius spiritus, id est vivida quaedam virtus, infundatur imagini, potissimum hominis tunc operantis spiritui consentanea. Adiuvari quoque suffumigationibus ad stellas accommodatis opus eiusmodi, quatenus suffumigationes tales aerem, radios, spiritum fabri, imaginis
materiam sic prorsus afficiunt. Ego vero odores quidem tanquam spiritui
aerique natura persimiles et, cum accensi sunt, stellarum quoque radiis con-
sentaneos arbitror, si Solares vel Iovii sunt, afficere aerem ac spiritum vehementer ad dotes Solis aut Iovis tunc dominantis opportune sub radiis capiendas; atque spiritum sic affectum, ita donatum, posse vehementiore quodam
affectu non solum in proprium corpus agere, sed propinquum, praesertim
natura conforme quidem, sed debilius, et consimili quadam afficere qualitate. Materiam vero imaginis duriorem ab odoribus et operantis imaginatione vix minimum quiddam suscipere posse puto; spiritum tamen ipsum ab
odore sic affici, ut ex ambobus unum conficiatur. Quod quidem ex eo patet
quod odor non agit ulterius in olfactum, postquam satis egit. Olfactus enim
et quodvis aliud a se ipso vel simillimo quopiam nihil patitur. Sed de his
alibi.

 Proinde imaginationis intentionem non tam in fabricandis imaginibus vel
medicinis vim habere, quam in applicandis et assumendis existimo, ut si
quis imaginem (ut aiunt) gestans rite factam, vel certe medicina similiter
utens, opem ab ea vehementer affectet, et proculdubio credat speretque fir-
missime, hinc certe quam plurimus sit adiumento cumulus accessurus. Nam
ubi vel virtus imaginis, si qua est, tangentis carnem penetrat calefacta, saltem virtus in electa eius materia naturalis, vel certe medicinae vigor intus
assumptae venis ac medullis illabitur, Ioviam secum ferens proprietatem,
spiritus hominis in spiritum eiusmodi Iovium affectu, id est amore, transfertur; vis enim amoris est transferre. Fides autem spesque non dubia spiritum
hominis iam ita percitum sistit in spiritu Iovio penitus atque firmat. Quod
si, quemadmodum Hippocrates et Galienus docent, aegrotantis amor fidesque
erga medicum inferiorem exterioremque ad sanitatem plurimum conferunt
(immo vero fiduciam hanc Avicenna plus inquit efficere quam medicinam),
quantum ad coelestem opem conducere putandum est affectum fidemque nobis erga coelestem influxum iam nobis insitum, agentem intus, viscera pene-
trantem? Iam vero amor ipse fidesque erga coeleste donum saepe coelestis

---

40 invida *P*   46 Iovi *z*   efficere *P*   aerem *om. P*   62 *post* virtus *add.* in electa eius materia *L*

stars through which the world-spirit acts. And when our spirit has been so joined, it too becomes a cause why (from the world-spirit by way of the rays) a particular spirit of any given star, that is, a certain vital power, is poured into the image—especially a power which is consistent with the spirit of the operator.[5] They say that a work of this kind is helped also by fumigations which have been adapted to the stars, because such fumigations thus directly affect the air, the rays, the spirit of the maker, and the material of the image. But I think odors—being very similar in nature to spirit and to air and consistent also, especially if they are burning [literally as incense or figuratively], with the rays of the stars—if they are Solar or Jovial, strongly influence the air and the spirit towards capturing the gifts of the Sun, or of Jupiter, whichever is then dominant, when the work is done opportunely under his rays; and I think that the spirit which has been so influenced and so gifted can act not only on its own body with a more powerful influence, but also, albeit less strongly, on one nearby, especially one similar to it in nature, and can influence it with a similar quality. The harder material of an image, however, can, I think, scarcely catch the least bit from odors and the imagination of the operator; but the spirit itself can be so influenced by an odor that the two become one. This last is clear from the fact that an odor acts no further on the sense of smell after it has registered.[6] For the sense of smell, like anything else, experiences nothing either from itself or from anything very similar to itself. But more of this elsewhere.

Accordingly, it is my opinion that the intention[7] of the imagination does not have its power so much in fashioning images or medicines as it does in applying and swallowing them. And so if anyone, as they say, wears an image which has been properly fashioned, or certainly if anyone uses a rightly made medicine, and yearns vehemently to get help from it and believes with all his heart and hopes with all his strength, he will surely get a great deal more help from it. For when either the heat-activated power of the image, if there is any such power (at least there is the natural power in its well-chosen material), penetrates the flesh of the person in contact with it, or certainly when the strength of medicine taken internally flows into the veins and marrow, carrying with it a Jovial property, then the human spirit is transformed into this Jovial spirit by an affect which is love; for love has the power to transform. Faith, too, and unwavering hope now calm the person's spirit which has been so excited by the Jovial spirit inside, and make it firm. But if, as Hippocrates and Galen teach, the love and faith of the sick person towards the doctor, a lower and external agent, are very conducive to health (or rather, as Avicenna says, this faith does more than medicine),[8] how much good for achieving help from heaven should we expect from our passion and faith in a celestial influence already implanted within us, working within and penetrating our vitals? Now the same love and faith toward a celestial gift are often the cause of celestial

adminiculi causa est, atque vicissim amor et fides hinc aliquando forsan proficiscitur, quod ad hoc ipsum iam nobis faveat clementia coeli. 75

De virtute verborum atque cantus ad beneficium coeleste captandum, ac de septem gradibus perducentibus ad coelestia.

Cap. XXI.

Verba praeterea quaedam acriore quodam affectu pronuntiata vim circa imagines magnam habere censent ad effectum earum illuc proprie dirigendum, quorsum affectus intenduntur et verba. Itaque ad duos ardentissimo quodam amore conciliandos imaginem sub Luna coeunte cum Venere in Piscibus vel Tauro fabricabant, multis interim circa stellas verbaque curi- 5
osius observatis, quae referre non est consilium; non enim philtra docemus sed medicinas. Probabilius autem est effectus eiusmodi vel per Venereos daemonas confici his operibus verbisque gaudentes, vel per daemonas simpliciter seductores. Nam et Apollonium Theaneum saepe lamias deprehendisse et prodidisse ferunt, daemonas scilicet quosdam salaces Venereosque, qui 10
formosas puellas simulent pelliciantque formosos quos, ut serpens elephantem ore, sic illi illos ore vulva pariter exsugant ac prorsus exhauriant. Sed haec Apollonius ipse viderit.

In verbis autem certis vim esse certam atque magnam Origenes asserit *Contra Celsum*, et Synesius atque Alchindus de magia disputantes; item Zoro- 15
aster vetans barbara verba mutari; Iamblichus quoque similiter. Item Pythagorici verbis et cantibus atque sonis mirabilia quaedam Phoebi et Orphei more facere consueti. Quod Hebraeorum antiqui doctores prae ceteris observarunt; omnesque poetae miranda canunt carminibus effici. Et gravissimus ille Cato in *Re rustica* in curandis bestiarum morbis aliquando barbaris can- 20
tionibus utitur. Sed praestat dimittere cantiones. Concentum vero illum quo adolescens David Saulem ab insania redimebat, nisi mysterium iusserit ad divinitatem referri, referet forte aliquis ad naturam.

Cum vero pro septem planetarum numero septem quoque sint gradus, per quos a superioribus ad inferiora fit attractus, voces medium gradum ob- 25
tinent et Apollini dedicantur. Infimum quidem tenent gradum materiae du-

---

3 suos *P*   4 imagine *Lw*^ac   6 observaris *P*   7 vel *om. z*   16 mutare *z*

aid; and love and faith in their turn perhaps sometimes get their start from this fact—that the kindness of the heavens is already befriending us for this very gift.

On the Power of Words and Song for Capturing Celestial Benefits and on the Seven Steps That Lead to Celestial Things.
Chap. XXI

In addition, they hold that certain words pronounced with a quite strong emotion have great force to aim the effect of images precisely where the emotions and words are directed. And so, in order to bring two people together in passionate love, they used to fashion an image when the Moon was above the horizon and was coming together with Venus in Pisces or Taurus, and they followed many precise directions involving stars and words which I will not tell you, for we are not teaching philters but medicine.[1] It is however more likely that an effect of this sort is achieved either by Venereal daemons who rejoice in such deeds and words or by daemons who are simply deceivers. For they say Apollonius of Tyana often caught and unmasked Lamiae, that is, lascivious and Venereal daemons who take the shape of beautiful girls and entice handsome men; as the serpent with its mouth sucks the elephant, so they likewise suck those men, using the genital opening as a mouth, and drain them dry. But I leave this to Apollonius.[2]

That a specific and great power exists in specific words, is the claim of Origen in *Contra Celsum*, of Synesius and Al-Kindi where they argue about magic, and likewise of Zoroaster where he forbids the alteration of barbarian words, and also of Iamblichus in the course of the same argument.[3] The Pythagoreans also make this claim, who used to perform wonders by words, songs, and sounds in the Phoebean and Orphic manner.[4] The Hebrew doctors of old practiced this more than anyone else; and all poets sing of the wondrous things that are brought about by songs.[5] And even the famous and venerable Cato in his *De re rustica* sometimes uses barbarous incantations to cure the diseases of his farm animals.[6] But it is better to skip incantations. Nevertheless, that singing through which the young David used to relieve Saul's insanity—unless the sacred text demands that it be attributed to divine agency—one might attribute to nature.[7]

Now since the planets are seven in number, there are also seven steps through which something from on high can be attracted to the lower things. Sounds occupy the middle position and are dedicated to Apollo. Harder materials,

riores, lapides atque metalla, ac Lunam referre videntur. Secundum in ascensu locum habent, quae ex herbis, arborum fructibus, gummis, membris animalium componuntur; respondentque Mercurio, si ordinem in coelo sequimur Chaldaeorum. Tertium pulveres subtilissimi eorumque vapores ex praedictis electi odoresque simpliciter herbarum et florum et unguentorum ad Venerem pertinentes. Quartum verba, cantus, soni, quae omnia rite dedicantur Apollini, musicae prae ceteris auctori. Quintum vehementes imaginationis conceptus, formae, motus, affectus vim Martiam referentes. Sextum rationis humanae discursiones deliberationesque consulte pertinentes ad Iovem. Septimum secretiores simplicioresque intelligentiae quasi iam a motu seiunctae, coniunctae divinis, destinatae Saturno, quem merito Sabath Hebraei nomine quietis appellant.

Quorsum haec? Ut intelligas quemadmodum ex certa herbarum vaporumque compositione confecta per artem tum medicam, tum astronomicam resultat communis quaedam forma, velut harmonia quaedam siderum dotata muneribus; sic ex tonis primo quidem ad stellarum normam electis, deinde ad earundem congruitatem inter se compositis, communem quasi formam fieri, atque in ea coelestem aliquam suboriri virtutem. Difficillimum quidem est iudicatu, quales potissimum toni qualibus conveniant stellis, quales item tonorum compositiones qualibus praecipue sideribus aspectibusque consentiant. Sed partim diligentia nostra, partim divina quadam sorte non aliter id assequi possumus, quam Andromachus in theriaca componenda diutissime fatigatus, ac tandem post diligentiam divina sorte consecutus theriacae virtutem. Quod quidem contigisse divinitus Galienus et Avicennna confirmant. Immo vero totam medicinam exordium a vaticiniis habuisse testis est Iamblichus atque Apollonius Theaneus. Ideoque Phoebum vatem medicinae praeponunt.

Tres vero potissimum regulas ad hoc afferemus, si prius admonuerimus, ne putes nos impraesentia de stellis adorandis loqui, sed potius imitandis et imitatione captandis. Neque rursum de donis agere credas, quae stellae sint electione daturae, sed influxu potius naturali. Ad quem profecto multiplicem et occultum ita nos exquisitis studemus modis accommodare, sicut quotidie ad manifestum Solis lumen caloremque salubriter excipiendum nos ipsos accommodamus. Aptare vero se ipsum ad occultas dotes eius atque mirificas solius sapientis est officium. Sed iam ad regulas cantum sideribus accommodaturas perveniamus. Prima est exquirere quas in se vires quosve ex se effectus stella quaelibet et sidus et aspectus habeant, quae auferant, quae ferant; atque verborum nostrorum significationibus haec inserere, detestari

---

32 omnium z 35 consultae z 50 confirmat z 55 mitandis x 58 exquisiti L; post exquisitis add. ex P 62 Primam x

stones and metals, hold the lowest rank and thus seem to resemble the Moon. Second in ascending order are things composed of plants, fruits of trees, their gums, and the members of animals, and all these correspond to Mercury — if we follow in the heavens the order of the Chaldeans.[8] Third are very fine powders and their vapors selected from among the materials I have already mentioned and the odors of plants and flowers used as simples, and of ointments; they pertain to Venus. Fourth are words, song, and sounds, all of which are rightly dedicated to Apollo whose greatest invention is music. Fifth are the strong concepts of the imagination — forms, motions, passions — which suggest the force of Mars. Sixth are the sequential arguments and deliberations of the human reason which pertain designedly to Jupiter. Seventh are the more remote and simple operations of the understanding, almost now disjoined from motion and conjoined to the divine; they are meant for Saturn, whom deservedly the Hebrews call "Sabbath" from the word for "rest."

Why all of this? To teach you that even as a certain compound of plants and vapors made through both medical and astronomical science yields a common form [of a medicine], like a harmony endowed with gifts from the stars; so tones first chosen by the rule of the stars and then combined according to the congruity of these stars with each other make a sort of common form [presumably a melody or a chord], and in it a celestial power arises. It is indeed very difficult to judge exactly what kinds of tones are suitable for what sorts of stars, what combinations of tones especially accord with what sorts of constellations and aspects. But we can attain this, partly through our own efforts, partly by some divine destiny; for Andromachus wore himself out for ages compounding theriac, and finally, after all that effort, he found the power of theriac by divine destiny. Both Galen and Avicenna confirm that this happened by divine aid.[9] Indeed, Iamblichus and Apollonius of Tyana testify that all medicine had its origin in inspired prophecy;[10] and therefore they make Phoebus the seer preside over medicine.

We will apply three principal rules for this undertaking, provided you be warned beforehand not to think we are speaking here of worshipping the stars, but rather of imitating them and thereby trying to capture them. And do not believe that we are dealing with gifts which the stars are going to give by their own election[11] but rather by a natural influence. We strive to adapt ourselves to this multifarious and occult influence by the same studied methods we use every day to make ourselves fit to receive in a healthy manner the perceivable light and heat of the Sun. But it is the wise man alone who adapts himself to the occult and wonderful gifts of this influence. Now, however, let us go on to the rules that are going to accommodate our songs to the stars. The first is to inquire diligently what powers in itself or what effects from itself a given star, constellation, or aspect has — what do they remove, what do they bring? — and to insert these into the meaning of our words, so as to detest what they

quae auferunt, probare quae ferunt. Secunda considerare quae stella cui loco maxime vel homini dominetur; deinde observare qualibus communiter hae regiones et personae tonis utantur et cantibus, ut ipse similes quosdam una cum significationibus modo dictis adhibeas verbis, quae sideribus eisdem studes exponere. Tertia situs aspectusque stellarum quotidianos animadvertere, atque sub his explorare ad quales potissimum sermones, cantus, motus, saltus, mores, actus incitari homines plerique soleant, ut talia quaedam tu pro viribus imiteris in cantibus coelo cuidam simili placituris similemque suscepturis influxum.

    Memento vero cantum esse imitatorem omnium potentissimum. Hic enim intentiones affectionesque animi imitatur et verba, refert quoque gestus motusque et actus hominum atque mores; tamque vehementer omnia imitatur et agit, ut ad eadem imitanda vel agenda tum cantantem, tum audientes subito provocet. Eadem quoque virtute quando coelestia imitatur, hinc quidem spiritum nostrum ad coelestem influxum, inde vero influxum ad spiritum mirifice provocat. Iam vero materia ipsa concentus purior est admodum coeloque similior quam materia medicinae. Est enim aer et hic quidem calens sive tepens, spirans adhuc et quodammodo vivens, suis quibusdam articulis artubusque compositus sicut animal, nec solum motum ferens affectumque praeferens, verum etiam significatum afferens quasi mentem, ut animal quoddam aerium et rationale quodammodo dici possit. Concentus igitur spiritu sensuque plenus, si forte tum secundum eius significata, tum secundum eius articulos atque formam ex articulis resultantem, tum etiam secundum imaginationis affectum huic sideri respondeat aut illi, non minorem inde virtutem quam quaelibet alia compositio traiicit in cantantem, atque ex hoc in proximum auditorem, quousque cantus vigorem servat spiritumque canentis, praesertim si cantor ipse sit natura Phoebeus, vehementemque habeat vitalem cordis spiritum atque insuper animalem. Sicut enim virtus ac spiritus naturalis ubi potentissimus est, mollit statim liquefacitque alimenta durissima atque ex austeris mox dulcia reddit, generat quoque extra se seminalis spiritus productione propaginem, sic vitalis animalisque virtus ubi efficacissima fuerit, ibi intentissima quadam sui spiritus per cantum tum conceptione agitationeque in corpus proprium potenter agit, tum effusione movet subinde propinquum; afficitque cum suum tum alienum siderea quadam proprietate, quam tum ex ipsa sui forma, tum ex electa temporis opportunitate concepit. Hac utique ratione Orientales Meridionalesque multi, praecipue Indi, admirandam feruntur in verbis habere potentiam, utpote qui magna ex parte Solares sunt. Vimque non naturalem dico, sed vitalem et animalem habent ferme omnium potentissimam; et quicunque in regionibus aliis maxime sunt Phoebei.

---

69 stupes *z*   animadverteret *z*   73 suscepturus *z*   74 Hinc *P*   78 hic *y*   81 et] etiam $Lw^{ac}z$
84 efferens *z*   87 articulo *x*   91 vehementerque $Lw^{ac}z$

remove and to approve what they bring. The second rule is to take note of what special star rules what place or person and then to observe what sorts of tones and songs these regions and persons generally use, so that you may supply similar ones, together with the meanings I have just mentioned, to the words which you are trying to expose to the same stars. Thirdly, observe the daily positions and aspects of the stars and discover to what principal speeches, songs, motions, dances, moral behavior, and actions most people are usually incited by these, so that you may imitate such things as far as possible in your song, which aims to please the particular part of heaven that resembles them and to catch an influence that resembles them.[12]

But remember that song is a most powerful imitator of all things. It imitates the intentions[13] and passions of the soul as well as words; it represents also people's physical gestures, motions, and actions as well as their characters and imitates all these and acts them out so forcibly that it immediately provokes both the singer and the audience to imitate and act out the same things. By the same power, when it imitates the celestials, it also wonderfully arouses our spirit upwards to the celestial influence and the celestial influence downwards to our spirit. Now the very matter of song, indeed, is altogether purer and more similar to the heavens than is the matter of medicine. For this too is air, hot or warm, still breathing and somehow living; like an animal, it is composed of certain parts and limbs of its own and not only possesses motion and displays passion but even carries meaning like a mind, so that it can be said to be a kind of airy and rational animal. Song, therefore, which is full of spirit and meaning—if it corresponds to this or that constellation not only in the things it signifies, its parts, and the form that results from those parts, but also in the disposition of the imagination—has as much power as does any other combination of things [e.g., a medicine] and casts it into the singer and from him into the nearby listener. It has this power as long as it keeps the vigor and the spirit of the singer, especially if the singer himself be Phoebean by nature and have in his heart a powerful vital and animal spirit. For just as the natural power and spirit, when it is strongest, not only immediately softens and dissolves the hardest food and soon renders harsh food sweet but also generates offspring outside of itself by the emission of the seminal spirit, so the vital and animal power, when it is most efficacious, not only acts powerfully on its own body when its spirit undergoes a very intense conception and agitation through song but soon also moves a neighboring body by emanation.[14] This power influences both its own and the other body by a certain stellar property which it drew both from its own form and from the election of a suitable astrological hour. For this reason in particular many dwellers in the East and South, especially Indians, are said to have an admirable power in their words, as these peoples are for the most part Solar.[15] I say that they are the most powerful of all, not in their natural, but in their vital and animal forces; and the same goes for all persons in other areas who are especially Phoebean.

Cantus autem hac virtute, opportunitate, intentione conceptus ferme nihil aliud est quam spiritus alter nuper penes spiritum tuum in te conceptus factusque Solaris et agens tum in te, tum in proximum potestate Solari. Si enim vapor et spiritus quidam aliquando per radios oculorum vel aliter foras emissus fascinare, inficere, aliterque afficere proximum potest, multo magis id valet spiritus ab imaginatione cordeque simul uberior profluens et ferventior motuque valentior; ut non omnino mirum sit, morbos quosdam animi atque corporis sic auferri posse aliquando vel inferri, praesertim quoniam spiritus eiusmodi musicus proprie tangit agitque in spiritum inter corpus animamque medium et utrunque affectione sua prorsus afficientem. Mirabilem vero in concitato canenteque spiritu vim esse concedes, si Pythagoricis Platonicisque concesseris coelum esse spiritum motibus tonisque suis omnia disponentem.

Memento vero totam procedere musicam ab Apolline; atque eatenus Iovem esse musicum, quatenus est cum Apolline concors; Venerem insuper et Mercurium musicam vicinitate Apollinis reportare. Item ad hos quattuor duntaxat attinere concentus; tres vero reliquos voces quidem habere non cantus. Iam vero voces tardas, graves, raucas, querulas Saturno tribuimus; Marti vero contrarias, veloces acutasque et asperas et minaces; medias vero Lunae. Concentus autem Iovi quidem graves et intentos dulcesque et cum constantia laetos. Contra Veneri cum lascivia et mollitie voluptuosos cantus adscribimus. Inter hos vero medios Soli tribuimus et Mercurio. Si una cum gratia suavitateque sunt venerabiles et simplices et intenti, Apollinei iudicantur. Si una cum iucunditate remissiores quodammodo sunt, strenui tamen atque multiplices, Mercuriales existunt. Tu igitur horum quattuor unumquemque cantibus tibi suis conciliabis, praesertim si competentes cantibus sonos adhibeas; adeo ut cum eorum more opportune canendo et sonando clamaveris, responsuri protinus videantur vel instar echo, vel sicut corda quaedam in cithara tremens, quotiens vibratur altera temperata similiter. Atque, ut vult Plotinus et Iamblichus, ita naturaliter id tibi continget e coelo, quemadmodum vel ex cithara reboatus sive tremor, vel ex opposito pariete fit echo. Profecto quotiens ex frequenti quodam usu harmoniae Ioviae vel Mercurialis vel Venereae factae videlicet his regnantibus, spiritus tuus ad hoc ipsum attentissime canens harmoniaeque conformatus evadit Iovius vel Mercurialis vel Venereus, interea Phoebeus evadit, siquidem Phoebi ipsius, musicae ducis, virtus in omni consonantia viget. Atque vicissim ex cantu sonoque Phoebeo ipse Phoebeus evadens virtutem Iovis interim tibi vendicas et Vene-

---

108 aliter] alter *P*   115 concede *x*   116 tonisque] rationisque *P*   129 Mercurialesque *P*   132 instat *P*   135 vel¹ *om. P*   136 Mercuriales *xyz*

Now song which arises from this power, timeliness, and intention is undoubtedly nothing else but another spirit recently conceived in you in the power of your spirit—a spirit made Solar and acting both in you and in the bystander by the power of the Sun. For if a certain vapor and spirit directed outwards through the rays of the eyes or by other means can sometimes fascinate, infect, or otherwise influence a bystander, much more can a spirit do this, when it pours out from both the imagination and heart at the same time, more abundant, more fervent, and more apt to motion. Hence it is no wonder at all that by means of song certain diseases, both mental and physical, can sometimes be cured or brought on, especially since a musical spirit of this kind properly touches and acts on the spirit which is the mean between body and soul, and immediately affects both the one and the other with its influence.[16] You will allow that there is a wondrous power in an aroused and singing spirit, if you allow to the Pythagoreans and Platonists that the heavens are a spirit and that they order all things through their motions and tones.[17]

Remember that all music proceeds from Apollo; that Jupiter is musical to the extent that he is consonant with Apollo; and that Venus and Mercury claim music by their proximity to Apollo [i.e., to the Sun]. Likewise remember that song pertains to only those four; the other three planets have voices but not songs. Now we attribute to Saturn voices that are slow, deep, harsh, and plaintive; to Mars, voices that are the opposite—quick, sharp, fierce, and menacing; the Moon has the voices in between. The music, however, of Jupiter is deep, earnest, sweet, and joyful with stability. To Venus, on the contrary, we ascribe songs voluptuous with wantonness and softness. The songs between these two extremes we ascribe to the Sun and Mercury: if with their grace and smoothness they are reverential, simple, and earnest, the songs are judged to be Apollo's; if they are somewhat more relaxed [than Apollo's or Jupiter's], along with their gaiety, but vigorous and complex, they are Mercury's.[18] Accordingly, you will win over one of these four to yourself by using their songs, especially if you supply musical notes that fit their songs. When at the right astrological hour you declaim aloud by singing and playing in the manners we have specified for the four gods, they seem to be just about to answer you like an echo or like a string in a lute trembling to the vibration of another which has been similarly tuned. And this will happen to you from heaven as naturally, say Plotinus and Iamblichus[19] as a tremor re-echoes from a lute or an echo arises from an opposite wall. Assuredly, whenever your spirit—by frequent use of Jovial, Mercurial, or Venereal harmony, a harmony performed while these planets are dignified—singing at the same time most intently and conforming itself to the harmony, becomes Jovial, Mercurial, or Venereal, it will meanwhile become Phoebean as well, since the power of Phoebus himself, the ruler of music, flourishes in every consonance. And conversely when you become Phoebean from Phoebean song and notes, you at the same time lay claim

ris atque Mercurii. Rursusque ex spiritu sic intus affecto similiter afficis animam atque corpus.

Memento vero orationem apte et opportune compositam et affectu sensuque plenam atque vehementem similem cantibus vim habere. Quantam in orando potentiam Damis et Philostratus habere sacerdotes quosdam Indos narrent, referre non expedit, nec etiam quibus verbis Apollonium evocasse manes Achillis affirment. Non enim loquimur nunc de numinibus adorandis, sed de naturali quadam potestate sermonis et cantus atque verborum. Esse vero Phoebeam medicamque in sono et eo quidem certo potentiam ex eo patet, quod qui in Apulia tacti phalangio sunt, stupent omnes semianimesque iacent, donec certum quisque suumque sonum audiat. Tunc enim saltat ad sonum apte sudatque inde atque convalescit. Ac si post annos decem similem audiverit sonum, subito concitatur ad saltum. Sonum vero illum ex indiciis esse Phoebeum Iovialemque coniicio.

Quomodo septem modis nos coelestibus accommodare possumus, et quibus Saturnus sit maleficus, quibus propitius; quos Iuppiter a Saturno defendat. Quomodo coelum agat in spiritum et corpus et animam.

Cap. XXII.

Quoniam vero coelum est harmonica ratione compositum moveturque harmonice, et harmonicis motibus atque sonis efficit omnia, merito per harmoniam solam non solum homines, sed inferiora haec omnia pro viribus ad capienda coelestia praeparantur. Harmoniam vero capacem superiorum per septem rerum gradus in superioribus distribuimus: per imagines videlicet (ut putant) harmonice constitutas, per medicinas sua quadam consonantia temperatas, per vapores odoresque simili concinnitate confectos, per cantus musicos atque sonos, ad quorum ordinem vimque referri gestus corporis saltusque et tripudia volumus; per imaginationis conceptus motusque concinnos, per congruas rationis discursiones, per tranquillas mentis contemplationes. Sicut enim corpus per harmoniam quotidie suam, id est per situm et habitum et figuram opportune lumini calorique Solis exponimus, sic et spiritum occultis stellarum viribus comparandis per suam quandam similem

---

150 somno *P*   151 qui] quae *z*   153 sudat *z*
    nos ante septem transp. *z*   possimus *yz*   quos] quibus *z*

to the power of Jupiter, Venus, and Mercury. And again, from your spirit influenced within, you have a similar influence on your soul and body.

Remember, moreover, that a prayer, when it has been suitably and seasonably composed and is full of emotion and forceful, has a power similar to a song. There is no use in reporting what great power Damis and Philostratus tell us certain Indian priests have in their prayers, nor in mentioning the words they say that Apollonius employed to call up the shade of Achilles.[20] For we are not now speaking of worshipping divinities but of a natural power in speech, song, and words. That there is indeed in certain sounds a Phoebean and medical power, is clear from the fact that in Puglia everyone who is stung by the phalangium [meaning one of various kinds of venomous spider] becomes stunned and lies half-dead until each hears a certain sound proper to him. For then he dances along with the sound, works up a sweat, and gets well. And if ten years later he hears a similar sound, he feels a sudden urge to dance. I gather from the evidence that this sound is Solar and Jovial.[21]

Seven Ways in Which We Can Accommodate Ourselves to Celestial Things. The Sorts of People to Whom Saturn is Malign, to Whom Propitious, and Whom Jupiter Defends from Saturn. How the Heavens Act on the Spirit, the Body, and the Soul. Chap. XXII

Since the heavens have been constructed according to a harmonic plan and move harmonically and bring everything about by harmonic sounds and motions, it is logical that through harmony alone not only human beings but all things below are prepared to receive, according to their abilities, celestial things. In the preceding chapter we distributed the harmony capable of receiving things above into seven steps: through images (as they believe) put together harmonically, through medicines tempered with a certain proper consonance, through vapors and odors completed with similar consonance, through musical songs and sounds (with which rank and power we wish to associate gestures of the body, dancing, and ritual movements), through well-accorded concepts and motions of the imagination, through fitting discourses of reason, through tranquil contemplations of the mind. For just as we expose the body seasonably to the light and heat of the Sun through its daily harmony, that is, through its location, posture, and shape, so also we expose our spirit in order to obtain the occult forces of the stars through a similar harmony of its own, obtained

harmoniam imaginibus (ut opinantur) et certe medicinis, odoribus harmonice compositis comparatam. Et denique per spiritum superis ita paratum, ut saepe iam diximus, animam eisdem exponimus atque corpus — animam, inquam, quatenus affectu ad spiritum inclinatur et corpus.

In anima vero nunc imaginationem, rationem, mentem ponimus. Potest utique imaginatio nostra vel propter qualitatem motumque spiritus, vel per electionem nostram, vel etiam utrinque ita disponi, componi, conformari Marti Solive, ut sit e vestigio proprium influxus Phoebei vel Martii susceptaculum. Similiter ratio vel per imaginationem spiritumque simul, vel per deliberationem, vel utrinque sic ad Iovem imitatione quadam comparare se potest, ut multo magis ob dignitatem propinquitatemque suam ipsa Iovem capiat et munera Iovis quam imaginatio sive spiritus, quemadmodum imaginatio spiritusque eadem ratione multo magis coelestia capiunt quam res et materiae quaevis inferiores. Mens denique contemplatrix quatenus se ipsam non solum ab his quae sentimus, verum etiam ab eis quae imaginamur communiter moribusque argumentamur humanis, sevocat, et affectu, intentione, vita ad separata se revocat, Saturno quodammodo se exponit. Huic soli propitius est Saturnus. Sicut enim Sol animalibus quidem nocturnis inimicus est, diurnis autem est amicus, ita Saturnus hominibus vel vulgarem palam vitam agentibus, vel fugientibus quidem vulgi consuetudinem, vulgares tamen affectus non dimittentibus est adversus. Vitam namque communem concessit Iovi, separatam vero sibi vendicavit atque divinam. Mentibus autem hominum re vera hinc pro viribus segregatis tanquam sibi cognatis quodammodo est amicus. Nam et spiritibus sublimem habitantibus aerem ipse Saturnus (ut Platonice loquar) est pro Iove, sicut Iuppiter hominibus communem agentibus vitam est iuvans pater. Nullis vero Saturnus est infensior quam hominibus contemplativam vitam simulantibus quidem nec agentibus. Hos enim nec Saturnus agnoscit ut suos, nec Iuppiter ipse, Saturni temperies, adiuvat eos qui communes hominum leges moresque et commercia fugiunt. Haec enim sibi Iuppiter usurpavit (ut aiunt) ligato Saturno, segregata Saturnus.

Quamobrem Lunares illi populi, quos Socrates in *Phaedone* describit, eminentissimam terrae superficiem et altiorem nubibus habitantes, viventes sobrii admodum frugibusque contenti et secretioris sapientiae studio religionique dediti Saturni felicitatem gustant; vitamque agunt ita prosperam, tam longaevam, ut non tam mortales homines quam immortales daemones habeantur, quos heroas multi nominant aureumque genus Saturnio quodam saeculo regnoque gaudens. Quod forsan astrologos Arabes voluisse puto, ubi aiunt ultra lineam aequinoctialem ad meridiem esse subtilissimos habitatores

16 iam *om. z*   20 confirmari *z*   21 Phoebeii *z*   22 vel[1]] ve *x*   34 non] num *z*   36 viribus *om. z*   cognitis *z*   39 Nullis *Lwy*; Nullus *Pxz*   42 adiuvet *z*   46 videntes *z*   50 heroes *z* genius *P*   52 aequinoctialem *om. P*

by images, as they believe, certainly by medicines, and by odors harmonically composed.[1] Finally, we expose our soul and our body to such occult forces through the spirit so prepared for things above (as I have often said)—yes, our soul, insofar as it is inclined by its affection to the spirit and body.

Now in the soul we locate the imagination, the reason, and the understanding. Our imagination is able to be so disposed, composed, and conformed especially to Mars or to the Sun (either on account of the quality and motion of our spirit or through our election or through both) that it might instantly be a proper receptacle for Martial or Phoebean influence. Similarly, our reason (either through the imagination and the spirit together, or through deliberation, or through both) by imitation is so able to adapt itself to Jupiter on account of its dignity and nearness to him that it can receive Jupiter and the rewards of Jupiter much more than the imagination or the spirit could, just as on this same principle the imagination and the spirit can capture celestial things much more readily than do inferior things and materials. Lastly, the contemplating intellect—insofar as it separates itself not only from things we perceive but even from those things which we commonly imagine and which we prove about human behavior and insofar as it recollects itself in emotion, in intention, and in life to supra-physical things—exposes itself somewhat to Saturn. To this faculty alone is Saturn propitious. For just as the Sun is hostile to nocturnal animals, but friendly to the diurnal, so Saturn is hostile to those people who are either leading publicly an ordinary life or even to those fleeing the company of the crowd but not laying aside their ordinary emotions. For Saturn has relinquished the ordinary life to Jupiter; but he claims for himself a life sequestered and divine. To the minds of those who are truly sequestered as much as possible, he is in a way friendly, as to his kinfolk. For Saturn himself is (to speak Platonically) in the place of Jupiter to the spirits inhabiting the sublime sphere, just as Jupiter is the helping father to people leading ordinary lives.[2] He is most hostile of all, however, to people professing the contemplative life and not practicing it. For neither does Saturn acknowledge these as his own nor does Jupiter, the temperer of Saturn, aid them since they are fleeing the ordinary laws, customs, and company of men. For Jupiter has taken over the latter, they say, in him who has been conjoined to Saturn; and Saturn has taken over the things which transcend the physical.

It is because of this that those Lunar people whom Socrates describes in the *Phaedo*, inhabiting that surface of the earth which is outermost and higher than the clouds, living very soberly, happy to be vegetarians, dedicated to the study of the more secret wisdom and to religion, taste the felicity of Saturn; and they lead a life so prosperous and long that they are held to be not so much mortals as immortal daemons whom many call "heroes" and the golden race enjoying a Saturnian age and kingdom.[3] I think perhaps the Arabic astrologers held this when they said that beyond the equinoctial line towards the South certain

quosdam daemonas, qui nec oriri videantur neque mori, ibique potestatem habere Saturnum Caudamque Draconis. Quod sane confirmare videtur Albumasar in libro *Sadar,* dicens quasdam Indiae regiones Saturno subiectas esse, ibique homines esse valde longaevos ac senio plurimum extremo decedere. Rationemque assignat, quoniam Saturnus non laedat domesticos sed externos.

Tu vero potestatem Saturni ne negligas. Hunc enim ferunt Arabes omnium potentissimum. Planetas sane vires eorum subire ad quos accedunt, omnes vero ad eum accedere potius quam vicissim, planetasque coniunctos illi natura illius agere. Est enim ipse inter planetas orbis amplissimi caput. Quilibet sane planeta sui orbis caput est et cor et oculus. Saturnus item stellis proximus est innumeris, primoque mobili quam simillimus; longum agit circuitum. Est altissimus planetarum, unde felicem eum vocant, cui ille feliciter aspiraverit. Et quamvis eum tanquam a communi vita hominum alienum plerumque maxime vereantur, placari tamen etiam communi vitae putant, si quando plurimam in ascendente potestatem dignitatemque habuerit, aut Iuppiter eum suus feliciter aspexerit, vel in suis finibus excellenter acceperit. Alioquin influxus illius importune susceptus in materia praesertim crassa fit quasi venenum, sicut et ovum putrefactione vel adustione fit venenosum, unde nascuntur vel evadunt immundi quidam, ignavi, tristes, invidi, daemonibus immundis expositi. Quorum commercium procul effugito. Nam Saturni venenum alibi quidem sopitum latet, ceu sulphur a flamma remotum. In viventibus vero corporibus saepe flagrat, atque ut sulphur accensum non comburit solum, sed vapore etiam noxio omnia circum implet atque inficit propinquantes. Contra influxum eius hominibus communiter peregrinum et quodammodo dissonum nos armat Iuppiter tum naturali qualitate sua, tum alimentis medicinisque certe suis atque (ut putant) etiam imaginibus, tum etiam moribus negotiisque et studiis atque rebus ad ipsum proprie pertinentibus. Noxium vero influxum Saturni effugiunt subeuntque propitium, non solum qui ad Iovem confugiunt, sed etiam qui ad divinam contemplationem ab ipso Saturno significatam tota mente se conferunt. Hoc enim pacto malignitatem fati devitari posse Chaldaei et Aegyptii atque Platonici putant. Cum enim coelestia nolint esse corpora vana, sed divinitus animata atque insuper mentibus recta divinis, nimirum illinc ad homines non solum quam plurima ad corpus et spiritum pertinentia, sed multa etiam bona quodammodo in animam redundantia proficisci volunt, non a corporibus in animam sed ab animis. Magis autem haec pluraque eiusmodi a mentibus superioribus coelo profluere.

---

61 plantasque *P*   62 plantas *P*   63 caput *om. P*   64 agit] ait *z*   70 opportune *z*   74 seu *z*

very insubstantial daemons live, who seem neither to be born nor to die, and that there Saturn and the Dragon's Tail hold sway. Indeed, Albumasar in his book *Sadar* seems to confirm this, saying that certain regions of India are subject to Saturn and that there people are very long-lived and die in extreme old age.[4] And the explanation he assigns is that Saturn harms outsiders, not his own household.

You certainly should not neglect the power of Saturn. For the Arabic writers say he is the most powerful of all; that we know planets submit their powers to those [planets] whom they are approaching, but that all approach him, rather than *vice versa* [because he is the slowest]; and that planets in conjunction with him act according to his nature. For he is of all planets the head of the widest sphere. (Certainly any planet is the head of its sphere and its heart and its eye.) Saturn is also neighbor to the innumerable [fixed] stars; and indeed, he is very similar to the Primum Mobile because he travels a lengthy circuit.[5] He is the highest of planets; hence they call that man fortunate whom Saturn fortunately favors. And although most people are terrified of him as alien from the ordinary life of man, nevertheless the Arabs consider he is agreeable even to the common life whenever he has very great power and dignity as he ascends, or his Jupiter [his temperer, see above] aspects him favorably or receives him well in his terms. Otherwise, unseasonably received in matter, particularly gross matter, his influence is like a poison, just as by putrefaction or adustion an egg may become poisonous. From such influence, certain people are born or become impure, lazy, sad, envious, and exposed to impure daemons. Flee far from the company of these. For in other places the poison of Saturn lies hidden and dormant like sulfur far from flame; but in living bodies it often blazes up and, like kindled sulphur, not only burns but fills everything around with noxious vapor and infects the bystanders. Against this influence of his, generally alien to, and in a way unsuitable for, human beings, Jupiter arms us by means of the following: with his natural quality, with certain foods and medicines of his, with images (as they think), and with behavior, business dealings, studies, and affairs properly pertaining to himself. But it is not only those who flee to Jupiter who escape the noxious influence of Saturn and undergo his propitious influence; it is also those who give themselves over with their whole mind to the divine contemplation signified by Saturn himself. The Chaldeans, Egyptians, and Platonists think that by this method one can avoid the malice of fate.[6] For since they believe the celestials are not empty bodies, but bodies divinely animated and ruled moreover by divine Intelligences, no wonder they believe that as many good things as possible come forth from thence for men, goods pertaining not only to our body and spirit but also overflowing somewhat into our soul, and not into our soul from their bodies but from their souls. And they believe too that the same sort of things and more of them flow out from those Intelligences which are above the heavens.

Inter haec si rationes omnes assignare volueris, quibus adductus Moses otium Sabbati mandavit Hebraeis, forsan ultra sublimiorem secretioremque allegoriam invenies Saturni diem actionibus civilibus bellicisque ineptum, contemplationibus aptum, eoque die divinum contra discrimina patrocinium obsecrandum. Quod quidem impetrari posse adversum Martis et Saturni minas Abraham et Samuel et plures Hebraeorum astrologi elevatione mentis in Deum votisque et sacrificiis confitentur, praeceptum illud Chaldaeum confirmantes: scilicet si mentem ad pietatis opus ardentem erexeris, corpus quoque caducum servabis. Consideratu dignum est illud Iamblichi, coelestia mundanaque numina vires quasdam in se superiores, nonnullas inferiores habere. Per has quidem effectibus nos fatalibus devincire, per illas autem vicissim solvere nos a fato, quasi claves, ut inquit Orpheus, ad aperiendum habeant et claudendum. Multo igitur magis divinitas mundo superior a fatali necessitate nos redimit. Exploratu quoque dignissimum est Hebraicum illud, in mactandis animalibus rebusque nostris sacrificio dissipandis mala coelitus imminentia a nobis ad nostra deflecti. Sed haec Pico nostro exploranda relinquimus.

Denique ubicunque dicimus coelestium ad nos dona descendere, intellige tum corporum coelestium dotes in corpora nostra venire per spiritum nostrum rite paratum, tum eadem prius etiam per radios suos influere in spiritum naturaliter vel quomodocunque illis expositum, tum etiam animarum coelestium bona partim in eundem spiritum per radios prosilire atque hinc in nostros animos redundare, partim ab animis eorum vel ab angelis in animos hominum illis expositos pervenire—expositos, inquam, non tam naturali quodam pacto quam electione arbitrii liberi vel affectu. Summatim vero quicunque voto, studio, vita, moribus beneficentiam, actionem, ordinem coelestium imitantur, eos existimato tanquam supernis similiores ampliores illinc dotes accipere. Homines autem artificiose coelestium dispositioni dissimiles atque discordes et clam esse miseros et denique palam infelices evadere.

---

94 actum *L*   97 Chaldaeorum *z*   99 mundana *z*   104 redemit *z*   114 illos *P*

BOOK THREE   CHAP. XXII   369

In the midst of these things, if you want to assign all the reasons which led Moses to command the Hebrews to be at leisure on the Sabbath, perhaps you will discover behind it a more sublime and secret allegory: the day of Saturn unfit for action in peace or war but fit for contemplation and for beseeching divine patronage on that same day against dangers.[7] Abraham and Samuel and most of the Hebrew astrologers testified that they were able to achieve this aid against the menace of Mars and Saturn by elevating their minds to God and by vows and sacrifices, thus confirming that rule of the Chaldeans: "If you lift your ardent mind to a work of piety, you will also preserve your weak body."[8] Noteworthy is that statement of Iamblichus: "The celestial and cosmic divinities include some powers higher than they are and some lower." Through the latter, they bind us to the effects of fate, but through the former in turn they free us from fate,[9] as if they have keys, as Orpheus says, for opening and closing.[10] Much more, therefore does a supercelestial divinity redeem us from fatal necessity. It would be very worthwhile to explore that Hebrew notion, namely that in ritual slaughter of animals and in the scattering of our possessions as a sacrifice, the evils menacing us from the heavens are deflected from us to our possessions. But we leave these things for our friend Pico to explore.[11]

Finally, whenever we say "celestial goods descend to us," understand: (1) that gifts from the celestial *bodies* come into our *bodies* through our rightly-prepared spirit, (2) that even before that, through their rays the same gifts flow into a spirit exposed to them either naturally or by whatever means, and (3) that the goods of the celestial *souls* partly leap forth into this our spirit through rays, and from there overflow into our souls and partly come straight from their souls or from angels into human souls which have been exposed to them — exposed, I say, not so much by some natural means as by the election of free will or by affection. In summary, consider that those who by prayer, by study, by manner of life, and by conduct imitate the beneficence, action, and order of the celestials, since they are more similar to the gods, receive fuller gifts from them. But consider too that men artificially made alien and discordant to the disposition of the celestials are secretly miserable and in the end become publicly unhappy.

*Ut prospere vivas agasque, imprimis cognosce ingenium,
sidus, genium tuum et locum eisdem convenientem.
Hic habita. Professionem sequere naturalem.*

Cap. XXIII.

Quicunque sanae mentis suique compos nascitur, est a coelo ad honestum aliquod opus et vitae genus naturaliter institutus. Quisquis igitur coelum optat habere propitium, hoc opus, hoc genus imprimis aggrediatur, hoc sedulo prosequatur, coelum enim suis favet inceptis. Ad hoc ipsum vero prae ceteris es natura factus, quod primum a teneris annis agis, loqueris, fingis, optas, somnias, imitaris; quod tentas frequentius, quod facilius peragis, quo summopere proficis, quo prae ceteris delectaris, quod relinquis invitus. Hoc est sane ad quod te coelum rectorque coeli genuit. Eatenus igitur tuis favebit inceptis et aspirabit vitae, quatenus genitoris ipsius auspicia prosequeris, praesertim si verum sit Platonicum illud, in quo tota consentit antiquitas, unicuique nascenti esse daemonem quendam vitae custodem ipso suo sidere destinatum, qui et ad hoc ipsum officium adiuvet, cui nascentem coelestia deputaverunt. Quicunque igitur per argumenta quae modo diximus suum ingenium perscrutatus ita naturale suum opus inveniet, invenerit simul suum sidus et daemonem. Quorum exordia sequens aget prospere vivetque feliciter, alioquin et fortunam experietur adversam et coelum sentiet inimicum.

Duo igitur sunt prae ceteris hominum infortunatorum genera: alterum eorum qui nihil professi nihil agunt, alterum eorum qui professionem ingenio alienam subeunt genioque contrariam. Illi quidem ignavia torpent interim ad actiones incitante coelo, semper agente. Hi dum aliena a patronis coelestibus agunt, frustra laborant supernis destituti patronis. Primum quidem antiquo proverbio confirmatur: dei adiuvant facientes, ignavis autem infensi sunt. Secundum proverbio simili: nihil agas invita Minerva. Ob hanc arbitror rationem Iovem in Pythagoricis carminibus obsecrari, ut vel ipse tot malis levet genus humanum, vel saltem quo duce daemone utamur ostendat.

Proinde operae pretium fuerit indagare, ad quam potissimum regionem habitandam et excolendam te tuum sidus daemonque tuus ab initio designa-

---

6 aptas *z*   8 est *om.* P   11 ipse *Lw*^{ac}

To Live Well and Prosper, First Know Your Natural Bent, Your Star, Your Genius, and the Place Suitable to These; Here Live. Follow Your Natural Profession.

Chap. XXIII

Whoever is born possessed of a sound mind is naturally formed by the heavens for some honorable work and way of life. Whoever therefore wants to have the heavens propitious, let him undertake above all this work, this way of life; let him pursue it zealously, for the heavens favor his undertakings. Assuredly for this above all else you were made by nature — the activity which from tender years you do, speak, play-act, choose, dream, imitate; that activity which you try more frequently, which you perform more easily, in which you make the most progress, which you enjoy above all else, which you leave off unwillingly. That assuredly is the thing for which the heavens and the lord of your horoscope gave birth to you. Therefore they will promote your undertakings and will favor your life to the extent that you follow the auspices of the lord of your geniture, especially if that Platonic doctrine is true (with which all antiquity agrees) that every person has at birth one certain daemon, the guardian of his life, assigned by his own personal star, which helps him to that very task to which the celestials summoned him when he was born.[1] Therefore anyone having thoroughly scrutinized his own natural bent [here he begins to use "ingenium" in its normal sense] by the aforesaid indicators will so discover his natural work as to discover at the same time his own star and daemon. Following the beginnings laid down by them, he will act successfully, he will live prosperously; if not, he will find fortune adverse and will sense that the heavens are his enemy.

Hence there are two kinds of people who are unfortunate beyond the rest: those who, having professed nothing, do nothing at all; others who subject themselves to a profession unsuited to their natural bent, contrary to their Genius. The do-nothings vegetate lazily when all the time the ever-moving heavens are continually inciting them to activity. The misfits, while they do things unsuited to their celestial patrons, labor in vain, and their supernal patrons desert them. The first sort confirms the ancient proverb: "The gods help those who are doing something; they are hostile to the lazy";[2] the second confirms another ancient proverb: "Do nothing with Minerva unwilling."[3] I think it is for this reason that the Pythagorean verses beseech Jupiter either that he himself would relieve the human race of its many evils or that at least he would show us what daemon we should adopt as our leader.[4]

Consequently it would be worthwhile to investigate exactly what region your star and your daemon initially designated you to dwell in and cultivate, be-

verit, ibi enim magis aspirant. Ea vero est in quam primum profectus spiritus tuus quodammodo recreatur, ubi sensus vegetior permanet, ubi corporis habitudo validior, ubi magis plerique favent, ubi vota succedunt. Haec igitur experire; hanc regionem elige; hanc cole feliciter. Hinc videlicet discessurus infelix, nisi et rediturus et ad similia pergas. Sed interea frequentibus in hac regione motibus te exerce, gyrosque quosdam coelestium instar agito, motu enim circuituque eiusmodi genitus similibus conservabere.

    Quantum praeterea ad habitationem pertinet, utiliter recordabere: sicut alimenta vitae necessaria rus quidem urbi suppeditat, urbs vero consumit, sic et ipsam vitam rusticatione frequenti, ubi taedium te minime coeperit, plurimum augeri, sed urbano cum otio tum negotio conteri. Quantum vero ad habitationem simul et professionem spectat, illud Orientalium astrologorum minime contemnendum: videlicet mutatione nominis, professionis, habitus, victus, loci coelestem influxum nobis tum in melius, tum in deterius permutari. Daemones quoque vel commutari, vel ad eosdem aliter hic et alibi nos habere Platonici iudicabunt. Daemonem vero uniuscuiusque custodem astrologi cum Platonicis geminum esse posse consentiunt: alterum quidem geniturae proprium, alterum vero professionis. Et quotiens professio cum natura consentit, eundem utriusque daemonem vel certe simillimum nobis adesse; vitamque inde nostram magis secum fore concordem atque tranquillam. Sin autem professio dissidet ab ingenio, daemonem acquisitum arte esse a genio naturali discordem, vitamque laboriosam atque sollicitam.

    Qualis autem unicuique daemon ab ipsa generatione praesit cupientibus invenire, Porphyrius regulam investigat ex planeta domino geniturae. Iulius Firmicus planetam geniturae dominum esse inquit, vel eum qui plures illic habeat dignitates, vel ex firmiori sententia potius eum cuius domicilium mox petitura sit Luna post signum quod homine nascente iam tenet. Sed daemonem non eadem regula putat investigandum, verum ex Chaldaeorum opinione a Sole potius aut Luna: a Sole quidem ad Lunam in nativitate diurna, a Luna vicissim ad Solem in nativitate nocturna, ut computato inter haec intervallo aequale spatium peragas ab ascendentis gradu descendens, et in quem terminum desinis animadvertas. Cuius enim stellae est ille terminus, eiusdem esse daemonem arbitrantur. Summatim vero a domino geniturae

30 tuus *om. z*   33 pergat *z*   38 ceperit *x*   50 ultamque *z*   53 Firmicus *z*; Firmius *LPwxy*
55 peritura *P*   57 a[1] *om. P*   60 Citius *z*

cause there they will favor you more. Assuredly, it is that region in which, as soon as you reach it, your spirit is somehow refreshed through and through, where your sense stays vigorous, where your physical health is stronger, where the majority favor you more, where your wishes come true. Learn about these things, therefore, by experience; select the region where you find them; inhabit it in good fortune. When you leave it, your fortune will be bad, unless you return and undertake similar activities. But while you are within this region, exercise by keeping constantly in motion and make various circular movements like those of the heavenly bodies [= Orphic dancing]. Since by their movings and circlings you were engendered, by making similar motions you will be preserved.

In addition, it will be useful for you to keep in mind what pertains to your dwelling-place. Just as the country supplies to the city the food necessary for life, but the city consumes it, so also you extend life itself by frequent residence in the country, where weariness will never begin for you; but in the city, you wear down your life as much by not working as by working [see also 2.15]. As far as pertains to dwelling and profession, that saying of the Oriental astrologers is by no means to be scorned, namely, that by change of name, profession, habits, manner of living, and place, the celestial influence can be changed in us as much for the better as for the worse. The Platonists will judge that daemons also are replaced or that we behave differently toward the same daemons in one place and in another. The astrologers agree with the Platonists that the guardian daemons of every individual whatsoever can be two, the one proper to his nativity, the other to his profession.[5] As often as our profession agrees with our nature, we are attended by the same daemon for each, or at least a very similar one; and our life will thence be more internally harmonious and tranquil. But if our profession sits ill with our natural bent, the daemon acquired by art is discordant with the natural Genius and the life troublesome and full of care.

For those who want to find out what sort of daemon attended every individual from his very begetting, Porphyry searches for a rule from the planet that is lord of the geniture.[6] Now the lord of the geniture, Julius Firmicus affirms, is either that planet who has the greater number of dignities at the time or else, on the basis of a sounder opinion, the one whose house the Moon will enter just after leaving the sign which she occupies when the man is born. But one's daemon, Julius Firmicus thinks, cannot be sought out from that same rule, but rather, according to the Chaldean opinion, from the Sun or the Moon. From the Sun to the Moon in a daytime nativity, conversely from the Moon to the Sun in a nighttime nativity: when you have computed the interval between these, you measure out an equal space descending from the degree of the Ascendant and you note in what term you stop. To whichever star that term belongs, they think your daemon belongs to it too. But in short, from

simul atque daemone tenorem vitae fortunamque perpendere solent. Fortunam adiunxi, quoniam nonnulli partem fortunae eadem ferme computant ratione.

Optabant veteres suum ad se daemonem ab aliquo coeli cardine descendisse: ab oriente videlicet vel occidente vel medio utrinque coelo, aut saltem ab undecima vel quinta plaga. Undecima quidem medio supra caput nostrum coelo succedit, ac bonus daemon cognominatur, et ascendentem ab oriente gradum aspicit ex sextili. Quinta vero coelo antipodum medio succedit, appellaturque bona fortuna, et ascendentem gradum contuetur ex trino. Optabant tertio loco daemonem, si modo a cadenti plaga venerit saltem, vel a nona venisse vel a tertia, nona enim appellatur deus, tertia vero dea; et illa ascendentem gradum ex trino, haec aspicit ex sextili. Cadentes vero duodecimam atque sextam exhorrebant, illam sane malum daemonem, hanc malam fortunam cognominantes.

Nos autem optare praeterita supervacuum arbitrati monemus easdem plagas, quas illi pro daemonibus fortunisque optabant, observari pro planetis et stellis ad opus efficiendum accommodandis, ut vel sint in angulis, aut in duabus quas diximus succedentibus, aut saltem in duabus duntaxat cadentibus quas antea nominavimus. Neque enim ab re Solem nona gaudere dicunt, Lunam tertia, Iovem undecima, Venerem vero quinta; hae namque gradum conspiciunt ascendentem.

Sed redeamus ad institutum. Sive igitur ab illa quam in superioribus narrabam experientia diligentiaque, sive ab hac arte quam modo recensui, primum investigemus naturae daemonisque instinctum, infortunatum esse censebimus, qui officium nullum profitetur honestum. Nam et ducem professionis re vera non habet, qui opus honestum non aggreditur; et ducem naturalem vix ullum habet, quoniam stellarum daemonumque sive angelorum ducum divinitus ad custodiam dispositorum officium est agere semper et excellenter atque latissime. Infortunatum insuper eum, ut supra diximus, qui professione naturae contraria diversum a genio subit daemonem. Memento vero pro dignitate professionum digniores gradatim accipi daemones, sive mavis angelos, atque in gubernatione publica etiam digniores; posse vero artem vitaeque tenorem accipi genio et ingenio non contrarium, neque longe diversum, etiam si ad excellentiora processeris.

Memento rursus familiaritatem eorum inire, quibus Gratiae coelestes afflant. Quod ex bonis animi, corporis, fortunae perpendes; sicut enim odor

---

73 descendentem *z* 74 illa *P* 77 observati *w* 79 in *om. P* 80 nova *z* 90 qui] quam *x*
96 coelestes *om. z*

the lord of the nativity together with the daemon, they usually assess your course of life and your fortune. I added "fortune" because some compute your Part of Fortune by nearly the same system.[7]

The ancients wished that their daemon would have descended to them from some cardine of the heavens, namely from the East or from the West, or from the mid-heaven either above us or below us, or at least from the eleventh or the fifth place. The eleventh, indeed, is succeedent to the mid-heaven above our heads and is called "the good daemon," and is in a sextile aspect with that degree which is Ascendant from the East. But the fifth place is succeedent to the mid-heaven beneath our feet and is called "good fortune" and is in a trine aspect with the degree of the Ascendant. As a third choice, if a daemon came only from a cadent place, they wished him to have come at least from either the ninth or the third. For the ninth place is called "god," the third, "goddess." And the former is in a trine aspect with the degree of the Ascendant, the latter, in a sextile. But they had a horror of the cadent twelfth and sixth places, naming the former indeed "bad daemon," the latter, "bad fortune."

We, however, thinking it superfluous to wish for things that have already happened, advise observing the same places which they wanted observed for daemons and fortunes, for the purpose rather of accommodating planets and stars for the effecting of some work, whether they be in the cardines, or in the two succeedent places which we listed, or at the very least in the two cadent places which we previously named. For it is not irrelevant what they say, that the Sun rejoices in the ninth place, the Moon in the third, Jupiter in the eleventh, Venus in the fifth. For these places aspect the degree of the Ascendant.

But let us return to the subject with which we began. Therefore let us first of all search out the inclination of our nature and of our daemon — whether by that experiment and careful attention which we narrated above, or by the astrological art which I have just now recounted. We will judge a person to be unfortunate who has professed no respectable employment; for he who does not undertake respectable work does not in fact have a daemonic guide in his profession, and he scarcely has a daemonic guide for his natural self either, for it is the duty of the stars and daemons (or guiding angels divinely stationed on guard) to act always, excellently, and on a grand scale. Still less fortunate is the person who, as we said above, subjects himself, by a profession contrary to his nature, to a daemon unlike his Genius. Now remember that you receive daemons or, if you will, angels, more and more worthy by degrees in accordance with the dignity of the professions, and still worthier ones in public government; but even if you proceed to these more excellent [levels], you can receive from your Genius and natural bent an art and a course of life neither contrary to, nor very unlike, themselves.

Once more, remember to go in the company of those to whom the celestial "Graces" are propitious. You will assess what people have from the goods of

ex musco, sic ex bono boni nonnihil exhalat in proximum, ac saepe perseverat infusum. Mirificus autem foret coetus trium felicium vel duorum inter se mirabiliter redundantium. Memento denique effrenatos et impudentes et 100 malignos ac infelices procul fugere. Hi namque malorum pleni daemonum vel radiorum malefici sunt, et tanquam leprosi pestilentesque non solum tactu nocent, sed propinquitate etiam et aspectu. Sane propinquitas ipsa corporum animatorum putatur esse contactus propter efficacem vaporum exhalationem foras a calore, spiritu, affectu manantem. Maxime vero pestilens erit 105 flagitiosorum familiaritas atque crudelium, si verum fuerit post vegetalem vitam mense Iovis, id est secundo, nobis infusam, deinceps mense Martis, id est tertio, sensualem animam infundi perturbationibus mancipatam. Sic enim qui perturbatione feruntur, Martis pleni Martiali contagione propinquos inficiunt. Contraria vero ratione consuetudo frequens contiguumque 110 commercium cum felicibus excellentibusque, ut diximus, prodesse mirifice consuevit. Apollonium Theaneum ferunt Ephesi deprehendisse senem, sub cuius figura lateret daemon, qui sola praesentia totam civitatem peste contaminabat. Quantum vero Socrates multis praesentia sola profuerit, Xenophon et Plato testantur. 115

Qua ratione litterati cognoscant ingenium suum,
sequanturque victum spiritui consentaneum.

Cap. XXIV.

Quoniam vero litterarum studiosis loquor, recordari unumquemque volo litterarum amore captum imprimis se esse Mercurialem; praeterea Solarem, quatenus ipse Mercurius est Solaris. Atque haec communis his omnibus est conditio. Proprie vero praeter naturam Mercurialem quisquis eloquii gratia, lepore, dignitate, venustate pollet, Apollinem in se agnoscat et 5 Venerem. Qui ad leges vel naturalem communemque philosophiam est propensior, non ignoret Iovem se habere patronum. Sed qui ad secretissima quaeque curiosius perscrutanda penitus instigatur, sciat se non Mercurialem solum esse, sed Saturnium, sub cuius etiam principatu sunt omnes in quovis studio usque ad finem seduli, praesertim in rebus aliis negligentes. Denique 10

99–100 inter se *post* mirabiliter *transp.* z   109 qui *om.* z
    5 cognoscat P   9 solum *om.* x   10 seculi z   aliis] diis z

soul, of body, and of fortune; for just as odor from musk, so something good exhales from the good man to his neighbor, and once infused, often persists. But a party of three fortunate ones would be wonderful, or of two, overflowing wonderfully into each other. And finally, remember to flee far away from the unbridled, the impudent, the malicious, and the unlucky. For these, being full of bad daemons or rays, are maleficent; and like lepers and people stricken with the plague, they harm not only by touch but even by proximity and by sight. Indeed, mere proximity of animate bodies is thought to constitute contact on account of the powerful exhalation of vapors emanating outward from bodily heat, from spirit, and from emotions. But most pestilent of all will be the company of the profligate and the cruel, if it is true that after the infusion of vegetable life in us in the month of Jupiter (that is, the second), next in the month of Mars (that is, the third) the sensual soul is infused, given over to agitation. For those who are carried away by agitation, being full of Mars, infect their neighbors with Martial contagion. By a contrary principle, however, the frequent company and close contact with the fortunate and the excellent, as we have said, usually does wonders for you. They say that Apollonius of Tyana apprehended an old man of Ephesus in whose shape lay hidden a daemon who by his presence alone was contaminating the whole city with a plague.[8] Xenophon and Plato testify how much Socrates profited many by his presence alone.[9]

By What System People Dedicated to Learning May Recognize Their Natural Bent and Follow a Manner of Life Suitable to Their Guardian Spirit.
Chap. XXIV

But since I am addressing people dedicated to learning, I want every single lover of letters to bear in mind that he is primarily Mercurial, and Solar besides, insofar as Mercury himself is Solar. And this is the condition common to all of them. Individually, however, aside from the Mercurial nature, a person who excels in the grace of eloquence, in amiability, in dignity, in charm, should acknowledge the Apollo in him and the Venus. A person who is more inclined to laws or natural and public philosophy, should be aware that he has Jupiter for a patron. But a person who is stimulated into scrutinizing curiously the depths of secret things, should know himself to be not only Mercurial but Saturnine. Under Saturn's leadership too are all those who delve as far as possible into any pursuit, especially those who neglect other affairs.

si verum est quod nonnulli tam physici quam astronomi tradunt, animam intellectu praeditam in conceptum humanum mense Solis, id est quarto, descendere, qui plurimum intellectu vivunt, et ab initio sunt praecipue et quotidie Solares evadunt. Horum itaque planetarum favor his hominibus auspicandus erit; sub eorum spiraculo medicinae conflandae; in eorum regionibus habitandum.

Verum ad Apollinem, Musarum ducem, imprimis vos, o litterati, Musarum cultores, advoco. Quicunque igitur inter vos, dilectissimi in Musarum amore fratres, ingenio multo magis longiusque quam corpore valent, ii profecto sciant in genitura quondam sua Phoebem quidem materiam suppeditasse perpaucam, Phoebeum vero spiritum infudisse quam plurimum; immo et quotidie humores alimentaque in corpore in spiritum maxima quadam ex parte resolvere. Unusquisque igitur vestrum totus est ferme spiritus — spiritalis, inquam, homo quidem terreno hoc corpusculo personatus, spiritum ante alios perpetuo quodam labore fatigans, ut ipsi prae ceteris sit assidue spiritus recreandus, et in senectute praeterea, in qua communiter crassior, ad subtilitatem propriam revocandus. Scitis profecto crassum corpus crassis elementis quattuor ali. Scitote igitur spiritale corpus suis quibusdam tenuibus elementis quattuor enutriri. Huic enim vinum est pro terra, odor ipse vini vicem gerit aquae, cantus rursum et sonus agit aerem, lumen autem praefert igneum elementum. His ergo quattuor praecipue spiritus alitur: vino, inquam, eiusque odore et cantu similiter atque lumine.

Sed nescio quomodo ab Apolline primum exorsi incidimus mox in Bacchum. Et merito quidem a lumine pervenimus in calorem, ab ambrosia in nectar, a veritatis intuitu in ardentem veritatis amorem. Fratres certe sunt individuique comites Phoebus atque Bacchus. Ille quidem duo potissimum vobis affert: lumen videlicet atque lyram; hic item praecipue duo: vinum odoremque vini ad spiritum recreandum, quorum usu quotidiano spiritus ipse tandem Phoebeus evadit et liber. Quamobrem ita vos ad excipiendum Solis lumen quotidie comparate, ut quatenus devitata destillatione quadam et exsiccatione fieri potest, frequentissime sub luce vivatis, saltem in conspectu lucis tum eminus, tum comminus, tum tecti, tum aperti, ad usum ubique vestrum vitalem Solis potentiam temperantes, atque igne referentes in nocte Solem, citharae cantusque interim non obliti. Spirate vero semper et vigilantes et dormientes aerem vivum, aerem luce viventem. Similiter habere vos oportet ad merum, Bacchi donum, Apollinis beneficio procreatum. Eadem igitur proportione qua lumen accipite vinum; abunde quidem quatenus nec destillatio, nec exsiccatio, qualem dixi, ebrietasve contingat. Atque praeter substantiam vini quotidie bis acceptam odorem eius frequentius haurite, par-

---

19 ii] in *y*   22 alimenta *P*   30 rursus *L*   31 ignem *z*   vino] uno *z*   34 in¹] ad *z*   36 potentissimum *z*   47 nec *om. z*   49 eius] vero *z*

Finally, if it is true, what some of both the natural philosophers and the astrologers report, that the soul endowed with intellect descends into the human foetus in the month of the Sun — that is, the fourth — then people who live very much by the intellect are principally Solar from birth and daily become more so. And so you should seek the favor of these planets for these people; under their influence medicines should be combined; in their regions such people should live.

But you, literary people, cultivators of the Muses, I summon especially to Apollo, leader of the Muses. Therefore, O beloved brothers in the love of the Muses, those among you who can work with their intelligence [here returning to his peculiar sense of "ingenium"] much more and longer than with their body, should be aware that at one time, in their nativity, Phoebe indeed supplied very little matter, but infused a great deal of Phoebus's spirit; indeed, that in their body humors and food daily resolve for the most part into spirit. Every one of you, therefore, is almost wholly spirit — "spiritual" man, I say, disguised in this little earthly body,[1] wearying his spirit with constant labor more than others do, so that more than theirs his spirit must be constantly renewed. Moreover in old age, when generally it becomes grosser, it must be recalled to its proper subtlety. You are fully aware that the gross body is fed with the four gross elements. You should know, therefore, that the "spiritual" body is nourished with its own four subtler elements. For to this body wine is in the place of earth, odor of wine takes the place of water, song and sound acts as its air, light represents the element of fire. By these four especially, the spirit is fed: by wine, I say, by its odor, by song, and similarly by light.

But somehow having started at first with Apollo, we immediately fall into mention of Bacchus. And justly indeed from light we proceed to heat, from ambrosia to nectar, from intuition of truth to ardent love of truth. For assuredly Phoebus and Bacchus are brothers and inseparable companions. Phoebus brings us principally two things, namely light and the lyre; just so, Bacchus brings us principally two things in particular, wine and the odor of wine to renew the spirit, by the daily use of which the spirit finally becomes Phoebean and liberated [pun on Bacchus as Liber].[2] Therefore prepare yourself daily for receiving the light of the Sun so that you live in the light as continually possible without sweating and dehydration, or at least in sight of the light, both at a distance and near, both covered and open to the sky, everywhere tempering the vital power of the Sun to your use, and in the night recalling the Sun by fire, meanwhile not forgetting the lute and song. Whether waking or sleeping, always breathe living air, air living with light. You ought to take a similar attitude toward wine, the gift of Bacchus, begotten by the kindness of Apollo. Take wine in the same proportion as light — abundantly, so long as neither sweat nor dehydration, as I said, nor drunkenness occurs. But besides the substance of wine taken twice daily, absorb more frequently the odor, partly indeed by

tim quidem os, ubi spiritus fuerit recreandus, colluentes mero, partim la- 50
vantes eodem manus, partim naribus et temporibus admoventes.
Satis iam fratres collocuti sumus satisque combibimus. Ergo valete.

Astronomica diligentia in liberis procreandis,
in praeparandis epulis, in aedificiis et habitatione
atque vestibus; et quantum curare talia liceat.

Cap. XXV.

Sed iuvat etiam parumper alloqui severum religionis antistitem. Dic age quidnam in astrorum usu damnas, antistes? Quicquid, inquies, arbitrio nostro detrahit; quicquid unius Dei cultui derogat. Eadem ego tecum non damno solum, sed etiam valde detestor.
 Exsecraris quinetiam scio, atque ego insuper perhorresco nonnullos qui, 5
cum Deum exoratum volunt, ad Iovem in medio coelo vastum illud Draconis Caput subeuntem tam miseri quam stulti confugiunt; ab ipso videlicet Dracone, qui quondam a coelo corruit, tertiam stellarum partem secum trahens, denique devorandi. Verum concedesne contractibus, matrimoniis, colloquiis, itineribus, similibusque operibus peragendis horas opportunas eli- 10
gere? Non facile te his assensurum video, nescio quid arbitrio metuentem. Ego igitur, etsi theologus ille magnus Albertus ista dabit et ratio quaedam forte dictabit, per electionem ipsam ad arbitrium pertinentem coelestia ita prudentiae nostrae usui subici, quemadmodum herbae medico subministrant, tibi tamen potius impraesentia credam. Et quam tu difficile nunc ea permit- 15
tis, tam facile ipse dimittam. Observationes vero Lunae ideoque aliarum stellarum ad morbos curandos et idcirco ad remedia praeparanda iamdiu (ut arbitror) permisisti. Concessum quoque abs te et insuper approbatum, crescente Luna eademque aucta lumine, nec aliunde infortunata, seminibus agros spargere, vites oleasque serere. 20
 Cur non igitur ad plantandum (ut cynice loquar) hominem utamur beneficio Lunae Iovisque et Phoebi? Nam Veneris quidem ad haec officio sem-

---

Astronomica] De astronomica *yz* 2 antistites *P* 3 diei *z* 5 insuper *ante* ego *transp. L* 6 exoratum *L* 8 qui] per *P* 13 ad *om. z* 20 vites oleasque] vitesque *z*

rinsing your mouth with wine, whenever you need to recreate your spirit, partly by washing your hands in it, partly by applying it to your nostrils and temples.

Now, brothers, I've conversed with you enough, and we've drunk together enough. Therefore, farewell.

Astronomical Care to Be Taken in Procreating Children, in Preparing Meals, in Buildings, and in One's Dwelling-place and Clothing; and How Much It Is Permissible to Care about Such Things.
Chap. XXV

But it will be useful to speak also for a moment with the severe ecclesiastical prelate. Go on, prelate, say, what do you condemn in the use of the stars? "Whatever detracts," you say, "from our free will; whatever derogates from the worship of the one God." With you I not only condemn these things but even bitterly curse them.

Furthermore, I know you curse — and I even have a horror of — some people, as pitiable as they are foolish, who, when they want to prevail on God with their entreaties have recourse to Jupiter in mid-heaven while he is in that vast Head of the Dragon. And by that Dragon, namely the one who once fell from heaven drawing after him one-third of the stars, they must finally be devoured.[1] But do you concede that people can elect suitable [astrological] hours for transacting contracts, marriages, conferences, journeys, and similar activities? I see you are not going to assent to this easily, fearing something or other for free will. Although that great theologian Albertus will allow all this[2] — and a certain reason will perhaps dictate that through the "election" pertaining to free will celestial things are just so subject to the use of our prudence as plants serve the physician — I therefore will still believe you for the present. And what you now permit with great difficulty I will dismiss with equal ease. But now for a long time you have permitted (I think) observations of the Moon and consequently of the other stars for the purpose of curing diseases and of preparing remedies for them. You have also allowed, and even approved, that people should scatter seed on the fields and plant vines and olives when the Moon is waxing and increasing in light and not made unfortunate from another source.

So why not use the favor of the Moon, or Jupiter, and of Phoebus for the planting (to speak in the manner of the Cynic philosophers) of man? For we always use Venus for this task — but more precisely I should have said just

per utimur — sed rectius modo dixissem: semper utuntur, nam ipsa mihi Venus est Diana.

Quid item de victu dicemus? Nonne licebit et proderit sub felici sidere tum autumno vinum, tum indies panem epulasque conficere? Ac si nequeamus in his praeparandis aspectus siderum expectare, expediet saltem ascendentes accipere, vel aliter angulares Solem, Iovem, Venerem atque Lunam. Sic enim omnia, quibus utimur, feliciter affecta coelitus feliciter nos afficient. Hactenus te video absque controversia concessurum, nisi forte dicas ita vitam nostram nihil fore aliud quam perpetuam servitutem. Ad haec ego subiciam frustra mortales cumulandis pecuniis et honoribus servituros, quibus sunt perpetuo mancipati, nisi interim diligentia physica dies vitae sibi plures accumulent. Aut igitur soli Deo serviant, quod quidem est potissimum, aut si cui praeterea servituri sunt, vitae tum validae, tum longae potius quam pecuniis honoribusque vanis indulgeant. Concordes ergo sumus.

Sed numquid vel domos fundabunt temere, vel infaustas habitabunt? Ubi contagiosa quaedam calamitas aedificii ferme sic inficit habitantem, ut venenosus pestilentiae vapor etiam ad biennium in pariete servatus, qualis etiam ex epidemia latens in veste, diu postea utentem inficit incautum atque perdit. At postquam hic in vestium incidimus mentionem, prohibebisne, pie pater, in veste conficienda, vel primum induenda spiraculum Veneris diligenter aucupari, quo quasi Venerea facta vestis, similiter prospera quadam corpus et spiritum afficiat qualitate? Nonne medici vetant vulpium pelles, agninas probant? Non aliter forte sidus indies quasi nascentes vestes afficit quam semel ab initio natas. Vestes quidem et cetera artis opera certam a sidere qualitatem accipere, Thomas Aquinas in libro *De fato* confirmat. Tu igitur affirmabis. Infectas vero vestes utentem inficere etiam, testis est scabies atque lepra. Denique si populi vitae consulis (ut opinor), ista permittes; atque ego permissione tua consulam observanda. Sin autem eiusmodi moribundae vitae curam non improbas quidem, sed negligendam mones, ego quidem negligo melioris vitae fiducia fretus, ceterisque similiter consulo faciendum. Vale.

---

38 venenose *L*   41 prohibebis me *z*   42 intuenda *z*   46 quidam *z*   50 promissione *P*
51 negligenda *P*

now,"*they* always use," for Venus herself is but Diana to me [i.e., as a priest I am celibate].

What in the same vein shall we say about food? Will it not be permitted, will it not be good, both to make wine in autumn and to make bread and fine foodstuffs day by day under a fortunate star? But if in preparing these things we cannot wait for the aspects of the stars, it will be expedient at least to take the Sun, Jupiter, Venus, and the Moon when ascending or else in the cardines. For thus everything we use, having been fortunately influenced by the heavens, will fortunately influence us. This much I see you are going to accept without controversy, unless perhaps you should say that our life would thus be nothing but perpetual servitude. To this I answer: in vain are mortals going to slave to accumulate money and honors, for which they are always sold into slavery, unless they meanwhile by medical care accumulate more days of life for themselves. Therefore either let them serve God alone, which indeed is best, or if they are going to serve something else besides, let them give themselves up rather to a life both strong and long than to money or empty honors. So, we are agreed.

But they aren't going to set up houses rashly or live in unfortunate ones, are they? They aren't going to live in houses where an epidemic disaster actually so infects the inhabitant of the building that the poisonous vapor of the plague — which can be retained in the partitions even for as long as two years, just as it lurks from the epidemic in a garment — infects long afterwards the unwary user and kills him. And since we happened to mention clothing here, will you forbid a person, pious Father, when making a garment or first wearing it, to take care to catch a little of Venus's breath by which the garment, becoming as it were Venereal, may likewise imbue the body and spirit with a beneficial quality? Don't doctors prohibit wolf-skins and recommend lamb-skins? Well, perhaps a star influences garments that are, as it were, born day by day [when they are put on] just as well as it does garments born once and for all from the start [on the lamb or wolf]. That clothing and other products of art do receive a particular quality from a star, Thomas Aquinas confirms in his book *On Fate*;[3] and you therefore will affirm it. But that infected clothing infects the user, even the scabies and leprosy testify. In conclusion, if you care for the life of the people (as I think you do), you will permit these things; and I with your permission will advise that they be practiced. If, however, while not disapproving indeed of the care of this dying life, you still admonish us to neglect it, I do indeed neglect it, relying on my confidence in a better life, and I counsel others to do likewise. Farewell.

*Quomodo per inferiora superioribus exposita
deducantur superiora, et per mundanas materias
mundana potissimum dona.*

Cap. XXVI.

Sed ne longius digrediamur ab eo quod interpretantes Plotinum instituimus ab initio, breviter ita collige: mundus ab ipso bono (ut Plato una cum Timaeo Pythagorico docet) quam optimus effici poterat, est effectus. Est igitur non solum corporeus, sed vitae insuper et intelligentiae particeps. Quamobrem praeter corpus hoc mundi sensibus familiariter manifestum latet in eo spiritus corpus quoddam excedens caduci sensus capacitatem. In spiritu viget anima; in anima fulget intelligentia. Atque sicut sub Luna nec miscetur aer cum terra, nisi per aquam, nec ignis cum aqua, nisi per aerem, sic in universo esca quaedam sive fomes ad animam corpori copulandam est ille ipse quem spiritum appellamus. Anima quoque fomes quidam est in spiritu corporeque mundi ad intelligentiam divinitus consequendam, quemadmodum summa quaedam in ligno siccitas ad penetraturum oleum est parata. Oleum huic imbibitum pabulum est ad ignem; ad calorem dico proxime. Calor ipse luminis est vehiculum, ac si lignum hoc eiusmodi sit, ut igne praesente fulgeat, non uratur, qualia quandoque vidimus. Iam hoc exemplo videbimus, utrum vel homo vel aliud quiddam sub Luna certis quibusdam praeparamentis, partim quidem naturalibus, partim arte quaesitis, vitalia atque etiam forte intellectualia quaedam bona opportune quodammodo desuper accipere possit.

Verum quod hic ad religionem spectat discutiemus alibi, ubi Plotinus in medium haec adducet. Quod vero ad naturales spectat influxus, qualescunque sint, desuper venientes, scito eos in nobis materiisque nostris ita demum per artem comparari posse, quando fomenta nobis nostrisque ad illos natura suggesserit, coelumque ad eosdem opportunius conspiraverit. Nonne in ipso fetu natura, fetus ipsius artifex, cum certo quodam pacto corpusculum affecerit figuraveritque hoc ipso statim praeparamento, velut esca quadam spiritum ab universo deducit? Perque hunc velut fomitem vitam haurit atque animam? Ac denique per certam animae speciem dispositionemque corpus ita vivens dignum est praesentia mentis tandem donatae divinitus.

Ubique igitur natura maga est, ut inquit Plotinus atque Synesius, videlicet certa quaedam pabulis ubique certis inescans, non aliter quam centro

---

9 sive] si *P*   20 ubi] ut *z*   22 scitu *z*   23 artem] aetatem *z*   24 celum *P*   29 *post* tandem *add.* iam *z*

How by Exposing Lower Things to Higher Things,
You Can Bring Down the Higher,
and Cosmic Gifts Especially through Cosmic Materials.

Chap. XXVI

But lest we digress too long from what we initially started to do, interpreting Plotinus, let us review it briefly as follows. As Plato teaches, echoing Timaeus the Pythagorean, the world has been produced by the Good itself the best it could possibly have been.[1] It is therefore not only corporeal but participating in life and intelligence as well. Accordingly, besides this body of the world, manifest habitually to our senses, a body that is spirit hides within it which escapes the capacity of our weak senses. In this spirit flourishes a soul; and in this soul shines an intelligence. And just as in this sublunary realm air is not mixed with earth except through water, nor fire with water except through air, so in the universe a sort of bait or kindling for linking soul to body is that very thing which we call spirit. Soul too is a sort of kindling in both the spirit and the body of the world so that they can attain to a divinely given intellect just as extreme dryness in wood prepares it to be penetrated by oil; and oil imbibed by this wood is fuel for the fire (I mean, for the heat in the first instance); and the same heat is the vehicle for light, as if this wood were of the sort which we sometimes see, a sort which when set on fire, glows but is not consumed. Now we will see by this example whether something beneath the Moon, be it a person or something else, can somehow receive by certain well-timed preparations (partly natural, partly sought out by art) certain vital and even perhaps intellectual goods from above.

But what in this concerns religion we will discuss in another and later place [in the commentary of which *De vita* was originally a part] where Plotinus will bring it up. But concerning natural influences coming from above, whatever they may be, you should know that art can only obtain them in ourselves and our materials thus: when nature shall have supplied to us and our materials the fomentations for them and when the heavens shall have seasonably arranged themselves for them. Is it not true that Nature in the foetus, as the artificer of the foetus, when she has disposed the little body in a certain way and shaped it, straightway by means of this very preparation, like a bait, leads down the spirit from the universe? And does the foetus not through this spirit as another fomentation absorb life and soul? And finally through a particular species and disposition of soul, the body thus animated is worthy at last of the presence of a divinely given mind.

Yes, everywhere nature is a sorceress, as Plotinus and Synesius say,[2] in that she everywhere entices particular things by particular foods, just as she attracts

terrae gravia trahens, Lunae concavo levia, calore folia, humore radices, ceteraque similiter. Quo quidem attractu secum ipso devinciri mundum testantur sapientes Indi, dicentes mundum esse animal passim masculum simul atque feminam, mutuoque membrorum suorum amore ubique coire secum, atque ita constare; vinculum vero membrorum inesse per insitam sibi mentem, quae totam infusa per artus agitat molem, et magno se corpore miscet. Hinc Orpheus naturam ipsam mundi Iovemque mundanum marem appellat et feminam. Usque adeo mutui partium suarum coniugii ubique mundus est avidus. Esse vero masculinum sexum feminino ubique commixtum, declarat illinc quidem ordo signorum, ubi praecedens perpetuo deinceps ordine masculinum est, subsequens femininum; hinc vero arbores atque herbae, quae etiam sicut animalia utrunque sexum habent. Mitto quod ignis ad aerem, aqua ad terram masculi vicem tenet ad feminam; ut non mirum sit membra inter se mundana et omnes eius articulos mutuum coniugium concupiscere. Quod et planetae conciliant, partim quidem mares, partim vero feminae, praecipue vero Mercurius masculus atque femina, Hermaphroditi pater.

Quod sane animadvertens agricultura praeparat agrum seminaque ad coelestia dona, et insitionibus quibusdam vitam plantae propagat, et ad speciem alteram melioremque perducit. Similia quaedam efficit medicus et physicus et chirurgicus in corpore nostro tum ad nostram fovendam, tum ad universi naturam uberius comparandam. Idem quoque philosophus naturalium rerum astrorumque peritus, quem proprie Magum appellare solemus, certis quibusdam illecebris coelestia terrenis opportune quidem nec aliter inserens quam insitionis studiosus agricola veteri recentem stipiti surculum. Quod et Ptolemaeus valde probat, affirmans eiusmodi sapientem sic astrorum opus adiuvare posse, quemadmodum agricola terrae virtutem. Subicit Magus terrena coelestibus, immo inferiora passim superioribus, ut proprias ubique feminas suis maribus fecundandas, ut ferrum magneti trahendum, ut camphoram aeri ferventi sugendam, ut crystallum Soli illuminandum, ut sulphur et sublimem liquorem accendendum flammae, ut ovi testam vacuam et impletam rore Soli elevandam, immo ut ovum ipsum gallinae fovendum.

Praeterea sicut nonnulli foventes ova, etiam sine animalibus vitam illis ex universo conciliant, et saepe materias quasdam opportune parantes, absque ovis manifestisque seminibus animalia procreant, ut ex ocimo scorpionem, apes ex bove, ex salvia avem merulae similem, vitam videlicet a mundo ma-

---

36 verum *L*   38 Hic *P*   45 articuli *Lw*^(ac)*x*   49 animadvertentes *z*   51 medicus *post* et *transp.*
z   52 chirurgus *z*   54 astrorum *x*   55 ne *x*   60 foecundas *x*   67 avem] autem *z*

heavy things by the power of the earth's center, light things by the power of the Moon's sphere, leaves by heat, roots by moisture, and so on. By means of this attraction, the wise men of India testify, the world binds itself together; and they say that the world is an animal which is masculine and at the same time feminine throughout and that it everywhere links with itself in the mutual love of its members and so holds together;[3] moreover, the bond of the members inheres through the ingrafted "Mind, which is blended through the limbs and moves the whole bulk and mixes itself with the great body."[4] Hence Orpheus called the very nature of the cosmos and the cosmic Jupiter masculine and feminine.[5] So eager is the world everywhere for the mutual union of its parts. That the masculine sex is truly everywhere mingled with the feminine, the order of signs testifies from up there, where successively in that unending order the preceding one is masculine, the subsequent one, feminine. Trees and plants testify it from down here: just like animals, they have one sex or the other. I pass over the fact that fire to air plays the role of masculine to feminine and so does water to earth, so that it is no wonder that the members of the cosmos and all its limbs yearn for mutual union among themselves. And this union is brought about by the planets, some of which are masculine, some feminine, but especially by Mercury, because he is masculine as well as feminine and the father of Hermaphroditus.

With this in mind, Agriculture prepares the field and the seed for celestial gifts and by grafting prolongs the life of the shoot and refashions it into another and better species. The doctor, the natural philosopher, and the surgeon achieve similar effects in our bodies in order both to strengthen our own nature and to obtain more productively the nature of the universe. The philosopher who knows about natural objects and stars, whom we rightly are accustomed to call a Magus, does the very same things: he seasonably introduces the celestial into the earthly by particular lures just as the farmer interested in grafting brings the fresh graft into the old stock. Ptolemy also strongly argues this, affirming that a wise man of this sort can help the work of the stars just as the farmer does the power of the earth.[6] The Magus subjects earthly things to celestial, lower things everywhere to higher, just as particular females everywhere are subjected to males appropriate to them for impregnation, as iron to a magnet to get magnetized, as camphor to hot air for absorption, as crystal to the Sun for illumination, as sulfur and sublimed liquor to a flame for kindling, as an egg-shell, empty and full of dew, to the Sun for elevation, or rather the egg itself to the hen for hatching.

Besides, some people by warming eggs even without animals win over to them life from the universe; and often, by seasonably preparing certain materials, they procreate animals even without any eggs or perceivable seeds, for example, the scorpion from basil, bees from an ox, a bird like a blackbird from sage,[7] that is, they supply them with life from the universe by particular

teriis certis opportunisque temporibus adhibentes; sic et ille sapiens ubi cognovit quae materiae sive quales partim incohatae natura, partim arte perfectae, etsi sparsae fuerint congregatae, qualem coelitus influxum suscipere possint, has eo regnante potissimum colligit, praeparat, adhibet sibique per eas coelestia vendicat. Ubicunque enim materia quaedam sic superis exposita est, sicut speculare vitrum vultui tuo pariesque oppositus voci, subito superne patitur ab agente videlicet potentissimo a potestate vitaque mirabili ubique praesente, virtutemque passione reportat, non aliter quam et speculum imaginem repraesentat ex vultu et ex voce paries echo.

His ferme exemplis ipse Plotinus utitur, ubi Mercurium imitatus ait, veteres sacerdotes sive Magos in statuis sacrificiisque sensibilibus divinum aliquid et mirandum suscipere solitos. Vult autem una cum Trismegisto per materialia haec non proprie suscipi numina penitus a materia segregata, sed mundana tantum, ut ab initio dixi et Synesius approbat — mundana, inquam, id est, vitam quandam vel vitale aliquid ex anima mundi et sphaerarum animis atque stellarum, vel etiam motum quendam et vitalem quasi praesentiam ex daemonibus. Immo interdum ipsos daemonas eiusmodi adesse materiis Mercurius ipse, quem Plotinus sequitur, inquit — daemonas aerios, non coelestes, nedum sublimiores — statuasque Mercurius ipse componit ex herbis, arboribus, lapidibus, aromatis naturalem vim divinitatis (ut ipse ait) in se habentibus. Adiungit cantus coelestibus similes, quibus ait eos delectari, statuisque sic adesse diutius et prodesse hominibus vel obesse. Addit sapientes quondam Aegyptios, qui et sacerdotes erant, cum non possent rationibus persuadere populo esse deos, id est, spiritus aliquos super homines, excogitasse magicum hoc illicium, quo daemonas allicientes in statuas esse numina declararent. Sed Iamblichus damnat Aegyptios quod daemonas non solum ut gradus quosdam ad superiores deos investigandos acceperint, sed plurimum adoraverint. Chaldaeos vero daemonibus non occupatos Aegyptiis anteponit — Chaldaeos, inquam, religionis antistites, nam astrologos tam Chaldaeorum quam Aegyptiorum quodammodo tentavisse daemonas per harmoniam coelestem in statuas fictiles trahere suspicamur. Quod significare videtur astrologus Samuel Hebraeus auctoritate Davidis Bil astrologi fretus, antiquos videlicet fictores imaginum fecisse statuas futura pronuntiantes. Harmoniam vero coelestium his accommodatam esse tradit; metallum fundere ad hominis pulchri formam die Mercurii, hora tertia scilicet Saturni,

---

70 qualem] qua- *x*   78 *post* sacrificiisque *add.* in *z*   79 autem *om. x*   87 arboribus *om.* P
88 Adiungunt *x*   91 hominibus *z*   92 illicitum *z*   98 suspicemus *z*   102 ab *z*

materials at the right times. Like all these, our wise man — when he knows what or what sort of materials (partly begun by nature, partly completed by art and, although they had been dispersed, grouped together) can receive what or what sort of influence from the heavens — assembles these materials when that influence is most dominant, he prepares them, he brings them to bear, and he wins through them celestial gifts. For whenever a material is thus exposed to the celestials, as a glass mirror to your face and as an opposite wall to your voice, immediately it experiences something from above from a most powerful agent, namely, the wonderful power and life everywhere present; and it gains power from that experience, just as from the face the mirror reproduces an image and from the voice the wall reproduces an echo.

Plotinus uses almost the same examples in that place where, paraphrasing Hermes Trismegistus, he says that the ancient priests or Magi used to capture in statues and material sacrifices something divine and wonderful.[8] He holds, moreover, with Hermes Trismegistus that through these materials they did not, properly speaking, capture divinities wholly separate from matter but deities who are merely cosmic [13.38], as I said from the beginning and as Synesius demonstrates[9] — cosmic, I say, that is, a life or something vital from the Anima Mundi and the souls of the spheres and of the stars or even a motion and, as it were, a vital presence from the daemons [8.24a, 13.37]. Indeed, the same Hermes, whom Plotinus follows, holds that daemons of this kind — airy ones, not celestial, let alone any higher — are themselves present all along in the materials and that Hermes himself put together statues from herbs, trees, stones, and spices, which had within themselves, as he says, a natural force of divinity [13.38]. He added songs resembling the heavenly bodies [as in 3.21]; he says the divinities take delight in such songs and so stay a longer time in the statues and help people or harm them. He adds that once the wise men of Egypt, who were also priests, since they were unable to persuade the people by reasoning that there were gods, that is, certain spirits [in the ordinary sense] superior to mankind, thought up this magical lure[10] through which they could allure daemons into the statues and thereby show that divinities exist [13.37]. But Iamblichus condemns the Egyptians because they not only accepted daemons as steps in the search for the higher gods but frequently also worshiped them. Rather than the Egyptians he prefers the Chaldeans, who were not preoccupied with daemons — the Chaldean priests of religion, I say, for I suspect the astrologers, both Chaldean and Egyptian, somehow tried to draw daemons through celestial harmony into earthen statues.[11] This is what the astrologer Samuel Hebraeus, leaning on the authority of David Bil the astrologer, seems to signify, namely, that ancient makers of images made statues which foretold the future. He says that the harmony of the heavenly bodies was accommodated to the statues. He says that they cast metal according to the form of a handsome man in the day of Mercury [Wednesday] in the third hour (i.e., that

quando Mercurius Saturnum in Aquario subit, in nona coeli plaga vaticinium designante; ascenditque Geminorum sidus, significans prophetas (ut aiunt), Mars a Sole comburitur, nec Mercurium intuetur; Sol tamen aspicit coniunctionis illius locum; Venus interea aliquem obtinet angulum, occidentalis est et potens; Luna ex trigono gradum aspicit ascendentem, similiterque Saturnus. Haec illi.

Ego autem primo quidem ex beati Thomae sententia puto, si modo statuas loquentes effecerint, non simplicem ipsum stellarum influxum ibi formavisse verba, sed daemonas. Deinde si forte contigerit eos in eiusmodi statuas ingredi, non arbitror hos ibi per coelestem influxum fuisse devinctos, sed sponte potius suis cultoribus obsecutos, denique decepturos. Nam et natura superior ab inferiore conciliatur quidem aliquando, sed cohiberi nequit. Et dispositio illa siderum paulo ante descripta concurrere forte non potest. Quamvis autem daemones astronomica ratione statuis non includantur, tamen ubi per cultum eis exhibitum praesentes extiterint, Porphyrius ait eos regulis astronomicis oracula reddidisse, atque ideo frequenter ambigua—et merito, quoniam Iamblichus probat prophetiam veram atque certam nec malis daemonibus convenire, nec humanis artibus vel natura, sed spiratione divina purgatis mentibus provenire.

Sed ad Mercurium, immo ad Plotinum iam revertamur. Mercurius sacerdotes ait accepisse virtutem a mundi natura convenientem, eamque miscuisse. Secutus hunc Plotinus putat totum id anima mundi conciliante confici posse, quatenus illa naturalium rerum formas per seminales quasdam rationes sibi divinitus insitas generat atque movet. Quas quidem rationes appellat etiam deos, quoniam ab ideis supremae mentis nunquam destituuntur. Itaque per rationes eiusmodi animam mundi facile se applicare materiis, quas formavit ab initio per easdem, quando Magus vel sacerdos opportunis temporibus adhibuerit formas rerum rite collectas, quae rationem hanc aut illam proprie spectant, sicut magnes ferrum, reubarbarum choleram, crocus cor, eupatorium spodiumque iecur, spica muscusque cerebrum. Fieri vero posse quandoque, ut rationibus ad formas sic adhibitis sublimiora quoque dona descendant, quatenus rationes in anima mundi coniunctae sunt intellectualibus eiusdem animae formis, atque per illas divinae mentis ideis. Quod et Iamblichus approbat, ubi de sacrificiis agit. Qua de re alibi nos opportunius

---

103 Saturno *L*   104 designare *z*   ascendit *P*   108 ille *z*   112 ibi] tibi *x*   116 non *om. z*
124 id] in *z*   *post* conciliante *add.* facile *xz*   128 anima *Lw*^{ac}*x*   132 vero *om. P*

of Saturn), when the heavens were disposed as follows: Mercury draws near to Saturn in Aquarius in the ninth mundane house which signifies prophecy; Mars ascends the constellation Gemini signifying prophets (as they say) and is combust by the Sun and does not aspect Mercury; the Sun aspects the place of the aforementioned conjunction [i.e., of Mercury and Saturn in Aquarius]; Venus meanwhile occupies a cardine and is west of the Sun and powerful; and the Moon is in a trine aspect with the degree of the Ascendant, and so is Saturn. This is what they say.[12]

But I think, in the first place, in accordance with the opinion of the blessed Thomas [Aquinas] that if they made speaking statues at all [8.24a, 13.37], it was not the mere influence of the stars itself that formed the words within, but daemons. Secondly, if by chance it happened that these daemons did enter into statues of this kind, I think they were not bound there by celestial influence but rather deliberately indulged their worshippers, intending to deceive them in the end. To be sure, a superior nature of this kind is sometimes won over by an inferior, but it cannot be constrained.[13] And that astrological arrangement described just above probably cannot happen all at one time.[14] And although daemons cannot be enclosed in statues by any astronomical principle, nevertheless where through worship proffered to them they have been present, Porphyry says they have rendered oracles by astronomical rules and therefore frequently ambiguously. Porphyry is right to say "ambiguously," since Iamblichus demonstrates that true and certain prophecy cannot come from such evil daemons, nor is it produced by human arts or by nature; it is only produced in purified minds by divine inspiration.[15]

But now let us get back to Hermes, or rather to Plotinus. Hermes says that the priests received an appropriate power from the nature of the cosmos and mixed it [i.e., its materials in the statues, 13.37]. Plotinus follows him and thinks that everything can be easily accomplished by the intermediation of the Anima Mundi, since the Anima Mundi generates and moves the forms of natural things through certain seminal reasons implanted in her from the divine. These reasons he even calls gods, since they are never cut off from the Ideas of the Supreme Mind. He thinks, therefore, that through such seminal reasons the Anima Mundi can easily apply herself to materials since she has formed them to begin with through these same seminal reasons, when a Magus or a priest brings to bear at the right time rightly grouped forms of things — forms which properly aim towards one reason or another, as the lodestone toward iron, rhubarb toward choler, saffron toward the heart, agrimony and spodium toward the liver, spikenard and musk toward the brain. Sometimes it can happen that when you bring seminal reasons to bear on forms, higher gifts too may descend, since reasons in the Anima Mundi are conjoined to the intellectual forms in her and through these to the Ideas of the Divine Mind.[16] Iamblichus too confirms this when he deals with sacrifices,[17] on which subject we

disputabimus, ubi etiam apparebit quam impura superstitio populi gentilis extiterit, contra vero quam pura pietas evangelica fuerit, quod magna ex parte in libro *De religione Christiana* iam fecimus.

FINIS

FINIS deest in P; post FINIS add. libri tertii et ultimi *y*

will dispute more seasonably at another place, where also it will appear how impure was the superstition of the heathen but how pure was the piety of the Gospel — which for the most part we have already done in our book *De religione Christiana*.

THE END

Apologia quaedam, in qua de medicina,
astrologia, vita mundi; item de Magis qui
Christum statim natum salutaverunt.

Marsilius Ficinus Florentinus dilectissimis suis in veritatis studio fratribus, tribus Petris, Nero, Guicciardino, Soderino, ter quaterque salutem. Rectius modo Tripetro quam tribus Petris fortasse dixissem. Sicut enim ubi palma est una, non faciunt plures in ea digiti manus ibi plures, sic vestra, amici, corpora tria nihil prohibere videntur, quominus unum efficiat Petrum una voluntas. Faber ille coelestis patriae Christus tam ingentem procreavit petram, ut immenso huic aedificio ecclesiae suae una haec petra fundando sufficeret. Ego quoque tam grandes nactus sum divina quadam sorte petras, ut tres nunc meo vel arduo satis aedificio faciant. Nunc vobis, amici, nunc, si nescitis, arx illa Palladis necessaria fore videtur, qua procul a nobis saevum impiorum gigantum impetum arceamus. Quamobrem vestra primum arce tribus constructa Petris trium liberorum meorum vitam vitae publicae succurrentium munire decrevi.

Scitis (ut arbitror) me *De vita* librum composuisse, in libellos tres divisum. Quorum primus *De vita sana*, secundus *De vita longa*, tertius *De vita coelitus comparanda* inscribetur. Igitur esca tituli tam suavis quam plurimos alliciet ad gustandum, sed in numero tanto ignorantes plerique futuri sunt (ut arbitror), maligni quoque non pauci. Alius ergo dicet: Nonne Marsilius est sacerdos? Est profecto. Quid igitur sacerdotibus cum medicina? Quid rursum cum astrologia commercii? Alius item: Quid Christiano cum magia vel imaginibus? Alius autem et quidem indignus vita vitam invidebit coelo. Cuncti denique sic affecti beneficio in eos nostro ingrati nimis erunt, atque adversus caritatem nostram, qua vitae prosperitatique publicae pro ingenii facultate consulimus, non pudebit esse crudeles. Communis igitur erit vobis iste labor, sed ut quodammodo levior sit, tres enim estis adversum tres hostes, distributum subite certamen. Nec invectiva (novi enim ingenium vestrum) confutabitis invectivam, sed alieni fellis amaritudinem (quae vestra suavitas est mirifica) vestri mellis dulcedine superabitis.

Apologia quaedam] Marsilii Ficini Apologia z   *post salutaverunt add.* agitur z   5 unum *om.* z
12 librorum xz   16 comparanda *scripsi; deest in Lwxyz*   23 prosperitateque z   24 nobis z

*An Apologia Dealing with Medicine,
Astrology, the Life of the World, and the Magi
Who Greeted the Christ Child at His Birth.*

Marsilio Ficino of Florence sends greetings again and again to his most beloved brothers in the pursuit of truth, the three Pieros: Nero, Guicciardini, and Soderini.[1] But perhaps I should more properly have said the tripartite Piero than the three Pieros. For just as when there is but one palm, the many fingers in the palm do not make many hands there, so, friends, your three bodies do not seem to prevent one will from making one Piero. Christ, that architect of the heavenly homeland, created a rock so great that this one rock was able to provide a foundation for the vast edifice of his church. I also have met, by some divine luck, with rocks so great that three are now sufficient for even this lofty edifice of mine. Now, friends, now, if you do not know it, it seems you need that citadel of Pallas, so that we may keep far from us the savage attack of impious giants.[2] For this reason, I have decided to fortify the life of my three children/books who are of service to everyone's life first with your citadel constructed upon three rocks.[3]

You know, I think, that I have written a book, *On Life*, divided into three little books. The first book will be entitled *On a Healthy Life,* the second, *On a Long Life,* and the third, *On Life from the Heavens.* The title will act as a pleasant bait, then, and will attract as many as possible to taste of it; but in such a great number, a good many will be ignorant, as I think, and not a few malicious to boot. Someone therefore will say: Marsilio is a priest, isn't he? Indeed he is. What business then do priests have with medicine or, again, with astrology? Another will say: What does a Christian have to do with magic or images? And someone else, unworthy of life, will begrudge life to the heavens. Finally, all who feel this way will be quite ungrateful for my service toward them; and they will not be ashamed to be cruel in the face of my charity, with which I looked to the life and prosperity of all citizens to the best of my ability. That labor of yours will, then, be a common one, but in order that the load may be somewhat lighter—for there are three of you against three enemies—fight an apportioned battle. You will not refute invective with invective, for I know your nature; but you are so charming that you will overcome the bitterness of another's gall with the wondrous sweetness of your honey.

Principio, candidissime Nere, respondeto primis antiquissimos quondam sacerdotes fuisse medicos pariter et astronomos. Quod sane Chaldaeorum, Persarum, Aegyptiorum testificantur historiae. Ad nullum praeterea magis quam ad pium sacerdotem pertinere singularis caritatis officia, quae quidem in maximo omnium beneficio quam maxime lucent. Officium vero praestantissimum est proculdubio, quod et maxime necessarium et imprimis ab omnibus exoptatum, efficere videlicet, ut hominibus sit mens sana in corpore sano. Id autem ita demum praestare possumus, si coniungimus sacerdotio medicinam. At quoniam medicina sine favore coelesti, quod et Hippocrates Galienusque confitentur et nos experti sumus, saepius est inanis, saepe etiam noxia, nimirum ad eandem sacerdotis caritatem astronomia pertinet, ad quam attinere diximus medicinam. Eiusmodi (ut arbitror) medicum honorari sacrae litterae iubent, quoniam propter necessitatem hunc Altissimus procreaverit. Et Christus ipse, vitae largitor, qui discipulis mandavit languentes toto orbe curare, sacerdotibus quoque praecipiet, si minus verbis, ut illi quondam, mederi possint, saltem herbis et lapidibus medeantur. Quae si minus ipsa sufficiant, opportuno quodam afflatu coeli conflare haec et aegrotis admovere iubebit. Nam et ipse eodem afflatu coeli animalia passim ad suam quaeque concitat medicinam, usque adeo vitae omnium abundantissime providet. Sic instinctu coelesti divinitus instigante, serpentes quidem marathro, hirundines autem chelidonia oculis medicantur; aquilae vexatae partu aetitem lapidem divinitus invenerunt, quo feliciter ova statim eniterentur. Itaque Deus ipse, qui per coelum animalia quaevis ad medicinas instigat, sacerdotes certe permittit, non mercede, inquam, sed caritate, medicinis coelitus confirmatis morbos expellere. His vero tu deinceps plura etiam, si expedierit, ingenii tui aculeis addes.

Surge post haec et tu, Guicciardine vehemens, atque curiosis ingeniis respondeto magiam vel imagines non probari quidem a Marsilio, sed narrari, Plotinum ipsum interpretante. Quod et scripta plane declarant, si aequa mente legantur. Neque de magia hic prophana, quae cultu daemonum nititur, verbum quidem ullum asseverari, sed de magia naturali, quae rebus naturalibus ad prosperam corporum valetudinem coelestium beneficia captat, effici mentionem. Quae sane facultas tam concedenda videtur ingeniis legitime utentibus, quam medicina et agricultura iure conceditur; tantoque etiam magis, quanto perfectior est industria, terrenis coelestia copulans. Ex hac officina Magi omnium primi Christum statim natum adoraverunt. Quid igitur expavescis Magi nomen formidolose? Nomen evangelio gratiosum, quod non maleficum et veneficum, sed sapientem sonat et sacerdotem. Quidnam profitetur Magus ille, venerator Christi primus? Si cupis audire, quasi quidam agricola est, certe quidam mundicola est. Nec propterea mundum

---

29 primis *om.* M   33 vere z   34 hominibus z   47 provideret M   49 aetitem] echitem $Lw^{ac}x$
55 et] es z   58 haec z

Reply first of all, whitest Nero, to the first, that the most ancient priests of long ago were doctors as well as astronomers, as indeed the histories of the Chaldeans, the Persians, and the Egyptians testify. Moreover, to no one more than to the pious priest did the duties of extraordinary charity pertain, which indeed shine forth as much as possible in the greatest service of all. The most outstanding duty without a doubt, most necessary and especially desired by all, is to see to it that men have a sound mind in a sound body.[4] This we can accomplish only if we join medicine with the priesthood. But since medicine is quite often useless and often harmful without the help of the heavens—a thing which both Hippocrates and Galen admit and I have experienced— astronomy certainly pertains to this priestly charity no less than does medicine.[5] The sacred Scriptures command us to honor such a doctor (as I think), "since for your need the Most High created him." And Christ, the giver of life, who commanded his disciples to "cure the sick" in the whole world,[6] will also enjoin priests to heal at least with herbs and stones, if they are unable to cure with words as those men did before. But if those things are not sufficient, he will command them to compound them with a seasonable breath of heaven and apply them to sick people. For with the same breath of heaven by which he incites animals everywhere, each to his own medicine, even so does he provide most abundantly for the life of all. Under the divine stimulus of such heavenly inspiration, snakes cure themselves with fennel;[7] swallows cure their eyes with chelidonia;[8] and eagles, when they have a hard time giving birth, have discovered by divine inspiration the eagle-stone with which they successfully bring forth their eggs right away.[9] Therefore God Himself, who through the heavens impels all animals to his medicines, certainly permits priests to drive out diseases, not, I say, for gain but out of charity, with medicines which are strengthened by the heavens. In addition to these arguments, you will then add even more, if it is expedient, through the keenness of your mind.

After this, you too rise, O mighty Guicciardini, and reply to intellectual busybodies that Marsilio is not approving magic and images but recounting them in the course of an interpretation of Plotinus. And my writings make this quite clear, if they are read impartially. Nor do I affirm here a single word about profane magic which depends upon the worship of daemons, but I mention natural magic, which, by natural things, seeks to obtain the services of the celestials for the prosperous health of our bodies. This power, it seems, must be granted to minds which use it legitimately, as medicine and agriculture are justly granted, and all the more so as that activity which joins heavenly things to earthly is more perfect. From this workshop, the Magi, the first of all, adored the new-born Christ. Why then are you so dreadfully afraid of the name of Magus, a name pleasing to the Gospel, which signifies not an enchanter and a sorcerer, but a wise priest? For what does that Magus, the first adorer of Christ, profess? If you wish to hear: on the analogy of a farmer, he is a cultiva-

hic adorat, quemadmodum nec agricola terram, sed sicut agricola humani victus gratia ad aerem temperat agrum, sic ille sapiens, ille sacerdos gratia salutis humanae inferiora mundi ad superiora contemperat; atque sicut ova gallinae, sic opportune terrena subicit fovenda coelo. Quod efficit semper ipse Deus, et faciendo docet suadetque facere, ut a superis infima generentur et moveantur atque regantur.

Denique duo sunt magiae genera. Unum quidem eorum, qui certo quodam cultu daemonas sibi conciliant, quorum opera freti fabricant saepe portenta. Hoc autem penitus explosum est, quando princeps huius mundi eiectus est foras. Alterum vero eorum qui naturales materias opportune causis subiciunt naturalibus mira quadam ratione formandas. Huius quoque artificii species duae sunt: altera quidem curiosa, altera necessaria. Illa sane ad ostentationem supervacua fingit prodigia, ceu quando Persarum Magi ex salvia sub fimo putrefacta, dum Sol et Luna secundam Leonis faciem occuparent, eundemque gradum ibi tenerent, generabant avem merulae similem serpentina cauda, eamque redactam in cinerem infundebant lampadi, unde domus statim plena serpentibus videbatur. Hoc autem tanquam vanum et saluti noxium procul effugiendum. Tenenda tamen species necessaria, cum astrologia copulans medicinam. Si quis autem pertinax ulterius instet, morem huic ita gerito, Guicciardine, ut ne legat haec nostra, nec intelligat, nec meminerit, nec utatur homo, si homo est tanto beneficio prorsus indignus. Multa sunt praeterea quae tu adversus ingratam ignorantiam in medium afferre tuo ingenio poteris.

Quidnam agis et tu, strenue Soderine noster? Tolerabis ne superstitiosos caecosque nescio quos futuros, qui vitam in animalibus vel abiectissimis herbisque vilissimis manifestam vident, in coelo, in mundo non vident. Iam vero si homunciones isti vitam minimis concedunt mundi particulis, quae tandem dementia est, quae invidia, nec nosse, nec velle totum vivere in quo vivimus et movemur et sumus? Quod quidem canit Aratus, Iovem manifeste significans communem corporis mundani vitam. Peropportune nunc in haec Arati verba nescio quomodo videor incidisse. Memini Lucam evangelistam, memini Paulum apostolum his verbis libenter uti, in quibus mundi vitam sapientes illi non horrent. At vero superstitiosus quidam his obiciet non facile convinci ex verbis eiusmodi, Paulum assentiri mundum habere animam, sed tantum subesse Deo ac nos in hoc ipso Deo vivere. Esto igitur. Ne nominemus in mundo, quando non placet, animam. Nomen anima sit propha-

---

74 regnantur *z*   75 eorum *om. M*   81 seu *z*   83 avem] autem *z*   86 tamen] tantum *M*
88 nostra] noxia *z*   90 adversum *L*   93 quos futuros *om. z*   103 vivente *x*

tor of the world. Nor does he on that account worship the world, just as a farmer does not worship the earth; but just as a farmer for the sake of human sustenance tempers his field to the air, so that wise man, that priest, for the sake of human welfare tempers the lower parts of the world to the upper parts; and just like hen's eggs, so he fittingly subjects earthly things to heaven that they may be fostered. God himself always brings this about and by doing, teaches and urges us to do it in order that the lowest things may be produced, moved, and ruled by the higher.

Lastly, there are two kinds of magic. The first is practiced by those who unite themselves to daemons by a specific religious rite, and, relying on their help, often contrive portents. This, however, was thoroughly rejected when the Prince of this World was cast out.[10] But the other kind of magic is practiced by those who seasonably subject natural materials to natural causes to be formed in a wondrous way. Of this profession there are also two types: the first is inquisitive, the second, necessary. The former does indeed feign useless portents for ostentation: as when the Magi of Persia produced a bird similar to a blackbird with a serpent's tail out of sage which had putrefied under manure, while the Sun and Moon occupied the same degree in the second face of Leo; they reduced the bird to ashes and poured it into a lamp, whereupon the house seemed as a result to be full of serpents.[11] This type, however, must be avoided as vain and harmful to health. Nevertheless the necessary type which joins medicine with astrology must be kept. If anyone obstinately insists further, however, gratify him, Guicciardini, to the extent that the man (if one wholly undeserving of such a benefit is a man) may never read these things of ours, nor understand, remember, or make use of them. There are many points besides which your own genius will be able to bring forward to oppose ungrateful ignorance.

Now, what are you to do, our vigorous Soderini? Will you tolerate it that there will be some men or other, superstitious and blind, who see life plain in even the lowest animals and the meanest plants, but do not see life in the heavens or the world? Now if those little men grant life to the smallest particles of the world, what folly! what envy! neither to know that the Whole, in which "we live and move and have our being," is itself alive, nor to wish this to be so. Aratus, indeed, sings this, showing clearly that Jupiter is the life which is common to the body of the world. Most fittingly I seem now to have lit somehow upon those words of Aratus. I remember Luke the evangelist, I remember Paul the apostle gladly using these words; those wise men do not fear the life of the world which they imply.[12] But some superstitious man will object that it is not easily shown from these words that Paul agrees that the world has a soul, but only that the world is subject to God and that we live in this God. Well, so be it. Let us not say that there is a soul in the world, since that is unacceptable. Let soul be a profane name. Will it not be permitted to say

num. Licebitne saltem vitam qualemcunque dicere? Quam Deus ipse, mundi faber, huic operi suo tam feliciter absoluto clementer inspiret, quandoquidem erga vilissima quaeque viventia non est avarus, et quotidie per coelum quam plurimis quae sunt in eo largissime praestat vitam. Dic amabo, nonne vides boves et asinos, o bos, o asine, qui tactu quodam ex se viventia generant, esse vivos? Si ergo haec praeterea ex se viva quaedam aspectu etiam generarent, an non multo magis haec vivere iudicares, si quod modo ipse iudicium, si quam vitam habes? Coelum, terrae maritus, non tangit (ut communis est opinio) terram. Cum uxore non coit, sed solis siderum suorum quasi oculorum radiis undique lustrat uxorem; lustrando fecundat procreatque viventia. Num ergo vitam vel intuendo largiens, ipsum in se propriam nullam habet vitam? Et quod dedit avi strutho vitam aspectumque vivificum, longe est hoc ipso deterius. His tandem adductis in medium, nisi persuaseris superstitiosum istum, mittito semivivum, immo vero non vivum. Proinde ut pluribus causam nostram patronis agamus, addito, Petre mi Nere, Amphionem illum nostrum, Landinum Christophorum, oratorem pariter et poetam. Ille noster Amphion suavitate mira celeriter lapidea hostium nostrorum corda demolliet. Tu vero, Guicciardine, carissime compater, ito nunc, ito alacer, Politianum Herculem accersito. Hercules quondam ubi periculosius certandum foret, vocitabat Iolaum. Tu nunc similiter Herculem. Nosti profecto quot barbara monstra Latium iam devastantia Politianus Hercules invaserit, laceraverit, interemerit; quam acriter expugnet passim, quam tuto propugnet. Hic ergo vel centum hydrae capita nostris liberis minitantia statim contundet clava, flammisque comburet. Eia, mi dulcissime Soderine, surge age, Picum salutato Phoebeum. Hunc ego saepe Phoebum appello meum, ille me Dionysium vicissim atque Liberum. Fratres ergo sumus. Nuntia Phoebo meo venenosum contra nos pythonem ex paludiamiam emergentem. Tendat arcum obsecra, precor; confestim spicula iaculetur. Intendet ille protinus, scio quid loquar, venenumque totum semel una nece necabit.

Valete iam feliciter, amatissimi fratres mei, non valetudine tantum felici, sed ipsa etiam felicitate digni; liberorumque meorum in lucem iam prodeuntium valetudinem felicitatemque curate.

XV. Septembris, MCCCCLXXXVIIII.   In agro Caregio

---

112 habet *z*   113 terra *z*   118 mitto *xz*   120 Laudinum *z*   pariter *om. z*   124 vocitabant *z*   125 quod *z*   126 laceraverit *z*   128 confundet $Lw^{ac}x$ 129 Phoebeum] Phoebum $L^{ac}z$ ergo *z*   Phoebeum *x*   130 Fratres] tres *M*   135 producentium *z*   137 *post* Caregio *add.* Apologiae finis *z*

that at least there is some sort of life? — a life which God himself, the maker of the world, so fortunately, perfectly, and gently breathes into this work of his, since he is not stingy towards the meanest of living things and daily through the heavens most bountifully bestows life on as many as possible of those things which it contains. Tell me, I pray, surely you see that oxen and asses are living, O ox, O ass,[13] who beget living things from themselves by a touch. If, moreover, these things were to generate living things from themselves by a look, would you not judge all the more that these things are living, if only you yourself have any judgment, if you have any life? Heaven, the husband of earth, does not touch the earth, as is the common opinion. It does not have intercourse with its wife; but by the rays of its stars alone as if with the rays of its eyes, it illuminates her on all sides; it fertilizes her by its illumination and procreates living things. If, therefore, it bestows life even by its glance, does heaven have no life proper to itself? And the fact that it gave life and a vivifying look to the sparrow is a thing far lower than this. After having brought forward these points, if you should fail in the end to persuade the superstitious man, dismiss him as half-dead, or rather as not even living.

Then, my dear Piero del Nero, in order that we may plead our case with more defenders, bring in that Amphion of ours: Christoforo Landino, orator as well as poet.[14] That Amphion of ours will quickly soften the stony hearts of our enemies with his wondrous sweetness. And you, Guicciardini, dearest godfather [of my books/children], go now, go quickly and summon Poliziano, our Hercules.[15] In those days, when Hercules was about to engage in a rather dangerous struggle, he used to call out "Iolaus."[16] Do you now similarly call out "Hercules." For you know how many barbarous monsters now devastating Latium Poliziano our Hercules has attacked, destroyed, and killed; how zealously he conquers everywhere, how securely he defends. This man, therefore, will immediately beat with his club and consume in flames even a hundred heads of the Hydra threatening our books/children.[17] Up, then, my dearest Soderini, rise and greet Pico, our Phoebus. I often call him my Phoebus and he in turn calls me Dionysius and Liber, for we are brothers.[18] Tell my Phoebus that the poisonous Python even now is rising from the swamp against us.[19] Let him stretch his bow, beg him, I beseech you. Let him shoot his arrows without delay. He will immediately bend his bow, I know whereof I speak, and with a single slaughter will once and for all destroy all the poison.

Farewell now fortunately, my most loving brothers, worthy not only of fortunate health but of good fortune itself. Take care of the health and good fortune of my children/books now coming forth into the light.

September 15, 1489   at Careggi

Quod necessaria sit ad vitam securitas et tranquillitas animi.

Marsilius Ficinus dilectissimis in veritatis venatione fratribus, Bernardo Canisiano, Ioanni Canacio, Amerigo Cursino salutem. Cum primis hic in verbis venationem quandam instituissemus, merito forsan canes statim adhibuimus et cursores. Apte quidem philosophantes appellavimus venatores, anhela semper veritatis indagine laborantes. Num etiam apte canes? Aptissime inquit in *Republica* Socrates: philosophantes enim vel legitimi sunt vel spurii; ambo canes. Illi quidem veritatem ipsam sagaciter investigant, mordicus inventam tenent, hi vero pro opinione latrant, mordent, lacerant. Tantum profecto canes inter philosophos sibi vendicant, ut non solum se ipsos in sectam aliquam inseruerint, sed etiam sectam ipsi suam nomine Cynicam quandoque confecerint.

Habet quinetiam suos academia canes. Huc ergo vos, sagaces academiae canes, huc vos, velocissimi cursores, advoco. Tres enim estis. Tres ergo nunc meos precor, defendite liberos adhuc teneriores, inter lupos (ut vereor) e vestigio prodituros. Currite, inquam, alacres, negotia enim nunc vobis optata mando, non curas. Georgium Benignum Salviatum cognoscitis meum, qui veritatem illam, per cuius nunc vos vestigia passim venando discurritis, iamdiu est sagaciter assecutus; qui et fratres suos, Solis instar, maior ipse minores illustrat. Huic igitur, si quem luporum ululatum audieritis, nuntiate. Fortissimus ille Georgius omnes facile fugabit lupos, qui et vastum draconem quandoque transfixit. Ille me igitur, ille sollicitudine simul et vos cura levabit.

Solet enim inter vos aliquis et quidem iam saepius dicere, nihil ad vitam salubrius experiri, quam magna cum securitate tempora deglutire; ceteri vero dicenti protinus arridere. Sed dic age, Canaci, quidnam hoc tuum est totiens repetitum: tempora devorare? Quid denique tibi vis? Non esse inquies, sed bibere potius; non mandere vel conterere, sed faucibus plenis ingurgitare, siquidem tempus ipsum natura quaedam est liquens (ut ita dixerim) atque labilis. Liquentium vero haec est conditio, ut si cohibeas in angustum, subito perdas, diffluunt enim coacta celeriterque diffugiunt. Si aquam spongiae imbibitam forte compresseris, exprimes eam statimque disperges; si latius hanc tenueris, retinebis—multo magis aerem ignemque et aetherem. Hinc apud poetas frustra contendunt qui ampla divorum maniumve simulacra ulnis capescere moliuntur. Late admodum accipienda sunt latissima; liquentia et amplissima sunt amplissime possidenda. Tunc certe graviter nos premit an-

---

1 dilectissimus *z*   2 *post* Canacio *add.* et *z*   8 modicus *z*   12-13 Huc—canes *om. M*
13 velocissimi] ut locissimi *z*   est *z*   22 iam] tam *z*   23 qui *M*   27 est *om. M*

That Freedom from Care and Tranquillity of Mind Are Necessary for Life.

Marsilio Ficino sends greetings to his most beloved brothers in the hunt for truth: Bernardo Canigiani, Giovanni Canacci, and Amerigo Corsini.[1] Since here with the first words I had begun a hunt, perhaps justly I immediately sent for dogs and runners. Aptly have I called men who philosophize "hunters," because they always labor, panting to encircle the truth. So are they aptly called dogs? "Most aptly," says Socrates in the *Republic*.[2] For people who philosophize are either legitimate or illegitimate, and both are dogs. The former, indeed, keenly track out the truth and, when found, hold onto it with their teeth. But the latter bark, bite, and mangle in defense of opinion. Among philosophers the dogs claim so much for themselves that not only have they infiltrated into any sect, but they have at some point made a sect of their own with their very name—"Cynic" [pun on Greek word for dog].

Furthermore, the Florentine Academy has its dogs. Hither, then, do I call you, the keen-nosed dogs of the Academy and the swiftest runners. There are three of you. Now, therefore, I pray you, defend my three children/books who are still young and are, I fear, just about to go forth among wolves. Run quickly, I say, for now I am enjoining upon you tasks you desire, not cares. You know my friend, Giorgio Benigno Salviati,[3] who has long keenly pursued that truth on the tracks of which you are now running here and there in your hunt, and who, being elder, illuminates his younger brothers like the Sun. Report to him, therefore, if you should hear any howling of wolves. The brave George, who once pierced a huge dragon,[4] will easily put to flight all the wolves. It is he, then, who will at one and the same time relieve me of worry and you of cares.

For one among you is accustomed to say, and indeed rather often, that he has found nothing more salutary for life than to "swallow down" time with extreme carelessness; moreover the rest straightway smile on the speaker. But tell me now, Canacci, what is this which you have so often repeated, to "devour" time? What finally do you mean? "Not to eat," you say, "but rather to drink." Not to chew or grind but to guzzle liberally, since indeed time itself has a nature that is liquid, so to speak, and fleeting. Now the condition of liquids is such that if you confine them narrowly you immediately lose them, for, having been compressed, they flow away and quickly disperse. If by chance you squeeze the water contained in a sponge, you will squeeze it out and immediately disperse it; if you hold it with a more open hand, you will retain it— much more so with air, fire, and aether. Hence those characters portrayed by the poets struggle in vain who try to hold in their arms the expanded apparitions of gods or departed spirits.[5] The widest things must be received quite widely; things which are liquid and very expanded must be most expansively possessed. Certainly confinement then oppresses us, when we have reduced

gustia, quando animum ipsum motumque eius naturaliter amplum redigimus 35
in angustum. Quicunque studia negotiaque pensitant examussim, et in minima quaeque semper exactissime deterunt, vitam interea suam, heu suam vitam, clam miseri conterunt. Recte igitur Pythagoras praecepisse videtur: cave ne quando in angustum forte cohibearis. Nihil coelo amplius, nihil est vitalius. Angustissima vicissim terra vitam habet in mundo quam minimam. 40
Denique si coelo temporeque vivimus, quanto haec latius absorbemus, tanto vivimus et diutius.

Vivite ergo lati ab angustia procul, o amici. Vivite laeti. Laetitia coelum vos creavit sua, quam suo quodam risu, id est dilatatione, motu, splendore declarat, quasi gestiens. Laetitia coelum vos servabit vestra. Ergo quotidie 45
impraesens vivite laeti, nam sollicitudo praesentium rapit vobis praesens praeripitque futurum. Curiositas futurorum celeriter in praeteritum vos traducit. Iterum igitur precor atque iterum, vivite laeti, nam fata sinunt, dum securi vivitis. Sed ut re vera sine cura vivatis, ne unam quidem hanc curam sumite, qua solliciti curetis unquam, qua potissimum diligentia curas effugi- 50
atis. Una enim cura haec mortalibus, heu miseris, omni cura cor urit. Negligite igitur diligentiam, negligentiam vero diligite; atque hanc etiam negligenter, quoad licet vobis, inquam, atque decet. Haec autem non tam ut sacerdos, amici, mando vobis quam ut medicus. Nam absque hac una tanquam medicinarum omnium vita medicinae omnes ad vitam producendam 55
adhibitae moriuntur.

XVI. Septembris, MCCCCLXXXVIIII.   In agro Caregio

                  Amerigus Corsinus

De triplici vita quem tu, Ficine, libellum
    Compositum in lucem mittere docte paras,
Imprimere hunc doctus gratusque Valorius ultro
    Curavit, doctis pabula grata viris.
Tresque Petri binique canes cursorque Amerigus
    Contendunt morsus pellere quisque feros.

---

35 redigemus *x*   37 exactissimae *w*   deserunt *M*   43 lati] laeti *xz*   46 vos *M*   47 vos *om.*
z   48 Iterum] Item *z*   57 XV. *M*   MCCCCLXXXVIIII *ante* XVI. Septembris *transp. x*   Careio
z; post Caregio *add.* Finis Apologiae *y*   *Amerigi Corsini versus desunt in yz*

to a narrow space the mind itself and its naturally expansive motion. Whoever ponders his pursuits and work precisely and threshes everything out right down to its smallest part, secretly wretched all the while, wears out his life, alas, his life! Pythagoras, then, seems to have rightly taught: beware lest you ever chance to be narrowly confined. Nothing is more expansive than the heavens, nothing more vital. Conversely, the earth is very small and it has the least life of anything in the cosmos. Finally, since we live by heaven and in time, the more widely we absorb these, the more and the longer do we live.

Live, therefore, O friends, uninhibitedly, far from confinement. Live joyfully. Heaven's joy has created you, which it expresses by its smile, that is, by its expansion, its motion, and its splendor, as if it were exulting. By your joy heaven will preserve you. Therefore, live joyfully in the present, day by day.[6] For worry about present circumstances both snatches the present from you and takes away your future. Anxious inquiry about the future quickly transfers you yourself into the past. Therefore, I beseech you again and again, live joyfully, for the fates indeed allow it when you live without care. But in order that you may truly live without care, do not even take this one care about which you ever nervously take care and by diligence in which you chiefly escape cares. This one care, indeed [presumably meaning care about one's health, enjoined in similar words in 1.2], burns the heart of wretched mortals, poor things, with every care. Therefore neglect diligence, but love negligence, and love it negligently, as long as you can and it is fitting. These things, however, my friends, I enjoin upon you less as a priest than as a doctor. For without this one item [presumably meaning freedom from care, as in 1 Proem 1] that is the life of all medicines, all medicines used to prolong life perish.[7]

September 16, 1489   at Careggi

Amerigo Corsini:

You, learned Ficino, composed a book on the triple life[8] which you now prepare to publish. A learned and gracious man, Valori, further financed its printing — pleasant food for the learned. The three Peters, the two dogs, and Amerigo the runner — each is striving to repel fierce bites.

COMMENTARY NOTES

WORKS CITED

INDICES

General Proem

1. Ficino makes Bacchus a priest of "sacris mysteriis" (line 7) because, in line with Plato's *Phaedrus* 265a, he always makes him, or his Greek counterpart Dionysus, the god of the divine frenzy known as *sacerdotium*. See Letter to Peregrino Agli, Dec. 1457, ad fin., citing Plato, *Phaedrus* 265a, *Op.*, p. 615, *Letters*, translated by members of the Language Department of the School of Economic Science, London, vols. 1-3 (London, 1975-1981), 1: 47-48; *Comm. Symp.*, 7.14 (*Op.*, p. 1361), ed. Marcel, p. 258; and Chastel, *Marsile Ficin et l'art* (Geneva, 1954), p. 130.

2. Ovid, *Met.* 3.317, "bis geniti Bacchi"; 4.12, "bimatrem"; Manilius, *Astronomica* 2.2. Epithets of this sort are often applied to Bacchus; for other examples, see Michael J. B. Allen, *The Platonism of Marsilio Ficino* (Berkeley, 1984), p. 31, n. 75. The "vindemiae fulmen" below corresponds to the fatal splendor of Jupiter's revealed godhead which killed Semele.

3. Melchisidech had no recorded parents; the author of Hebrews dwells on this lacuna so as to make him a type of Christ, 7:1-4, citing Gen. 14:18; see also Ps. 110:4; Heb. 5:6,10; 6:20; 7:1-17.

4. Word-play on "medicus" and "Medici"; for a similar word-play, see Letter of 11 November 1490 to Bartolomeo Scala, Kristeller, *SF*, 1.60. He was ordained (*pace* Corsi's *Vita*) in 1473, Della Torre, pp. 594-95. "Ficinum medicum" is Diotifeci Ficino of Figline in Val d'Arno, personal physician, or so Ficino always claimed, to Cosimo de' Medici. Originally called Diotifeci d'Agnolo di Giusto, he took the name "Ficino" only after being summoned to Florence by Cosimo, probably even after Marsilio's birth, Marcel, *MF*, pp. 124-25. See "The Author in the Work." Cosimo was of course the grandfather of Lorenzo and the founder of the ruling dynasty.

5. See Phillip De Lacy, "Galen's Platonism," *American Journal of Philology* 93 (1972): 27-39.

6. In 1462, Cosimo had commissioned the young Marsilio to translate the works of Plato, Kristeller, *Phil MF*, p. 16.

7. The translation of Plato was finished around 1468 (see Kristeller, *Phil MF*, p. 17) but not published until 1484. The next item to be mentioned, "decem atque octo de animorum immortalitate libros et aeterna felicitate," Ficino's major original work, better known as the *Theologia Platonica* after Proclus's book of the same title, was written 1469-1474, though not published until 1482; see Kristeller, *Phil MF*, pp. 17-18.

8. Ficino here gives the false impression that Book 2 was composed second whereas it was composed last, after Book 3 (see above, "Editorial Introduction," ad init.).

9. While all of the authorities consulted agree that musicians are born under Venus, none of them, not even Ficino himself elsewhere, straightforwardly attributes doctors to Venus; see Letter to Antonio Canigiani similarly justifying his dual profession of music and medicine, *Letters*, 1: 141–44 (*Op.*, p. 650,4). Ptolemy says that Venus produces druggists; Venus and Mercury, physicians who employ drugs in their treatments, *Tetrabiblos*, 4.4 (Venice, 1484). Thus Venus gives birth to doctors only under certain conditions, not "equally." For the possible presence of such a combination in Ficino's own horoscope, which would explain his overstatement here, see "The Author in the Work."

10. In Books 1 and 2, Ficino seems to use *anima* and *animus* interchangeably; here—for one and the same entity—he so uses "animus iste meus" with "ex mea . . . anima" above it and "per suam . . . animam" below it. "A clear distinction between *animus* and *anima* is not always observed, though the ancients attempted to draw one," writes James Tatum, adducing examples of the confusion even in Cicero, "The Tales in Apuleius's *Metamorphoses*," *TAPA* 100 (1969): 509, n. 54. See above, Introduction, "Principles of Translation."

11. Cf. Augustine *De Genesi ad litteram* 12.35 entitled "Resurrectio corporum ad perfectam beatitudinem animae cur sit necessaria," *PL* 34: 483. The union of body and soul referred to in this metaphor is primarily that of the final Christian resurrection, as in the quotation from Augustine—even though "Cuius artubus in unam formam iam compactis, vita protinus adsit" sounds like the stages of gestation. As a compliment to Lorenzo, Ficino equates his home with Paradise. In this life, of course, for Ficino as for any good Platonist, it is precisely the body which disquiets the soul; see for example, *Theologia Platonica*, 14.7, ed. Marcel (hereafter referred to simply as ed.) 2: 273 (*Op.*, p. 317).

12. An extended pun on words for "breath" (*afflatu, aspira,* and *spiritu*) and on the function—celebrated in *De vita*—of the medical spirit to link body and soul.

Proem to Book 1

1. A play on *probo* begins here. Both dedicatees were members of Ficino's Academy; both were associated with Lorenzo. Ficino had submitted to them, among others, his translation of Plato for correction, as his "Praefatio ad lectorem" of that work acknowledges, ed. Kristeller, *SF*, 2: 105; see also *SF*, 1: 111–12, and *Letters*, 1: 224, 233, and 2: 114. Giorgio Antonio Vespucci was the uncle and teacher of that Amerigo for whom America is named; see E. H. Gombrich, *Symbolic Images*, p. 43 and p. 81, n. 47; Della Torre, pp. 772–74.

2. Mt. 11:28; John 14:6.

1.1

1. Jupiter, the major benefic or "greater Fortune," is missing here, though included in similar lists, e.g., 3.24, *Op.*, p. 568. Saturn, by convention the worst planet of all, is omitted here but introduced as early as 1.4, *Op.*, p. 496, and included, last and defensively, in the list in 3.24. One of the contributions of *De vita* is to establish Saturn as another planet not only characteristic of scholars but beneficial to them; see "Traditional Material and Innovations," hereafter "Traditions," and "The Author in the Work." The mention of the planets at this early point proves that Book 3 or something like it was part of Ficino's plan from the outset.

2. Since no individual can select his own natural father, either a second and spiritual father of the sort mentioned in Gen. Proem must be uppermost in Ficino's mind, or else "nostra diligentia" here must mean that of humankind at large.

3. Education is of course a central concern of the *Republic*. As for the father, while Plato's ideal commonwealth places no trust whatever in the natural parents of potential *savants* (transferring all infant guardians to the collective wardship of the State, *Rep.* 457-65), Socrates himself in the same work praises one individual historical father—Ariston, father of two of his interlocutors Adeimantus and Glaucon, and probably also of Plato himself, *Rep.* 367e. More to Ficino's purpose, *Laws* 5.729 and 6.781a specify duties of fathers in training sons.

4. A comprehensive discussion of education, including the parents' role, forms the apparently truncated conclusion of Aristotle's *Politics* 7.13-8.7 (1331b-1342b). The duties of fathers and teachers toward children are also mentioned in 1.12-13 (1259a-1260b), et passim.

5. The father is central, being in fact the addressee, throughout the first essay in the *Moralia* (1A-14C), the *De liberis educandis*, now considered to be of doubtful authenticity but in the Renaissance constitutive of educational theory, first through Guarino's translation of 1411 and then through Vittorino's "first great school of the Renaissance," J. E. Sandys, *A History of Classical Scholarship*, vol. 2 (1908. Reprint. New York, 1958), p. 53; William Harrison Woodward, *Studies in Education . . . 1400-1600* (Cambridge, 1924), p. 7.

6. *Institutes* 2.2; 3; 8; 9; indeed, the entire *Institutes* centers on education. Although the father is less prominent than the teacher, being mentioned as the employer of the teacher (2), the Proem to 6 records Quintilian's past concern for his own son's mental growth, now rendered vain by death. The complete text of Quintilian's *Institutes* had been discovered by Poggio in 1416 and had likewise influenced humanist education, Woodward, op. cit., p. 8.

7. This is not to deny that scholars have been cursorily mentioned as patients in medical treatises before; Plutarch, for example, has much to say about the health of scholars in his "De sanitate tuenda," in *Moralia* 122B-137E. Still closer to Ficino, Antonio Guaineri of Pavia (fl. 1412-1448), in his *Practica* (Venice, 1517), Tr. 15.2, lists among the causes of melancholy "assiduitas studii," fol. 23, col. a; and Constantinus Africanus likewise "nimia cogitatio," etc., *Della melancolia*, ed. and trans. M. T. Malato and U. De Martini (Rome, 1959), p. 54 (Latin) and 1.3, p. 89 (Italian); see also KP&S, p. 82, and "The Author in the Work."

8. A pun on Minerva as "minuens nervos" begins here, and see below, 2.3, ad fin.

1.2

1. Unless otherwise noted, Ficino in *De vita* uses the word *spiritus* only in the scientific sense; see Introduction, "Habits." Ficino's initial definition of spirit here coincides almost exactly with the typical Renaissance version of the doctrine as summarized by D. P. Walker, "The Astral Body in Renaissance Medicine," *JWCI* 21 (1958): 120, quoted in "Habits." The subdivision into natural, vital, and animal, which applies not only to *vires* and *virtutes* but to spirit itself, recurs rarely, e.g., in 3.6 (*Op.*, p. 537), and in 3.21 (*Op.*, p. 563). Each serves as raw material for the next and higher one. The adjective *animal* means not "animal" but "of or pertaining to soul." See also in general, Gérard Verbeke, *L'évolution de la doctrine du pneuma du Stoicisme à S. Augustin* (Paris, 1945), e.g., p. 212, attributing to Galen the idea that the spirit is the "instrument" of soul; Marielene Putscher, *Pneuma, Spiritus, Geist: Vorstellung vom Lebensantrieb in ihren geschichtlichen Wandlungen* (Wiesbaden, 1973), esp. pp. 43, 187, 188-99, and 194; and on the threefold subdivision, E. Ruth Harvey, *The Inward Wits* (London, 1975), pp. 16-18, citing Haly Abbas.

2. On the interior senses, see *Theol. Plat.* 11.3, ed. 2: 98 (*Op.*, p. 242); cf. 6.2, ed. 1: 225-26 (*Op.*, p. 157), and Harvey, *Inward*, pp. 23-24; see also below, 2.15 and note 1.

3. One of Ficino's favorite metonymies for the brain, probably a reminiscence of *Iliad* 6.88 and 297, which reads, in Spondanus's Latin translation, "in templum . . . Minervae in arce summa." KP&S helpfully paraphrase his meaning here as: "generated by, or even contained in, the blood, but working only in the brain," p. 265, except that they wrongly (for Ficino) call spirit a fluid.

1.3

1. Here Ficino introduces his central doctrine of the four humors and especially of melancholy. As with Saturn and spirit, his point of departure is the traditional doctrine; see KP&S, especially, in the present context, p. 10. The last sentence is modeled on Horace, *Epistle* 1.1.106-8.

1.4

1. On Mercury, see for example Haly Albohazen, son of Abenragel (fl. ca. 1016-1040), *Liber de iudiciis astrorum*, translated from Arabic into Spanish by Judah ben Moses and thence into Latin by Egidius de Tebaldis of Parma and Petrus de Regio (ed. pr. Venice, 1485), 1.4, "De naturis planetarum," "De Mercurio," calling him hot and dry and linking him in patronage of intellectuals not with Saturn but with Jupiter, see also notes on 3.6 and 3.18; and *Guidonis Bonati Foroliviensis mathematici de astronomia tractatus X* (Basel, 1550), Part 1, Tract. 3, chap. 6, cols. 112, 114. They do not associate Mercury with melancholy but with a variable and in itself neutral nature. On Saturn, see Bonatti, 1.3.1, col. 98; the attribution to

him of cold, dryness, black bile, and melancholy and hence of perseverance and tenacious memory, is standard; see KP&S, p. 127; see for example Haly Albohazen, 1.4, "De Saturno." Thus Ficino is enhancing Saturn by arrogating to him some of the intellectual functions of Mercury and of Jupiter.

2. *Timaeus* 90c–d; see also Ficino's *Appendix commentariorum in Timaeum* at this approximate point, *Op.*, pp. 1484, 1483.

3. 87–88a. Plato here speaks only of the bad effects on the body; by conflating this passage with 90c–d about the good effects on the soul, Ficino makes it more optimistic.

1.5

1. Ps.-Aristotle, *Problem* 30.1 (953a).
2. Plato, *Theaetetus* (subtitled *De scientia*, see Kristeller, *SF*, 2: 106) 144a–b; see also *Rep.* 503c–d. In both dialogues, Plato prefers that rare person who represents a mean, whereas Ficino accepts joyfully the excesses of the agile-minded.
3. Democritus of Abdera, fifth century B.C., in Diels-Kranz, *Fragmente der Vorsokratiker*, chap. 68, B 17–18. Closer to Ficino in wording is Cicero, *De divinatione* 1.37.80 (Diels calls it 38); and *De oratore* 2.46.194. Cf. Ficino's Letter of 1 Dec. 1457 on divine frenzy to Peregrino Agli, *Letters* 1: 42–8 (*Op.*, p. 612).
4. *Phaedrus* 245a, for an accessible ed. of which in Ficino's translation, see M. J. B. Allen, *Marsilio Ficino and the Phaedran Charioteer*, p. 52; cf. Ficino's *In Platonis Iovem* [sic, for *Ionem*] . . . *epitome*, *Op.*, pp. 1281 ff.; see also Letter to Agli, op. cit.; and for the arts in general, *Theol. Plat.* 13.2, ed. 2: 202 (*Op.*, p. 287).
5. Cf. *In Platonis Ionem* . . . *epitome*, cited above and, in more detail, *Comm. Symp.* 7.3, ed. Marcel, p. 245 (*Op.*, p. 1357), denying to that alienation of mind caused by disease any part in divine madness.
6. In actuality, this categorical assertion is unique to Ficino, although Guaineri cites melancholy as one possible condition for inspiration, 15.4, fols. 23v–24v, see below; see KP&S, p. 259.
7. Democritus and Plato do not even connect melancholy with apparent divinity; only Ps.-Aristotle does, and that without stressing divinity. This, Ficino's truly original idea, he fathers upon respectable ancients.
8. Ficino claims originality only in discovering the causes for the alleged benefits of melancholy. "Aristotle's" cause is rightly judged by Ficino to be insufficient — that black bile like wine simply exaggerates any qualities the patient may already possess. Guaineri, however, had already attempted to assign causes, 15.4, fol. 24r–v, col. a; though Platonic and astrological, they are not much like Ficino's, so that Ficino's claim to originality may be sincere. Briefly, Guaineri says that melancholy by suspending the senses returns the soul to a state like that both of its preexistence, when it knew everything by intuition as do the angels, and of its moment of birth when its natal star influenced it without impediment. Allen praises Platonic "furor" (which as we know is one result of melancholy) as facilitating anamnesis by returning us to our antenatal condition, but without specific Ficini-

an proof-texts (*Platonism*, p. 61); and Ficino certainly does not so explain it in *De vita*.
    9. Cf. Guaineri, 15.2, fol. 23r, col. b.
    10. Cf. Guaineri, 15.3, fol. 23v, col. a.
    11. For Guaineri's somewhat different definition of melancholy properly so called, see 15.1, fols. 22v-23r.
    12. For a somewhat different formula, see Ficino's *App. comm. in Tim.* (*Op.*, p. 1481). Ps.-Aristotle says only that the amount of heat should be moderated, 954a-b, and Guaineri prescribes only symptomatic cures, 15.7-12, fols. 25v-26v.
    13. On the proper proportion of heat, see *App. comm. in Tim.* (*Op.*, p. 1481) and Ps.-Aristotle, 954a-b. The extremism of melancholy is summed up at the end of *Problem* 30.1. The comparison to wine runs throughout the *Problem*, and Ficino's comparison to iron was suggested by the brief comparison to steel.
    14. Heraclitus, sixth to fifth century B.C., in Diels-Kranz, *Fragmente der Vorsokratiker*, chap. 22, B 118, which was also cited, in connection with light, not dryness, in *Theol. Plat.* 6.2, ed. 1: 237 (*Op.*, p. 162).

1.6

1. Democritus, Diels-Kranz, chap. 68, B 21 and 112. These authorities are summoned again, I take it, to support a newly emphasized benefit of melancholy — prophecy.
    2. *Phaedrus* 244.
    3. *Problem* 30.1 (954a). As KP&S have pointed out, p. 37, Ps.-Aristotle does indeed link what sounds like Plato's prophetic madness to melancholy, thus providing the germ of this entire section of *De vita* 1, but he sees such divine inspiration as only a minuscule part of his portrait of the melancholic, not as the crowning glory of the temperament. Cf. also Guaineri, 15.4, fol. 23v, col. b. Prophecy was a real and important phenomenon to Ficino; see Kristeller, *Phil MF*, pp. 213, 309, 312. The philosophic and the prophetic represent two of Ficino's four *furores* whereby one can re-ascend to the divine; see *In Platonis Ionem . . . epitome*, pp. 1281-82. Medical causes such as melancholy are the facilitators of intellectual excellence, but not its efficient causes, in *Theol. Plat.* 13.2, ed. 2: 202, 203 (facilitators not causes), 219 (*Op.*, pp. 286-94, especially 287, 294).
    4. Avicenna (ibn Sina, 980-1037), *Liber de philosophia prima sive scientia divina* or *Metaphysica*, translated into Latin by Gerard of Cremona and Dominicus Gundissalinus (Venice, 1495, repr. Louvain, 1961), Lib. 10, chap. 3, "De cultu dei et utilitate eius in hoc mundo et in futuro." This chapter is billed in the preceding chapter as telling "quae aptos naturaliter moveant ad inquisitionem sapientialem." It contains all Ficino's ideas here expressed, along with much that is different. A new critical edition is forthcoming; see *Liber de philosophia prima sive scientia divina I-IV*, ed. S. van Riet (Louvain and Leiden, 1977).
    5. Avicenna, *Liber de anima seu sextus de naturalibus IV-V*, ed. S. van Riet, Intro. G. Verbeke (Louvain and Leiden, 1968), Quarta Pars, chap. 2; Quinta Pars, chap. 6, esp. pp. 148-53. Ficino equated the Intellectus Agens with the Christian God. For an assessment of Ficino's debt to Avicenna, see Marian Heitzmann, "L'agostinis-

mo avicenizzante e il punto di partenza della filosofia di Marsilio Ficino," *Giornale critico della filosofia italiana* 16 (1935): 295–322; 460–80; 17 (1936): 1–11. Avicenna nowhere credits these gifts to melancholy.

6. This Serapion is Serapion the Elder (9th century), *Practica Johannis Serapionis dicta Breviarium* (Venice, 1503), Tract. 1, chap. 22, "De melancolia," fol. 7, col. 4.

7. *Liber canonis*, translated into Latin by Gerard of Cremona (Venice, 1507, repr. 1964), Lib. 3, Fen 1, Tract. 3, chap. 18, "De melancholia," fol. 188, col. 3. Ficino's breakdown of melancholy according to its various humoral origins (1.5) is also duplicated in this work, Lib. 1, Fen 1, Tract. 4, chap. 1.

1.7

1. Ficino is mistaken in ascribing this judgment to Hippocrates, a mistake he made also in *Consiglio contro la pestilenza*, chap. 5, Latin translation *Op.*, p. 580. According to Galen, *Commentary* 1.4 on Hippocrates' *Epidemia* 3 (Kühn 17.1: 521), it was Democritus who judged sexual intercourse to be like epilepsy. "It is remarkable that with regard to 'Venerei coitus' the Platonist Ficino departs from the views of the clinicians—to which, in this respect, even Hildegard of Bingen subscribed—and associates himself with the ascetic advice given by authors of a monastic and theological tendency," KP&S, p. 267, n. 81. Ficino himself, however, qualifies his remarks: "especially if it proceeds even a little beyond one's strength" (1.7.13–14) and "especially if you have intercourse immediately on a full stomach or while hungry" (1.11.35–36). For intercourse as beneficial, see Constantinus Africanus, *Opera* 1: 293, 303.

2. *De animalibus*, translated into Latin by Michael Scot (Venice, 1508, repr. Frankfurt am Main, 1961), 3.3, p. 32, col. 1a.

3. Diogenes Laertius 3.33, which in turn quotes the epigram now known as *Anth. Pal.* 9.39, on all of which see James Hutton, *The Greek Anthology in Italy* (Ithaca, NY, 1935), pp. 110–11.

4. See St. Jerome, *Contra Jovinianum* 2.11: "Heia discite a Platonico Galieno impossibile esse animam sanguine et adipe suffocatam coeleste aliquid cogitare." The passage from St. Jerome is given word for word, although without citation, in Ficino, *Epistolae* 5 (*Op.*, p. 786,1).

5. See Guido Bonatti, *De astronomia*, 1.2.5, col. 75: "Duodecima quidem significat carceres."

6. See Arnald of Villanova, *De conservanda bona valetudine*, which is his commentary on the *Regimen Salernitanum* (Paris, 1555), chap. 3, "De diurno sive meridiano somno," pp. 18–20. See also Avicenna, *Liber canonis*, 1.2.2.10.

7. See Arnald of Villanova, *Speculum medicinae*, chap. 78, in *Opera* (Lyons, 1504); and Avicenna, *Liber canonis* 1.2.2.13 and 3.1.3.1 and 4.

8. *Cratylus* 411b. See also Ficino, *Theol. Plat.*, 14.10, ed. 2: 288 (*Op.*, p. 323), although here Ficino seems to be saying that the passage comes from the *Theaetetus*.

9. *Oeconomica* 1.6.5 (1345a).

10. See Pss. 30:5 and 57:8.

1.8

1. See Galen, *De sanitate tuenda* 2.3, quoting Hippocrates, *De officina medici* (Kühn 6: 93); also Celsus, *De medicina* 2.14.2.
2. See Avicenna, *Liber canonis* 1.3.2.4: "De fricatione."
3. See Guido Bonatti, *De astronomia* 1.2.5, col. 73 on the ninth place: "Et dixit Alchabicius quod significat sapientiam"; and 1.2.11, col. 93: "Sol gaudet in nona quae est domus religionis." See also Albertus Magnus, *Speculum astronomiae*, eds. Stefano Caroti, Michela Pereira, and Stefano Zamponi, under the direction of Paola Zambelli (Pisa, 1977), chap. 12, p. 36.63-65 (= Borgnet 10: 644a). Albertus quotes from Albumasar, *Introductorium* 6.26: "Domus quoque nona vocata est domus peregrinationis et motionis fidei quoque atque operum bonorum, propter reversionem eius ad Iovem, etc." The Sun was in the ninth place in Ficino's own natal chart; see "The Author in the Work."

1.9

1. See Arnald of Villanova, *De conservanda bona valetudine*, chap. 14: "De aere," pp. 70-72; also Avicenna, *Liber canonis* 1.2.2.5.

1.10

1. Ficino's list of things which increase black bile can also be found in Arnald of Villanova, *De conservanda bona valetudine*, chap. 7: "De cibis vitandis"; Constantinus Africanus, *De melancholia*, ad init.; and Guaineri, *Practica*, Tract. 15: "De melancholia et mania." See KP&S, p. 267, n. 84: "Here (*De vita* 1.10-11 and 2.6-7), Ficino's agreement with school medicine appears particularly clearly; he brought little of his own to the usual prescriptions for eating and drinking." See also KP&S, pp. 82-86, for a discussion of Constantinus Africanus and traditional school medicine.
2. Plato, *Laws* 2.666b-c, and see below, *De vita* 2.7.66-68. Aristotle, *Problem* 3.16 (873a); also cf. 3.28 (875b) and 30.1 (954b).
3. See also below, 2.18.
4. See also 3.21. Cf. Hermes Trismegistus, *Asclepius* 38, where music played to the animated statues is imitative of the music of the spheres; and *Corpus Hermeticum*, Tract. 18, on music and musicians in general. Pythagoras, in Iamblichus, *De vita Pythagorica* 15.64-67 and 25.110-14. Plato, *Charmides* 157a-c and *Timaeus* 47d.
5. 1 Sam. 16:14-23.
6. See also below, 2.14 et passim.

1.11

1. Myrobalans are an astringent and plum-like fruit, once used in pharmacy but now chiefly in tanning, and they grow on trees of the various species of *Terminalia*.

Only this fruit comes in the kinds elsewhere specified by Ficino: emblic, chebule, and belleric or belliric; see for example, 1.20, *Op*, p. 505; 2.7, *Op.*, p. 515; 2.8, *Op.*, p. 516; 2.17, *Op.*, p. 524; 2.18, *Op.*, p. 527. Another possible meaning is the palm-nut or ben-nut, but it does not come in the above varieties; Ficino could say only of a fruit, not of a nut, what he says of myrobalans, "Memineritis autem myrobalanos conditas meliores esse; siccas vero saltem diem integrum oleo amygdalarum dulcium vel butyro vaccino prius infundite quam confletis" (below, 2.18.134-36); and besides, when Ficino refers to the ben, or horseradish-tree, he does so explicitly; see "been," 1.12.18, *Op.*, p. 503, and "radicum been" in 3.11.111, *Op.*, p. 546, see Index of Materia Medica.

1.12

1. Theriac or treacle is a name given to a popular class of antidotes. Most kinds were made from a large number of ingredients, a feature which becomes important in Book 3.

1.13

1. See Galen, *De locis affectis* 4.2 (Kühn 8: 224); *De sanitate tuenda* 6 (Kühn 6: 429); and *De methodo medendi* 12 (Kühn 10: 857).
2. Mesue the Younger (d. 1015), *Antidotarium* or *Grabadin medicinarum universalium*, in *Opera omnia* (Venice, 1561), Distinctio 10, chap. 10: "De pillulis," p. 151.3E. Cf. Stephen Blancardus, *Lexicon medicum renovatum* (Lyons, 1756), "alephanginae."
3. *Antidotarium*, Dist. 10, chap. 10, p. 152.3H.

1.16

1. *Antidotarium*, Dist. 1, Part 2: "De electuariis," p. 105.4E-G.

1.17

1. *Antidotarium*, Dist. 4: "De conditis," pp. 118.4-119.1; and Dist. 6: "De syrupis," p. 126.2-3.

1.18

1. Cf. Hippocrates, *Aphorism* 4.22 (Littrè 4:510) and Galen, *De crisibus* 1.6 (Kühn 9: 571).

1.19

1. An electuary is a medicinal paste, made from various powdered ingredients mixed with honey, jam, or syrup; see 1.23 for specific recipes.

1.20

1. The gifts of the Magi were, of course, gold, frankincense, and myrrh, all employed in the recipe below. See also 2.19 and "Apologia," 63-67.
2. For the Armenian stone, probably azurite, see Dioscorides, *De materia medica*, ed. M. Wellmann (Berlin, 1906-1914), 5.90.105, and Pliny *HN* 35.12.30 and 35.28.47; cf. also Burton, *Anatomy of Melancholy*, 2.4.1.4, and below, 3.19 and n. 5.
3. See Pliny, *HN* 25.21.52; Valerius Maximus, *Factorum et dictorum memorabilium libri novem*, ed. Karl Kempf (Leipzig, 1888), 8.7.5; Martianus Capella, *De nuptiis Philologiae et Mercurii*, ed. Adolph Dick, rev. Jean Préaux (Stuttgart, 1925, repr. 1978), 4.327.
4. Cf. Mesue, *Antidotarium*, Dist. 6: "De syrupis," p. 134.1D-2A. Gentile da Foligno (d. 1348), who taught at various schools in Italy, wrote a number of commentaries on Avicenna as well as various medical *Consilia*. See Thorndike 3: 233-52 and Nancy Siraisi, *Taddeo Alderotti and His Pupils* (Princeton, 1981), p. xxi.

1.21

1. *Timaeus* 89b-c.

1.22

1. See 1.6.
2. See 1.2.
3. Lev. 17:10 ff.

1.23

1. Rhazes (al-Rāzi, 865-932, active in Baghdad), *Liber ad Almansorem* (translated into Latin by Gerard of Cremona) in his *Opera parva* (Lyons, 1511), 9.13: "De melancholia," p. 150: "ex electuario quod vocatur letificans."
2. *Liber de viribus cordis*, translated into Latin by Arnald of Villanova, and pub. together with his *Liber canonis* (Venice, 1507, repr. Hildesheim, 1964), 2.4, p. 552.
3. *Antidotarium*, Dist. 1: "De electuariis," pp. 94.4H-95.1A.
4. *Antidotarium*, Dist. 1, p. 95.4E-G.
5. *Antidotarium*, p. 94.2C-D: "Electuarium de gemmis."
6. Peter of Abano (d. c.1316), professor of philosophy, astrology, and medicine at Padua, and a voluminous writer, see Thorndike 2: 874-947.

1.25

1. Archigenes was a physician at Rome during the reign of Trajan (98-117). Andromachus, the physician of Nero (emperor, 54-68), was credited with being the discoverer of theriac; see below, 3.21.48-50. Theodotion, a Hellenistic physician, was better known for his eye-salves (Celsus 6.6), than for his hiera.
2. The Jew is Isaac Judaeus or Israeli (c. 832-c. 932). See his *Liber primus practice*

Pantegni 10.49: "De diversis descriptionibus pilularum," in *Opera omnia* (Lyons, 1515), fol. 137v ff.

3. *Grabadin medicinarum particularium*, in *Opera omnia* (Venice, 1561) sec. 1, summa 3, chaps. 5 and 8, pp. 186.2D and 187.2A.

4. *Antidotarium*, Dist. 1, Part 2, p. 107.4F.

5. *Grabadin*, sec. 1, particula 1, summa 3, chap. 23: "De diminutione memoriae," p. 189.1B-C. The son of Zacharias is Rhazes, on whom see 1.23, n. 1.

1.26

1. Plato, *Charmides* 156e–157a, and *Rep.* 3.403d. See also Ficino, *Theol. Plat.* 13.1, ed. 2: 198–99, *Op.*, p. 285, and *Epistolae* 4, *Letters* 3: 24 (*Op.*, p. 760).

2. Plato, *Apology* 21a.

3. Plato, *Phaedo* 64d–67b.

4. *Rep.* 6.507d–509a, equating Plato's Idea of the Good with God. See also Ficino, *Epistolae* 4 (*Op.*, p. 760), and *Letters* 3: 22.

5. Jn. 1:9; Ps. 36:9.

6. *Phaedo* 64d–67b and *Timaeus* 90b–c.

Proem to Book 2

1. Filippo Valori bore the expense of publishing both his translation of Plato, 1484, and *De vita*, Della Torre, pp. 623–24, 734. See also 3 Proem and Corsini's poem at the end of the work.

2.1

1. Hippocrates, *Aphorism* 1.1 (Littrè 4.458).

2. Plato, *Rep.* 3.406a–b; Aristotle, *Rhetoric* 1.5.10 (1361b). Ficino repeats the citation in his *Comm.* on *Enn.* 3.1.3 (*Op.*, p. 1683) and in his *Disputatio contra iudicium astrologorum*, ed. Kristeller, *SF*, 2: 67.

3. Plutarch, *De liberis educandis* (*Moralia* 2C–E), and see above, n. 5 on 1.1.

2.3

1. Ps. 119:105.

2. The lamp metaphor, which Ficino has developed by this striking prosopopoeia, was a commonplace "of post-Avicennan medical thought in the West"; see Michael McVaugh, "The *Humidum Radicale* in Thirteenth-Century Medicine," *Traditio* 30 (1974): 259–83, esp. 264, 266–67.

3. A pun, as in 1.1, on the etymology of Minerva as "minuens nervos."

2.4

1. *Liber canonis* 4.7.1.16.
2. See Roger Bacon, *Fratris Rogeri Bacon De retardatione accidentium senectutis cum aliis opusculis de rebus medicinalibus*, eds. A. G. Little and E. Withington (Oxford, 1928), *Liber de conservatione iuventutis*, pp. 131-32; also *De retardatione accidentium senectutis*, chap. 2, p. 10.4-7, where Avicenna and Galen are cited. In their note on this citation, p. 209, Little and Withington say that Bacon has mistaken Haly's *Commentary* (on which see note 11 to 2.18, below) on Galen's *Ars medica* (= the *Microtegni*) 3.30 for Galen's text.

2.5

1. Roger Bacon, too, in his *De retardatione accidentium senectutis*, chap. 3, pp. 34-38, also praises *euchima*, which according to Pliny restores the natural moisture.
2. *Liber divisionum* 108.
3. *Liber canonis* 4.7.1.16; and cf. *De viribus cordis* 1.8. See Roger Bacon, *Liber de conservatione iuventutis*, in Little and Withington, p. 131.11-14, who also quotes this passage of Avicenna.
4. The Latin word for "starch" is *amilum*. Ficino has used *amidum*, which is the Romanic-influenced form of the word. See Index of Materia Medica.

2.6

1. Cf. *Aphorism* 2.9 (Littrè 4: 472).
2. See Porphyry, *De abstinentia animalium* (ed. A. Nauck, 1886) and Ficino's selective translation (*Op.*, p. 1932). See also Iamblichus, *De vita Pythagorica* 30.186.
3. Cf. *Aphorism* 2.20 (Littrè 4: 476).
4. *Liber canonis* 4.7.1.16.
5. Galen, *De alimentorum facultatibus* 3.2 (Kühn 6: 663); cited also in Arnald of Villanova, *De conservanda bona valetudine*, chap. 7, fol. 48v.
6. *De viribus cordis* 2.3, fol. 550v.
7. See *De vita* 1.7, n. 6 to Arnald and Avicenna.

2.7

1. Cf. *De conservanda bona valetudine*, chap. 14: "De aere," fols. 70v-72r. More to the point, however, is Roger Bacon, *De retardatione accidentium senectutis*, chap. 3, pp. 36-39.
2. Ficino repeatedly uses *pomum Persicum* in contexts which show he means "peach," calling it "golden" (3.11.129-30, *Op.*, p. 546), and listing it along with the pear (2.18, *Op.*, p. 526). In the sources, the story is a commonplace, but it is told of various fruits, none of which is a peach (*pomum Persicum*), though each is associated

with a word beginning *pers-*. According to Pliny, this is the fruit of the "persea," an entirely different tree. It concerns an unidentified Persian tree in Roger Bacon, *De retardatione accidentium senectutis*, chap. 2, p. 21.12–15, see his editors' note on p. 210: "Possibly explained by the fact that στρύχνον μανικόν (belladonna) was also called πέρσειον." This indicates that the bad effects alleged for the "persea" (or, in Ficino, the *pomum Persicum*) when it was transplanted into Persia were in actuality the effects of a different substance with a similar name, *perseion*.

3. *Politics* 7.11 (1330a).
4. *Phaedo* 111a–b.
5. What Ficino thought Hesiod said is not found in Hesiod himself, but rather in Varro, *De re rustica* 1.23.3.
6. On this work, see Introduction, "*De vita* in the Canon."
7. Isaac Judaeus, *Liber dietarum particularium*, in his *Opera omnia* (Lyons, 1515), fols. 151–52. This same passage is also quoted in Roger Bacon, *De retardatione*, chap. 3, p. 39.21–26.
8. *Liber dietarum particularium*, fol. 151v; cited also by Roger Bacon, *De retardatione*, chap. 7, p. 61.11–17.
9. Commentary on Hippocrates's *Aphorism* 7.56 (Kühn 18.1:169); cited also in Roger Bacon, *De retardatione*, chap. 7, p. 60.22–26. Little and Withington say in their note, p. 211, that this citation is actually taken from Avicenna, *Liber canonis* 1.3.2.13.
10. *Laws* 2.666b–c; see also above, *De vita* 1.10.27–29.
11. See *De vita* 3.4–6, 22. In general, 2.6–7 largely repeat 1.10–11 and the relevant doctrines of school-medicine.

2.8

1. Cf. Avicenna, *Liber canonis* 4.7.1.17 and 4.7.2.2.
2. This passage seems to be deliberately obscure. "Puerile non esse puerile" may be a simple pun on "puerile" in the unfavorable sense, but we have another explanation. Alternatively, Ficino's obscurity may have been motivated by a fear of public scandal or ridicule, see the conjecture of Little and Withington as to a similar fear on the part of Roger Bacon, Introduction, *De retardatione*, pp. xl–xli. This fear would be justified if "puerile fomentation . . . made . . . by David, but perhaps made too late" refers to the famous passage in 1 Kings 1.1–4 about the young virgin Abishag who slept with David in his declining years so that her body heat might warm the old king. If so, it is "not for the young" because it would incite them to lust.
3. On Democritus, see Diogenes Laertius 9.43 and below, *De vita* 2.18.84–87.
4. *Liber ad Almansorem* 5.9.
5. *Liber ad Almansorem* 3.27.
6. *Liber canonis* 4.7.1.16. The reference to Avicenna, as well as the two references to Rhazes, can also be found in Roger Bacon, *De retardatione*, chap. 6, p. 51.7–17.

2.9

1 For the Tree of Life, see Gen. 3:22. Ficino makes the same conjecture about myrobalans in 3.12.51-53, *Op.*, p. 547. For a similar connection of myrobalans with longevity see OED, s.v. "Myrobalan," 1, Bullein (1579): "Who so useth to eate often of Myrobalans, being condite, shall not seem old, saith Mesue."

2. This word is also used in 3.15.30, *Op.*, p. 551, and 3.16.95, *Op.*, p. 554; it is defined by the Arabic word *karabe* in a textual variant to 1.12.16, and also in one to 1.20.11; it probably means "amber," but Ficino's usual word for that is *ambra*, which is used just below, line 20, as if he did not realize that they are essentially the same substance. A similar oddity is *olibanum*, below, line 18, for frankincense, instead of his usual word *thus*. The two words for amber could be distinguished if Benesch is correct in saying that *ambra* means "ambergris," *Marsilio Ficino's 'De triplici vita' (Florenz, 1489) in deutschen Bearbeitungen und Übersetzungen* (Frankfurt a. M., 1977), Glossar, Substanzen aus dem Tier- und Menschenreich, s.v. "ambra," p. 307, but in context this meaning seems unlikely.

3. Isaac Judaeus, *Liber febrium*, Part 3, chap. 2; also cited in Roger Bacon, *De retardatione*, chap. 1, p. 11.15-16.

4. *Liber canonis* 4.1.3.1; this passage too is in Bacon, *De retardatione*, chap. 1, p. 11.19-22.

5. *Liber virtutum simplicium medicinarum* (Lyons, 1512), chap. 262, p. 52.3-4.

2.10

1. For the important role of gold in the Middle Ages in the prolonging of life, see Gerald J. Gruman, *A History of Ideas about the Prolongation of Life: The Evolution of Prolongevity Hypotheses to 1800*, in *Transactions of the American Philosophical Society*, New Series, vol. 56, Part 9 (December, 1966): 65-66.

2.11

1 See Ovid, *Fasti* 6.131-43.

2. At this, the French translator Guy Lefèvre de la Boderie protests: "This method of using human blood is not humane." Roger Bacon in *De retardatione*, chap. 7, pp. 57-60, recommends, in the words of the editors, "the restoration of youth by the exhalations or effluvia of healthy young persons, and other products *animalis nobilis*.... There can be little doubt that Bacon's 'lapis quadratus nobilis animalis' is human blood," Introduction, *De retardatione*, pp. xl-xli. Bacon, to be sure, is nowhere as specific as Ficino.

3. This citation is not from Galen but from Dioscorides, *Liber virtutum simplicium medicinarum*, chap. 595: "De sanguine diversorum animalium," p. 102.3. This Serapion is Serapion the Younger, an Arab physician of the twelfth century. See his *Liber aggregatus in medicinis simplicibus*, translated into Latin by Simon Cordo of Genoa (Venice, 1503), chap. 450: "De sanguine," p. 164.1.

2.12

1. Socrates lived to an advanced age and maintained close friendships with youths such as Alcibiades. Ficino saw such friendships as models for his own friendship with Giovanni Cavalcanti. Ficino says they kept Socrates young (*Op.*, p. 1362). He prefixes the epithet "chaste" as assurance to the reader that they remained above the perversely physical; for a similar assurance about Socrates, see the story recounted by the character Alcibiades in the end of the *Symposium*; Ficino's *Comm. Symp.* 7.2, ed. Marcel, p. 242, *Op.*, p. 1356; 7.16, ed. Marcel, pp. 260-62, *Op.*, pp. 1362-63; and *Vita Platonis*, i.e., *Letters* 3.19, p.37, *Epistolae* 4, *Op.*, p. 765.

2.13

1. Plato, *Apology* 21a; and see above, 1.26.9-12.
2. On the virtues of which, see, of all places, the heading of this chapter in the Table of Chapter Headings.
3. Not comprised of mummified corpses, Benesch assures us, but of the pitchy substance by which mummies were preserved, *Marsilio Ficino's 'De triplici vita,'* Glossar, Substanzen aus dem Mineralreich, s.v. "mumia," p. 309.

2.14

1. In view of the context, I here leave *crocus* as the flower; elsewhere I translate it as its product, "saffron." This entire speech is deliberately obscure, as befits an "oraculum."
2. See Ps.-Aristotle, *Problem* 31.19, 959a.

2.15

1. See 1.2 and note ad loc. On the interior senses in general, including an operational classification into four, see *Theol. Plat.* 11.3, Marcel ed. 2: 98 (*Op.*, p. 242). The interior senses are three according to doctors, five according to philosophers. In them, Ficino customarily includes *phantasia* and the faculty variously designated *imaginatio* or the *virtus imaginativa* or *cogitativa*, and he would presumably have included memory. The remaining two are the *sensus communis* and the *virtus aestimativa*. See E. R. Harvey, *Inward Wits*, esp. pp. 23-24; and Avicenna, *Liber canonis* 1.1.6.5.
2. Perhaps alluding, besides the obvious physical resemblance, to Homer's comparison of the old men of Troy to cicadas, *Iliad* 3.150-55, or to the lovers of song metamorphosed into cicadas, *Phaedrus* 259b.
3. As elsewhere in this book, Ficino is pursuing the problem of replacing the radical moisture, here, after it has been lost in the form of semen through sexual

activity. The material remaining after the fourth digestion, or, as it is sometimes designated, the final stage of the third digestion, is semen, see McVaugh, "*The Humidum Radicale,*" p. 280. Seeking foods with the same "qualitas," he fastens on those which have to do with reproduction.

4. The conventional planetary scapegoats, see Introduction, "Traditions," both for this and for the astrological references which follow.

5. Alluding to Jupiter as the most temperate planet, to Pythagoras's proverb "Nothing to excess" (quoted above, on which see "Quod necessaria sit" and note 6), and to Plato's *Timaeus* which admonishes in 88–90 (alluded to in 1.5) that the soul should not be promoted at the expense of the body or *vice versa*, but that each should receive its proper "nourishment."

6. On music, see also 3.21 and the cross-references listed there.

7. Ps. 103:5.

2.17

1. This Chaldean "rule" is given in Roger Bacon, *De retardatione*, chap. 3, p. 40.17–24, which is probably Ficino's proximate source. Ficino also quotes one or another Chaldean rule from the *Oracula Chaldaica* in 3.22, below, which see for bibliographical information, and in *Theol. Plat.* 13.4, ed. 2: 235 (*Op.*, p. 301).

2. For the Medea and Pelias story, see Ovid, *Met.* 7.297–349; see also below, 3.20 and note 1.

2.18

1. See Plato, *Phaedo* 111a–c; Pliny, *HN* 7.2.25; and below, 3.11, n. 4; on the *astomi* or apple-smellers in general, see John Block Friedman, *The Monstrous Races in Medieval Art and Thought* (Cambridge, Mass., 1981), pp. 27–28, 132, 184.

2. *De viribus cordis* 1.9.

3. Cf. Galen, *De placitis Hippocratis et Platonis* (Kühn 5: 605), and his *Commentary* on Hippocrates's *De humoribus* 3.3 (Kühn 16:357–63).

4. Aristotle, *Historia animalium* 7.4 (584b), and Avicenna, *De animalibus* 9.5. See also below, "Ad lectorem," and n. 2.

5. Ps.-Nicolas Peripateticus is the author of *Quaestiones Nicolai Peripatetici*, an unedited work which exists in 10 MSS of the 13th-15th cs. under varying titles and ascriptions, see Charles Lohr, "Medieval Latin Aristotle Commentaries," *Traditio* 28 (1972): 299–300. Alexander the Peripatetic may be Ps.-Alexander of Aphrodisias, confused with the great commentator on Aristotle of the second and third centuries, but really a physician of the Pneumatic school, who wrote *Problemata* and *De febribus*, both translated into Latin by Giorgio Valla at about this time, see George Sarton, *Introduction to the History of Science* I (Washington, DC, 1927): 619. Ficino owned a MS containing a work of "Alexander Aphrodisiensis," *SF*, 1: LIII. Galen in the work cited above (Kühn 16: 359) says that bad odors debilitate the spirits but not that good odors nourish them. Ficino's idea seems a natural extension of

both this idea and the idea of people nourished by odors alone.
   6. See also below, 3.11, *Op.*, p. 544, n. 1. For the chameleon, see Pliny, *HN* 8.51.122; for the salamander, see Petrarch, *Rime*, 191.10-13; cf. Pliny, *HN*, 10.86.188; and 29.23.76, echoed by many medieval bestiaries.
   7. Diogenes Laertius 9.43; and see above, *De vita* 2.8.26-27.
   8. *De vita* 3.12 (*Op.* p. 547), and 3.16 (*Op.*, p. 554). On the *Consiglio*, see Introduction, "*De vita* in the Canon."
   9. *Liber canonis* 4.7.1.16.
   10. *Conciliator* (Venice, 1521), Differentia 113, fol. 159M.
   11. This Haly is Haly Abenrudian, Arabic ʿAli ibn Ridwān (998-1061 or 1069), *In parvam Galeni artem commentatio* (Venice, 1557), 3, p. 217A. See also note 2 to 2.4 above.

2.19

   1. Mt. 2:1-12. On the medical significance of the gifts of the Magi, see also 1.20, above, ad init., and "Apologia," 63-67.

2.20

   1. Conceived as multiples of 7 (7, 14, 21, etc.), the climacteric years designated critical stages in human life. See Claudius Ptolemaeus (fl. 127-48), *Tetrabiblos* or *Quadripartitum* 3.10.141. Aulus Gellius, *Noctes Atticae* 3.10.9, quotes the Chaldeans; and see Pliny, *HN* 7.49.50.161, and Bouché-Leclercq, pp. 526-32.
   2. Ps.-Ptolemy, *Centiloquium*, translated into Latin by John of Seville or Hugh of Santalla (Venice, 1484), 5 and 8. The *Centiloquium* or *Fructus* is an abridgement of Ptolemy's *Quadripartitum* or *Tetrabiblos*. See Charles Homer Haskins, *Studies in the History of Mediaeval Science* (Cambridge, Mass., 1927), pp. 68-72.
   3. *Conciliator*, Diff. 113, fols. 158H-160C. By contrast, Gerald J. Gruman in his 1966 study, *A History of Ideas about the Prolongation of Life*, pp. 9-10, 15-17, cites Aristotle, Galen, and Avicenna to the effect that man has a natural span of life which is unable to be prolonged by any medical recourse.
   4. Ps.-Ptolemy, *Centiloquium* 9; and see Ps.-ʿAli ibn Ridwān, really Aḥmad ibn Yūsuf ibn al-Dāya (d. ca. 951, on whom see Plessner, p. 237), *Commentary* on *Centiloquium*, translated into Latin by Hugh of Santalla (Venice, 1484), Aphorism 9, sig. f8v.
   5. Meaning, respectively, *De vita* 3 and 1. See *SF*, 1: CXXVI-CXXVII, no. 14 for inclusive dates of entire Plotinus commentary. The commentary on images here specified, that on *Enn.* 4.3.11 which became Book 3, had in reality already been composed even before Book 2, but Ficino pretends the books were written in the order in which they now stand, see Clark's "Editorial Introduction," ad init.
   6. Tibullus 1.4.37-38.
   7. Hills exposed to the Sun were recommended to old people in 2.12. Cf. Gen. Proem on Bacchus as a healer even better than Phoebus. Besides equating wine and

sunlight in therapeutic value, the interdependence of Phoebus and Bacchus may be explainable as a personal compliment, since they are the nicknames of Ficino and of his "alter idem," Pico della Mirandola, see "Apologia," ad fin. The interdependence of these gods is discussed and related to Ficino's favorite metonymy of the Three Graces in Edgar Wind, *Pagan Mysteries in the Renaissance*, 2nd rev. ed. (London, 1968), "The Medal of Pico della Mirandola," p. 39, n. 14; on Dionysius/Bacchus and Apollo, see also pp. 172-75, 196, n. 21.

8. In Greek mythology, the Fates or Moirai, Latin *Parcae*, spun the threads of human destiny. Clotho spun the thread, Lachesis measured it out, and Atropos cut it off. See Hesiod, *Theogony* 217-22 and 904-6; cf. Tibullus 1.7.1-2 and Juvenal 12.64-66.

9. See Ficino's translation of the Pythagorean *Symbola* or precepts in *Op.*, p. 1979. For a full discussion of these collected maxims and sayings, see Walter Burkert, *Lore and Science in Ancient Pythagoreanism*, trans. Edwin L. Minar, Jr. (Cambridge, Mass., 1972), pp. 166-92.

Proem to Book 3

1. Matthias Corvinus, king of Hungary, 1458-1490, and a renowned patron of the arts, to whom Ficino also dedicated books 3 and 4 of his *Epistolae*. See *Letters* 2: 107-8 for a brief biographical note, repeated in *Letters* 3: 123-24. A letter from Ficino to him is printed in *Op.*, p. 902.

2. On Democritus's having lived for more than 100 years, see Diogenes Laertius 9.39. On Pythagoras's having lived to 80 or 90, see Diogenes Laertius 8.44. For Apollonius of Tyana, the Pythagorean sage of the first century A.D., see below 3.2, 3.3 and 3.8, n. 19.

3. Plato, *Statesman*, 272e-73.

4. Meaning, from his horoscope. As it turned out, King Matthias died within a few months, see *SF*, 1: XXII and "Editorial Introduction," above.

5. Literally, its number "among the rest of our commentaries on him" is "Cap. XI," but its text is found only in MS *P*, see "Editorial Introduction." On the filiation with Ficino's *Commentary* on Plotinus, *Ennead* 4.3.11, see also 3.1 and n. 1; "Editorial Introduction"; and "*De vita* in the Canon"; see also *Enn.* 4.4.30-43 for fuller treatments of the same subjects; and D. P. Walker, p. 3, n. 2 and p. 41; and *SF*, 1: LXXXIV. Other clear references to this lemma occur above, 2.20.34-38, *Op.*, p. 528; "Ad lectorem," 34, p. 530; 3.1 title, p. 531; 3.26, pp. 570-71; and "Apologia," 57, p. 573.

6. Filippo Valori, dedicatee of Book 2, see Proem 2, p. 509 and n. 1. For the sake of the pervasive pun on "valor," Ficino refers to him as if he were "Valor itself," i.e., the personification Valor.

Ad lectorem

1. This is the first mention of artificial astrological images in this book. The next explicit one comes in chap. 13, as if he were postponing the topic out of fear or uncertainty. They have been mentioned prospectively at the end of Book 2 (chap. 20.31-35, *Op.*, p. 528). On Ficino's caution about them here and elsewhere, see Walker, p. 42, Yates, p. 62, and Kaske, "Ficino's Shifting Attitude Towards Astrology" in *Marsilio Ficino e il ritorno di Platone* (Florence, 1986), pp. 371-80.
2. See also above, 2.18 and n. 4. In his note to Aristotle, *Historia animalium* 7.4 (584b) translated in vol. 4 of *The Works of Aristotle*, ed. J. A. Smith and W. D. Ross (Oxford, 1910), D'Arcy Wentworth Thompson says, "According to the mediaeval astrologers the eighth month was under the rule of Saturn, and for this reason dangerous."

3.1

1. On the original identity of Book 3 with Ficino's *Commentary* on Plotinus, *Ennead* 4.3.11, see also Proem, n. 5; "Editorial Introduction"; and "*De vita* in the Canon"; for the divergence from it, see the textual notes, passim.
2. Ficino means primarily that in the descending order of the hypostases she is the first to partake of motion; he may also mean that she is the soul or Intelligence (the first term is Platonic, the second Aristotelian and scholastic), who moves the sphere called the Primum Mobile. She is called the "Primum Mobile" in Proclus, *Elements of Theology*, hereafter *ET*, prop. 200. Ficino calls her the *media rerum* both in *Comm. Tim.*, chap. 28, *Op.*, p. 1453, and in his Preface to his translation of Theophrastus's *De anima* and Priscian's commentary thereon, *Op.*, p. 1801, in which "medicina" is clearly a misprint (due to incorrect expansion of a ligature) for "media," as Marcel indeed emends it, *MF*, p. 352. Kristeller says the mediatorial function of the World-soul is a fundamental tenet both of Ficino and of other Renaissance Platonists, *Phil MF*, pp. 106-7, 120; it is one of the main points of *Enn.* 4.3.11.
3. Not in 4.3.11, but frequently elsewhere in Plotinus, e.g. 3.2.2, ad fin., 4.4.40, the universe is one animal united by the World-soul. Many points in the above paragraph which are not in *Enn.* 4.3.11 are in the Neoplatonist Synesius of Cyrene (c. 370-413), *De insomniis*, ed. N. Terzaghi in *Synesii Cyrenensis hymni et opuscula* (Rome, 1944), inferior but more available ed. in *PG* 66 under Psellus, in Ficino's Latin translation, *De somniis*, *Op.*, pp. 1968ff., especially the fourth section, not numbered but entitled "Solum quod mundo connexum est, a mundanis trahi potest." From here on, he sticks more closely to 4.3.11, except where noted.
4. Not in 4.3.11. On this operation with the added help of the daemons mentioned in the next sentence, see the end of this chap. and Proclus, *De sacrificio et magia*, trans. Ficino, *Op.*, p. 1929. The seminal reasons which figure so largely in 3.1 were invented by the Stoics and reached Ficino chiefly through Plotinus, who gives them a major role as the lowest agent of the Ideas. In the individual, they can be pictured as performing roughly the same function as does the genetic code according to modern science. Conceived on analogy with the seeds and sperm

of organic life, they all reside without extension in the World-soul (*Enn.* 2.3.14; 4.3.10). For Plotinus, they respectively inhere in the individual beings which they are essentially responsible for forming, even to the differing shapes of people's noses (5.9.12, 4.3.10, though of course they are variously modified by the receiving matter, 4.9.15, see also 4.4.39). For Ficino, however, as the present passage indicates, they correspond to and form through the constellations only the species and its characteristics (species have "rationes . . . proprias"), whereas the individuals, as he explains elsewhere, are shaped not only by them but also by other necessary causes, by contingent causes, and by free will, *Comm. Plot.*, "De fato," = *Enn.* 2, *Op.*, p. 1676. Presumably Ficino would trace the differing shapes of people's noses to "situ stellarum et habitu motionum aspectuumque planetarum." After the Stoics, these λόγοι σπερματικοί also came to be regarded as a dynamic and vital force linking all natural objects and enabling them to return via the series to the one, and thus as facilitators of magic; see F. E. Peters, *Greek Philosophical Terms* (New York, 1967), s.v. dýnamis, sections 8-11. These reasons are transmitted through the celestial figures; on this important notion also affirmed below at n. 8, see *Enn.* 4.4.35, ad init., and Ficino's comment thereon, *Op.*, p. 1746. For other discussions of the role of seminal reasons in Ficino's thought, see Introduction, "Habits", n. 14; Copenhaver, "Renaissance Magic and Neoplatonic Philosophy: *Ennead* 4.3-5," in *Marsilio Ficino e il ritorno di Platone*, pp. 353-69; Heitzmann, "La libertà," Part 1, pp. 360-61; and on the notion in general, Peters, *Greek Philosophical Terms*, and E. O'Brien, *The Essential Plotinus* (Indianapolis, Ind., 1975), "Glossary," s.v. "seminal reasons."

5. The renunciation is not explicit in *Enn.* 4.3.11; rather Plotinus simply affirms that Soul and not Mind can be attracted, though in 3.26, on which see below, a renunciation something like this will be ascribed to Plotinus. The higher powers in this distinction, the "numina quaedam penitus a materiis separata," originated in Plotinus as the rare differentiation νόες within Plotinus's second hypostasis or first emanation from the One, the νοῦς — Mind, Intelligence, or Intellect — see for example *Enn.* 6.7.17; Joseph McAllister, ed., *The Letter of Saint Thomas Aquinas 'De Occultis Operibus Naturae,'* Catholic University of America Philosophical Studies 42 (Washington, D.C., 1939), p. 176; and M. J. B. Allen, "The Absent Angel in Ficino's Philosophy," *JHI* 36.2 (1975): 225. These later proliferated into the supramundane or supercelestial gods, henads, or Intelligences of Iamblichus, Sallustius, and Proclus (*ET*, nos. 113-14; nos. 164-65); see Dodds, ed., "Commentary," p. 283). In these thinkers, the "numina quaedam penitus a materiis separata" are either "intellectuals," mediators to and from the Ideas, like the celestial figures and the seminal reasons, though higher than either on the ontological scale, or "intelligibles," personified versions of them; for in effect the Ideas, as McAllister puts it, "are not merely thoughts of Intelligence, but at the same time are relative individualities, for which the name Intelligence was used," p. 176.

See Ficino's parallel rejection in 3.26.77 ff., *Op.*, p. 571, citing Plotinus and Synesius, who is also relevant here, of "numina penitus a materia segregata" in favor of daemons. As if in parallel and contrast, the astrological "numina" whom Ficino does invoke without reservation here and in Book 3 at large are called "coelestia mundana numina" in 3.22.99-100, *Op.*, p. 565. This distinction derives from the

distinction he draws in the opening sentences of this chapter between the Intellect in which these "numina" reside, which is immaterial and therefore impassive, and Soul. Soul embraces the Proclan "animate world" of the *Phaedrus* commentary, chap. 11, which includes any and all rational souls, not only human but planetary and daemonic; while above matter, it is not "penitus a materiis separata" in that it is in fact invariably found to be connected with a body, and it is somewhat passible (e.g., daemonic souls have emotions) and hence attractible. As Ficino once wrote, among self-subsistent beings, "aliquod non vivificat materiam, ut intelligibilia et intellectualia pura; aliquod vivificat per presentiam, ut anima que, licet materie aliquomodo uniatur, tamen non desinit esse abstractam, quia non coextenditur," ed. H. D. Saffrey, "Notes Platoniciennes de Marsile Ficin dans un manuscrit de Proclus," *Bibliothèque d'Humanisme et de Renaissance*, 21,1 (1959): 170. For Ficino's indirect invocation of supercelestials, besides this chapter, see the "superioribus" in the title he supplies in his translation of *Enn.* 4.3.11, quoted in its entirety below, 3.13, *Op.*, p. 549, and 3.15, p. 552, speculating whether "supercoelestes" can also be attracted by way of the "coelestes." True, he does twice (3.22, pp. 565–66) affirm that they can be attracted directly; see "Repercussions," ad fin. His authority on these matters is usually Iamblichus. Synesius in the cited and very similar passage (*Op.*, p. 1969.4) goes on to say that supercelestials can be influenced by worship, but that his fidelity to civil law prevents his treatise from dealing with this matter, presumably because such worship, however high-minded, would be pagan; and this would be the motive for Ficino's renunciation as well. Ficino's sentence, especially the word "numina," also echoes the language of Iamblichus in Ficino's epitome, where it is used generically for personal beings, whether gods, angels, or daemons, though Ficino reverses the sentiment from endorsement to renunciation. Instead of trying vainly to manipulate "numina . . . immaterialia" by means of "a celestial figure," Iamblichus urges the priest to make himself like them and get friendly with them, in other words, to worship them, *De mysteriis, Op.*, p. 1888,2.

While Ficino's employment of the pagan term "numina" indicates he is making no particular effort to syncretize the Platonic with the scholastic entity, these supercelestials are roughly equatable with the *substantiae separatae*, Aquinas's word for angels, though the latter can be fallen as well as unfallen. Matter entails passivity; hence Aristotle lays down separation from matter as a condition for all true thinking (*De anima* 3.5, 430a17; on this whole point, see Ludwig Schütz, *Thomas-Lexikon*, 2nd ed., repr. New York, 1957, s.v. "substantia," section 6; and *Enn.* 5.9.3), hence their other name "Intelligences." Another similarity is as follows: Aquinas reports that the separated substances were closely linked by Plato to the species (*ST* 1a, q. 50, art. 3, contra; cf. Aristotle, *Metaphysics* 1.6 (987b7); 7.1 (1042a25); in a passage recounting a Platonic ladder similar to that in 3.1.56–62, below, he agrees with "the Platonists" that the "separated substances" are the agents closest to God in that chain of causes which "mediante virtute et motu corporum coelestium imprimunt formas apud se intellectas in materiam corporalem. Et quia actiones et virtutes corporum naturalium ex formis specificis causari ostendimus, consequens est quod ulterius reducantur sicut in altiora principia in corpora coelestia, vel in virtutes coelestium corporum et adhuc ulterius in substantias separatas intellectuales," *De occultis operibus naturae*, ed. McAllister, paragraphs 9–11, also discussed

and quoted by Copenhaver, "Scholastic Philosophy," p. 537 and n. 37. Unlike Aquinas, Ficino regards the supercelestials as incapable of evil, equating the fallen angels with fallen daemons; since for him the daemons have subtle but nonetheless corporeal bodies, he groups daemons not among "numina . . . separata" but below them in the animate world (see Allen, *Platonism*, p. 9, nn. 19 and 20). He then protests that "numina separata" will not be employed in his magic and daemons will. For Ficino, then, the term "numina separata" is not really equatable with anything in the scholastic system; despite the verbal similarity, it could not possibly mean the daemons but it is roughly equatable with angels in their aspect as Intelligences; the heresy to be feared in using them would be the "worshiping of angels" condemned by St. Paul in Col. 2:18. Again, Ficino may be renouncing the "numina separata" either because some of their scholastic counterparts, the fallen "substantiae separatae," are castigated by Aquinas as agents of bad magic (*SCG* 3.104-6, cited in *De vita* 3.18), and he wants to seem exempt from Aquinas's condemnation (see also "Repercussions," ad fin.), or, more likely, because he wants to join Synesius in renouncing Iamblichan higher theurgy.

6. For the story of Zoroaster, as well as his alleged connections with the Chaldean Oracles, see J. Bidez and F. Cumont, *Les Mages hellénisés* (Paris, 1938) 1: 36 ff. For the *iynges* of Zoroaster and the Chaldeans, which Ficino translates as *illices*, see Michael Psellus, the Byzantine Neoplatonist (1018-c.1098), *Expositio in Oracula Chaldaica* (*PG* 122.1123-50) in *Oracles chaldaïques*, ed. Édouard des Places (Paris, 1971), 1133a4-b4, pp. 170-71, commenting on frag. no. 206, and 1149a10-b11, pp. 185-86, commenting on frag. no. 77. A *iynx*, Hans Lewy explains, "is a term applied to the magical top, which is spun by the conjurers who wish to compel gods or spirits to appear," *Chaldaean Oracles and Theurgy*, rev. ed. Michel Tardieu (Paris, 1978), p. 132, and further, pp. 132-37 and 249-52, as well as pp. 473-79 on Psellus and the Chaldeans; also Thorndike 1: 265-67. For a description of a *iynx*, taken from Psellus 1133a5-8, p. 170, see below, 3.13 and note 7. Synesius, *De insomniis* 132C3-4 (= *PG* 66: 1285a) is translated by Ficino as using the word, "illecebrae," section 3, *Op.*, p. 1969.

7. The "ratio exemplaris" is equatable with the "formas in mente . . . animali" (3.1, below), also with the "intellectualibus eiusdem animae formis" (3.26 ad fin., see n. 11, below). Besides the seminal reasons, directed towards matter, the World-soul has a mind, directed towards things above, and this contains the exemplary reasons to help her know the Ideas in the intelligible world. "Exemplum," Ficino explains in his introduction to Proclus in MS Riccardiana 70, means "above the subject," i.e., the model after which the subject was made, as opposed to "imago," which is "within the subject" ("Notes Platoniciennes," ed. Saffrey, p. 169). For the relation of the seminal reasons to other levels and another scheme, see n. 11, below.

8. See, for example, Plotinus: she made "domiciles for gods," *Enn.* 4.3.10. Ficino inserts this parenthetical ascription because, as he explains in 3.4, *Op.*, p. 535, Christians believe that God made the stars directly, see our n. 1 ad loc. Ficino qualifies this passage and disavows the whole idea of celestial figures as operative units in his later letter to Poliziano, *Epist.* 12, *Op.*, p. 958, 1, on which see Kaske's "Ficino's Shifting Attitude Towards Astrology," pp. 373-74.

9. Probably thinking of the "faces" or decans though perhaps of the single degrees.

10. These are the 48 constellations of Ptolemy, *Syntaxis mathematica*, popularly known as the *Almagest*, in *Opera*, vol. 1, part 2, ed. J. L. Heiberg (Leipzig, 1898-1903), 7-8. I am grateful to David Pingree for this reference and for most of my many explanatory interpolations in this paragraph.

11. The four degrees of unity on this Platonic ladder correspond roughly to the four Neoplatonic "worlds" or levels of being Ficino endorses in the *Phaedrus* commentary, see Allen, *Phaedran Charioteer*, pp. 66-69. Even in the *Phaedrus* commentary, however, Allen notes, Ficino tends to demote the intellectual gods from the supercelestial place, and to create a gulf between it and the "heavens" to which he demoted them, the boundary of the "animate" or mundane order (*Platonism*, pp. 252-53). In *De vita*, by a similar change, Ficino collapses the Intellectuals into a part, albeit a distinct part, of the World-soul, her intellectual forms or exemplary reasons, see n. 7 above. For the highest level here, see Proclus, *ET*, no. 113 and *Enn.* 4.3.11, ad fin., which reads in Guthrie's translation: "Indeed, intelligible things are not separated from each other; they are distinguished only by their difference and their constitution. Each of them remains within itself, without any relation to locality; they are simultaneously united and separate." For the highest three, see 3.26.134-35: "rationes in anima mundi coniunctae sunt intellectualibus eiusdem animae formis, atque per illas divinae mentis ideis"; see also Aquinas, *De occultibus operibus naturae*, paragraphs 9-11, quoted above. Since figures are never returned to or led back to the poles, but revolve around them, I translate "rediguntur" in its less central but still attested meaning "diminish to a point"; figures which diminish to a point at the poles are of course the degrees and in a sense the 12 zodiacal figures which are sometimes seen as marking out whole segments of the celestial sphere. This represents the last clear reference in this chapter to *Enn.* 4.3.11.

12. *Enn.* 4.3.11 mentions the Sun, though in another connection. For a similar sentiment, see *De Sole*, *Op.*, p. 970. The other thinker is doubtless the Emperor Julian the Apostate, who evolved his sun-worship from such texts as *Enn.* 4.3.11; see O'Brien's note ad loc., *The Essential Plotinus*, p. 140. Although Julian does not stress the World-soul or the World-spirit, he did make available to Ficino the notion in the next paragraph of an aetherial quintessence pervading all things and "culminating" in the Sun, *Works of the Emperor Julian*, ed. W. C. Wright, vol. 1 (London, 1913), Oration 4, "Hymn to the Sun," 132c, p. 358. See the explicit reference to him, 3.6 and n. 5; Julian's hymn underlies much of Ficino's thinking in Book 3. Ficino also refers to it in his *Commentary* on Plotinus, *Enn.* 4.4.30 (*Op.*, p. 1745); for further information, see Walker, p. 18.

13. The idea that some sort of planetary spirit pervades all things but is concentrated in certain ones, is found in *Picatrix*, 3.5, German translation by Ritter and Plessner, hereafter "translation," p. 190 = ed., p. 180. For further bibliographical data, see "Magic," n. 1.

14. This phrase means: "when the Sun has the most dignities in the total configuration of the sky at a given moment."

15. See textual note. For the use of human components in magical recipes, cf. the *Flos naturarum* of Geber incorporated into the Latin *Picatrix* as 3.11.58-112 of David Pingree's forthcoming edition.

16. On the "motacilla," which on balance seems to refer to the wagtail, although

it could be part of a larger class of birds employed as *iunges* in theurgy, see Copenhaver, "Iamblichus, Synesius and the *Chaldean Oracles* in Marsilio Ficino's *De vita libri tres*: Hermetic Magic or Neoplatonic Magic?" in a Festschrift, forthcoming, n. 14; see also our n. 6, above. On this entire chap., see Garin, *Lo zodiaco della vita*, pp. 18 ff., and "Le 'elezioni'," *L'età nuova*, p. 19. As Yates explains (pp. 64-66), Ficino's chapter contains the same two topics—an outline of Neoplatonic theory and a discussion of physical receptacles for capturing the World-soul—as does *Enn.* 4.3.11, but in reverse order, and with different receptacles. For more on the latter topic and Ficino's source for it, see chap. 26 and notes ad loc.; but I must here point out that Ficino postpones Plotinus's statues, mentioning only the raw materials, nor does he mention representations of any sort until chap. 13, presumably to postpone the subversive aspect of his therapy as long as possible, see Kaske's article, "Ficino's Shifting Attitude Towards Astrology," pp. 379-80.

I quote here the entire chapter from Ficino's Latin translation, employing the rather more modern punctuation of the Basel, 1580 ed.:

> 11. *Magica trahit vim proprie ab anima mundi, Diisque mundanis per haec a superioribus.* Atqui mihi videntur veteres sapientes quicunque optabant sibi adesse deos, sacra statuasque fabricantibus in ipsam universi naturam mentis aciem direxisse, atque inde animadvertisse naturam animae ubique ductu facilem admodum pronamque esse, omniumque facillime posse capi, siquis fabricaverit aliquid, quod facile ab ipsa pati possit, patiendoque portionem aliquam ab ipsa sortiri. Facile vero patiens est quod qualicunque modo imitationi aptum est, velut speculum speciem quandam arripere potens. Etenim universi natura omnia mirabili quodam artificio fabricat ad illorum imitationem, quorum in se possidet rationes: cumque sic unumquodque fiat, certe ratio in materia, quae secundum rationem materia superiorem formata est, conjuncta est illi Deo [sc. Intelligentiae], secundum quem genita fuit, et in quem suspexit anima, habuitque dum faceret. Proinde neque possibile erat hic aliquid fieri divinitatis expers, neque rursus illam ad ista descendere. Illa siquidem mens ipsa est, ceu sol divinus qui nobis esto rationis exemplar: proxima vero huic succedit anima, suspensa intellectui manenti manens: dat enim haec terminos suos ad solem hunc vergentes eiusmodi soli, efficitque per se velut mediam, ut illic iterum sequentia religentur, velut interpres tum eorum quae inde huc deducuntur, tum eorum quae hinc illuc reducuntur, quantum per animam recurrit in mentem. Neque enim longe semotum aliquid est ab aliquo, rursusque semotum per differentiam quandam et mistionem: sed est in seipso, neque tamen secundum locum, et quodlibet ibi conspirat, simulque permanet et distinctum. Dii vero hi sunt, quatenus ab illis nunquam destituuntur, atque animae prodeunti ab initio suspenduntur: animae tamen velut inde hucusque sese diffundendo quodammodo iam abeunti. Hac autem ratione quatenus et sunt, et quod respicere dicuntur ad intellectum, divini dicuntur, ipsa videlicet anima non alioquin illuc semper suspiciente,

Plotini . . . *Enneades* (1st ed. Florence, 1492), Sig. bb iii, fol. 252 and (Basel, 1580), pp. 380-81.

For English translations, see S. MacKenna, rev. B. S. Page (London, 1962), p. 270; preferably, the more literal one, rearranged according to the order of composition, by K. S. Guthrie (Alpine, N. J., 1918) 2: 407-8; and A. H. Armstrong in the Loeb Classical Library, although his translation departs both from the literal sense and from what Ficino made of it. Although Yates and Garin were not using Ficino's translation, their parallels hold good for it.

3.2

1. Plato, *Timaeus* 30c-31a. Plotinus, *Enn.* 4.4.32. See also n. 9, below.
2. Compagni says that hiding under references to "astrologi Arabes" is Ficino's debt to *Picatrix*, "Picatrix latinus," pp. 260-61, n. 3; but she fails to pinpoint any specific parallel to this particular notion, that the human species is distinctively Solar.
3. On marcasites of gold and silver, see below and Index of Materia Medica.
4. "Term" = that part of any sign of the zodiac which is ruled by the planet; every sign was variously divided among the planets, omitting the Sun and the Moon, see chap. 9, below. "Cardine" = the four main points of the zodiac in relation to the horizon at any given moment, sometimes less correctly called Angles by Ficino and others; strictly speaking, they are the Ascendant, the Descendant, the Medium Coeli (M. C.) and the Imum Coeli (I. C.), mentioned also in chap. 6 below. The M. C. and I. C. should not be confused with the zenith and nadir, nor with the "cardinal points" of the compass, North and South, though they could be called the cardinal points, north and south, of the ecliptic; see Bouché-Leclercq, pp. 258, n. 1, 272. "Direct in motion," i.e., not retrograde. "Burned path" = an unfortunate part of the zodiac; for Ficino's version of what degrees it occupies, see 3.6. On all of these terms, see "Traditions."
5. Briefly, at the end of the preceding chapter.
6. Ficino did once hold the astrological view, *Consiglio contro la pestilenza*, *Op.*, p. 577; Letter to Cavalcanti, *Letters* 2: 33-34 (*Op.*, pp. 732-33); he here espouses, like his friend Cavalcanti, *Letters* 2: 31-32 (*Op.*, p. 732), the Neoplatonic view; see "The Author in the Work," ad fin.
7. Aphorism 10.
8. See Philostratus, *Vita Apollonii*, hereafter *VA*, 3.15, and *De vita*, below, 3.21 and n. 4.
9. *Timaeus* 30b; Plotinus, *Enn.* 2.9.5; 3.2.3; 4.3.7; 4.4.32.
10. This idea—that magic finds its natural basis in the continuity between our medical spirits and the spirit of the cosmos—has already been announced in 3.1 ad fin. in a paragraph which adumbrates this one. Although it is by no means apparent in "Platonic" sources (cf. *Enn.* 4.4.26 and Ficino's commentary thereon, *Op.*, p. 1744, for a vague adumbration of it), Ficino is perhaps referring to the cosmic pneuma of the prophet, on which see below, 3.3, citing that possessed by Apollonius of Tyana, Philostratus, *VA* 3.42; see also Dodds, ed., Proclus, *ET*, Appen-

dix 2. Cf. Copenhaver on Ficino's use of *Enn.* 4.4.26, "Scholastic Philosophy," p. 550, n. 67; and "Renaissance Magic," p. 354, for the precedent Ficino found in *Enn.* 4.3.8 according to his commentary, *Op.* p. 1736. He does not consider the Arabic writers. Although Ficino fathers it upon Platonists and Arabic writers, it is really one of his more original ideas; see 3.20, n. 4, and "Magic." "Arab astrologers" usually means *Picatrix*; and for one physical receptacle for capturing the pneuma of the cosmos, see *Picatrix* 3.5(5), pp. 193-96 = ed. 183-86, referred to explicitly in *De vita* 3.18.

3.3

1. Philostratus, *VA* 3.34.
2. Certainly thinking of fire, one of the two elements classified since the Stoics as "active," and perhaps also of the other one, air.
3. For a somewhat similar definition of Elixir, cf. *Picatrix* 1.2, translation, pp. 8-9 = ed., pp. 7-8 = forthcoming ed. of D. Pingree, 1.1.2. Ficino's description of this basic alchemical operation is standard, see textual note and Verbeke, *Pneuma*, "Les écrits alchemiques," pp. 338-40. This is the closest Ficino comes in *De vita* to mentioning alchemy, see "Magic."
4. "Plotinically" refers to procreation or procession, a distinctively Neoplatonic mode of creating things, see for example *Enn.* 4.3.6, see also 2.9.4; 4.8.6 — one which does not preclude the Christian God also creating everything *ex nihilo*; see below, 3.4, n. 1. As a matter of fact, even the Holy Spirit of Christian theology "proceeded from the Father" by way of this Neoplatonic procreation, see the Nicene Creed. As for the World-soul procreating the World-spirit and using it to procreate the stars, there is no such statement in Plotinus. See Zanier, p. 28, and Verbeke, *Pneuma*, "Plotin," pp. 352-62.
5. On the different kinds of fire, subterranean, ordinary/terrestrial, and stellar, see 3.12.43; 3.16.10 ff.; for Ficino's occasional identification of our spirit too as quintessence or stellar fire, see textual variants to this passage in *L*; 2.14, ad fin.; Introduction, "Habits"; and Walker, p. 13.
6. Meaning the proportions of the natures in the World-spirit, cf. *Timaeus* 31-32.
7. Vergil, *Aen.* 6.726, see also below, 3.26.36-37 and n. 4.
8. Philostratus, *VA* 3.42.

3.4

1. Plotinus, *Enn.* 4.3.6, see also 2.9.4. Timaeus of Locri (Timaeus the Pythagorean) may have been simply a name made up by Plato as a fictitious source; then in the first century A.D., someone composed the paraphrase of the *Timaeus, On the Soul of the World and of Man*, and he or someone else ascribed it to Timaeus of Locri. Christian writers and the *Timaeus Locrus* ascribe creation to an eternal "God," and within creation, the latter includes the World-soul, 95e-96d. For Ficino's reconciliation of these two cosmogonies as two stages of creation, see *Summa* 42, "Quae

a Deo proxime, et quae per media fiant," in his commentary on *Timaeus* 41-42, *Op.*, p. 1463.

2. *Timaeus* 36b-d (World-soul), 43a-44d (human soul), echoed by Ficino, *Comm. Tim.*, chap. 28, *Op.*, p. 1453.

3. Avicenna, *De viribus cordis* 1.1-2. *De vita* 1.6; 23.

4. *Harmonicorum sive de musica libri tres* (Venice, 1562), 3.15; in *Die Harmonienlehre des Klaudios Ptolemaios*, ed. Ingemar Düring, *Göteborgs Högskolas Årsskrift* 36.1 (1930), it is 3.16, pp. 110-11. The information which follows is also found in *Tetrabiblos* 1.4-5; see also below, 3.12, n. 1.

5. This margin of error is called the "orb" of the planet. See "Traditions."

3.5

1. Yates, p. 63, suggests that Ficino may have derived "the equation of beneficent astral influences with the three Graces" from Julian's "Hymn to the Sun" 148D, p. 406, referred to above, 3.1, n. 12, and cited by Ficino in 3.6.47-48. Ficino calls these planets the Three Graces in 3.7.11, 3.10.74, et passim, and in *Letters* 2: 4. On Ficino's employment of the image for various other themes, see Edgar Wind, *Pagan Mysteries in the Renaissance*, "The Medal of Pico della Mirandola," pp. 36-41. In Ficino's use of it here, which Wind does not mention, the middle Grace seems to correspond to Jupiter.

2. For the astrological terms in this paragraph — conjunction, aspect (already explained by Ficino in the end of 3.4), reception, signs, triplicities, mansions of the Moon, and dignities essential (i.e., those of zodiacal house, exaltation, and, according to some authorities, term, face, triplicity, and mutual reception by house) and accidental (those of place, i.e., mundane house, of elevation, i.e., being the planet in the eastern hemisphere which is closest to the M. C., and, according to some authorities, of aspect and a few other dispositions) — see "Traditions." This is the first detailed treatment since 3.1 (which has something of the nature of an introductory overview) of astrological figures, which he was to renounce in his letter to Poliziano of 1494 (*Op.*, p. 958,1) and reaffirm in his *Apologia* against Savonarola of 1498 (ed. Kristeller *SF*, 2: 77). Ficino seemingly postponed the topic this long in favor of topics he was more certain about, namely the World-soul, the *spiritus mundi*, and the magical substances which preoccupy him in chapters 2, 3, and most of 4.

3.6

1. See the Orphic fragment in honor of Zeus, cited below, n. 11.

2. On the natural, vital, and animal spirits, see Introduction, "Habits." Plato, *Phaedrus* 250b; *Sophist* 216c. Ficino also cites this passage in *Epistolae* 12 (*Op.*, p. 947,2) and in *Theol. Plat.* 13.2, ed. 2:202 (*Op.*, p. 286).

3. Homer, *Od.* 18.136-37.

4. He takes on the qualities of any planet with which he is associated, see below; and his synodical period is only about 116 days.

5. Iamblichus, *De mysteriis* 7.3 and in Ficino's epitome, *Op.*, 1901-1902, see also on the general importance of the Sun, his *De vita Pythagorica*, chaps. 25 and 35. Although Plessner, p. 233, identifies this Julian with either Julian the astrologer from Laodicea or Julian the theurgist, it is more likely to be Emperor Julian the Apostate, for full data on whom see the note on him at 3.1, "Hymn to the Sun," in *Works* 134b, pp. 362-65, esp. 364-65; 143b-144c, pp. 390-95. Proclus, *In Remp.*, ed. W. Kroll (Leipzig, 1901), 2.220.11; *In Tim.*, ed. E. Diehl (Leipzig, 1906), 3.63.21 ff.; 132.32 ff.; "Hymn to the Sun," esp. 8 ff., in E. Vogt, ed., *Hymni* (Wiesbaden, 1957), pp. 27-28. See also Ficino, *De Sole*, *Op.*, p. 970.

6. For Jupiter as "helping father," see Cicero, *De natura deorum* 2.25.64; repeated below, 3.22.38-39.

7. For his neutralizing medicine by strengthening the patient's nature, see Ps.-Ptolemy, *Centiloquium*, Aphorism 19.

8. Perhaps Albumasar (c. 787-886), *Introductorium in astronomiam*, translated into Latin by Hermann of Dalmatia (Venice, 1489), Book 6, sig. g3. See also Richard Lemay, *Abu Ma'shar and Latin Aristotelianism in the Twelfth Century*, American University of Beirut, Publication of the Faculty of Arts and Sciences, Oriental Series No. 38 (Beirut, 1962), esp. pp. 109-13, speaking of *Introductorium* 3 which "deals with the paramount influence of the two luminaries, Sun and Moon [acting as instruments of God], upon the physical changes occurring in the lower world" (p. 42).

9. These are the four natural faculties of organic parts; see O. Temkin, *Galenism*, p. 89, originally elaborated by Galen, *On the Natural Faculties*, Book 1. The generative function of the *virtus naturalis* Ficino here and elsewhere (see below in 3.6.129-31) incorporates into digestion, somewhat as do Constantinus Africanus and Arnald of Villanova as summarized in W. C. Curry, *Chaucer and the Medieval Sciences*, pp. 140-49.

10. Astrologers tell the fortune of the year in somewhat the same way as they tell the fortune of an individual, from the "figure" or total arrangement of the sky when it begins, see 3.19 and n. 3.

11. Ps.-Empedocles, *Sphaera* 2.5, in Ernst Maass, *Commentariorum in Aratum reliquiae* (Berlin, 1898), pp. 170-71. Orpheus, ed. Otto Kern, *Orphicorum fragmenta* (Berlin, 1922 repr. 1963), Frag. 168.5, p. 201. This Orphic passage was especially popular among the Neoplatonists; see the testimonia in Kern, pp. 202-7.

12. Ps.-Ptolemy, *Centiloquium*, Aphorism 20; cf. 3.10.49-52 (*Op.*, p. 543), below.

13. This Haly is Haly Albohazen, son of Abenragel (fl. c. 1016-1040; for full data see the note on him at 1.4), *De iudiciis astrorum*, 1.2, "In terminis"; see also on Mercury, terms, and aspects, Introduction, "Traditions."

14. Achates was the faithful companion of Aeneas; see Vergil, *Aen.* 1.312 and throughout the poem. His name became proverbial for a loyal comrade.

15. On circular motion and other Orphic dancing, see also below, 3.11, p. 544, and 3.23, p. 566. "Orphic" means using the activity as a ritual to get something from the heavens, as in "Orphei more" in 3.21; see n. 4. As this example shows, Orphic activities do not make the heavens do anything out of the ordinary but rather accommodate the performer to influences already available everywhere.

3.7

1. Lit., "to elect the Moon directed to." These astrological terms will occasionally be employed for brevity. "Elect a planet doing something" means "wait to act until a planet is doing something"; and "directed to" means "approaching by way of its annual motion." Though the verbs the astrologers use—such as "erigo," "dirigo," and "colloco"—are manipulative, they really mean them passively in the sense of "wait until the thing is so disposed."

3.8

1. Mercurius (Hermes) Trismegistus, *Quadripartitus* or *De quattuor partibus* (commonly *De quindecim stellis, quindecim lapidibus, quindecim herbis et quindecim imaginibus* or *figuris*), ed. Louis Delatte, in *Textes latins et vieux français relatifs aux Cyranides*, Bibliothèque de la Faculté de Philosophie et Lettres de l'Univ. de Liège, fasc. 93 (Liège and Paris, 1942), pp. 241-75. This work, in its variant versions, is ascribed to Hermes, Enoch, or Thebit. See Lynn Thorndike, "Traditional Medieval Tracts Concerning Engraved Astrological Images," *Mélanges Auguste Pelzer* (Louvain, 1947), pp. 221-27; and also Francis J. Carmody, *Arabic Astronomical and Astrological Sciences in Latin Translation: A Critical Bibliography* (Berkeley and Los Angeles, 1956), p. 56. A.-J. Festugiére, *La Révélation d'Hermès Trismégiste* 1: 160-86, esp. pp. 165-69 and 175, lists the 15 fixed stars of the Hermetic text, their modern equivalents, planetary correspondences, stones, herbs, and images. Ficino omits the Hermetic images but does include a brief description of their respective powers. He also adds three stars to the Hermetic list: the *Umbilicus Andromedae*, the *Ala Corvi*, counted twice (*dextra* and *sinistra*), and the *Humerus Equi*. These additional stars can be found in a list of seventeen stars (*Spica* is missing) in Cornelius Agrippa of Nettesheim, *De occulta philosophia* 2.31, a list taken from Ficino, which Festugiére (p. 169) compares to the Hermetic text. In the notes below, the few discrepancies between the Hermetic text and Ficino are mentioned, including the Arabic star names as compared to the Latin ones. The order in which Ficino presents his eighteen stars accords with the usual order of the twelve signs of the zodiac, from Aries to Pisces.

2. Caput Algol, a bright star in the constellation Perseus. The head is that of the Gorgon, Medusa, pictured as held aloft by Perseus. The Hermetic text has black hellebore for the herb rather than mugwort; the version ascribed to Thebit does have mugwort, see Thorndike, "Traditional Medieval Tracts," p. 223.

3. Pleiades in the constellation Taurus; the Hermetic Alchoraya has Venereal for Martial.

4. Aldebaran, a star of the first magnitude in the constellation Taurus.

5. Hircus or Capella, a star of the first magnitude in the constellation Auriga; the Hermetic Alhaiot.

6. Canis Major or Sirius, the Dog Star, brightest star in the constellation Canis Major; the Hermetic Alhabor.

7. Canis Minor or Procyon, a star of the first magnitude in the constellation Canis Minor.

8. Cor Leonis or Regulus, the royal star, of the first magnitude in the constellation Leo.
9. Cauda Ursae Majoris; Hermetic Benenays.
10. Its stone is onyx according to the Hermetic text.
11. Spica, star of the first magnitude in the constellation Virgo; Hermetic Alchimech Alaazel. The herb *promarulla* associated with it we cannot identify, but it resembles *primula*, identified by the OED as a cowslip, field daisy, or primrose.
12. Alchameth or Arcturus, star of the first magnitude in the constellation Boötes; Hermetic Alchimech Abramech, classified there as Martial and Jovial.
13. Elpheia (Cornea), star in the constellation Corona Borealis; Hermetic Alfeca, classified there as Mercurial not Martial.
14. Cor Scorpionis or Antares, star of the first magnitude in the constellation Scorpio.
15. Vultur Cadens or Vega, very bright star in the constellation Lyra.
16. Humerus Equi in the constellation Pegasus, who is pictured according to mythology as a winged horse; like the *Ala Corvi* and the *Umbilicus Andromedae*, it is lacking in the Hermetic text.
17. Our identifications of the above substances are only conjectural, see Introduction, "Scope of the Notes." By "Thebit," Ficino may be referring to that Hermetic treatise cited above, n. 1, which in a variant version entitled *De proprietatibus quarundam stellarum et convenientia earundem cum quibusdam lapidibus et herbis* is ascribed to Thebit. See Thorndike, "Traditional Medieval Tracts," pp. 223-24, and Carmody, *Arabic Sciences*, p. 56. Perhaps Ficino also has in mind Thebit ben Korah, *De imaginibus*, referred to below, 3.18 and n. 29.
18. See Philostratus, *VA* 3.41. Damis, the disciple and companion of Apollonius in his travels, is said by Philostratus, the early third-century author of the life of Apollonius, to have written memoirs upon which Philostratus based his biography. Apollonius in his ascetic wanderings performed many miraculous deeds and visited the Magi of Persia and the Brahmans of India, whose chief sage was named Hiarchas (Iarchas). See also above, Proem 3, lines 10-12.
19. Hiarchas's grandfather (*VA* 3.30) and Apollonius (*VA* 8.29) lived to a ripe old age, but this longevity is not described in Philostratus as due to the wearing of rings.
20. Aquinas, *SCG* 3.92, citing (Ps.?-)Aristotle, *Magna moralia* 2.8-9 (1206b-1207b).

3.9

1. The Chaldean order is also mentioned below, 3.21.29-30. Ficino invokes the Chaldean order whenever in the concentric order of the spheres he places Venus next to the Sun and Mercury next to the Earth. See Allen, *Platonism*, p. 118, n. 17, saying it is sometimes simply called the Ptolemaic order and listing the other possibilities. According to Bouché-Leclercq (pp. 107-10), this notion is not distinctive to the Chaldean order but variable within it, e.g., in different works of Cicero (see 110, n. 1), whereas the real innovation of the Chaldean order in the

history of science was the placement of the sphere of the Sun as the middle one of the seven planetary spheres.

3.10

1. I take *oras*, "zones," to be a typically Ficinian elegant variation for *plagas*, "regions," his precise technical term for the mundane houses or places which he is about to describe. There is, however, a slight chance that *oras* is a medieval variant spelling for *horas*, yielding a verbal parallel with Manilius's phrase, "propriasque ascribere in horas," *Astronomica* 3.298, in which case the translation should read "in accordance with the hours [of the day]." Since the subject is the places, and a given heavenly body enters a new place every two hours, the underlying sense is the same in either case.
2. Ps.-Ptolemy, *Centiloquium*, Aphorism 57.
3. "Thighs" here is out of place both anatomically and with respect to other accounts of the "zodiacal man" (zodiacal topothesia), including Ficino's own account in "Epitome" to *Laws*, 5(745), *Op.*, p. 1502. Since the word is repeated in its proper place exactly one line below, I suspect it is a scribal error. Literally, in both instances its number is singular, but context demands a plural.
4. An electuary is a moist, semi-solid medicine made from powder mixed with honey, jam, or syrup, see 1.23 for recipes.
5. Ptolemy's precept is *Centiloquium*, Aphorism 21.
6. Galen, *Quod optimus medicus sit quoque philosophus* (Kühn 1: 53); *De diebus decretoriis*, on astrology, see chap. 3.1–7 (Kühn 9: 901–15); on the Moon, Saturn, and Mars, see in particular 3.6 (Kühn 9: 911–12). Cf. Galen, *De Hippocratis et Platonis placitis* 9.8 (Kühn 5: 789–91). See also Thorndike's discussion of Galen and astrology, 1: 178–80.

3.11

1. The thing living in fire would be the salamander; see 2.18, (*Op.*, p. 526) and n. 6.
2. This "fact" about the sparrow is repeated in "Apologia," 116, *Op.*, p. 574 and in *Theol. Plat.* 13.4, ed. 2: 234–35 (*Op.*, p. 300). The stars as here described resemble eyes, which, according to Plato's and Ficino's optics, both emit and receive rays.
3. On Orphic or astrologically efficacious dancing, see 3.6, n. 9.
4. Gen. 2.4 and 3.22. Plato, *Phaedo* 111a–c and 114c. Pliny, *HN* 7.2.25.
5. The Latin word for starch is *amilum*. Ficino has used *amidum*, which is the Romanic-influenced form of the word. See Index of Materia Medica.

3.12

1. *Tetrabiblos* 1.4–5.
2. *Tetrabiblos* 1.9.

3. For a discussion of the occult properties of the stone bezoar (the modern Latinate form of an Arabic-Persian word), see Thorndike 2: 909-10 citing Pietro d'Abano, and 4: 224-25, citing Antonio Guaineri.

4. Galen was the first to mention the efficacy of the peony amulet to cure epilepsy, *De simplicium medicamentorum temperamentis et facultatibus* 6.3.10 (Kühn 11: 858-61); his account was widely repeated.

5. Although "illusio" and its verb do not mean "delusion" in classical Latin, this meaning is well attested in ecclesiastical Latin, where it is a standard word for nocturnal emission; see Du Cange, s.v. "illudo." For a description of some of the delusions induced by black bile, see Ficino, *Comm. Symp.*, 7.3, ed. Marcel, p. 245 (*Op.*, p. 1357).

6. On myrobalans, see 1.11, n. 1, and especially, in this connection, 2.9 and n. 1.

7. Serapion the Younger (12th c.), *Liber aggregatus in medicinis simplicibus*, chap. 398, pp. 156.4-157.1-2. Professor Copenhaver informs us that Latin *hyacinthus* could mean any number of gem-stones, such as sapphire, aquamarine, or zircon. Elsewhere, Ficino uses the word to denote the flower, see Index of Materia Medica.

8. Also mentioned in "Apologia," 49-50. On the eagle-stone, see Pliny, *HN* 36.39.149-51; said to help eagles in bringing forth their eggs, 30.44.130; cf. *Picatrix* 4.8(7), translation, p. 404.13 ff. For Rhazes and Serapion confirming its efficacy, see Rhazes, *Continens* 37.2.17 (Venice, 1509), p. 63, cited by Serapion, *Liber aggregatus in medicinis simplicibus*, chap. 402, p. 157.1-2. Lucina, the goddess of childbirth, is usually identified with Juno or Diana.

9. Ps.-Plato, *Alcibiades I*, 104c-d. Pythagoras in Iamblichus, *De vita Pythagorica* 30.182; and cf. Aristotle, *Metaph.* 985b23-30 and 1078b23. Socrates and the Pythagoreans are cited by Proclus, *In Alc. I*, 120-21, ed. L. G. Westerink (Amsterdam, 1954), pp. 54-55.

10. Plato, *Rep.* 8.546a; Pythagoras in Iamblichus, *De vita Pythagorica* 30.180-83. Both citations are also made by Proclus, *In Alc. I*, 121, p. 55.

11. *Centiloquium*, Aphorism 2.

12. *Speculum astronomiae*, chap. 15, p. 45.2-5 (= Borgnet 10: 648b). See also Thorndike 2: 692-717 for a discussion of the *Speculum* and the question of authorship.

3.13

1. Ps.-Ptolemy, *Centiloquium*, Aphorism 9.

2. Ps.-ʿAlī ibn Riḍwān (on this work and its real author, see 2.20, n. 3; for data on the supposed author, see 2.18, n. 11), *Commentary* on Ps.-Ptolemy, *Centiloquium* 9 (Venice, 1484), sig. f8v. Cf. also *Picatrix*, 2.1 (1-2), translation, p. 56 = ed., p. 55. D. Pingree informs us that the story was widely known.

3. Serapion the Younger, *Liber aggregatus in medicinis simplicibus*, chap. 396, p. 156.1-2, cites the physician Hahamed. Ficino also prescribed this image and credited it to Serapion and Hahamed in *Consiglio contro la pestilenza*, in the Latin translation, *Contra pestem*, chap. 24 (*Op.*, p. 605).

4. Ps.-ʿAlī ibn Riḍwān, *Comm. Centiloquium* 9, sig. f8v. For Archytas of Tarentum, a Pythagorean of the fourth century B.C., see Aulus Gellius 10.12.9.10; also

cited in Ficino, *Theol. Plat.* 13.3, ed. 2: 223 (*Op.*, p. 295). The mechanical flying dove manufactured by Archytas was an example of a wondrous machine whose operations were associated with those of natural magic, see F. Yates, *Giordano Bruno*, pp. 147-49.

5. *Asclepius* 37 in *Corpus Hermeticum*, ed. A. D. Nock and A.-J. Festugiére (Paris, 1945), 2: 347-49. This is Ficino's first explicit reference to the major statue-animating passage from the *Asclepius*, a translation of which can be found in "Magic." Others are 3.20, p. 561, and 3.26, p. 571.

6. The analogy of figurate talismans to the Prometheus myth is repeated in *Comm. Plot.*, "In Cap. 13 et 14 [sic]," *Op.*, p. 1738, just one page after the place where *De vita* originally appeared as "In Cap. 11." For Prometheus the creator who fashioned man out of clay which he animated with fire from heaven, see Raymond Trousson, *Le thème de Prométhée dans la littérature européene* (Geneva, 1964), 1: 47-48.

7. This description of a iynx or magical top is taken from Psellus, *Expositio Orac. Chald.*, 1133a5-8, in Des Places ed., p. 170; see above 3.1, n. 6. Copenhaver notes it belongs not to natural magic but to theurgy, "Iamblichus," forthcoming.

8. See above note and Psellus, *De daemonibus* 4-7, *PG* 122: 880-81, in Ficino's translation, *Op.*, 1941. Copenhaver notes that Psellus calls the entire operation silly, "Iamblichus," forthcoming.

9. Porphyry, *Letter to Anebo* 24 and 29; and Iamblichus, *De mysteriis* 3.23-29; in Ficino's epitome, *Op.*, p. 1894. Since Porphyry's *Letter to Anebo* was not edited until the seventeenth century, Ficino may have known it only through the quotations in Iamblichus's reply; this is the only explicit mention of it in *De vita*; see also 3.23, n. 6.

10. Cf. Iamblichus, *De mysteriis* 5.12 and 23, in Ficino's epitome, *Op.*, p. 1899.

11. Proclus, *De sacrificio et magia*, trans. Ficino, *Op.*, pp. 1928-29; see also Proclus, *ET*, Prop. 145. Synesius, *De insomniis*, 132B1-D13 (*PG* 66: 1285a-b), section 3 in Ficino's translation, *Op.*, p. 1969. The above passages from Proclus continue to be echoed throughout the next paragraph in the dominant idea that magic is the conflation of forces which in nature are widely separated.

12. Iamblichus, *De mysteriis*, in Ficino's epitome, *Op.*, p. 1887. The passage should exist also in the original *De mysteriis* 3.14-15, but the relevant sentence seems to exist only in Ficino. To this sentence, Compagni sees a similarity in the Paris MS of the Latin *Picatrix*, 4.4, discussing the force of talismans made out of stone ("Picatrix latinus," pp. 260-61, n. 3).

13. *De vita* 2.14, ad fin.

14. For the stone "pantaura" or "pantarbe," see below, 3.14.41, 3.15.21 and n. 2, 3.16.112.

3.14

1. The closest he has come to this so far in the *De vita* is "From these well-ordered forms all those lower forms depend," 3.1.56-57, *Op.*, p. 532; perhaps he means in his translation of Proclus, *De sacrificio et magia*, in Ficino's translation, *Op.*,

pp. 1928-29, which provides the philosophical framework for all but the last paragraph of this chapter.

2. "Asterion" is perhaps the adjectival form for "aster"; see Pliny, *HN* 27.19.36 for the aster which has little heads on top with rays like stars and is good for problems of the groin. For the Cor Scorpionis or Antares, see above, 3.8 and n. 14.

3. Proclus, *De sacrificio*, in Ficino's translation *Op.*, p. 1929.

4. Ibid.

5. For the Cor Leonis, see above 3.8 and n. 8.

6. Ficino's description of the lotus is taken from Proclus, *De sacrificio*, in Ficino's translation, *Op.*, p. 1928 (and see Pliny *HN* 13.32.108); that of the palm and the laurel from p. 1929.

7. Ficino's description of the stone "elitis" or "helitis" and the stone "Solis oculus" is taken from Proclus, *De sacrificio*, in Ficino's translation, *Op.*, p. 1928. For the stone "pantaura" or "pantarbe" see below, 3.15 and n. 2.

8. "Perforata" or "fuga daemon," better known as "hypericum," St. John's wort. It is mentioned in *Consiglio contro la pestilenza*, the Latin translation, chap. 6 (*Op.*, p. 584).

9. Ficino seems to have had in mind not the *Asclepius* nor the *Hermetica* he translated but some medieval treatise attributed to Mercurius (Hermes) Trismegistus, as in 3.8, ad init. See Roger Bacon, *De retardatione*, chap. 6, p. 56.11-15, who also describes the herb according to Hermes; the herb is described with reference to the Emperor Alexander the Great in Ps.-Albertus Magnus, *De virtutibus herbarum, lapidum et animalium quorundam libellus*, ed. Michael Best and Frank H. Brightman (Oxford, 1973), p. 19; the translators suggest that the herb may be chickweed (*stellaria media*). For the question of the latter work's authorship, see Thorndike 2: 233-34.

3.15

1. Proclus, *De sacrificio*, trans. Ficino, *Op.*, p. 1928.

2. Philostratus, *VA*, 3.46, speaking of the wondrous powers of the stone "pantarbe," which among its other properties can act as a magnet. "The latter Herculean stone" means the magnet or lodestone; it "rapit nos ad se contemplandum" as it "rapit" iron.

3. The magnetized needle is obviously a primitive compass. The statement about the compass parallels Ficino's own marginalia to *De sacrificio* in MS Vallicellianus F 20, fol. 139r as transcribed by Copenhaver, "Hermes Trismegistus, Proclus," forthcoming. Ficino's word for amber here is "succinum." Since in a pharmaceutical context, he uses "ambra" (see Index of Materia Medica), he may not have realized they are essentially the same substance. Textual variants to totally unrelated words in pharmaceutical chapters 1.12.16 and 1.20.11 say "karabe id est succinum."

4. Cf. Psellus, *De daemonibus* 6, *PG* 122:880c-d; see also Porphyry, *De abstinentia* 2.36-43 and Proclus, *In Tim.* 1.77. Jer. 1:14; Is. 14:13. There is a fuller citation of the direction from which daemons emanate in Ficino, *Theol. Plat.* 10.2, ed. 2: 56 (*Op.*, p. 223).

5. Aquinas, *SCG* 106-7. Iamblichus, *De mysteriis* 2.10, 3.13, in Ficino's epitome, *Op.*, pp. 1881, 1886. See below, 3.18.157-60 and nn. 31-36.
6. This statement parallels Ficino's own marginalia to *De sacrificio* in MS Vallicellianus F 20, fol. 139r as transcribed by Copenhaver, as above.
7. Pietro d'Abano, *De venenis* (Venice, 1521), chap. 4, p. 249.2-3. See also Gentile da Foligno, *Contra pestilentiam* (Salamanca, c. 1515), sig. b2v.
8. Dioscorides, *Liber virtutum simplicium medicinarum*, chap. 360, p. 68.1-2; Pliny, *HN* 37.54.144.
9. *Liber virtutum*, chap. 359, p. 68.1; and see Pliny, *HN* 37.54.155.
10. This Platonic saying is taken from Proclus, *De sacrificio*, in Ficino's translation, *Op.*, p. 1928, which in turn forms the basis of the next two sentences; see also Proclus, *ET*, Prop. 145, *In Tim.* 1.444-45, and Ficino, *Theol. Plat.* 10.2, ed. 2: 58 (*Op.*, p. 224).

3.16

1. Although the fire Ficino speaks of is inside the earth, his imagery in this paragraph seems to owe something to the Pythagorean doctrine of the central fire in the cosmos around which the planets revolved, see Aristotle, *De caelo* 293a18 ff. This central fire was called the hearth of the universe or Hestia (the Roman Vesta), see Plato, *Tim.* 40b-c, *Phaedrus* 247a, and Plutarch, *Numa* 11, who mentions the perpetual fire in the temple of Vesta, as well as the Pythagoreans and Plato; also Chalcidius, *In Tim.* 122 and Proclus, *In Tim.* 3.133 ff.; see also D. R. Dicks, *Early Greek Astronomy to Aristotle* (Ithaca, N. Y., 1970), pp. 65-66, 114-15; and W. Burkert, *Lore and Science in Ancient Pythagoreanism*, pp. 231-33, 337-42, and Allen, *Platonism*, p. 141. The description of "ignem infernum" as "incendium quoddam luminis expers" would seem to be the source of the fire that gives "no light, but darkness visible" in Milton's Hell, *Paradise Lost* 1.62-64; for other analogues, see John Carey and Alastair Fowler, eds., John Milton, *Complete Poems* (London, 1968), Fowler's note ad loc.
2. Ficino, *Comm. Symp.* 7.4, *Op.*, p. 1358.
3. Pliny, *HN* 28.23.82, mentions that the glance of a menstruous woman tarnishes a mirror. See also Aristotle, *De insomniis* 459b23-460a32.
4. Pliny, *HN* 7.2.16-17; also cited in Ficino, *Theol. Plat.* 13.4, ed. 2: 234 (*Op.*, p.300).
5. On the catoblepas, apparently a beast like a gnu, see Pliny, *HN* 8.32.77, and on the "regulus" or "basiliscus," 8.33.78; both mentioned by Ficino, *Theol. Plat.* 13.4, ed. 2: 234 (*Op.*, p. 300). On serpents fascinating people as an analogy explaining how magicians influence the stars, see *Enn.* 4.4.40. On fascination in Ficino, see also 3.21, n. 16.
6. For the torpedo-fish, see Pliny, *HN* 32.2.7; for the echinus, or rather "echeneis," 9.41.79-80 and 32.1.1-6; and for the phalangium-spider, 29.27.86.
7. The "scopa" and "arbutus" are problematic; I am grateful to Prof. Copenhaver for the tentative translations. For answers to these rhetorical questions about them, see 3.18 ad fin.

8. Serapion, *Liber aggregatus in medicinis simplicibus*, chap. 399, p. 157.1.
9. *Consiglio contro la pestilenza*, chap. 6, in *Op.*, p. 583, and chap. 24, pp. 604–5.

3.17

1. "Up there" must mean in the ontological levels higher than the visible heavens, since Ficino has just entertained the notion that the stars are fire of some sort, i.e., matter. Aristotle fits this description insofar as he says there is no weight in the visible heavens, but he does maintain there is matter (quintessence or aether, *De caelo* 269b18–270a12). It is the supercelestial heavens which Aristotle believed to possess no matter, i.e., nothing which occupies space, only light, *De caelo* 279a. A realm which fits this description appears in Ficino's own statement (though he is no Peripatetic) that the "animate world" as such has nothing corporeal, only color and shape, *Comm. Phaedrus*, chap. 11, *Op.*, p. 1372, ed. Allen, *Phaedran Charioteer*, text, pp. 124–25, and see Allen's summary of the four Neoplatonic levels of being, "Headnote," pp. 66–69, especially p. 67. This "animate world," while separable in theory from matter, the next lower level, is in fact always found in a body, however tenuous; among its possible bodies are the visible heavens, the stars and planets; they represent the bodies of the celestial souls. See also Apuleius (though he is no Peripatetic either), *De Platone et eius dogmate* in his *Opuscules philosophiques*, ed. Jean Beaujeu (Paris, 1973), 1.9, section 199.

2. Ficino's defensive tone betrays the fact that in this chapter he is using statements by Plotinus and Al-Kindi to refute in advance Aquinas's negative views on figurative talismans, *SCG* 105, ad fin.—views which Ficino will cite in the next chapter and which are negative insofar as Aquinas denies any natural force to figure as such. Space permits only an assemblage of Plotinian passages which parallel, and Aquinian passages which contrast with, *De vita* 3.17. For ease of comparison, in this chapter I will quote the passages, first in English, then in the original. Line numbers are those of the original Greek in Henry-Schwyzer and the Loeb; but since the question is what Ficino made of Plotinus, I will quote not the original Greek but Ficino's Latin translation of it from the *editio princeps,* Florence, 1492, modernizing orthography and punctuation and correcting the chapter numbers (most of the relevant chapter numbers are five less than they ought to be, e.g., for 29 read 34, etc., a confusion compounded by the fact that the commentary precedes rather than follows the lemma). Garin ("Le 'elezioni,' " p. 29-437) affirmed the indebtedness of Ficino's doctrine of the intrinsic efficacy of shape to Plotinus, specifying *Enn.* 4.4.40, and meaning no doubt lines 14–15, which read, in Ficino's translation, "Besides, [magicians] use figures having specific powers," "Praeterea figuris utuntur vires certas habentibus;" see also Ficino's commentary thereon, reprinted in *Op.*, p. 1748. *De vita* 3.17 in general parallels *Enn.* 4.4.35; there Plotinus asks "How then do these forces dispose themselves? . . . What is the difference between one triangle and another? How does the one dispose itself and act towards the other, and why, and how far does it go?" "Quo igitur modo hae vires se habent? . . . quidnam differentiae habeat triangulus ad triangulum comparatus, quidve hic habeat agatve ad illum et secundum quid hoc agat, et quousque?" *Enn.* 4.4.35.1–4;

see also 4.4.34.9-33, and Ficino's commentary thereon, reprinted in *Op.*, p. 1746. Plotinus answers this question in direct contrast to Aquinas (true, Plotinus is talking for the moment about the powers of celestial figures on us rather than of our figures on the stars as he does in 4.4.40.14-15 — and as Aquinas does all along — but he uses human postures as an analogy to them, implying that the principle is transferrable to human agents): ". . . so that figures themselves also have force. For according to this or that disposition, different consequences follow," "adeo ut ipsae quoque figurae vim habeant. Nam secundum ipsum, quod ita vel ita se habeat, aliter agit, aliterve agitur," *Enn.* 4.4.35.44-46. And he ends his chapter (35) with the points with which Ficino begins this chapter, the association of these powers with those of color and their distinction from elemental powers of heat and cold, *Enn.* 4.4.35.64-66.

Aquinas's statements in *SCG* 3 are opposable to these statements in that with regard to efficacy, he speaks of figure in the abstract; he draws no distinction here between celestial and terrestrial figures (though he does elsewhere affirm that constellations influence natural objects and that they cause in particular the occult qualities as distinct from the elemental ones, by way of the substantial forms, Copenhaver, "Scholastic Philosophy," esp. pp. 535-46). Contrast this entire chapter, then, with Aquinas's statement:

> Natural matter is not in any way disposed toward form by figures. So the bodies on which these figures are put have the same readiness to receive the celestial influence as any other bodies of the same species. . . .
>
> Per figuras non disponitur aliqualiter materia naturalis ad formam, . . . Corpora igitur in quibus sunt impressae huiusmodi figurae, sunt eiusdem habilitatis ad recipiendam influentiam caelestem cum aliis corporibus eiusdem speciei. . . .
> *SCG* 105, Leonine ed. 331a.12-16; Bourke sec. 10, 3.2: 96

Contrast with Ficino's first paragraph in particular, Aquinas's statement:

> In the practices of this art they use certain symbols and specially shaped figures. Now, shape is the principle of neither action nor passion; if it were, mathematical bodies would be active and passive. Hence it is not possible to dispose matter by special figures so that it will be receptive to a natural effect. So, the magicians do not use figures as dispositions. . . .
>
> In observationibus huius artis utuntur quibusdam characteribus et figuris determinatis. Figura autem nullius actionis principium est neque passionis: alias, mathematica corpora essent activa et passiva. Non ergo potest per figuras determinatas disponi materia ad aliquem effectum naturalem suscipiendum. Non ergo utuntur magi figuris aliquibus quasi dispositionibus. . . .
> *SCG* 105, Leonine ed. 330b.18-25, Bourke sec. 7, 3.2: 95-96

Bourke suggests, 3.2: 89, n.1, that Al-Kindi's *Theorica artium magicarum* (now better known as *De radiis*), which Ficino will cite in 3.21, forms the background of the relevant chapters (104-5), of *SCG*; and Ficino got the ideas which he tacitly opposes to Aquinas partly from Al-Kindi, *De radiis*, ed. M.-T. d'Alverny and F. Hudry, *Archives d'histoire doctrinale et littéraire du moyen âge* 41 (1974), chap. 8, p. 252; so that both sides are arguing about the same sort of magic.

3. See Plotinus: "For [star] figures are each made according to a reason and to specific numbers." "Praeterea figurationes omnes secundum rationem fieri, certisque singulas numeris," *Enn.* 4.4.35.12-14.

4. See *Comm. Phaedr.* chap. 11, ed. Allen *Phaedran Charioteer*, pp. 124-25, on the Intelligible world as characterized by unparticipated light.

5. Plotinus: "For what would be the sense in admitting that colors have force and activity and yet denying the same power to figures?" "Qua enim ratione fatebimur colores habere vim atque facere, figuras vero non confitebimur?" *Enn.* 4.4.35.59-61.

6. The analogies in these two paragraphs of the influence of celestial figures to the sympathetic effects produced in people by music and by facial expressions come at least ultimately from Plotinus; see for example, "For there is an attractive force inherent in charms and songs, and in a particular sound and posture [lit. *figura*] of the operator himself; for these things have a wonderful power of attraction, as do plaintive words and accents and sad postures." "Insita enim traducendi vis est carminibus cantibusque, et certo cuidam sono figuraeque ipsius agentis: nam talia quaedam mirabiliter attrahunt, sicut flebiles quaedam voces et accentus miserabilesque figurae. Trahitur vero anima, sed quo pacto? neque enim electio, neque ratio, sed irrationalis anima musica demulcetur," *Enn.* 4.4.40.20-24; ". . . since indeed the fact that figures in themselves also have pwers can be seen here below. For why are some figures terrifying to those who see them though those who are terrified have had no experience of evil from them before?" ". . . quandoquidem et figuras secundum se vires habere in rebus quoque nostris licet aspicere. Cur enim aliae figurae cernentibus sunt terribiles, ubi etiam nihil passi antea fuerint, qui terrentur?" *Enn.* 4.4.35.49-53; see also Ficino's *Comm. Plot., Op.*, p. 1746 on 4.4.35 ad fin.

7. The analogy of two lutes or lyres (λύρα) to explain how our magical figures gather the influence of the stars, comes from *Enn.* 4.4.41.6-8, although Plotinus here speaks of magical analogies in general, including shape, without specifying man-made figures. The analogy of a mirror is elaborated from Plotinus' brief comparison of a statue or other man-made receptacle for the World-soul to a mirror, *Enn.* 4.3.11.6-8. This example confirms that Plotinus does envision figure as operating upwards toward the heavens as well as downwards.

8. The description of diaphanous objects (corresponding to Plotinus's τὸ διαφανὲς, translated by Ficino as *perspicuum corpus*) as passive, but particularly receptive to light and hence to other celestial influences, resembles *Enn.* 4.5.42-49. It may also derive ultimately from Aristotle's *De anima* 418b4-13; see Copenhaver, "Scholastic Philosophy," p. 529.

3.18

1. Albumasar, *Introductorium*, see also Arabic ed. with German translation, Boll, *Sphaera* (Leipzig, 1903), pp. 491-93; what follows is a digest of 6.1-2 combined with its repetition (with no acknowledgement except to the Indians) in *Picatrix*, 2.2, translation pp. 59 ff. Yates comments on this and ensuing pages, pp. 70-1. Plessner says the source for many of the prescriptions which follow is unknown. Although the summary of them given by Gundel, *Dekane und Dekansternbilder*, Studien der Bibliothek Warburg no. 19 (Glückstadt and Hamburg, 1936), pp. 280-81, contains misreadings, it rightly assesses Ficino's qualified acceptance of them, and the background information is helpful.

2. Albumasar, cf. *Introductorium*, 6.2; Boll, *Sphaera*, p. 513. This is the only decan-figure cited, i.e., one that denotes a "face"; because of its figure, this face is also invoked by Ficino in *De stella Magorum*, *Op.*, p. 491, as the probable location of the comet which was the star of Bethlehem. Ficino must have felt authorized to include it because according to Albertus Magnus, whom he later cites, it contains an explicit reference to Christ's virgin birth, *Speculum astronomiae*, chap. 12, pp. 36-37 = Borgnet ed. 10.644b-645a. Garin says that Albumasar's remarkable statement was echoed also by Abraham ibn Ezra, Roger Bacon, and Pierre d'Ailly, "Introduzione," Giovanni Pico della Mirandola, *Disputationes adversus astrologiam divinatricem* (Florence, 1946), 1:12.

3. Ficino will outline the "formam ad coeli similitudinem . . . rotundam" in 3.19. One "recent authority" who advocates such an image is Al-Kindi, who says in *De radiis*, chap. 8, "De imaginibus," "Imago autem animalis, quia [aliter, que] est simulacrum animalis quod habet centrum et unitatem regitivam ad equalitatem propius accedentem, sicut mundus, habilior est ad recipiendam virtutem. . . . Hec enim maiorem portant in se et radiis suis similitudinem cum mundo—qui est perfecte equalitatis," p. 253, see also chap. 9, p. 255, recommending round creatures for sacrifices on the same grounds. Minor differences are that Al-Kindi believes images emit as well as attract rays, and that Ficino ignores the living creature and focuses on the geometrical shape. Al-Kindi will be cited by Ficino in 3.21.

4. On the geometrical appropriateness of straight-lined talismans for capturing rays, and the general concept of a progression from point to line to "superficies" to "corpus," see *Picatrix* 2.7, translation, pp. 101-3 = ed., pp. 96-97.

5. *Picatrix* 3.5 (5), translation, pp. 193-96 = ed., pp. 183-86. In view of this unique and sometimes almost verbatim similarity, we agree with Compagni (pp. 260-61, n. 3) and Plessner, ad loc., that "Das *Arabum collegium* . . . könnte also *Picatrix* sein, den Ficino begreiflicherweise nicht zu erwähnen wagt." Even here, however, Ficino omits from *Picatrix* both the subdivision of the spirit into seven according to the planets and special features such as the hollowness of the cross, its two feet, and the extra images upon which it is normally set. The alternative "formam ad coeli similitudinem . . . rotundam" is not in *Picatrix*.

6. Not in *Picatrix* 3.5 (5). See Rufinus, *Historia ecclesiastica* 2.29, *PL* 21:537. Ficino and Rufinus are referring to the *ankh*, the Egyptian symbol of life, a figure like a cross and indeed called an "ansate cross," *crux ansata*, or "handled cross," having a loop instead of an upper vertical arm. See also André Chastel, "Il 'signum crucis'

del Ficino," in *Marsilio Ficino e il ritorno di Platone*, ed. Giancarlo Garfagnini (Florence, 1986), pp. 216-19.

7. Unless otherwise noted, the *Picatrix* citations which follow will be from 2.10 (15). *Picatrix*, translation, p. 127.24 ff. = ed., p. 120. Plessner corrects Ficino's gloss: a Feyrizech is not a sapphire but a turquoise.

8. This image seems to be composed of elements from *Picatrix*, translation, p. 118.13 ff. = ed., p. 111; p. 128.26 ff. = ed., p. 121; and p. 129.14 ff. = ed., p. 122.

9. *Picatrix*, translation, p. 118.18-23.

10. *Picatrix*, translation, p. 115.14 ff., with elements from p. 119.8 ff.

11. Although Plessner can find no source for this image in his ed. of the original *Picatrix*, Yates, p. 71, claims to find one in the less authentic though better-known Latin version, 2.10, Sloane MS 1305, fol. 45, whose purpose is political, not medical. Libra and Taurus are the houses of Venus, Pisces her exaltation.

12. See also n. 11. In this and the next three sentences, Ficino's attention confusedly jumps back and forth between Mercury and the Moon. The image of the Moon is described in one place in *Picatrix*, its purpose and astrological hour somewhat (indeed, in this case, ten pages) later, see nn. 11 and 13; and so it is in *De vita*. For this image of Mercury, see *Picatrix*, p. 116.12 ff.; Plessner says the staff in the right hand of this image is probably in reality the same object as the reed in the right hand of the other Mercury below. In the Sala dei Mesi of the Palazzo Schifanoia, completed well before 1489 — see Eberhard Ruhmer, *Francesco del Cossa* (Munich, 1959), p. 73 — the decan image for the first face of Gemini is likewise a man holding a staff or "tela," though other details differ, pls. 18 and 43. See also Marco Bertozzi, *La tirannia degli astri: Aby Warburg e l'astrologia di Palazzo Schifanoia* (Bologna, 1985). As for the other decan-figures in these frescoes, contrary to Yates's implication, p. 57, and to Plessner's note, p. 240, n. to p. 146.26 ff., none of the images Ficino describes, whether or not borrowed from *Picatrix*, resemble them strongly enough to establish Ficino's indebtedness to them.

13. An unspecified image of the Moon is prescribed in *Picatrix*, translation, p. 126.15 ff., for the purpose not of *augumentum* but of driving out scorpions.

14. This second image of Mercury, including his reed, is derived principally from *Picatrix*, pp. 123-24; see also p. 116.12-28 = ed., p. 109, "wo vier verschiedene Merkurbilder angegeben sind, aus deren jedem etwas in unserem Text vorkommt," Plessner, ad loc., p. 241.

15. This image is specified for the Moon in *Picatrix*, translation, pp. 116.30-117.5.

16. Plessner finds no source for this prescription; but since the astrological hour is practically the same, presumably the image is that of Saturn described at n. 5, above (for which there is a source), here turned to a new application.

17. A highly creative conflation of various Sun-images owing something to *Picatrix*, pp. 115.14 ff., 119.8 ff., and 120.10 ff., in Pingree's edition, 2.12.39 and 44, after which (in some MSS, see his Appendix 21) Pietro d'Abano is likewise cited for this image (with the lion gazing at stones placed before him, which is the closest available analogue to him rolling one under his feet) and precise astrological hour. Lions in gold were common on astrological images; see Thorndike, 4: 122-27, citing at second hand Ficino's supposed model for Book 2, Arnald of Villanova, and an ecclesiastical condemnation thereof; 576; 578; 580 ff.

18. *Conciliator*, Diff. 10; fol. 16P: "Et ego quidem fui expertus figuram leonis impressum in auro, sole existente in medio celi cum corde leonis Iove aut Venere aspiciente: ac malis infortunatis et cadentibus dolorem renum afferre," also cited with further significant detail in some MSS of *Picatrix*, see preceding n.

19. Mengo Bianchelli da Faenza, "a distinguished physician," was present at a dinner given in June, 1489, at Lorenzo's house, with Ficino, Pico, Poliziano, and others, Della Torre, p. 813. It may have been at this time that he told Ficino the story of Giovanni Marliani's cure. Marliani was a famous lecturer on medicine at Pavia, Thorndike, 4: 207-8; his cure was later recounted by Girolamo Torella, Thorndike, 4: 577-78.

20. *Conciliator*, Diff. 113, fol. 158M-O. No source has been found for the talisman preceding this one.

21. The talismans of the mansions of the Moon. Mansion 14, *Picatrix* 1.4 (15), p. 18.32-19.7 = ed., p. 19.

22. Mansion 22, *Picatrix* 1.4 (23), p. 20.21 ff. = ed., pp. 21-22.

23. Mansion 23, *Picatrix* 1.4 (24), p. 20.28 ff. = ed., p. 22.

24. Mansion 27, *Picatrix* 1.4 (28), p. 21.19 ff. As Ficino professes, he has indeed selected those positions possessing medical significance and avoided those which interfere with free will and which are destructive. The mansions of the Moon are also found in the next author Ficino cites, Albohazen Haly filius Abenragel, *De iudiciis astrorum*, Part 7, chap. 101; but they are purely elective, no talismans are mentioned (see "Traditions"), and even the fostered activities are only vaguely similar, thus confirming Ficino's indebtedness to *Picatrix* here.

25. *De iudiciis astrorum* 1.4: "In naturis planetarum," "De Sole," sig. A3v.

26. For destruction of a city, alienation of minds, and other transitive, malicious, and sometimes psychological effects, see for example Mansion 4, *Picatrix* 1.4 (5), p. 16.23-30 = ed., p. 16.

27. Porphyry, *Life*, Section 10, Ficino's translation, *Op.*, p. 1541. As to whether Olympius used images, Porphyry does not say.

28. Albertus, full title, *Liber dictus Speculum astronomicum Alberti Magni de libris licitis et illicitis*, which we have been calling *Speculum astronomiae*, chaps. 11, p. 32.103-39 = Borgnet 10: 642a-b) and 16, p. 47.1-21 = Borgnet 10: 649b-650a). All the material down to "Pietro d'Abano" comes directly from Albertus.

29. For Thebit's patronymic "Benthorad," Ficino meant to say Ben Korah and he should have said Ibn Qurra, 834-901, who wrote in Baghdad (on whom see also above, 3.8 and n. 17), *De imaginibus* 5-10, 21, and 36, in Francis J. Carmody, *The Astronomical Works of Thabit b. Qurra* (Berkeley, 1960), pp. 181-84 and 186. Ps.-Ptolemy, *De imaginibus super facies signorum*, translation Gundel, *Dekane*, pp. 394-401, meaning the entire work. An edition of the Latin version of this work is in preparation by D. Pingree, who informs us that it exists in some 22 MSS and that out of these, three Latin MSS are presently in Florence. On the work, see Lynn Thorndike, "Traditional Medieval Tracts" (see above, 3.8, n. 1), pp. 256-59.

30. Pietro, *Conciliator,* Diff. 113, fol. 158M-N: " . . . ut recitat Thebit de Fedice qui imaginem construxit regionem destruentem"; see Thebit, *De imaginibus*, 14, in *Astronomical Works*, p. 182. The astrologer Phedix, possibly Felix, has not been identified.

31. Aquinas, *SCG* 3.104-7. The very grudging exculpation of figures is chap. 105, ad fin.; on its importance for Ficino's magic, see Copenhaver, "Scholastic Philosophy," pp. 533-34; for Aquinas' basically negative attitude towards figures, see notes to *De vita* 3.17.

32. 4 ad fin., ed. Fretté and Maré, 27: 462; the arguments against Aquinas's authorship, which include the untypicality of the very endorsement of astrology Ficino quotes, are given by Thorndike, 2: 614-15. For a more typical statement, see also the genuine *De occultis operibus naturae*, ed. cit., 24: 504b, and on the work in general, Joseph McAllister, ed. (Washington, D. C., 1939) Catholic University of America Philosophical Studies, 42. Copenhaver warns that McAllister's discussion omits the very part of the work Ficino cites here.

33. *SCG* 104, section 6.

34. *De occultis operibus naturae*, p. 507.

35. Iamblichus, *De mysteriis* 2.10, in Ficino's epitome, *Op.*, p. 1881; 4.7, *Op.*, p. 1891; see also above, 3.15 and n. 5.

36. *De mysteriis* 3.28-30, *Op.*, p. 1891.

37. Ps.-Ptolemy, *Centiloquium*, Aphorism 10. Ps.-ʿAlī ibn Riḍwan, *Comm. Centiloquium*, ad loc.

3.19

1. Ficino's model of the universe recalls that transparent sphere through which one should view "first the Sun and the other stars together, then the sea, the earth, and all living beings," suggested by Plotinus as an "experiment," *Enn.*, 5.8.9, with a roughly similar though not identical psychological aim.

2. The metals in this sentence are problematic. *Aes* is ambiguous; elsewhere I have translated it in its newer meaning "brass," because it is qualified as is brass by "yellow" or "red"; here, however, its use as a stamp on other metals requires hardness and indicates bronze. *Argenti lamina . . . aurata*, cf. 3.15.12, *Op.*, p. 551, *argento . . . deaurato*.

3. The precise meaning of this sentence is a bit unclear; its general aim is to refute the pagan notion that the world is eternal. The horoscope of the world is the Thema Mundi or conjectured position of every planet at the beginning of the world. For another version of the widespread notion of the Thema Mundi or birthday of the world, see Firmicus Maternus, *Mathesis*, eds. W. Kroll, F. Skutsch, and K. Ziegler (1897, repr. Stuttgart, 1968), 3.1. For an example of telling the fortune of the world for a given year on its birthday, an example of general astrology, see Ficino, *Consiglio contro la pestilenza*, *Op.*, p. 578: even old men were subject to this plague because "Saturn retrograde was lord of the year." I translate "sors" as "Lot" in the sense Manilius gives it in *Astronomica* 3.75-159, as a part of a scheme analogous to the "places" of the dodecatropos, each of which governs an activity of human life, see Goold, ed., Introduction, pp. lxii-lxviii, and *Oxford Latin Dictionary*, s.v. "athlum."

4. A pun on "genesis" and the biblical book of Genesis. Ficino means Pico's *Heptaplus*, 1489, a commentary on Genesis, ed. E. Garin (Florence, 1942). Nothing

particular in this paragraph is borrowed from the *Heptaplus*. On the contrary, in his *Disputationes adversus astrologiam divinatricem* 2.5, 1: 132-34, Pico was to rebuke Roger Bacon for precisely this astrological explanation for resting on the Sabbath (see Garin, ed., n. 2 ad loc.) on the grounds that it reduced a divine mystery to an astrological motive.

5. For the Armenian stone, see above, 1.20 and note 2.

6. Vesta is the God of the earth in the Neoplatonic alignment of the Twelve Great Gods with the twelve spheres. Archimedes, see Cicero, *Disp. Tusc.* 1.25.63 and *Rep.* 1.21-22, also mentioned by Ficino, *Theol. Plat.* 4.1, ed. 1: 157-58 (*Op.*, pp. 157-58) and 13.3, ed. 2:223 (*Op.*, p. 226). For Lorenzo della Volpaia, see Chastel, pp. 95-97, nn. 15-17, echoed by Yates, p. 75, n. 1, with important qualifications; also, Prof. Chastel now believes, as he kindly informs me, that the clock in the Museo Civico of Florence is not necessarily the precise object to which Ficino here refers, but at least it exemplifies the type of object. All three images — the ceiling-painting, the clock, and the mental image — are artistic embodiments of the Platonic notion that the heavens are a redemptive subject of study because, being free from corruption, they retain the pristine "archetypal" form they received from the hand of the Creator executing his "Idea"; see "Habits." Ben Jonson's *Haddington Masque*, 265 ff., calls for a large planetarium as a stage-prop; Spondanus in his edition of Homer (1584), alludes in a note at *Iliad* 18, pp. 340-41, to one described by Cardano in his *De subtilibus machinis*. On the connection of such wondrous machines with talismanic magic, see Yates, pp. 147-49.

7. Plato, *Rep.* 1.335d. The two possibilities in the preceding sentence are both affirmed by Ficino in *Comm. Tim.* chap. 24, *Op.*, pp. 1448-49.

8. Abraham ibn Ezra (ca. 1089-1167), *Liber rationum*, translated into Latin by Pietro d'Abano, in *Abrahe Avenaris Judei astrologi peritissimi in re judiciali opera* (Venice, 1507), p. 38. See also his *Introductorium in iudicia astrorum quod dicitur principium sapientie*, chap. 4, pp. 18v-19; and *Tractatus in tredecim manieriebus planetarum*, p. 88. Ficino also cites this opinion of Abraham on Saturn in his *Argumentum* to Plotinus's *Enn.* 2.3.6, *Op.*, p. 1617. For a discussion of Pietro d'Abano and his translation of Abraham, see Raphael Levy, *The Astrological Works of Abraham ibn Ezra* (Baltimore, 1927), pp. 32-46.

3.20

1. For Medea and her herbs, see Ovid, *Met.* 7.159-349; referred to also in Roger Bacon, *De retardatione*, chap. 3, p. 41; see also above, 2.17, n. 2. Medea made a statue of Artemis-Hekate with herbs in it; and she promised to make an old man young again; what Ficino does not notice here, though he does in 2.17, is that both measures were mere pretense, see Diodorus Siculus, *Bibliotheca* 4.51, trans. C. H. Oldfather, Loeb (Cambridge, Mass., 1933) 2: 504-7. In this reference the Magi have not been identified; they could be the reputed authors of the *Chaldean Oracles*, ascribed to the Magi; perhaps frag. no. 128, quoted in 3.22 (see our n. 8) translating σῶμα ῥευστόν, "corpus caducum" not as "weak body," as I have done there, but as "body which is passing away," i.e., "aging."

2. For Egyptians, see *Asclepius* 24a and 37-38, more explicitly cited in 3.26, see n. 7 there; for Arabs, see *Picatrix* 3.5(5), translation, pp. 193-97. The otherwise unficinian subdivision of the cosmic spirit into spirits of individual planets in this chapter (see Introduction, "Principles of Translation" and "Magic") probably betrays the distinctive influence of Al-Kindi and the *Picatrix*, even though other sources too occasionally mention more than one divinity.

3. Unlike its English cognate "mundane," "mundanus" in this context distinguishes the "fire" in question as celestial, opposed both to the subterranean fire which burns, not shines, and to ordinary terrestrial fire, see 3.16, ad fin.; moreover, since it is separate from and co-ordinate with the stars, Ficino is probably thinking in particular of the so-called elemental sphere of fire. For more discussion of the word "mundanus," see Introduction, "Principles of Translation."

4. See 3.13, p. 548; 3.26, p. 571; and "*De vita* in the Canon." On this paragraph Copenhaver comments: "Having once again [as in 3.13] established the *efficacy* of talismans, imputing it either to material or demonic agency, Ficino then raises the issue of *legitimacy* by comparing the animation of statues to demonic possession and by identifying an obviously evil motivation for the activity of the demons, "Iamblichus, Synesius, and the Chaldaean Oracles," forthcoming.

5. The stress on the psychology of the user and operator in the latter part of this chap. may be from *Picatrix*, cf. the "Entschluss des Ausführenden," mentioned 3.5, ad init., p. 190 = ed., p. 180. Al-Kindi, who will be cited in 3.21, devotes even more space and emphasis to the "desiderium," "fides," and "ymago in mente concepta," in the (medical) spirit of the operator as themselves emitting rays which have a power analogous to that of the stars, p. 230, both to move external objects, pp. 231-33, and to shape the wills of the victims, pp. 238-46. Compagni says the unknown author of *Picatrix* knew and used Al-Kindi's *De radiis* and cites this resemblance, "Picatrix latinus," pp. 276-77. Walker has shown that this contact of the human medical spirit with the cosmic spirit is the key doctrine in Ficino's entire system of spiritual magic. Ficino rather over-generously credits it to the "Arabs," i.e., Al-Kindi and the various authors represented in the *Picatrix*. *Picatrix* is responsible for the synthesis to the extent that all the elements of it are juxtaposed in the space of about a dozen pages in the conclusion of 3.4 and in 3.5, translation, pp. 185-97, first the medical "Geist" and then the "Pneuma des Menschens" are juxtaposed to the "pneumata" of the planets, to their rays, and to the general "pneuma" of the cosmos. These sources seem to have provided the raw materials of Ficino's synthesis, which remains unprecedented in its explicit and direct contact between the two corporeal spirits—the human and the general but impersonal cosmic spirit.

6. Lit., "acted enough"; i.e., the sense soon ceases to be aware of a smell, showing that the smell has become one with the perceiving spirit. I owe this interpretation to Michael J. B. Allen.

7. Al-Kindi frequently employs the term "intentio" in his parallel discussion, but he does not do so in quite the same sense as Ficino's, since he connects it more with the will. "Intentio" in Ficino, however, is a technical term for what the "imaginatio" produces. Ficino later speaks of a parallel "imaginationis conceptus" (3.21.33-34). In this definition, in its earlier, Avicennan form, an "intentio" represents a primitive "stage of universalization from sense impressions," one with-

in the capacity of a beast (Walker, p. 10, n. 1; Harvey, *Inward Wits*, p. 42). "Intentio" is more often located in the "fantasia," i.e., the "vis imaginativa" or "vis cogitativa," a higher power than the "imaginatio" (which, strictly speaking, is simply the storehouse of sense-impressions, see Walker, p. 6, n. 3; Harvey, pp. 46, 59). In his use of the term here for images of anticipated events deliberately summoned up, Ficino seems to have followed this general practice as exemplified in Aquinas in lumping the "intentiones" and their receptacle the "imaginatio" with the higher "phantasmata" and their receptacle the "fantasia," in that this faculty has also the power to recombine the "intentiones" into previously unperceived images at will, see Harvey, pp. 55, 59-60, Kristeller, *Phil MF*, pp. 324-34, 360, 369.

8. See Galen, *Comm.* 4.4.9 on Hippocrates's *Epidemics* (Kühn 17.2:146); Galen's *Comm.* 1.2 on Hippocrates's *Prognosticon* (Kühn 18.2:3); and Avicenna, *Liber canonis* 1.2.3.1, who cites Galen on the *Prognosticon*. The citations of Avicenna and Galen are also made by Roger Bacon, *De diebus criticis*, in Little and Withington, eds., *De retardatione*, p. 187.

3.21

1. Compagni compares this lunar talisman of love to one described in *Picatrix* 1.5, presumably meaning one or both of those described in translation, p. 31 = ed., pp. 32-33, though *Picatrix* does not mention Pisces.

2. Philostratus, *VA* 4.25, recounts the tale that Apollonius exposed a lamia or lady-vampire (the word is a direct transliteration of Philostratus's Greek) at Corinth who was fattening up a young man in order to suck his blood, see also Thorndike 1: 263. The story was repeated by Burton, *Anatomy of Melancholy* 3.2.1.1, which inspired John Keats's poem *Lamia*.

3. Origen, *Contra Celsum* 1.25; also 5.45 and 8.37. Synesius, *De insomniis*, 132C3-7 (*PG* 66: 1285a-b), section 3 in Ficino's translation, *Op.*, p. 1969. Al-Kindi, *De radiis*, chap. 6, "De virtute verborum," pp. 233-50 (note similarity of his and Ficino's chapter titles). For Zoroaster, see fragment no. 150 of the *Chaldean Oracles*, in Des Places (above, 3.1 and n. 6), p. 103, and in Wilhelm Kroll, *De oraculis Chaldaicis* (1894, repr. Hildesheim, 1962), p. 58; and Psellus, *Expos. Orac. Chald.* 1132c, in Des Places, pp. 169-70. Iamblichus, *De mysteriis* 7.4-5, in Ficino's epitome, *Op.*, p. 1902.

4. For Pythagoreans, see Iamblichus, *De vita Pythagorica*, chaps. 15.64-67 and 25.110-14, and see above, 3.2 and n. 8; Proclus too performed miracles by words, songs, and sounds—see Marinus's account of him, *Vita Procli*, chaps. 19 and 26-27. On magical words in general, see Walker, p. 37; on musical effects in general, see also above, 1.10 and nn. 4 and 5. "Orphei more" means using them as an incantation, prayer, or ritual to get something from a given star and its deity; "Phoebi more" perhaps means the same thing by way of Apollo's association with charms, see Gen. Proem. We are unable to identify the Hebrew doctors.

5. Vergil, *Aen.* 4.487-91; Horace, *Epod.* 5.45-46.

6. Cato, *Agr.* 160.

7. I Sam. 16:14-23, see also above, 1.10 and n. 5. Scripture is called "mysterium" in *Comm. Phaedr.* chap. 2, *Op.*, p. 1364, ed. Allen, *Phaedran Charioteer*, pp. 76-77.

8. For the Chaldean order, see above, 3.9, n. 1 ad loc., and Bouché-Leclercq, pp. 107-10. Copenhaver, "Scholastic Philosophy," observes that the substances are here ranked on a typically Neoplatonic ladder from inorganic matter to the highest faculties of the mind, pp. 529-30. Sounds here dedicated to Apollo will themselves be parceled out between him and three other planets, below, 3.21 ad fin., *Op.*, pp. 563-64.

9. Andromachus, physician to the Emperor Nero, discovered theriac by adding viper's flesh to the antidote of Mithridates; see above, 1.25 and n. 1, also Thorndike 1: 171. See Galen, *De antidotis* 1.1 (Kühn 14: 2-3); and Avicenna, *Liber canonis* 5.1.1.1 and *De viribus cordis* 2.4. Roger Bacon cites Andromachus and Avicenna in his *Antidotarius*, in Little and Withington, eds., *De retardatione*, p. 108.5-9. Neither Galen nor Avicenna say that Andromachus's discovery was divinely inspired, although Ficino in his *Consiglio contro la pestilenza*, Latin translation, chap. 6 (*Op.*, p. 582), says that Galen thought the power of theriac to be divine. See Galen, *Ad Pisonem de theriaca* 3 (Kühn 14: 224-25).

10. Cf. Iamblichus, *De mysteriis* 3.3, in Ficino's epitome, *Op.*, p. 1883. For Apollonius, see Philostratus, *VA* 3.44.

11. Ficino employs the word "electio" for any act of will; it is not astrological elections which he is rejecting here. Astrological elections are affirmed, for example, in the last sentence of 3.12 and passim, every time he says, "at the right time" or "opportunely" or specifies the correct astrological hour for performing some work; he mentions them two paragraphs on in this very chapter. On those, see Garin, "Le 'elezioni'," and Introduction, "Traditions." By denying "electio" here, he means to say with Plotinus, *Enn.* 4.4.42, whom he cites below, that the stars respond to prayers or magic not by an act of will but naturally and spontaneously.

12. Since the idea is complicated, I paraphrase with the help of Walker, p. 17: Third, observe what effects a given star causes in terms of human speeches, songs, etc., and if you want to obtain some further influence from this star, offer such speeches, songs, etc., back to it in your song.

13. On "intentiones" see 3.20, n. 7.

14. Ficino reasons by analogy from one kind of medical spirit to another. On the three kinds of medical spirit, see Introduction, "Habits of Mind," and 1.2, n. 1. He adds this argument to bolster the idea, which he found in Al-Kindi (see below), that words can move bodies. The precise meaning of "effusione" is unclear; my "emanation" follows Prof. Copenhaver's suggestion that it is the Latin equivalent of ἔλλαμψις, literally, "a raying forth," a Plotinian word for that emanation whereby the Neoplatonic hypostases bring lower things into being.

15. Cf. the geographical astrology in Ptolemy, *Tetrabiblos* 2.1-5.

16. Similarly, Al-Kindi says that when a desired image is vividly pictured "in spiritu ymaginario," then "spiritus emittit radios moventes exteriora," especially if helped by some external aid such as words, chap. 5, pp. 231, 233. On fascination, see above, 3.16, nn. 2 and 5. For the medical spirits as aery and hence as able to be fascinated, whether by words or by objects, see Al-Kindi, chap. 6, p. 240 and notes t and x.

17. For Pythagoras, Plato, and the harmony of the spheres, see Iamblichus, *De vita Pythagorica* 15.65, Aristotle, *De caelo* 290b12 ff., Plato, *Rep.* 530d, 531c, and 617b, *Tim.* 36d, and the discussion in Burkert, *Lore*, pp. 350-57.

18. On the various voices pertaining to the various planets, cf. Al-Kindi, chap. 6, p. 234.
19. *Enn.* 4.3.12; 4.4.41; Iamblichus, *De mysteriis* 3.9, in Ficino's epitome, *Op.*, p. 1885.
20. Philostratus, *VA* 4.16.
21. Walker, to whose section on Ficino's music I am particularly indebted in this chapter, wittily subjoins, p. 20, "presumably he had not heard a Tarantella."

3.22

1. For the Pythagorean sources of this idea, see above, 3.21, n. 17. Their being "harmonica ratione compositum" is opposed to being "compositum" with an overplus of some quality, an idea refuted in 3.19, *Op.*, p. 560. In speaking of the music of medicines, odors, vapors, and sun-bathers, Ficino is employing the recognized and philosophically charged metaphors of "musica mundana" for the order of the visible universe and "musica humana" for the moral and prudential ordering of human affairs, see Leo Spitzer, *Classical and Christian Ideas of World Harmony* (Baltimore, 1963), pp. 34 et passim.
2. Ficino is thinking ahead to the Platonic Lunar people, on which see the next note.
3. See Plato, *Phaedo* 110b-111c, although these people are not said to be Lunar, Saturnian, or heroic.
4. This is a widely known quotation from *Albumasar in Sadan* (not *Sadar*), which is the Latin version of the Greek abbreviated version of an Arabic treatise by Abū Saʿid Shādhān; see D. Pingree, "Abū Maʿshar," in *Dictionary of Scientific Biography* 1, esp. p. 39. The work has never been edited. In the two manuscripts, the quotation occurs as follows: Bodleian MS Laud. Misc. 594, of the l4th c., fols. 137a-14lva; and BN MS 7302, of the 15th c., fols. 109a-130va. See Lynn Thorndike, "Albumasar in Sadan," *Isis* 45 (1954): 22-32, esp. pp. 28-29 for his citation of the relevant passage here. As to why Ficino called it *Sadar* (a simple mistake), he may have had in mind Sabor, King of the Medes and addressee of a treatise by Avicenna, cited in Book 4 of his Epistles (*Op.*, pp. 759-60), entitled "In Praise of Medicine," *Letters* 3: 23.
5. All planets approach Saturn rather than *vice versa* because he is the slowest planet. Compagni notes that the importance of Saturn here can be compared to its treatment in *Picatrix* 2.6. While Saturn is not credited with so much as she implies, being introduced there largely by way of example, he is credited with being slow, more powerful than most planets, and close to, and hence allied with, the spheres of the fixed stars and of the Primum Mobile.
6. See Psellus, *Expos. Orac. Chald.*, *PG* 122.1132b, ed. Des Places, p. 169, on fragment no. 164, and the commentary in Hans Lewy, *Chaldaean Oracles and Theurgy*, pp. 293-94.
7. On Saturday as the day of rest, see also above, 3.19.
8. Ficino also quotes Abraham ibn Ezra for this statement in his *Comm.* on Plotinus, *Enn.* 4.4.42, *Op.*, p. 1748. The astrologer Samuel has not been identified.

For the Chaldean rule, see fragment no. 128 of the *Chaldean Oracles*, in Des Places ed., p. 97; Psellus, *Expos. Orac. Chald.*, *PG* 122: 1140b, Des Places ed., p. 177; and Kroll, *De Oraculis Chaldaicis*, p. 54. Ficino also quotes one or another Chaldean rule in his *Theol. Plat.* 13.4, ed. 2: 235 (*Op.*, p. 301), as well as above, 2.17.

9. Iamblichus, *De mysteriis* 8.6-7, in Ficino's epitome, *Op.*, p. 1904, also cited by Ficino in his *Comm. Phaedrum cum summis capitulorum*, summa 9 (*Op.*, p. 1374), ed. and trans. Allen, *Phaedran Charioteer*, p. 139, where, however, this is done not by the supercelestial or even the celestial gods but by the good daemons, the rulers of the world. On the supercelestial gods freeing the theurgist from fate, see the passages from Iamblichus and the Chaldean Oracles quoted and cited in E. R. Dodds, *The Greeks and the Irrational* (Berkeley, 1951), p. 291. In this passage, Ficino violates his usual avoidance of higher theurgy.

10. Orpheus says Love possesses the keys of the universe, "Hymn to Eros," ed. E. Abel, *Orphica* (Leipzig, 1885), p. 89, no. 58.4. This idea is also cited by Ficino in his *Comm. Phaedrum cum summis capitulorum*, summa 9 (*Op.*, p. 1374), ed. Allen, *Phaedran Charioteer*, p. 139; the *Comm. Symp.*, Ded., ed. Marcel, pp. 134-35, not found in the *Op.*; and 3.3, p. 164 (*Op.*, p. 1330). Otto Kern, *Orphicorum fragmenta*, pp. 324-25, cites this passage from *De vita* 3.22, but refers it wrongly to Orphic Hymn no. 1.7 (Abel ed., pp. 58-59), an Orphic text which is also cited by Proclus, *In Remp.* 614b, ed. Kroll, 2.121.8-11 — wrongly in that this hymn identifies Hecate as possessing the keys of the universe.

11. Cf. *Heptaplus*: against astrological determinism, Expositio 2.7, citing Chaldeans; the precise notion of sacrifices deflecting a bad fate onto our possessions is not present here, but it is in the spirit of the Chaldean Oracles.

3.23

1. Plato, *Phaedo* 107d-108b and *Rep.* 10.617d-e, 620d-e. For the doctrine of the *genius* in Latin literature, see Horace, *Ep.* 2.2.187-89, Tibullus 2.2.5, and Apuleius, *De deo Socratis* 15; and cf., for a Christian and hence derogatory version, Lactantius, *Institutiones divinae* 2.15. See also Allen, *Platonism*, pp. 8-28.

2. Varro, *De re rustica* 1.4; and see A. Otto, *Die Sprichwörter und sprichwörtlichen Redensarten der Römer* (Leipzig, 1890), p. 111.

3. Cicero, *De officiis* 1.110, Horace, *Ars poetica* 385; and see Otto, *Sprichwörter*, p. 225.

4. See Ficino's translation of the *Golden Verses of Pythagoras, Aurea verba*, *Op.*, p. 1979.

5. See Proclus, *In Remp.* 617d-e, ed. Kroll, 2.271-73.

6. Porphyry, *Letter to Anebo* 39 and Iamblichus, *De mysteriis* 9.2, in Ficino's epitome (*Op.*, 1905). On the *Letter*, see 3.13, n. 9.

7. Julius Firmicus Maternus, *Mathesis*, 4.19.2. See also 4.17-18, on the Part of Fortune and place of the daemon. The discussion of the dodecatropos or twelve places is also found in Firmicus, 2.19-20; see Bouché-Leclercq, pp. 289-96.

8. Philostratus, *VA* 4.10.

9. Xenophon, *Memorabilia* 1.2.3 and 24-25; Ps.-Plato, *Theages* 128b-c. See also Proclus, *In Alc.* 1.86-87, pp. 38-39.

3.24

1. Ficino could be describing himself, for he was slight of build.
2. Similar whimsical fantasies about Phoebus and Bacchus are found in Gen. Proem — including both a pun on Bacchus as Father Liber and his devotee as *liber*, "free," and a similar analysis of the author's own chains of association — and 2.20.

3.25

1. Ficino here equates the astrological Head of the Dragon, the Moon's ascending node, with the Biblical Dragon, Rev. 12:4, who represents Satan.
2. Albertus Magnus, *Speculum astronomiae*, chap. 15, p. 45.2-5 (= ed. Borgnet 10:648b).
3. Ps.-Aquinas, *De fato* 4, ad fin., *Opera.*, ed. Fretté and Maré, 27: 462. See also the genuine *De occultis operibus naturae* in Fretté and Maré, 27: 504b. The legitimate uses of astrology appealed to by Ficino early in 3.25 resemble those endorsed in this work and in *SCG* 3.92 as well as those endorsed in the spurious *De fato*.

3.26

1. The Demiurge in the *Timaeus* 29d-30a, apparently conflated on the basis of his goodness with the Good itself in *Rep.*; God in *Timaeus Locrus* 93-95a; see also Ficino, *Theol. Plat.* 11.4, ed. 2: 120, *Op.*, p. 252.
2. Plotinus, *Enn.* 4.4.40, which pervades this entire paragraph; Synesius, *De insomniis*, 132D10-13 (= *PG* 66: 1285a-b), in Ficino's translation, section 3, *Op.*, p. 1969. These authors are in turn following Plato's *Symposium*, see Introduction, "*De vita* in the Canon"; see also Ficino's *Comm. Symp.*, ed. Marcel, p. 220.
3. See Philostratus, *VA* 3.24, where Hiarchas the Indian sage is speaking.
4. *Aen.* 6.726-27.
5. Orpheus, frag. no. 168.3, ed. Kern, *op. cit.*, p. 201; also cited in *Letters* 1: 47, *Op.*, 614.
6. Ps.-Ptolemy *Centiloquium*, Aphorism 8, cited above, 3.24 and below, "Apologia." Also said by Ps.-Aquinas, *De fato*, 4 ad fin., ed. Fretté and Maré, 27: 462. The comparison of magic to some such agricultural operation is also found in *Enn.* 4.4.40.16,. The verb ἐξάπτω which Plotinus employs here has been translated "cross-fertilizes" (Guthrie), "trains toward one another" (MacKenna), "trains together" (Armstrong) and "joins together separated shoots" (Geoffrey Lewis's translation of Book 6 of the Arabic paraphrase known as the *Theologia Aristotelis* in Henry-Schwyzer, *Enneads* 2:137).
7. Scorpion from basil, Pliny, *HN* 20.48.119; bees from an ox, Vergil, *Georgics* 4.281-314, Varro, *De re rustica* 3.16.4, and Pliny, *HN* 11.23.70. For recipes promising to make animals by magic, see *Picatrix* 4.9 (19-20), and see also below, "Apologia," and note 11.
8. *Enn.* 4.3.11. For the example, see n. 6, above; it is not in exactly the same

place, just in the same *Ennead* (4). There are really two god-making, or better, statue-animating, passages in *Asclepius*, 24a and 37-38, also cited above in 3.13, p. 548, and 3.20, p. 561; see "Magic," where the later and longer passage is quoted and translated in its entirety. Ficino's interweaving of these will be traced hereafter by parenthetical refs. in text. As for the topic discussed below, what rank of divinity was employed, Plotinus asserts with uncharacteristic boldness that the World-soul herself was captured; Hermes says terrestrial daemons, 37 (cf. 24 and Ficino's aery daemons — who are at least of the same rank, elementals — not celestial gods), 38. For a similar preference for the lower ranks, see *De vita* 3.1, p. 531; 3.22, p. 565.

9. Synesius, *De insomniis*, 133A6-C2 (= *PG* 66: 1285c-d), section 4 in Ficino's translation, *Op.*, p. 1969.

10. The unavailability of an accurate text led Yates, p. 67, and Walker, p. 42, to think that the magic here described was "illicit"; see textual note. An alternative translation of *magicum illicium* would be "magical charm."

11. Iamblichus, *De mysteriis* 6.7, in Ficino's epitome, *Op.*, p. 1901. Ficino misrepresents Iamblichus here in that Iamblichus is not condemning the Egyptians as compared to the Chaldeans on grounds of their worship of daemons but of their use of threats addressed to the higher gods. Again, Ficino does not use the word *gradus* ("steps"); but at least the notion is present in daemons being ἐν τάξει ("in series") with the gods at 6.6.247.11-6.7.248.2, cf. Ficino's translation: "Ordo deorum immobilis permanet in eisdem [sc. daemonibus, though in the Greek the antecedent is the mysteries guarded by the daemons]. . . hanc enim ob causam mundi partes in ordine permanent, quod beneficio potestas Osiridis syncero permanet," p. 1901; cf. 246.19; the notion occurs more explicitly in Ficino's *Comm. Plot.*, "In librum de amore," chap. 5, "De daemonibus," *Op*. p. 1715, where daemons are "mediators" to those planetary gods which are Ficino's prime concern here.

12. The astrologer Samuel (also cited above, 3.22) has not been identified. "David Bil the astrologer" may be a scribal error for "David Bilia the astrologer."

13. Aquinas, *SCG* 3.104-6; see also 3.18, above, and D. P. Walker on this passage, p. 42.

14. The predicate could be translated as "cannot be a chance coincidence," but that would make no sense in context, since the distinction between chance and non-chance is inapplicable to the motions of the heavens; my translation, on the other hand, voices what would be a logical reaction to the aforementioned "dispositio siderum," namely, that it is too complicated for all its conditions to be met at one time.

15. Porphyry, *Letter to Anebo* 25; see Ficino's epitome of Iamblichus, *De mysteriis* 3.30, *Op.*, p. 1891. Iamblichus, *De mysteriis* 3.1 and 3.4-5, and in Ficino's epitome, *Op.*, pp. 1883-84. For information on Porphyry's *Letter*, see 3.13, n. 9.

16. *Enn.* 4.3.11. Ficino imported the reference to the Magus manipulating substances from *Enn.* 4.4.40. He apparently added the specific substances himself.

17. Iamblichus, *De mysteriis* 5.1-26, in Ficino's epitome, *Op.*, pp. 1894-1900, talks about sacrifices, but does not say about them what Ficino does.

Apologia

1. Piero del Nero (d. 1512), Della Torre pp. 623, 728; Piero Guicciardini, Della Torre, pp. 623, 727-28; Piero Soderini (1452-1522), Della Torre, pp. 623, 726-27. In the opening of his "Apologia," Ficino plays with the meaning of the name "Piero" or "Peter," which in Latin (*petra*) means "rock," cf. Matt. 16:18. When he later addresses Nero as *candidissime* ("whitest") he is punning on the Italian meaning of Nero as "black."
2. According to one legend, the Greek goddess Athena received the title Pallas because she killed a giant of that name, see Apollodorus, *Bibliotheca* 1.37. On Ficino's figurative use of the "arx Palladis," see *De vita* 1.2, n. 3. A pun on the etymology of "arx" from "arceo" begins here.
3. Here and below, passim, there is word-play on *libri* and *liberi*, "books" and "children"; for a similar conceit, see *Op.*, p. 916,2. See Plato, *Phaedrus* 275a, where writing, invented by the Egyptian god Theuth, is said to be his offspring, and 277e-278b, where Socrates says that not written discourses but only discourses on the instruction of justice, honor, and goodness, which are written in the souls of the listeners, can be considered a person's legitimate children.
4. See Juvenal 10.356: "mens sana in corpore sano." The expression became proverbial.
5. "Astronomy" is used in this sentence as a synonym for "astrology." Hippocrates, *De decoro* (Littré 9: 234-36). Galen, *Quod optimus medicus sit quoque philosophus* (Kühn 1: 53); *De diebus decretoriis* on astrology, see chap. 3.1-7 (Kühn 9:901-15); cf. Galen, *De Hippocratis et Platonis placitis* 9.8 (Kühn 5:789-91). Cf. above, 3.10 and n. 5. See also Thorndike's discussion of Galen and astrology, 1: 178-80. For the dependence of Ficino's own medical practice on astrology, see "Ad lectorem," p. 530.
6. Ecclus. 38:1; see also 38:7, 12, 15. Luke 9:1; Matt. 10:1. Cf. Ficino's *Letters* 1: 127-28, *Op.*, p. 645.
7. Pliny, *HN* 8.41.99.
8. Pliny, *HN* 25.50.89; Dioscorides, chap. 359, cited above in 3.15.78-79.
9. Pliny, *HN* 36.39.149-51, it helps eagles to bring forth their eggs, 30.44.130. Also cited above in 3.12.56-58, see n. 8 ad loc.
10. Jn. 12:31.
11. Recipes for making animals by magic are found in *Picatrix* 4.9 (19-20), translation, pp. 418-19 = ed. 411-12; and see above, 3.26 and n. 7.
12. Aratus of Soli in Cilicia, third c. B.C. The first eighteen lines of his *Phaenomena* are an ode to Zeus. For Jove as the *animus* and *spiritus mundi*, see also Ficino, *Letters* 1: 47, *Op.*, p. 614. In his speech to the Athenians, Acts 17:28, Paul does indeed quote from line 5 of Aratus's *Phaenomena*, "For we are also His [God's] offspring." Luke the Evangelist is the author of Acts; see also his Gospel, 20:36 "children of God." The words directly quoted by Ficino, "for in Him we live and move and exist," are also in Acts 17:28, but they are generally ascribed not to Aratus but to Epimenides of Crete, sixth c. B.C. See *The Beginnings of Christianity, Part 1: The Acts of the Apostles*, vol. 5, eds. Kirsopp Lake and Henry J. Cadbury (London, 1933), pp. 246-51.

13. As it happens, the ox and the ass are melancholic animals; see William of Conches, *Philosophia mundi*, in *PL* 172: 55.

14. Cristoforo Landino (1424-1504), a member of Ficino's Academy, see Della Torre, p. 623, et passim.

15. Angelo Poliziano (1454-1494), see Della Torre, pp. 623, 657-58, et passim.

16. Iolaus was the nephew and faithful companion of Hercules to whom Hercules called out for help in his battle with the Hydra, see Apollodorus, *Bibliotheca* 2.5.2.

17. One of Hercules' labors was the killing of the Hydra of Lerna. The Hydra had many heads which, when cut off, grew back. Iolaus cauterized the several necks with a firebrand to prevent the heads from growing back. See Apollodorus, 2.5.2.

18. Pico della Mirandola, see Della Torre, p. 623, et passim.

19. According to legend, the god Apollo killed the dragon Python at Delphi, see Homeric Hymn no. 2, "To Pythian Apollo," 300 f.

Quod necessaria sit

1. See Della Torre, esp. pp. 623-24, 732. Ficino is playing on the similarity of the names of "Canigiani (*Canisianus*), "Canacci" (*Canacius*), and "Corsini" (*Cursinus*) to the Latin words for dog (*canis*) and runner (*cursor*). Plato does not distinguish the legitimate from the illegitimate dogs.

2. Plato, *Rep.* 2.376a-b.

3. See Della Torre, esp. pp. 623, 812.

4. A reference to the legend of St. George in which he slays a dragon.

5. *Iliad* 23.97-104; *Od.* 11.206-8; *Aen.* 2.792-94; 6.700-702; Dante, *Purgatorio* 2.79-81; "expanded" alludes to the belief that one way in which a spirit can be told from a mortal is by its greater size, *Aen.* 2.772-73.

6. Pythagoras's precept to avoid excess. See the *Golden Verses of Pythagoras*, 18-21; Ficino's translation of *Aurea verba, Op.*, p. 1979; Diogenes Laertius 8: 9 and 23. This was essentially the motto inscribed around the walls of the Academy at Careggi, which concluded: "Avoid excess and troubles, be joyful in the present" — see Ficino's *Letters*, 1: 39-40 (*Op.*, p. 609,2); see also the *Select Sentences of Sextus the Pythagorean*, "To neglect things of the smallest consequence, is not the least thing in human life," in Iamblichus, *Life of Pythagoras*, trans. Thomas Taylor (London, 1818), p. 268.

7. This second letter, especially the last two paragraphs, is so personal and allusive that its relevance is difficult to divine. On the literal level, Ficino is exploring the paradox that "care" to avoid illness can itself bring on illness and shorten the life it seeks to save. On this level he is arguing, as in Gen. Proem ad init. and 3.25 ad fin., against hygienic scrupulosity (as is indicated by his echoing words and ideas from 1.2, which advocates scrupulosity) and thus downgrading *De vita*. "Less as a priest than as a doctor," however, indicates that he is also arguing against religious scrupulosity and hence against the detractors of *De vita*. He may want the detractors to read it as the former; his friends, as the latter.

8. Kristeller convincingly argues that Corsini's erroneous phrase gave rise to the traditional title of the book, *De vita triplici*; see "Editorial Introduction," n. 1; for another and not necessarily competing explanation of it, see Plessner, p. 260, n. 1.

Works Cited

Primary Sources

Standard works by classical and English authors are omitted.

Abano, Pietro d'. *Petri de Albano* [sic] *Expositio in Problematis Aristotelis*. Edited by Hieronymus Faventinus. Mantua, 1475.
———. *Conciliator*. Venice, 1521.
———. *De venenis*. Venice, 1521.
Abraham ibn Ezra. *Abrahe Avenaris Judei astrologi peritissimi in re judiciali Opera*. Translated by Pietro d'Abano. Venice, 1507.
Albertus Magnus. *Speculum astronomiae [Liber dictus Speculum astronomicum Alberti magni de libris licitis et illicitis]*. Edited by Stefano Caroti, Michela Pereira, and Stefano Zamponi, under the direction of Paola Zambelli. Pisa, 1977.
Ps. Albertus Magnus, *The Book of Secrets [De virtutibus herbarum, lapidum et animalium quorundam libellus]*. Anonymous sixteenth-century translation edited by Michael R. Best and Frank H. Brightman. Oxford, 1973.
Albohazen Haly, filius Abenragel = Abū al-Hasan Álī ibn Abī al-Rijāl (fl. 1016-1040). *Liber de iudiciis astrorum*. Translated from Arabic into Spanish by Judah ben Moses and thence into Latin by Egidius de Tebaldis of Parma and Petrus de Regio. 1st ed., Venice, 1485.
Albumasar = Abū Ma'shar. *Albumasar in Sadan*. MS Oxford Bodl. Laud. Misc. 594, fols. 137ra-141va, 14th c.; MS Paris BN 7302, fols. 109ra-130va, 15th c.
———. *Introductorium in astronomiam*. Translated into Latin by Hermann of Dalmatia. Venice, 1489.
———. *Introductorium* 6.1. Arabic edited and translated into German by K. Dyroff in F. Boll, *Sphaera: Neue griechische Texte und Untersuchungen zur Geschichte der Sternbilder*. Leipzig, 1903. Reprint. Hildesheim, 1967. Pp. 482-539.
Al-Kindi, see under Kindi.
Apollonius, see Philostratus.
Aponensis, Petrus, see Abano, Pietro d'.
Apuleius (of Madaura). *Asclepius*. See Hermes.

———. "De Platone et eius dogmate." In *Opuscules philosophiques et fragments*. Edited by Jean Beaujeu. Paris, 1973.

Aquinas, St. Thomas. *Summa contra Gentiles*. Vols. 13–15 of *Opera omnia*. Leonine ed. 47 vols. Rome, 1882–1971.

———. *De occultis operibus naturae*. Edited by Joseph McAllister, Catholic University of America Philosophical Studies, 42. Washington, D.C., 1939.

Ps.-Aquinas. *De fato*. In *Opuscula*. Edited by S. E. Fretté. Vol. 27 of *Opera*. Edited by Fretté and P. Maré. 34 vols. Paris: Vivés, 1874–1889.

Aratus of Soli. *Phaenomena*. Edited by Ernst Maass. 2nd ed. Berlin, 1955.

Arnald of Villanova. *De conservanda bona valetudine* = his commentary on the *Regimen sanitatis Salernitanum*. Paris, 1555.

———. *De conservanda iuventute et retardanda senectute*. In *Opera*. Lyons, 1509.

———. *Speculum medicinae*. In *Opera*. Lyons, 1504.

Asclepius. See Hermes, supposed author.

Augustine, Aurelius. *De Genesi ad litteram*. PL 34: 483 ff.

Avicenna (ibn Sina, 980–1037). *Liber de anima seu sextus de naturalibus*. Edition of the medieval Latin translation by S. van Riet. 2 vols. Louvain and Leiden, 1968–72.

———. *Liber canonis*. Translated into Latin by Gerard of Cremona. Venice, 1507. Reprint. Hildesheim, 1964.

———. *Liber de animalibus*. Translated into Latin by Michael Scot. In *Opera*. Venice, 1508. Reprint. Frankfurt a.M., 1961.

———. *Liber de viribus cordis*. Translated into Latin by Arnald of Villanova and published together with *Liber canonis*, which see.

———. *Metaphysica sive eius prima philosophia [Liber divinorum]*. Translated into Latin by Gerard of Cremona and Dominicus Gundissalinus. Venice, 1495. Reprint. Brussels and Louvain, 1961.

Bacon, Roger. *Fratris Rogeri Bacon De retardatione accidentium senectutis cum aliis opusculis de rebus medicinalibus*. Edited by A. G. Little and E. Withington. Oxford, 1928. Contains all the works of Roger Bacon which we cite.

Blancardus, Stephanus. *Lexicon medicum renovatum*. Lyons, 1756.

Bonatus (= Bonatti), Guido. *De astronomia tractatus X*. Basel, 1550.

Breton, Nicholas. *Melancholike Humours*. Edited by G. B. Harrison. London, 1929.

Bright, Timothy. *A Treatise of Melancholy*. London, 1586.

Celsus, Aulus Cornelius. *Medicinae libri octo ex recensione Leonardi Targae . . . indices materiae medicae Celsianae rerumque*. Edited by Edward Milligan. 2nd rev. ed. Edinburgh, 1831.

Chaldean Oracles. *De Oraculis Chaldaicis*. Edited by Wilhelm Kroll. 1st ed., 1894. Reprint. Hildesheim, 1962. See also Psellus, Zoroaster.

———. *Oracles Chaldaïques*. Edited and translated by Édouard des Places. Paris, 1971.

Constantinus Africanus. *Della melancolia.* Latin and Italian. Translated and edited by M. T. Malato and U. de Martini. Rome, 1959.

———. *Libri duo de melancolia.* Arabic and Latin. Edited by Karl Garbers. Hamburg, 1977.

———. *Opera.* Basel, 1536.

Corpus Hermeticum. See Hermes.

Diels, H. and W. Kranz. *Die Fragmente der Vorsokratiker.* 6th ed. 3 vols. Berlin, 1951–1952.

Diogenes Laertius. *Lives of Eminent Philospohers.* Loeb Classical Library. 2 vols. 1938.

Dioscorides. *Liber virtutum simplicium medicinarum.* Lyons, 1512.

———. *De materia medica.* Edited by M. Wellmann. Berlin, 1906–14.

Ps.-Empedocles. *Sphaera.* In *Commentariorum in Aratum reliquiae.* Edited by Ernst Maass. Berlin, 1898.

Ficino, Marsilio.

Editions and translations of *De vita* used and/or discussed; for those of purely textual interest, see "Editorial Introduction."

———. *The Book of Life.* Translated by Charles Boer. Irving, Tex., 1980.

———. *Das Buoch des Lebens Marsilius Ficinus . . . mit vil nüwen zu satzen der quinta essentia. . . .* Translated by Johannes Adelphus Müling. Strassburg, 1515.

———. *De vita.* [Editio princeps.] Florence, 1489.

———. *Marsilio Ficino's 'De triplici vita' (Florenz 1489) in deutschen Bearbeitungen und Übersetzungen: Ed. des Codex palatinus germanicus 730 und 452.* Edited by Dieter Benesch. Frankfurt a.M., 1977. Both MSS omit *De vita* 3.

———. *De vita libri tres.* Edited posthumously by Felix Klein-Franke from the manuscript by Martin Plessner, text a facsimile of Venice, 1498. Hildesheim, 1978.

———. *Delle tre vite, cioè, A qual guisa si possono le persone letterate mantenere in sanità, Per qual guisa si possa l'huomo prolungare la vita, Con che arte, e mezzi ci possiamo questa sana, e lunga vita prolungare per via del cielo* (= only the first two, despite title), translated by Lucio Fauno [Giovanni Tarcagnota]. Venice, 1548. Reprint. Milan, 1969.

———. *Les trois livres de la vie. . .* translated by Guy Lefèvre de la Boderie. Paris, 1582 [Colophon, 1581].

Other works composed, translated, or commented upon by Ficino:

Ficino, Marsilio. *De amore.* See under his translations and commentaries, below, Plato, *Symposium.*

———. "Disputatio contra iudicum astrologorum." Edited by P.O. Kristeller in *SF* 2: 11–76.

———. *Lessico Greco-Latino: Laur. Ashb. 1439: Vocabula excerpta ex Julio Polydeuca graeca et latina.* Edited by Rosario Pintaudi. Lessico intellettuale europeo, 15. Rome, 1977.

———. *Letters*. Translated by the Members of the Language Department of the London School of Economic Science. Vol. 1 = *Epistles* 1, London, 1975; vol. 2 = *Epistles* 3, London, 1978; vol. 3 = *Epistles* 4, London, 1981. American edition (3 vols.) New York, 1985. The page numbers of vol. 1 are 28 pages less than the page numbers of the London edition, which we cite.

———. *Opera omnia*. 4 vols. Edited by M. Sancipriano and P. O. Kristeller. Basel, 1576. Facsimile. Turin, 1959.

———. (Marsile Ficin). *Théologie platonicienne de l'immortalité des âmes*. Edited by Raymond Marcel. Vols. 1-2, Paris, 1964; vol. 3, Paris, 1970.

———, translator. Iamblichus, *De mysteriis Ægyptiorum*; Proclus, *De sacrificio et magia*; Psellus, *De demonibus*; Synesius, *De somniis* et al. (= "Platonici"). Venice, 1503. Reprint. Frankfurt a.M. 1972. The Venice, 1516 ed. of this includes also the entire *De vita*.

———, translator. *Platonis opera*. Florence, 1484.

———, (Marsile Ficin), commentator. *Commentaire sur le Banquet de Platon*. Edited and translated into French by Raymond Marcel. Paris, 1956.

———, commentator. *Commentary on Plato's Symposium on Love*. Newly translated and annotated by Sears Jayne. Dallas, 1985.

———, commentator. *Marsilio Ficino and the Phaedran Charioteer*. Edited and translated by M. J. B. Allen. Berkeley, 1981.

———, commentator. *Marsilio Ficino, the Philebus Commentary*. Edited and translated by M. J. B. Allen. Berkeley, 1975.

———, translator. *Plotini . . . Enneades*. Florence, 1492.

———, translator. *Plotini . . . Enneades*. Basel, 1580.

Firmicus Maternus, Julius. *Mathesis*. 2 vols. Edited by W. Kroll, F. Skutsch and K. Ziegler. Leipzig, 1897-1913.

Galen. *Opera omnia*. 20 vols. Edited by C. G. Kühn. Leipzig, 1821-1833.

Guaineri, Antonio (fl. in Padua, 1412-1448). *Practica*. Venice, 1517.

Haly Abenrudian = Ālī ibn Riḍwān (998-1061 or 1069). *In parvam Galeni artem commentatio*. Venice, 1557.

Ps.-Haly Abenrudian, really Aḥmad ibn Yūsuf ibn al-Dāya (d. ca. 951). *Commentary* on Ps.-Ptolemy, *Centiloquium*. Translated into Latin by Hugh of Santalla. In Ptolemy, *Liber centum verborum*, Venice, 1484, which see.

Haly Albohazen, see Albohazen.

Hermes Trismegistus, supposed author. *Corpus Hermeticum*. 4 vols. Edited and translated by A. D. Nock and A.-J. Festugière. Paris, 1945-1954.

———. *Hermetica*. 4 vols. Edited by Walter Scott. Oxford, 1924-1936.

———. *Quadripartitus* or *De quattuor partibus*. Edited by Louis Delatte. In *Textes latins et vieux français relatifs aux Cyranides*. Bibliothèque de la Faculté de Philosophie et Lettres de l'Univ. de Liège. Fasc. 93 (1942): 241-75.

Hippocrates. *Oeuvres complètes*. 10 vols. Edited by É. Littré. Paris, 1839-1861.

Homer. *Homeri quae extant omnia. . . . cum Latina versione*. Translated and edited by Iohannes Spondanus. Basel, 1583.

Iamblichus. See Jamblichus.
Isaac Judaeus = Isaac Israeli (ca. 832-ca. 932). *Liber primus practice Pantegni.* In *Opera omnia.* Lyons, 1515.
———. *Liber dietarum particularium.* In *Opera omnia.* Lyons, 1515.
Jamblichus. *De mysteriis Ægyptiorum,* etc. In Ficino's epitome, *Opera,* pp. 1873-1908. Edited and translated by Édouard des Places, *Jamblique: Les mystères d'Egypte.* Paris. 1966.
———. *De vita Pythagorica liber.* Edited by L. Deubner. Teubner ed. Leipzig, 1937.
Julian, Emperor, the Apostate. *Works of the Emperor Julian.* Edited by W. C. Wright. London, 1913.
Al-Kindi. *De radiis.* Edited by M.-T. d'Alverny and F. Hudry. In *Archives d'histoire doctrinale et littéraire du moyen âge* 41 (1974): 139-260.
Manilius, Marcus. *Astronomica.* Edited by G. P. Goold. Loeb Classical Library. Cambridge, Mass., 1977.
Martianus Capella. *De nuptiis Philologiae et Mercurii.* Edited by Adolph Dick, revised by Jean Préaux. Stuttgart, 1925. Reprint. 1978.
Mercurius. See Hermes.
Mesue the Younger (d. 1015). *Antidotarium = Grabadin medicinarum universalium.* In *Opera omnia.* Venice, 1561.
———. *Grabadin medicinarium particularium.* In *Opera omnia.* Venice, 1561.
Migne, J. P., editor. *Patrologiae cursus completus . . . Series graeca.* 161 vols. Paris, 1857-1866. Abbreviated *PG.*
———. *Patrologiae cursus completus . . . Series latina.* 1st ed. 221 vols. Paris, 1844-1864. Abbreviated *PL.*
Orpheus, supposed author. *Orphica.* Edited by E. Abel. Leipzig, 1885. Reprint. 1971.
———. *Orphicorum fragmenta.* Edited by O. Kern. Berlin, 1922. Reprint. 1963.
[*Picatrix*] Ps.-Maǧrīṭī. *Das Ziel des Weisen.* Edited by Hellmut Ritter. Studien der Bibliothek Warburg, 12. Berlin, 1933.
Picatrix. Das Ziel des Weisen von Pseudo-Maǧrīṭī. Translated into German from the Arabic by Hellmut Ritter and Martin Plessner. Studies of the Warburg Institute, Vol. 27. London, 1962.
Picatrix. Medieval Latin text edited by David Pingree. Warburg Institute. London, forthcoming.
Philostratus, Flavius. *Vita Apollonii.* In vol. 1 of *Opera auctiora.* 2 vols., edited by C. L. Kayser. Leipzig, 1870-1871.
Pico della Mirandola, Giovanni. *Disputationes adversus astrologiam divinatricem.* 2 vols. Edited and translated into Italian by E. Garin. Florence, 1946.
———. *Opera omnia.* 2 vols. Edited by Cesare Vasoli. Basel, 1557-1573. Facsimile. Hildesheim, 1969.
Plotinus. *Complete Works in Chronological Order.* 4 vols. Translated by K. S. Guthrie. Alpine, N. J., 1918.

———. *Enneads*. Translated by S. MacKenna. London, 1962. Includes Porphyry's *Life*.

———. Translated by Marsilio Ficino. See Ficino. *Plotini Enneades*.

———. *Opera*. 3 vols. Edited by P. Henry and H.-R. Schwyzer. Paris, 1951.

———. *Plotinus*. Translated by A. H. Armstrong. Loeb Classical Library. Cambridge, Mass., 1966–87. Line numbers in the Greek are the same as in the Henry-Schwyzer ed., with an occasional deviation of one due to textual emendation.

Porphyry. For Ficino's translations, see Ficino.

———. *De abstinentia*. In *Porphyrii philosophi Platonici opuscula selecta*. Edited by A. Nauck. Leipzig, 1886.

———. *Vita Plotini*. In vol. 1 of *Plotini Enneades*. 2 vols. Edited by R. Volkmann. Leipzig, 1883–1884.

Proclus. *Elements of Theology*. Edited and translated by E. R. Dodds. Oxford, 1933. 2nd ed. 1963.

———. *Hymni*. Edited by E. Vogt. Wiesbaden, 1957.

———. *De sacrificio et magia*. For Ficino's translation, see *Opera*, pp. 1928–29. For an edition of the original Greek, see Joseph Bidez, et al. *Catalogue des manuscrits alchemiques grecs*. Vol. 6, *Michael Psellus*. Appendix, "Proclus sur l'art hiératique," pp. 148 ff. Brussels, 1928. For an edition of Ficino's translation, Bidez's text (but not all of his notes), and an English translation, see Copenhaver, "Hermes."

———. *Théologie platonicienne*. 2 vols. Edited and translated into French by H. D. Saffrey and L. G. Westerink. Paris, 1968.

———. *Commentary on the First Alcibiades of Plato*. Edited by L. G. Westerink. Amsterdam, 1954.

———. *In Platonis Rem Publicam commentarii*. 2 vols. Edited by W. Kroll. Leipzig, 1899–1901.

———. *In Platonis Timaeum commentaria*. 3 vols. Edited by E. Diehl. Leipzig, 1903–1906.

Pseudonymous authors. See supposed author.

Psellus, Michael. *Expositio in Oracula Chaldaica*. In *PG* 122:1123–1150.

———. *De daemonibus*. In *PG* 122:876B–881; for Ficino's translation, see *Opera*, pp. 1939–1945.

Ptolemy, Claudius. *Liber centum verborum [Centiloquium] cum expositione Haly; liber quadripartiti [Quadripartitum]*. Venice, 1484.

———. *Harmonicorum sive de musica libri tres*. Venice, 1562.

———. *Die Harmonienlehre des Klaudios Ptolemaios*. Edited by Ingemar Düring. *Göteborgs Högskolas Årsskrift* 36.1 (1930): 110–11.

———. *Syntaxis mathematica*. In *Opera omnia*, vol. 1, parts 1–2. Edited by J. L. Heiberg. Leipzig, 1898–1903.

———. *Tetrabiblos* or *Quadripartitum*. See *Liber centum verborum*, above.

Ps.-Ptolemy. *Centiloquium*. Commented by Ps.-Haly Abenrudian, which see. Translated into Latin by Hugh of Santalla.
———. *De imaginibus super facies signorum*. Translation by W. Gundel in *Dekane und Dekansternbilder*. p. 394-401.
Pythagoras. *Aurea verba*. For Ficino's translation, see *Opera*, p. 197.
Rhazes (al-Rāzi, 865-932, active in Baghdad). *Continens*. Venice, 1509.
———. *Liber ad Almansorem*. Translated into Latin by Gerard of Cremona. Lyons, 1511.
Rowlands, Samuel. *Democritus: or, Dr. Merry-man his medicines against melancholy humours*. First ed. London, 1607.
Savonarola, Girolamo. "Contra li astrologi," in *Scritti filosofici*. Edited by E. Garin and G. Garfagnini. Edizione Nazionale delle Opere di Girolamo Savonarola, vol. 1. Rome, 1982.
Serapion the Elder (fl. 9th c.). *Practica Johannis Serapionis dicta Breviarium*. Venice, 1503.
Serapion the Younger (fl. 12th c.). *Liber aggregatus in medicinis simplicibus*. Translated into Latin by Simon Cordo of Genoa. Venice, 1503.
Synesius, of Cyrene. *De insomniis*. In *Synesii Cyrenensis hymni et opuscula*, edited by N. Terzaghi. Scriptores graeci et latini, consilio Academiae Lynceorum editi. Rome, 1944. For Ficino's translation, called *De somniis*, see Ficino, *Opera*, pp. 1968-1978.
Thabit B. Qurra. *Astronomical Works*. Edited by Francis J. Carmody. Berkeley and Los Angeles, 1960.
Thebit, see Thabit.
Valerius Maximus. *Factorum et dictorum memorabilium libri novem*. Edited by Karl Kempf. Leipzig, 1888.
William of Conches (Ps.-Honorius Augustodunensis). *Philosophia mundi libri quattuor*. *PL* 172:39-102.
Zoroaster, see also Chaldean Oracles. *Oracula magica Zoroastris cum scholiis Plethonis et Pselli*. Edited by Johannes Opsopoeus. Paris, 1607.

Secondary Sources

Since standard works are nowhere listed, references specifically to the editors of such works, even primary sources, appear here. If a work already appears in "Primary Sources," however, references to its editor are not repeated here.

Ackerman, Robert. *Backgrounds to Medieval English Literature*. New York, 1966.
Allen, D. C. *The Star-Crossed Renaissance*. Durham, N. C., 1941.
Allen, Michael J. B. "The Absent Angel in Ficino's Philosophy," *Journal of the History of Ideas* 36.2 (1975): 219-40.

———, editor and translator. *Marsilio Ficino, The Philebus Commentary*. Berkeley, 1975. Reprint. 1979.
———, editor and translator. *Marsilio Ficino and the Phaedran Charioteer*. Berkeley, 1981.
———. Review of *Marsilio Ficino. The Book of Life*, translated by Charles Boer. *Renaissance Quarterly* 35 (1982): 69-72.
———. *The Platonism of Marsilio Ficino: A Study of His "Phaedrus" Commentary, Its Sources and Genesis*. Berkeley, 1984.
Anastos, Milton V. *Pletho's Calendar and Liturgy*, pp. 185-269. *Pletho and Islam*, pp. 270-305. In Dumbarton Oaks Papers 4. Cambridge, Mass., 1948.
Arnaldi, Francesco, and P. Smiraglia. *Latinitatis italicae medii aevi . . . lexicon imperfectum*. vol. 1. Brussels, 1939; vol. 2. Brussels, 1951-1953; vol. 3. Turin, 1970.
Armstrong, A. Hilary. "Was Plotinus a Magician?" *Plotinian and Christian Studies*. London, 1979. Pp. 73-79.
Babb, Lawrence. *The Elizabethan Malady: A Study of Melancholia in English Literature from 1580-1642*. East Lansing, Mich., 1951.
Baron, Hans. "Willensfreiheit und Astrologie bei Marsilio Ficino und Pico della Mirandola." In *Kultur- und Universalgeschichte, Festschrift für Walter W. Goetz*. Leipzig, 1927. Pp. 145-70.
Bertozzi, Marco. *La tirannia degli astri: Aby Warburg e l'astrologia di Palazzo Schifanoia*. Bologna, 1985.
Bidez, J., and F. Cumont. *Les Mages hellénisés*. Paris, 1938.
Boll, Franz; Carl Bezold; Wilhelm Gundel. *Sternglaube und Sterndeutung: Die Geschichte und das Wesen der Astrologie*. Edited and revised by W. Gundel, 1931. Reprint. Stuttgart, 1966.
Bouché-Leclercq, Auguste. *L'Astrologie grecque*. Paris, 1899.
Bregman, Jay. *Synesius of Cyrene, Philosopher-Bishop*. Berkeley, 1982.
Bruno, Maria. *Il lessico agricolo latino*. 2nd ed. Amsterdam, 1969.
Burkert, Walter. *Lore and Science in Ancient Pythagoreanism*. Translated by Edwin L. Minar, Jr. Cambridge, Mass., 1972.
Canavero, A. Tarabochia. "Il 'De Triplici Vita' di Marsilio Ficino: una strana vicenda ermeneutica." *Rivista di filosofia neo-scolastica* 69 (1977): 697-717.
Carmody, Francis J. *Arabic Astronomical and Astrological Sciences in Latin Translation: A Critical Bibliography*. Berkeley and Los Angeles, 1956.
Cassirer, Ernst, translated by Mario Domandi. *The Individual and the Cosmos in Renaissance Philosophy*. Philadelphia, 1972. First published as *Individuum und Kosmos in der Philosophie der Renaissance*. Studien der Bibliothek Warburg 10, 1927. Translation first published 1963.
Chastel, André. *Art et Humanisme à Florence au temps de Laurent le Magnifique*. Publications de L'Institut d'Art et d'Archéologie, 4. Paris, 1961.
———. *Marsile Ficin et l'art*. Travaux d'Humanisme et Renaissance, 14. Geneva, 1954.

———. "Il 'signum crucis' del Ficino." In *Marsilio Ficino e il ritorno di Platone*. 2 vols. Edited by Giancarlo Garfagnini. Florence, 1986.

Clark, John R. "Marsilio Ficino Among the Alchemists." *Classical Bulletin* 59 (1983): 50-54.

———. "The Manuscript Tradition of Marsilio Ficino's *De vita libri tres*." *Manuscripta* 27 (1983): 158-64.

———. "Roger Bacon and the Composition of Marsilio Ficino's *De vita longa*." *JWCI* 49 (1986): 230-33.

———. "Two Ghost Editions of Marsilio Ficino's *De vita*." *Papers of the Bibliographical Society of America* 73 (1979): 75-79.

"The College of General Practitioners." *British Medical Journal*, 20 December, 1952, p. 1344.

Collins, Ardis B. *The Secular is Sacred: Platonism and Thomism in Ficino's Platonic Theology*. International Archives of the History of Ideas, no. 69. The Hague, 1974.

Compagni, Vittoria Perrone. "Picatrix latinus. Concezioni filosofico-religiose e prassi magica." *Medioevo. Rivista di storia della filosofia medievale* 1 (1975): 237-337.

———. "La magia ceremoniale del *Picatrix* nel Rinascimento." *Atti dell'Accademia di Scienze Morale e Politiche* 88 (1977): 279-330.

Copenhaver, Brian P. "Hermes Trismegistus, Proclus and the Question of a Theory of Magic in the Renaissance." Washington, D. C., Proceedings of Conference on Hermetism, Folger Shakespeare Library, forthcoming. Contains translation of Proclus' *De sacrificio* into English.

———. "Iamblichus, Synesius and the *Chaldaean Oracles* in Marsilio Ficino's *De Vita Libri Tres*: Hermetic Magic or Neoplatonic Magic?" In a Festschrift, forthcoming.

———. "Renaissance Magic and Neoplatonic Philosophy: *Ennead* 4.3-5 in Ficino's *De vita coelitus comparanda.*" In *Marsilio Ficino e il ritorno di Platone*. 2 vols. Edited by Giancarlo Garfagnini. Florence, 1986.

———. "Scholastic Philosophy and Renaissance Magic in the *De vita* of Marsilio Ficino." *Renaissance Quarterly* 37, 4 (Winter, 1984): 523-54.

Corsini, Andrea, "Il 'De vita' di Marsilio Ficino." *Rivista di storia critica delle scienze mediche e naturali* 10 (1919): 5-13.

Csapodi, Csaba, Klára Csapodi-Gárdonyi, and Tibor Szántó, *Bibliotheca Corviniana: The Library of King Matthias Corvinus of Hungary*. Translated by Zsuzsanna Horn, translation revised by Alick West. New York, 1969.

Curry, Walter Clyde. *Chaucer and the Medieval Sciences*. 2nd ed. New York, 1960.

Curtius, Ernst R. *European Literature and the Latin Middle Ages*. Translated by Willard Trask. London, 1953. Originally published as *Europäische Literatur und lateinische Mittelalter*. Bern, 1948.

Davies, Hugh William. *Devices of the Early Printers, 1457-1560:* Their History and Development. London, 1935.

De Lacy, Phillip. "Galen's Platonism." *AJP* 93 (1972): 27-39.
Delcorno Branca, Daniela. "Un discepolo del Poliziano: Michele Acciari." *Lettere italiane* 28 (1976): 464-81.
Dell, Floyd, and Paul Jordan-Smith, editors. Robert Burton. *The Anatomy of Melancholy*. New York, 1927.
Derolez, Albert. *The Library of Raphael de Marcatellis, Abbot of St. Bavon's, Ghent, 1437-1508*. Ghent, 1979.
Dicks, D. R. *Early Greek Astronomy to Aristotle*. Ithaca, N. Y., 1970.
Dodds, E. R. *The Greeks and the Irrational*. Berkeley, 1951.
Festugière, A.-J. *La révélation d'Hermès Trismégiste*. 4 vols. Paris, 1949-1954. Vol. 1^2 1950.
Flashar, Hellmut. *Melancholie und Melancholiker in den medizinischen Theorien der Antike*. Berlin, 1966.
Friedman, John B. *The Monstrous Races in Medieval Art and Thought*. Cambridge, Mass., 1981.
Gandillac, Maurice de. "Astres, anges et génies chez Marsile Ficin." In *Umanesimo e esoterismo*, edited by Enrico Castelli. Padua, 1960. Pp.85-109.
Garfagnini, Giancarlo, editor. *Marsilio Ficino e il ritorno di Platone*. 2 vols. Florence, 1986. Individual articles cited are also listed separately in this bibliography.
Garin, Eugenio. "La diffusione di una manuale di magia." In *La cultura filosofica del Rinascimento italiano*. Florence, 1961. Pp. 159-65.

———. "Le 'elezioni' e il problema dell'astrologia." In *L'età nuova*. Naples, 1969. Pp. 421-47. First published in *Umanesimo ed esoterismo*. Edited by E. Castelli. Padua, 1960. Pp. 17-37.

———. *Lo zodiaco della vita: la polemica sull'astrologia dal Trecento al Cinquecento*. Bari, 1976. Translated as *Astrology in the Renaissance: The Zodiac of Life* by Carolyn Jackson, June Allen and Clare Robertson. London, 1983.

———. *Medioevo e Rinascimento*. Bari, 1954. "Magia ed astrologia nella cultura del Rinascimento" is translated by Peter Munz in *Science and Civic Life in the Italian Renaissance*. New York, 1969.

———. "Postille sul ermetismo del Rinascimento." *Rinascimento*, Ser. 2:16 (1976): 245-49.

———, editor. *Prosatori latini del Quattrocentro*. Milan, 1952. Reprint. Turin, 1977.

———. "Recenti interpretazioni di Marsilio Ficino." *Giornale critico della filosofia italiana* 21 (2nd ser., vol. 8) (1940), nos. 1-2: 299-318.

———. *L'Umanesimo italiano*. Bari, 1952.

Gentile, S., S. Niccoli, and P. Viti, comps. *Marsilio Ficino e il ritorno di Platone: Catalogo, Mostra di Manuscritti, Stampe, e Documenti*. Florence, 1984.
Gesamtkatalog der Wiegendrucke. Edited by the Kommission für den Gesamtkatalog der Wiegendrucke. 2nd ed. Vol. 8. Stuttgart and Berlin, 1978.

Gombrich, E. H. *Symbolic Images: Studies in the Art of the Renaissance.* London, 1972. 2nd ed. Oxford, 1978.
Graeser, Andreas. *Plotinus and the Stoics.* Leiden, 1972.
Gruman, Gerald J. *A History of Ideas about the Prolongation of Life: The Evolution of Longevity Hypotheses to 1800. Transactions of the American Philosophical Society,* New Series, vol. 56, part 9 (December, 1966).
Gundel, Wilhelm. *Dekane und Dekansternbilder.* Studien der Bibliothek Warburg, no. 19. Glückstadt and Hamburg, 1936.
Harvey, E. Ruth. *The Inward Wits: Psychological Theory in the Middle Ages and the Renaissance.* Warburg Institute Surveys, 6. London, 1975.
Haskins, Charles Homer. *Studies in the History of Medieval Science.* Cambridge, Mass., 1927.
Heitzmann, Marian. "L'agostinismo avicenizzante e il punto di partenza della filosofia di Marsilio Ficino." *Giornale critico della filosofia italiana* 16 (1935): 295-322; 460-80; 17 (1936): 1-11.
———. "La libertà e il fato nella filosofia di Marsilio Ficino." *Rivista di filosofia neo-scolastica* 28 (1936): 350-71; 29 (1937): 59-82.
Hooper, Robert, and Samuel Akerly. *Lexicon Medicum or Medical Dictionary.* 2 vols. in one. 16th American ed. New York, 1856.
Hutton, James. *The Greek Anthology in Italy.* Ithaca, N. Y., 1935.
———. "Some English Poems in Praise of Music." In *Essays on Renaissance Poetry.* Edited by Rita Guerlac. Ithaca, N.Y., 1980. Pp. 17-73. First published in *English Miscellany* 2 (1951): 1-63.
Jayne, Sears. "Ficino and the Platonism of the English Renaissance." *CL* 4 (1952): 214-38.
———. *John Colet and Marsilio Ficino.* Oxford, 1963.
———, translator and editor. *Marsilio Ficino's Commentary on Plato's Symposium.* Univ. of Missouri Studies in Language and Literature, vol. 19, no. 1 (1944). Employed solely for its notes.
Kahl, Wilhelm. "Die älteste Hygiene der geistigen Arbeit, die Schrift des Marsilius Ficinus *De vita sana sive de cura valetudinis eorum qui incumbunt studio litterarum (1482)." Neue Jahrbücher für das klassische Altertum, Geschichte und deutsche Literatur und für Pädagogik,* N. S. 18, no. 9 (1906): 482-91; 525-46; 599-619.
Kaske, Carol V. "Marsilio Ficino and the Twelve Gods of the Zodiac." *JWCI* 45 (1982): 195-202.
———. "Ficino's Shifting Attitude Towards Astrology in the *De vita coelitus comparanda,* the Letter to Poliziano, and the *Apologia* to the Cardinals." In *Marsilio Ficino e il ritorno di Platone.* 2 vols. Edited by Giancarlo Garfagnini. Florence, 1986. Pp. 371-80.
Klibansky, R. *The Continuity of the Platonic Tradition during the Middle Ages.* London, 1939.
Klibansky, R., E. Panofsky, and F. Saxl. *Saturn and Melancholy.* London, 1964.

First published by the two last in a shorter version as *Dürers "Melencolia. I."* *Eine quellen- und typengeschichtliche Untersuchung.* Leipzig, 1923.

Kristeller, P. O. "L'Etat présent des études sur Marsile Ficin." In *Platon e Aristote à la Renaissance.* Pp. 59-77. XVIe Colloque International de Tours. Paris, 1976.

―――. *Iter Italicum.* 3 vols. Leiden, 1963, 1967, 1983.

―――. "Marsilio Ficino as a Beginning Student of Plato." *Scriptorium* 20, 1 (1966): 41-54.

―――. *Il pensiero filosofico di Marsilio Ficino.* A revised, Italian version of *The Philosophy of Marsilio Ficino,* which see. Biblioteca storica del Rinascimento, N. S., 3. Florence, 1953.

―――. "Philosophy and Medicine in Medieval and Renaissance Italy." In *Organism, Medicine, and Metaphysics: Essays in Honor of Hans Jonas,* edited by Stuart F. Spicker. (Dordrecht, 1978). Pp. 29-40.

―――. *The Philosophy of Marsilio Ficino.* Translated by Virginia Conant. New York, 1943.

―――. *Die Philosophie der Marsilio Ficino.* Frankfurt a.M., 1972. German translation of *The Philosophy of Marsilio Ficino* by the author.

―――. *Studies in Renaissance Thought and Letters.* Rome, 1956. Collected articles.

―――. *Supplementum Ficinianum Marsilii Ficini Florentini philosophi Platonici opuscula inedita et dispersa.* 2 vols. Florence, 1937-1945. Reprint. 1973.

Lake, Kirsopp, and Henry J. Cadbury, eds. *The Beginnings of Christianity: Part 1: The Acts of the Apostles.* Vol. 5. London,1933.

Lapidge, Michael. "Stoic Cosmology." In *The Stoics,* edited by John M. Rist. Berkeley, 1978. Pp. 161-85.

Lemay, Richard. *Abū Maʿshar and Latin Aristotelianism in the Twelfth Century.* American Univ. of Beirut, Publications of the Faculty of Arts and Sciences, Oriental Series, no. 38. Beirut, 1962.

Levy, Raphael. *The Astrological Works of Abraham ibn Ezra.* Baltimore, 1927.

Lewis, C. S. *The Discarded Image.* Cambridge, 1964.

Lewy, Hans. *Chaldaean Oracles and Theurgy.* Rev. ed. by Michel Tardieu. Paris, 1978.

Litt, Thomas, O.C.S.O. *Les corps célestes dans l'univers de Saint Thomas d'Aquin.* Philosophes Médiévaux, 7. Louvain, 1963.

Lohr, Charles. "Medieval Latin Aristotle Commentaries." Traditio 23 (1967): 313-413; 24 (1968): 149-245; 26 (1970): 135-216; 27 (1971): 251-351; 28 (1972): 281-396; 29 (1973): 93-198.

Lovejoy, A. O. *The Great Chain of Being.* Baltimore, 1961.

Lyons, Bridget Gellert. *Voices of Melancholy: Studies in Literary Treatments . . . in Renaissance England.* London, 1971. Reprint. New York, 1975.

Marcel, Raymond. *Marsile Ficin, 1433-1499.* Paris, 1958.

Masai, F. *Pléthon et le Platonisme de Mistra.* Paris, 1956.

Mazzeo, Joseph. *Renaissance and Revolution.* New York, 1965.

McVaugh, Michael. "The *Humidum Radicale* in Thirteenth-century Medicine." *Traditio* 30 (1974): 259-83.
Merlan, Philip. "Plotinus and Magic." *Isis* 44 (1953): 341-48.
Monfasani, John. *George of Trebizond: A Biography*. Leiden, 1976.
O'Brien, E., editor. *The Essential Plotinus*. New York, 1964. Reprint. Indianapolis, Ind., 1975. Employed solely for its notes.
Otto, A. *Die Sprichwörter und sprichwörtlichen Redensarten der Römer*. Leipzig, 1890.
Park, Katharine, *Doctors and Medicine in Early Renaissance Florence*. Princeton, 1985.
Pellechet, Marie. *Catalogue général des incunables des bibliothèques publiques de France*. Vol. 3. Paris, 1909.
Perrone Compagni. See Compagni.
Peters, F. E. *Greek Philosophical Terms: A Historical Lexicon*. New York, 1967.
Pingree, David. "Astrology." In *New Encyclopedia Britannica*. 15th ed. *Macropedia* 2: 219-23.
―――. "Astrology." In *Dictionary of the History of Ideas*. Vol. 1.
―――. "Between the *Ghāya* and *Picatrix* I: The Spanish Version." *JWCI* 44 (1981): 27-56.
―――. "Some of the Sources of the Ghāyat Al-Ḥakīm." *JWCI* 43 (1980): 1-15.
―――, editor. *Picatrix: The Latin Version of the Ghāyat Al-Hakīm*. Studies of the Warburg Institute, 39. London, forthcoming.
Pintaudi, Rosario, see "Ficino" in Primary Sources.
Putscher, Marielene. *Pneuma, Spiritus, Geist: Vorstellung vom Lebensantrieb in ihren geschichtlichen Wandlungen*. Wiesbaden, 1973.
Ritter, H. "Picatrix, ein arabisches Handbuch hellenistischer Magie." *Vorträge der Bibliothek Warburg 1921-1922* (1923): 94-124.
Ruhmer, Eberhard. *Francesco del Cossa*. Munich, 1959.
Saffrey, H. D. "Notes platoniciennes de Marsile Ficin dans un manuscrit de Proclus," *Bibliothèque d'Humanisme et de Renaissance* 21, 1 (1959): 161-84.
Saitta, Giuseppe. *Marsilio Ficino e la filosofia dell'umanesimo*. 3rd ed. Studi di Filosofia e di Storia della Filosofia, vol. 1. Bologna, 1954.
Sambursky, Samuel. *Physics of the Stoics*. London, 1959.
Sandys, J. E. *A History of Classical Scholarship*. Vol. 2. Cambridge, 1908. Reprint. New York, 1958.
Saxl, F. "Die antike Astrologie als dämonisch-bewegende Macht in der Kultur der Frührenaissance." Section 3 of "Il Rinascimento dell'Antichità." *Repertorium für Kunstwissenschaft* 43 (1922): 227-36.
Sarton, George. *Introduction to the History of Science*. Vol. 1. Washington, D. C., 1927.
―――. "The Scientific Literature transmitted through the Incunabula." *Osiris* 5 (1938): 41-245.

Schmitt, Charles B. Review of Marsilio Ficino, *Letters* 2. *Times Literary Supplement*, no. 3, 982 (July 28, 1978): 864d.
Schütz, Ludwig. *Thomas-Lexikon: . . . in sämtlichen Werken des h. Thomas von Aquin.* 2nd, rev. ed. New York, 1975.
Seznec, Jean. *The Survival of the Pagan Gods.* Translated by Barbara Sessions. New York, 1953. Reprint, 1961.
Shumaker, Wayne. *The Occult Sciences in the Renaissance: A Study in Intellectual Patterns.* Berkeley, 1972.
Siraisi, Nancy. *Taddeo Alderotti and His Pupils: Two Generations of Italian Medical Learning.* Princeton, 1981.
Sleeman, J. H., and Gilbert Pollet. *Lexicon Plotinianum.* Leiden, 1980.
Spitzer, Leo. *Classical and Christian Ideas of World Harmony: Prolegomena to the Interpretation of the Word "Stimmung."* Baltimore, 1963.
Tarabochia, see Canavero.
Tatum, James. "The Tales in Apuleius's *Metamorphoses*." *Transactions of the American Philological Association* 100 (1969): 487–527.
Taylor, H. O. *The Medieval Mind.* 2 vols. 4th ed. Cambridge, Mass., 1949.
Temkin, Owsei. *Galenism: Rise and Decline of a Medical Philosophy.* Ithaca, N.Y., 1973.
———. "On Galen's Pneumatology." *Gesnerus* 8 (1951): 180–89.
Thomas, Keith. *Religion and the Decline of Magic.* New York, 1971.
Thorndike, Lynn. "Albumasar in Sadan." *Isis* 45 (1954): 22–32.
———. *A History of Magic and Experimental Science.* 8 vols. 2nd ed. New York, 1923–1958.
———. *Science and Thought in the Fifteenth Century.* New York, 1929.
———. "Traditional Medieval Tracts Concerning Engraved Astrological Images." In *Mélanges Auguste Pelzer.* Louvain, 1947.
Torre, Arnaldo della. *Storia dell'Accademia Platonica di Firenze.* Florence, 1902.
Trinkaus, Charles. *In Our Image and Likeness: Humanity and Divinity in Italian Humanist Thought.* 2 vols. Chicago, 1970.
Trousson, Raymond. *La Thème de Prométhée dans la littérature européenne.* Geneva, 1964.
Ussery, Huling E. *Chaucer's Physician: Medicine and Literature in Fourteenth-Century England.* Tulane Studies in English, no. 19. New Orleans, 1971.
Vasoli, Cesare. "L'Analogie dans le langage de la magie à la Renaissance." Translated by D. Lesur. In *La Magie et ses langages,* edited by Margaret Jones-Davies. Travaux et Recherches, Université de Lille 3. Lille, 1980.
Verbeke, G. *L'Évolution de la doctrine du Pneuma du Stoicisme à S. Augustin.* Paris, 1945.
Walker, D. P. "The Astral Body in Renaissance Medicine." *JWCI* 21(1958): 119–33. Reprinted with the original pagination in D.P. Walker, *Music, Spirit, and Language in the Renaissance,* edited by Penelope Gouk. London, 1985.

---. "Orpheus the Theologian and Renaissance Platonists." *JWCI* 16 (1953): 100-120. Reprinted in *The Ancient Theology: Studies in Christian Platonism from the Fifteenth to the Eighteenth Century*. Ithaca, N. Y., 1972.

---. *Spiritual and Demonic Magic from Ficino to Campanella*. London, 1958; Notre Dame, Ind., 1975.

---. "Marsilio Ficino and Astrology." *Marsilio Ficino e il ritorno de Platone*. 2 vols. Edited by Giancarlo Garfagnini. Florence, 1986. Pp. 341-9.

Wallis, R. T. *Neoplatonism*. London, 1972.

Wetherbee, Winthrop. *Platonism and Poetry in the Twelfth Century: The Literary Influence of the School of Chartres*. Princeton, 1972.

Wind, Edgar. *Pagan Mysteries in the Renaissance*. 1st pub. New York, 1958; rev. ed. London, 1968.

Wittkower, R. and M. *Born under Saturn, the Character and Conduct of Artists: A Documented History from Antiquity to the French Revolution*. London, 1963.

Woodward, William H. *Studies in Education during the Age of the Renaissance, 1400-1600*. Cambridge, 1924.

Yates, Frances. *Giordano Bruno and the Hermetic Tradition*. Chicago, 1964.

Zambelli, Paola. "Platone, Ficino, e la magia." In *Studia Humanitatis: Ernesto Grassi zum 70. Geburtstag*. Edited by E. Hora and E. Kessler. Munich, 1973. Pp. 121-42.

Zanier, Giancarlo. *La medicina astrologica e la sua teoria: Marsilio Ficino e i suoi critici contemporanei*. Rome, 1977.

Index to the Introduction

Pseudonymous, putative, and doubtful authors are listed under their pseudonyms. Except where there might be confusion of persons, I have used initials for forenames. Addressees of Ficino's letters are indexed. Translators of modern works are not indexed as such. An older author (e.g., Plato) can appear in the index in three ways: as a person, as the author of a work, as an author whom Ficino translated or on whose work he commented. The heading "Daemons" makes no effort to distinguish bad demons and devils. Names of Olympians may designate the god, the planet, or both; such entries should be consulted in addition to the entries "Gods" and "Planets." Since free will and determinism are topically inseparable, all references have been listed under "Determinism." If the reader does not find a high-level abstraction, he should drop down to the next level of generality or to one or more of the particulars covered by the abstraction.

Acciaiuoli, Zanobi 55, 87
Acciari, Michele 45, 46, 85
Ackerman, Robert 82
Agriculture 58, 88
Agrippa, Cornelius 48, 54
Albertus Magnus 54
Alchemy 46, 53–55, 74
Allen, D. C. 4, 59, 62, 72, 77, 87–89
Allen, Michael J. B. 3, 5, 12, 62, 72, 73, 75 79, 83
Alphonso the Wise 45
Amulets: *see* Talismans
Analogy 22, 26, 29, 32, 37, 40, 43, 44, 48, 49, 52, 60, 83
Anastos, M. V. 89
Ancient theology 39
Angels 15, 39, 47, 59, 62–65, 68, 89; *see also* Supercelestials, Intelligences
Anima Mundi 4, 14, 25, 26, 43; *see also* World-soul
Anima, translation of 14, 75

Animate world 42
Animus, translation of 14, 75
Antiquari, Jacopo 53, 86
Antoninus, St. 87
Antonio da San Miniato 76
Apollo 39
Apollonius of Tyana 16
Apuleius 14, 75
Aquarius 20, 21, 33, 35, 77
Aquinas: *see* Thomas Aquinas
Arabic authors and language 5, 15, 17, 19, 45, 46, 50, 51, 69, 70, 78, 84–86
Aragon 34, 77
Aretino, Matteo 19
Aries 21, 33, 35
Aristotle 18, 22, 23, 31, 41, 43, 50, 81; — Pseudo-Aristotle 22, 83
Armstrong, Arthur Hilary 80, 84
Arnald of Villanova 7, 73, 75
Arnaldi, F. 15
Art, visual 23; *see also* Statues

Artist 23, 55
ascendant, lower-case, the point where the Zodiac intersects the Eastern horizon 35, 36; Ascendant, the sign which is on this point 35, 36
Asclepius 26, 28, 29, 47, 52, 80, 84, 86
Aspect (astrological term) 15, 20, 21, 35, 40
Aspicio, translation of 15
Astral body: *see* Vehicle
Astrologers 21, 22, 36, 39, 58, 65
Astrology 4, 18-22, 27, 28, 31-40 (especially 33-38), 43, 44, 48, 51, 55-60, 63, 64, 68, 70, 79-83, 86-90; *see also* relevant names and terms
Astrology, semiological 38, 58, 59, 88
Astronomy 32-33, 42
Athenagoras 65
Augustine 27, 29
Auvergne, William of 54

Babb, L. 78
Bacchus, Dionysus, Liber 78
Bacon, Francis 54, 55
Bacon, Roger 16, 57, 73
Bailey, Cyril 75
Bandini, Francesco, bibliographer 9
Barbaro, Ermolao 56
Baron, H. 88
Basin, Bernard 57, 62
Baurmeister, Ursula 74-75
Beaufilz, Jean 12, 75
Benesch, Dieter 12, 75
Benivieni, Antonio 19
Bessarion, Cardinal 77
Bezold, K. 82
Bible 17, 27, 65, 89
Bidez, J. 80
Black bile 4, 23, 29, 31, 38, 40
Bleeding, phlebotomy 36, 54
Blood 18, 29-31, 43
Boderie: *see* Lefèvre de la Boderie
Boer, Charles 5, 12, 72
Boethius 75
Boll, F. 82
Bouché-Leclercq, A. 82, 83

Brahmans 16
Bregman, J. 90
Breton, Nicholas 24
Bright, Timothy 24
Bruni, Leonardo 77
Bruno, Giordano 3, 54
Bruno, Maria 15
Burton, Robert 24

Canavero: *see* Tarabochia
Cancer, constellation, 20, 21, 32, 33, 35
Caponsachi, Piero, biographer of Ficino, 76
Capricorn 20, 32, 33, 35
Carducci, Filippo 88
Cassirer, E. 38, 58, 59, 87, 88
Castelli, E. 79
Cavalcanti, Giovanni 10, 20-22, 30, 55, 77
Celestial world 41, 63, 67, 69, 70, 83
Ceremonial magic, ceremonies 48, 53; *see also* Worship, Theurgy
Chain of Being, Great (Scale of Nature), for purposes of this Index equated with Neoplatonic *series* 41, 64, 66, 69, 83
Chaldean Oracles 28, 66, 67, 89
Chapman, George 24
Character (glyph) of a planet, sign, etc. 35, 37
Chastel, A. 78
Choler 31, 33
Christ 18, 61; *see also* Bible
Christianity 39, 42, 49, 52, 61-70, 85, 87-90; *see also* Bible, Christ, God
Church 18, 52, 55, 57, 61-63, 65, 66, 70; *see also* Curia
Cicero 14, 16, 75
Clark, John R. 4, 5, 15, 16, 25, 53, 55, 56, 74
Coelum, coelestis, coelitus translation of 15
Colet, John 24, 89
Collins, Ardis 90
Combust (position of a heavenly body) 35

Compagni: *see* Perrone Compagni
Conjunction 34-35
Constantinus Africanus 23
Copenhaver, B. 5, 47, 48, 50, 61, 67, 79, 80, 86, 88-90
Corpus Hermeticum 28, 29, 44, 48, 55, 63, 64, 83, 84, 86
Corsi, Giovanni, biographer of Ficino 19, 87
Corsini, Amerigo 9, 11, 72
Corsini, Andrea 3, 71, 72
Corvinus: *see* Matthias Corvinus
Cosimo de' Medici 18
Cratylus, Plato's 14, 89
Csapodi, Csaba, et al., eds. 74
Curia, Papal 56, 57, 59, 66, 69, 70
Curry, W. C. 81, 82
Curtius, E. R. 77
Cyprian, George the 19

Daemons 14, 28, 39, 47, 49, 50, 52, 53, 59, 60, 62-70, 80, 89, 90
D'Alverny, M. T. 50, 86
Dancing 4, 26, 49, 60
Dante 27, 29, 33, 67
Davies, Hugh William 74
Debility, astrological 35
De Colines, Simon 75
Deities: *see* Gods
Delcorno Branca, Daniela 19, 45, 85
Dell, Floyd, and Paul Jordan-Smith 24, 78
Della Porta, Giambattista 48
Della Torre, Arnaldo 17, 76
Democritus 24, 75
Demon, bad 28, 62
Derolez, A. 74
De Scepper, Cornelius 74
Determinism (restriction of free will) 4, 38, 46, 49, 52, 57-60, 67, 70, 79, 83, 88
Devils 89; *see also* Demon, Daemons
De vita 5, 6; — composition 6-8; — date of Book I 73; — editions 3, 5, 8, 9, 11-13, 16, 72, 74, 75; — manuscripts 6-11, 73, 74, 79; — title 72, 73; — title of Book I 73; — title of Book II 72, 73; — translations 3, 5, 12, 75
Dignity, astrological 20, 35, 54
Dikearchus 75
Dionysius the Areopagite, Ps. 65
Dionysus: *see* Bacchus
Direct motion of a planet 33
Divinities, divine beings: *see* God, Gods, Supercelestial gods / world, Intellectual gods, Angels, Anima Mundi, World-soul, Seminal reasons, Mundane gods, Heroes
Dodds, E. R. 79, 80, 86
Dodecatropos 36
Dürer 23

Egyptian religion: *see Corpus Hermeticum*, Hermes Trismegistus, Iamblichus
England 24, 78, 82, 86
Enneads 7, 10, 25-28, 49, 58, 64, 65, 73, 78-84, 88, 89; *see also* Plotinus
Erasmus 3
Exaltation, astronomical term 21, 35, 38
Exemplary reasons 42

Face, decan, one-third of a zodiacal sign 35, 46
Fauno, Lucio 12, 15, 72, 75
Female 29, 34, 35
Festugière, A.-J. 80, 83, 86
Ficino, Alessandra 20
Ficino, Diotifeci 18, 20, 76
Ficino, Marsilio: life 17-23, 76, 77, 87; — Works: Catalogues of his works 81; *Consiglio contro la Pestilenza* 3, 9, 24, 25, 61; *De vita*, see separate entry; Dedicatory Epistle to translation of Plotinus 81; "De triplici vita et fine triplici" 72-73; *Disputatio contra iudicium astrologorum* 31, 81; *Epistolae* 6, 34, 54, 71-73, 76, 77, 81, 87, 89; *Theologia platonica* (*Platonic Theology*) 18, 22, 63, 66, 75, 82, 84; — Commentator: on *Cratylus* 89; on *Phaedrus* 42, 71, 77; on *Philebus* 26, 73, 79; on Plotinus's *Enneads* 7, 78, 79, 81, 84; on

Romans 65; on *Symposium* 24, 78, 81, 82, 90; on *Timaeus*, 19; — Translator: "Platonici" 24, 28; *Corpus Hermeticum* 28, 63; Dante, *De monarchia* 28; Iamblichus, *De mysteriis Aegyptiorum* 24, 28; Proclus, *De sacrificio* 24, 28; Psellus, *De daemonibus* 24, 28; Synesius, *De somniis* (Ficino calls it *insomniis*) 24, 28
Figures 26, 40, 61
Firmicus Maternus, Julius 22, 82, 88
Fixed stars, 32, 33
Flashar, Hellmut 78
Free will: *see* Determinism
Furores, the four Platonic 23, 30, 77

Galen 31, 43, 76, 81, 83
Galileo 19, 77
Garbers, Karl, ed. 78
Garfagnini, G. 87
Garin, E. 3, 14, 15, 25, 26, 39, 40, 45, 49, 50, 52-54, 57-59, 71, 72, 75, 76, 79, 80, 82-88
Gemini 33, 35
Gentile, S. 76
George the Cyprian, Doctor 19
Gerson, Jean 61, 88, 89
Giles of Rome 50
God, the supreme being 15, 22, 29, 37, 42, 44, 49, 55, 57, 59, 62, 63, 65, 66, 68, 70, 89, 90
Gods 14, 22, 26, 28, 39, 40, 42, 44, 46, 47, 52, 63-70, 79, 82, 84, 86, 89, 90; *see also* Supercelestial gods, individual gods
Gods, mundane 26, 39, 44, 67, 84
Gombrich, E. 78
Grace, divine 67
Graces, the Three 21, 34
Graeser, A. 80
Gray, Thomas 24
Greek language 14-16, 40, 47, 51, 80, 83
Guaineri, Antonio 16, 23, 30, 54, 78, 84
Gundel, W. 82

Harmony 41, 47, 49, 53, 83; *see also* Musica mundana
Heitzmann, Marian 27, 79, 88
Heninger, S. K. 82
Heresy 29, 56, 57, 60-63, 65-67, 70, 85, 87-90; *see also* Determinism, Idolatry, Polytheism)
Hermaphroditic planet, i.e., Mercury 34
Hermes Trismegistus, supposed author of *Corpus Hermeticum* and *Asclepius* (q.v.) and of the medieval Hermetica 50, 51, 80, 86
Heroes 23, 39, 63, 65
Hippocrates 85, 86
Hippocratic Oath 86
Homo, translation of 14
Hora, E., ed. 81
Horoscope 19-22, 24, 27, 34-37, 46, 55, 58, 68, 77, 79
Hour, astrological 20
House, zodiacal 13, 20
Hudry, F., ed. 50, 86
Humors 14, 21, 23, 31, 33, 81; *see also* Phlegm, Choler, Black Bile, Blood
Hutton, James 83

Iamblichus (Jamblichus) 24, 28, 51-53, 63, 64, 66-69, 88, 89
Ideas 15, 41, 42, 44, 65, 66, 68, 82, 83, 90
Idolatry 4, 51, 60, 65; *see also* Polytheism
Image 25, 37, 39, 40, 42, 45, 46, 49, 60, 61, 72, 82, 86, 88
Ingenium, translation of 14
Innocent VIII, Pope 56
Intellectual gods 42, 90; *see also* Supercelestial Gods / World
Intellectual, learned person 3
Intelligences 39, 62, 63
Intelligible world 41, 42, 66, 90
Intermediaries 40-44, 49, 53, 59, 60, 62, 63, 66, 69, 83, 90
Interrogations, astrological 37

Jayne, Sears 24, 78, 89

John of Burgundy 81
John of Hungary 55, 59, 77
Jupiter 10, 20-22, 33, 34, 38, 77

Kahl, Wilhelm 12, 71, 72, 75
Kaske, Carol V. 4, 5, 82, 87
Keats, John 24
Kessler, E., ed. 81
Al-Kindi 28, 46, 50, 51, 83, 86
Klein-Franke, F., ed. 5, 71
Klibansky: *see* KP&S
KP&S (Klibansky, Panofsky, and Saxl, *Saturn and Melancholy*) 3, 4, 22, 24, 26, 28, 31, 50, 71, 72, 77-79, 82, 83
Kristeller, Paul Oskar 7-9, 16-19, 25, 28, 30, 37, 41, 53, 55, 59, 71-76, 79, 81, 83, 85-88, 90
Kühn, Karl G., ed. 81

Lapidge, M. 51, 83
Lathiére, A.-M. 75
Leenius, Andreas 9, 12, 74
Lefèvre d' Étaples, Jacques 86
Lefèvre de la Boderie, Guy 12, 15, 57
Leo 21, 33, 35, 77, 83
Leoni, Pierleone, of Spoleto 19
Lewis, C. S. 31, 82
Liber Almansoris 11
Libra 20, 21, 33, 35
London School of Economic Science, Members of Language Department of, translators and editors of Ficino's *Letters* 76, 77
Lorenzo de' Medici 7, 10, 19, 74, 75, 78
Love 23, 24, 29, 30, 40, 49, 78, 81
Lovejoy, A. O. 41, 83
Lover 23, 24, 29, 30
Lucas, amanuensis of Ficino 10, 79
Lucretius 14, 75
Lull, Ramon 19
Lyons, Bridget Gellert 78

Macrobius 27
Magic 3-5, 16-18, 23, 25-29, 31, 37, 38, 40, 42, 44-55, 57, 61-64, 67-70, 79-84, 86, 87, 89

Maǧrīṭī, Pseudo 84
Malato, M. T., ed. 78
Manilius, Marcus 84
Marcel, Raymond 17, 19, 29, 30, 55, 64, 72, 73, 75-77, 80-82, 87, 89, 90
Marescalchi, Francesco 76
Mariotto di Nicolo, Doctor 76
Marrasio, Renaissance poet 77
Mars 20, 21, 33, 34, 37, 46, 67, 77
Marston, John 24
Martelli, Braccio 65, 89
Martellini, Lorenzo 19
Martini, U., ed. 78
Matthias Corvinus, King of Hungary 7, 10, 58, 74
Mazzeo, J. 55, 86
Medici 7, 9, 10, 18, 19, 74, 75, 77, 78; *see also* Cosimo, Lorenzo
Melancholy 3, 4, 16, 20-25, 29, 30, 33, 38, 77, 78, 82, 84
Mercury 20, 21, 33, 34, 39, 88
Merlan, P. 79, 80
Mid-heaven 36
Milton, John 24, 89
Mind, the Angelic, the Intellect, second hypostasis 39, 42, 43, 49, 65
Minerva 39
Modern science 40, 42
Moon 20, 29, 32-36, 38, 39, 44, 46, 49
Müling, Johannes Adelphus 12, 15
Mundanus, translation of 14
Mundus, translation of 14
Music 4, 22, 26, 40, 43, 47, 49, 51, 53, 60, 77, 83
Musica mundana 40, 41
Myth 3, 39

Neoplatonism 3, 15, 27, 28, 30, 34, 39-41, 44, 46-49, 52, 53, 55, 62, 64, 65, 66, 68-70, 80, 86, 88
Niccoli, S. 76
Nock, A. D., ed. 83, 86

Occult science / qualities / properties 19, 28
One, the, first hypostasis 39, 49, 66, 68

Opposition, astrological 20, 25, 35
Orbs 35
Oricellario (Rucellai), Bernardo 73
Origen 65
Orphic music / dancing / lyre / song 49, 60, 90
Orsini, Rainaldo, Bishop 56, 77
Overburian Characters 24

Paganism 52; *see also* Polytheism, Idolatry
Panofsky: *see* KP&S
Paracelsus 54, 55
Park, Katharine 75
Part of Fortune 21, 58, 77
Paul 65; — Pauline epistles 65; *see also* Bible
Pellechet, Marie 74
Peripatetic 82; *see also* Aristotle
Perrone Compagni, Vittoria 45, 46, 84, 85
Petrarch 3, 23
Phaedrus, Plato's 42, 64, 71, 77, 78, 89
Philebus, Plato's 26, 41, 73, 79
Phlegm 31
Physicians 16, 18, 19, 61, 66, 76, 82, 86; *see also* name of physician
Picatrix 5, 16, 17, 19, 28, 45-47, 50, 51, 53-55, 61, 69, 70, 84-87
Pico della Mirandola, Giovanni 20, 41, 50, 56, 57, 61, 67, 72, 73, 77, 82, 86, 87-88
Pietro d'Abano 23, 61, 78
Pintaudi, Rosario 15
Pisces 33, 35
Place, mundane house, *plaga*, in dodecatropos 20, 21, 35, 36, 38
Planets 21, 22, 27, 32-35, 38, 40, 41, 45, 46, 50, 56, 69, 77, 82; *see also* individual planets
Plato 14, 15, 18, 20, 22, 25, 30, 41, 42, 44, 55, 65, 66, 73, 78, 81, 83, 84, 87, 89; *see also* individual dialogues
Platonism 18, 30, 42, 60, 63-65, 67-69, 71, 77, 81, 83, 87, 89, 90
Plessner, Martin 3, 5, 39, 45-47, 71, 72, 74, 82, 84, 85

Pletho, Georgius Gemisthus 66-69, 77, 89, 90
Plotinus 7, 8, 10, 18, 22, 25-29, 38, 40, 43, 44, 48-53, 55, 56, 58, 59-61, 64, 65, 70, 78-84, 86, 88, 89; *see also* Enneads
Poet 66, 77, 84
Poliziano 19, 39, 50, 56, 85, 87, 90
Pollet, G. 80
Polytheism 63, 65-67, 90; *see also* Idolatry
Porphyry 65
Prayer 68, 86
Preninger, Martinus Uranius 19-21, 25, 28, 73, 77, 81
Primum Mobile 29, 33
Proclus 22, 24, 28, 42, 46-51, 53, 66, 67, 69, 80, 86, 90
Prophecy 22, 29
Psellus, Michael 24, 28, 80
Ptolemy 21, 33, 77, 82
Putscher, Marielene 3, 39, 50, 60, 71, 83

Quintessence 34, 46

Rabelais 45
Raleigh, Sir Walter 24
Raphael de Marcatellis 8, 11, 74
Renouard, Philippe 75
Retrograde motion of a planet 33
Rhetoric 39, 57
Rist, J. M. 83
Ritter, Hellmut 45-47, 84
Rowlands, Samuel 24

Sagittarius 33, 35
Saints 39, 62, 65
Saitta, Giuseppe 17, 21, 77
Salernitan medicine 16
Salvinus, Sebastianus 10
Sambursky, S. 81
Sarton, George 3, 71
Saturn 3, 4, 19-22, 33-35, 37, 38, 46, 55, 58, 59, 67, 72, 77, 82, 88
Savonarola, Girolamo 57, 81, 87

Saxl, Fritz 39, 45, 84; *see also* KP&S
Schmitt, Charles 3
Scholarios, George 66
Scholasticism 41, 62, 68, 76
Scorpio 20, 21, 33, 35, 39
Scott, Walter, ed. 47
Seminal reasons 27, 28, 42, 65, 68, 83
Semiological Astrology 38, 58, 59, 88; *see also* Astrology
Sensible world 41, 69
Sexuality 29, 30
Seznec, Jean 22, 39, 40, 77, 82, 84
Shakespeare 24
Shape 40, 42, 46
Shumaker, Wayne 3, 4, 36, 48, 53, 71, 82
Siraisi, N. 76, 82, 86
Sleeman, J. H. 80
Smiraglia, P. 15
Soderini, Piero 84
Soul, human and/or cosmic 14, 26-30, 39, 40, 42-44, 49-51, 59, 60, 63, 68, 70, 79-81, 83, 90; *see also* Anima Mundi, World-soul
Species 42, 61, 64, 83
Spenser, Edmund 24
Spheres 32, 33, 39, 40, 44, 49, 50, 63
Spicker, S. F., ed. 76
Spifame, Jacques Paul 74
Spinoza 44
Spirits (incorporeal, human medical, planetary, and cosmic; on the last *see also* World-spirit) 4, 14, 27, 29, 45-47, 49-53, 59, 60, 62, 64, 66, 69, 70, 72, 80, 83, 84, 86, 89; — natural, vital, animal 43, 60; — major treatment 42-44
Spiritus, translation of 14, 72
Spitzer, L. 83
Star-souls 39, 59, 62, 63, 68-70
Statues 26, 28, 29, 47, 51, 52, 64, 69, 70, 79
Stoics 27, 29, 43, 51, 80, 81, 83
Substance 31, 41, 45, 48, 52
Substantiae separatae 68, 89
Succeedent, astrological term 36

Sun 20, 21, 32-39, 44, 80
Supercelestial gods / world 39, 40, 42, 65-70, 90; *see also* Angels, Ideas, Intelligible world
Supercoelestis, meaning of 15
Surgeon 54, 76
Sympathy 37, 38, 40, 48, 49, 52, 53, 64, 66, 69, 79; *see also* Magic, Harmony
Syncretism, religious 39, 60
Synesius 24, 28, 40, 68, 69, 83, 89, 90

Talismans 4, 26, 38, 41, 46, 47, 51, 60-62, 69, 88
Tarabochia Canavero, Alessandra 12, 74, 75
Tatum, James 75
Taurus 33, 35
Temkin, O. 83
Temperaments, the four 23; *see also* Melancholy
Termini, astrological, also called *fines* 35
Terrestrial world 41
Theurgy 28, 46, 47, 51-53, 60, 66, 67, 69, 70, 80
Thomas Aquinas 49, 52, 55, 56, 58, 61-64, 66, 70, 87, 89
Thomas, Keith 52, 81, 82, 88
Thomson, James, *City of Dreadful Night* 24
Thorndike, L. 45, 52, 54, 57, 61, 62, 76, 79, 81, 84, 88, 89
Three worlds, of Pico 41
Timaeus, Plato's 19, 30, 44, 81, 83, 84
Trebizond, George of 66, 77, 89
Trinity 39, 65
Triplicities 35
Twain, Mark 24

Under the Sun's rays, astrological term 35
Ussery, H. 61, 86, 88

Valeri, Tommaso 19
Valla, Lorenzo 39
Valori, Filippo 7, 9, 10, 20, 45, 59, 77, 85, 88

Vehicle, in special sense, astral body 27, 50, 66, 80, 83, 86
Venus 20, 21, 33, 34, 39, 77
Verbeke, G. 80, 83
Vesta 39
Virgin Mary 39
Virgo 21, 33, 35, 77
Viti, P. 76

Walker, D. P. 3, 4, 15, 26, 42–44, 47–50, 52–54, 59, 60, 62, 63, 65, 70, 71, 73, 80, 81, 83, 86–88, 90
Warburg, A. 3, 39, 45, 46, 73, 83, 84
Wetherbee, Winthrop 81
Witchcraft 48, 54
Wittkower, R. and M. 78
Words, spoken or sung in magic 48, 51, 52, 61

Wordsworth 39
World-soul 27, 28, 30, 39, 42–44, 49, 51, 63, 68, 70, 79–81, 83, 90; *see also* Anima Mundi
World-spirit 4, 27, 28, 43–46, 49, 51–53, 60, 69, 80, 86
Worship 28, 45, 47, 52, 57, 59, 60, 62–70

Yates, Frances 3, 4, 26, 28, 45, 54, 71, 80, 84, 86–88
Young, Edward, *Night Thoughts* 18, 20, 24, 28, 30, 87

Zambelli, Paola 29, 40, 49, 53, 54, 84, 87
Zanier, G. 19, 49, 50, 59, 70, 72, 77, 79, 82, 83, 88
Zodiac 13, 33, 35, 36; *see also* individual constellations
Zoroaster 89; *see also Chaldean Oracles*

Index auctorum et nominum propriorum

The index is keyed to book, chapter, and line number of the Latin text. The following abbreviations have been used: GP for the introductory proem, P1 for the proem to Book 1, and P2 and P3 for the proems to Books 2 and 3 respectively; V for the second proem to Book 3 entitled *Verba ad lectorem*; A for the *Apologia*; Q for the second apology beginning *Quod necessaria sit*; t when the word occurs in the title to a chapter.

Abraham astrologus Hebraeus 3.19.83; 3.22.96
Achates 3.6.165
Achilles 3.21.148
Aegyptus 2.7.14; 2.18.44; 3.4.29; 3.13.7, 24; — Aegyptii 3.10.70; 3.13.14; 3.18.6, 9, 30, 33; 3.20.21; 3.22.84; 3.26.90, 93, 97; A.31
Ala Corvi dextra 3.8.23
Ala Corvi sinistra 3.8.24
Albertus Magnus 3.12.121; 3.18.127; 3.25.12; — *Speculum* 3.12.122; 3.18.128
Albumasar 3.6.79; 3.18.8; 3.22.54; — Sadar (*for* Sadan) 3.22.55
Alchameth 3.8.27
Alchindus (Al-Kindi) 3.21.15
Aldeboran 3.8.9
Alexander peripateticus 2.18.51
Algol, *see* Capot Algol 3.8.4
Amphion A.120, 121
Andromachus 1.25.7; 3.21.48
Andromeda (*see* Umbilicus Andromedae) 3.8.3
Anticyra 2.7.15
antiqui/antiquiores 1.1.20; 2.6.17; 2.7.61; 3.1.43; 3.6.11; 3.12.68; 3.13.t, 2; 3.15.t, 103; 3.18.t, 17, 93; 3.21.18; — antiquitas 3.23.11; — *see also* prisci 1.19.3; 3.8.49; *and* veteres 3.23.65
Apollo 1.7.9, 11; 1.26.9; 2.13.1; 2.15.46; 3.10.14; 3.21.26, 33, 118, 119, 120; 3.24.5, 17, 33, 46; *see also* Phoebus; — Apollineus 3.21.127
Apollonius Theaneus (Apollonius of Tyana) P3.10-11; 3.3.39-40, 41; 3.8.52, 53, 55; 3.15.21; 3.21.9.13, 52, 147; 3.23.112
Apulia 3.16.65; 3.21.151
Aquarius 2.15.75; 3.5.29; 3.6.130, 155; 3.7.16; 3.8.38; 3.9.1, 24, 29; 3.10.48, 61; 3.18.68, 110; 3.26.103
Aquinas, Thomas 3.8.67; 3.18.141; 3.25.47; 3.26.109; — *Contra gentiles* 3.8.68; 3.18.146, 154; — *De fato* 3.18.149; 3.25.47; — *De occultis naturae operibus* 3.18.153-54
Arabes 1.20.24; 3.2.14, 89; 3.3.23; 3.12.36; 3.18.18; 3.20.21, 36; 3.22.51, 59; — collegium Arabum 3.18.18
Aratus A.97, 99
Arcadicus 1.5.39

Archigenes 1.25.7
Archimedes 3.19.48
Architas 3.13.13
Argivi 2.15.53
Aries 2.10.14; 3.4.27; 3.6.127; 3.7.2; 3.8.2; 3.9.3, 4, 10, 29, 33; 3.10.43, 55, 56; 3.14.23; 3.15.3; 3.18.3, 106; 3.19.6, 17
Aristoteles 1.1.22; 1.5.4, 14, 16; 1.6.29; 1.7.113; 1.10.27; 2.1.14; 2.7.15; 2.18.45; 2.20.22; 3.8.71; — *Oeconomica* 1.7.113; — *Politici* 1.1.22; — *Problemata* 1.5.4; 1.6.29
Arnaldus philosophus (Arnald of Villanova) 2.7.4
astrologi GP.37; 2.1.10; 2.16.1; 2.20.28; P3.22, 23; 3.2.14, 89; 3.3.23; 3.4.55; 3.5.6; 3.6.8, 95; 3.8.1; 3.10.26; 3.11.135; 3.12.24, 115; 3.13.24; 3.14.32; 3.15.103, 109; 3.17.26; 3.18.35, 92, 121, 128, 131; 3.19.6, 11; 3.20.6, 15; 3.22.51, 96; 3.23.40, 45; 3.26.96; — astrologus 2.18.141; 2.20.17; 3.15.93; 3.18.124, 140; 3.19.83; 3.26.99; — astrologia 2.20.26; 3.10.69; 3.13.33; 3.18.127, 160; A.t, 20, 87
astronomi 1.4.5; 1.7.45; 1.8.19; 2.8.3; 2.20.1, 11; 3.15.50; 3.16.3; 3.24.11; A.30; — astronomia 2.20.32; A.39
Avicenna 1.6.29, 35; 1.7.18; 1.23.2; 2.4.11; 2.5.39; 2.6.24, 49; 2.8.23, 60; 2.9.37; 2.18.18, 45, 137; 3.4.17; 3.20.70; 3.21.50; — *De anima* 1.6.30; — *De animalibus* 1.7.18; — *De viribus cordis* 1.23.2; 3.4.17-18; — *Liber divinorum* 1.6.29

Babylonia 3.4.29
Bacchus D.1, 4, 11, 13, 15; 1.7.8; 2.15.108; 2.20 *passim*; 3.24.33, 36, 46; *see also* Dionysius, Liber
Boninsegnius, Ioannes Baptista (Giovanni Battista Buoninsegni) P1.1-2
Brachmanes 3.2.63

Canacius, Ioannes (Giovanni Canacci) Q.2, 24
Cancer 3.6.131, 135, 136; 3.7.3; 3.8.13; 3.9.2, 5. 15, 30; 3.10.44, 57, 65; 3.15.7; 3.18.62, 108
Canis Maior 3.8.14
Canis Minor 3.8.15
Canisianus, Bernardus (Bernardo Canigiani) Q.1-2
Capricornus 3.6.129, 138; 3.8.35; 3.9.1, 3, 23, 29; 3.10.48.60; 3.18.97, 98, 109; — *Cauda Capricorni* 3.8.38
Caput Algol 3.8.4
Caput Draconis (see *Draco*) 3.25.6
Carneades phanaticus 1.20.25
Cato 3.21.20; — *Res rustica* 3.21.20
Cauda Capricorni (*see* Capricornus) 3.8.38
Cauda Draconis (*see* Draco) 3.22.54
Cauda Ursae Maioris (*see* Ursa Maior) 3.8.20
Ceres 1.7.8; 3.19.45
Chaldaei 2.17.1; 3.9.34; 3.18.6; 3.21.30; 3.22.84, 97; 3.23.56; 3.26.95, 96, 97; A.30
Charybdis 1.3.3; 1.7.6
Christus 1.26.12; 2.19.1; 3.18.33, 35; A.t, 6, 42, 64, 67; — Iesus 3.18.37, 38; — Dominus 2.19.3
Christianus/Christiani 3.18.36; 3.26.139; A.20
Circe 2.15.55
Clotho 2.20.57
Cor Leonis (*see* Leo) 3.8.17; 3.14.29-30; 3.18.71
Cor Scorpionis (*see* Scorpio) 3.8.32; 3.14.2-3
Cornea 3.8.30
Cosmus Medices (*see* Medices) GP.18, 25
Cupido 1.7.23
Cursinus, Amerigus (Amerigo Corsini) Q.2; *final poem* (secta) Cynica Q.10; — cynice 3.25.21

Damis 3.8.49; 3.21.146
David 1.7.116; 1.10.51; 1.26.23; 2.8.23; 3.21.22

Index nominum 487

David Bil astrologus 3.26.99
Democritus 1.5.7, 13, 15; 1.6.28; 2.8.26; 2.18.85; P3.10
Deus GP.3; P1.13; 1.1.18, 29, 32; 1.5.17; 1.7.117; 1.26.21, 27; 2.13.29; 2.20.66; P3.14, 17; V.5, 29; 3.15.113, 117; 3.19.21; 3.22.97; 3.25.3, 6, 34; A.51, 73, 103, 105; — Altissimus A.41; — deus/dei 2.20.43; 3.6.12; 3.23.23, 72; 3.26.91, 94, 127
Diana 2.15.20, 46; 2.19.14; 3.19.29; 3.25.24
Dionysius A.130; *see also* Bacchus, Liber
Dioscorides 2.9.46; 3.15.77
Draco 3.15.58, 59, 61; 3.25.8; — *Caput Draconis* 3.25.6; — *Cauda Draconis* 3.22.54

Elpheia 3.8.29
Empedocles 3.6.97
Ephesus 3.23.112

Ficinus, Marsilius GP.t, 21; P1.1; P2.1; P3.1; V.t, 13; A.1, 18, 56; Q.1; — *Contra pestem* 3.14.63; 3.16.100; or *Contra pestilentiam* 2.7.26; 2.18.121; — *De amore* 3.16.58; — *De animorum immortalitate* GP.24, 45–46; — *De religione Christiana* 3.26.139; — *De vita* GP.t; A.14; — *De litteratorum valetudine curanda* GP.26; or *De curanda valetudine litteratorum* 2.1.19; or *De curanda litteratorum valetudine* 2.20.37; 3.4.18; or *De curandis litteratis* 3.14.60; or *De litteratorum cura* 3.5.2; or *De vita sana* A.15; — *De vita longa* GP.28; P2.t; 3.5.2; 3.11.116; 3.14.60; A.15; — *De vita tum valida tum longa coelitus comparanda* GP.30; — *De vita coelitus comparanda* A.15
Ficinus pater, medicus GP.18; 2.4.39
Firmicus, Iulius 3.23.52–53
Florentia P3.34; V.27; 3.15.53; — Florentinus GP.t; P1.1; P3.1; 3.t; 3.19.48; A.1

Fulginas, Gentilis (Gentile da Foligno) 1.20.35–36

Galienus GP.19, 21; 1.7.32; 1.13.2; 1.18, 5; 2.4.12, 14; 2.6.33; 2.7.64; 2.11.24; 2.18.29, 51; 2.20.23; 3.10.69; 3.20.68; 3.21.50; A.38
Gemini 3.6.130; 3.8.9; 3.9.5, 14, 30, 37; 3.10.44; 3.18.58, 107; 3.26.104
Graecia 2.18.44; — Graeci 1.3.5; 1.5.24; 1.20.23; 2.5.1; 2.13.1; 2.20.11; 3.6.7; 3.9.32
Gratia/Gratiae 1.1.9; 3.5.t, 5, 6, 17; 3.7.11, 13, 17; 3.10.74; 3.11.136, 141, 153, 154, 156; 3.12.1, 37; 3.14.64; 3.19.32, 41; 3.23.96
Guicciardinus, Petrus (Piero Guicciardini) A.2, 55, 88, 122

Hahamed physicus 3.13.11
Haly (Haly Abenrudian) 2.18.142; 2.20.23; 3.13.4, 13; 3.18.183; — (Haly Albohazen, son of Abenragel) 3.6.159; 3.18.111
Hebraei 3.13.23; 3.15.50; 3.21.18, 37; 3.22.92, 96, 104
Hecate 1.7.9; 3.13.20
Heraclitus 1.5.74
Hercules 1.7.10, 11; A.123, 124, 125; — Herculeus (lapis) 3.15.24
Hermaphroditus 3.26.47
Herodicus 2.1.13
Hesiodus 2.7.20
Hesperus 2.14.15
Hiarchas Indus 3.3.40; 3.8.50, 53
Hippocrates P1.20; 1.7.16; 1.8.5; 1,26.9, 11; 2.1.7; 2.6.7, 22; 2.17.12; 2.18.29; 3.20.68; A.37
Hircus 3.8.10
Homerus 3.6.10
Humerus Equi 3.8.41

Iamblichus 3.6.47; 3.13.29, 55; 3.15.52; 3.18.157; 3.21.16, 52, 134; 3.22.99; 3.26.93, 119, 135
Illyrici 3.16.60

India 3.15.54; 3.22.55; — Indi 3.3.2; 3.8.50; 3.15.20; 3.18.5; 3.21.100, 146; 3.26.34
Iolaus A.124
Iris 1.6.6
Isaach Iudaeus (Isaac Israeli) 1.25.7; 2.7.53, 61; 2.9.36
Isis 3.13.16; 3.15.17
Iudaei 3.13.26
Iudaeus, *see* Isaach Iudaeus
Iulianus 3.6.48
Iuppiter (Iovis) GP.6; 1.20.4; 2.3.3; 2.7.73; 2.10.3, 14; 2.13.2, 4.6, 9, 17, 19, 20; 2.14.13, 14; 2.15.46, 83, 114; 2.16.19; 2.17.19, 20; 2.19.4, 15; 2.20.7; 3.1.111, 112, 3.2.22, 30, 73, 79, 86; 3.4.t, 51, 53, 56, 57, 61, 63, 65; 3.5.t, 4, 9, 17, 30; 3.6 *passim*; 3.7.18, 19; 3.8.4; 3.9 *passim*; 3.10, 8, 11, 31, 72; 3.11 *passim*; 3.12 *passim*; 3.13.42, 44, 70; 3.14.7, 61; 3.15.80; 3.16.100, 113, 115, 117, 118; 3.18.48, 50, 73, 75, 80, 115, 117; 3.19.29, 34, 35, 39, 56; 3.20.47; 3.21.36, 118, 124, 141 3.22 *passim*; 3.23.25, 81, 107; 3.24.7; 3.25.6, 22, 28; 3.26.38; A.97; — Iovialis 2.10.5; 2.14.65; 2.17.40; 3.1.112, 114, 118; 3.2.20, 65; 3.4.t, 59, 64; 3.5.24; 3.8.17, 41; 3.11.95; 3.12.86; 3.14.5; 3.21.155; — Iovius 3.2.25, 31; 3.4.47, 59; 3.5.1, 22; 3.6.60; 3.8.10, 32; 3.11.55, 62, 72, 135; 3.12.99; 3.15.40, 52; 3.16.99; 3.19.37; 3.20.46, 64, 65, 67; 3.21.136, 138

Landinus, Christophorus (Cristoforo Landino) A.120
Latium A.125; — Latini 1.20.23
Laurentius Florentinus 3.19.48
Laurentius Medices (*see* Medices) GP.t, 33, 44, 49; P1.8; P2.12; P3.24, 27
Leo 2.10.13; 3.4.27, 30; 3.6.127; 3.7.3, 15; 3.8.17; 3.9.3, 16, 28; 3.10.45, 58; 3.14.22; 3.15.3; 3.18.53, 70; A.82
Liber, pater GP.9; 2.14.7; 2.15.108; 2.20.52; A.130; *see also* Bacchus, Dionysius
Libra 2.15.75; 3.6.110, 130; 3.8.22; 3.9.1, 4, 19, 28; 3.10.46, 59; 3.18.56, 108
Lucas evangelista A.99
Lucifer 2.14.15
Lucina 3.12.57
Luna 2.10.13; 2.11.5, 19; 2.17.18; 2.20.5, 6, 10, 29; 3.2.28, 41, 42, 46, 76; 3.4.27, 54, 62, 64, 68; 3.5.7, 8, 22, 25, 27; 3.6 *passim*; 3.7.t, 7, 10, 12, 13, 16, 18, 19; 3.8.45; 3.9.5, 7, 9, 27, 29, 30, 36; 3.10 *passim*; 3.11.65, 83, 123; 3.12.5, 6, 7, 8, 13, 14, 57; 3.13.5, 6, 25; 3.14.67; 3.15 *passim*; 3.16.113, 118, 124; 3.17.2, 15; 3,18.11, 61, 79, 93, 95, 106, 113, 115; 3.19.33; 3.21.4, 27, 123; 3.23.55, 57, 58, 81; 3.25.16, 19, 22, 28; 3.26.7, 16, 32, 107; A.82; — Lunaris 3.8.6, 20; 3.11.67; 3.14.66, 68; 3.15.9, 10, 15, 18, 42; 3.22.45

Maecenas P1.11
Magi 1.20.3; 1.26.7; 2.19.t, 1, 7; 3.2.63; 3.13.19; 3.15.65, 109; 3.20.4, 15; 3.26.78; A.t, 64, 65, 81; — Magus 3.18.102, 124; 3.26.54, 58, 129; A.67
Marlianus, Ioannes (Giovanni Marliani) 3.18.76
Mars 1.7.23; 2.15.48; 2.20.7; 3.2.28, 48, 53, 57, 62, 73; 3.4.50; 3.6.107, 111, 136, 167, 170; 3.9 *passim*; 3.10.4, 8, 10, 28, 33, 37, 73; 3.11.65, 87, 142; 3.12.4, 5, 9, 10, 12, 15; 3.13.26; 3.18.51, 52; 3.21.122; 3.22.21, 95; 3.23.107, 109; 3.26.105; — Martialis 3.10.29; 3.11.69; 3.15.49; 3.23.109; — Martius 3.4.49; 3.8.6, 9, 16, 18, 23, 29, 32, 41; 3.13.69; 3.15.51; 3.21.34; 3.22.21
Medea 2.17.11; 3.20.4

Medices (the Medici) P2.5, 6, 8;
— Cosmus Medices (Cosimo de' Medici) GP.18.25; — Laurentius Medices (Lorenzo de' Medici) GP.t, 33, 44, 49; P1.8; P2.12; P3.24, 27
medici GP.11; 1.2.12; 1.4.7; 1.5.18; 1.7.90; 1.12.4; 1.22.1; 2.1.10; 2.2.19; 2.6.19, 33; 2.7.26; 2.8.30; 2.11.9; 2.15.87, 92; 2.16.22; 2.20.26, 28; P3.22, 24; V.17; 3.2.59, 61; 3.10.27; 3.12.114; 3.13.33, 47; 3.14.5; 3.15.116; 3.16.38; 3.19.38; 3.25.44; A.30; — medicus GP.19, 21, 25, 34, 38; 1.1.16, 24, 28, 31; 1.12.1; 1.26.1; 2.4.39; 2.15.93; 2.16.35; 2.18.142; 2.20.18, 40; 3.6.39; 3.8.73; 3.10.28, 29, 69; 3.15.92; 3.18.83, 103; 3.20.69; 3.25.14; 3.26.51; A.40; Q.54
Medusa 3.16.123
Melchisedech GP.16
Mengus physicus 3.18.74
Mercurius 1.1.5, 6, 11; 1.4.3, 5, 7; 1.6.22; 1.7.42; 2.15.t, 3, 19, 120; 2.17.46; 2.20.6; 3.2.20, 30, 74, 78, 80; 3.5.7; 3.6 *passim*; 3.9 *passim*; 3.10.11, 14; 3.11.74, 77, 105, 123, 138, 139, 141; 3.12.6, 8, 9, 51, 53; 3.13.16; 3.16.113; 3.18.11, 12, 13, 57, 58, 59, 62, 81; 3.21.29, 120, 126, 142; 3.24.3; 3.26.47, 102, 103, 105; — Mercurialis 3.2.17, 24, 31; 3.8.3, 15, 25, 36, 38; 3.10.11, 12; 3.11.63, 64, 72, 94; 3.15.41; 3.21.129, 136, 138; 3.24.2, 4, 8
Mercurius Trismegistus 1.10.49; 3.8.1; 3.13.14; 3.14.67; 3.26.77, 79, 85, 86, 122
Meridionales 3.21.100
Mesues 1.13.2, 8; 1.16.10; 1.17.10; 1.20.35; 1.23.3, 17, 45; 1.25.7, 10; — *Antidotarium* 1.25.10
Minerva 1.1.27, 30; 1.7.20; 2.3.t, 2, 29; 3.23.24
Moses 3.11.50; 3.19.25; 3.22.91

Musae P1.12; 1.1.2, 5, 16; 1.2.8; 1.5.1; 1.7.20, 21, 23; 1.8.20, 21; 3.24.16, 17

Neptunus 1.7.9, 11
Nicolaus peripateticus 2.18.51

Oceanus 3.6.34
Olympius Magus et astrologus 3.18.123
Orientales 3.21.100; 3.23.40
Origenes 3.21.14; — *Contra Celsum* 3.21.15
Orpheus 3.6.98; 3.21.17; 3.22.102; 3.26.38
Osyris 3.13.16; 3.15.16

Pallas 1.2.19; 1.7.10; 2.3.13, 22; 2.15.53; A.10
Pannonia P3.1
Paulus apostolus A.100, 102
Pelias 2.17.11
Peripatetici P1.3; 3.6.20; 3.17.9; — Peripatetice 3.19.61
Persia 2.7.14; — Persae 3.15.65; A.31, 81; — Persicus 1.21.5
Perseus 3.16.122
Petrus Aponensis (Pietro d'Abano) 1.23.19; 2.18.140, 148; 2.20.22; 3.15.69; 3.18.72, 83, 138;
Petrus Nerus (Piero del Nero) A.2, 29, 119-20
Phedix astrologus 3.18.140
philosophi 1.6.24; P3.2; 3.3.2; 3.6.10; Q.9; — philosophus V.31; 3.8.42, 54; 3.26.53
Philostratus 3.8.49; 3.21.146
Phoebe 3.15.17; 3.24.20
Phoebus GP.5, 11, 14, 35; 1.1.7, 11; 1.8.20, 22; 2.13.3, 4, 5, 7, 17, 25; 2.14.13; 2.16.19; 2.19.15; 2.20.41, 42, 44, 45, 46, 47, 50, 55; 3.12.59; 3.13.16; 3.15.16; 3.17.59; 3.21.17, 52, 139; 3.24.36; 3.25.22; A.129, 131; — Phoebeus 2.15.102; 2.19.5; 3.2.65; 3.12.46, 86; 3.13.66; 3.14.11, 13, 24, 26, 33, 35, 37;

3.15.1; 3.21.91, 104, 139, 141, 150, 155; 3.22.21; 3.24.21, 39; *see also* Apollo
physici 1.5.11; 3.3.20; 2.12.53; 3.16.86; 3.24.11; — physicus 3.18.74; 3.26.51
Picus Mirandula, Ioannes (Giovanni Pico della Mirandola) 3.19.25; 3.22.106; A.129
Pisces 3.6.131, 134, 136; 3.8.41; 3.9.2, 4, 25, 29; 3.10.49, 61, 65; 3.18.56, 100; 3.21.5
Plato GP.20, 21, 22, 45; 1.1.21; 1.4.43; 1.5.9, 13, 16; 1.6.27; 1.7.112; 1.10.27, 49; 1.21.22; 1.26.7, 18, 29; P2.2, 4, 7, 11; 2.1.14; 2.7.17, 67; 2.15.83; 3.6.10; 3.11.50; 3.12.107; 3.23.115; 3.26.2; — *Alcibiades* 3.12.105; — *De legibus* 1.1.22; — *De republica* 1.1.22; Q.6; — *De scientia* 1.5.5–6; — *Phaedo* 3.11.50; 3.22.45; — *Phaedrus* 1.5.9; — *Timaeus* 1.4.43; 1.21.22; — Platonici 3.1.42; 3.15.49; 3.16.4; 3.18.156; 3.21.115; 3.22.84; 3.23.44, 45,; — Platonicus GP.19; 1.5.5; 1.7.21; P2.6, 9; 3.2.88; 3.15.81; 3.19.81; 3.23.10; — Platonice 3.3.29; 3.14.1; 3.22.38
Pleiades 3.8.6
Plinius 3.11.50
Plotinus 2.20.35; P3.24, 25; V.34; 3.1.t; 3.4.6; 3.15.109; 3.18.123, 124, 125, 126; 3.21.134; 3.26.1, 20, 30, 77, 85, 122, 124; A.57; — Plotinice 3.3.29
Plutarchus 1.1.23; 2.1.15
poetae GP.1; 1.8.20; 2.20.40, 59; 3.21.19; — poeta GP.35; 1.7.3; 1.10.51; A.121; Q.32
Politianus A.123, 125
Porphyrius 2.6.17; 3.4.6; 3.13.26; 3.18.122; 3.23.52; 3.26.117; — *Epistola ad Anebonem* 3.13.26
posteriores/postremi 1.13.8; 3.18.6; — cf. recentiores 1.19.4
Priapus 1.7.8
Proculus 3.6.48; 3.12.105; 3.13.32; 3.14.13, 27; 3.15.5

Prometheus 3.13.18
Psellus Platonicus 3.13.23
Ptolemaeus 2.20.20, 32; 3.2.59; 3.4.53; 3.6.67; 3.10.29, 64; 3.12.10, 118; 3.13.1; 3.18.130, 183; 3.26.56; — *Centiloquium* 3.2.59; 3.12.119; 3.13.1; — *Quadripartitum* 3.12.11
Pythagoras 1.10.49; 2.15.83; 2.20.62; P3.10; 3.12.105, 107; Q.38
Pythagorei/Pythagorici 2.6.17; 3.2.63; 3.16.4; 3.21.16, 115; 3.23.25

Quintilianus 1.1.23

Rasis 1.23.1; 2.5.37; 2.8.58; 3.12.58; — = filius Zachariae 1.25.11
Roma 3.18.124
Sabath (Sabbatum) 3.19.20; 3.21.37; 3.22.92
sacerdotes GP.1, 15; 1.2.8; 1.5.1; 3.12.68; 3.21.146; 3.26.78, 90, 122, A.19, 30, 43. 51; — sacerdos D.2, 3, 17; 3.26.129; A.18, 32, 39, 66, 70; Q.54
Sagittarius 2.10.14; 3.6.127; 3.7.4; 3.8.32; 3.9.2, 21, 28; 3.10.47
Salviatus, Georgius Benignus (Giorgio Benigno Salviati) Q.16, 20
Samuel astrologus Hebraeus 3.22.96; 3.26.99
Saturnus 1.4.3, 8, 18; 1.6.23; 2,8.2; 2.13.6, 11, 19, 22; 2.14.9; 2.15.48, 49, 67, 72, 75; 2.16.1, 4, 6, 19, 28, 30; 2.19.6; 2.20.5, 7, 9; V.28; 3.2.26, 47, 54, 57, 60, 64, 72; 3.6.107, 111, 136, 171; 3.8.4; 3.9 *passim;* 3.10.4, 8, 9, 27, 32, 37, 73; 3.11.46, 65, 84, 87, 142; 3.12.6, 10, 13, 15, 51, 69; 3.14.7; 3.18.43, 45, 67, 68; 3.19.20, 23, 27, 37, 83; 3.21.37, 122; 3.22 *passim;* 3.26.102, 103, 108; — Saturnalis 3.11.69; 3.15.48; — Saturnius 2.8.4; 2.16.13, 18, 24; 3.8.10, 23, 38; 3.10.29; 3.22.50; 3.24.9
Saul 1.10.51; 3.21.22

Index nominum 491

Scorpio/Scorpius 3.6.110, 131, 135, 136; 3.7.16; 3.8.29; 3.9.3, 20, 28; 3.10.47, 59, 65; 3.13.6, 25; 3.15.63; 3.16.102; 3.18.52
Scylla 1.3.3; 1.7.6
Scythia 3.16.61
Semele GP.5
Serapio 1.6.35; 2.11.24; 3.12.54, 58; 3.13.11; 3.16.96
Serapis 3.18.32
Serpens/Serpentarius 3.13.5; 3.14.6; 3.15.63, 69
Sirius 3.14.11
Socrates P1.20; 1.26.10, 11, 13; 2.12.27; 2.13.1; 3.12.105; 3.22.45; 3.23.114; Q.6
Soderinus, Petrus (Piero Soderini) A.2, 92, 128
Sol 1.4.6; 1.7.35, 42, 44, 47, 51, 61, 67, 93; 1.8.2, 3, 17, 19; 1.26.17, 19; 2.7.6, 54; 2.10.2, 14; 2.17.54; 2.19.5; 2.20.6, 49, 51; 3.1.72, 74, 95, 98, 99, 100; 3.2.30, 41, 55, 56, 74, 77, 79, 85; 3.4 *passim;* 3.5 *passim;* 3.6 *passim;* 3.7.18; 3.9.3, 7, 9, 27, 30, 34, 35, 38; 3.10.24, 31, 41; 3.11.30, 54, 74, 126, 136, 138, 139; 3.12.4, 5, 9, 12, 16, 76; 3.13.42, 44, 70; 3.14 *passim;* 3.15.3, 11, 13, 14, 16, 39; 3.16.112, 115; 3.18 *passim;* 3.19.5, 11, 13, 16, 22, 28, 34, 39; 3.20.47; 3.21.59, 126; 3.22.12, 21, 31; 3.23.57, 58, 80; 3.24.12, 40, 43, 44; 3.25.28; 3.26.61, 63, 105; A.82; Q.18; — Solaris 2.10.4; 3.1.95, 99; 3.2.14, 24, 30; 3.4 *passim;* 3.5.1, 24; 3.6.60, 165; 3.10.14; 3.11 *passim;* 3.12.99; 3.13.66; 3.14 *passim;* 3.15.14, 18, 20, 76; 3.20.46; 3.21.101, 107; 3.24.2, 3, 14
Spica 3.8.25
Synesius 3.1.31; 3.13.32; 3.21.15; 3.26.30, 81
Syrenes 2.15.54

Taurus 3.6.129, 138; 3.7.16; 3.8.3; 3.9.4, 6, 12, 29, 35; 3.10.44; 3.15.8; 3.18.3, 57; 3.21.5
Thebit Benthorad 3.8.42; 3.18.130, 140
Theodotion 1.25.7
theologi GP.48; 3.15.52; — theologus 3.18.134; 3.25.12
Timaeus Pythagoricus 3.4.7; 3.26.3
Triballi 3.16.60
Umbilicus Andromedae 3.8.2-3
Ursa 3.15.27, 28, 29, 34, 35, 45; — Ursa Maior 3.15.62; — Cauda Ursae Maioris 3.8.20; — Ursa Minor 3.15.62

Valor, Philippus (Filippo Valori) P2.1, 6; P3.31, 33
Venus GP.37; 1.1.9, 12; 1.7.8, 21, 23, 42; 1.20.4; 2.8.2; 2.13.2, 4, 6, 11, 18, 20; 2.14.t, 1, 2, 81, 82; 2.15 *passim;* 2.16.1, 4, 6, 20, 28, 29; 2.20.6; 3.1.120; 3.2.28, 42, 43, 75, 79; 3.4.54; 3.5.t, 4, 9, 15, 16, 18, 19, 20, 25; 3.6 *passim;* 3.7.18. 19; 3.9 *passim;* 3.10.7, 11, 31, 72; 3.11.47, 104, 114, 123, 138, 139; 3.12.5, 7, 8, 13, 14, 48, 57; 3.13.25, 70; 3.16.113, 118; 3.18.55, 56, 57, 73, 79, 80; 3.19.23, 32, 35; 3.21.4, 32, 119, 125, 141; 3.23.81; 3.24.6; 3.25.22, 23, 28, 42; 3.26.106; — Venereus 1.7.13, 22; 2.8.4; 2.16.9, 15, 17, 24; 3.5.3, 24; 3.6.60; 3.8.3, 9, 14, 20, 25, 29, 36; 3.11.58, 59, 62, 72, 93; 3.12.70; 3.14.58; 3.15.40; 3.21.7, 10, 137, 139; 3.25.43
Vespuccius, Georgius Antonius (Giorgio Antonio Vespucci) P1.1
Vesta 3.16.12, 13; 3.19.45; — Vestalis 3.16.12
Virgo 3.6.129; 3.7.4; 3.8.20; 3.9.5, 18, 28; 3.10.46; 3.18.7, 11, 13, 14, 95
Vultur Cadens 3.8.35

Xenophon 3.23.114
Zacharias (*see* Rasis) 1.25.11
Zoroaster 3.1.30; 3.13.19; 3.21.15

Appendix: angelus, anima, animus, daemon, deus, spiritus

angelus 3.22.113; 3.23.88, 93
anima GP.43. 50, 52; 1.5.74; 2.15.84; 2.18.66, 67; 2.20.45; 3.1 *passim;* 3.2.87, 91; 3.3 *passim;* 3.4.2, 4, 5, 7; 3.8.57, 60, 79; 3.11.9, 27, 28; 3.13.15; 3.18.126; 3.21.113, 142; 3.22.t, 16, 18, 88, 89, 111; 3.23.108; 3.24.11; 3.26 *passim;* A.102, 104
animus GP.22, 24, 46, 47; P1.20; 1.1.4, 7, 13, 25; 1.2.14; 1.3.8; 1.4.11, 15, 35, 37, 44; 1.5.30, 38; 1.6.4, 16, 19, 21, 24; 1.7.32; 1.8.27, 28; 1.10.43, 49; 1.26.6, 8, 11; 2.4.4, 28; 2.5.50; 2.6.65; 2.7.47; 2.8.14; 2.17.57; 3.2.67; 3.4.13, 15, 24, 39; 3.8.34; 3.11.63, 78, 146, 150, 152; 3.12.66; 3.16.66; 3.17.29; 3.18.119; 3.19.49; 3.20.3; 3.21.75, 111; 3.22.113; Q.t, 35
daemon 1.6.34; 3.1.t, 24, 37, 39, 41; 3.4.3, 4; 3.8.8, 34 (daemonia), 62; 3.13.15, 28, 31; 3.14.3, 7, 11, 20, 27, 64, 65; 3.15.49, 51, 53; 3.18.135, 148, 152, 156, 159; 3.20.24, 26, 28, 33; 3.21.7, 8, 10; 3.22.49, 53, 73; 3.23 *passim;* 3,26 *passim;* A.58, 76
deus 2.20.43; 3.6.12; 3.23.23, 72; 3.26.91, 94, 127. For Deus *see* Index auctorum et nominum propriorum.
spiritus GP.51; 1.2.t, 11, 15, 18, 21, 23; 1.3.1; 1.4.27, 35; 1.5.30, 37, 40; 1.6.8, 11; 1.7 *passim;* 1.8.26; 1.9.4; 1.10.26, 29; 1.12.t, 2, 6, 34; 1.13.10, 11; 1.18.3; 1.19.7; 1.20.5; 1.21.18; 1.22.2; 1.23.20, 24; 1.26.t, 1, 4; 2.2.12; 2.5.22, 24, 25; 2.6.50; 2.8.8, 10, 12, 20, 27; 2.9.5.27; 2.10.5; 2.12.10; 2.14.18, 19; 2.14 *passim;* 2.15.99, 104, 105, 107; 2.16.5, 6, 8, 24, 26, 38; 2.17.35; 2.18 *passim;* 2.19.21; 3.1.75, 77, 78, 87, 89, 94; 3.2.16, 67, 87, 90, 92, 93; 3.3 *passim;* 3.4 *passim;* 3.5.27; 3.6 *passim;* 3.8.58, 63; 3.10.74; 3.11 *passim;* 3.12 *passim;* 3.13.20; 3.14.t, 51; 3.15.8, 10, 15, 22, 59; 3.16.44, 65; 3.17.29, 33, 36; 3.18.29; 3.19.71; 3.20 *passim;* 3.21 *passim;* 3.22 *passim;* 3.23.29; 3.24.t, 21, 22, 23, 24, 26, 31, 38, 50; 3.25.44; 3.26.6, 7, 10, 26, 91

Index materiae medicae

The present index of *Materia medica* contains a glossary of medical terminology in addition to a list of all the various flora and fauna mentioned by Ficino in the *De vita*, whether in a medical context or not. I have attempted to identify the various plants by the modern classification of genus and species, although such identifications must not be pressed too far. The problems connected with the identification of plant names in Latin are notoriously difficult. It is also doubtful whether Ficino himself always knew precisely what he or his authorities had in mind. Thus the index is meant to lead the reader back to the text of Ficino rather than to serve as a guide to Renaissance medicine.

The following works have been most usefully consulted (with abbreviations in parentheses): Lewis and Short, *A New Latin Dictionary;* *The Oxford Latin Dictionary* (*OLD*); *The Oxford English Dictionary* (*OED*); J. Innes Miller, *The Spice Trade of the Roman Empire: 29 BC to AD 641* (Oxford, 1969); H. L. Gerth van Wijk, *A Dictionary of Plant Names* (Vaals-Amsterdam, 1971); Dieter Benesch, "Glossar," pp. 301–15 in his *Marsilio Ficinos De triplici vita (Florenz 1489) in deutschen Bearbeitungen und Übersetzungen* (Frankfurt am Main, 1977) (*Benesch*); Jacques André, *Les noms de plantes dans la Rome antique* (Paris, 1985) (*André*).

The following abbreviations have been used: GP for the general proem to the entire work; P1, P2, P3 for the respective proems to the individual books; V for the second proem to Book 3 entitled *Verba ad lectorem;* A for the *Apologia;* Q for the second apology beginning *Quod necessaria sit;* t when a word occurs in the title to a chapter.

absinthium: absinthe, wormwood (*Artemisia absinthium*) 1.17.19

acetum: vinegar 1.11.16; 1.15.5; 1.17.9, 18, 20; 1.24.13; 2.6.53; 2.7.45; 2.18.115; 3.15.56, 57, 59, 61; 3.18.173

(*lapis*) *achates*: the agate stone 3.2.33; 3.8.16; 3.12.53

acorus: an aromatic plant; sweet flag or calamus (*Acorus calamus*); see *calamus aromaticus*. 1.25.17

adamas: adamant, diamond 3.8.4

aes: brass 3.2.44, 53; 3.20.12; bronze at 3.19.4

(*lapis*) *aetites*: the eagle-stone, said by Pliny to help eagles in bringing forth their eggs 3.12.57; A.49

agaricum: agaric, a type of tree fungus, such as the larch fungus (*Polyporus officinalis*) 1.13.4; 1.20.18; 2.17.24

agnus: lamb 2.6.33; 3.1.118; 3.25.45

agnus castus: chaste-tree (*Vitex agnus-castus*) 3.12.69

(*lapis*) *albugedes* (*albugis?*): a stone simi-

lar to the jacinth, described by Serapion 3.16.97

(*lapis*) *alectorius*: the cock-stone, said to be found in a cock's gizzard 3.15.76

alimentum: food 1.4.32, 44; 1.9.6; 1.11.4; 1.14.6; 2.3.28; 2.4.9, 25; 2.5.2, 16, 34, 48, 51, 67; 2.6.45; 2.7.5, 2, 10, 24, 37, 46; 2.10.5; 2.15.32, 85; 2.17.4, 7, 51, 55; 2.18.4, 9, 11, 16, 18, 24, 26, 31, 47; 3.1.87, 91, 92; 3.4.36; 3.21.93; 3.22.79; 3.23.37; 3.24.22

allium: garlic (*Allium sativum*) 1.10.5

aloe: properly a plant (genus *Aloe*) from whose juice a bitter drug is procured 1.12.15, 18, 32; 1.15.5; 1.17.7; 1.20.12, 20, 30; 2.7.28; 2.15.90; 2.17.13, 16, 21, 25; — *lignum aloes*: lign-aloes, aloe-wood, the aromatic resin or wood of the aloes tree (*Aquilaria agallocha*) 1.1039; 1.20.9; 1.23.11; 2.9.17; 2.13.8; 3.1.103; 3.14.47

althaea: marshmallow (*Althaea officinalis*) 2.13.21

amaracum (from the Greek): an aromatic plant, another name for the plant marjoram, especially sweet marjoram (*Origanum majorana*); see *maiorana*. 1.14.5; 1.25.20, 27; 2.13.5

ambra (an Arabic loan-word): amber or ambergris; see *succinum*. 1.10.39; 1.12.29; 1.23.10, 30, 43; 1.25.18; 2.8.41; 2.9.20, 25, 43; 2.13.8, 27; 2.15.90; 2.17.32; 2.18.128; 3.1.102; 3.11.134; 3.14.47

amethistus: amethyst 3.8.33

amidum (Romanic-influenced form for *amylum*): starch 2.5.57; 2.8.56; 2.13.21; 3.11.109

amomum: an eastern spice plant, perhaps the same as cardamom (*Amomum cardamomum*) 1.24.7

amygdala: almond (*Prunus amygdalus*), in particular the sweet almond 1.10.20; 1.23.33; 2.5.57; 2.8.37, 38; 3.11.109, and its oil 1.24.11; 2.5.57; 2.18.135; — *lac amygdalinum*: almond milk 1.10.46; 1.24.11, 21; 2.8.56; 2.17.39

anacardus: anacard, the cashew-nut (*Anacardium occidentale*); esp. its honey 1.25.17; 2.18.138; — *anacardina*: name for a confection described by Mesue; the chief ingredient is anacard, the cashew-nut. 1.25.9, 10

anguilla: eel 2.5.32

animalia: animals 1.10.22; 2.5.59; 2.6.18, 19, 55; 2.7.1; 2.12.23; 2.18.57; 3.1.93, 96, 118; 3.2.34, 43; 3.3.13; 3.13.42, 67; 3.14.29, 44; 3.15.73, 75; 3.19.68; 3.21.29; 3.22.31, 105; 3.26.43, 64, 66; A.46, 51, 93

anisum: anise (*Pimpinella anisum*) 2.18.110

anser: goose 2.6.51; 2.13.25, 26

antidotum: antidote V.18

antimonium: antimony 1.16.3

aper: wild boar 2.6.44

apis: bee 2.1.23; 2.12.11; 3.26.67

aqua: water 1.5.59; 1.6.9; 1.9.10; 1.10.28, 37, 46, 55; 1.12.11, 21, 27; 1.13.5; 1.14.6; 1.15.5; 1.16.2, 3, 6; 1.19.14, 18; 1.20.37, 39; 1.21.3; 1.23.5, 7, 18, 37; 1.24.13, 15; 2.3.27; 2.4.36; 2.5.9, 18, 58, 62; 2.6.10, 52; 2.7.7, 18, 30, 42, 43, 44, 52, 54, 60, 68; 2.8.42; 2.9.27; 2.10.15, 16, 18, 23; 2.11.20; 2.12.16; 2.13.15; 2.14.33, 39, 40, 41, 42, 44; 2.15.111; 2.17.32, 37; 2.18.61, 115, 134; 2.19.17; V.26; 3.11.9, 11, 16; 3.14.59; 3.16.22; 3.24.30; 3.26.8, 44; Q.29; — *aqua vitae* or *aqua vitis*: name for an ardent spirit, a strong alcoholic liquor such as brandy 1.6.9

aquila: eagle 2.15.119; 3.1.119; 3.12.57; 3.18.49, 63; A.49

aranceum: orange (*Citrus aurantium*) 1.10.34, 40; 3.11.130

arbor: tree 2.10.21; 2.11.2, 3; 2.12.20;

Index materiae medicae 495

2.11.4, 24; 3.12.52; 3.14.45; 3.21.28; 3.26.42, 87
arbutus: the wild strawberry (*Arbutus unedo*) 3.16.67; 3.18.174
argentum: silver 1.10.30; 1.23.29, 38, 41, 43, 2.9.7; 2.14.64; 3.1.112; 3.2.32, 46; 3.11.124; 3.15.7, 12; 3.16.114, 117, 118; 3.18.12, 78; 3.19.4;
— *argentum vivum*: quicksilver 3.2.32;
— *argenteus*: silver, silvery 1.10.32; 3.8.44; 3.15.7
aries: ram 3.1.103
aristolochia longa: long birthwort (*Aristolochia longa*) 3.8.33
(*lapis*) *Armenus*: the Armenian stone, perhaps azurite, a blue carbonite of copper, said to be useful as a purgative. 1.20.19, 27; 3.19.39
aroma (*aromaticum*): spice 1.9.14; 1.19.15, 16; 2.6.9, 11; 2.8.52; 2.9.t, 9, 29, 31; 2.14.58, 60; 2.15.95; 2.18.26, 27; 3.1.103; 3.12.89, 114; 3.26.87
artemisia: mugwort (*Artemisia vulgaris*) 3.8.5, 11, 14, 21, 26, 39
arundo: reed (*Phragmites communis*) 1.24.16
asinus: ass A.109
(*herba*) *asterion*: an unidentified herb, probably based on the aster herb (*Aster amellus*) described by Pliny as having a star-like top and used as a remedy for problems of the groin. 3.14.4
astur: hawk 3.1.103; 3.13.67; 3.14.25
auripigmentum: orpiment, the trisulfide of arsenic, with a yellow color resembling gold 3.1.100
aurum: gold 1.6.3, 5; 1.10.30; 1.12.30; 1.20.8; 1.23.13, 29, 37, 41, 43; 2.8.43, 47, 62; 2.9.7; 2.10 *passim;* 2.14.64; 2.15.118; 2.17.33; 2.18.132, 139; 2.19.2, 4, 12, 19; 3.1.82, 86, 100, 117; 3.2.52, 55; 3.3.21, 22; 3.13.68; 3.14.39, 42, 45; 3.15.2, 67; 3.16.114, 115, 117, 118; 3.18.68; 3.19.38, 39; — *auri folia*: gold leaves 1.10.30; 1.20.8; 2.8.43, 47; 2.10.17, 19; 2.15.118; 2.18.132; 2.19.12; 3.14.45; — *auri squama*: gold scales 2.8.62; 2.18.139; — *aureus*: gold, of gold 1.10.32; 1.20.2; 2.10.t, 16, 19; 2.17, 36, 37; 2.19.14; 3.1.101; 3.8.43; 3.11.124, 125, 129; 3.13.20, 24; 3.14,39; 3.15.66; 3.19.31, 34, 38, 44; 3.22.50; — *auratus*: 2.10.25; 3.19.5
(*nux*) *vellana*: filbert or hazel nut (*Corylus avellana*), named after Abella (Avella), a town in Campania 2.8.39; 3.11.109
avis: bird 1.2.7; 1.10.20; 2.6.45; 2.12.8; 2.20.49; 3.1.35; 3.26.67; A.83, 116

balsamum: balsam, balm (*Commiphora opobalsamum*) 3.1.82, 102; 3.13.67; 3.14.47, 49 *opobalsamum*: particularly the balm of Gilead or Mecca (*Commiphora opobalsamum*) 2.13.17
been (*behen* or *ben;* from the Arabic): on the one hand, ben or ben-nut, the winged seed of the Horse-radish tree (*Moringa pterygosperma*), a whitish nut useful for its oil; on the other hand there is the white behen and the red behen, two varieties of plants which the old herbalists had received from Arabic sources but which were identified by different authors with different plants. The root of the behen was thought to possess astringent and strengthening qualities. 1.12.18; 1.20.10; 1.23.38; 1.25.24; 2.8.50; 2.9.12; 2.13.10; 3.11.111
berillus: beryl 3.1.113; 3.8.14
betonica: betony (*Stachys betonica*) 2.12.14
(*lapis*) *bezaar*: the bezoar-stone, an Arabic word for the stone found in the stomach of various animals; renowned for its occult properties as an antidote. 3.12.36; 3.13.9; 3.16.99
bos: cow, ox 1.10.3; 2.6.40; 3.19.85; 3.26.67; A.109

borago: borage (*Borago officinalis*) 1.10.45; 1.19.9; 2.10.12
brassica: cabbage (*Brassica oleracea*) 1.10.5
bubo: owl, horned owl 1.7.98
buglossa: bugloss or ox-tongue (*Anchusa officinalis*) 1.10.45; 1.19.9, 18; 1.21.4; 1.23.5, 26; 2.10.12; 2.13.9
butyrum: butter 2.18.137, 139

calamus aromaticus: sweet calamus, sweet flag, an aromatic plant (*Acorus calamus*); see *acorus*. 3.1.102; 3.14.47
camoinum: the cameo? 3.2.52
camomilla: camomile (*Matricaria chamomilla*) 1.24.17; 2.5.71; 3.6.78
camphora: camphor (*Dyrobalanops aromatica* and *Cinnamomum camphora*) 1.10.37; 1.24.11, 12; 2.18.116; 3.17.71; 3.26.60
canis: dog 1.2.4; 2.11.24, 26, 28, 32; 3.2.35; 3.12.61; 3.16.66; Q.3, 5, 7, 9, 12, 13
cantharis: a beetle; the scarab beetle? 3.1.104
capillus Veneris: maiden-hair (*Adiantum capillus-veneris*); Benesch has white maiden-hair (*Asplenium ruta muraria*). 1.19.10
capo: capon 2.6.41; 2.10.16, 22; 2.17.14
capparis: caper (*Capparis spinosa*) 1.11.16; 1.17.18; 2.12.14; 2.13.19
capreolus: roebuck 2.6.43
carbunculus: carbuncle, "a name variously applied to precious stones of a red or fiery color," also "a mythical gem said to emit a light in the dark," *OED*. 1.23.42; 3.1.101; 3.13.68; 3.14.41; 3.16.111; 3.17.71
cariota (for *carota*): carrot (*Daucus carota*) 1.10.5
caro: flesh 1.10.3, 20; 2.6 *passim;* 2.8.11; 2.10.24; 2.18.82; 3.11.110; 3.12.38, 46; 3.19.85; 3.20.62
casseus: chese 1.10.4, 20; 2.6.44; 2.12.13
cassia: the plant cassia (*Cassia fistula*), whose pods produce a pulp used as a laxative; see also *sena*. 1.21.7; 2.13.21
(*oleum*) *castoreum*: castor-oil, an unctuous substance obtained from the inguinal glands of the beaver 1.25.25; 2.18, 140
catoblepas: the down-looker, a small wild animal of Africa 3.16.62
cepa: onion (*Allium cepa*) 1.10.5; 3.18.172
cerasium: cherry (*Prunus cerasus*) 1.10.24
cerotum: a wax ointment 2.13.13
cervus: deer 2.6.53
chalcidonius: chalcedony, a precious or semi-precious stone, a type of quartz 3.2.52; 3.8.39; 3.12.47
chameleon: 2.18.62
chelidonia: celandine, the swallowwort (*Chelidonium majus*). Pliny (25.50.89-90) says that swallows use the plant to cure the eyes of their young just as humans use its juice in an eye-salve. 1.16.2; 3.8.18; A.49
(*lapis*) *chelidonius*: the swallow-stone, said to be found in the stomach of swallows (Pliny 11.79.203) 3.15.78
chrysolitus: chrysolite, a greenish gem, in spite of the etymology of its name. In antiquity *chrysolitus* referred to the modern topaz, a yellowish gem, while *topazius* meant a kind of chrysolite. Ficino may also have been confused about their identifications. 3.1.101; 3.8.35
cibus: food 1.7.27, 29, 82, 85; 1.8.16; 1.9.10; 1.10.2, 15, 32, 45; 1.11 *passim;* 1.12.12, 23; 1.14.6; 1.17.16; 1.18.8; 1.23.15; 1.24.4; 2.4.14, 17, 20, 23, 24, 27; 2.6.24, 58; 2.8.34, 56; 2.12.12; 2.18.15, 91; — *cibaria*: food 3.1.105
cicada: 2.15.26, 27
cichorea: chicory (*Cichorium intybus*) 1.11.16; 2.13.18; 3.1.110; 3.8.21
cicuta: hemlock (*Conium maculatum*) 2.18.123
cinnamum or *cinnamomum*: cinnamon

(genus *Cinnamomum*) 1.9.15; 1.10.18, 38; 1.11.3; 1.12.17, 24; 1.17.5, 16; 1.19.13, 17; 1.20.9; 1.23.11, 27, 38, 50; 2.5.65; 2.7.35; 2.9.30; 2.10.25; 2.13.9; 2.14.59; 2.17.29, 38; 2.18.109, 114, 127; 3.1.86, 103, 117; 3.11.131; 3.14.48

ciperus: the plant cyperus, with an aromatic root; native both to India and to the Mediterranean; see the English galingale (*Cyperus longus*). 1.25.17

citraria: the aromatic herb balm (*Melissa officinalis*), same as *melissa* 1.12.18; 2.8.42; 2.10.13; 2.13.8

citrus: citron (*Citrus medica*) 1.10.38, 40; 1.12.17, 28; 1.17.15; 1.19.13; 1.20.9; 1.23.26, 31, 37, 48; 2.9.16, 18; 2.13.9; 2.17.32; 2.18.116; 3.14.48

clyster: an enema to empty the bowels 1.22.12, 14; 2.17.13; 3.10.59

(*pilulae*) *cocchiae*: pills of cochee; name applied to an unspecified composition of pills. 1.25.5

collyrium: an eye-salve 1.16.2, 6

columba: a pigeon, dove 2.6.42; 3.1.120

condimentum: condiment 2.7.40; 2.18.93

confectio: confection; in general it means anything made up with sugar. A soft, solid mix of ingredients mixed with sugar or honey. 1.12.22, 33; 1.15.2; 1.17.10; 1.23.32, 43; 1.24.6; 1.25.9, 10; 2.8.46, 61; 2.17.28; 2.18.138; 3.18.105

corallus: coral, esp. *corallus ruber*, red coral, which seems to have been regarded as a plant which turned into a stone when taken from the sea (see Pliny 32.11.22). 1.11.16, 27; 1.12.26; 1.17.14; 1.20.11; 1.23.28, 39; 2.5.52; 2.9.7; 2.13.5; 2.14.64; 3.1.112; 3.2.44; 3.12.47; 3.14.66

cordialia: cordials; "a medicine, food or beverage which invigorates the heart and stimulates the circulation; a comforting or exhilarating drink," *OED*. 2.9.t, 15, 17, 30, 33, 40; 2.10.7; 2.14.57; 3.4.36

coriandrum: coriander (*Coriandrum sativum*) 1.11.24; 1.14.6; 2.5.52; 2.6.36, 52; 2.9.16; 2.13.12; 2.18.116

corneola: carnelian, a reddish-colored variety of chalcedony 3.2.43

corvus: raven 3.14.25; 3.18.54

crocodillus: crocodile 3.1.104; 3.14.25

crocus: saffron crocus (*Crocus sativus*) 1.9.15; 1.10.18, 39; 1.12.17, 25; 1.16.3; 1.19.14, 17; 1.20.9, 17; 1.21.11; 1.23.29, 40, 50; 1.24.4, 7, 12; 2.5.64; 2.7.36; 2.8.41; 2.9.30, 41; 2.10.25; 2.13.8, 27; 2.14.12, 13, 59; 2.15.34; 2.17.31; 2.18.114, 128, 140; 3.1.102, 117; 3.8.33; 3.11.135; 3.12.75, 76; 3.14.47; 3.26.131

crystallum: crystal 3.1.113; 3.2.47; 3.8.6; 3.16.23; 3.26.61

cucumis: cucumber (*Cucumis sativus*), esp. its seeds 1.10.19; 1.23.34; 2.8.39; 2.13.21

cucurbita: gourd (*Cucurbita pepo*) 1.10.23

cucurbitula: cupping-glass 1.16.15; 1.25.26; 3.10.50

cuscuta: dodder (*Cuscuta epilinum*); see *epithymum*. 1.19.10

(*pomum*) *cydonium*: quince, fruit of *Pyrus cydonia* 1.11.15, 24; 1.14.7; 2.5.53, 57, 63; 2.13.12; 2.18.116

cygnus: swan 3.14.25

dactylus: date, date palm; fruit of *Phoenix dactylifera* 2.12.13

dia-: This prefix was frequently used for medicinal compounds from the Greek pharmacopoeia; "consisting of" plus the name of the chief ingredient. Ficino employs these compounds in his elecutaries.

diabuglossa: a compound with bugloss as the chief ingredient.; — *saccharum diabuglossatum*: a sugar mixed with this compound 1.23.52

diacatholicon: a compound of general ingredients 1.21.4

diacedon: the name of an unidentified herb 3.8.6

diacitonites: a compound with an unknown ingredient 1.17.12, 17

diacoloquintis: a compound with the colocynth or bitter-apple (*Citrullus colocynthis*) as its chief ingredient 1.25.6

diacori: a confection with sweet flag (*acorus*?) as its chief ingredient 1.15.2; 1.25.18

diacydonion: a compound with quince as its chief ingredient 2.5.53

diaeta: diet or medical regimen 2.3.17; 2.8.t, 12; 2.12.t; 2.16.37; 2.17.t, 13; 2.20.28

diamarenaton: a compound with an unknown ingredient 1.17.11

diambra: a confection with amber as its chief ingredient 1.15.2; 1.25.18

diamuscus: a compound with musk as its chief ingredient 1.23.17, 52

diaprunis: a compound with plum as its chief ingredient 1.23.54

diasena: a compound with senna as its chief ingredient 1.21.4

Cretaea dictamus: dittany (*Origanum dictamnus*), named after Mt. Dicte on Crete where the herb grew. 3.12.60

doronicum: name for a genus of plants, such as leopard's bane (*Doronicum pardalianches*), a kind of aconite. 2.9.18; 2.13.8; 2.17.30; 2.18.110, 127; 3.1.118; 3.11.131; 3.14.48

draco: snake, dragon 3.14.9; 3.15.54, 74; 3.18.46, 49, 65; Q.20

lapis draconitis: the stone draconite, a precious stone said to be taken from the head of a dragon (Pliny 37.57.158). 3.14.9; cf. 3.15.54, 73-74

dracontea: perhaps the plant dragons or dragonwort (*Dracunculus vulgaris* or *Arum maculatum*) 3.8.15

echinus (*echenais* or *echeneis*): echinus; "the sucking-fish believed to delay ships, the remora." *OLD* 3.16.64

electrum: an alloy of gold and silver 2.14.64

electuarium: electuary, a medicinal paste, formed by mixing various ingredients with honey and syrup. 1.19.6; 1.21.6; 1.23.t, 1; 2.8.37; 2.18.125, 131; 3.10.58; 3.13.34, 36; 3.14.46

elephans: elephant 3.21.11

elephanginae: the name given by Mesue to medicinal pills he had concocted. 1.13.2

lapis elitis: the sun-stone; Ficino found this stone in Proclus, *De sacrificio*. 3.14.39

endivia: endive (*Cichorium endivia*) 1.10.46; 1.19.10; 2.13.18; 3.1.110

epithymum: epithyme or dodder (*Cuscuta epithymum*), a parasitic plant growing on thyme; see *cuscuta*. 1.19.11, 14, 16; 1.20.19

equus: horse 1.2.7

eruca: rocket (*Eruca sativa*), a plant of the mustard family 1.10.5

euchima: a Greek word for foods which are wholesome and productive of healthy humors 2.5.2

eufrasia: eye-bright (*Euphrasia officinalis*) 1.16.13

eupatorium: agrimony (*Agrimonia eupatoria*) or hemp agrimony (*Eupatorium canabinum*), esp. good for the liver. "Through confusion as to the application of *Eupatoria* and *Liverwort*, old names of Agrimony, the name has been, with or without qualification, extended to other plants," *OED*. 2.13.17; 3.1.110; 3.26.131

euphorbium: gum plant (*Euphorbia resinifera*) of the Spurge genus, useful for its milky juice. 1.25.24; 3.2.62

exhilarans: the name for an unspecified electuary concocted by Rhazes 1.23.1

faba: bean (*Vicia faba*) 1.10.4; 2.7.23

feniculum: fennel (*Foeniculum vulgare*); see also *marathrum*. 1.13.5; 1.15.4; 1.16.2; 3.8.7

ferrum: iron 1.5.55; 1.10.28; 2.5.62; 2.7.68; 3.2.54; 3.10.50; 3.12.60; 3.15.20, 24, 28, 31, 32, 35, 46; 3.26.60, 131; — *squama ferri*: iron scales 2.8.61; 2.18.139

lapis de Feyrizech: Arabic for the same stone as the sapphire 3.18.44

ficus: fig (*ficus carica*) 1.10.24; 2.12.13; 2.14.11

flores: flowers 1.10.39; 1.19.9; 1.23.26; 2.10.12; 2.15.55; 2.18.89, 90; 3.1.99; 3.2.45; 3.11.24; 3.14.38, 45; 3.18.55; 3.21.31

fomentum: fomentation. "The application to the surface of the body either of flannels etc., soaked in hot water, whether simple or medicated, or of any other warm, soft, medicinal substance," *OED*. 2.4.22; 2.8.21, 23, 24; 2.9.40; 2.18.8, 42; 2.20.55; V.18; 3.1.108, 109; 3.15.95; 3.26.23

fraxinus: ash-tree (*Fraxinus excelsior*); Pliny (16.24.64) speaks of its power against poison. 3.14.34

fructus: fruit 2.5.13; 2.6.8, 59; 2.7.12; 2.12.22; 3.14.44; 3.21.28

fruges: field produce 2.7.5; 2.18.3

fuga daemon: see *perforata*.

fumus terrae: fumitory (*Fumaria officinalis*) 1.16.6; 3.8.36

fungus: mushroom (*Agaricus campestris*) 2.6.9

gallina: hen 2.5.60; 2.6.47, 51; 2.10.22; 2.17.8, 9; 3.26.63; A.72; — *gallinaceus pullus*: young hen or cock, chicken 1.10.20–21; 2.6.41; 3.11.110

gallus: cock 3.1.103; 3.13.67; 3.14.12, 25, 26, 28; 3.15.74, 76; 3.18.63

gariophylus (*c(h)ariophyllus*); clove (*Eugenia caryophyllata*) 1.10.38; 1.25.20; 2.6.36; 2.9.18, 22; 2.13.9; 2.18.114; 3.11.133; 3.14.49

gentiana: gentian (*Gentiana lutea*) 3.12.61

glycyrrhiza (from the Greek): licorice-root (*Glycyrrhiza glabra*); see *liquiritia* (in Book 1 the late Latin spelling is used) 2.5.56; 2.7.44, 69; 2.8.53, 54; 2.13.20; 3.6.76, 78; 3.11.109

granatum: garnet 3.8.18

gummi: gum, a viscid secretion from certain trees 2.12.19; 3.21.28

haedus: young goat, kid 2.5.60; 2.6.44

haematites: haematite, a reddish iron-ore 3.15.66

hamech: the name applied to an unspecified electuary 1.21.6

hedera: ivy (*hedera helix*) 3.8.31

helioselinon: an unidentified gem described by Proclus, *De sacrificio*, having both solar and lunar properties. 3.15.11

heliotropium: heliotrope. As a stone, the bloodstone; also the name of the genus of plant which turns its flowers and leaves to the sun. 3.1.100

helleborus: hellebore, name for a genus of plant with poisonous and medicinal properties; see *veratrum*. 2.7.15; 2.17.5, 8; 3.2.62; 3.16.72, 73; 3.20.1, 10

hepatica: "the old name in the herbalists for Common Liverwort (*Marchantia polymorpha*)," *OED;* perhaps *Anemone hepatica*. 2.13.18; 3.1.110

hepar (*-atis*): the liver? things pertaining to the liver? 3.1.100

lapis Herculeus: the stone of Hercules refers to the magnet or lodestone (Pliny 36.25.127). 3.15.24

herbae: herbs GP.14, 36; 1.10.23; 2.5.14; 2.6.8, 59; 2.7.5; 2.8.6; 2.15.91; 2.18.3; 2.20.56; 3.8.74; 3.11.4, 24; 3.12.89, 114; 3.14.38, 45, 62, 65, 66; 3.18.144; 3.20.5; 3.21.28, 31, 39; 3.25.14; 3.26.42, 36; A.44, 93

hiera (from the Greek): literally "holy" or "sacred," a word given to various

medicines in the Greek pharmacopoeia 1.13.4

hierapicra: literally "holy bitters," a medicinal compound composed by Galen 1.13.2

hiera Andromachi: the hiera composed by Andromachus 1.25.7

hiera Archigenis: the hiera composed by Archigenes 1.25.7

hiera diacoloquintidos: a hiera with the colocynth as its chief ingredient 1.25.6

hiera Theodotionis: the hiera composed by Theodotion 1.25.7

hieralogodion: the name given to an unspecified medicinal compound 1.20.28; 1.25.6

hierobotanum: literally "sacred planet"; in the classical period, vervain. Ficino, however, (1.10.44) qualifies it as *sclarea silvestris*, the scariole or broad-leaved endive (*Cichorium endiva* or *latifolium*) 1.10.44

hircus: goat 3.18.172

hirundo: swallow 3.15.74, 48; A.49

hirudo: leech 2.11.16

hyacinthus (*iacintus*): jacinth, a gem-stone. "Among the ancients, a gem of blue colour, probably sapphire. In modern use, a reddish-orange gem, a variety of zircon; also applied to varieties of topaz and garnet," OED. 1.10.43; 1.23.41; 2.14.65; 2.15.91; 3.1.112; 3.12.35, 54; 3.16.97, 104. Also a plant (hyacinth); "according to Ovid a deep red or 'purple' lily (?*Lilium Martagon*), but variously taken by authors as a gladiolus, iris, or larkspur," OED. 1.10.43? 2.15.91?

hydra: a water-serpent killed by Hercules A.127

hysopus: hyssop, an aromatic herb (*Hyssopus officinalis*) 2.12.14

iaspis: jasper 3.2.51; 3.8.28; 3.12.70

(*pilulae*) *Indae*: Indian pills, name applied to unspecified pills; Benesch says they are compounded from Indian salt, lapis lazuli, and vegetable drugs. 1.20.27; 1.25.5

inula: elecampane (*Inula helenium*), esp. its roots 2.8.50; 3.11.111

iuleb: julep, a sweetened drink 1.17.14; 1.20.38, 45; 2.10.17; 2.15.112

ius: broth, soup, juice 1.10.31; 2.10.24; 2.17.14

iusquiamus (*hyoscyamus*): henbane (*Hyoscyamus niger*) 3.8.23

iuvencus: a young bull, bullock 3.1.119

lac: milk 1.10.20; 1.16.7; 1.24.18; 2.6.8; 2.9.45; 2.17.51; — *lac amygdalinum*: almond milk, see *amygdala*; — *lac caprinum*: goat's milk 2.15.34; — *lac humanum*: human milk 2.11.t, 5, 6, 7; 2.15.34; — *lac suillum*: pig's milk 2.15.34

lacca: lac, a dark-red resinous substance secreted on certain trees by various insects, esp. a species (*Laccifer laca*) of India. 3.2.34

lachrymae: gumdrops 2.12.19

lactuca: lettuce (*Lactuca sativa*) 1.10.46; 1.24.4, 5, 7, 16

lapathium: sorrel (*Rumex acetosa*); André has patience, a species of dock (*Rumex patientia*). 3.8.23

lapilli: stones, gems 3.1.95, 99; 3.13.53; 3.14.14, 19, 46, 66; 3.15.1, 5, 73, 74; 3.16.110, 111

lapilli pretiosi: precious stones 1.23.43; 2.9.7–8; 2.14.65; 2.15.91; 3.1.82–3

lapides: stones, gems 2.20.33; 3.3.16; 3.8.74; 3.11.5, 6, 127; 3.12.116; 3.14.42; 3.18.178; 3.21.27; 3.26.87; A.44

lapis lazuli: an azure-blue, semi-precious stone 1.20.19, 27; 1.23.12; 3.2.44; 3.19.36 (lapis lazulus)

laurus: laurel, sweet bay (*Laurus nobilis*) 2.14.72; 3.13.68; 3.14.34, 50, 55

legumen: pulse, any legume 1.10.4

lenticula: lentil (*Lens esculenta*) 1.10.4
leo: lion 3.1.104; 3.14.12, 25, 26, 28; 3.18.68
lepus: hare 1.10.3; 2.6.40; 3.19.85
lignum aloes: aloe-wood; see *aloe*.
lilium: lily (*Lilium candidum*) 2.13.9; 2.14.12, 13; 3.11.122
limax: slug, snail 2.5.61
limon: lemon (*Citrus medica* or *limonum*) 1.12.28; 1.17.15; 1.23.31, 37
lingua ranae: frog-tongue? There is a species of crowfoot (*Ranunculus lingua*), great spearwort. 3.8.24
liquiritia: licorice-root; see *glycyrrhiza* (the Latinate form of the Greek word is used in Books 2 and 3). 1.10.33; 1.19.12; 1.20.38; 1.21.11
lotos: lotus, described in Proclus, *De sacrificio*, and in Pliny; the water lily of Egypt (*Nymphaea lotus* or *Nelumbium speciosum*). 3.14.35
(*pilulae*) *lucis*: pills of light? an unspecified composition of pills, good for weak eyes. 1.16.4–5
herba Lunaris: an unidentified herb, supposedly described by Hermes Trismegistus 3.14.66
lupinus: lupin (*Lupinus albus*) 1.10.28; 2.7.23, 68
lupus: wolf Q.14, 19, 20

macis: the spice mace, from the dried outer covering of the nutmeg (*Myristica fragrans*) 1.11.3; 2.9.18; 2.13.6; 2.18.140; 3.14.49
magnes: magnet, lodestone, a strongly magnetic variety of the mineral magnetite 3.2.51; 3.8.21; 3.15.20, 24, 26, 27, 31, 32, 35, 45; 3.26.60, 131
maiorana: marjoram, esp. sweet marjoram (*Origanum majorana*); see also *amaracum*. 1.14.5; 1.15.4; 1.16.2; 3.8.39
malum: apple (*Pyrus malus*), esp. sweet apples; see also *pomum*. 1.10.22; 1.24.12

malva: mallow (*Malva rotundifolia* or *silvestria*) 1.24.16; 2.13.21
(*vinum*) *malvaticum*: see *vinum*.
mandragora: mandrake (*Mandragora officinarum*), a poisonous plant, having emetic and narcotic properties. 3.2.62; 3.8.11, 26, 39
manna: a sweet, gummy juice condensed from the bark of the manna-ash tree (*Fraxinus ornus*) and useful as a laxative. 1.21.8; 2.13.21; 2.17.13, 14; 3.11.113
marathrum (from the Greek): fennel (*Foeniculum vulgare*); see also *feniculum* at 1.13.5. Pliny too (8.41.99; 20.95.254) says that snakes use fennel to slough off their old skins. 1.16.8, 12; 1.25.20; 2.9.46; A.48; — *marathrum dulce*: sweet fennel (*Foeniculum dulce*) 2.9.44; 2.11.5, 7; 2.13.7; 2.18.110, 134; 3.11.131
marcassita: marcasite, a pyrite, a metallic sulfide. "The marcasites of gold and silver seem to have been specimens of copper and iron pyrites with the lustre of gold and silver, and hence wrongly supposed to contain traces of those metals," *OED*; — *marcassita aurea*: golden marcasite 3.2.52–53; — *marcassita argentea*: silver marcasite 3.2.32–33, 47
margarita: pearl; see also *unio*. 1.23.13, 29, 39
mastix: mastic, a gum or resin from the bark of the mastic tree (*Pistacia lentiscus*). 1.11.15, 27; 1.15.3; 1.20.31; 2.5.62, 63; 2.7.31; 2.9.18; 2.13.4; 2.17.17; 3.8.18; 3.14.48, 49; 3.16.104
matrisilva (Italian dial.): honeysuckle (*Lonicera periclymenum*); or possibly the woodruff (*Asperula odorata*). 3.8.13
medicamen: medicament, remedy 1.21.23
medicina: medicine GP.11, 22, 29, 33, 35; 1.1.25; 1.13.t; 1.17.3; 1.21.t, 11, 13; 1.22.12; 1.26.t, 9; 2.5.14; 2.7.32;

2.8.t; 2.13.3, 28; 2.15.t, 115; 2.17.t, 3, 12, 52; 2.19.t; V.8, 10, 15, 23, 25; 3.4.19; 3.6.70, 134; 3.8.47, 77; 3.9.t; 3.10.t, 7, 57, 60, 61, 64; 3.11.87; 3.13.t; 3.14.59; 3.15.t, 112; 3.18.103, 105, 114, 162, 163, 177; 3.20.20, 58, 59, 63, 70; 3.21.7, 51, 52, 81; 3.22.6, 14, 79; 3.24.15; A *passim*; Q.55

mel: honey 1.13.5; 1.17.4; 1.20.37; 1.21.11; 1.23.9; 1.25.17; 2.6.9; 2.12.11, 12; 2.13.27; 2.15.34, 117; 2.18.87, 88, 89, 90, 131, 138; 3.1.102, 114; 3.14.49; A.28

melissa: the aromatic herb balm (*Melissa officinalis*); see *citraria*. 1.10.39, 45; 1.12.18; 1.19.10; 1.20.9, 17; 2.8.42; 2.10.13

melongia: perhaps the eggplant (*Solanum melongena*). Benesch has melon (*Cucumis melo*); a legume? 1.10.4

menta: mint (*Mentha viridis*) 1.10.39; 1.11.15, 27; 1.17.5, 19, 20; 1.20.10; 2.8.25; 2.13.4, 10; 2.14.9, 10; 2.15.90; 2.18.117; 3.1.117; 3.8.11; 3.12.65

merula: blackbird 3.26.67; A.83

merum: wine, unmixed with water GP.6; 1.5.65; 1.6.10; 1.11.22; 1.12.9, 19; 1.20.13; 2.7.67; 2.15.110; 2.17.37; 2.19.14, 16; V.26; 3.24.46, 50

mespilum: medlar, fruit of *Mespilus* or *Pyrus germanica* 1.11.25

metalla: metals 2.20.33; 3.1.95; 3.2.56; 3.3.16, 22; 3.11.5, 127; 3.12.115; 3.13.53, 68; 3.14.14, 19, 42; 3.16.25, 110, 113; 3.18.178; 3.21.27

mithridatum: a multi-ingredient electuary prepared in the first century BC for the King of Pontus, Mithridates the Great. It was said to have made him impervious to poison. 1.12.12, 13

morum: black medick (*Medicago lupulina*)? Benesch has mulberry (*Morus nigra* or *alba*); a legume? 1.10.5

motacilla: white water-wagtail 3.1.120

mumia: mummy, dried meat 2.13.25

(*nux*) *muscata*: nutmeg (*Myristica fragrans*) 1.9.14; 1.11.3; 1.14.4; 1.25.20, 27; 2.9.18; 2.13.3; 3.11.133; 3.14.49

muscus: musk; in the classical period, *muscus* meant moss. 1.10.39; 1.12.29; 1.23.14, 30, 43; 1.25.18; 2.8.41; 2.9.20, 43; 2.13.8, 27; 2.15.90; 2.17.32; 2.18.128; 3.1.101; 3.11.134; 3.14.47; 3.23.98; 3.26.132

myrobalanus: myrobalan, "the astringent plum-like fruit of species of *Terminalia*" (*OED*), brought from the East Indies; not the North African ben-nut tree of Pliny 12.46.100. 1.11.20; 2.5.53; 2.7.31; 2.8.47, 60, 62; 2.9.1, 6, 15, 42; 2.14.60; 2.15.90; 2.17.14; 2.18.135, 144, 146; 3.1.83; 3.11.113; 3.12.49, 72; 3.20.6; — *myrobalanus bellirica*: belliric myrobalan, the roundish or oblong fruit of *Terminalia bellerica* 2.8.58; 2.17.29; 2.18.127; — *myrobalanus chebula*: chebule myrobalan, the large, dried prune-like fruit of *Terminalia chebula* 1.12.16, 24; 1.16.11; 1.17.12-13; 1.20.12, 17, 30; 1.23.27; 1.25.17; 2.8.62; 2.13.26-27; 2.15.115; 2.17.16, 29; 2.18.126, 131, 134, 139; 2.19.18; — *myrobalanus emblica*: emblic myrobalan, the round fruit of *Phyllantus emblica* 1.12.17, 25; 1.17.13; 1.20.12, 17, 30; 2.7.34-35; 2.8.58; 2.15.117; 2.17.16, 28; 2.18.126, 131, 138; 2.19.19; — *myrobalanus Inda*: Indian or black myrobalan, also the fruit of *Terminalia chebula*. Because it has no stone, it was supposed to be gathered unripe. 1.20.12, 18; 2.8.58, 59; 2.13.27; 2.17.29; 2.18.126, 138

myrrha: myrrh, gum resin of *Commiphora myrrha* 1.20.9, 16; 2.13.6; 2.17.49; 2.19.3, 6, 12, 19; 3.1.101

myrtus: myrtle (*Myrtus communis*) 1.10.37; 2.5.71; 2.9.17, 43; 2.13.7, 11; 2.14.15; 2.17.49; 2.18.115

Index materiae medicae 503

nardus: see *spica nardi*
nenufar: nenuphar, white water-lily (*Nymphea alba*); in particular, its oil. 1.24.11
nepita: catnip or catmint (*Nepeta cataria*). André says calamint (*Calamintha nepeta*). 3.8.39
noctua: owl 1.7.92, 93
nutrimentum: nourishment 1.11.32; 2.4.18, 42; 2.5.3; 2.6.49; 2.8.28, 30, 51; 2.9.40, 44; 2.12.1, 6; 2.18.t, 7, 13, 74, 83, 98

ocimum: basil (*Ocimum basilicum*) 2.13.10; 2.18.61; 3.26.66
(*lapis*) *Solis oculus*: the stone called "the eye of the Sun." Ficino found this stone in Proclus, *De sacrificio*. 3.14.40
olea: olive (*Olea europaea*); see *oliva*. 3.25.20
oleum: oil 1.15.5; 1.24.10, 11; 1.25.23, 24; 2.2.2; 2.3.1, 2, 5, 8, 16, 20, 22; 2.5.32, 33, 36, 57, 58, 62; 2.7.42, 70; 2.12.20; 2.13.13; 2.17.48; 2.18.136; 3.6.76, 78; 3.14.49; 3.26.12, 13
olibanum: olibanum, frankincense (*Boswellia carterii*); see also *thus*. 2.9.18
oliva: olive (*Olea europaea*); see also *olea*. 2.5.32; 2.14.72; — *olivetum*: olive grove 2.12.18
olor: swan 3.1.103
opium: the juice of the poppy (*Papaver somniferum*); used medicinally as a stupefying agent to relieve pain and induce sleep. 3.2.62
opobalsamum: balm; see under *balsamum*
ovis: sheep 2.12.8
ovum: egg 1.10.21; 1.16.7; 2.6.47, 51; 58; 2.8.9; 2.10.20, 25; 2.15.33, 36; 3.11.110; 3.22.71; 3.26.62, 63, 64, 66; A.50, 71
oxymel: a mixture of vinegar and honey 1.13.5
oxysaccharum: a compound of vinegar and sugar 1.17.8

paeonia: peony (*Paeonia officinalis*) 1.20.16; 2.13.5; 3.12.46; 3.14.36
palma: palm tree (*Phoenix dactylifera*) 3.14.33
panis: bread 1.16.12; 1.24.4; 2.5.16; 2.6.16, 30, 58; 2.8.24, 26; 2.15.110; 2.17.37, 39; 2.18.81, 86, 89, 115; 3.25.26
pantaura: the stone pantaura or pantarbe. Philostratus, *VA* 3.46, describes its wondrous properties. A stone of the sun, it is said to act as a magnet to attract other precious stones. 3.13.68; 3.14.41; 3.15.21; 3.16.112
papaver: poppy (*Papaver somniferum*) 1.24.7, 9, 10, 16
(*uva*) *passula* (from *uva passa*, "dried grape"): raisin, the dried fruit of *Vitis vinifera*. 1.10.46; 1.11.15; 1.19.12; 1.20.37; 1.21.11; 2.8.57; 2.12.14; 2.13.18; 3.11.109
pavo: peacock 2.6.41; 3.1.118; 3.11.110; 3.18.64
pentaphyllon: the plant cinquefoil (*Potentilla reptans*), with compound leaves each of five leaflets 3.12.66
pepo: watermelon (*Citrullus vulgaris*) or other gourd 1.10.19, 22
perdix: partridge 2.6.42, 51; 3.11.110
perforata or *fuga daemon* (daemon-router): better known as *hypericum*, the name for a genus of plant; esp. St. John's wort (*Hypericum perforatum*) 3.14.63–64
(*pomum*) *Persicum*: peach, fruit of *Prunus persica* 1.10.22; 1.11.25; 1.17.9; 2.7.13–14; 2.18.81; 3.11.130
phalangium: phalangium-spider; "a name given to various venomous spiders," *OED*. 3.16.65; 3.21.151
pharmacum: drug 1.21.23; V.18; 3.6.68; 3.15.106
phasiana: pheasant 2.6.42, 51; 3.11.110
pilula: pill 1.12.19, 22, 35; 1.13.1, 3, 6, 7, 8; 1.14.2; 1.16.4, 5; 1.19.5, 19; 1.20 *passim;* 1.21.2; 1.25.5, 7; 2.17.18, 23, 24, 26; 2.19.14

pinus: pine (*Pinus pinea*) 2.12.19, 20; 2.14.72; — *pina* (for *pinea*?): pine-nut, pine-cone? 2.13.20; — *nucleus pineus*: pine-nut, the edible seed or kernel of the pine tree 1.10.19; 1.23.33; 2.5.56; 2.6.31; 2.8.29, 33; 2.12.15; 3.11.109; — *pinucleatum*: pine-cone? 2.8.35; — *pinetum*: pine grove 2.12.18

piscis (*pisciculus*): fish 2.6.8, 59; 2.18.61; 3.1.35; 3.16.64; 3.18.48

pistacium: pistachio nut (*Pistacia vera*) 2.5.56; 2.8.38; 2.12.15; 2.13.17; 3.11.109

placenta: cake 2.10.25

planta: plant 1.24.14; 2.12.9; 2.15.96; 3.1.96; 3.2.76; 3.3.12; 3.11.20, 22; 3.13.42, 67; 3.14.14, 19, 33, 55; 3.19.67, 69; 3.20.16; 3.26.50

plantago: plantain (*Plantago major*) 3.8.28

plisarchoticon: the name given to an unspecified medicinal confection. Benesch says it is a compound of drugs, spices, musk, camphor and sugar. There is an *electuarium pleres archonticon* described in Arnald of Villanova's *Antidotarium*, ch. 13. 1.15.3; 1.25.18

polypodium: polypody, a kind of fern (*Polypodium vulgare*) 1.19.10; 1.20.19; 1.21.10

pomum: fruit, sometimes apple 1.10.40; 1.12.17; 1.19.12; 1.23.4; 2.7.5; 2.18.3, 81; 3.11.24, 49; 3.14.36; 3.18.55

porrum: leek (*Allium porrum*) 1.10.5

portulaca: purslane (*Portulaca oleracea*) 1.24.16

potus: drink 1.9.10; 1.11.4, 6, 30, 31; 1.17.18; 2.3.10; 2.4.20, 23; 2.6.10, 24, 58, 59, 60; 2.10.20, 27; 2.11.11, 24; 2.18.149; 2.19.16; 3.13.9

prassium: horehound (*Marrubium vulgare*) 3.8.11

promarulla: an unidentified herb; perhaps a distortion of *primula*, the name given to early spring flowers such as the cowslip (*Primula officinalis*) 3.8.26

pruna Damascena: plums from Damascus, damson plums (*Prunus domestica*) 1.10.22; 1.19.11

pulegium: pennyroyal (*Mentha pulegium*) 3.8.16

pullus: chicken 2.10.22

pulpa: flesh 2.13.25

pulver: powder 1.16.12; 1.23.11; 2.7.34, 36; 2.8.25; 2.11.6; 3.13.34, 36; 3.14.46; 3.21.30

malum or *pomum Punicum*: pomegranate, fruit of *Punica granatu* 1.10.33; 1.11.17, 25; 1.17.9, 20; 2.12.14

pyrum: pear, fruit of *Pyrus communis* 1.10.22; 1.11.25; 1.17.9; 2.6.9; 2.18.81; 3.11.130

python: 3.12.59; A.131

quadrupes: quadruped 1.10.21

radicula: radish (*Raphanus sativus*) 1.10.5

rana: frog 3.16.77

(*serpens*) *regulus*: regulus, a kind of serpent 3.16.62

remedium: remedy GP.29; 1.1.32; 1.9.2; 1.19.2; 1.25.4, 22; 2.5.43; 2.15.50; 2.16.16, 20, 37; 2.20.19; V.19; 3.6.97; 3.10.53; 3.25.17

reubarbarum: rhubarb (*Rheum palmatum*) 1.13.7; 1.17.8; 2.17.21, 22, 25; 3.26.131

rosa: rose (*Rosa gallica* or *damascena*) 1.10.37; 1.11.16, 27; 1.20.18, 32; 1.23.49; 1.24.16; 2.5.52, 71; 2.7.30, 32; 2.9.16, 43; 2.13.11; 2.14.14; 2.15.112; 2.17.49; 2.18.115; 3.1.86; 3.11.122; 3.14.5, 59; — *rosa purpurea*: purple or red rose 1.12.16, 25; 1.20.10, 32; 2.17.17, 30; — *acetum rosaceum*: rose-vinegar 1.17.18; 2.7.45; 2.18.115; — *aqua rosacea*: rose-water 1.10.37; 1.12.11, 21, 27; 1.16.6; 1.23.5, 18, 37; 1.24.13; 2.5.58; 2.7.30, 44; 2.8.42; 2.10.15; 2.13.15; 2.17.32, 37; 2.18.115, 134;

2.19.17; — *aromaticum rosaceum*: rose-spice 1.17.3-4; 1.23.50, 51; — *mel rosaceum*: rose-honey 1.13.5; 1.17.4; 1.21.11; — *oleum rosaceum*: rose-oil 1.15.5; 2.7.70; 3.6.76, 78; — *saccharum rosaceum*: rose-sugar 1.17.4, 11; 1.23.25, 51; 2.5.53; 2.8.46-47; 2.15.116; 2.18.129

rosmarinus: rosemary (*Rosmarinus officinalis*) 3.8.31

rubinus: ruby 3.8.13; 3.12.35

ruta: rue (*Ruta graveolens*) 1.15.4; 1.16.3; 1.25.20; 3.12.63

saccharum: sugar (*Saccharum officinarum*) 1.11.16, 24; 1.12.27; 1.16.6, 12; 1.17.4, 8, 11, 19; 1.19.16; 1.23 *passim;* 1.24.8, 19; 1.25.15; 2.5.53; 2.6.38; 2.7.44; 2.8.40, 42, 46, 56, 59; 2.10.15, 24; 2.11.6, 18, 19, 20; 2.15.33, 116; 2.17.33, 38; 2.18.109, 129, 134; 3.1.82, 85, 113; 3.11.112, 132; — (*saccharum*) *candum*: candy 1.23.34

sal: salt 2.6.37, 52; 2.10.24

salamandra: salamander 2.18.62

salix: willow, osier (genus *Salix*) 1.24.16

salvia: sage (*Salvia officinalis*) 1.11.15; 2.9.19, 47; 2.17.49; 3.8.25; 3.12.65; 3.26.67; A.81

sambucus: elder tree (*sambucus ebulus* or *nigra*) and in particular its oil (*oleum sambucinum*); cf. Pliny 24.35.51. 1.25.23

sandalum: sandal (also sandalwood or sanders, *Santalum album*) 1.10.18, 37; 2.5.52; 2.7.35; 2.9.16; 2.13.11; esp. *sandalum rubrum* or *rubeum*, red sanders (*Pterocarpus santalinus*), the wood of an East Indian tree "formerly employed in medicine as an astringent and tonic," *OED*. 1.12.17, 26; 1.17.13; 1.19.13; 1.20.11; 1.23.28, 39; 2.17.31; 2.18.116, 130

lapis sanguineus: bloodstone 3.2.54

sanguis: blood 1.2.12, 13, 15, 16, 17, 22; 1.4.28, 29, 33; 1.5.20, 21, 31, 39, 40, 50, 51, 68; 1.7.19, 32, 52, 56; 1.10.15; 1.16.16; 1.21.16; 1.22.t, 1, 2, 3, 5, 9, 12; 2.4.1, 12; 2.5 *passim;* 2.6.34, 37, 50; 2.8.8,10; 2.11 *passim;* 2.13.16; 2.18.24, 75; 3.8.28; 3.10.57; 3.11.56; 3.12.70; 3.14.24, 44; 3.18.67

sapphyrus: sapphire; in antiquity, the word referred to the lapis lazuli. 1.23.42; 3.1.113; 3.2.43; 3.8.10; 3.11.124; 3.12.35; 3.13.21; 3.16.113; 3.18.45; 3.19.32, 35, 36, 42

sardonius: sardonyx 3.8.33

satureia: savory (*Satureia hortensis*) 3.8.35

savina (*herba Sabina*, Sabine herb): savin, a shrub (*Juniperus sabina*) 3.8.14

scabiosa: the herb scabious (genus *Scabiosa*) 2.12.14

sclarea silvestris: scariole or broad-leaved endive (*Cichorium endivia* or *latifolium*); see *hierobotanum*. 1.10.44

scolopendria: a fern scolopendrium or hart's-tongue (*Phyllitis scolopendrium*) 2.13.19

scopa: the shrub broom (genus *Genista* or *Cytisus scoparius*)? 3.16.67; 3.18.174

scorpio or *scorpius*: scorpion 3.13.6, 8, 10; 3.14.3; 3.16.103; 3.26.66

selenites: selenite, the moonstone 3.15.5

sena: senna (*Cassia acutifolia*); its leaves were used as a cathartic and emetic. See also *cassia*. 1.19.10; 1.20.19

sericum: silk 2.14.65; 3.11.126; 3.15.3; — esp. raw silk of a reddish hue 1.20.9; 1.23.3, 7, 28, 40

serpens: snake, serpent 2.9.46; 3.12.62; 3.13.4, 5; 3.14.8; 3.15.63, 64; 3.16.62; 3.18.66; 3.21.11; A.48, 84, 85

(*herba*) *serpentaria*: the herb serpentaria, snake-root (*Dracunculus vulgaris*) or snakeweed (*Polygonum bistorta*); see also *dracontea*. 3.14.9; 3.15.67

lapis serpentinus: the stone serpentine 3.14.10

sesamum: sesame (*Sesamum indicum*); in particular, the oil extracted from its seeds (*oleum sesaminum*). 2.5.58
simia: monkey, ape 3.2.35
sinapis: the mustard plant (genus *Brassica*) 1.10.5
sine quibus: the name of an unspecified pill 1.13.8
smaragdus: emerald 1.23.42; 3.2.34; 3.8.25; 3.12.35; 3.16.105, 113
(*lapis*) *Solis oculus*: see under *oculus*. 3.14.40
solsequium: a plant of the genus *Heliotropium*, such as the turnsole (*Heliotropium europaeum*); see also *heliotropium*. 3.8.16
spelta: spelt (*Triticum spelta*) 2.6.52
spica or *spica nardi*: spikenard (*Nardostachys jatamansi*) 2.13.6; 3.1.102; 3.14.48; 3.26.132; — its oil 2.13.13; 3.14.50
spodium: a metallic oxide produced by calcination. Benesch calls it a preparation containing zinc oxide. 2.9.7; 2.13.18; 2.14.64; 3.1.110, 113; 3.26.132
stannum: tin 3.2.32; 3.18.12
stichas (-*ados*) *Arabicus*: stechas or stechados, French lavender (*Lavandula stoechas*) 1.20.16
struthum: sparrow 3.11.14; A.116
succinum: amber (see also *ambra*); — as an aromatic 2.9.15; — with the power of attraction 3.15.30; 3.16.95 (see Pliny 37.12.48)
succus: juice 1.10.33; 1.12.28; 1.17.15, 20; 1.23.4, 5, 31, 49; 2.5.15, 56; 2.7.30, 44; 2.8.53; 2.9.16; 2.17.32; 2.18.4; 3.14.59; 3.18.172
sulphur: sulfur 3.1.38; 3.2.53; 3.16.89, 94; 3.22.74, 75; 3.26.61
sus: pig 2.6.32; 2.11.21, 22; 2.15.34
syrupus: syrup 1.13.6; 1.17.5, 10, 19; 1.19.t, 5, 9, 17; 1.20.35, 42; 1.21.3, 10, 12; 1.24.9, 10

tamariscum: tamarisk (*Tamarix gallica*) 2.13.20

taurus: bull 3.18.65
terebentus: terebinth or turpentine tree (*Pistacia terebinthus*); in particular its oleoresin 2.5.33
testudo: tortoise, turtle 2.5.60
theriaca: theriac or treacle, name given to a popular class of medicinal compounds. Originally the word referred to an antidote against venomous bites and poison in which viper's flesh was an essential ingredient. 1.12.5, 12, 22, 32; 1.14.4; 1.17.6; 1.25.21; 2.7.61; 2.8.48; 2.9.23; 2.18.120; 3.12.63, 79, 84, 85, 94; 3.21.48, 49
thus: frankincense, an aromatic gum resin of the *Boswellia carterii*. See also *olibanum*. 1.14.3; 1.20.8, 17; 1.25.16, 19, 27; 2.13.5, 8; 2.15.90; 2.19.2, 5, 12, 19; 3.1.101; 3.12.64; 3.13.9; 3.14.47; 3.16.104
titimallus (*tithymallus*): tithymal, an old name for the spurge and its genus *Euphorbia;* see also *euphorbium*. 3.8.13
topazius: topaz; but see *chrysolitus*. 3.1.112; 3.8.31; 3.12.35; 3.16.104
torpedo: torpedo-fish, the electric ray 3.16.63
triasandalum: an unspecified medicinal compound (three parts sandalwood?) 1.17.8
trifolium: trefoil, name for a genus of plant (*Trifolium*) with triple or trifoliate leaves 3.8.25, 31
triphera: the name applied to a medicinal compound in which myrobalans are the chief ingredient (2.18.144) 1.16.9; 1.21.5; 2.8.58, 60; 2.18.143, 144
triticum: wheat, wheat flour (*Triticum vulgare*) 2.6.30; 2.7.t, 48; 3.11.112
trochiscus: troche, a small, round or lozenge-shaped pill 1.13.4; 1.20.18; 2.17.5, 24
turtur: turtle-dove 3.1.120
tutia: tutty, a crude oxide of zinc 1.16.7

unguentum: ointment, unguent 1.18.9;

Index materiae medicae 507

V.19; 3.1.105; 3.13.34, 36; 3.14.46; 3.15.107; 3.21.31
unicorni cornu: unicorn's horn; the horn of the rhinoceros, narwhal, or other animal. 3.12.36
unio: a large white pearl; see also *margarita*. 1.23.13; 3.2.47
uva: grape (*Vitis vinifera*); see also *uva passula*, raisin. 1.10.24

veratrum: hellebore (*Veratrum album*); see also *helleborus*. 1.20.25
verbena: vervain (*Verbena officinalis*) 3.12.62
vervex: wether, a castrated male sheep 2.6.43
vespertilio: bat 1.7.98
vinum: wine; see also *merum*. G.P.4, 6, 13; 1.7.26; 1.10.2, 25, 27, 40; 1.11.20; 1.12.21; 1.17.9; 1.20.20, 32, 36, 45; 1.23.15; 1.24.4, 10; 2.5.60, 61, 70; 2.6.14, 31; 2.7 *passim;* 2.8.9, 10, 13, 45; 2.10.16, 19, 27; 2.11.18, 22; 2.12.20; 2.13.14; 2.14.8; 2.15.89, 112; 2.17.23, 36, 48, 51; 2.18 *passim;* 2.20.51, 54; 3.1.82, 85, 113, 117; 3.6.76; 78; 3.11.111; 3.12.67; 3.15.59; 3.24.29, 30, 31, 37, 38, 47, 49; 3.25.26; — *vinum malvaticum*: malmsey wine, a strong, sweet wine 2.8.25; 2.15.110; 2.17.18; 3.11.130; — *vinum vernaceum*: vernage wine, a strong, sweet white wine 2.15.110; 3.11.130
viola: violet (*Viola odorata*), but the word was used to refer to several fragrant spring flowers. 1.10.37; 1.19.10; 1.20.39; 1.23.54; 1.24.11, 12; 2.14.11, 14; 2.18.115; 3.11.122; 3.14.59
vipera: viper 2.17.5
vitis: vine, grapevine (*Vitis vinifera*) G.P.5, 32; 1.24.16; 2.12.18; 2.14.7; 3.25.20
vitulus: calf 2.6.43; — *vitulus aureus*: the golden calf 3.13.24; — *vitulus marinus*: seal 3.14.29
vulpis: fox 3.25.44

zedoaria: zedoary (*Curcuma zedoaria*), with an aromatic root 2.9.17, 23; 3.12.63; 3.14.48
zinziber: ginger (*Zingiber officinale*) 1.9.15; 1.17.5; 1.25.15; 2.8.41; 2.9.20, 48; 2.15.90, 116; 2.18.139; 3.11.131; 3.12.61; 3.14.48
ziziphum: jujube, fruit of *Zizyphus sativa* or *jujuba* 2.12.14

Three Books on Life is a treatise on the health of the intellectual. It anticipates Burton's *Anatomy of Melancholy* in subject, in its various styles, and in sophistication and importance for cultural history. Though one of "the strangest and most complex" of Ficino's works (Garin), it was immensely popular in the Renaissance. Its magic is of particular interest at the present moment as historians of society, of religion, and of the arts, at both scholarly and popular levels, erect magic into a topic worthy of study in its own right. Yet primary magical documents are difficult of access. *On Life* is "the charter of natural magic" (P. Zambelli), but up to now the only reliable edition has been the facsimile of the Venice, 1498 edition by the late Martin Plessner which, besides being expensive, includes only a sketchy and eclectic apparatus and no translation.

The present edition includes a substantial introduction with its own notes and index, a critical text, a translation, notes, a general index, an index of *materia medica*, and a list of primary and secondary works cited. The introduction addresses two sections — on the scientific background and on Ficino's habits of mind — to a broader audience, and other sections — on the work's textual history, for example, on its degree and kind of heterodoxy, and on its indebtedness to Plotinus and the *Picatrix* — to a scholarly audience. The critical text is based on the first edition of 1489 and its errata sheet; it gives every variant from the MSS which has any claim to being authorial. The translation, since it appears facing the Latin, tries less to reproduce the aesthetic effects of Ficino's style than to remain as faithful as is consistent with formal written English. The rich notes aim to give the source of every explicit citation but not to trace unacknowledged sources. The substantial indices allow specialists of various sorts to select what they want to read; in particular, the index of *materia medica* with tentative identifications will enable historians of science to pursue their interests in *De vita* — interests which are only touched on in the present edition, as in the editions of other works of Ficino by Michael J. B. Allen, Sears Jayne, and Raymond Marcel.

Carol V. Kaske is Associate Professor of English at Cornell University. She has published on Ficino, Spenser, and related subjects, in *Renaissance Quarterly, Dante Studies, English Literary Renaissance, Anglia,* and other journals. She has also been the recipient of fellowships at Washington University, Smith College and Johns Hopkins University, as well as several grants-in-aid.

John R. Clark is Associate Professor and Chair of the Classics Department at Fordham University. He has held a research fellowship from the Wellcome Institute and several grants-in-aid, and has published on Ficino in *Classical Bulletin, Papers of The Bibliographical Society of America, Manuscripta,* and *Journal of the Warburg and Courtauld Institutes.*

mRts

medieval & renaissance texts & studies
is the publishing program of the
Center for Medieval and Early Renaissance Studies
at the State University of New York at Binghamton.

mRts emphasizes books that are needed —
texts, translations, and major research tools.

mRts aims to publish the highest quality scholarship
in attractive and durable format at modest cost.

www.ingramcontent.com/pod-product-compliance
Lightning Source LLC
Chambersburg PA
CBHW070056020526
44112CB00034B/1399